The Economic Consequences
of U.S. Mobilization for
the Second World War

THE ECONOMIC CONSEQUENCES OF U.S. MOBILIZATION FOR THE SECOND WORLD WAR

Alexander J. Field

Yale UNIVERSITY PRESS   NEW HAVEN AND LONDON

Published with assistance from the Louis Stern
Memorial Fund.

Yale University Press books may be purchased in quantity
for educational, business, or promotional use. For
information, please e-mail sales.press@yale.edu (U.S. office)
or sales@yaleup.co.uk (U.K. office).

Set in 10/14 ScalaPro by Newgen North America.
Printed in the United States of America.

Library of Congress Control Number: 2022930067
ISBN 978-0-300-25102-9 (hardcover : alk. paper)
ISBN 978-0-300-27671-8 (paperback)

A catalogue record for this book is available
from the British Library.

10 9 8 7 6 5 4 3 2 1

Contents

Preface and Acknowledgments

We cannot zero-base our beliefs about every aspect of the world every morning. And so we necessarily rely on conclusions reached by others, or conclusions that we ourselves have reached in the past. Coming to or accepting a position relaxes us. It feels good. It requires less intellectual and sometimes emotional energy than maintaining uncertainty and doubt. Once we hold views with a high degree of confidence, there are often very high bars to dislodging them, and indeed we may forcibly resist encouragements to reconsider. But now and again curiosity or an accumulation of discordant data loosens a settled position and moves it back to the unsettled realm, where logic, doubt, and critical thinking can again operate to full effect. As a result, some of our views, some of the time, do change.

This book is the result of a reexamination and ultimate rejection of beliefs I long held about the economic effects of U.S mobilization for war between 1941 and 1945. You may find that you start with views similar to those I once held. If so, rest assured you are in good company. The positions I endorsed are those held today by most economists and many historians. They have been reinforced over multiple decades from many sources—both scholarly and popular—including print, film, and television.

When an original interpretation is proposed, skeptics typically advance one of two objections: either it is wrong or we already knew this. An author proposing something new must anticipate each of these possible critiques. This requires a balance between developing the evidence supporting the new arguments and defending against the claim one has set up a straw man. It is easy to be novel and easy to be right, but much more difficult to be both.

This book's organization reflects a search for that balance. The first chapter lays out the central thesis, along with some of the evidence that the beliefs against which the argument is counterposed are indeed pervasive. But we can quickly tire of claims that what is proposed is new. We also want legitimately to know whether what an author has to offer makes any sense, and what the evidence for it is. And so chapter 2 moves directly into the central empirical finding of the book, the poor productivity performance of U.S. manufacturing during the war, and proceeds in the chapters to follow to explore its causes and implications. Manufacturing productivity went down because of resource shocks from enemy action, including curtailed access to natural rubber and, on the Eastern Seaboard, petroleum. But most importantly, it was depressed by sudden, radical, and temporary changes in the output mix. The war forced a shift away from producing goods in which the country had a great deal of experience toward those in which it had little. Learning by doing was only a partial counterbalance to the intermittent idleness and input hoarding that marked a shortage economy. The conflict distorted human and physical capital accumulation and once it ended, America stopped producing most of the new goods. In the interim, the war shut down basic scientific research and the ongoing development of civilian goods, trends reflected in patent data. There may well have been longer-term gains from logistical learning. But the case for manufacturing is much weaker. U.S. world economic dominance in 1948 owed less to the experience of making war goods and more to the country's productive potential in 1941, along with the damaged state of the economies of other combatant nations.

In the concluding chapter I return to the conventional wisdom, examining its origins and why it continues to have such a firm hold on so many people. During the war business spent millions of tax-deductible dollars cementing a triumphalist narrative which was then picked up by authors and other influencers after it ended. The desire to accentuate the positive and, in a victorious country, to celebrate, is understandable, and these efforts found fertile ground. The consequence is that we now have a large body of literature stretching over multiple decades making the same basic arguments, with authors gaining confidence by referencing what has been said before.

The truth is that the celebratory imperative has clouded our thinking about the economic history of the war and its aftermath. To talk repeatedly of miracles dulls our ability to think critically and crowds out efforts to find out what really happened. It creates a penumbra that shades and colors the interpretation of the supply-side consequences of the war. It can make data showing sharp declines in manufacturing productivity or depressed wartime patenting rates seem surprising.

This book reflects several years of intensive work exploring and excavating the details of U.S. mobilization for the Second World War. It reflects as well more than two decades of research on the history of U.S. production and productivity during the second quarter of the twentieth century. Special thanks to my wife, Valerie, for indulging, or at least tolerating, the preoccupations that help make an academic career both stimulating and meaningful.

The ideas developed here benefited from presentations at the All-UC Group in Economic History Conference, Tenaya Lodge, California, March 25, 2017; the New Economic School, Moscow, Russia, June 29, 2017; Santa Clara University, October 11, 2017; the ASSA meetings in Philadelphia, January 8, 2018; the NYU–Abu Dhabi Conference on Economic Convergence and Divergence, Abu Dhabi, U.A.E, February 25, 2018; the University of California, Davis, February 27, 2018; the World Economic History Conference, Cambridge, Massachusetts, August 3, 2018; Rutgers University, April 29, 2019; the ASSA meetings in San Diego, January 4, 2020; the University of California, Berkeley, February 10, 2020; the University of Michigan, March 30, 2021; and the Abramovitz Lecture at Stanford University, December 6, 2021. Thanks to all who participated for their input.

I am also grateful for comments on earlier working papers and draft chapters from Naren Agarwal, Michael Edelstein, Price Fishback, Robert Gordon, Peter Lindert, Deirdre McCloskey, Paul Rhode, Hugh Rockoff, Peter Rousmaniere, Richard Sylla, Thomas Weiss, Mark Wilson, Gavin Wright, and two anonymous readers for the press.

My father, Mark George Field, served as an intelligence officer in the United States Army in 1944 and 1945, providing liaison with the Soviet forces advancing eastward into Germany. This was one of the formative experiences of his life, and he never stopped talking about it. His time in the military delayed his graduation from Harvard but influenced the trajectory of his academic pursuits (and was likely responsible for his meeting my mother). It provided a rapid path to U.S. citizenship on which, as a stateless refugee from Nazism, he placed inestimable value. I would very much have appreciated and valued his reading of this manuscript, although my focus is on a set of issues different from those with which he was principally engaged. In his honor, out of love, and in recognition of his scholarly achievements, I dedicate this book to him.

ABBREVIATIONS

ASF	Army Service Forces
BEA	Bureau of Economic Analysis
Benelux	Belgium, Netherlands, Luxembourg
BLS	Bureau of Labor Statistics
CKD	Completely knocked-down
CMP	Controlled Materials Plan
CPFF	Cost plus a fixed fee
DDB	Double declining balance
DPA	Defense Production Act
DSC	Defense Supplies Corporation
FAT	Fixed Asset Table
FTE	Full-time equivalent workers
GDP	Gross Domestic Product
GNP	Gross National Product
GR-S	General-purpose synthetic rubber
IRC	Intercontinental Rubber Company
IRS	Internal Revenue Service
KL	Capital Labor method of calculating TFP
KLEMS	Capital Labor Energy Materials Services method of calculating TFP
kWh	Kilowatt hours
MFP	Multifactor productivity; synonym for TFP
MIT	Massachusetts Institute of Technology
NBER	National Bureau of Economic Research
NDAC	National Defense Advisory Commission
NIPA	National Income and Product Accounts
OECD	Organization for Economic Cooperation and Development
OPA	Office of Price Administration

OPEC	Organization of Petroleum Exporting Countries
OPM	Office of Production Management
OWM	Office of War Mobilization
PAW	Petroleum Administration for War
PCE-S	Personal consumption expenditures—services
PDE	Private domestic economy
PNE	Private nonfarm economy
POW	Prisoner of war
R&D	Research and development
RFC	Reconstruction Finance Corporation
RRC	Rubber Reserve Company
SPAB	Supply Priorities and Allocation Board
TEL	tetraethyl lead
TFP	Total factor productivity
TUP	Twin-unit pack
VE Day	Victory in Europe Day (May 8, 1945)
VJ Day	Victory over Japan Day (August 14 or 15, 1945)
WAA	War Assets Administration
WPA	Works Progress Administration
WPB	War Production Board

1 • The Impact of War Mobilization
on Economic Potential

This is a book about the economic consequences of U.S. mobilization for World War II. It is about what happened between 1941 and 1945 and about the longer-run economic legacy of that experience. The focus is only partly on the mobilization of the men who actually did the fighting or provided direct support for them through participation in the armed forces of the United States. The central emphasis is on the mobilization of workers, materiel, and physical capital to produce the goods needed to wage war: the planes, ships, tanks, trucks, guns, and ammunition, as well as the food, blankets, boots, medicine, and fuel needed to keep men and equipment moving, both on the home front and in the theaters of war. This book deals with numbers, economic concepts, and some macroeconomic theory, as well as the historiography of the era and the legacy of various efforts at persuasion. Its intent is to overturn a conventional wisdom broadly shared by economists, many historians, and the general public.

The initial aim of this book is to document what for many will surely be the surprisingly disappointing record of manufacturing productivity growth during the war. A second objective is to understand the effects of the war on the level and rate of growth of potential output in the postwar period. Getting a fix on that is what matters when we ask whether or to what degree the war laid the foundations for growth in the years after 1948. It is true that part of the economic and political legacy of the conflict was a permanently higher level of military spending, which provided a buffer and some insurance against the possibility of a decline in aggregate demand such as had caused and prolonged the Depression. But a high level of total spending in the economy is only a necessary, not a sufficient, condition for growth over the longer run.

Economic growth can mean not just recovery from recession and depression as output gaps close in response to higher spending, but also advance reflecting an increase in economic potential. If the supply-side underpinnings of higher output are not there—that is, if growth in labor, physical capital, or knowledge is absent—spending per se cannot increase real output or real output per person beyond a certain point. And so the question comes down to asking what was the effect on the labor force, the physical capital stock, and the country's technological, scientific, and organizational capability of U.S. participation in the Second World War.

It is commonly argued that the influence of war on these factors, as well as political and institutional conditions conducive to growth, will, on balance, be positive. In the title of his 2006 book, *Is War Necessary for Economic Growth?*, the economist Vernon Ruttan posed a provocative question that he answered affirmatively: "It is difficult to overemphasize the importance of the historical role that military procurement has played in the process of technology development" (Ruttan, 2006, p. 3).[1] Without war, he suggested, the R&D spending necessary to develop new technologies would simply not be forthcoming.

Recent treatments by historians of the economic consequences of the Second World War reflect a similar robustness of the thesis as applied to that conflict. In *Warfare State* (2011) James Sparrow wrote that "the war brought opportunities for 'creative destruction' on a scale that has yet to be matched" (Sparrow, 2011, p. 7). The reference was not to artful bombing, but rather to an alleged Schumpeterian dynamic in which wartime innovation devalued older assets and businesses and sometimes led to their demise. Maury Klein, in *A Call to Arms: Mobilizing America for World War II*, focused less on the standard learning-by-doing narratives, and instead on new products, enumerating a range of innovations he argued originated in the war and benefited the postwar economy: "jet planes, radar, magnetic tape recording, early computers, and a host of electronic innovations" (Klein, 2013, pp. 1–2). In *Freedom's Forge: How American Business Produced Victory in World War II*, Arthur Herman gave as much credit as he could to America's business leaders (not labor or government) for the success of American war mobilization, arguing that captains of industry both transformed the American military and "laid the foundations for a postwar prosperity that would extend across three decades into the 1970s, and fuel the economic growth of the planet" (Herman, 2012, p. x). We may or may not accept Herman's grant of heroic status to America's captains of industry. But in each of these instances, we see endorsement of positive and persisting supply effects as a consequence of the experience of war production, either generally or with specific reference to World War II.[2]

The views of economists on these matters have been buttressed by a series of widely accepted stylized facts about wartime productivity growth. Productivity, it must be emphasized, is not the same as production. Productivity is a ratio of output to one or more inputs, most commonly either labor or a combined measure of labor and physical capital services, as in measures of total factor productivity (TFP). In 1986 William Baumol, based on his reading of Angus Maddison's data, took World War II's contribution to higher (labor) productivity growth during and after the war as a given: "It is noteworthy . . . that the duration and amplitude of the great leap above historical U.S. productivity growth in the war and early postwar years were just about as great as the previous shortfalls during the Great Depression" (Baumol, 1986, pp. 1081–82). In his influential 2016 book, Robert Gordon restated the thesis insofar as it applied to the Second World War and used macroeconomic data on TFP growth to bolster his narrative (Gordon, 2016, ch. 16).

Evaluating the evidence in support of these interpretations is important not only for our understanding of mid-twentieth-century U.S. economic history, but also because of its relevance to the broader claims about the effect of war and military spending on technological and economic progress. Since the impact of the war on labor supply available in the immediate postwar period was clearly negative (roughly 407,000 mostly prime-age males did not return alive; another 671,000 were wounded), and since the effect of the war on available physical capital was neither obviously positive nor negative (more on this later), the main contested issue involves the claim that learning by doing in producing war goods led to persisting advances in sectoral and economy-wide efficiency, which are reflected in data on levels and rates of growth of productivity.

The empirical sections of this book will show, inter alia, that both labor productivity and TFP in manufacturing declined during the war in comparison with 1941 and grew relatively anemically after the war. How do we reconcile these data with the widely recounted learning-by-doing narratives—the cost reductions as output of Liberty ships, C-47s, B-24s, and other durables increased? One solution is simply to say that the sectoral productivity numbers are wrong in their underlying data or in their construction. My intent is to persuade that the story told by the numbers is basically correct, and to explain why the fascination with and continued repetition of the learning stories have misled. One argument is simple: levels matter as much as and sometimes more than growth rates. If a firm switches temporarily from making goods in which it is experienced to those in which it is not, and its productivity declines, a high subsequent growth rate will not necessarily return it to where it started.

The State of the U.S. Economy in 1941

It has been easy to conflate the World War II U.S. record with respect to production (output) and that associated with productivity (output per unit input). They are, of course, not the same. Manufacturing output can go up sharply while productivity declines—which is what in fact happened. A focus on the starting conditions—the output gap remaining in 1941, along with the very rapid growth of TFP in manufacturing during the interwar period, which affected the level of technical, scientific, and organizational knowledge at the start of the war—is essential in understanding U.S. success in producing large increases in military (and total) product between 1941 and 1945.

Studies of long-run productivity growth in the United States began with the work of Moses Abramovitz (1956), Robert Solow (1957), and John Kendrick (1961). Solow's memorable conclusion (based on Kendrick's then-unpublished data) was that a remarkably small fraction of output growth between 1909 and 1949 could be accounted for by the growth of inputs (labor and capital) conventionally measured. In other words, the residual—the difference between real output growth and a weighted average of the growth rates of the two key inputs—accounted for a large portion of output growth over these four decades. Subsequent studies with access to longer runs of data have confirmed that the second and third quarters of the twentieth century experienced particularly strong TFP growth, but there remain important differences about when within those decades the most rapid advance occurred (Abramovitz and David, 2000a, 2000b; Field, 2003, 2011; Gordon, 2016). I situated it in the 1930s (specifically, measuring between 1929 and 1941), but in his most recent work Gordon located it in the 1940s.[3] Whereas Gordon accepted my revisionism regarding (at least moderate) productivity advance between 1929 and 1941, he retained (repackaging it as new) the "economic miracle" interpretation of the supply-side effects of the war, arguing that TFP growth across the war years "perhaps" greatly exceeded that during the Depression.[4]

World War II confirmed the fundamental Keynesian prediction that massive fiscal stimulus combined with expansionary monetary policy could bring a depressed economy to full employment and beyond within a very short time.[5] But for decades it has also been argued that the war was associated with a permanent boost on the supply side, particularly because of its effect on the growth of TFP.[6]

Only in the United States is it common to argue that mobilization contributed positively to levels and rates of growth of productivity in the postwar period.[7] In the historiography of no other major World War II combatant is this true. That is one reason we should proceed carefully before accepting these claims insofar as they apply to the United States. It is also the case that none of the other major combatants began mobilization with as large a gap between actual and potential output as did the United States. A large output gap did not characterize the economies of England, Germany, Japan, or the Soviet Union at the time they entered the war, nor was this true for the U.S. economy at the onset of participation in World War I, Korean, or Vietnam conflicts. There is likely a connection between these observations.

The record of U.S. manufacturing output during the war is indubitably impressive. In contrast, the record with respect to productivity is disappointing, whether we look at the manufacturing sector alone (chapter 2) or the total economy (chapter 8), and whether we consider only the period of war mobilization and demobilization, or the years that followed as well.

Between 1942 and 1945, the United States mobilized economically the way it would wage war on the battlefield: by directing a firehose of men and women and material at the targets. Efficiency improvements in the production of a radically changed output mix were low on the country's list of priorities, the quantity of output and the speed with which it could be produced far outranking them. With learning and experience, productivity in the manufacture of well-known military capital goods eventually improved. But this only partially counterbalanced the negative influences of disruptions in resource supply inflicted by the Japanese and Germans and the initial sudden, forced, and radical change in the output mix, an echo of which was experienced in 1944 as the war (for the United States) entered its bloodiest and most brutal phase. Throughout the war, these effects were reflected in and augmented by shortages of materials, machine tools, subassemblies, and ultimately manpower that were persisting features of the wartime industrial economy. These disorders were worsened by the behavioral pathologies and compliance burdens that accompanied the systems of non-price rationing of producer and consumer goods to which these shortages gave rise.

The analysis in this book builds on arguments developed in Field (2008). In that earlier work (see also Field, 2011, ch. 3), I explored the contrast between aggregate (private nonfarm) TFP growth during the periods 1929–41 and

1941–48, and provided a detailed analysis of the wrenching changes associated with industrial mobilization for war (1941–43) and demobilization (1943–48) by identifying sectors acquiring and releasing full-time equivalent workers (FTEs) during these two periods, and the magnitudes of the manpower flows involved.[8] This book focuses not only on aggregate and sectoral evidence that the contribution of war mobilization to the growth of TFP and potential output was negative, but also more extensively on the issue of why.

A principal argument can be stated succinctly: TFP in manufacturing fell during the war because the conflict forced a wrenching shift away from products and processes in which manufacturers had a great deal of experience toward the production of goods in which they had little. Enormous quantities of new physical capital—both buildings and machinery—were constructed and deployed in this effort, and the portion of the manufacturing and total labor force working on war production grew considerably. The exigencies of war demanded that this be done quickly and it was. Raw material shocks, shortages of machine tools, components, and subassemblies, and ultimately a severe scarcity of manpower created additional and continuing disruptions, all aggravated by producer hoarding. This concatenation of negative influences retarded productivity advance in manufacturing. We will be concerned both with the immediate issue of why manufacturing productivity declined during the conflict and with the longer-run question of why the learning experienced in war production did not have more persistent positive influences on productivity growth after the war.

Economic Growth and Growth Accounting

Economic mobilization for war refers to the period during which an economy transitions from a largely peacetime footing to the point where it devotes its maximum effort to producing military goods. Understood in these terms, U.S. mobilization for the Second World War took place during the twenty-one months from February 1942 through November 1943, after which production for the military dipped slightly, though it remained at a high plateau until the end of the conflict in Europe (May 1945).

One of many misconceptions about this period is the belief that, because of Lend-Lease and aircraft orders from Britain and France before its fall, the United States was already nearly fully mobilized by the time of Pearl Harbor. Military spending and head count had indeed grown from low points in 1939 and 1940. Government construction of training camps, aircraft assembly plants, and such facilities as the Detroit Tank Arsenal began and were in some cases completed before the Japanese attack. And planners were, after considerable resistance, able to implement a 20 percent cutback in booming civilian vehicle production effective August 1941.

But on the morning of December 8 the economy was not close to fully mobilized for war. U.S. production of civilian automobiles did not cease until February 1942, thirty months after the German invasion of Poland and almost twenty months after the fall of France. Of the more than 300,000 aircraft produced in the country between 1940 and 1945, barely 25,000 had been manufactured by the end of 1941. The quantitative impact of Lend-Lease, construction, and aircraft orders from Britain and France was small compared with what would subsequently be experienced.[9]

The challenge facing the country after Pearl Harbor was to mobilize labor, capital, and materials to produce goods for U.S. allies, for its own military, and for the civilian population, while at the same time accommodating the manpower demands of the armed forces. Responding to that challenge was made somewhat easier for the United States because in 1941 there remained a gap between the output of the economy and its potential, and therefore a substantial reservoir of labor in the form of the unemployed and those who could easily be drawn into the labor force.[10] But a rise in output reflecting the closing of an output gap due to growing aggregate demand should be distinguished from one based on an increase in an economy's potential. Realizing a country's economic potential is not the same as increasing it.

Economists consider the evolution of a macroeconomy to be the consequence both of its internal structure and of the perturbations to which it is subject over time. Among the latter, the most fundamental distinctions are between aggregate demand shocks (positive or negative) and aggregate supply shocks (positive or negative). Aggregate demand refers to flows of spending from all sources: consumption by households, private domestic investment (business spending on plant and equipment and intended net acquisition of inventories), government spending on goods and services, and, finally, spending by our trading partners on our goods or services (exports) less what we spend on theirs (imports). The sum of these flows is what we mean by aggregate demand.[11] When the economy is operating below potential, fluctuations in aggregate demand can exercise a determining influence on actual output and employment. Insufficient levels of aggregate demand were the main cause of the twelve year-long Great Depression in the United States that began in 1929, during which actual output was persistently below potential, and unemployment levels and rates were elevated. This has also been true for most of the postwar recessions, with the notable exception of 1973–75, triggered by the first OPEC oil shock.

During the Second World War the U.S. economy experienced powerful disrupters of both types. First and most obviously, the country was hit with large positive demand shocks because of the increase in government spending on munitions, on the facilities to produce them, and on the infrastructure necessary to train and administer a much-expanded military. The stimulus from such spending was only partly offset by increases in tax rates, which, along with rationing, kept consumption in check, as well as a diminution in private-sector capital formation in sectors not closely related to the war effort. These fiscal effects were complemented by Federal Reserve actions that expanded the monetary base and kept interest rates low. Combined fiscal and monetary stimulus rapidly closed the gap between actual and potential remaining in 1941 and by 1943 had driven the civilian unemployment rate below 2 percent, almost unimaginably low, where it remained on an annual basis through 1945. Much new physical capital was added, new pools of labor (including more women, teenagers, and older individuals) entered the labor force, and the average number of hours worked per week increased, while millions of men were drawn into the military. The continuing high levels of aggregate demand fueled inflationary pressures, contained during the war by rationing, restrictions on what could be produced, price controls, and efforts to encourage saving through government bond drives.

The inflationary pressures, however, were only partly the result of demand stimulus. Potential output, determined in the realm of aggregate supply, was negatively affected by disruptions in raw material availabilities, by the need to produce a radically altered final product mix, by the compulsory withdrawal of millions of men from the civilian labor force into the armed forces, and, most generally, by endemic shortages. Limitations on the size of an economy's potential reflect the fundamental economic problem of scarcity. Below potential, aggregate demand may well limit what can be sold and therefore profitably produced. But for any economy, the ability to produce goods ultimately faces constraints on the supply side. Because of a range of developments and conditions specific to the war, these got much tighter for the United States in 1942.[12]

The effects of aggregate demand shocks on the U.S. economy during the war have been widely studied and are well understood (Rockoff, 2012, ch. 6).

They are not the main focus of this study. Rather, the emphasis is on the supply-side consequences of mobilization, both during the war and after. The existing historiography, as noted, overwhelmingly emphasizes positive effects. There were some, although most were transitory and were more than counterbalanced by those that were negative.

The textbook definition of potential is the highest level of output an economy can sustain without being so stimulated by rises in aggregate demand that an acceleration in the inflation rate ensues, in which case actual may temporarily rise above potential. The level and rate of growth of potential output depend principally on three kinds of supply constraints, beginning with the amount and quality of labor that will be voluntarily supplied at different wage rates. Work-leisure preferences can have some influence here, as can the legal, institutional, and cultural environment. But ultimately demographic factors, such as the size and age distribution of the population, are the main limiting factors.

A second constraint is the quantity of physical capital inherited from the past. This includes buildings (residential and nonresidential), equipment and machinery, and inventories. These stocks emit service flows, which, combined with labor services, produce output (goods and services). The physical capital stock—and the service flows from them—grow over time when resources are devoted to building or producing such assets rather than satisfying immediate consumption needs. The existing stock also experiences wastage because of deterioration, obsolescence, or other forms of depreciation. Service flows from the stock may also deteriorate over time. This is not the same as, although it is related to, depreciation in asset values. In addition to more normal forms of deterioration and depreciation, the economic value of the existing stock and its service flows can be adversely affected when assets are specialized to the production of specific goods and the product mix changes, an important concern during the periods of both mobilization and demobilization. This dynamic applied particularly to special-purpose machine tools and some buildings. It also affected human capital when workers acquired product-specific skills building certain goods that were then no longer produced, or when temporary entrants to the labor force exited after the war.

A third supply-side constraint is a society's level of technological, scientific, and organizational knowledge: the known recipes that can be used to combine the services of the labor force and the physical capital stock to produce goods and services. Improvements in knowledge make it possible for an economy to produce more output from the same set of inputs, or the same output with reduced flows of inputs. Legal, environmental, political, and cultural factors also influence potential and help explain the wide cross-national variation in economic performance. For a country for which such factors can be considered relatively stable, however, trends in labor, physical capital, and knowledge provide a useful starting point in explaining changes over time in output.[13]

Decomposing output growth into the respective contributions of these three factors is the essence of what economists call growth accounting. When we say that the growth of potential output is determined by changes in aggregate supply, we are principally referring to changes in these variables, and are thus abstracting from or holding constant other influences.[14] When we quantify such contributions with actual data, we typically try to do so between peaks in business activity, when we can assume the economy is at or close to potential, and measures of productivity growth will not be influenced by cyclical demand factors affecting levels at the beginning or end of the period.[15]

Negative supply shocks result from the death, incapacitation, or unavailability for paid work of members of the labor force, from destruction, contamination, or obsolescence of plant or equipment, or from loss of access to or relevance of technological, scientific, or organizational knowledge. Obviously, labor or physical capital can become unavailable or unusable, but can this also happen to knowledge? Such a development might appear fanciful—generally, knowledge accumulates and does not decay. Yet history offers many instances in which productive knowledge retreated. One example is the reversal occurring after the collapse of the Roman Empire, eventually followed by the Renaissance, in which classical knowledge was rediscovered. More immediately germane to U.S. mobilization and its aftermath: product-specific knowledge, like special-purpose machine tools and structures, experienced a loss of value in 1942, when the production of many consumer durables was shut down. A similar loss was experienced after 1945, when goods produced during the war were never manufactured again.

The change in the output mix that accompanied mobilization for war also meant that the U.S. economy was vulnerable to materials shortages and inflationary pressures at lower levels of total employment and output than would have been the case had aggregate demand growth more closely mirrored the structure of final demand in a peacetime economy. Stated another way, supply bottlenecks arose sooner than if the stimulus had been due simply to an across-the-board tax cut, sustained rise in the monetary base, revival of private-sector business optimism, or government spending programs of a size and composition similar to what had prevailed in the 1930s (highways, bridges, airports, tunnels, hydroelectric facilities, and other public infrastructure).

The economic mobilization for war that began in earnest in February 1942 and continued to accelerate at breakneck speed through November 1943 was anything but a "normal" expansion. The desired product mix simultaneously featured large increases in demands for naval and maritime ship construction, aircraft assembly plants and the machine tools to fill them, plants to manufacture synthetic rubber, additions to and reconfigurations of refineries to allow the production of more aviation fuel, and many other new production and cantonment facilities to allow the training of a much-expanded military. This was on top of enormous orders for conventional guns, ammunition, tanks, trucks, and jeeps. And the product mix continued to change, sometimes dramatically, during the course of the war.

The increase in record-keeping and reporting requirements that inevitably accompanied price control and rationing was a related retardant. Managers in both favored and unfavored sectors spent hours engaged in competitive expediting and complying with wartime regulations. Dealing with shortages, priorities, ration coupons, thirty-five-mile-per-hour speed limits, and the host of other obstacles and requirements resulting from what was close to a command economy consumed both managerial and worker energy.

Planned economies are good at mobilizing industrial production. Regulations helped restrain inflation and meet the production targets required for the prosecution of the war. Controls divided the economy into favored sectors, which had little incentive to economize on materials, physical capital, or labor because, even if such resources were in short supply, these sectors had priority (although not guaranteed) access to them. The rest of the economy faced greater struggles to obtain the resources needed. The machinery of control and the nature of the contracts used to elicit production of war goods reduced incentives for productivity improvement, pushing efficiency far down the list of economic priorities, a lesson evident in the history of Soviet-era economies and the United States during the war.

Perhaps most insidiously in terms of its effects on production and productivity, manufacturing during World War II faced both the fear and reality of endemic shortages, first of materials, then of complementary components, and finally of labor itself. Input unavailability, aggravated by producer hoarding, periodically caused manufacture of specific items to slow down or stop. For some firms and sectors, the uneven and unpredictable arrival (and departure) of war orders contributed additionally to intermittency. There can be little more corrosive of productivity advance than the cessation of production and the enforced idleness, even if temporary, of labor and capital.

The Effects of Process and Product Changeovers during Peacetime

The deteriorating supply conditions for materials, components, and equipment, however, formed only part of a panoply of challenges facing an economy striving to produce a radically altered mix of goods and services. Consideration of two earlier transitions gives us insight into the adverse initial consequences of process and product mix changeovers.

The first involves the electrification of the internal distribution of power within factories during the early decades of the twentieth century. The process of shifting away from the mechanical shafts and belts that were a feature of the nineteenth-century steam- or waterpower–driven factory delivered extraordinary increases in both labor productivity and sectoral TFP between 1919 and 1929, and these gains were remarkably similar across all industries at the two-digit Standard Industrial Classification level of aggregation (Devine, 1983; Field, 2003, 2011). But as Boyan Jovanovic and Peter Rousseau show (2005, p. 1190, fig. 4), the largest percentage point increases in electrification took place in the preceding decade (1909–19), during which TFP and labor productivity growth in the sector were both anemic.[16] In every one of the fifteen industries examined, the percentage of horsepower electrified began to plateau or in two cases actually declined slightly in the 1920s. Yet it was only in the 1920s that the big productivity gains were realized. For TFP growth within the sector, for which Kendrick provides data only for benchmark years, we have 5.18 percent annually between 1919 and 1929, compared with .29 percent per year between 1909 and 1919, and .72 percent per year between 1899 and 1909 (Kendrick, 1961, appendix tables D-I and D-II). The initial effect of electrification of the internal distribution of power within factories was to depress TFP growth within manufacturing, although subsequently big gains were realized.

A second and particularly interesting case is Ford's 1927 shift from producing Model Ts to Model As. The Model T was introduced in 1908. Sales peaked in 1923 as Ford confronted growing competition from other automakers offering more options and higher horsepower. On May 26, 1927, the 15 millionth Model T rolled off the assembly line, and Ford plants worldwide shut down for retooling. Most of the existing special-purpose machine tools were scrapped, and Ford engineers designed and ordered new ones, which they eventually installed. On October 21, 1927, the company completed its first pilot Model A but did not begin selling to the public until December 22 of that year (Krebs, 1993). For almost five months, both labor productivity and TFP in Ford's plants were effectively nil. U.S. passenger car production fell from 357,000 in May to 106,000 in December.[17] Some of this was seasonal (the series is not seasonally adjusted), but much can be attributed to Ford's transition to the new product. The decline in production and productivity can be thought of as the result of a temporary negative supply shock—a reduction in potential output as resources were devoted to designing, building, and installing new machine tools, transferring production from Highland Park to the new River Rouge plant, reorganizing production lines, and accustoming workers to new machines and tasks.

The arithmetic of the productivity drop is easily comprehended. Labor inputs declined somewhat as production workers were furloughed, while, on net, most capital input flows persisted and had to be paid for, even if they were not used in production. These are in the denominator of a TFP calculation. In the numerator is output, which was close to nonexistent for almost half a year. The transition, at the time unprecedented in its cost (between $100 and $250 million), contributed to prolonging the recession that began in October 1926 and ran through November 1927. Ultimately, of course, production and productivity revived and grew rapidly (not difficult if one starts from a level close to zero). Ford eventually produced over 5 million Model As before retiring the model in 1931, during the depths of the Depression.

The initial effect of each of these changeovers was to slow the growth rate of or actually depress the level of productivity; gains were experienced only after a lag. Electrification of the internal distribution of power in American factories required retrofitting existing structures and rethinking the organization of production flow. It led to design changes in new factory buildings, including a shift away from multistoried to single-storied structures. It differed from the Model T to Model A changeover in that it affected the entire manufacturing sector and involved alterations in processes rather than a dramatic change in the output mix. Neither transition, however, was markedly affected by the urgency of wartime mobilization, and both paled in comparison to the adjustments forced on the U.S. manufacturing sector after Pearl Harbor. Electrification of the internal distribution of power in plants ultimately resulted in very substantial gains. But in contrast to the changes in product mix during the Second World War, which persisted only for a very few years, those design and process changes endured.

The two cases show that changes in the composition of output or technique can slow the growth and in some instances depress the level of productivity. The larger, the more urgent, and the more disruptive the transition, the greater the potential for the temporary depression of production and productivity. Economic mobilization for war involved the construction or modification of hundreds of plants and facilities—many of the new ones very large— and a fifty-fold increase in the annual production and installation of machine tools. It forced a switch to the development and refinement of processes and the production of products new to most of those who were making them. Many of these goods were extraordinarily complex, involving tens, in some cases hundreds of thousands, and, in a few cases, millions of parts. The gains eventually made in the production of the new products were enjoyed only for a short time because the change in the final product mix was for the most part temporary (see chapter 6).

Both of these earlier transitions took place when the economy did not face the shortages of materials, machine tools, subassemblies, and ultimately labor that characterized the U.S. economy during the war. Ford's transition to making aircraft engines and B-24 bombers in the first half of the 1940s was much more challenging than its shift from making Model Ts to Model As in the 1920s. The number of parts in a B-24 was two orders of magnitude larger than in a passenger car. The government spent hundreds of millions of dollars on the huge new Willow Run facility, for which ground was broken in April 1941. Ford received $224 million for aircraft facilities expansion through 1944; it contributed just $11.3 million of its own funds (Aircraft Industries Association of America, 1953, table 1-6). The company hired tens of thousands of workers. But it was not until well into 1943 that B-24s began rolling off the assembly line on anything like a regular basis (although some components were produced during the interim). In 1942, a year in which American industry built 47,386 aircraft, Ford is credited with just 24. Ford was eventually able to mass-produce the bombers, although only after relaxing its opposition to using subcontractors for some of the components. In 1944 Ford built 3,990 out of a total of 96,319 aircraft (4.1 percent), accounting for 9.6 percent of airframe construction by weight (Aircraft Industries Association of America, 1953, tables 2-13 and 2-14).

We are perhaps naturally inclined, given U.S. victory in the war, to focus on the eventually beneficial effects of manufacturing the new products at scale (even here there are qualifications that will be discussed in chapter 6), so much so that we lose sight of the adverse effects of the transition and the reality that the glory was short-lived. When Ford finally hit its stride in 1944, the army slashed orders in favor of the B-29, a plane whose manufacture was also repeatedly delayed by production problems, and a weapon system that ultimately would become the most expensive of the war. In 1941 Ford built automobiles with an efficiency and at productivity levels honed through years, indeed decades, of experience. In 1942 Ford shifted to airplanes (it had constructed about two hundred Trimotor aircraft between 1925 and 1933 before exiting the business); its large increases in labor and capital services input had very little to show on the output side. (The company did somewhat better with aircraft engines). The output improvements in late 1943 and continuing into 1944 moved firm productivity back toward where it had been in 1941, but the upward trajectory was blunted with the cutbacks in orders as B-29 development and production ramped up.

Iconic photographs from 1944 show assembly lines of partially completed planes in the huge Willow Run plant stretching into the horizon almost as far as the eye can see. One must resist the temptation to look at these images and conclude that mobilization for war must obviously have improved productivity within the manufacturing sector. It did not. If response to adversity and learning allowed a firm's productivity to return partway to where it had been before the shift in product mix, it was not necessarily at a higher level than before experiencing the shock. Ford's bumpy transition and that of many other firms are important parts of the explanation of the steep sectoral drop in both labor productivity and TFP between 1941 and 1942. These metrics moderated their rates of decline in 1943 but then descended sharply again in 1944 and 1945.

Eventually, managers and workers gained experience, solved problems, and overcame bottlenecks. Production and productivity of specific war goods increased. But for the Second World War we have been mesmerized by stories of those subsequent increases and lost sight of the depression in the level of productivity associated with the initial transitions. The historical balance sheet might look different if the U.S. economy had shifted permanently to building 100,000 aircraft and thousands of merchant ships a year. But economic mobilization for World War II was a one-off, unique event, never again to be repeated. A few short years after mobilization began, it was unwound. In 1948, after demobilization was more or less complete and the output mix reverted to something resembling what had prevailed in 1941, total factor productivity in manufacturing was lower than it had been before Pearl Harbor.

The much-celebrated learning by doing never overcame the initial negative effects of transition and became largely irrelevant after the war. Almost all the products enjoying the reduction in unit costs with cumulated output ceased production in 1945 or shortly thereafter. The country would never again mass-produce military hardware in such a compressed interval. The spillovers from military production to postwar civilian and military production were limited. And the focus on military production shut down learning and R&D in the civilian sector for at least thirty months.

In contrast to the optimism and enthusiasm expressed by many authors, I argue that the war retarded the growth of potential output. It did so not just by slowing the growth of TFP, but also by destroying human capital on the battle-field and distorting its acquisition within production in ways that reduced its relevance after the war. Product-specific skills were of little value after 1945 if the products were no longer produced. The more general skills acquired as the result of higher female labor-force participation were dissipated as many women embraced or were forced into domesticity and raising the boomer generation. And finally, although the war did not reduce overall physical capital acquisition, it distorted its trajectory of accumulation, channeling it in ways appropriate for the wartime product mix but not necessarily for that to which the economy would largely return in peacetime. The war was associated with a decline in the level of TFP in manufacturing and a reduction in its growth rate in the private domestic economy.

William Greider in 1987 enthusiastically endorsed the conventional wisdom about the long-term effects of mobilization: for America, the "economic consequences of World War II were . . . extraordinarily bountiful." He described how the government "force-fed the rapid development of new productive facilities across many industrial sectors [that] would become the basic industries of America's postwar prosperity," thus "laying the groundwork for an abundant future." It was, he suggested, little short of an "industrial revolution" (Greider, 1987, pp. 323–24).

With equal enthusiasm, V. R. Cardozier described wartime manufacture as "an astonishing feat of productivity, accomplished in a short period" (Cardozier, 1995, p. 134). But that is not quite right. If *production* appeared astounding, it was largely because, before Simon Kuznets made his calculations (see chapter 2), the full extent of the growth in potential between 1929 and 1941 had not been understood or appreciated. Productivity within manufacturing never recovered from the negative effects of the product mix and resource shocks accompanying mobilization. Considered in its totality, wartime manufacture did not benefit from a productivity miracle.

Not all the conventional wisdom has been wrong. The war was good for business in the sense that profits were high. The war spending and associated monetary stimulus closed the output gap remaining in 1941 and thus completed the country's exit from the Great Depression. The longer-run question is whether the learning and innovation associated with mass-producing military hardware or the responses to the resource shocks laid the foundation for economic growth in the postwar period. Here the answer is much more nuanced.

Mobilization dramatically and rapidly altered the structure of the U.S. industrial base. But the changes were mostly temporary and had questionable relevance or carryover for the postwar period. Most of the supply side foundations for the golden age (1948–73) were already in place in 1941. Indeed, those foundations were part of what made it possible for the United States successfully to prosecute the war.

2 • Manufacturing Productivity Before, During, and After World War II

If the thesis that war benefits aggregate supply is correct, it is in manufacturing that we should most likely see efficiency gains from the experience of economic mobilization. Mechanized conflict required huge increases in the production of airplanes, tanks, ships, and many other types of ordnance, and the plant, equipment, materials, energy, and intermediate goods necessary to make and (where applicable) operate them. This in turn was associated with an increase in the shares of the nation's labor force devoted to manufacturing, which reached an all-time high during the war, and within manufacturing, an increase in the share of output directly and indirectly supporting the military. The sector is the locus of all the well-known learning-by-doing narratives: the Liberty ships, the destroyer escorts, the C-47s, the B-24s, the Oerlikon and Bofors antiaircraft guns (Nelson, 1946; Walton, 1956; Arrow, 1962; Alchian, 1963; Gemery and Hogendorn, 1993; Thompson, 2001; Thornton and Thompson, 2001).[1] The narratives emphasize and imply that experience producing those goods generated sharp and persisting increases in efficiency, persisting in the sense that they moved the sector to permanently higher productivity levels. That emphasis draws attention away from the low initial productivity levels experienced as a consequence of the sudden, forced change in product mix. The argument also requires that the economy kept making the goods, or goods similar to them, or that the learning was broadly applicable to the manufacture of a range of products.

This chapter explores levels and rates of growth of manufacturing productivity from 1899 through 2019 in the United States, with special attention to growth rates between 1941 and 1948 compared with what took place during the interwar period and after demobilization was complete. It will make the empirical case that output per unit of input in manufacturing fell dramatically between 1941 and 1945, recovered only partially between 1945 and 1948, and, during the golden age (1948–73), advanced at a rate substantially below what had been achieved between 1919 and 1941. Later chapters will explain *why* productivity and efficiency declined so much between 1941 and the peak years of war mobilization, and why the much-vaunted spillovers from learning by doing did not do more to boost productivity in the sector after 1948.

The United States entered the war with a high, indeed world-leading, level of manufacturing productivity, the result of experience gained and capabilities refined during the Roaring Twenties and the Great Depression. It also entered the war with a negative output gap, the tail end of a more than decade-long depression. That gap was more apparent in sectors other than manufacturing, but it meant that reserves of labor were available to help increase output within manufacturing, above and beyond what could be gained on the labor input side from patriotic appeals and encouragements to women, teenagers, and older individuals to enter or reenter the labor force.

These preconditions meant that the sector could absorb a variety of adverse supply shocks and still, in the context of increases in labor and capital input and restrictions on the manufacture of metal-using consumer durables, achieve large increases in the output of goods destined for the military and U.S. allies. That achievement does not require or imply increases in sectoral productivity, or that advances in producing specific military capital goods benefited aggregate supply in the postwar period. Increases in output were achieved in spite of rather than because of overall movements in sectoral productivity. Localized learning by doing was insufficient to offset forces depressing productivity and did not by and large persist when the economy stopped making the goods whose cumulative production experience had given rise to them. The bulk of the gains from learning by doing in making aircraft, ships, tanks, and guns was experienced in 1943. The gains were already dissipating in 1944 as military production shifted toward heavier, more advanced, and more complex capital goods, as new goods such as the B-29 and the Pershing tank replaced B-24s and Shermans. Once again factories retooled, suffering through agonizing production setbacks and initial low productivity levels.

To understand the production achievement that allowed the United States to defeat its adversaries and the development of the capabilities that permitted the country to dominate the world economy in the postwar period, appreciation of the advance of productivity prior to the war is essential. Table 2.1

**Table 2.1: Total Factor Productivity Growth in
U.S. Manufacturing, 1899–2019 (percent per year)**

1899–1909	.72
1909–1919	.29
1919–1929	5.18
1929–1941	3.05
1941–1948	−1.40
1949–1973	1.49
1973–1989	.57
1989–2008	1.39
2008–2019	−.12

Sources: 1899–1929: Kendrick (1961), p. 464, table D-I;
1929–48: see table 2.3, below, and text; 1949–89: U.S.
Bureau of Labor Statistics (2004), table 2; 1989–2019:
https://www.bls.gov/data/#productivity (accessed
February 2, 2022).

reports growth rates of TFP within manufacturing for different time intervals
between 1899 and 2019. These data show that the years of mobilization were
preceded by more than two decades of very rapid advance followed by rates of
postwar productivity growth considerably lower than had been realized in the
twenty-two years before Pearl Harbor. TFP in the sector was 88 log percentage
points higher in 1941 than it had been in 1919—a continuously compounded
growth rate of 4 percent a year over the period. There is nothing comparable in
U.S. economic history at any other time. This rate of advance compares with
1.49 percent a year between 1949 and 1973.

Growth accounting, which gives rise to these TFP estimates, is, at its core,
quite simple. It posits that changes in output are the consequence of changes
in labor input, changes in capital services input, and changes in productivity (output per unit of combined input). TFP growth is a residual: the difference between the growth rate of output and a weighted average of the growth
rates of the two key inputs (the growth rates of labor and capital services are
weighted by their respective shares of national income). TFP can be considered the secret sauce of economic growth. Its uncertain origins are described
as "manna from heaven" in a reference widely attributed to Robert Solow.[2]

The following variable definitions and formulas summarize the key relationships. Capital letters represent levels, lower-case letters, annual average

rates of continuously compounded growth. β = capital's share in national income.

Y = real output
N = labor hours
K = capital service flow
Y/N = labor productivity
y–n = labor productivity growth
Y = $AK^{\beta}N^{1-\beta}$ = production function (Cobb-Douglas, constant returns to scale)
A = $Y/(K^{\beta}N^{1-\beta})$ = TFP
a = $y - \beta k - (1-\beta)n$ = growth rate of TFP
y = $a + \beta k + (1-\beta)n$ = growth rate of output and its decomposition
y–n = $a + \beta(k-n)$ = growth rate of labor productivity and its decomposition

With some important exceptions, the beginning and end points of the intervals in table 2.1 correspond to peaks in peacetime business activity, years in which unemployment was low and the economy close to potential output. The reason for preferring these intervals rather than, for instance, simply measuring between census years, is the well-documented procyclicality in measures of productivity, particularly TFP (Field, 2010). Periods in which census data are collected will not necessarily center on business cycle peaks, and measuring from trough to peak or peak to trough could give a misleading estimate of the trend growth rate of efficiency. To the extent possible, the measures that follow are peak to peak, although the paucity of annual data before 1929 makes it difficult for the three earliest intervals.

After examining the data collection procedures for those intervals, Creamer et al. (1960) concluded that the first benchmark poses a problem. Canvassers gathered information between June 1, 1899, and May 31, 1900. June was a business cycle peak, but the remainder of the collection interval included the better part of a contraction that went on for a year and half, bottoming out in December 1900. Because much of the information was collected during a contraction phase, the twelve-month interval should be thought of as closer to a trough than a peak. It is therefore likely that the trend growth rate between 1899 and 1909 in table 2.1 is overstated because the 1899 level experienced a greater reduction attributable to cyclicality than did the 1909 level.

Data for 1909 and 1919 were assembled mostly during months of expansion and are thus more easily comparable with later years such as 1929 and 1948, identified using annual data as business cycle peaks. Census takers collected the 1909 numbers from January through December, which included the last two-thirds of an expansion peaking in January 1910. Similarly, enumerators collected the 1919 data during that calendar year, which included a period of contraction through April but then an expansion through the remainder of 1919 that peaked in January 1920 (Creamer, Dobrovolsky, and Borenstein, 1960, pp. 17–18).

The year 1941 also requires comment. Although unemployment declined during the year, it still averaged close to 10 percent. Nevertheless, 1941 is the closest we can get to potential before the disruptive effects of full-scale war production kicked in and is therefore the best peacetime year to compare with other peacetime peaks. Although the entire economy may not yet have been operating at capacity, manufacturing was close to it, given the constraints imposed on the sector by its then-installed capital stock. Physical capital in 1941 had increased only 23 percent since 1929, but real manufacturing output was 70 percent above where it had been in 1929, and 3.4 times what it was in 1933. The growth from 1933 reflected recovery from the worst year of the Depression (hours had almost doubled since the trough), productivity gains, and a modest net increase in manufacturing structures and equipment (tables 2.2–2.4). While the output gap remaining in 1941 justifies a cyclical adjustment to productivity measures for broad aggregates such as the private nonfarm economy (PNE, everything except government and agriculture) or the private domestic economy (PDE, everything except government) (Field, 2003, 2011), there is less warrant for one for manufacturing.[3]

Without significant new investments in physical capital, there were limits in 1941 to how much real output could have increased. The move to a radically altered product mix after Pearl Harbor imposed additional constraints that would not have been experienced if output had increased without changing its proportionate composition. About 8 percent of manufacturing capacity, forced to shut down by limitation orders, would ultimately prove unable to participate in war production. And the altered final product mix meant changed derived demands for materials. The supply capabilities of the U.S. economy were optimized for the prewar product mix, and supply chains were not necessarily well suited or prepared to provide what was now needed. This aggravated shortages beyond those resulting from the simple increase in overall manufacturing output and beyond those consequent upon the abrupt reductions in the availability of natural rubber from Southeast Asia and deliveries of petroleum products to the East Coast.

Total manufacturing output nevertheless grew by more than one-third—36 percent—between 1941 and 1943. This was made possible by large infusions of the services of new physical capital—buildings and equipment—paid for mostly by the government, along with even larger increases in labor input. Capital service flows increased 32 percent as the result of the construction of new facilities and the production and installation of new machine tools. Labor hours grew 47 percent because of growth in average weekly hours along with inflows of workers from other sectors and those (including women) not previously in the labor force (Field, 2008). TFP declined because output grew more slowly than a combined input measure. Labor productivity declined because TFP declined and capital shallowed: labor input grew more rapidly than capital service flows.

For the postwar period, 1948 was clearly a peak. Demobilization was largely over and the economy, now on a civilian footing, was close to potential, as evidenced by the low—3.8 percent—unemployment rate. It is generally accepted that 1973 was the end of the postwar boom, the last year before the economy was hit with the oil shocks and the unemployment and rising inflation that ensued during the remainder of that decade. The period 1989–2008 experienced most of the benefits of the information technology productivity boom, the years in which the Solow paradox (computers are showing up everywhere except in the productivity statistics) finally resolved itself. That period is a noticeable oasis in a post-1973 productivity desert, but its record is dwarfed by what occurred during the interwar years. After hesitating during the height of the financial crisis of 2007–9, manufacturing TFP reached a peak in 2010 but declined subsequently. In 2019, before the pandemic, sectoral TFP remained 1.3 percent below its 2010 level.

We move now to compare rates of advance within manufacturing over the period 1941–48 with those experienced between 1929 and 1941. For the two decades spanned by these intervals we present annual data on levels, not just for the benchmark years, but also for those intervening. This enables us to examine productivity performance within the war period and across it. Let us begin by reviewing the historical context. For the 1920s (1919–29), Kendrick has TFP growth in manufacturing at 5.18 percent per year (see table 2.1), a figure accepted by Abramovitz and David (2000a, 2000b), Field (2003, 2011), and Gordon (2016). That extraordinary rate of advance, never again equaled, was fueled in part by a shift from mechanical to electrical means of distributing power within factories, a move away from the overhead metal shafts, pulleys, and leather belts that were the signature of nineteenth-century power-driven factories.

That transition, which accelerated (from low levels) after 1905, proceeded rapidly between 1909 and 1919, particularly in transport equipment and fabricated metals. It was stimulated and facilitated by sharp decreases in the cost of electric power and the development of smaller fractional horsepower electric motors. The price of a kilowatt hour (kWh) dropped precipitously between 1905 and 1917 before rising somewhat and then declining modestly between 1922 and 1929. The rise in the share of manufacturing horsepower powered by electricity tracks this decline closely in the 1909–19 period: as noted earlier, the percentage point increase in the share of electrified horsepower was considerably greater in those years than it was in the decade following (Jovanovic and Rousseau, 2005, pp. 1188, 1197, figures 2, 10). The payoff appeared with a lag, during the 1920s. According to table 2.1, TFP in manufacturing grew more slowly in 1909–19 compared with 1899–1909, although the 1899–1909 increase is probably overstated because of the cyclical effect previously discussed. By the end of the 1920s, electricity fueled almost two-thirds of manufacturing horsepower.

This, then, was the recent history as the manufacturing sector entered the two decades of depression, economic mobilization for war, and demobilization on which we now focus. A note about data. After 1947 we can turn to the full set of national income and product accounts maintained by the Bureau of Economic Analysis (BEA), and after 1948 we can rely on the productivity calculations made by the Bureau of Labor Statistics (BLS), although the productivity data for manufacturing, as opposed to total economy measures, only begin in 1949. Before 1947 the available data are not as extensive, although some of the government statistical series do extend earlier, and we will exploit them where they are available. Kendrick (1961) is the go-to source with which to begin any consideration of productivity in the United States before the second half of the twentieth century. Because it is the starting point for inquiries of this nature, we will compare estimates appearing in his book with those developed in this chapter.

Estimating Labor Productivity Growth

Calculating a growth rate of labor productivity requires estimates of real output growth and labor input growth. The most intuitively appealing procedure compares the number of units of a physically undifferentiated product with the number of hours of physically undifferentiated labor or the number of undifferentiated workers. In the numerator one avoids or abstracts from variation in the nature or quality of the output or the need to aggregate different kinds of products, and in the denominator one avoids or abstracts from variation in the motivation, education, skill, training, or health of the workers providing the labor power. Common examples are tons of pig iron produced annually per worker, numbers of first-class letters delivered per year per Post Office employee, or, to give an example that was calculated and widely used during and after the war, pounds of airframe produced per worker per month or year (see Hagen and Kirkpatrick, 1944, p. 477, n. 3; Aircraft Industries Association of America, 1953, table 2-15, based on BLS data).

Even within an individual plant, of course, production may consist of different physical commodities. The aircraft industry continued to use poundage as an aggregated measure of output throughout the 1950s and the 1960s (Aerospace Industries Association of America, 1971, pp. 30–31). This ignored output heterogeneity (airplane models were not all the same), although the numbers were obviously thought useful as a productivity metric applicable to the largest single category of World War II spending.

The most straightforward way to deal with heterogeneous output is to aggregate the different goods using market prices and then divide by the sum of labor inputs in the various product lines. If one lacks price data but has access to output quantities and labor input by product line, it is still possible to calculate productivity growth. Suppose an industry or firm produces different goods, each of which is stable in its characteristics. Construct time series where the annual observation for each product is the ratio of physical output (in units) to hours (or workers). From these series calculate labor productivity growth rates and then aggregate with weights equal to the shares of total hours used in the production of each good. Since the shares may change over time, average the shares at the beginning and end of the interval, and normalize so that the sum of the shares equals 1.[4]

This recipe was used in the National Research Project on Reemployment Opportunities and Recent Changes in Industrial Techniques conducted under the auspices of the Works Progress Administration (WPA) in the late 1930s, efforts described in Magdoff (1939) and Block and Burns (1986, pp. 769–70). The WPA project was concerned with technological unemployment—the extent to which increases in labor productivity and corresponding reductions in unit labor costs might be aggravating the Depression-era unemployment problem.

In the process the project succeeded in producing productivity growth estimates that were based on physical quantities alone for roughly half the manufacturing sector measured by employment. Some of the materials underlying labor productivity estimates for manufacturing in Kendrick (1961) are also based on physical quantities alone.

Unfortunately, reckoning productivity growth in this way does not deal well with a situation where the economy experiences a major change in its output mix. A 1946 Bureau of Labor Statistics report documented labor productivity advance between 1914 and 1941 using this method and then again during the rapid output growth and high output levels in the sector between 1941 and 1945, but it eschewed comparisons between the two periods: "Since the production pattern changes radically when the United States began its war program, it is not possible to measure the change in manufacturing efficiency from peace to war. To do this would require, for example, some equating of ships, planes, and munitions, against automobiles, vacuum cleaners or typewriters . . . hence it is not possible to state whether physical output per manhour increased or decreased when the automobile industry converted to war equipment" (U.S. Bureau of Labor Statistics, 1946, pp. 896–97). Labor productivity series in manufacturing relying on physical output measures during and preceding the war cannot simply be spliced together. One needs prices.

The development of a framework for national income and product accounts led, in the postwar period, to the availability of data on income originating in the different sectors of the economy. These data combine heterogeneous outputs based on their value; deflators are used to adjust the value series over time for the effects of price changes, as well as, where necessary and feasible, of quality improvements. It would be wrong, however, to suggest that the problems posed by the change in the product mix are thereby fully resolved. They are not. Nevertheless, an approach using such data offers some promise of moving beyond the pessimism expressed in the 1946 BLS report.

For Kendrick's manufacturing output series, I substitute one based on data first provided by the Office of Business Economics (precursor to the BEA) in 1966. That volume, which built on supplements to the *Survey of Current Business* in 1947, 1954, and 1958, extended national income and product data back to 1929. These data have been carried forward essentially unchanged in subsequent government publications and still represent the most detailed available analysis from the government statistical offices of income and product originating in different sectors of the economy during the years of concern here, 1929 through 1948.

The output measure is value added, not gross sales. Value added is the difference between gross sales and purchased materials, energy, and business services. Purchased inputs will show up in a manufacturing firm's gross output and revenue, but they represent the contributions of other firms' employees and owned capital to GDP, not those of the entity in question. Thus, an in-house attorney would contribute to a firm's value added, but contracted services from a law firm would not (although they would contribute to the law firm's value added). Similarly, equipment or buildings owned by a company would generate service flows contributing to that firm's value added, but machines rented from an equipment service provider or buildings rented from a company specializing in such transactions would not, although they would contribute to the business service providers' value added. The same would be true for purchased energy.

It is value added, not gross sales, that represents an organization's contribution to gross domestic product and to gross domestic income. A firm uses the services of its employees and owned capital to add value to its purchased materials, energy, and business services. It is that flow of additional value (revenue exceeding the cost of purchased inputs not including employed labor) that enables the firm to pay its wage and salary workers (including management), a return to the owners of and those who have provided financing for the firm's owned capital, and its tax liabilities. Because of the dual role of value added in contributing to both gross income and gross product, data on nominal income originating in a sector can stand in for value added. Value added for the manufacturing sector as a whole is the sum of value added by individual firms.

To estimate the growth of real output over time in a sector, one must remove the effects of price changes, a procedure unnecessary if output measures are restricted to physical quantities. I convert nominal income in the durables and nondurables subsectors (U.S. Department of Commerce, 1966, table 1.12, lines 13 and 24) into real value added using deflators for each subsector, also provided in the same source (table 8.6, lines 2 and 14; 1958 = 100). Summing across durables and nondurables to create annual levels enables calculation of a growth rate of manufacturing output of 4.43 percent per year between 1929 and 1941, and 1.98 percent per year between 1941 and 1948. This and all annual growth rates in this book, unless otherwise noted, are continuously compounded, calculated by taking the difference between the natural logarithm of the end year and the natural logarithm of the beginning year (or, equivalently, the natural logarithm of the ratio of the two years) and dividing by the number of years in the interval.

Table 2.2: Index of Manufacturing Output, 1929–48 1929 = 100.0

	1 Kendrick	2 Field	1/2 Ratio
1929	100.0	100.0	1.00
1930	85.6	86.8	1.01
1931	72.0	68.6	0.95
1932	53.8	47.4	0.88
1933	62.8	49.5	0.79
1934	69.1	64.5	0.93
1935	82.8	76.7	0.93
1936	96.8	93.2	0.96
1937	103.3	106.6	1.03
1938	80.9	84.8	1.05
1939	102.5	101.9	0.99
1940	118.6	125.6	1.06
1941	157.9	170.2	1.08
1942	197.2	198.4	1.01
1943	238.1	231.4	0.97
1944	232.5	219.2	0.94
1945	196.5	181.2	0.92
1946	160.6	164.4	1.02
1947	178.3	180.9	1.01
1948	184.2	195.5	1.06

Sources: Kendrick, 1961, pp. 465–66, table D-II; see text.

Kendrick did not have access to the 1966 Department of Commerce numbers when he published in 1961 (although his pioneering work probably helped the agency put them together). Table 2.2 compares the resulting series of levels with that provided by Kendrick (1961, appendix D, pp. 465–66). The real (inflation-adjusted) manufacturing series I construct tracks Kendrick's closely over the entire period, although there are some differences. Both are normalized to start at 100 in 1929, and the 1947 levels of the indexes are within 1 percent of each other. Because the level of Kendrick's index is 8 percent lower than mine in 1941, however, output growth using Kendrick is lower between 1929 and 1941 (3.8 percent per year versus 4.43 percent), but higher between 1941 and 1948 (2.20 percent versus 1.98 percent per year). My numbers show a considerably sharper decline during the worst years of the Depression (particularly 1932 and

1933), recovery to a higher level in 1937, and higher levels in 1940 and 1941. The Kendrick series, however, rises more sharply between 1941 and 1943, and falls off less rapidly through 1945 before plunging in 1946.

To obtain a series on person hours input, I begin with data on full-time equivalent workers (FTEs) in the sector drawn from the BEA's National Income and Product Accounts table 6.5a (available online at https://apps.bea .gov/iTable/index_nipa.cfm). These numbers are identical to those in Department of Commerce 1966, table 6.4, line 11, except for small downward revisions for 1947 and 1948. I combine these with data from *Historical Statistics of the United States* (Carter et al., 2006, series Ba4580) that show average weekly hours declining from 44.2 in 1929 to 40.6 in 1941 to 40.0 in 1948, although they rose sharply, albeit temporarily, during the war, peaking at 45.2 in 1944.

I estimate the growth rate of hours across particular intervals by adding the growth rate of weekly hours to the growth rate of FTEs, which will equal the growth rate of their product. Based on these calculations, hourly labor input in U.S. manufacturing grew at 1.22 percent per year between 1929 and 1941, and at 2.18 percent between 1941 and 1948. These are very close to growth rates based on Kendrick's man hours series for manufacturing, and between 1929 and 1947, inclusive, the levels of the indexes are never more than 1 percent apart. The biggest variance is for 1948, where my index for hours is 1.4 percent higher. Combining data on the growth of sectoral output and hours yields continuously compounded labor productivity growth (their difference) of 3.22 percent per year between 1929 and 1941 and .04 percent per year between 1941 and 1948.

The changes in labor productivity, however, cannot all be attributed to improvements in efficiency. Some may be the consequence of equipping each worker with more (or less) physical capital (capital deepening or shallowing).[5] Getting closer to what we mean by changes in efficiency requires an estimate of the growth rate of TFP. This requires an annual series on capital services input and the respective shares of labor and capital in national income with which to weight the growth rates of labor and capital services.

This in turn necessitates consideration of a complex, often confounding set of issues involved in the estimation of capital service flows. In proceeding along this route I have two different audiences in mind: those who are skeptical about TFP calculations, and those who are not. Excavating and describing these little-understood procedures can help those in the first group to better understand the aims and promise of the methodology and lead those in the second to better appreciate its limitations. What follows examines how U.S. statistical agencies approach the problem, what they aim to achieve, and the challenging conceptual and statistical terrain within which these efforts are undertaken. Understanding these issues helps in evaluating how our traditional reliance on wealth stocks as a proxy for service flows may bias our estimates of the latter.

Capital Services Input

Kendrick, as did most of the pioneers of growth accounting, treated capital service flows within the manufacturing sector as proportional to the value of capital stocks. He did not offer a complete annual series, reporting levels for 1919, 1937, and 1948 based on Creamer et al. (1960), but nothing for the intervening years. These lacunae are testimony to the greater conceptual and statistical challenges involved in calculating a series for capital services input as compared with output and hours. Some perspective on these challenges can be obtained by considering the very different types of data available for capital and labor, particularly as this applies to stocks as compared with flows, and the procedures in the case of capital for inferring the latter from the former.

In production function estimation and growth accounting, the services of labor and physical capital input are often treated symmetrically. But, of course, they are not. First, whether in active use or not, all physical capital is owned by some entity and can be bought and sold in primary and secondary markets. For stocks of labor power (able-bodied humans), this has simply not been the case since the abolition of slavery. Second, although every individual human is different, and labor services have different values, they have a natural metric: a person hour (or, historically, man hour). There is nothing comparable for physical capital.[6] Some writers talk about a machine hour, but machines are a small portion of the overall physical capital stock (structures dominate), and the hourly services of a drill press are clearly very different from those of an aircraft or a warehouse. An airplane is not simply a more efficient drill press or a warehouse with more education or experience.

These realities are reflected in the types of data available for the two classes of inputs. This is most apparent when considering the value of input stocks. For capital we have data on the prices of new assets when installed. Again, this is not applicable to labor, because labor cannot be owned (except in the sense of self-owned), and what is not owned is not bought and sold. For capital we also have used asset prices from secondary physical asset markets. These data are analogous to those generated in the used car market and available from Kelley Blue Book (www.kbb.com) by make and model, age, condition, mileage, and region. An important difference is that the market for used cars (the most important consumer durable) is for standardized products with a limited number of options. Producer durables, in contrast, are often custom-built and intended for a very specific use. The resale market for producer durables is much thinner. Data from sales in secondary markets are sparse, and there is some concern in the literature about the lemons problem: in thin markets sellers may be retaining the "good" assets and disposing of the stinkers (Hulten, 1990, p. 143). Again, in the case of labor, used "asset" prices are not available and the concept is not applicable.

When it comes to service flows, the situation is quite different. For labor, we have extensive information on the values of labor services that can be decomposed into quantities (hours worked) and prices (wage rates). For physical capital, we have data on the prices of service flows only for the few types of structures and equipment with active rental or operational lease markets. These include buildings, several types of transport equipment, including aircraft, and some types of construction equipment, but not machine tools or other types of production equipment, many of which are made for a specific purpose and often custom-designed. Even where good data on rental charges exist, they can be only an approximation for user cost, since they will also include the labor and capital costs of running the leasing operation itself (see OECD, 2009, p. 65), and will thus be somewhat higher than the true user cost of employing owned capital in production.

Finally, we have estimates of average service lives for each type of asset and retirement distribution functions. None of this is directly relevant for labor.

To summarize, we have excellent data for the value of labor service flows, broken down into quantities and prices, and only limited data on the value of stocks; such data arise sporadically from litigation or cost-benefit analyses where lawyers or economists are (controversially) compelled to come up with the remaining value of a human life or ability to work cut short. For physical capital, the statistical environment is almost the reverse. Comprehensive data are available on the values of assets, at least when they are new (the data on used assets are limited), and scattered data on the value of service flows. A consequence is that, unlike labor, the estimation of capital service flows and their growth continues to begin (and must necessarily begin) with estimates of the value of stocks. There are, however, different types of stock estimates, and which concept one uses matters. In particular, the task of constructing stocks whose value will grow at the same rate as the service flows they give rise to is different from simply asking what assets of different types and different vintages would command in the marketplace and then aggregating.

The OECD's *Measuring Capital* manual states that "there is now wide agreement that the contribution of capital to production should be measured in terms of the *flow of services* produced by capital assets rather than by the *stock* of these assets" (2001a, p. 9; emphases in original). Fair enough, but, as noted, in contrast with labor, the route to measuring these flows continues to run through stock estimates. These are not, however, the more familiar wealth or market value estimates. It is common for scholars to use data on net wealth stocks and assert or assume implicitly that service flows are proportional, and that the aggregate service flows change pari passu with the value of the stocks. The use of such proxies is often necessary, particularly in historical work, but the assumption is almost always questionable. What are desired are stocks specifically constructed so that service flows from them grow at the same rate as do the stocks themselves. The OECD and the U.S. Bureau of Labor Statistics call these *productive stocks*. Understanding the differences between wealth and productive stocks is essential in identifying whether service flows are likely to be under- or overestimated when wealth stocks are used in lieu of productive stocks.

The task of building productive stock estimates for different asset categories and then combining them so that the aggregate will grow at the rate of real capital services poses serious challenges. Different national statistical bureaus have resolved them differently. In describing current practices in estimating capital services input, my reference points will be the OECD manuals *Measuring Capital* (2001a; second edition, 2009) and *Measuring Productivity* (2001b), and various publications of the U.S. BLS (1997, 2007a, 2007b, 2017). The procedures described in these publications build on the work of statistical pioneers such as Raymond Goldsmith and John Kendrick. Practices have also been influenced by the theoretical work of such scholars as Robert Hall and Dale Jorgenson, although national statistical offices have not always followed all their recommendations or embraced all their assumptions. There is much confusion and few good descriptions about how capital service input is actually or ideally should be reckoned, which contributes to an opaqueness about this key input, and in turn, I think, to skepticism about TFP estimates and growth accounting methods in general.

In some circles that skepticism is a legacy of the Cambridge controversies that raged in the 1960s and early 1970s (Cohen and Harcourt, 2003). Economists based in Cambridge, England, critiqued mainstream (neoclassical) thinking about physical capital, where mainstream referred to economists domiciled in Cambridge, Massachusetts, mostly at Harvard and MIT. The critiques called into question—indeed denied—the possibility of calculating an aggregate of different types of capital goods, let alone their service flows, and raised important questions about the marginal productivity theory of income distribution, particularly as it applied to capital.

If Cambridge, England, had limited itself to pointing out that income distribution takes place within an institutional and historical context, it should not have been controversial. But although participants made references to the importance of history and politics, proponents evidenced relatively little interest in empirical or historical economics, or in statistical procedures that could be useful in understanding the course of development. The arguments were developed at a highly abstract level, were unremittingly critical, and in some instances descended into an almost celebratory nihilism. Although infrequently mentioned in recent decades, the controversy continues to exercise an influence on efforts to measure capital, capital service flows, and TFP.

The productivity programs developed by national statistical offices represented, in a sense, an attempted rejoinder to the various claims voiced during the controversies about what was and was not possible. Michael Harper (1999, p. 329) in fact described BLS procedures as having "gradually emerged" after (and in part in response to) that debate. Since the productivity calculations in this chapter and the data underlying them are a starting point for the argument of this book, I describe how the U.S. statistical agencies approach the challenge of estimating capital service inputs so that readers can understand both how my estimates for the years 1929 through 1948 are similar and how they differ from those constructed using more complete data for the postwar period, and what biases these differences may introduce.

Productive Stocks and Why They Differ from Wealth Stocks

A nation's or sector's productive stock, whose growth will track the growth of its service flows, will in almost all instances differ from a wealth stock. The monetary value of a nation's fixed assets—the wealth reflected in its capital—can be measured using the perpetual inventory method, cumulating gross investment additions and depreciation (capital consumption) subtractions. In a gross stock calculation, capital consumption is recorded when an asset is withdrawn from service; for a net stock, it is debited on an annual basis. Unfortunately, only under restrictive and unrealistic assumptions can a measure of the wealth stock for an asset type—particularly a net wealth stock—stand in for its value considered as a productive stock.

The reason is that for any particular asset type, service flow deterioration in most cases will progress more slowly than depreciation. The posited rate at which each takes place for an asset type is reflected for depreciation in an *age-price* profile and for deterioration in an *age-efficiency* profile. The distinction between the two is important and little understood. Hall (1968, p. 37) alluded to the ease of confusion between the two, and Hulten and Wykoff noted that "the general non-equivalence between the age-price profiles and the age-efficiency profile . . . is probably the most misunderstood relationship in all of depreciation theory" (Hulten and Wykoff, 1981, p. 90; see also Hulten, 1990, and Triplett, 1997).

A productive stock is built so that its growth rate will track the growth rate of its service flows. For a given asset type, different vintages will be weighted in accordance with the type's age-efficiency profile. In contrast, in a net wealth stock, different vintages are weighted by their market values, in accordance with the type's age-price profile.

Physical capital goods possess exceptional heterogeneity beyond differences attributable to the age of an asset within a category. In 2022 the U.S. Bureau of Labor Statistics constructed productive stocks for over one hundred different asset types, including multiple types of equipment, nonresidential structures, and residential structures (U.S. BLS, 1997, p. 92; 2017, pp. 2–3, table 1). Productive and wealth stocks differ both because of how the different vintages within an asset category are weighted, and because of how the stocks and growth rates of different asset types are combined.

We start with the first aggregation. The productive stock for an asset type will include multiple vintages. The service flows from earlier vintages will be lower because of declines in such flows during the interval between when the assets are installed and when they are retired according to differences reflected in the type's age-efficiency profile. These declines will be due to some combination of rising maintenance and repair costs, physical deterioration of the service flow, or obsolescence (Harper, 1982, p. 22). Generally accepted accounting procedures define repair and maintenance as expenses incurred to restore an asset to its earlier condition or to keep it performing at its current level. Such activity may enable the asset (when working) to yield the services it did when new, but the need for these expenditures and the downtime for maintenance or repair still reflect a decline in efficiency. After a certain point, repair and maintenance may no longer be capable of restoring the asset to a point where its service flow when working is like new. For a machine employed in manufacturing, for example, deterioration may be reflected in an increasing number of defective units produced (OECD, 2001a, p. 66). Service flow may also decay if the asset becomes obsolete because a newly developed asset type superior in performing the required function becomes available, because technological advance makes it incompatible with other complementary inputs, or because a change in the product mix reduces or eliminates the need for it.

Note that service flow decay could, temporarily, be negative in initial years, as a piece of machinery is run in or operators become familiar with its use. The key point is that both physical deterioration in the service flow when operating and increases in repair and maintenance costs and downtime contribute to declines in efficiency, as does possible obsolescence. A final set of factors to be considered in aggregating vintages within an asset category has to do with service lives—both their average and variance—the statistical distribution of withdrawals or scrappage rates.

In the United States the BEA calculates net wealth stocks by adding to last year's stock an estimate of gross investment and subtracting an estimate of depreciation; depreciation represents the decline in market value of each vintage of each physical asset type from one year to the next. The problem for productivity measurement is that regardless of the asset type, depreciation is unlikely to run at the same rate as the decline in service flow: indeed, it is likely to be more rapid.

A canonical illustration is a lightbulb. Suppose the bulb has a five-year life span and will not fail before then.[7] A user interested in annual lighting services should be completely indifferent between a two-year-old bulb and a four-year-old bulb and were there an established rental market for assets capable of generating flows of lighting service, the annual cost of renting should be identical. At the same time, the value of a four-year-old lightbulb, were it sold on a secondary market, would be considerably less than that of a two-year-old bulb because the potential buyer of the former would understand that the bulb had fewer useful hours remaining. One-hoss-shay deterioration is an extreme form of hyperbolic deterioration: efficiency deteriorates little or not at all initially, and then declines by larger amounts as the asset ages and, in the extreme case, all at once at the end of its useful life.[8]

Many household consumer durables come close to exhibiting such profiles, including electronics and small electric appliances. As for automobiles, the value of the service flow from a late-model vehicle remains relatively unchanged for a number of years after its purchase. Yet as the car ages, the percentage decline in the value of the asset will be greater than the percentage decline in the rental price of the service flow because buyers know that an older vehicle has fewer remaining years of reliable service before physical deterioration and higher repair and maintenance costs kick in. Consequently, the percentage decline in the value of the car between year 2 and year 3 will generally be greater than the percentage decline in the real services it can offer in year 3 as compared with year 2. As was true in the lightbulb example, the asset value will decline more rapidly than the annual rental value. Car rental companies charge the same for use of a two-year-old and a three-year-old vehicle, but the market values of cars of different vintages will differ: those that are older, with more mileage, will be lower. The same is true in the rental market for ski equipment.

Newly installed assets represent additions both to an asset type's productive stock and to its wealth stock. The following year, if the price of the type has increased, new gross investment must be deflated so that the stock is measured in dollars of similar purchasing power. If the newly installed goods are deemed to be of higher quality, the real value of that asset type's investment can be increased by adjusting the price deflator downward. As new investment adds to the wealth stock, depreciation (declines in market value) of older vintages subtracts from it; after debiting annual depreciation, we arrive at a net wealth stock estimate.

As new investment adds to the productive capital stock of an asset type, deterioration in the service flow from older vintages causes their weight to decrease, according to posited age-efficiency profiles. Except under the restrictive assumption that both deterioration and depreciation decline geometrically and at the same rate, age-efficiency profiles will differ from the age-price profiles reflecting depreciation. In the lightbulb example, the former profile is flat (horizontal) and then drops precipitously at the end of its service life. The age-price profile of the bulb will be different. The price (value) of the lightbulb, were it traded in secondary asset markets, would decline each year during the interval between when it is installed and when it fails and is retired.[9] Thus, the bulb's market value is depreciating throughout the interval between installation and retirement, even though its service flow remains unchanged—until the very end. The same was true throughout the one-hundred-year service life of Oliver Wendell Holmes's one-hoss shay.

A number of economists (in particular Jorgenson and Griliches, 1967, p. 255) have argued strongly for assuming geometric deterioration, which means that the service flow deteriorates by a constant fraction (percentage) of its previous end-of-year value. Double declining balance (DDB) deterioration is one instance. Under straight-line deterioration, an asset with a service life of ten years would find the value of its service flow dropping 10 percent from its first-year starting value. DDB deterioration would, in this case, mean a decline of 20 percent the first year, and then 20 percent of the value of the service flow in year 2, and so on. Note that in straight-line deterioration (or depreciation), the absolute amount of the decline is the same each year, but the percentage decline increases each year.

An inconvenient feature of geometric deterioration is that the service flow never drops completely to zero, as happens when the lightbulb burns out. Of greater concern is the realism of the assumption for assets (of which there are many) in which the real service flows drop slowly at first but by larger absolute amounts as the asset ages. For geometric deterioration, in contrast, the largest absolute declines occur when the asset is new. The main appeal of geometric deterioration is that, assuming that the constant annual deterioration fraction is the same as the constant annual depreciation fraction, it produces an age-efficiency profile in which the deterioration profile will approximate the more familiar depreciation profile. The age-price and the age-efficiency profiles for an asset category will be similar or, in the case of infinitely lived assets, identical.[10]

The assumption that both service flow and depreciation decline at the same geometric rate greatly simplifies matters because it eliminates the distinction between a productive stock and a wealth stock. It means that time series of real net stocks of capital as estimated by the BEA (where the subtractions from the perpetual inventory stock each year are based on depreciation) can be used for an asset class to approximate the profile over time of the service flow from that category. The question faced by statistical agencies is how much the appeal of convenience and computational simplicity should trump realism in dictating assumptions. At the present time there is a lack of consensus. Statistics Canada makes no distinction between the age-efficiency and age-price profiles, assuming geometric decline for both, but the U.S. Bureau of Labor Statistics opts for hyperbolic age-efficiency profiles (small absolute declines in efficiency during initial years, larger thereafter) that, its statisticians believe, more closely track the actual deterioration of service flow from physical assets. Thus the (productive) capital stocks used by the BLS in productivity calculations differ from the wealth stocks calculated by the BEA based on depreciation, an untidiness that bothers some economists (OECD, 2001a, p. 19; 2009, p. 92).

Apart from one-hoss-shay deterioration, almost all posited age-efficiency profiles are consistent with depreciation profiles that are convex to the origin under a reasonable range of assumed discount rates. For example, if we assume that the age-efficiency profile for an automobile exhibits small declines in service flows in initial years (is concave to the origin), this is easily consistent with age-price data that show relatively higher depreciation in initial years (convex to the origin). An age-price profile estimated from used asset data suggesting geometric depreciation is, therefore, not necessarily evidence that age-efficiency profiles also reflect geometric deterioration .

The OECD's 2001 *Measuring Productivity* manual declaimed strong prescriptive ambitions on this matter (2001b, p. 7), but the second edition of *Measuring Capital* (OECD, 2009), at least in some sections, pushed much more forcefully in the direction of standardizing on an assumption that both deterioration and depreciation proceed geometrically, on the basis of a new argument that the age-efficiency profile of an *individual member* of a cohort was not necessarily a good guide to the age-efficiency profile of an *entire cohort* (Hulten, 1990, p. 126). Even if one accepted the stylized fact for an individual asset (concavity to the origin of its age-efficiency profile), deterioration profiles for an entire cohort of an asset type might still be geometric (convex to the origin). Conclusion: "The **Manual therefore recommends the use of geometric patterns for depreciation** because they tend to be empirically supported, conceptually correct and easy to implement" (OECD, 2009, p. 12; boldface in the original).[11] The statement follows the claim that age-efficiency and age-price profiles are similar, and what is not stated, but should have been, is that the authors are also recommending the assumption of geometric, and similar, patterns for deterioration as well. The intent and motivation is made clear later in the manual: "As geometric efficiency and depreciation patterns immensely facilitate computational procedures for capital stocks and capital services, this is an important practical consideration" (OECD, 2009, p. 42).

Assuming similar geometric declines in both service flows and market values over time gives rise to age-efficiency and age-price profiles for an asset type that are equivalent, an equivalence that clearly facilitates estimation of service flow, given that one may be more likely to have data of the latter type. The question is how strong are other arguments in favor of the assumption. The cohort claim is based on the idea that if n identical copies of an asset with an average service life of t years are installed in a given year, not all will be withdrawn from service exactly t years later. The distribution of withdrawals can be particularly wide for transport equipment, for example, which is subject to statistically foreseeable accidents that will lead to the retirement of vehicles even when they are, as it were, in the prime of life. The illustrations in section 13 (OECD, 2009, pp. 105–22) make the connection appear more compelling than it is, and the extent to which this argument justifies the manual's recommendation that statisticians assume similar age profiles for deterioration of service flow and depreciation of market value remains questionable.[12]

Hard evidence on age-efficiency profiles is scarce because it depends on the existence of active and thick rental markets for asset service flows. The data we do have, such as rental rates for late-model cars of different vintages, suggest limited efficiency drop-off in initial years. Hyperbolic age-efficiency profiles are concave to the origin because efficiency deteriorates only slowly in the initial years. They have considerable intuitive appeal because they conform with our individual experience with automobiles and other consumer durables.

For these reasons and others, the case for universal adoption of geometric deterioration/depreciation, although prosecuted vigorously by influential economists, has not been universally accepted, particularly within the statistical agencies. This is reflected in a 1982 BLS working paper by Harper and at multiple points in more recent OECD and BLS manuals. That said, positions on either side of the issue lack strong empirical foundation. Indeed, a 1983 BLS bulletin stated frankly that the assumed age-efficiency profiles were "a 'prior' based on cursory observations and informed discussions with businessmen" (U.S. Bureau of Labor Statistics, 1983, p. 45).

A productive capital stock can be thought of as equivalent to the number of newly installed units of an asset type that would be needed to generate service flows equivalent to what can be generated with an existing stock consisting of different vintages. The application of the estimated age-efficiency profiles to previously installed vintages in constructing the stock ensures this equivalence. The OECD manuals refer to *standard efficiency units* as the annual physical services that can be provided by one new unit of the asset type, and thus the time series for a productive capital stock of an asset type is reckoned in these units. Given the current price of one new investment good of this type, the stock can be assigned a monetary value, which in most cases will differ from the monetary value of the stock considered as wealth.

Combining Asset Type Productive Stocks into an Aggregate

We turn now to the other main dimension of heterogeneity, that involving different types, rather than different vintages of the same type. Time series of productive stocks for each asset class must be combined to create index numbers for the levels of an aggregate productive stock consistent with its growth rate. To arrive at the aggregate growth rate, the growth rate of the productive stock of each asset type is weighted by the type's share in total capital compensation. As noted, the productive stock for an asset category can be thought of as consisting entirely of new units, or standard efficiency units. Capital compensation shares are determined, for each type, by answering this question: How much revenue could the rental of one such unit, or $100 worth of this stock, bring in during a year? This will vary according to the type, mostly because some asset types suffer much more depreciation in value and (ultimately) deterioration in service flow per year of life than others. An owner of a capital asset will derive an annual return, either by using it in her own production or by renting it out. In equilibrium, this will equal user cost, which will consist of two main components. In addition to returning to its owner compensation for the opportunity cost of immobilizing financial capital in it, it must, over its lifetime, recover the ravages of depreciation.

For the few types with active used asset markets, annual depreciation can be approximated from data on transactions in these markets, just as, for those few asset types with active rental markets for different vintages, annual deterioration in service flow can be estimated from those markets. Unfortunately, both types of data are rare: for most producer durables we lack anything analogous to the numbers available for automobiles. Residential house values and rental rates are widely available on sites such as Zillow.com, but there is little comparable for commercial properties, which turn over much less frequently. Nevertheless, the BEA does its best to estimate depreciation, and a government or corporate bond rate can be used to approximate what might otherwise have been earned by the financial capital invested in the asset stock. And the BLS does its best to estimate service flow deterioration

Note again that, except where one accepts identical geometric rates of decline of both depreciation and deterioration, the annual percentage depreciation of an asset will not equal the annual percentage decline in what the service flow can sell for. Market value will, instead, in equilibrium reflect the decline in the discounted present value of the annual service flows remaining until retirement. Thus, returning to the lightbulb example, before failure and retirement there will be no decline from one year to the next in the service flow from the bulb or what its annual rental will cost for the renter or fetch for its owner. But the asset value will depreciate from year to year as the remaining number of annual rental cycles shrinks. The service flow remains the same but the shares of user cost representing depreciation as opposed to compensation for the opportunity cost of immobilizing financial capital will vary over the bulb's lifetime (for a formal mathematical treatment, see Hulten, 1990, pp. 127–30).

By construction, the productive stock for each category will have associated with it a service flow proportional to it, which implies that service flows for an asset type will grow at the same rate as its productive stock. But the proportionality factors will differ across asset types, which must be taken into account in building a time series of index numbers for an aggregate stock that will reflect its growth rate. The main influence on those differences will be differences in asset lives: shorter-lived assets, regardless of the shape of their age-efficiency profile, must recover each year, on average, more depreciation than longer-lived assets. Differences in the depreciation rates will be the principal drivers of differences in the user costs of different types of assets, and one of two main influences on the share of an asset type in capital compensation. Higher overall rates of return can soften these differences but not change the most important influence on them. Robert Barro stated the obvious, given the definition of user cost: "For a given required rate of return on capital, the rental price . . . is higher if the depreciation rate is higher" (1998, p. 4).

Wealth stocks for asset types can be added together to create an aggregate wealth stock. But although each of the individual productive stocks can be given a dollar value, they cannot simply be summed to produce an aggregate stock whose growth rate will track the service flows from it. The growth rates of a type's productive stock and its service flows will be equivalent. But the ratio of the service flow to the productive stock will differ among the different types, principally because some asset categories have shorter service lives and therefore, on average, incur more annual depreciation.

Shares in capital compensation are the product of a type's productive stock measured in standard efficiency units and its (implicit) rental price (user cost) divided by total capital compensation. These shares are used to weight the growth rates of the different productive stocks to produce an aggregate index. The BLS uses a Törnqvist procedure, which weights the log percentage increase for each type's productive stock between adjacent years by the type's average share of capital compensation in the two years. The end product is a time series of index numbers reflecting the growth of an aggregated productive capital stock that will also track the growth of the aggregated annual service flows emanating from it.

If all the individual asset type productive stocks increased at the same annual rate, there would be no need to create a weighted average in figuring an
aggregate growth rate. The growth rate of any would give us the growth rate of
the aggregate. But since they do not all grow at the same rate, weighting matters. For example, when the productive stock of shorter-lived equipment rises
more rapidly than productive stocks of longer-lived asset types, capital services
input will increase more rapidly than would be indicated by an unweighted
average of the growth rates of the different subclasses of the productive stock.

The procedures used by the BLS in calculating aggregate capital service input introduce additional complexity by allowing for the possibility that different asset classes have associated with them different risk-adjusted opportunity
costs. The agency allocates BEA property income to different asset classes and
then subtracts depreciation. The residual represents the net return, which is
divided by the asset type's net wealth stock, yielding the type's rate of return.[13]
This procedure has, however, a downside. In a year in which gross operating
surplus is low, it can result in the anomaly of negative user costs. For details,
see Harper (1999) and BLS (2007a).

An alternative and simpler approach, now preferred by the BLS, is to use a
government or corporate bond rate to measure the opportunity cost of tying
up financial capital in a physical asset, adding to that estimates of the rate of
depreciation in market value (capital consumption) (see OECD, 2001a, pp. 88–
89). Between the two methods, the OECD manual states, "no strong conclusion has been reached on the matter and much speaks for solutions that are
governed by data availability" (OECD, 2001a, p. 89). The objective in either case
is to construct an aggregated productive stock that will grow at the same rate
as its aggregated service flows.

The procedures described above represent contemporary thinking about
how best to measure changes in capital input over time. They do not address
all the concerns raised by Cambridge, England, in the 1960s and 1970s. In particular, the role of an aggregated capital stock in determining the overall rate
of return—and thus capital's share—remains murky. It is often stated that
given an age-efficiency profile for an asset type, and an average asset life and
a distribution of retirements, one can determine an age-price profile. But as
the second edition of the OECD's *Measuring Capital* manual repeatedly notes,
moving from one to the other requires an externally specified rate of return
(this was less clear in the first edition). Without that, or the imposition of
identical geometric rates of service flow deterioration and market value depreciation, there is "a possible circularity when the rate of return is computed

endogenously and when the age-price profile is derived from the age-efficiency profile: a rate of return is needed to compute the age-price profile and hence depreciation. But the rate of depreciation is needed to compute the endogenous rate of return" (OECD, 2009, p. 102).

Another concern, given the underlying heterogeneity of assets, is that defining the number and boundaries of asset types involves some degree of arbitrariness. Even with a number of asset types exceeding one hundred, there will remain substantial nonvintage heterogeneity within each type, rendering the identification of an appropriate deflator for annual additions even more fraught than it already is, given the challenges of dealing with quality change.

In 1981 John R. Hicks described the measurement of capital "as one of the nastiest jobs that economists set to statisticians" (Hicks, 1981, p. 204, quoted in Hulten, 1990, p. 119). One can surely say the same about capital services, as Hulten's 1990 survey repeatedly attests, and as readers will almost certainly agree. That said, the writing of macroeconomic history requires asking and answering questions such as whether more physical capital services were devoted to the U.S. manufacturing sector in 1943 than was true in 1941. Growth accounting and the estimation of TFP require measures of capital service inputs, and so the issue comes down to whether the approaches described in this chapter, and the data sources supporting them, despite their limitations, allow insights that might otherwise be unattainable. I believe they do, and that they often suggest a narrative that can point us in the direction of other evidence, both quantitative and qualitative, that may qualify, confirm, or refine it. That is the motivation (and justification) for the approach followed in Field (2003, 2011), and in this work.

Estimates of Capital Input and TFP Growth, 1929–48

I now describe construction of a capital input series in manufacturing during the years 1929–48, which, along with series on output and labor input described earlier, underlie estimates of TFP. The intent here is to develop capital input numbers that are based on a limited number of transformations and then discuss possible biases introduced by the statistical sources used and how sensitive the resulting TFP estimates might be to them. In historical work we are often forced to use wealth stocks as a proxy for capital service flows in lieu of the more conceptually appealing productive stocks. It is important to understand up front that this practice is quite likely to understate the growth of capital service flows and, consequently, overstate TFP growth. The reasons for this, as well as other possible biases in the estimates, are discussed in the following section.[14]

As in so much historical work, productive stock estimates are not available. We must begin with wealth stocks and then consider whether they are likely to lead to an under- or overestimate of capital service flow and how that affects estimated TFP growth rates. The starting point here is the BEA's Fixed Asset Table (FAT) 4.2, line 9, which provides chain type quantity indexes for the net stock of private fixed assets in the sector going back to 1925 (the Fixed Asset Tables are available at https://apps.bea.gov/iTable/index_FA.cfm). A reminder again: net wealth series may not accurately proxy trends in capital service flow in ways outlined in the previous section and considered in the next.[15]

The BEA adopted chained index methods for measuring growth rates in 1996 and has applied them to output and, as in this case, to fixed assets. For each of two adjacent years the various vintages of the assets are valued first in the prices of the initial year, and then in the prices of the second year (see Landefeld and Parker, 1997). Growth rates are calculated using initial-year prices (a Laspeyres measure) and second-year prices (a Paasche index), and a geometric average of the two is taken. The output of this calculation is used to increment the index number for the capital stock, creating a Fisher ideal index (both the Törnqvist and the Fisher ideal index are discrete time approximations of a Divisia index, a method for aggregating continuous-time growth rates of variables).

This series shows that private-sector manufacturing capital grew across the Depression years (1929–41) at 1.11 percent per year and at 3.90 percent per year between 1941 and 1948.

The series does not include government-owned manufacturing capital operated by contractors. These plants and facilities were funded largely by the Defense Plant Corporation, a subsidiary of the Reconstruction Finance Corporation, and played a crucial role in American manufacturing beginning in 1941. As has been noted, the federal government spent almost a quarter of a billion dollars ($223.6 million), for example, building the Ford Motor Company's massive Willow Run facility. We can be sure that the BEA series does not include such capital because it shows the net stock of privately owned manufacturing capital *declining* between 1942 and 1943, whereas it is certain the total stock in use increased substantially in those two years. The prices contractors were able to charge the government for the output they manufactured included a return on the employed (but not necessarily owned) capital, which, as Gordon observed, was registered in the national income and product data, along with the wages and salaries paid by the contractors (Gordon, 1969, p. 222).

It is imperative that some proxy for the services provided by the government capital be included in the TFP calculations.[16] Their value cannot be measured directly, so as is always the case with capital, one begins with evidence on the value of stocks. To create a combined measure of both privately owned and government-owned capital used in manufacturing during the war, I have first cumulated government expenditures on manufacturing plant and equipment (1958 dollars) and subtracted retirements as summarized in Gordon (1969, table 4). I have then converted the time series for current-cost net stock of privately owned manufacturing capital (U.S. BEA FAT 6.1, line 12) into 1958 values for each year between 1941 and 1948 by multiplying each annual value by the ratio of the implicit GDP deflator for nonresidential fixed investment in 1958 to its value in the year in question (U.S. BEA NIPA table 1.1.9, line 9). This values everything in 1958 prices and enables calculation of the ratio of government-owned to privately owned manufacturing capital in each year during the war. Finally, I go back to the chained index series for private-sector manufacturing capital and augment it by multiplying by 1 plus that ratio for each year. This increases manufacturing capital by about 8 percent in 1941, 27 percent in 1942, 41 percent in 1943, 50 percent in 1944, and 32 percent in 1948, and increases the 1941–48 growth rate of manufacturing capital to 6.75 percent per year.[17]

Combining this series with data on output and labor input in the fundamental growth accounting equation, and weighting capital growth by .3 and labor input growth by .7, yields manufacturing TFP growth of 3.05 percent per year between 1929 and 1941, and −1.40 percent per year between 1941 and 1948 (see table 2.1).[18] These numbers differ from the 2.76 per year between 1929 and 1941 and -.35 percent per year reported by Field (2011).[19]

Note again that in this calculation we are measuring from premobilization to the first fully employed post-demobilization year. By 1948 the economy was once again on a largely civilian footing. We are ultimately interested in whether wartime manufacturing experience positively influenced sector-wide rates of productivity growth between 1941 and 1948 and in subsequent years. That said, an important intervening question is whether productivity increased from 1941 to 1942, to 1943 (the peak of wartime industrial production using monthly data), to 1944 (the peak using annual data), or to 1945. The data show that labor productivity and TFP within the sector fell sharply during the war years.[20]

Table 2.3: Indexes: U.S. Manufacturing, 1929–48 1929 = 100.0

	LP	TFP	Output	Hours	Capital
1929	100.0	100.0	100.0	100.0	100.0
1930	102.1	96.6	86.8	85.0	102.1
1931	98.9	88.3	68.6	69.4	101.4
1932	85.4	71.9	47.4	55.5	98.6
1933	83.2	71.8	49.5	59.5	97.3
1934	102.7	90.2	64.5	62.8	96.9
1935	108.5	98.6	76.7	70.7	97.1
1936	113.6	107.3	93.2	82.0	99.1
1937	120.2	115.0	106.6	88.7	102.8
1938	120.2	107.3	84.8	70.5	103.1
1939	125.9	116.9	102.7	81.5	104.4
1940	139.7	131.9	125.6	90.0	108.9
1941	147.1	144.3	170.2	115.7	123.4
1942	138.8	137.5	198.4	142.9	147.6
1943	136.2	138.1	231.4	169.9	162.3
1944	131.1	129.3	219.2	167.2	175.3
1945	126.4	117.9	181.2	143.3	181.0
1946	129.8	117.5	164.4	126.7	176.5
1947	135.7	122.3	180.9	133.4	188.6
1948	147.5	133.4	195.5	130.8	198.0

Note: LP = labor productivity; TFP = total factor productivity.
Source: Table 2.1; see text.

Between 1941 and 1943, real manufacturing output rose 15.4 percent a year, and hours by 19.2 percent a year; labor productivity fell at a rate of 3.8 percent per year. Of that decline, 1.66 percentage points can be attributed to capital shallowing, and the remainder to declining TFP (see below). Capital services grew more slowly than hours: 13.7 percent per year. Bringing these numbers together, TFP declined at a rate of –2.18 percent per year between 1941 and 1943. Between 1941 and 1944, decline was at –3.66 percent per year, and between 1941 and 1945 at –5.05 percent (see table 2.3). This contrasts with the two years before mobilization (1939–41), during which manufacturing TFP grew at 10.5 percent per year, reflecting strong secular TFP growth across the Depression years along with the predictable effects of a cyclical recovery. The decline of manufacturing productivity between 1941 and 1945 almost completely wiped out the gains made between 1939 and 1941.

Between 1945 and 1948 TFP recovered at 3.5 percent a year, but this was from the very low levels of 1945 and 1946, which were also affected by the disruptive effects of demobilization. This immediate postwar recovery still left the 1948 level substantially below where it had been in 1941. Reconversion required unwinding many of the wartime changes as the economy returned to a peacetime product mix. One should again note the importance of including government-owned plant and equipment in calculating manufacturing TFP. Its inclusion reduces the index number for sectoral TFP for 1942 from 147.7 to 137.5; for 1943 from 150.0 to 138.1; for 1944 from 146.0 to 129.3, and for 1945 from 132.9 to 117.9 (the latter numbers appear in table 2.3). Absent the upward adjustment in capital services input, manufacturing TFP would show a more moderate decline between 1941 and 1948.

Figure 2.1 displays the evolution of labor productivity and TFP over the years 1929 through 1948. During this two-decade period, the U.S. manufacturing

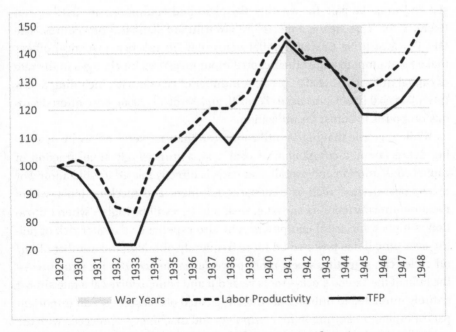

Figure 2.1. Indexes of labor productivity and TFP, U.S. manufacturing, 1929–48; 1929 = 100.0. Source: Table 2.3.

sector experienced two sharp four-year declines in productivity. During the first, between 1929 and 1933, TFP in the sector fell more than 28 percent, coinciding with the worst years of the Depression. During the second, between 1941 and 1945, TFP declined 18 percent, coinciding with the war. The causes of these two episodes were, however, very different.

The Depression-era collapse was largely the result of a decline in aggregate demand and, correspondingly, output and employment. Measures of TFP are highly procyclical in peacetime (see Field, 2010). Various explanations have been advanced, the most popular of which has been labor hoarding. Because of the costs of hiring and training workers, firms initially retain workers, even if they are underused. Output falls more than recorded and paid man hours, which mean that both labor productivity and TFP decline. But this dynamic is unlikely still to have been operative by the time we reach 1933, so it is unpersuasive as an explanation of the steep productivity drops between 1929 and 1933.

In contrast with what is true for labor, the private sector considered as an aggregate can't lay off its physical capital stock: most capital service flows persist and must be paid for whether the plant and equipment are used or not (Field, 2010). This view is reflected in government statistical procedures. The OECD's *Measuring Capital* manual notes that "in practice, statistical offices make no attempt to adjust their capital input measures for changes in the rate of capital utilization" (2001a, p. 84). A number of economists, including Solow (1957), Massell (1960), and Basu, Fernald, and Kimball (2006), have offered various proposals to adjust for utilization.

While it is true that higher utilization can increase service flow by increasing depreciation, a component of user cost, a surprisingly small fraction of capital consumption and overall user costs is directly related to utilization. For mechanical devices such as transport equipment and machine tools, where metal-on-metal friction is an issue, wear and tear will be higher when utilization is higher. Electrical equipment may also experience a higher risk of failure over time if it is powered on more frequently, although the number of on/ off cycles can sometimes be a more powerful influence. But for structures—the bulk of the capital stock—roofs wear out and paint oxidizes at a rate almost entirely unrelated to utilization. And anticipated obsolescence—an important part of capital consumption for computers and machinery—proceeds with the pace of technological advance and, for special-purpose tools or facilities, the change in the product mix. Neither is likely to be affected much by downtime resulting from deficiencies in aggregate demand.

Again, to quote the OECD's *Measuring Capital* manual, "In order to be counted as part of the capital stock all that is required is that assets are present at production sites and capable of being used in production or that they are available for renting by their owners to producers" (2001a, p. 31). The first part of this sentence might be said to be applicable to salaried workers—their hours are considered labor input whether they're browsing Facebook or ordering from Amazon while at their desks. But the second half of the sentence is clearly not applicable to labor in non-slave systems. The relevant difference between capital and labor from the employer's standpoint is that labor can be laid off, in which case its maintenance is the problem or responsibility of no business enterprise. When aggregate demand goes down, utilization of both labor and capital declines. But labor can be let go, which means the user costs from the standpoint of employers mostly vanish. Almost all the user costs of capital, on the other hand, continue irrespective of utilization. Capital service flows continue to be counted in the productivity calculations, and TFP declines. This should not be dismissed as a statistical artifact. The broader OECD *Measuring Productivity* manual notes that on the issue of adjusting capital input measures for utilization, "a generally accepted solution—*if desirable*—has yet to crystallize" (2001b, p. 56; emphasis added). My position is that, on balance, it is not desirable.

This idea can be made more concrete by considering a second home—a vacation house. The user costs of owning this asset will include the opportunity cost of holding wealth in this form (the monetary value could have been held in stocks or government bonds) and the depreciation on the building and its contents along with the maintenance and repair required to forestall depreciation. True, the stove and refrigerator and dishwasher and microwave may wear out a little more quickly if they are used more often than if they are not, but the computer in the house is becoming obsolete at the same rate, the roof is wearing out at the same rate, the exterior stain is oxidizing at the same rate, irrespective of the number of days of occupancy. Selling the asset merely transfers these user costs to another owner.

It is common to see TFP rise more slowly or actually decline during business downturns, as it did between 1929 and 1933. It is not common to see such outcomes when aggregate demand is growing rapidly. And for this reason, it is obviously not possible to explain the sharp decline in productivity between 1941 and 1945 in the same way. In spite of tax increases and controls on consumption and private investment, aggregate demand between 1941 and 1945 rose sharply because of growth in federal government spending and monetary ease. Inflationary pressures were contained through rationing and price controls. Output was above potential.

A key contributor to declining manufacturing TFP between 1929 and 1933 was idle capacity. Idle capacity also played a role between 1941 and 1945, but for entirely different reasons. Wartime declines in manufacturing productivity were the consequence of disrupted supply conditions resulting in part from the forced requirements of absorbing large amounts of new plant and equipment and labor in a historical environment where there was tremendous pressure to manufacture an altered product mix quickly. Approximately 8 percent of the 1941 manufacturing capital stock, although shut down by limitation orders, never successfully transitioned to use in defense production. The Japanese conquest of Singapore in February 1942 almost eliminated imports of natural rubber, and German U-boat predation in 1942 had a similar effect on crude oil and petroleum deliveries to the Eastern Seaboard. Selective Service manpower demands exhausted labor reserves and by the end of 1943 had precipitated a shortage of industrial labor more severe than any the country had previously experienced.

Endemic shortages caused manufacturing labor and capital periodically to stand idle or be less than fully utilized, a syndrome aggravated by producer hoarding in response to anticipated shortages. Throughout the period many manufacturers struggled as they shifted from producing goods in which they had a great deal of experience to those in which they did not. Buffeted by adverse supply shocks, the economy was nonetheless able to increase output substantially because those shocks were more than counterbalanced by the increase of capital and labor inputs. Production increased while productivity declined, in spite of the learning by doing in producing some products that eventually ensued.

In an October 9, 1945, report, *Wartime Production Achievements and the Reconversion Outlook,* J. A. Krug, the final chairman of the War Production Board (WPB), was in a celebratory frame of mind: "This country has just demonstrated a degree of resourcefulness, of strength, of productivity far greater than many of us dared imagine a few years ago."[21] He argued that productivity (output per man hour) increased sharply between 1939 and 1944, and he went on to claim that we "superimposed war production on our normal production job, instead of substituting guns for butter" (U.S. War Production Board, 1945a, p. 1). What he chose not to emphasize was the very substantial output gap existing in 1939. That meant that part of an increase in output composed of both guns and butter reflected a northeast movement from within the production possibility curve toward its frontier.

Manufacturing employment increased from 10.2 million in 1939 to 16.6 million in 1944, while the sector's share of the civilian labor force grew from 19 to 26 percent. By 1944, 57 percent of manufacturing employment was in war work, compared with 1 or 2 percent in 1939 (U.S. War Production Board, 1945a, p. 5). Considering the growth in the sector overall, this meant that manufacturing employment in work that was not war-related declined roughly 30 percent (10.2 million to 7.2 million) over that five-year period.

When new products or processes are introduced, new facilities must be constructed and old ones reconfigured, and labor must develop new capabilities. We have already mentioned the effect on automobile production (and indeed GNP) of Ford's switch from Model T to Model A assembly in 1927. Jovanovic and Rousseau, as we have seen, have documented this dynamic as it applied to the internal distribution of power within U.S. factories during the first three decades of the twentieth century. They have also suggested, along with others, that slow productivity growth in the 1970s resulted from the initial stages of computerization, although the application of the argument in that instance is less persuasive, given the two massive oil shocks that marked that decade and the small share of information technology in the economy at the time. But the dynamic they describe does help us understand one of the forces depressing productivity in U.S. manufacturing between 1941 and 1945.

Consider another thought experiment. Suppose a group of economics professors is told that for reasons of national security they must shift from teaching economics to teaching Arabic or Mandarin Chinese, and they must do so as soon as possible. (This is obviously a far-fetched example, since it is well-known that economics instruction is indispensable.) Some, echoing Henry Ford, will announce that teaching Arabic or Mandarin Chinese is not different in principle from teaching economics and will plunge ahead. Regardless of their initial confidence and bravado, most will discover that this is not true, and that although there is some overlap in terms of what is needed in the classroom, the "products" are quite different. To assist in the effort, the government funds and builds hundreds of state-of-the-art labs specialized for instruction in these languages. Massive amounts of new investments in human capital are also required, and it will be months before any of the new classes can be taught, a period during which output (learning outcomes) will be dramatically depressed, even though inputs of both labor and capital service flows will be high and rising. Economics instruction will have largely ceased during this time; as a consequence, measured teaching productivity will have declined dramatically.

Eventually the new courses will be rolled out, and faculty will, with experience, become more proficient at what they are doing. Gradually learning outcomes (output) will improve. Then, roughly three years later, the national emergency ends, and the faculty are told to go back to teaching economics. Cognitive dissonance and a search for silver linings will lead many to identify ways in which the experience was positive and had caused them to rethink their pedagogy, with persisting benefits. They will marvel at how they went from being unable to teach Arabic or Mandarin Chinese to being able to do so reasonably well. But the brute fact is that whatever side benefits may have come from this experience—and there will be some—will be dwarfed by the opportunity costs: a hiatus in economics instruction, a three-year gap in economics research programs, and the limited attention these faculty have been able to devote to the progression of the field during this national emergency. The economic value of the human capital accumulated to teach the foreign languages will be almost entirely written off because these faculty will never be asked to teach those classes again. The labs, optimized for the teaching of these two languages, gather dust and are eventually scrapped.

This thought experiment, unrealistic though it may be, helps illustrate one of the dynamics retarding U.S. manufacturing productivity during and after the war. The narrative history of U.S. wartime productivity has focused almost entirely on the eventual productivity recoveries that took place, ignoring the negative shocks and losses associated with the altered product mix and the intermittently idled capacity resulting from shortages and hoarding of scarce materials, components, and sometimes labor. Subsequent chapters will detail how, after the war, most of what firms learned producing B-24s and Sherman tanks, and most of the special-purpose machine tools manufactured to facilitate their production, was scrapped, written off, or vastly reduced in value because the country stopped making most of the products. This lopsided attention to the equivalent of eventually getting good at teaching Arabic or Mandarin Chinese has obscured the sharp reduction in efficiency resulting from the altered output mix mandated by wartime exigency, then reversed almost as quickly as it had been imposed.[22]

Looking closely at the progression of manufacturing labor productivity between 1941 and 1945, one sees that the largest percentage decline took place between 1941 and 1942. In addition to the challenges of trying to produce unfamiliar products, this can be attributed to the severe materials shortages that developed during 1942, which gave rise to what came to be known as priorities unemployment. Many firms subject to limitation orders ceased making metals-using consumer durables but had great difficulty or were simply unable to obtain the materials and machine tools they needed to start producing the new goods. Machine tools did not go to the highest bidder but had been allocated (rationed) by the Defense Plant Corporation starting in December 1940, a year before Pearl Harbor (Hyde, 2013, p. 41).

In 1943 labor productivity declined less and TFP eked out a small increase, reflecting the eventual gains in mass-producing important military capital goods, including planes, ships, and tanks. In 1944 and 1945 productivity resumed its sharp downward trajectory, as additional major changes in the output mix coincided with the heaviest fighting of the war by U.S. forces and as manpower scarcity added to continuing materials and component shortages to drag down productivity. Numbers for 1945 were further reduced by disruptions associated with demobilization. Plants had to pivot from struggling to meet wartime production quotas, still driven by the expectation of a protracted and bloody land invasion of Japan, to scrambling to unclog production facilities by clearing out unfinished goods in process, inventories, and specialized machine tools to make way for the resumption of civilian production, all of this complicated by a historically unprecedented strike wave after the war ended.

In *National Product in Wartime* (1945), Simon Kuznets struggled with how to combine war goods with the rest of the economy to obtain measures of real national product. Working within a rudimentary national income and product statistical apparatus, he despaired of valuing the output of munitions at administered prices, instead doing so based on measures of resource inputs, adjusted according to his judgment about the relative efficiency of input use in 1943 as compared with 1939. He allowed that evidence on this matter was scarce, "scattered" information consistent with a rise in labor productivity in aircraft and merchant ships, but also, suggesting movement in the opposite direction, "fragmentary data on loss of labor time paid for due to labor hoarding, difficulties of obtaining a smooth flow of materials and components, and troubles arising from rapid modifications in technical specifications due to fluid conditions of modern warfare." He made clear that there was no contradiction between allowing for a rapid growth in efficiency following its initial sharp depression, and a conclusion that the 1943 level of productivity was below prewar levels (Kuznets, 1945, pp. 49, 51).

Kuznets experimented with several assumptions about the productivity trend, but his preferred premise was that efficiency in the war industries was

20 percent below what it had been in 1939. He quickly noted that this should not be taken as a negative verdict on the country's production achievements. At the same time, "it would be misleading to ignore the patent fact that resources were not used as economically as they might have been had more efficient methods feasible with slower growth under more normal competitive conditions been possible. . . . Assigning to war production a lower level of relative efficiency in the first half of 1943 than existed in similar industries before the war is decidedly more justifiable than putting it at the same or higher level." Elsewhere he spoke of the "haste and waste of wartime."

His views on productivity trends within munitions and the relative priorities accorded to speed and efficiency in war production echo those advanced here for the manufacturing sector as a whole (Kuznets, 1945, pp. 41, 56). Indeed, Kuznets' views regarding decline are even starker than those suggested in table 2.3 or figure 2.1, particularly because 1939 productivity was almost certainly depressed by a substantial remaining output gap in the sector. Table 2.3 has labor productivity in 1943 7.4 percent below where it had been in 1941, although 8 percent above where it had been in 1939. Since more than half of U.S. manufacturing was in war work by the end of 1943 (which is what Kuznets focuses on), a very high growth rate of labor productivity in the remainder would be necessary to make these numbers consistent with his suggestion of a 20 percent decline in efficiency in the war industries between 1939 and 1945. Given the difficulties faced by non-war manufacturing in obtaining access to materials and machine tools, such a high growth rate is unlikely to have obtained. The important point here is that Kuznets' intuition about the direction of productivity change in U.S. munitions manufacturing is generally consistent with the numbers in table 2.3, which apply to the entire sector.

Biases in the TFP Estimates

We turn now to ways in which biases in any of the three series underlying the calculations summarized in table 2.3 could affect calculated TFP growth. If output growth has been under- or overstated, TFP growth will be as well, and by the same amount. If the growth of either labor or capital inputs has been under- or overstated, TFP growth will be affected in the opposite direction. I limit myself to considering the direction of possible biases, and how they might change the main conclusion reflected in figure 2.1.

Consider output first. The output measure is fixed weight, using 1958 prices. Compared to series constructed using chained index methods, fixed weight measures usually understate growth before the base year and overstate it for years after (see Landefeld and Parker, 1997, p. 60). The reason is substitution bias. The output categories that have grown most rapidly are likely to be those whose relative prices have declined. This covariance diminishes the effect of rapidly growing categories of goods on the calculated growth rate. Consequently, use of 1958 prices will tend to understate output growth before that year.

Landefeld and Parker (1997) found that for the entire economy between 1929 and 1987, the use of fixed 1987 price weights as compared with chained index measures understated real growth by an average of .4 percentage points per year. Understating growth before a base year is not, however, inevitable. The wrenching changes in output within manufacturing over the years 1941–48 reflected the imperatives of war and then demobilization in the context of an administered economy. They were not driven by the evolution of income-weighted consumer preferences communicated through the price mechanism.

In the same article, Landefeld and Parker also examined growth over seven postwar expansions occurring within or (almost entirely within) the 1949–87 period, comparing real output increase using 1987 prices and growth calculated using chained index methods. In six of the seven expansions, the estimated growth using fixed weight is lower than with chained index, as expected. The one exception is the 1949Q4–1953Q2 expansion, which includes the ramp-up of military production for the Korean War. This finding suggests that what is generally true during peacetime may not be true during war, when the increased production of military goods is driven by imperatives other than consumer response to prior declining prices. If so, a switch from fixed weight (1958 prices) to chained index measures of manufacturing output, assuming it could be implemented, might increase the absolute value rather than reverse the sign of the (negative) productivity growth for 1941–48 reported in table 2.1, despite what would otherwise be expected from the operation of substitution bias.

KL versus KLEMS

A second issue concerns the comparison of prewar TFP growth estimates with those from 1949 onward. There are two widely used methods for estimating TFP growth in a subsector. The first, the Capital Labor (KL) method, takes value added as the output measure and examines by how much its growth exceeds or falls short of a weighted average of the growth rates of the two key inputs. That is the approach described in the text. The second, which the BLS has adopted for its postwar TFP (MFP) productivity program, uses *gross* output as the output measure, and examines how much its growth exceeds or falls short of a weighted average of the growth of physical capital services (K), labor hours (L), and other purchased materials or services, specifically, energy (E), materials (M), and business services (S). The weights of the input growth rates are their respective shares in compensation, assumed to reflect the marginal products of these different inputs. The methodology is known by the acronym KLEMS, each letter standing for one of the five input categories. This means that the procedures underlying the postwar numbers in table 2.1 are not the same as those used for the World War II period and before.

The differences between KL and KLEMS estimates can be large when examining an individual industry because the share of intermediates in gross output can be large. For manufacturing as a whole, the share in gross output of intermediates (purchases from sectors other than manufacturing) will be smaller. For total or near-total economy aggregates, such as the private domestic economy, the value added, or KL, method is always used because almost all the production of what would be intermediate goods purchases in a smaller sector or subsector will already be included in the output measure.

That said, manufacturing did and does purchase energy, materials, and contracted business services from firms outside the sector. Evidence from the postwar period shows that the KL approach generates a manufacturing TFP growth rate higher than one constructed using the KLEMS approach. For the 1949–73 period, Gullickson and Harper (1987, p. 19) got 2.1 percent per year using KL, as compared with 1.5 percent per year using KLEMS (the latter number is reflected in table 2.1).

Why the higher number for the postwar period using KL? The KL method would attribute to TFP growth within manufacturing any effect on output of increases in the ratios of energy, materials, or purchased business services to employed labor or owned capital in the sector. In a peacetime economy, this would probably reflect TFP advance in sectors other than manufacturing, advance that cheapened energy, purchased materials, or business services, or anything else that led to a decline in their relative price, inducing increases in their use relative to employed labor and owned capital.[23] Using similar logic, any deterioration in efficiency in the production of purchased inputs or anything else making them relatively more expensive would most likely in peacetime lead to reduced ratios of these inputs relative to labor or owned capital.

Using the KL method, this would show up as lower estimated efficiency growth within manufacturing. In either instance, the estimated changes in manufacturing efficiency using KL could be viewed as misleading because they would reflect changes in supply conditions outside the manufacturing sector itself.

Table 2.1 shows an almost 3 percentage-point difference between the estimated TFP growth rates for the 1941–48 and 1949–73 intervals. The Gullikson and Harper numbers suggest the difference might have been .6 percentage points *more* if KL were used for the postwar estimate as well, reflecting a KL to KL comparison and widening the gap between the two intervals. What would be the effect of using KLEMS for the earlier period (thus enabling a KLEMS to KLEMS comparison)? Would such a switch be likely to make the estimated manufacturing TFP growth between 1941 and 1948 less negative, thus narrowing the gap between the growth rates in the two intervals? Under peacetime conditions this would require deteriorations in supply conditions in purchased inputs like energy and materials that increased their relative price and reduced their use relative to employed labor and owned capital. The KL method would "unfairly" penalize the manufacturing TFP estimate for lower purchased input (E, M, and S) intensity.

But the economy operated differently during war. Consider energy. Overall, the country was awash in cheap energy (E) before the war, during the war, and after it. The 1943 coal strike threatened (although it did not actually curtail) steel production. The WPB discussed rationing of coal, but the crisis subsided and the fuel was never formally rationed. Neither, except for a few brownouts, was electricity. Electric power production in the economy increased by more than one-third over the course of the conflict, from 15.35 billion kWh in December 1941 to a peak of 20.49 billion kWh in January 1945.[24] As for oil, until near the end of the war, there was more than enough domestically produced petroleum in the country to satisfy all household, business, and military demands, including those of our allies. In the 1940s the United States was the world's leading producer and consumer of petroleum. Gasoline was indeed rationed, but the main motivation was to extend the life of the nation's installed stock of rubber tires. Rationing, including that of fuel oil, was tighter on the East Coast because of shortages resulting from U-boat warfare (see chapter 4), but "nonessential" household use bore most of the brunt. It is unlikely that changes in the energy intensity of manufacturing would contribute to differences in KLEMS and KL measures of TFP growth in the sector.

Because of its relative abundance, energy was responsible at midcentury for a small fraction of the value of gross manufacturing output: just 2 percent in 1949. The same can be said for purchased business services (S), responsible in 1949 for only 5.2 percent of the value of gross output (Gullickson and Harper, 1987 p. 25). It is only in the postwar period that the shares of both began steadily to rise.

Materials from outside of manufacturing, on the other hand, accounted for 30.2 percent of the costs of gross output in 1949, substantially more than physical capital (20.9 percent). So deteriorating supply conditions for materials, had the economy been operating according to peacetime rules, could have driven a KL measure down relative to KLEMS by forcing reductions in materials intensity. But, again, the wartime economy did not operate according to peacetime rules. There certainly were disruptions of materials supply, but this did not produce smooth alterations in input ratios across the board. Rationing resulted in the paradoxical coexistence of severe shortages and almost unlimited access, depending largely upon where a firm was situated relative to the needs of the war economy, which led to conditions in many respects similar to anecdotal descriptions of Soviet-era and other controlled economies. When purchased inputs were in short supply, some activities were simply shut down, either by fiat (limitation orders) or because of inability to obtain necessary inputs, while other activities often (but not always) got everything or even more than they needed. The goods favored with allocations were those likely to be produced, and they dominated the output flows.

U.S. military forces, for which most of the war goods were destined, had a reputation for profligacy in their use of materials and energy that astounded allies. This casual attitude toward conservation was reflected as well in the prioritized wartime manufacturing undertaken to supply them. If you were favored, and if you were producing, there was little incentive to economize, since the priorities system and ultimately the Controlled Materials Plan aimed to give war industries first claim, even in the face of severe scarcity. Much of the economizing was done with blunt instruments: the production of metal-using (and therefore resource-competing) consumer durables was simply prohibited, the production of nylon stockings ceased so there would be plenty of the new synthetic fiber for parachutes and mosquito netting, and producers of men's clothing were ordered to eliminate cuffs and pockets so as to ensure a plentiful supply of cloth for uniforms. There is little evidence that prioritized manufacturers in the United States were engaged in any serious efforts to economize on energy or materials. With respect to materials, firms directed their efforts at obtaining more than was needed and then sitting on it. The most dangerous shortage was rubber, and for critical uses there were almost no possibilities for substitution. If one had it, however, one used it. For the war industries, controls were intended to ensure abundant supplies, which they succeeded in doing except when they did not, which led to hoarding, which, worsening the underlying scarcities, led to curtailment or halts in production.

It is unlikely that the use of KL before 1948 is the key to understanding the negative wartime trend in manufacturing TFP, or, stated another way, that switching to KLEMS would reverse or weaken it, thus moving the 1941–48 growth rate closer to that estimated using KLEMS for the postwar period. Man- ufacturing productivity declined during the war because of the switch to the production of unfamiliar products and because of the shortages that caused labor and capital in the sector to stand intermittently idle. Those were the prox- imate causes. Readers should nevertheless be aware of the difference between KLEMS and KL methods when comparing the postwar rates of TFP growth from the BLS with those calculated for World War II and earlier decades.

Capital Input

There are several reasons why the capital series in table 2.3 might under- state the true growth of service flows. First, the share of the manufacturing capital stock composed of shorter-lived equipment was rising. Second, be- cause of its rapid overall growth, the stock was getting much younger. Third, the depreciation rate was abnormally high, particularly for equipment, not just or even principally owing to the operation of double or triple shifts, but because of the unusually rapid rate of obsolescence.

Figure 2.2 shows that the ratio of the current cost stock of privately owned equipment to structures in the entire economy was flat from 1929 through 1941 and indeed through 1947.[25] If trends within manufacturing echoed those in the broader private economy, the use of a wealth rather than productive capital stock for the sector probably would not, on this account, understate the growth of capital service flows from the privately owned portion of the stock. It is only in the postwar period that the equipment-to-structures ratio in the private sector rose sharply, increasing to a plateau of about 60 percent start- ing around 1977 and continuing through 1999 at that level before declining to around 45 percent from 2008 onward.

For the war years, however, one must also consider the composition of the government-owned portion of the stock. Dividing the government assets

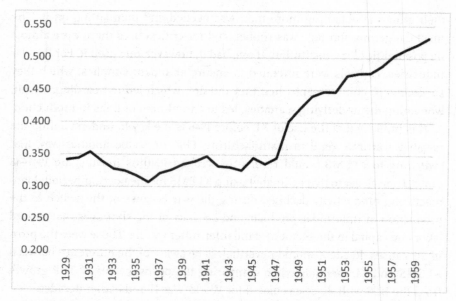

Figure 2.2. Ratio of current cost private equipment to nonresidential structures, United States, 1929–59. Source: BEA Fixed Asset table 1.1.

into two gross stocks serving as proxies for productive capital stocks, one for structures and the other for equipment, figure 2.3 shows a sharp change in composition between 1941 and 1945: an initial dominance of structures yields to a growing preponderance of equipment. The increase within the government-owned portion means that the share of equipment was rising in the combined stock, which suggests an underestimate of the growth of capital service flow on this account. Why?

A correctly estimated productive stock would register higher growth than a wealth stock, since the equipment components whose shares were increasing had shorter lives, higher average annual depreciation, and therefore higher average annual user costs or rental rates, and would receive increasing weight in constructing the aggregate growth rate of the productive stock. This is the underlying logic of the upward adjustment Gordon has made in multiple venues for a growth rate of capital services proxied by net wealth stock measures during periods when the share of equipment in the total is increasing (Gordon, 2000; 2016, data appendix).

The manufacturing capital stock was also getting much younger. The huge government expenditure on industrial facilities between 1940 and 1943, and the

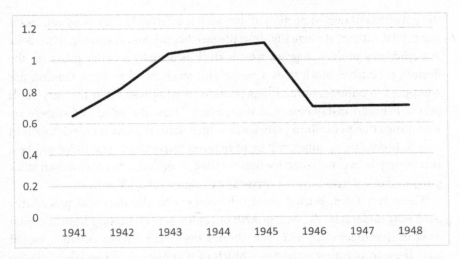

Figure 2.3. Ratio of gross stock of government-owned equipment to structures, U.S. manufacturing, 1941–48 (1958 dollars). Source: Gordon (1969), table 4.

more than an order-of-magnitude increase in machine tool production over the same period resulted in the rapid growth of that stock and big changes in its vintage demography. Assuming hyperbolic age-efficiency profiles, with little drop-off in the initial years after installation, reduction in the average age of assets because of rapid growth, independent of changes in the shares of different asset types, would normally mean that the use of a wealth stock to serve as proxy for a correctly calculated productive stock will understate the growth of service flows. Because depreciation runs faster than the decline in efficiency (service flow), an increase in the share of younger vintages means the productive stock would rise faster than a net wealth stock.

These two dynamics underlie the conclusions of OECD researchers Arnaud and his colleagues: "From comparisons at the total economy level it would appear that in most cases measures of capital services grow quicker than the net capital stock. In other words, using the net capital stock as a substitute for a measure of capital services is likely to entail an underestimation of contribution of capital to economic growth, and by implication an overestimation of MFP" (2011, p. 5; MFP, or multifactor productivity, is a term used synonymously with TFP).

In the calculations for the war years, however, we can be somewhat less concerned about the second effect (the effect of the equipment stock becoming younger). That is because the utilized measure of capital service input for the government-owned portion of the stock is effectively a gross wealth stock. For capital with an abnormally short life (see below), and assuming hyperbolic age-efficiency profiles, a gross wealth stock is actually a better proxy for the desired productive stock than a net wealth stock. Neither I nor Gordon has attempted to subtract annual depreciation in what was often the very short period between installation and retirement. Thus, the effects of vintage re-weightings due to declining efficiency, which drive the second mechanism in a stock becoming younger, will be of reduced importance, and there will be a smaller gap between the service flow implied by the use of a gross wealth stock proxy and one derived from a correctly calculated productive stock.

There is a third, related reason, however, why the data and procedures used may understate the true growth of capital service flows. Physical capital used in manufacturing had even shorter lives than almost certainly would have been true during peacetime. Much of it consisted of special- or single-purpose tools that were (as anticipated) scrapped quickly after the war, when the products to whose production they were specialized were no longer produced. User costs for given types of capital were therefore unusually high during the war, an effect that was, again, particularly pronounced for equipment. Much of this new capital was in use for only two or three years, installed in the second half of 1942 or in 1943 and withdrawn and scrapped by 1946. This anticipation of a truncated life was one of the arguments business used in pressing either for government financing and ownership or for the right, in calculating tax liabilities, to greatly accelerate depreciation on the equipment and buildings they installed on their own account: straight-line depreciation over five years, "or, if the emergency lasted a shorter time, during the period of the emergency."

After the fact, these provisions were criticized as excessive. During the Korean War, defense contractors were again offered five-year straight-line depreciation on new buildings or equipment they paid for themselves, but without the option of even quicker write-offs if the conflict ended sooner (Aircraft Industries Association of America, 1953, p. 9). Whether or not the World War II provisions are now viewed as too generous, the argument and expectation that most of this equipment and many of the structures would have little value once hostilities ceased and the economy's output mix again changed had considerable merit.

Economic depreciation depends significantly on an asset's useful life, which is a function not just of wear and tear, but also of obsolescence. In the case of computers, for example, obsolescence often results from rapid improvements in the attributes of more recently produced units as well as complementary inputs such as software. But assets can also become obsolete if they can only be used in the production of particular goods or the operation of particular processes and if those goods or processes, for whatever reason, cease to be produced or operated. This means that the use of peacetime assumptions about the useful lives of asset types during wartime poses a problem. Actual depreciation was more rapid, which meant higher user costs. Thus, the abnormally high rate of obsolescence augments the impacts of the growing share of equipment and the decline in the capital stock's average age. This effect complements, although it is not the same as, Robert Higgs' emphasis on the accelerated depreciation associated with running double and triple shifts during the war (2004, 2010).[26]

By increasing equipment's share of overall capital compensation, unusually rapid obsolescence increases the weight put on the faster-growing productive stocks of equipment in producing an aggregated productive stock whose growth proxies the growth of capital services. An extraordinary quantity of equipment was, over a very short period and for a very short period, thrown into the production battle. As a result of mobilization for war, annual machine tool output in the United States grew dramatically. Production during the Depression years was approximately 7,000 individual tools per year, generated by roughly two hundred specialized firms. In 1940, 110,000 units were produced, and in 1941, 185,000. At the peak of production in August 1942, machine tools were generated at an annual rate of 365,000, although by 1944, more than a year before the war ended, production had already fallen back to less than half the peak rate (Walton, 1956, p. 229; see also Ristuccia and Tooze, 2013, table 1).

These data refer to production of new tools (investment flows). As for cumulated stocks, the U.S. War Production Board (1945b, p. 5) reported that the number of installed machine tools rose from 934,000 at the end of 1939 to just under 1.4 million in 1943 (this count included mothballed units). Close to 40 percent of the government-owned equipment stock—much of it special-purpose and custom-built—was withdrawn and scrapped during 1945 and 1946 (Gordon, 1969, table 4). These dynamics applied to a lesser degree to manufacturing structures built during the war, many of which, if not exactly special-purpose, were designed and built during the war in strategic locations with particular uses in mind, and in some cases not expected to last more than a few years.

Labor Input

The quality of the manufacturing labor force during the war probably experienced little overall change. The local boards making Selective Service System decisions understood the need to consider the requirements of war industry along with those of the military. It did no good to fully staff the armed services if there were insufficient workers remaining to produce guns, ammunition, planes, tanks, jeeps, and ships. At the same time, there was considerable skepticism about the justification for many occupational deferments, as well as strong support among the local boards and within Congress for protecting fathers and those in the farm sector (see chapter 5). Multiple crosscurrents affected the composition of industrial labor.

By 1943 aircraft and aircraft-engine production had become the number one manufacturing industry in the United States, having risen from a prewar rank of forty-four, and data from that industry illustrate some features of the sector's wartime labor force. Within the manufacture of aircraft and engines, production workers constituted about 80 percent of the industry's prime contractor labor force in 1943 (Aerospace Industries Association of America, 1962, pp. 61–67). The one "fact" almost everyone knows about World War II manufacturing is that the share of women workers in its labor force increased. As a percentage of prime contractor employment in the aircraft industry, women peaked at 36.9 percent in July 1944.

Anecdotal evidence suggests that women were often considered superior for jobs requiring dexterity or the ability to crawl into or through small openings (dwarfs were also employed in aircraft construction). More than three times as many women worked in airframes as in engine manufacture: they made up 40 percent of the workforce in airframes and 30.7 percent in engines (Aircraft Industries Association of America, 1945, table 3-7). Women were paid less than men, but not by a large margin. In August 1943 their hourly wage in aircraft-engine plants was 87.1 percent of male wages. Data for 1944 for prime contractors in airframe, engine, and propeller plants show that both quits and separations were much higher for women than men: 74.3 quits per 100 employees for women, versus 40.7 for men; 92.3 separations for women per 100 employees versus 63 for men (Aircraft Industries Association of America, 1945, table 3-18). On the other hand, quits and separations for both genders were elevated during the war, which reflected both the pressures of the jobs and the tight labor market (see chapter 5).

Women, on average, brought less work experience to their jobs. But because of the change in the output mix, previous experience was less important than it might otherwise have been in influencing productivity. Skills specific to the manufacture of consumer durables no longer being made were at least temporarily devalued—another reflection of the negative supply shock caused by the change in the output mix. Both male and female production workers often needed to master the operation of processes or the production of products that were entirely new and in which they lacked experience. It would be a mistake to conclude that increased feminization necessarily represented a deterioration in the quality of the labor force.

The manufacturing labor force also included (in addition to production and clerical workers) engineers, scientists, technical workers, and managers. A study based on data from the Terman longitudinal study at Stanford University found that individuals in those occupational categories faced a much higher probability of getting a draft deferment than, for example, other professionals like physicians and lawyers, who had value for the military but were less essential for war production (Dechter and Elder, 2004). One of every four males aged eighteen to forty-four in professional and semiprofessional occupations was ultimately drafted, but the deferments are evidence of the differential attention paid by the Selective Service System to retaining critical nonproduction workers on the home front. The Terman study included mostly middle- and upper middle-class California men who were in the data set because they scored well on tests administered in high school. This study does not, however, appear to document class-based discrimination in the granting of deferments, since physicians and lawyers did not benefit from the same preference.

Gordon (2016) used the Goldin and Katz (2008) measure of educational quality improvement to adjust labor hours for quality improvement (see chapter 8). There is virtually no difference in the rate of growth of that measure for 1915–40 and for 1940–60 (about .5 percent per year for each of the two intervals), although the rate was probably lower during the war as teenagers dropped out of high school to work, and college students were drafted into the military.

In sum, a significant drop in the "quality" of the manufacturing labor force is unlikely to be the explanation for the measured productivity decline during the war. For reasons previously discussed, however, it is likely that the rise in capital services input has been understated and output growth may possibly have been overstated. Taken together, these considerations strengthen the conclusion reflected in figure 2.1: both labor productivity and TFP declined sharply between 1941 and 1945. If the conclusion about capital services is correct, then the capital shallowing in manufacturing reported may be less important than the initial calculations suggest. More, perhaps most, of the drop in labor productivity is to be attributed simply to a sharp drop in TFP.

That decline would have been greater without the learning that eventually kicked in and moderated productivity declines in 1943. Unfortunately, like the machine tools specialized to produce particular war goods, this learning represented the acquisition of human capital, much of which was of little value after the war because the country stopped producing most of these goods in 1945 or shortly thereafter. Whatever relevant experience women production workers gained was also largely written off, as only a fraction remained in the labor force. By and large, wartime production involved the application of known organizational blueprints to the manufacture of already developed but not yet mass-produced goods. The challenge was to apply these blueprints, which dictated massive numbers of special-purpose machine tools in special-purpose industrial facilities to a new set of products—and the transition took time and was sometimes painful. The wartime achievement of labor in the sector—both production workers and managerial, engineering, and technical talent—was learning how to produce military ordnance such as airplanes and tanks at scale.

Some technological paradigms ripe for exploitation—particularly atomic energy—did receive large infusions of government R&D money. But the Manhattan Project was the exception. Producing a B-24 Liberator, which had first flown on December 29, 1939, was not a moonshot. Producing at scale was the challenge. Because of the difference between military and consumer durables, this involved the adjustment, alteration, and refinement of templates developed in the production of automobiles, radios, and refrigerators during the interwar period. For military production the magnitude of the eventual flows was unlike anything that had been seen before, and on first pass it seems reasonable to suggest that some of what was learned might have been more generally applicable to ordnance or other durables after the war.

The problem with this suggestion is that the manufacturing experience in World War II was, when all is said and done, sui generis. Consider again aircraft production. In all the years subsequent to 1946, combined civilian and military output, including small general aviation aircraft, broke 20 percent of peak 1944 production (barely) in only three years: 1966, 1967, and 1968, at the height of the Vietnam conflict. Postwar military production of aircraft tended to be low volume and high unit cost, quite different from what was true during the war. The industry never again attempted the level of mass production Ford eventually achieved in its Willow Run plant. The share of production workers in the industry labor force in 1944, which was not very different from what it had been in automobiles in 1941 (about 80 percent), by 1960 had fallen to below 60 percent, reflecting the increased employment of engineering and scientific workers and the growing technical complexity of the products (Aerospace Industries Association of America, 1971, pp. 87–88). The B-17, which first flew on July 28, 1935, required 200,000 engineering hours to get from conception to the first flight of a production model. The B-52, which first flew on April 15, 1952, required 4,085,000 engineering hours to make the same transition (Aerospace Industries Association of America, 1958, p. 48).

Conclusion

From the perspective of macroeconomic history, one of the unique features of war production was the clear exogeneity of the changes in the product mix and the rate and composition of physical capital accumulation within manufacturing. Since the concept of TFP came into sharper focus in the late 1950s, much discussion has centered on how we can or should understand its growth rate. In peacetime we often view it as a crude measure of the rate of scientific, technological, and organizational advance. A recurring concern, however, has been that input growth, particularly of capital, cannot necessarily be taken as exogenous, and in fact may be partly a function of that advance. If the availability of new blueprints improves the return to capital, and if this elicits higher saving and thus higher growth of the private capital stock, calculation of TFP growth as a residual will understate the combined (direct and indirect) impact of technological advance on output and output per hour, because some of the gains in the former would be attributable to more capital and in the latter to capital deepening (rises in the capital-to-labor ratio) induced by improved techniques (see David, 1977; Oliner and Sichel, 2000).

This dynamic requires a positive elasticity of saving with respect to the real interest rate, an empirical response questionable if one believes that income effects roughly balance out the substitution effects, as they do in the aggregate for labor supply. For World War II, however, it does not matter whether we believe this. First, the increases in private saving that helped fund the widening government deficit were not a response to a higher return consequent upon newly available blueprints. Thanks in part to the Federal Reserve, government bond rates and interest rates in general were historically low, particularly given the repressed inflation. The saving that took place was encouraged by the carrot of patriotic appeals and enforced by the sticks of rationing and the unavailability of most metal-using consumer durables. Second, the manufacturing capital stock increased because government investment responded to military necessity, not technological advances that increased the return to investment. The increase in capital services was truly exogenous from an economic standpoint.

But if sharp advance in TFP growth during the Depression years between 1929 and 1941 can be interpreted as evidence of technological progressiveness, what of declines across the war period? Negative TFP growth in manufacturing reflected wartime reductions in efficiency due to struggles to mass-produce new goods and periodic idleness of facilities and labor resulting from shortages and producer hoarding. Mass production of military goods required the learning of new skills, the manufacture of hundreds of thousands of new machine tools, and the construction of specialized facilities, which in many cases became permanently obsolete after the war.

The productivity declines are not evidence of technological regressiveness in the literal sense that somehow the economy forgot, lost, or suffered destruction of blueprints to which the country previously had access. At the same time, disruptions in materials supply, the canonical instance of which was rubber, had consequences similar to those experienced in the hypothetical case of a loss of production technology. Just as the 1973–74 oil shock represented, for the United States, the deterioration of a "technology" for transforming soybeans and plywood into oil, so too did Japanese military success in the Far East and German submarine predation in the Atlantic damage the productive capability of the economy. Similarly, the sudden and radical alteration in the product mix meant not that access to blueprints for making passenger cars, refrigerators, and washing machines was lost, but rather that they were temporarily obsolete in the sense that, along with a large stock of mothballed specialized machine tools, they could not be used for several years.

Understanding the true course of manufacturing productivity during the war is important in challenging conventional narratives about its contribution to the level and rate of growth of potential output in the postwar period. But it is also relevant for our understanding of the history of the war itself. If labor productivity in manufacturing had remained at its 1941 level through 1944, 1.8 million fewer workers would have been needed for war production in the latter year.[27] Those individuals could have contributed to civilian production or provided additional head count for the armed forces. In resisting calls for national service legislation and denying that there was ever a true national shortage of men and women for defense production, organized labor never departed from claiming that the problem was poor management and utilization. The success in improving productivity in Boeing's B-17 plant in Seattle gives some credence to these views (Flynn, 1979, p. 69). Nevertheless, although better management and utilization might have weakened the decline in productivity, it could not have eliminated it, and its effect was to heighten the challenges of balancing the direct manpower needs of the military and the requirements of war production.

3 • What Kind of Miracle Was the U.S. Synthetic Rubber Program?

The U.S. economy experienced powerful negative supply shocks during World War II that drove down potential output and adversely affected productivity. One of the earliest and most consequential was the loss of 90 percent of the country's natural rubber supply after the Japanese overran Singapore in February 1942. The United States had accumulated what was, compared with its annual consumption, only a small stockpile of natural rubber, and there were no substitutes for pneumatic tires, effectively no domestic sources of latex, and very limited opportunities for importing the raw material from Latin America or Africa. Japan's advance into Southeast Asia, particularly the Dutch East Indies, eliminated its prewar dependence on the United States for 80 percent of its oil. In a stunning reversal, the Japanese achievement in the Pacific now posed an existential threat to the U.S. economy and its military capabilities. In response, the federal government, working with oil and chemical firms, developed a domestic industry that produced an imperfect substitute.

Redressing the loss of Southeast Asian rubber imports was more important than the Manhattan Project in making Allied victory possible. Without the atomic bomb, the country would eventually have prevailed over Japan, as it had already done throughout the Pacific, although at the cost of greater loss of American and arguably Japanese lives.[1] Without rubber, the country would almost certainly have lost the war. The U.S. synthetic rubber industry was built almost entirely from scratch beginning in 1942, and, unlike the bulk of facilities financed by the Defense Plant Corporation, most of it remained government-owned although contractor-operated until 1955. And it was expensive. The new plants alone cost nearly $700 million, easily a third of the total cost of the atomic bomb program.

A commemorative pamphlet celebrating the designation of the U.S. Synthetic Rubber Program as a "National Historic Chemical Landmark" described it as "an industrial and scientific miracle" (American Chemical Society, 1998, p. 1). The word *miracle* is used with great frequency in treatments of U.S. industrial mobilization during the Second World War. We would be better served if the term were banned from the lexicon from which descriptors of U.S. World War II production efforts are drawn. "Stripped of the mythology that has grown up around it," wrote one of its most knowledgeable chroniclers, the synthetic rubber program "was a scandalous, a complete, a nearly catastrophic foul up" (Solo, 1980, p. 31).

The initiative was hampered both by flawed design and by prewar denialism that the United States would or should become involved in the war, which led to delays in facilities construction. The program could have been conducted differently. It could have used different processes, relied on a different mix of feedstocks, and rolled out on a different timetable. A smaller program might have been adequate if coupled with other actions to mitigate the risk and ultimate reality of cutoff, including the acquisition of a larger stockpile of natural rubber before the Japanese attacked, or the embarkation earlier on an agricultural program to develop alternative domestic sources of latex such as guayule.

The actual course of history tends to acquire an aura of inevitability, and it is important not to lose sight of different possibilities. That said, there is no gainsaying that with the fall of Singapore, the United States faced a problem with far-reaching implications and consequences for economic mobilization, for the conduct of the war, and for the daily lives of Americans.

The main cause of the decline of labor productivity and TFP in manufacturing detailed in chapter 2 was the radical change in the output mix that forced firms to shift from making goods in which they had a great deal of experience to making those in which they had little. But there were other mechanisms in play as well. The assembly of military goods was the final stage—the very visible peak—of a complex infrastructure requiring the production of intermediate goods and, at its base, the supply and refining of raw materials. Supply chains at the end of the 1930s were optimized to meet the needs of the prewar output mix. Large product-mix changes accelerated the arrival of materials shortages as the output gap closed. Because it exacerbated bottlenecks in material supply, the change in what was made meant earlier arrival at inflationary waypoints—both for familiar materials like steel, aluminum, and copper, and for many less familiar, including several of the ferroalloys. When complementary inputs were simply not available, their price became effectively infinite, and both labor and capital stood idle.

Shortages, however, reflected not only changes in the derived demands from the new final product vector but also the role of enemy military action in disrupting the flow of strategically important inputs from abroad, most importantly rubber, and to a lesser degree Manila hemp, tin, and other minerals, and between regions of the country, in the case of deliveries of petroleum and petroleum products to the East Coast. The resource shocks interacted with and potentiated the effect of the product-mix shock, together helping to drive down productivity levels within manufacturing. If a forced change in output mix can be in its effects *like* a negative supply shock, a sudden cutoff or decrease in supply of a critical raw material *is* the canonical instance of such a disruption.

The first of these shocks, and the most serious, resulted from Japanese success in eliminating U.S. access to almost all its supplies of natural rubber. The effect of that event is dramatically evident in statistics on imports, which dropped from 1,029,007 long tons in 1941 to 55,329 long tons in 1943, a decline of almost 95 percent (Herbert and Bisio, 1985, p. 127, table 11.1).[2] The other major resource shock, addressed in the next chapter, was Germany's success, during the first half of 1942, in cutting off 90 percent of the supply of petroleum and petroleum products to the Eastern Seaboard of the United States.

There were other proximate contributors to declining labor productivity in manufacturing during the war. Among these were increases in the length of the average workweek, difficulties getting to and from work, and limited housing in centers of war production, all of which contributed to high rates of absenteeism and labor turnover. Later in the war, as the result of accelerating draft calls and the shrinkage of the civilian labor force, employer difficulties in obtaining and retaining the quantity and quality of labor desired, labor-management conflict, unauthorized work stoppages, and wartime plant seizures aggravated the downward pressures. The rubber shortages contributed to a number of these, including the squalid living conditions near such facilities as Willow Run. Ford planned for his workers to live in Detroit and commute, but tire and gasoline rationing made that difficult, and the conditions in trailer parks and makeshift housing near the plant contributed to a labor turnover rate of 100 percent per month in 1942 (Albrecht, 1995, pp. 114–17). Several wartime controls, including tire rationing, nationwide gasoline rationing, and the thirty-five-mile-per-hour speed limit, were the direct consequence of the loss of Southeast Asian rubber. By 1943 civilian consumption of rubber had been forced down to just 10 percent of 1941 levels. Combined civilian and military consumption dropped 60 percent between 1941Q2 and 1942Q4 (Wendt, 1947, p. 218). The loss of access to natural rubber seriously constrained U.S. military options in 1943, helping to delay the planned cross-Channel invasion in Europe by at least a year.

It is true that in response to a negative shock, producers often innovate, in the sense that they are forced or inspired to learn how to operate processes or produce products with which they were previously unfamiliar. Ford was eventually able to produce both Model As and B-24s at scale. Organizations get better at dealing with the new circumstances, which is what the learning-by-doing stories and the data underlying them document. We are inclined to celebrate successful responses to adversity.

It is commonly argued that the response to adversity can leave a nation or an industry better off than would have been the case had the shock not occurred. The appeal of the proposition reflects a natural human tendency to search for silver linings and the attractiveness of what may seem to be counterintuitive or surprising outcomes. Counterintuitive arguments, nevertheless, need to be applicable to cases other than the exceptional. The positive influence of such innovation rarely has a greater absolute influence on productivity than the initial negative shock, even in the longer run. If the contrary were true, we might, as a policy to encourage growth, deliberately inflict product mix or resource supply shocks and additional regulatory burdens on our most important industries. Negative shocks generally leave an economy worse off than would have been true without them. That is why we describe them as negative.[3]

The U.S. synthetic rubber program started late, failed to meet production targets before the last quarter of 1943, produced an imperfect substitute for natural rubber, and involved hundreds of millions of dollars of unnecessary expenditure. Because of delays and unforced errors, its success remained highly uncertain until the final quarter of 1943. In the wake of a politicized battle over what feedstock should be used in the program, and after his veto of the Rubber Supply Act of 1942, President Roosevelt appointed a committee (formally, The U.S. Special Committee to Study the Rubber Situation) and instructed it to examine the perilous economic, military, and political situation in which the country then found itself. The committee consisted of James Conant, Karl Compton, and Bernard Baruch (chair). Conant, a chemist, was then president of Harvard. Compton, a physicist, headed MIT. Both were experienced and respected academic leaders and scientists and had worked together on the National Defense Research Committee and within the Office of Scientific Research and Development (Conant, 1947). Baruch, perennial advisor to presidents, had helmed the War Industries Board in the final year of the First World War. He also knew a good deal about rubber because of his role in establishing and overseeing the Intercontinental Rubber Company's operations cultivating and refining guayule in Mexico in the first decades of the twentieth century (more on this below).

The crisis that brought the committee into existence and the substance of its September 1942 *Report of the Rubber Survey Committee*, henceforth referred to as the Survey Committee Report, are discussed at various points in this chapter. The report was treated as authoritative when released, and most of its recommendations were at least initially adopted. Its production forecasts from the vantage point of mid-1942 were unvarnished and pessimistic. It noted that "there are many more circumstances which might arise to change the figures *unfavorably* than there are to change them favorably" (U.S. Special Committee to Study the Rubber Situation, henceforth cited as U.S. Rubber Survey Committee, 1942, p. 27; emphasis in original). The committee cautioned that beyond the challenge of mass-producing the key input, the need to blend synthetic with natural rubber in the production of most military tires would require additional time and effort, resulting in "about a one third-loss in efficiency" (U.S. Rubber Survey Committee, 1942, p. 13).

The greater difficulties of working with this substitute raw material were also referenced a year later in a report on the rubber program to the War Production Board at its August 10, 1943, meeting, which noted that "synthetic rubber requires more milling and processing than crude rubber" (U.S. Civilian Production Administration, 1946a, p. 233). GR-S—what the United States called its general-purpose synthetic rubber—lacked plasticity and tack (stickiness) and was lower in tensile strength and tear resistance, and tires made from it deteriorated more rapidly when overheated than those made from natural rubber. The product was more sensitive to temperature fluctuations during milling, and it took longer to cure (U.S. Senate, Committee on Military Affairs, 1945, p. 5). To compensate, since synthetic rubber did not adhere well to cotton cord, and for other reasons, truck tires would need the substitution of high-tenacity rayon cord for cotton cord. If the country was going to rely on synthetics to keep its civilian and military economies operating, there was no avoiding these negative influences on productivity in the fabrication of final products. But one is also struck, in studying the processes used to manufacture the synthetic raw material and its key feedstocks, by how very far down the list of priorities of an economy mobilized for war was improved efficiency.

During World War II in the United States, economic activities were roughly segregated into those for which cost was no object—these were the high-priority activities—and those that had to shut down or scramble for resources. The means for enforcing this was nonprice rationing. This included the flat prohibition of production of many consumer durables along with the requirement that civilians proffer both ration tickets and cash to purchase other items. Regulation of consumption was coupled with regulation of production, a key feature of which was the administrative prioritization or allocation of critical metals, raw materials, and, starting as early as December 1940, machine tools. This was done initially through a set of priority grades, which were a more elaborate system of rationing for producers, who needed a high rating and cash to get the equipment or materials they desired. The system broke down eventually because of widespread inflation of priority levels, and, following an abortive experiment with a burdensome Production Requirements Program, was replaced in 1943 by the Controlled Materials Plan (CMP). The CMP was a more transparent system for allocating limited supplies of steel, copper, and aluminum among claimants, one less subject to political pressure and gaming, and one that had the great merit of requiring less paperwork (Landon-Lane and Rockoff, 2013).

Because they had protected access to what they needed on the input side, and because they were generally compensated on a cost-plus-fixed-fee basis, the operating firms in the high-priority sectors had little incentive to economize on labor, materials, or physical capital services.[4] The starved sectors may have had such incentives, but those sectors declined in relative importance. Sectors favored because they were critical for U.S. military capability grew substantially as a share of manufacturing and the overall economy. According to the standard narratives (see chapter 6), it is in these sectors that we are supposed to have reaped the benefits of efficiency improvements. But the improvements from experience with initially unfamiliar goods, enjoyed for just a short period, only partly compensated for the effect of the initial negative shocks.

What of the possible longer-run benefits from innovations induced by the adverse shocks? These would have value for future productivity levels and growth if the products or services affected continued to be demanded and produced. If not, and if spillovers were limited, or if innovations emerged in reaction to an unusual set of factor prices or input availabilities that proved temporary, they would leave little imprint on the future trajectory of productivity advance. The legacy of wartime synthetic rubber production is more favorable on this account than was the corresponding inheritance for aircraft and aircraft engines.[5] But it is still a mixed picture.

If the sectoral productivity numbers are correct in the impression they convey, we ought to be able to interpret the synthetic rubber program and what led to its creation in ways consistent with the data, that is, as one of a range of factors contributing to declining manufacturing productivity during the war. This will require historical background on the sourcing of natural rubber as well as some understanding of the chemistry of making synthetics and the different routes available to address what was demonstrably a critical economic and military challenge for the country.

Prior to Pearl Harbor, it was well understood that if war broke out in the Pacific, the United States would be vulnerable to a disruption or complete cutoff of access to its sources of natural rubber from Southeast Asia. Because of the lack of adequate substitutes, particularly in the fabrication of pneumatic tires, this possibility represented a threat to the national security of the United States. Beyond suppression of nonessential demand, there were, before cutoff, three main routes whereby, by enhancing supply, the threat might be addressed. The first was to develop plant-based sources of latex within the United States or within countries unlikely to be overrun by or allied with enemies. The second was to stockpile large quantities of natural rubber as insurance against the possible interruption of imports. The third was to develop an industry that could manufacture a synthetic substitute based on advances in organic chemistry. Each of these mitigation strategies would be expensive and might after the fact be viewed as wasteful, particularly if foreign supply continued to be widely available.

The primary natural rubber plant, *Hevea brasiliensis,* is native to South America, where it grows wild and at low density in forest environments. Products made directly from its milky sap become hard and brittle in the cold and melted and sticky in the heat and were therefore in limited demand. In the 1830s the United States imported less than a thousand tons of crude rubber a year. Charles Goodyear's 1839 invention of vulcanization improved the quality of rubber goods, making the harvesting of latex from *H. brasiliensis* more profitable, although in 1854 the United States still imported relatively small quantities (2,150 long tons) (Fisher, 1956, p. 75).[6]

Vulcanization heated the natural rubber in the presence of sulfur, which cross-stitched the polymerized isoprene molecules in the latex with sulfur atoms, improving the rubber's resistance to degradation over a range of temperatures and controlling its elasticity, depending on the amount of sulfur introduced. Once vulcanized or cured, rubber can no longer be molded, rolled, extruded, or otherwise formed into specific thicknesses or shapes, but it remains elastic, and if stretched will return to its original state.

Between 1880 and 1910 the exploitation of Brazilian wild rubber in the Amazon erupted into a frenzy, as the production of bicycles and eventually automobiles rolling on pneumatic tires increased both overall demand and its price inelasticity (Stocking and Watkins, 1946, pp. 59–60). The most opulent manifestation of the boom and the attendant creation of wealth was the ornate opera house constructed in the city of Manaus, in the heart of the rain forest, nine hundred miles upstream from where the Amazon River flows into the Atlantic. Construction on this extraordinary building began in 1884 and was completed in 1896. Unfortunately for opera lovers, but perhaps fortunately for many of the indigenous workers who were brutally exploited (Tully, 2011, ch. 6), the rubber boom collapsed in 1910 with the introduction onto world markets of large quantities of crude rubber from Southeast Asian plantations.

In 1876 Sir Henry Wickham spirited out of Brazil 70,000 seeds, a few thousand of which successfully germinated in the Royal Botanical Gardens greenhouses in England. A quarter century later, as rubber prices soared along with bicycle and automobile production, seedlings were transplanted from England into environments favorable to their growth elsewhere in the world. *H. brasiliensis* began to be cultivated extensively in Southeast Asia, beginning in Ceylon and continuing into areas controlled by Great Britain and the Netherlands, including the Malay Peninsula, Thailand, the Indonesian island of Sumatra, and, eventually, French Indochina and parts of Africa as well. Rubber's rising price overcame initial resistance in some areas to shifting out of coffee cultivation, and the latex-producing plant came to be grown by native cultivators, generally on small plots, and on large plantations owned and managed by Europeans.[7] By 1910 Southeast Asia was the dominant supplier to the world, and by the late 1930s, 90 percent of the U.S. supply of natural rubber came from that region. In spite of the development of synthetics, natural rubber remained an important commodity in international trade in the 2020s, accounting worldwide for more than 40 percent of raw material input in the rubber products industry; Southeast Asia continued to provide most of the supply.

The history of rubber sourcing in the United States is quite different from that of oil, another key input in a modern industrial economy, and one where vulnerability to supply disruption can create similar national security concerns. Without either oil or rubber, the economy and military capabilities of an industrialized country face severe degradation. In the 1930s and the 1940s, the United States was almost entirely self-sufficient in petroleum and petroleum products, and indeed a major exporter. It was only in the second half of the twentieth century that the country became dependent on imports, in particular from the Middle East, a dependency from which it partially emerged in 2019, becoming again a net exporter of petroleum and petroleum products.

As far as natural rubber is concerned, however, the United States was not in 1941, is not now, and never has been remotely close to self-sufficiency. As the Survey Committee Report stated in September 1942, we were (and are) a "have not" nation. The threats to economic activity and military capability of losing access to most of its supply became very real on February 15, 1942, with the fall of the supposedly impregnable British fortress of Singapore. By the end of March of that year, the Japanese controlled all the areas of rubber cultivation in Southeast Asia and the sea-lanes to and from ports accessing them, and the last imports arrived in April. During the remainder of the Second World War, *no Southeast Asian supplies of natural rubber reached the United States.*[8]

Relatively little had been done at the national level in anticipation of this likelihood, apart from some halting initiatives by the federal government to build a strategic reserve. In 1939 the United States imported a half million tons of rubber, by value the country's largest single commodity import. Imports that year benefited from a barter deal with Britain in April whereby the United States swapped 500,000 bales of cotton for 90,000 tons of rubber (Wendt, 1947, p. 203). Imports doubled over the next two years, to 1,029,007 long tons, under the stimulus of economic recovery and government-led efforts to increase stocks, which by the end of 1941 had grown to 533,344 long tons (Herbert and Bisio, 1985, pp. ix, 126, 127). The U.S. appetite for rubber—the country then consumed half the world's annual supply—was driven largely by the automobile industry. Seventy percent of U.S. rubber consumption went into tires (American Chemical Society, 1998, pp. 1–3), so demand grew hand in hand with output of cars, trucks, and buses, consumption varying according to the state of the business cycle.

The 1941 end of year inventory stock for the United States represented almost a fourfold increase over 1939, which at year end stood at just 125,800 long tons, down from 231,500 at the end of 1938 (Herbert and Bisio, 1985, pp. 9–10). Well into the third quarter of 1943, that 1941 stockpile would be the chief and indeed almost only bulwark against the potentially catastrophic consequences of a possible and, in the event, actual cutoff of Southeast Asian supplies of crude rubber.

Given the likelihood of war and the prewar state of synthetic rubber and guayule production, the failure to accumulate a much larger national stockpile was, in retrospect, a serious mistake. Why was more not done to prepare for what would become a crisis? Part of it came down to economics: given availability of a reliable and relatively cheap foreign supply, it was costly and apparently inefficient for domestic firms or the federal government to hold large buffer stocks.[9] Protecting against the threat of supply disruption required alternative sources of natural rubber from *Hevea* or plant-based substitutes, large-scale investments in physical plant and equipment for a synthetic rubber capacity that might never be needed or used and whose development path was highly uncertain, or the holding of substantial inventory stocks.

Resistance to accumulating a larger strategic reserve was fueled by beliefs that the threat of disruption had been exaggerated. Part may be attributed to isolationist thinking, reinforced by the relative calm that prevailed for seven months following the German invasion of Poland. The Phony War, or Sitzkrieg, as British newspapers waggishly referred to it, lasted from September 1939 through the spring of the following year. In June 1939, Roosevelt had managed to squeeze out an appropriation to stockpile strategic materials (the Strategic and Critical Materials Stockpiling Act). But in May 1940, as the Sitzkrieg came to an end, just $13 million of the $100 million appropriated had actually been spent: Jesse Jones, head of the Reconstruction Finance Corporation (RFC), had insisted on keeping his eye out for bargain prices, and his caution (which he justified as a desire not to waste taxpayer dollars) continued even after the formation of the Rubber Reserve Company in June (Nelson, 1946, p. 39; Janeway, 1951, pp. 80–82).[10]

On April 9, 1940, Germany invaded Norway by sea and air and (in six hours) conquered Denmark. A month and a day later, on May 10, usually taken as the "official" end of the Phony War, Germany invaded France, Belgium, the Netherlands, and Luxembourg. On June 22, 1940, the defeated French signed an armistice that marked the cessation of large-scale military operations on the ground in France and the Benelux countries for almost four years, until the D-Day invasion of June 6, 1944. But fierce combat in the air continued, as the Battle of Britain commenced on July 10 and raged through the end of October, followed by nighttime air attacks (the Blitz) through the end of May 1941.

The period of the Phony War encouraged a hope and belief that perhaps the worst was over and the United States could avoid being drawn into the conflict. Whatever the reasons, very little was in place to address the threat of an almost complete loss of rubber supplies until the "Twilight War," as

Churchill described it, ended. Private corporations had been reluctant to accumulate and hold large inventories of natural rubber because it was expensive and risky, given large historical fluctuations in price. By default, it fell to
government to address the threat to the manufacture of rubber products—and
national security—posed by the possibility of an interruption in supply. Seven
weeks after the German attack on France and the Benelux countries, two and
a half weeks after the end of the ignominious British cross-Channel retreat at
Dunkirk, and following the June 22, 1940, armistice marking the fall of France,
the U.S. Congress acted, strengthening the powers of the Reconstruction Finance Corporation (RFC) to increase the strategic reserve. The German military successes and the commanding position that country now held on the
European continent placed England in dire straits but also made the precarious position of the United States more difficult to ignore, particularly in the
event it faced a war on two fronts.

The RFC was a Depression-era creation originally charged with providing
aid to agriculture, trade, and industry by making loans to banks and credit
agencies. On June 25, 1940, Congress amended the original authorizing act,
increasing the agency's authority. Its powers and responsibilities now included financing the production of airplanes, tanks, and guns, the construction, equipping, and operation of plants for so doing, and the stockpiling of
strategic metals and materials. Three days later, on June 28, the RFC created
the Rubber Reserve Company (RRC), half its equity subscribed to by the RFC
and the other half by rubber products manufacturers. The RFC then loaned
its subsidiary $140 million to finance purchases (U.S. Tariff Commission,
1940, p. 27). The RRC's main efforts would be to procure and stockpile natural
rubber on government account, store it in warehouses, and distribute it to
qualified users. On the same day, the RFC also created the Metals Reserve
Company, which aimed to procure, stockpile, and subsidize the domestic production of strategic metals and minerals. It would be most active in acquiring
bauxite, chromium, copper, diamonds, lead, manganese, mica, quartz, silver,
and zinc, and it heavily subsidized the domestic production of copper, lead,
and zinc. It also procured and stockpiled smaller quantities of more valuable
strategic minerals and metals, and it built a tin smelter in Texas City, Texas,
which remained in government hands until 1957 (U.S. Secretary of the Treasury, 1959, pp. 123–27).

The creation of these RFC subsidiaries reflected the correct anticipation,
seventeen months before Pearl Harbor, that, particularly in the case of a two-
front war, the United States was likely to face serious materials shortages that

had the potential to interrupt production, adversely affect productivity, and, in the worst case, bring the war effort and the U.S. economy to a halt. In rubber the concern was the likely loss of foreign supplies of an input for which the country had almost no domestic sourcing, and for which, in important uses, there were simply no substitutes.

Two months later, the RFC formed two additional subsidiaries: on August 23, 1940, the Defense Plant Corporation, which would contract for the construction and equipage of government-owned defense plants, and the Defense Supplies Corporation, on August 29, 1940, which would contract for their operation. In the rubber program, the builders and operators of the plants were usually the same private firms.

The Rubber Reserve Company ultimately played a large role in the design, magnitude, and timing of the synthetic program, but its initial remit was the accumulation of a large strategic stockpile of natural rubber that would be purchased, stored, and ultimately disbursed by the new government entity. Before it was created, only the Treasury or War or Navy department procurement officers could buy rubber on government account. In June 1941, a year after it was set up, Rubber Reserve became the sole purchaser, public or private.[11] Inventories grew to 288,864 long tons at the end of 1940 and then, as noted, nearly doubled to 533,344 long tons by the end of 1941, three weeks after Pearl Harbor. Inventory stocks peaked in April 1942 at 634,152 long tons, with the arrival of shipments on the way to the United States before the Japanese completely cut off supplies (Rubber Reserve Company, 1945, pp. 5, 16; Herbert and Bisio, 1985, pp. 14–15).

In the context of domestic rubber consumption of 775,000 tons in 1941, this reserve was still dangerously inadequate, *even* were civilian consumption to be drastically curtailed. In the four calendar years 1942–45, the United States managed to import a total of 583,053 long tons, as compared with the 1,023,631 long ton inflow in 1941 alone. At the end of 1944, natural rubber inventories stood at just 93,650 long tons. Import flows were lowest in 1943 but year-end inventory stocks reached their lowest point in December 1944. During World War II the United States never escaped the threat of running out of rubber, which stood as a sword of Damocles over the entire economic and military effort. In 1944 it almost ran out.

Some of the consequences were described in the 1945 *Annual Report* of the Army Service Forces (ASF), responsible for procurement for the ground forces: "It was necessary during the last 3 months of 1944 and first 2 months of 1945 to place in effect stringent restrictions on the use and issue of tires for military vehicles in zone of the interior [the 48 states] . . . . Only vehicles in special categories were allowed to be equipped with spares." Tires were removed from all vehicles in storage and undergoing repair and shipped overseas. Finally, "Vehicles were accepted from manufacturers without spares, and it was necessary to accept a considerable number of vehicles without any tires on them" (U.S. Army Service Forces, 1945, p. 199).

In his retrospective from the vantage point of October 1945, Julius Krug, the second and last director of the War Production Board, emphasized how dicey the situation remained, in spite of the large volumes of synthetic rubber that were by then being produced, because for many critical purposes some quantity of natural rubber still had to be blended with the synthetic to make a satisfactory product: "This residual technological dependence on natural rubber meant that our precarious supply outlook for that raw material persisted to the very end of the Japanese war. Forward demand estimates for 1945 and 1946 under the stepped-up military tire schedules for those years had indicated exhaustion of our reserve stocks during the first half of 1946" (U.S. War Production Board, 1945a, p. 94).

Before Pearl Harbor it was clear to anyone who looked at the problem seriously that access to natural rubber would be seriously impaired were the country to become embroiled in a conflict with Japan. Supply lines might be jeopardized by a shortage of shipping, by submarine predation, or, worst of all, by a complete cutoff if the producing areas came under Japanese control, as in fact happened. Even if consumer demand could be (as it eventually was) repressed through the imposition of a nationwide thirty-five-mile-per-hour speed limit along with gasoline rationing, and the forced cessation of the production of passenger vehicles, the derived demand for rubber from the production of military goods simply could not be satisfied by African, Latin American, or Ceylonese (still under British control) supplies of natural rubber alone, even if augmented by possible domestic plant substitutes for natural rubber or reclaimed rubber.

A Sherman tank, of which almost 50,000 were produced, required half a ton of rubber. A heavy bomber (almost 35,000 produced) required almost a ton. A battleship took eighty tons. Additional rubber would be needed to equip soldiers with gas masks (26.6 million produced), boots (26.3 million pair), and other rubber-using equipment and clothing (Finlay, 2009, p. 171). Add to that commitments to supply allies with rubber and rubber goods as well as maintain the existing domestic fleet of cars, buses, and trucks and satisfy critical industrial, medical, and electrical industry needs, and one begins to appreciate how precarious the situation could and would become. In addition to the 27 million cars and 5 million trucks, there were 1.6 million tractors and 142,000 buses in operation at the time of Pearl Harbor, along with earth-moving and heavy construction vehicles, most of which also rolled on rubber tires (U.S. Petroleum Administration for War, 1946, p. 9).

During the First World War the United States never experienced a serious shortage of rubber, aside from one sometimes created by limited shipping capacity. But there had been a short period starting in November 1914 during which England temporarily curtailed access to supplies from the East Indies, a reminder of U.S. vulnerability. The British intent, successfully achieved, was to pressure the then-neutral United States for a commitment not to reexport natural rubber to Germany (Finlay, 2009, p. 34).

In the recession of 1920–21 that followed the war, rubber prices cratered. British colonial producers, with help from the British government, moved to cartelize production through the Stevenson Plan, a system of export licenses designed to control the worldwide quantity of shipments. In spite of the inability to secure cooperation from producers in areas under Dutch control, the efforts contributed, in the context of rising demand from the U.S. automobile industry, to a tenfold increase in the price of natural rubber, from under 12.5 cents a pound in August 1922 to $1.23 a pound in July 1925. The United States, which in that year consumed 76 percent of world production (Howard, 1947, p. 5), responded by developing a reclaimed (recycled) rubber industry, whose output was an inferior material usable only in low-grade products, and with several types of initiatives intended to reduce dependence on Southeast Asian supplies.[12] In one category were attempts to develop large *Hevea* plantations outside the United States but under the control of U.S. private investors.

Attempts to Develop Alternative Plant-Based Sources of Latex

Goodyear and U.S. Rubber moved forward, developing their own plantations in Malaya and Sumatra, respectively, but access to them would of course be lost following the fall of Singapore. The most famous effort was Henry Ford's attempt to integrate backward into the cultivation and production of rubber—a key raw material required by the cars rolling off his assembly lines. Ford built Fordlandia, a rubber plantation and transplanted midwestern factory town in the heart of the Amazon, on a land grant more than three times the size of Rhode Island (2.5 million acres). Ford began work on the project in 1928 and abandoned it in 1934. He tried again at a location about eighty miles downstream. Twenty million dollars later, both efforts were failures because of labor shortages, poor choices of location, and, most devastatingly, leaf blight (Grandin, 2009).[13]

Plantation cultivation of Hevea never succeeded in South America because of the microorganism (Microcyclus ulei) that causes the blight and eventually kills the trees. The wild trees survive because they are dispersed, on average about one per acre; in plantations, close together, they invite attack. Remarkably, the infestation did not spread to Southeast Asia. Almost all the rubber trees in the region were and are genetically identical to those growing wild in Brazil; this lack of biodiversity makes them vulnerable.[14]

Harvey Firestone had more commercial success in Africa. In 1925 he negotiated with the Liberian government a lease on 200,000 acres with a ninety-nine-year option on an additional 800,000 acres (Stocking and Watkins, 1946, p. 73). Firestone's Liberian operations, which became the world's largest rubber plantation, began in 1926. It has continued to operate, sometimes at reduced capacity depending on the state of the world rubber market and Liberian internal political conflict; operations have been mired in recent decades in allegations of child labor and the company's cooperation with the murderous guerilla leader Charles Taylor. After Pearl Harbor, Rubber Reserve contracted with Firestone for the entire output of his Liberian operation. U.S. imports from that country almost tripled during World War II, and in 1943, the year of the United States' lowest imports, these holdings supplied almost a quarter (23 percent) of a greatly reduced flow of imports, although this was never enough to account for more than about 2 percent of overall U.S. consumption (Herbert and Bisio, 1985, p. 18; Wendt, 1947, p. 208).

Both Henry Ford and Harvey Firestone were also keenly interested in the search for plants that could be grown in the United States or areas under U.S. political control that might be commercially viable sources of polymerized isoprene, supporting research or in the case of Ford actually conducting experimental cultivation. It was their close friend and camping companion Thomas Edison, however, who pursued this exploration most aggressively. Edison devoted the last four years of his life (1927–31) to the systematic search for plants that could be grown rapidly in the United States (so that a rubber supply might be quickly accessed in an emergency), were suitable for mechanical harvesting, and from which relatively high yields of rubber could be extracted. At the time of his death, he was focused on goldenrod.

Many other plants were and have been considered. These included kok-saghyz, a Russian dandelion with over 10 percent rubber content (versus about .2 percent in common dandelions), *Cryptostegia grandiflora,* a vine native to Madagascar, which was the basis of a wartime project involving hundreds of thousands of acres in Haiti, and guayule (*Parthenium argentatum*), a shrub native to Mexico and the southwestern United States.[15] Few people are familiar with this plant. But at the turn of the twentieth century, wild guayule already had a record of successful commercial exploitation by the Intercontinental Rubber Company (IRC), which numbered among its investors a pantheon of Wall Street notables, included Nelson Aldrich, Bernard Baruch, Daniel and Sol Guggenheim, Jacob Schiff, and John D. Rockefeller Jr. The IRC operation in Mexico, through its operating subsidiary, the Continental Mexican Rubber Company, harvested and then, using capital-intensive and patented processes, extracted rubber from the plants. Polished stones in rotating drums crushed the leaves and stalks. The output was placed in settling tanks, where the rubber floated to the top and was then dried in sheets (van Harmelen, 2021, p. 70). In 1910 guayule was the source of almost one-fifth (19 percent) of U.S. rubber consumption. The IRC controlled over 3.8 million acres in Mexico, which gave it a practical monopoly of the shrub's natural habitat.

Beginning in 1910, Mexican revolutionaries repeatedly disrupted operations at the Torréon, Mexico, facility, and in 1916 the IRC took seeds to the United States with the intent of converting the wild plant into a domesticated cultivated crop, planting acreage near San Diego, California, and south of Tucson, Arizona, and, in 1926, in Salinas, California. Over five months during the spring of 1930, U.S. Army Major Dwight D. Eisenhower toured IRC operations in California, Arizona, and Mexico as part of a two-man team. He recommended in a confidential report that the government subsidize 400,000 acres of guayule cultivation in the United States, replanting a quarter every year to ensure a renewable supply of about 71,000 long tons per year, a fifth of annual consumption during the 1930s, and just under a tenth in 1941. This production flow would have exceeded the entirety of U.S. rubber imports in 1943 and would have substantially relaxed wartime constraints.

Nothing came of the proposal, largely because Southeast Asian rubber at the time was so cheap. Profits eluded the IRC in the worst years of the Depression, but the broader recartelization of the international industry in 1934 with the International Rubber Regulation Agreement lifted prices and helped keep the firm afloat. Salvation came in March 1942, with the passage of the Emergency Rubber Act (also known as the Guayule Act), which empowered the federal government to "buy up all properties, rights, and patents of the Intercontinental Rubber Company" (U.S. Senate, 1942, p. 41). In 1942 and 1943 the federal Emergency Rubber Project funded the planting of 33,000 acres of guayule on irrigated land in California and Arizona, and between 1942 and 1945 the project imported an average of 6,000 tons of rubber from Mexican wild guayule.

The minutes of the May 18, 1943, meeting of the War Production Board indicate that the "need for food" had dictated "curtailing to a minimum the production of guayule on irrigated food producing lands" (U.S. Civilian Production Administration, 1946a, p. 227). This anodyne notation papered over contentious economic and political conflicts. U.S. farmers chafed under pressure from the Emergency Rubber Project to sign long-term contracts to grow guayule. Farmers had become accustomed to Agricultural Adjustment Act payments for food crops and cotton, which were jeopardized by the guayule contracts pressed on them by the Project (Finlay, 2009, p. 203). On May 14, 1945, a bill that would have encouraged private cultivation of guayule by setting the price at 28 cents a pound through 1956 passed the House of Representatives but did not become law. In 1946 farmers plowed under guayule plants that, had they been allowed to reach maturity, would have been capable of producing 20,000 long tons of rubber (Wendt, 1947, pp. 206–8; van Harmelen, 2021, pp. 88–89). Cultivated guayule yielded only about 1,000 long tons of rubber before the wartime program was terminated.

Guayule is not an ideal emergency rubber source. Edison had never been enthusiastic about it because, after planting, it took at least two and ideally four years to yield significant rubber content. At its optimum age for harvesting (four years), guayule, excluding its leaves, contains about 22 percent latex (U.S. Army Industrial College, 1946b, p. 15). So it would have been better to start on a crash program before 1942, as Eisenhower had recommended in the early 1930s. About $45 million was nevertheless spent on the Emergency Rubber Project during World War II. The project was headquartered in Salinas, California, at the IRC facilities bought by the Department of Agriculture, and over a thousand agricultural scientists participated.

In a separate research operation championed by Dr. Robert Emerson of Caltech, interned Japanese American agronomists at the Manzanar relocation camp demonstrated the advantages of planting and propagation using cuttings, made progress on hybridization, developing strains that could better survive in semi-arid conditions, and improvised more efficient processes for extracting the rubber (Wendt, 1947, p. 208; Finlay, 2009, pp. 199–201; U.S.

Department of Agriculture, 2017; van Harmelen, 2021, p. 76). Their research was strongly supported by Eisenhower's brother Milton, the first director of the War Relocation Administration (he resigned after three months) and subsequently associate director of the Office of War Information. The Manzanar project was ultimately shut down, in part because of conflict with the Agriculture Department scientists in Salinas, who saw the Manzanar lab as competition and spread baseless rumors that the internees were shipping seeds to Japan (van Harmelen, 2021, p. 81).

Another revival of interest in guayule took place in the 1970s, when surging oil prices undermined what had always been the case for producing synthetic rubber from a petroleum feedstock. In November 1978 Congress passed the Native Latex Commercialization and Economic Development Act to support research, development, and demonstration production of guayule rubber. In the 1990s researchers discovered that guayule rubber, although similar to rubber from *Hevea*, is hypoallergenic, and therefore of value to those allergic to latex; this created a niche market for surgical gloves made from the product. Corporate-backed projects to develop domestic sources of guayule for use in tire production, reflecting the United States' continuing dependence on natural rubber, continued in the twenty-first century. In 2017 the country consumed 965,000 metric tons of natural rubber, 23 percent more than it had in 1941.[16] In 2020 it remained the second-largest importer of natural rubber after China.

Whatever hopes there may have been for domestic plant-based solutions to the country's rubber vulnerability, and whatever limited imports might be drawn from Firestone's Liberian or the IRC's Mexican operations, or RRC contracts with Central American or South American governments, most notably Brazil,[17] for access to the latex in wild plants, it was obvious in 1940, given the failure to act on Eisenhower's proposal, and as the United States prepared for the likelihood of a two-front war, and given the unwillingness or inability at that late date to accumulate a larger strategic reserve, that a U.S. synthetic rubber program would have to be part of the solution. Between 1941 and 1943, imports from Asia (including Ceylon) fell 98 percent, from 1,007,600 to 20,100 long tons. Imports from Africa (the Firestone Liberian operations) increased from 10,600 to 13,600 long tons, and from Latin American wild cultivation increased from 10,800 to 26,200 long tons. But these were just drops in the bucket compared to the loss of Southeast Asian rubber (Wendt, 1947, p. 208). The plug was pulled on the $45 million domestic guayule program before it could contribute significant supplies.

Without domestic sources of rubber, with an inadequate domestic stock-pile, and given the Japanese stranglehold on U.S. imports of natural rubber. the United States faced a disaster of monumental proportions unless it could quickly produce large amounts of synthetic rubber. Suppressing nonessential demand could buy some time but could be only part of the solution. Four days after Pearl Harbor (December 11, 1941) the Office of Price Administration (OPA) temporarily halted all sales of tires, while it worked to set up 5,600 local ration boards. Starting on January 5, 1942, each board received an allotment based on the number of local vehicle registrations and rationed tires according to criteria specified in OPA guidelines.

As the war progressed, the problem was not simply the military needs for tires, tank treads, radiator hoses, seals, gaskets, grommets, and innumerable other rubber products used in the manufacture and maintenance of military trucks, jeeps, tanks, planes, and ships and the outfitting of soldiers. In the face of rationing and very limited availability of replacements, the existing tires on the country's 27 million passenger vehicles and 5 million trucks were wearing out "at a rate eight times greater than they are being replaced," the Survey Committee Report warned in September 1942. "If this rate continues, by far the larger number of cars will be off the road next year [1943] and in 1944 there will be an all but complete collapse" (U.S. Rubber Survey Committee, 1942, p. 5).

A May 27, 1942, report of the Petroleum Industry War Council had estimated that without reductions in average speed and mileage, and in the absence of more rubber, 18 million passenger vehicles would be off the road by the end of 1943, and 26 million (in other words, almost all of them) by the end of 1944 (U.S. Bureau of the Budget, 1946, p. 167). For some critically important prod-ucts made from rubber, there were simply no substitutes. A joint committee of automotive engineers and tire specialists, desperate for substitutes, studied possible alternatives, but concluded in 1943 that "an automobile simply could not be kept on the road and in useful service by any known device save the rubber tire" (Howard, 1947, p. 207).[18]

The United States depended, more than other nations, on vehicles rolling on pneumatic tires to get its workforce to and from work and to distribute raw materials, inventories, and finished products for both civilian and military uses. Heavy rail, light rail, and trolleys could take up some of the slack, but even these vehicles depended on rubber for electrical insulation and many other components.

Reliance on synthetics rather than increased domestic supplies of natural rubber as the primary supply enhancement meant that the scientific effort would be led primarily by industrial chemists and petroleum engineers rather than by botanists or agronomists. This did not, however, resolve important questions of what feedstocks should be dominant in the program, when and if construction should begin on the plants, and what their capacity should be. Perhaps it was inevitable, given the situation in 1941, that the country would rely on synthetic rubber rather than alternative sources of *Hevea* (which could not be grown in the continental United States) or other plant sources for natural rubber, such as guayule, which needed more lead time. But within the synthetic program, the choice of feedstocks, the types of synthetics produced, and the processes used to turn the former into the latter were by no means inevitable. Nor were the dates on which plant construction would actually begin.

The United States did develop a synthetic rubber industry, which by 1944 produced large quantities, indeed, more in that year than the military could use, because of dwindling stocks of natural rubber, which remained a complementary input. And the industry persisted, ultimately commercially viable and fully privatized by 1955. In 1957 U.S. reliance on synthetics far exceeded that of any other Western country (Canada was the closest), partly because the United States did not have a significant interest in protecting the exports of rubber-producing colonies or former colonies (Phillips, 1960, p. 331). So it is easy to fall into the celebratory language of the American Chemical Society ("an industrial and scientific miracle"). But there are reasons to resist that urge.

Although the private companies operating the fifty-one government-owned plants had little initial experience with a number of the processes chosen, the chemistry allowing rubber to be created synthetically, based mostly on European research, had been understood for at least two decades. It was also known that there were two main pathways to achieving this result, the most important distinctions involving which feedstocks were used, petroleum or alcohol, and that along each pathway there were multiple routes or byways. By 1939 Germany had a well-developed industry using brown coal (lignite) to produce gasoline, industrial alcohol, and synthetic rubber. During World War I, the Soviet Union produced synthetic rubber from plant sources (mostly potatoes and wheat) and continued to do so during World War II.

A small part of the synthetic program consisted of neoprene and butyl. These were specialty rubbers that had been developed in the 1930s by DuPont and Standard Oil of New Jersey, respectively. Neoprene, but not butyl, had been produced and sold commercially before the war. Specialty rubbers commanded a price premium and were used in relatively small quantities in applications where their properties were of particular value. The fact that the country continued to be able to make these products in modest quantities after Pearl Harbor was not a miracle.

The major component of the synthetic rubber program was GR-S, the U.S. label for what the Germans called Buna S. The real challenge was to develop the ability to produce large quantities of general-purpose rubber, which could substitute for much of the natural rubber in such critical applications as tire treads and carcasses. The objective, and ultimately the big achievement of the program, was to mass-produce GR-S. Was it miraculous for the United States ultimately to produce a product, Buna S (GR-S) rubber, which Germany and the Soviet Union had been making for years? True, the United States eventually synthesized much of it using petroleum as a feedstock, a departure from German and Soviet practices. And it produced much more than these other countries. Germany was poorly endowed with petroleum and relied on the alcohol pathway, albeit using a different byway than that favored by the USSR. What the United States achieved can appear miraculous only if one has a poor view of U.S. war-planning, organizational, and engineering capabilities. One cannot both have a decent opinion of the latter and claim a miracle.[19]

The Feedstock Question: Why So Much Emphasis on Petroleum?

The history of the German and Soviet industries underlines the reality that there were different routes to synthesizing rubber, and in the case of the United States, the decisions about which to emphasize had implications for production, productivity, and the ability to prevail in the military conflict. In 1942 the military situation was perilous for the country, and long-run considerations were of little relevance if the U.S. economy ground to a halt and its military capabilities collapsed. The decisions made with respect to the timetable and overall design of the synthetic rubber program, combined with earlier decisions to stint on the stockpile program and not fund guayule cultivation, came close to precipitating a disaster in 1943. The substantial shortfall of synthetic output relative to target seriously constrained military options and threatened the U.S. domestic economy as it depleted its nonreplenished stock of installed pneumatic tires.[20] By 1943 tire tread remaining on the 27 million passenger vehicles in the country was down to 40 percent of normal (Wendt, 1947, p. 220).

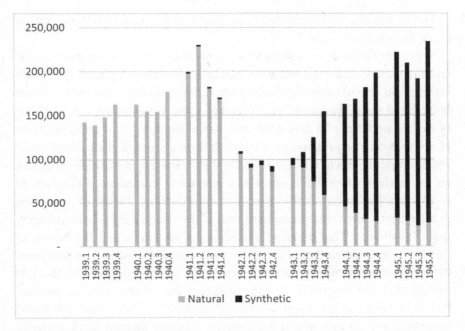

Figure 3.1. U.S. rubber consumption, quarterly, 1939–45 (long tons). Source: U.S. War Production Board, 1945a, p. 95.

The severity of constraints placed by the rubber situation on the economy can be appreciated by examining quarterly data on consumption of natural and synthetic rubber (Figure 3.1). This figure reveals several striking realities. First, as far as rubber is concerned, following peak consumption in 1941Q2, the United States embarked on a starvation diet.[21] By the fourth quarter of 1943, consumption had declined 60 percent and would not recover until after the end of the war. Second, synthetic production was negligible until well into the second half of 1943. Synthetic rubber of all types constituted only 7.6 percent of consumption in 1943Q1 and only 16.2 percent in 1943Q2. In 1943Q3 it rose to 40.4 percent and, finally, in the last three months of 1943, it exceeded 50 percent for the first time.

Some of the obstacles overcome by U.S. chemists and engineers could have been avoided through a different design of the program or an earlier start to plant construction—or both. And the prewar acquisition of a larger stockpile of natural rubber would have relaxed many constraints. So, too, would the adoption of the Eisenhower proposal. Even had all of this been done, the country would have taken a hit on productivity in the fabrication of rubber products. But the miscalculations and bad bets regarding synthetic supply made the situation worse.

Whatever the feedstocks chosen for the program, in retrospect it was a mistake not to have embarked earlier on building the necessary plants. The delays represented one of several gambles with national security that many argued beforehand were ill-advised. In this instance the bet was that U.S. supplies of rubber would not be disrupted, and so the country could avoid the costs of a very expensive program or, if supplies were disrupted, the country could quickly produce lots of GR-S at scale, or, if that was not possible, it could rely on the strategic stockpile. It was also a mistake to embark on a program so heavily emphasizing (initially exclusively emphasizing) the use of petroleum as a feedstock to produce butadiene, one of the two key ingredients in making GR-S rubber. That decision wasted scarce resources and manpower in constructing facilities that, during the war, were not needed. The processes used to produce butadiene from petroleum refinery byproducts required more complicated and expensive capital equipment than that needed to produce butadiene from alcohol. There was little experience with the petroleum-based processes, and no one within the industry expected them to work perfectly from the start. The plant construction program, designed principally around the petroleum pathway, resulted in conflicts with the aviation fuel program for scarce valves, pumps, heat exchangers, and motors (Wendt, 1947, p. 212). Once in operation, the butylene needed to make the butadiene conflicted with the needs for producing 100-octane aviation fuel.

Defenders of the emphasis on petroleum can argue that the key decisions, basically made by November 1940, were correct from the standpoint of the longer run. But the hard reality is that the program failed to deliver promised production in the critical year 1943, and it then produced more than could be used in 1944, in the process having consumed resources that could have been better employed elsewhere in the war effort. Defenders can say with some reason that these problems would not have been as serious had plant construction started earlier. Government decision makers, especially Jesse Jones, bear responsibility here. But Jones does not deserve all the blame. Proceeding along a petroleum route might have been easier and more defensible had Standard Oil of New Jersey in the 1930s moved more aggressively to encourage development of a synthetic rubber capability through its licensing policies and its own research.

Synthetic rubber was far from a smooth creation from scratch of an industry necessary for economic survival and military victory. The economics and the politics of the country, the delays in initiating construction, and the imperfect navigation by government officials of the conflict between the commercial interests of private U.S. corporations and the national interest in defeating adversaries led to a development path that jeopardized military capabilities in 1943 and could arguably have led to the loss of the war had the Soviets not prevailed at Stalingrad. There is unanimity among historians that Stalingrad was a turning point. What that conclusion implies, had the outcome been different, involves exercises in counterfactual history that are inherently speculative. What is not speculative is that shortfalls in synthetic rubber production seriously constrained Allied military options in 1943.

The Output Mix and the Basic Chemistry

In contrast to wartime aircraft manufacture, the final products being produced, such as tires, were not radically different for many of the firms making them. The big challenges involved producing an adequate substitute for the natural rubber that otherwise would have been imported and used as the principal input in rubber products manufacture and learning how to use and blend synthetic with natural rubber in the fabrication of familiar end products. The government-funded synthetic rubber program in the United States produced three different types of rubber during the war. The vast bulk of program output was GR-S (general-purpose synthetic) rubber, the American designation for what the Germans had trademarked as Buna S. The rest was neoprene and butyl. The main use of GR-S was and is in the manufacture of tire treads and carcasses.

Butyl rubber had been developed by researchers at Standard Oil of New Jersey in 1937. Butyl differs from GR-S in having high gas impermeability, which made it desirable for the manufacture of inner tubes. It is also highly resistant to ozone, the enemy of natural and many other forms of synthetic rubber. The record of producing butyl during the war, however, was disappointing. Standard Oil of New Jersey, the sole government contractor for this part of the program, had great difficulty getting its processes to operate at scale, and it never met production targets. The reasons for this are unclear (references in the literature are typically to unspecified "technical problems"), but the process Standard had developed in the 1930s required copolymerization at 100 degrees below zero Fahrenheit, which likely turned out to be much more difficult to manage and control in large batches. In his memoir, Standard's vice president in charge of research, patents, and chemical development simply states that the processes were not behaving "consistently" (Howard, 1947, pp. 191–92). Even moderate success was not achieved until June 1944 (Solo, 1959, p. 91).

Although Standard had high hopes for butyl, it remained largely a specialty product. The material was ideal for most inner tubes (90 percent of butyl was used for this purpose in 1953), but with the diffusion of the tubeless tire, introduced in 1954 and standard on new passenger vehicles starting in 1955, demand tanked. Several years later, after the development of chlorinated and brominated butyl made it possible to bond butyl to GR-S or natural rubber, butyl began to be used for the inner liner in tubeless tires, where its high gas impermeability again served well.

The main marketing disappointment, however, was that all-butyl tires were inferior to those made from natural rubber or GR-S or a blend of the two. The reason was poor tread wear. This was a conclusion reluctantly reached by the military after National Bureau of Standard tests conducted in 1943 (Roth and Holt, 1944). In 1959 Standard, Firestone, and U.S. Rubber again tried selling all-butyl tires, but the products failed for the same reason they had been rejected by the military in 1943: poor tread wear (Herbert and Bisio, 1985, pp. 200–201). As a specialty rubber, butyl rubber is used (aside from as a tire liner) wherever airtight seals are needed (as in gas masks), in heavy rubber gloves where gas impermeability is a necessity (for example, in the nuclear industry), as a binder in C-4 explosives, and in chewing gum. And bicycle inner tubes continued to be made from it in the 2020s.

Finally, there were smaller amounts of neoprene, the most expensive of the synthetics. The pioneer research on acetylene chemistry that led to the development of this product was conducted by Julius A. Nieuwland of Notre Dame University. DuPont bought the patent rights from Notre Dame and in 1930, under the direction of Wallace Carothers, created the new synthetic rubber.[22] Neoprene is characterized by high oil resistance and is thus particularly suitable for hoses used in fueling vehicles with gasoline. It also has relatively good resistance to ozone. In its foamed version (suffused with nitrogen bubbles) it is familiar in wetsuits, ski masks, mouse pads, and laptop and tablet cases.

How did the United States approach the manufacture of GR-S, the main output of the synthetic rubber program? Since Germany was making Buna S using coal as a feedstock, and the Soviet Union was producing it using potatoes or grain as a feedstock, the product can clearly be synthesized from quite different raw materials. In 1942 the primary national objective for the United States, and the rationale for asking government to shoulder the burden of building plants that industry was reluctant to fund, was to ensure the survival of the country by maintaining and expanding its military capabilities while allowing the domestic economy to continue to function. Leaders of the firms operating the plants, however, always had in the back of their minds the design of an industry that might (but might not) be commercially viable after the war. The decision to structure the program around an almost exclusive emphasis on petroleum as a feedstock worked at cross-purposes with the immediate objective of winning (or at least not losing) the war.

Petroleum Refineries, Hydrocarbon Chemistry, and Synthetic Rubber

To understand how synthetic rubber is produced along the petroleum pathway, one must start with how crude oil is refined. That process begins by heating the raw material until it vaporizes, after which it enters a distillation tower, where the oil separates into lighter and heavier fractions, depending on their boiling points. The lighter fractions, including gases such as propane (known to consumers as a fuel for camping and RV stoves) and butane (familiar in small cigarette lighters), rise to the top of the tower and are drawn off. Below them, light distillates, such as gasoline and kerosene, condense and can be drawn off. And below those, medium distillates such as diesel fuel condense, and then toward the bottom one finds heavier and less volatile distillates such as heating oil (for homes) and bunker oil (for ships). At the very bottom are carbon black feedstock and asphalt for sealing roofs and paving roads. Distillation involves the physical separation of compounds present in the crude oil but not their transformation through chemical reactions. The various fractions resulting from distillation are referred to in the industry as straight-run, as in straight-run gasoline or straight-run fuel oil.

Following distillation, some of the fractions can be further refined through cracking, which requires the application of heat and pressure, sometimes in the presence of catalysts, to the straight-run outputs of distillation. The ability to break down some of the heavier, longer-chain hydrocarbons into shorter molecules means that the percentage of different products derived from a barrel of crude oil can be changed from what results from a straight run. In particular, cracking can produce from the heavier fractions some of the lighter fractions that emerge "naturally" from the distillation process. Thus, for example, while simple distillation of crude oil could produce about one barrel of gasoline from four barrels of crude, cracking allowed the yield to be much higher. Gasoline yield was less important when the main demand was for kerosene for heating and illumination (indeed, the more volatile fuel was often simply discarded), but that changed with the growing importance of internal combustion engines.

Cracking dates from the patenting of the Shukhov process in 1891. The development of the Burton process in 1911 at Standard Oil of Indiana (patented in 1913) allowed a gasoline yield from crude to approach 50 percent. These were similar energy-intensive thermal cracking processes, relying on high heat and pressure to break heavier into lighter fractions. During the 1920s German researchers at BASF (which became part of the IG Farben conglomerate) discovered catalysts that allowed much quicker and cheaper extraction of gasoline from brown coal and in principle allowed the yield from a barrel of crude to approach 100 percent (Howard, 1947, pp. 15–16).[23] Catalytic cracking was cheaper than the earlier thermal cracking methods, requiring lower temperatures and pressures, and yielded a gasoline base stock whose octane could more easily be boosted with blending agents. During the 1920s and the 1930s a French chemist, Eugène Houdry, developed a successful semi-batch catalytic process. During the Second World War, Standard perfected a continuous-flow fluid catalytic process (based on the BASF–IG Farben patents), which, because of its lower cost for large volumes, ultimately supplanted the Houdry units in the postwar period. Houdry also developed a separate catalytic process for making butadiene from butane (American Chemical Society, 1996, p. 4).

Butane, butylene, and isobutylene gases, which figure in the production of both GR-S and butyl rubber, are all hydrocarbons and are all byproducts of the refining of crude oil. Butane gas, as noted, is obtained from the initial (straight-run) distillation process and is also abundant in natural gas. Butane (C_4H_{10}) is a saturated hydrocarbon, an alkane with single bonds connecting the hydrogen and carbon atoms. Butylene, also known (this is confusing) as butene (C_4H_8), is an unsaturated alkene with a double bond between two of the carbon atoms.[24] Isobutylene is an isomer of butylene (same chemical formula; different structure and properties). Although small amounts of butylene and isobutylene are present in crude oil, most is obtained through the further refinements (cracking) of heavier fractions that emerge from the distillation process (and in some cases by dehydrogenating butane).

There are two essential ingredients in the Standard Oil–IG Farben recipe for making GR-S rubber. The first, and most important by weight, is butadiene (C_4H_6). Butadiene can be manufactured from industrial alcohol (C_2H_6O), adding carbon and removing the oxygen, or by dehydrogenating (removing hydrogen from) butane (C_4H_{10}) or butylene (C_4H_8), which, as we have seen, are obtained from the distillation of crude oil and further refinement (cracking) of distillation products. The molecular formulas elucidate the logic of the hydrocarbon chemistry which, stated in its simplest terms, required the application of heat or pressure (or both), sometimes along with catalysts, to add or subtract one or more of the elements in these compounds, thus transforming them into different compounds.

There are multiple byways along either the petroleum or the alcohol pathway. The original process for manufacturing butadiene from ethanol (industrial or grain alcohol) was developed by the Russian chemist Sergei Lebedev before World War I and was the foundation of both the Soviet and German programs. Lebedev also produced polymerized butadiene, which, however, was too soft to be used in tires. In 1929 the chemists Walter Bock and Eduard Tschunker at IG Farben perfected a process for copolymerizing butadiene with styrene, creating Buna S rubber.

Styrene (C_8H_8) is commonly obtained by compressing ethylene (C_2H_4) and benzene (C_6H_6) in the presence of a catalyst, producing ethylbenzene (C_8H_{10}), which is then, under heat and pressure and in the presence of a catalyst, dehydrogenated (losing two hydrogen atoms). The material is a key ingredient in making many plastics (polymerized styrene—polystyrene—is the chief plastic in model airplane kits; foamed polystyrene is familiar as Styrofoam). Both ethylene gas and benzene are produced in the petrochemical industry as the result of distillation of crude oil and further refinement (cracking) of distillation products. Ethylene can also be produced from ethyl alcohol (ethanol), and this turned out in fact to be the dominant route used during the war for obtaining it (Rubber Reserve Company, 1945, p. 26). Styrene, unlike butadiene, had been manufactured commercially before the war, admittedly at a relatively small scale, and only by one company, Dow Chemical (Howard, 1947, p. 160).

GR-S rubber was made by copolymerizing butadiene gas and styrene liquid in a ratio of 3:1. In an enclosed, glass-lined reaction vessel, butadiene and styrene were emulsified in water using small amounts of soap flakes along with two catalysts. The result was a milky latex that, when stirred in the presence of acids, formed curds, which were subsequently washed, dried, pressed, and sheeted. Natural rubber and filler and extenders such as carbon black and other compounds were then blended (compounded) with the synthetic in large Banbury mixers before the final product (such as a tire) was cured or vulcanized.

The main question, which erupted into a full-blown political crisis in the United States in 1942, was where the butadiene was to come from. The Lebedev process derived it from ethanol, which could be obtaining by fermenting plant material (corn, other grains, potatoes, sugar refinery byproducts) or from coal or petroleum. Ultimately (and only after substantial protest and political resistance), out of 630,000 short tons per year of rated butadiene capacity built by the government, only three plants with a total of 220,000 short tons of rated capacity were designed and built to use alcohol rather than petroleum as a feedstock. These were the Union Carbide plant in Institute, West Virginia (80,000 short tons rated annual capacity), the Union Carbide plant in Louisville, Kentucky (60,000 short tons), and the Koppers plant in Kobuta, Pennsylvania (80,000 short tons).

These plants made butadiene quickly and in quantity in 1943 and 1944, when it was most needed, as table 3.1 shows. In 1943 they produced 129,685 short tons, 58.9 percent of the combined rated capacity of the three plants. That represented 82 percent of the butadiene produced from all sources in that year. In 1944 these three plants delivered 361,731 short tons, 164.4 percent of rated capacity, and 65 percent of the butadiene produced from all sources in that year. The 1945 figures are lower since immediately after V-J Day in August 1945, all the alcohol-based plants were put on standby because the marginal cost of alcohol feedstock was by then higher than the butylene from petroleum.

Based on the number of employees at the end of 1944, physical labor productivity in the plants using alcohol was 199.0 short tons per employee in the peak year of production. Capital productivity, based on the cost of constructing the plants, was 3.175 tons per thousand dollars of installed annual capacity. In both cases these numbers substantially exceeded those observed in the plants using petroleum as the feedstock. That the alcohol plants were so successful in quickly producing large quantities of butadiene at scale is not surprising. Although the United States had little experience with either alcohol- or petroleum-based processes, the ethanol-to-butadiene route had been successfully exploited for more than two decades in the Soviet Union, Germany, Poland, and other countries. The same can be said for the copolymerization of butadiene and styrene into Buna S or GR-S rubber.

But it cannot be said for the petroleum-to-butadiene route. The chemistry of working through either butane or butylene (butene) to butadiene was understood, and there was confidence either of these byways could eventually be made to work. But no country had produced butadiene from petroleum on a large scale before, so there was little experience in running the reactions and in increasing the yields. One could not expect these processes to operate at scale immediately. Above and beyond the reasonable anticipation of the

Table 3.1 Inputs to GR-S Rubber: Butadiene and Styrene Production, 1943–45
Butadiene from Alcohol

Contractor	Location	Plant Cost $ millions	Number Employed Dec. 44	Rated Capacity (short tons)	Output as % of Rated Capacity		
					1943	1944	1945
Union Carbide	Institute, W.V.			80,000	96.8	176.2	112.4
Union Carbide	Louisville, Ky.			60,000	42.6	156.8	94.9
Koppers	Kobuta, Pa.			80,000	33.4	158.4	108.1
TOTAL FROM ALCOHOL		$113.95	1,818	220,000	58.9	164.4	106.1
Labor productivity, alcohol (tons per employee)					71.33	198.97	
Capital productivity, alcohol (tons/$1,000 installed capacity)					1.14	3.17	

From Petroleum Feedstock:
Butadiene from Butylene (Butene)

Contractor	Location	Plant Cost $ millions	Number Employed Dec. 44	Rated Capacity (short tons)	1943	1944	1945
Cities Service	Lake Charles, La.			55,000		12.0	60.4
Humble Oil	Baytown, Tex.			40,000	15.5	73.7	98.8
Neches Butane	Port Neches, Tex.			100,000		48.3	98.0
Shell Union	Torrance, Calif.			55,000	3.0	56.2	77.3
Sinclair Rubber	Houston, Tex.			50,000		38.3	91.0
SONJ	Baton Rouge, La.			15,000	77.0	118.7	110.2
TOTAL				315,000	6.2	48.4	87.4

Butadiene from Butane

Contractor	Location			Rated Capacity	1943	1944	1945
Phillips	Borger, Tex.			45,000	8.7	51.7	70.9
Sun Oil	Toledo, Ohio			15,000		16.5	60.3
SOCA	El Segundo, Calif.			18,000		22.1	48.6
TOTAL				78,000	5.0	38.1	63.7

Butadiene from Naphtha

				22,500	19.5	61.5	75.8
TOTAL FROM PETROLEUM		$221.23	5,670	415,500	6.7	47.1	82.3
Labor productivity, petroleum (tons per employee)					4.89	34.55	
Capital productivity, petroleum (tons/$1,000 installed capacity)					0.13	0.89	
TOTAL BUTADIENE FROM ALL SOURCES (% of rated capacity)					24.8	87.7	90.6

Styrene

Contractor	Location	Plant Cost $ millions	Number Employed Dec. 44	Rated Capacity	1943	1944	1945
Union Carbide	Institute, W.V.			25,000	23.7	76.2	67.1
Dow	Los Angeles, Calif.			25,000	43.3	52.4	76.2
Dow	Velasco, Tex.			50,000	18.2	96.2	123.2
Koppers	Kobuta, Pa.			37,500	15.6	85.4	78.3
Monsanto	Texas City, Tex.			50,000	31.1	95.3	106.7
TOTAL STYRENE		$77.3	2,162	187,500	25.2	85.3	96.1

Notes: Humble Oil is a subsidiary of Standard Oil of New Jersey. SONJ = Standard Oil of New Jersey; SOCA = Standard Oil of California.

Sources: Herbert and Bisio, 1985, tables 11.5, 11.6, 11.8, 11.9; original data from Rubber Reserve Company, 1945.

equivalent of bugs and crashes, it was clear, given the late start, that the petro-leum-based butadiene plants would compete with the aviation fuel program (among others) for needed plant, equipment, and construction materials, and, finally, once operational, that there would be conflicts with aviation fuel over the butylene (butene) needed to make the butadiene.

Military and war planners knew in 1942 that the military situation in 1943 would continue to be perilous particularly if, as was then expected, the So-viet resistance at Stalingrad collapsed. So at a time when large quantities of butadiene were urgently needed, it was risky, indeed arguably imprudent, to continue to proceed with a synthetic program designed so heavily around this pathway.[25] The Rubber Survey Committee acknowledged as much but basi-cally said that by the time of its inquiry (August 1942) the train had left the sta-tion, and that, aside from a few adjustments at the margins, the only reason-able path forward was to "bull through" to the targeted destination.

The committee may have been right in terms of the possible disruptive consequences of trying to make major changes at that point. Beyond the accumulation of an inadequate stockpile of natural rubber, and the failure to embark on a government guayule program before 1942, the public policy mistake had been to allow a heavy and initially exclusive emphasis on pe-troleum as the feedstock to get baked into the structure of the program as early as November 1940, and then, even if that was the wrong decision, to delay starting to build the necessary plants until well into 1942. By the time of the Rubber Survey Committee's deliberations, political pressure had at least succeeded in designating three of the scheduled thirteen butadiene plants to use alcohol, which turned out to be of tremendous importance in 1943.[26] It is possible to compare the output of the three alcohol plants with that of the six facilities built to produce butadiene from butylene (butene), the petroleum refinery byproduct. In contrast to the former group, performance of the latter group in 1943 was abysmal. Three of the six petroleum-based plants produced nothing—zero output—in all of 1943. The remaining three provided a total of 19,427 short tons, 6.2 percent of their combined rated capacity of 315,000 short tons. The three alcohol plants manufactured 6.6 times as much. On August 19, 1943, William Jeffers, the rubber czar appointed after the Survey Committee Report, wrote to Baruch with this evaluation: "By and large, butadiene from petroleum is a pretty sick picture" (Finlay, 2009, pp. 194, 295). Only in 1945 did petroleum-based butadiene production surpass that from the alcohol plants, in part because the latter were shut down almost immediately after V-J Day (see table 3.1).

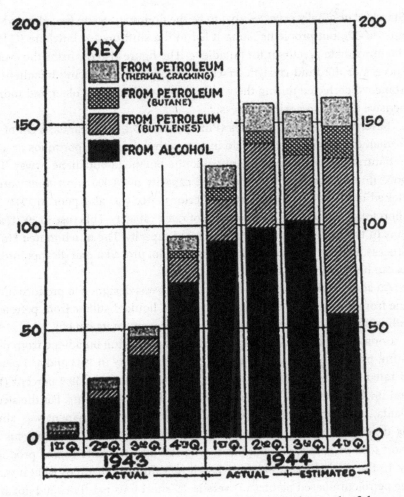

Figure 3.2. Butadiene production by source, quarterly, 1943–44 (thousands of short tons). Source: Howard, 1947, p. 298.

Figure 3.2, excerpted from the memoir of Standard's vice president for research, provides data at higher (quarterly) frequency on butadiene production and also illustrates the effects of the repeated delays and a program design heavily emphasizing the petroleum pathway. It again shows the poor performance of the program in 1943, saved only by the alcohol pathway, and the dominance of alcohol-based butadiene until the final quarter of 1944. It also shows the relative failure of the butane byway along the petroleum pathway, which involved proceeding directly from butane (C_4H_{10}) to butadiene (C_4H_6).

Standard originally expected that to be the dominant route (see Howard, 1947, pp. 136–37), but problems along it led to the shift toward butylene (C_4H_8) as the immediate precursor for butadiene. The figure also confirms the eventual success of the fluid catalytic cracking process for producing butadiene that Standard perfected during the war (as compared with the older and more expensive thermal cracking process).

Several of the oil companies (Phillips, Sun Oil, and Standard Oil of California), for reasons having to do in part with their patent portfolios or access to natural gas, remained committed to the butane-to-butadiene byway. Three government plants with a total rated capacity of 78,000 short tons were designed to operate along this route. Performance was also poor in 1943: 3,930 short tons of output, or just 5 percent of rated capacity. This rose to 29,717 short tons in 1944, still under 40 percent of rated capacity. The much-touted Houdry process, used at the Sun Oil facility in Toledo, proved a real disappointment, as can be seen in table 3.1.

An additional 22,500 tons of rated capacity was designed to produce butadiene from straight-run naphtha, a volatile but liquid distillate from petroleum, falling somewhere between gasoline and kerosene in its density.

Considering all three categories of plants producing butadiene from petroleum, production was at 6.7 percent of rated capacity in 1943 and 47.1 percent of rated capacity in 1944, which compares with output of 58.9 percent (1943) and 164.4 percent (1944) of rated capacity for the alcohol plants. For the alcohol plants, labor productivity based on December 1944 employment was almost six times the comparable figure for the petroleum plants: 199.0 versus 34.6 short tons of output per employee. One can also calculate capital productivity. In the alcohol-based plants in 1944 it was almost four times what it was in the petroleum-based plants: 3.17 versus .89 short tons per thousand dollars of installed capacity.

Robert Solo described the performance of the petroleum-based butadiene plants (and Standard's butyl plants) in this fashion: "These processes were untried, untested, complex, requiring relatively large amounts of critical components. These processes were brought into operation only after repeated delays, experimental trials, failures, and readjustments, so that substantial quantities of synthetic rubber were produced by these processes only in the closing months of 1944 after the critical phases of the military struggle were behind us" (Solo, 1954, p. 67).

One can perhaps quibble with some of the nuances of Solo's narrative, but the data on output in table 3.1 and figure 3.2 are clear on this trajectory.

Defenders of the decision to base the program so heavily on petroleum emphasize that such plants would *eventually* be cheaper to operate, particularly for large volumes, and that the petroleum feedstock would *eventually* be cheaper, helping make the marginal cost of using the petroleum plants lower, once we got to 1945 and beyond. Military imperatives, however, the justification for the government financing of synthetic rubber plants in the first place, were that the country needed rubber and needed it quickly, particularly in 1943 and in 1944. Those were the critical years, when imports were at their lowest, stocks of natural rubber were at their lowest, and U.S. military capability and the civilian economy were most at risk from shortages of rubber products.

Delays in Building Butadiene Capacity

At the time the Rubber Survey Committee began its work (August 1942), a total of only 401 short tons of GR-S had been produced, none of it in the government-owned plants then planned or under construction. Not much more in total (2,241 long tons) had been manufactured by the end of 1942 (Rubber Reserve Company, 1945, pp. 59, 62). Construction on two of the three alcohol-to-butadiene plants started in February and March 1942. The first alcohol plant was not operational until January 29, 1943, although all the capacity was operational by the end of the year. Jeffers, the rubber czar, had worked with the WPB to assign the highest priorities to the equipment needed to finish the alcohol plants, "because of lesser requirements of critical materials and shorter time for completion" (Rubber Reserve Company, 1945, p. 7). Ground was not broken on any of the butylene-to-butadiene plants until May and June 1942, when work was started on four of them. Four of the seven eventually built would not be operational until sometime in 1944.

The committee's decision not to recommend changes in the basic structure of the construction program then planned or under way, in particular its balance between alcohol and petroleum as feedstocks, represented a judgment that the disruptions and delays associated with abandoning some of the petroleum capacity in favor of alcohol would outweigh the possible benefits of more rapidly obtaining large quantities of butadiene from additional alcohol capacity once installed. The overriding objective was to get a great deal of butadiene as soon as possible. The Survey Committee Report in September 1942 emphasized how disastrous the situation would be if this did not happen. In the letter of transmittal to Roosevelt signed by Conant, Compton, and Baruch, the language describing the threat was stark: "We find the existing situation to be so dangerous that unless corrective actions are taken immediately this country will face both a military and civilian collapse. . . . Of all critical and strategic materials, rubber is the one which presents the greatest threat to the safety of the Nation and the success of the Allied cause. . . . If we fail to secure quickly a large new rubber supply, our war effort and our domestic economy will collapse" (1942, p. 23).

Gas Rationing to Save Rubber

In advocating a nationwide program of gas rationing, the committee argued that it was "the only way of saving rubber." Gasoline was not in fact in short supply: "The limitation on the use of gasoline is not due to shortage of that commodity—it is wholly a measure of rubber saving. That is why the restriction is to be nationwide. Any localized measure would be unfair and futile" (U.S. Rubber Survey Committee, 1942, p. 6). The report hoped that if the synthetic program could fulfill "reasonable expectancy," gasoline rationing could be curtailed "before the end of 1943." That was not to be. After resistance in Congress fueled by complaints from drivers in the Midwest and West, where distances were long and gasoline was in plentiful supply, Roosevelt went ahead by executive order and instituted nationwide gas rationing on November 26, 1942, effective December 1, 1942.

Roosevelt, who had earlier seemed, at least in public, unconcerned about the gathering crisis in rubber availability, had encouraged those who thought a scrap rubber drive and voluntary conservation might substitute for the rationing of gasoline in husbanding the rubber inventories held on vehicle axles. And, mindful of opposition from Harold Ickes at the Office of the Petroleum Coordinator and western and midwestern voters, he was probably happy to delay implementation until after the 1942 midterm elections (Tuttle, 1981, p. 47).

Seventeen eastern states had already introduced gas rationing, but this was in response to a regional shortage created by the sinking of tankers moving from the Gulf Coast to eastern ports (see chapter 4). That disruption, which arose from U-boat predation, would be partially mitigated in 1943 and 1944 by the completion of the Big Inch and Little Big Inch pipelines, which brought crude oil and refined products from East Texas to New Jersey and Philadelphia.

Submarine warfare did not threaten shipments from East Texan and Californian refineries to the Midwest and West, and gasoline was abundant in those regions. A spokesperson for the regional OPA office in Cleveland complained, in answer to critics of the rationing program, that citizens were not taking the rubber shortage seriously: "Ohio State and Illinois played to an estimated 68,000 in Cleveland . . . Notre Dame and Michigan drew a crowd of 57,000 in South Bend. People did not walk to these games. Traffic conditions in the host cities indicated that they rode to and from on critical rubber" (*New York Times*, November 27, 1942, p. 32).

The Rubber Survey Committee's report made clear several times that it was not in favor of sacrifice for sacrifice's sake, and it recommended substantial increases in tire production for the domestic automobile fleet in 1944, although, when supplies of natural rubber remained tight in that year, the domestic fleet, as residual claimant, lost out. The committee also explicitly acknowledged past errors, including the failure to place a greater emphasis on alcohol feedstock: "Why not earlier? Why so late? The answers to these queries lie in the past. These errors, growing out of procrastinations, indecisions, conflict of authority, clashes of personalities, lack of understanding, delays, *and early non-use of known alcohol processes*, are not to be recounted by us, nor shall we go into the failure to build a greater stockpile of crude rubber. We are concerned with the past record only insofar as it has seemed to cast light on problems of future administration" (U.S. Rubber Survey Committee, 1942, p. 7; emphasis added). The committee also noted that it "appreciates that it is asking the public to make sacrifices because of mistakes that have been made and for which the people are not to blame. But wrong things done in the past cannot be cited as a defense for making mistakes in the future" (p. 22). The report laid down markers: "If our hopes are realized, the production of Buna S and Neoprene . . . will total 425,000 tons by the end of 1943." But it allowed that "the figure might easily fall to less than half that amount if delays occur" (U.S. Rubber Survey Committee, 1942, p. 7).

Delays did occur, and the more pessimistic forecast turned out to be accurate. Consider Conant and Compton's more pessimistic forecast as an estimate of total cumulated output between September 1942 and December 1943. The data underlying table 3.2 show that combined output of GR-S and neoprene over those two years was 209,672 long tons. The committee considered what might be the consequences, given the anticipated military situation in 1943, of such a shortfall: "With only 200,000 tons of Buna S produced, our supplies would be exhausted. The successful operation of our mechanized army would be jeopardized" (U.S. Rubber Survey Committee, 1942, p. 7). In U.S. government-owned plants the program produced 183,711 long tons of Buna S in 1942 and 1943 combined (Rubber Reserve Company, 1945, p. 59).[27]

The authors reemphasized how important was production for 1943: "The year 1943 is so critical for the rubber situation that the production of 100,000 or 200,000 tons of Buna S may be the determining factor in the success of our military program." And again: "The Committee must emphasize once again that the critical time for the country, as far as the military effort is concerned, is the third quarter of 1943 and the quarters immediately following." And again: "The Committee wishes to emphasize and reemphasize the absolute necessity of having the maximum amount of synthetic rubber produced in the year 1943" (U.S. Rubber Survey Committee, 1942, pp. 17, 34, 48).

Other knowledgeable war planners expressed a similar urgency. Ferdinand Eberstadt had written to Baruch in May 1942 that "unless synthetic rubber is available in quantity by the time the crude stockpile is exhausted, around July 1 [1943], we would appear to have no alternative but to call the whole thing off" (quoted in Tuttle, 1981, p. 38). By "the whole thing," he meant the U.S. military effort in World War II. Eberstadt, the developer of the Controlled Materials Plan, served as chair of the Army and Navy Munitions Board and vice chair of the WPB between September 1942 and February 1943, when he was forced out. It is most likely that his letter to Baruch was prompted by a report of the Advisory Subcommittee on Rubber Economics to the Committee on Synthetic Rubber of the Petroleum Industry War Council submitted on May 27, 1942. Discussed at a June 2, 1942, meeting of the War Production Board, the report, as mentioned earlier, forecast that at then-current rates of wear, the number of operable cars would decline from 27 million to 9 million by the end of 1943 and to 1 million by the end of 1944 (U.S. Civilian Production Administration, 1946a, p. 77).

The U.S. synthetic rubber program eventually succeeded in meeting and exceeding production targets. But it did so at great cost, and it failed to do so in 1943, which exposed the U.S. economy and nation to grave danger. In early 1941 Standard Oil of New Jersey reviewed multiple techniques for producing butadiene (Howard, 1947, p. 136). It zeroed in on two main byways along the petroleum pathway that required either butylene (butene) or butane (as an additional nuance, butylene could be and sometimes was produced with butane as the precursor). A further complicating factor in the use of petroleum as a means of obtaining butadiene: butylene (the main byproduct ultimately used to make it) was also a critical ingredient in producing 100-octane aviation fuel.

Octane measures the ability of gasoline fuel to avoid premature ignition, known popularly as knocking, which occurs when, as the result of heat and pressure, fuel explodes in an engine cylinder before the sparkplug fires.

Table 3.2 Synthetic Rubber Output, 1942–45
GR-S Copolymerization Plants

Contractor	Location	Plant Cost $ millions	Number Employed Dec. 44	Capacity (short tons)	Output as % of Rated Capacity			
					1942	1943	1944	1945
Firestone	Akron, Ohio			30,000	3.1	80.7	131.3	103.3
Firestone	Lake Charles, La			60,000		9.1	77.2	110.5
Firestone	Port Neches, Tex.			60,000		1.1	84.3	105.8
Goodrich	Louisville, Ky.			60,000	0.2	49.5	96.6	103.7
Goodrich	Berger, Tex.			45,000		15.0	88.1	107.8
Goodrich	Port Neches, Tex.			60,000		9.4	83.7	105.7
Goodyear	Akron, Ohio			30,000	2.9	56.8	123.9	99.0
Goodyear	Houston, Tex.			60,000		2.6	75.9	106.7
Goodyear	Los Angeles, Calif.			60,000		11.7	48.8	49.6
US Rubber	Naugatuck, Conn.			30,000	1.1	39.1	92.0	101.2
US Rubber	Institute, W.V.			90,000		40.9	125.5	108.7
US Rubber	Los Angeles, Calif.			30,000		4.3	71.3	112.7
Copolymer	Baton Rouge, La.			30,000		65.8	127.0	109.5
General	Baytown, Tex.			30,000		27.9	123.7	108.9
NSR	Louisville, Ky.			30,000		18.1	118.4	106.0
TOTAL		$152.06	8,105	705,000	0.3	25.7	94.9	101.8
Neoprene								
DuPont	Louisville, Ky.	$37.39	1,887	60,000		41.0	78.8	
Butyl								
SONJ	Baton Rouge, La.			38,000		4.7	37.7	
Humble Oil	Baytown, Tex.			30,000			15.2	
TOTAL		$50.94	1,694	68,000		2.6	27.8	

Notes: Humble Oil is a subsidiary of Standard Oil of New Jersey (SONJ). Butyl output for 1943 and 1944 includes 408 and 442 tons of special polymers, respectively.
Sources: Herbert and Bisio, 1985, tables 11.2, 11.3, 11.8, 11.9; original data from Rubber Reserve Company (1945).

Knocking, which can seriously damage an engine, can be avoided either by using a low-compression design, which limits the attainable horsepower, or by using a specially blended high-octane fuel that can withstand pressure and heat without premature combustion.

In mid-1936 the U.S. Army Air Forces standardized on 100-octane fuel to allow for the development and use of high-compression aircraft engines. By the time of the attack on Pearl Harbor, the United States was a leader in the production of such fuel, and it exported considerable quantities to Britain, which gave British aircraft an edge over their German adversaries in the struggle for supremacy over the skies of Britain between July and October 1940.

With U.S. entry into the war, the country urgently needed more plants to produce 100-octane fuel, and the emphasis on petroleum as the feedstock for the rubber program set up a conflict between the crude oil products (butylene) that would be needed either to produce the butadiene for synthetic rubber or to make isooctane, a blending agent used to increase octane levels in gasoline to 100. There were other routes to raising octane—adding tetraethyl lead—but they had disadvantages, necessitating more frequent maintenance (U.S. Petroleum Administration for War, 1946, p. 197), and possibly endangering pilot health. The likelihood of this conflict was anticipated in congressional and other testimony. And, during the plant-construction phase in 1942, friction developed between Rubber Reserve and the Office of the Petroleum Coordinator as well as the War Department as to which program should have higher priorities for scarce materials and critical components. That conflict was part of what lay behind the Rubber Survey Committee's recommendation that the WPB appoint a rubber czar who could play the advocacy role that Ickes did as Petroleum Coordinator.

The Interest of the U.S. Oil Industry in Using Petroleum to Produce Rubber

Standard Oil of New Jersey's patent-sharing agreements with the German firm IG Farben, along with its own decisions, delayed development of synthetic rubber in the United States during most of the 1930s. Starting in 1939, however, Standard began efforts to interest the U.S. government in subsidizing the development of a synthetic rubber industry at a time when many in the government, including Jesse Jones, believed that this was neither necessary nor desirable. Because of its prewar collaboration with IG Farben, and additional agreements with that company after war broke out in Europe, Standard had both the legal right and a strong commercial interest in developing or, ideally, having the federal government pay for the development of a synthetic rubber program centered on the production of Buna S *and based on the use of petroleum as a feedstock*. Aside from specialty rubbers, neither Standard nor any other private company was prepared to make large-scale investments toward this end using its own funds because of the uncertainty about postwar natural rubber supplies and prices. If, at the conclusion of the war, natural rubber again flowed freely and cheaply to the United States, the investments in physical capital and know-how in producing general-purpose synthetic rubber might well be worthless. This same dynamic—the unique ways in which wartime forced drastic and often temporary changes in the output mix, here aggravated by the likely disruption of raw material supply—probably played a role in the earlier establishment of government-owned and government-operated armories and naval yards.

There was the possibility, however, that after the war, synthetic rubber *might* be profitable, in which case a synthetic rubber industry producing for the military and civilian markets could be a valuable source of demand for byproducts of Standard's petroleum refining operations (in particular butane or butylene to make butadiene). This was particularly so because the company's patent position put it in a commanding position to extract royalties that would be paid by those (presumably tire companies) actually manufacturing the synthetic rubber in the copolymerization plants and then using the material in making final products such as radiator hoses and tires. Standard was taking the long view but wanted the government to shoulder the burdens associated with the risks and uncertainty just described.

Standard was correct in emphasizing the threat to national security posed by the possible cutoff of natural supplies of rubber. If one believed, as did Roosevelt, that war was inevitable, the failure to move expeditiously on bulking up alternative sources for rubber, which could include a synthetic rubber program, was, given conditions in 1939 and 1940, a costly and dangerous mistake, acknowledged as such by the Rubber Survey Committee. But Standard's advocacy for the petroleum route to butadiene, while understandable from the standpoint of its long-run commercial interest, was not necessarily in the national interest. Following the attack on Pearl Harbor, government officials showed little interest in developing the in-house technical knowledge needed to evaluate different pathways, instead subcontracting the planning of the industry, particularly the choice of feedstock and processes, to large private corporations whose interests were not necessarily coincident with those of the nation. The national interest was in deploying scarce resources effectively in preparation for war, to wage war, and, ultimately, to win.

Jones, having dragged his feet in building up the rubber stockpile, also delayed moving forward with construction of plants, particularly those that would produce the butadiene that would be needed in the synthetic program. Roosevelt himself apparently thought that if war in the Pacific came, the

Japanese could be quickly beaten, that reserve stocks of natural rubber along with scrap rubber drives could enable the country to weather any temporary disruption of imports, and that, if synthetic plants were to be built, this should be done by the rubber, oil, and chemical firms themselves, using and risking private capital that, as noted, they were generally unwilling to do (Tully, 2011, pp. 320–22, citing Chalk, 1970, pp. 238–39, 251–52; Tuttle, 1981, p. 46).

Because of negotiations that took place after its 1927 and 1929 patent-sharing agreements with IG Farben, Standard ended up owning the U.S. rights to the processes developed in 1929 by its partner for copolymerizing butadiene with styrene to make Buna S rubber. The original agreements specified that IG Farben had the rights to all of the two companies' patents in the chemicals area anywhere in the world, and that Standard had the rights to all of the two companies' patent rights in oil anywhere in the world *except* Germany. Eighty percent of royalties on oil patents were to go to Standard, and 20 percent to IG Farben. Patents in areas difficult to classify (neither strictly oil nor chemical), including synthetic rubber, were housed in another corporation, Jasco, owned fifty-fifty by the parent companies, but the right to develop remained with the originator of any process.

During the 1930s Standard Oil had worked either without great success (Howard, 1947) or without great interest (Finlay, 2009) in developing processes for producing butadiene at scale from oil or natural gas.[28] In exchange for worldwide dominance in oil (except for Germany), the company for a decade respected barriers to its development of synthetic rubber processes in the United States using German patents even though it had a financial stake in them. Standard made no protest when in the early 1930s IG Farben refused to grant Buna S licenses to other companies except on onerous terms. In 1937 and 1938, when Standard asked for permission itself to pursue synthetic rubber in the United States, IG Farben declined, claiming it could not do so because of opposition from the German government, and in 1939 the company declined again on the grounds of "military expediency."

By this point, Standard was concerned that other U.S. companies were making independent progress, and it therefore felt some urgency to move forward in the area. Since IG Farben had (as the result of political pressure) not fulfilled its obligations under the previous agreements, Standard would have been justified in abrogating them. The company continued to cooperate, however, turning over information on its butyl product to its German partner in 1938, an action for which it was subsequently (and legitimately) faulted.

It was only under pressure from the Army and Navy Munitions Board fifteen months later, after the fall of France, that Standard made butyl technical knowledge more generally available to the U.S. rubber industry (Stocking and Watkins, 1946, pp. 98–101).

In 1939, after war broke out in Europe, Standard's Executive Vice President Frank Howard met with IG Farben representatives at The Hague, and they struck a new agreement specifying that the rights to develop synthetic rubber patents in the United States and the British and French empires would now go to Standard, although IG Farben would retain exclusive rights in the rest of the world (obviously including Germany) (U.S. Senate, 1942, pp. 50–53). But Standard failed to obtain access to technical information on the actual operation of the Buna S copolymerization processes. What had ultimately happened was that an American commercial enterprise was negotiating with a firm (IG Farben) that had effectively become an arm of a totalitarian state. Stocking and Watkins concluded, "The Americans gave the fruit of American technological progress, such as they were, to their German cartel partner, but received only empty promises and barren patent specifications in return." These authors viewed the Standard–IG Farben agreements as another instance of the baleful influence of international cartels: "The record is plain: the cartel system retarded the development of a domestic synthetic rubber industry, and in so doing, jeopardized national security" (1946, p. 117).

By the end of 1939, the Germans already had one operating synthetic rubber plant and had started work on another but refused to share plans for the plants. They were obtaining their butadiene from brown coal using processes similar to those used in the Soviet Union (differences related to the means of obtaining the industrial alcohol). As a result of its 1939 agreement with IG Farben, Standard could proceed with developing Buna S in the United States, but it lacked the requisite technical know-how. It had little interest, in any event, in following IG Farben down the alcohol pathway, which would not offer an additional market for Standard's refinery byproducts even if in the wartime context it might produce butadiene more cheaply and certainly more quickly than could be done with petroleum.

As the United States entered the war, the situation facing the country was this. Total synthetic rubber production in 1941 was 8,383 long tons, almost all specialty rubbers, which had higher gas impermeability, were more resistant to oil, or had other desirable features, but were more expensive and inferior to natural rubber for tire treads and carcasses. Two-thirds of this consisted of

DuPont's neoprene, and almost all the rest was some form of Buna N (Herbert and Bisio, 1985, p. 38). Buna N copolymerized butadiene with acrylonitrile (C_3H_3N), rather than styrene.[29] It was far more expensive than Buna S because the acrylonitrile was more expensive than styrene, but it had much better oil-resistance properties, and versions of it had been the focus of Goodyear's and Goodrich's prewar research efforts.

The United States, in close cooperation with private corporations, faced the prospect of building a synthetic rubber industry with a major emphasis on Buna S with confidence that the basic chemistry was sound, but with little practical experience using either the petroleum or alcohol pathways to butadiene. Nor did the tire companies have experience in using the synthetic product, which would need to be blended with natural rubber in a process that, as noted, would require more facility time and labor input per unit of output in this final stage of manufacture.

Although it turned out not to be true, the situation appeared initially to be somewhat more favorable with respect to butyl rubber, the gas-impermeable synthetic preferred for inner tubes. In 1932 IG Farben had developed polymerized isobutylene (C_4H_8), which it found could be used to vary the viscosity of motor oils. Because of its earlier patent-sharing agreements, Standard had access to this technology, and starting in 1933 it marketed Vistanex as a viscosity regulator for motor oil. By 1935 it had built on the technology and developed means of more cheaply producing isobutylene from refinery operations and converting it to di-isobutylene (C_8H_{16}), an important ingredient in making 100-octane aviation fuel. In 1937 Standard copolymerized isobutylene with small amounts of butadiene (C_4H_6), eventually switching to small amounts of isoprene (C_5H_8), thereby creating butyl rubber. The main ingredient in butyl rubber is isobutylene gas (98 percent), which as we have seen, results from the distillation of crude oil or additional cracking of heavier fractions.

The final recipe for butyl copolymerized isobutylene with about 2 percent isoprene, a substance naturally produced by plants (natural rubber results from the polymerization of isoprene in the bark of the rubber tree). Isoprene can also be produced industrially by cracking products of petroleum distillation such as naphtha (like gasoline, naphtha is a blend of hydrocarbons). But unlike neoprene, butyl had not progressed to commercial sales before the United States entered the war.

Note again that the byproduct (isobutylene gas) needed to manufacture either GR-S or butyl rubber was also needed to produce 100-octane fuel. This foreseen conflict was one source of the dangerous shortfalls in synthetic rubber production in 1943. Standard's advocacy for a petroleum pathway was, therefore, partly responsible for a course of development that involved limited and delayed production of synthetic rubber, conflicts with the 100-octane program, and serious limitations on U.S. military options well into early 1944.

From 1939 onward, Standard bears somewhat less responsibility for the late start in building a U.S. synthetic capability. Additional contributing factors were differences among government officials and legislators regarding the probabilities that the Southeast Asian supply would in fact be cut off, combined with the hope and belief that recycling or an adequate strategic reserve of crude rubber could protect against any possible interruption. In May 1938 representatives of the Army and Navy Munitions Board expressed concern about the level of natural rubber inventories, recommending a stockpile of 500,000 long tons. On June 7, 1939, as previously noted, Congress passed the Strategic and Critical Materials Stockpiling Act, authorizing $100 million for the accumulation of reserves. On May 28, 1940, two and a half weeks after the end of the Phony War, and a month before the formation of the Rubber Reserve Company, Roosevelt reestablished by executive action a National Defense Advisory Commission (NDAC) to provide some institutional structure for planning economic mobilization for a war that Roosevelt viewed as probable if not inevitable.

In 1940, however, the U.S. economy had little immediate use for synthetic rubber, which was or would under most scenarios be more expensive than natural rubber and bring with it the need for adjustments of uncertain difficulty in working with a new and unfamiliar material in the fabrication of products like tires. Key policy decisions were: Should the government rely on a strategic reserve of natural rubber, or subsidize the preemptive development of a synthetic industry that might not in the event be needed? If so, what should be its capacity, what types of synthetics should it produce, and should the emphasis be on petroleum or alcohol from molasses or grain as the feedstock?

U.S. rubber consumption had grown from 437,000 long tons in 1938 (a recession year) to 592,000 long tons in 1939. As the economy's output gap closed, consumption increased further to 648,500 long tons in 1940 and 775,000 in 1941 (U.S. War Production Board, 1945a, p. 45). For planning purposes, peacetime civilian demand was placed at between 500,000 and 1,000,000 long tons per year, depending presumably on the state of the business cycle. Demand for natural rubber might be reduced by recycling, lower speed limits, gasoline rationing, or shutting down automobile production. Should the country build a synthetic industry based on worst-case forecasts? Combine a small standby program with the accumulation of a strategic reserve of natural rubber to cover the time necessary to build out a full-scale program if needed? Resistance to subsidizing a large-scale program rested on concerns that those now pushing for it (such as Standard) had a commercial interest in having the government build plants for them that they would ultimately end up acquiring (probably on the cheap) if conditions were right, hopes that, as in the First World War, crude rubber supplies would not be interrupted, and finally, concerns that, if successful, a synthetic rubber industry might adversely affect colonial economies of Dutch and British allies (Howard, 1947, p. 141).

Britain's concern with the possible effects of increased supply on rubber prices and the earnings of colonial producers in Southeast Asia was very real. Rubber Reserve's 1940 agreements with the International Rubber Regulation Committee to purchase 430,000 tons included the provision that in the absence of U.S. entry into the war, the rubber could not be released for use until 1944, and then only in 100,000-ton increments. The cotton-rubber barter deal with Britain in 1939 included similar provisions (Stocking and Watson, 1946, p. 83).

Jesse Jones Drags His Feet on Output Targets and Plant Construction

The initial output targets for a synthetic industry were formulated not by government planners, but simply by querying large petroleum, chemical, and tire companies, asking them what types of synthetic (or inputs to it) they might like to produce and how much capacity they might be interested in operating (none of the companies was offering to build new facilities on their own account). Under the auspices of the NDAC, a Synthetic Rubber Committee, chaired by Clarence Francis, president of General Foods, began to meet. On July 17, 1940, the Francis committee announced a goal of 108,000 long tons of synthetic of all types per year, later increased to 150,000 long tons when two more tire companies stepped forward, and cut back to 120,000, when Standard reported it was having difficulties operating its butyl manufacturing process at scale. To obtain government funds, committee members approached Jesse Jones, head of the RFC. Jones was skeptical about the need for the program, as apparently was Roosevelt, and in November 1940 Jones cut the NDAC target by two-thirds, to 40,000 long tons, which he thought was the right balance between committing taxpayer funds and providing opportunities for large oil, chemical, and tire companies to get "educational" experience with the new processes and materials. But this was apparently still too much for Jones. In February 1941 he completely canceled the program. Then, following protests from both Standard and the rubber companies, he backtracked and agreed to fund four 2,500-long-ton copolymerization plants, for a total annual capacity of 10,000 long tons.

In eight months, Jones had managed to cut the annual production target from 120,000 to 10,000 long tons. In May 1941 he testified before the Banking and Currency Committees of both houses of Congress. The "ensuing discussion in the Senate Committee indicated that the threat of curtailment of the Far East supply of natural rubber seemed not sufficiently imminent to warrant an extensive extension of synthetic rubber facilities" (Rubber Reserve Company, 1945, p. 20). The same logic apparently justified his decision to go slowly on building a stockpile.

As war approached, the challenge was not to embark on a crash program to decipher the chemistry of synthetic rubber. Rather, *if* one agreed that synthetic would be necessary, it was to decide what types of rubber to produce, and particularly for GR-S, which of several competing approaches to employ in making its ingredients, especially butadiene, and then to build or make preparations to build quickly the production capability needed to address demands that might explode under the collision of war production with the likely cutoff of 90 percent of the supply of natural rubber. The implementation of the program would not in fact begin until well into 1942, but in retrospect its basic design had been agreed on by November 1940. The copolymerization plants (those combining the butadiene and styrene to make GR-S rubber) were to be paid for by the government but built and operated by the Big Four rubber companies—Goodyear, Goodrich, Firestone, and U.S. Rubber—which would also use the synthetic rubber, along with natural rubber, to make final products. Standard had already licensed the latter two companies to produce Buna S, and they were committed to obtaining their butadiene from Standard, which would, along with other oil and chemical companies, operate one of several to-be-determined petroleum byways for making the butadiene.

Goodyear and Goodrich were initially committed to making their own synthetic rubber, which they had trademarked, respectively, as Ameripol and Chemigum. Standard viewed these both as versions of Buna N, to which, thanks to its agreements with IG Farben, Standard also claimed U.S. rights, and it threatened a patent infringement suit. Goodyear and Goodrich backed off and agreed to manufacture Buna S for tire carcasses and treads under license from Standard. Thus, the wartime production of the main synthetic rubber product (GR-S) would be standardized (no pun intended), although the processes for producing one of the two key ingredients (butadiene) would not. For their butadiene, the four tire companies would rely not just on Standard Oil of New Jersey but also on Union Carbide, which intended to use ethanol derived from petroleum, and Phillips Petroleum, which hoped to exploit the butane in its natural gas supplies to make the butadiene, and eventually other companies as well.

On December 9, 1940, the RFC issued a request for proposals to build the copolymerization facilities necessary to make the reduced 40,000-long-ton annual output of GR-S then on the table, proposals to be submitted by January 15, 1941. The proposals came in, and then Jones reconsidered. The panic induced by the end of the Phony War, the fall of France, and the likelihood of an invasion of Britain had once again yielded to complacency, buttressed by the belief that an (inadequate) strategic reserve could ensure against worst-case scenarios. Given the uncertainties about the technologies, Jones did not want to waste government money on "expensive plants," except in an "extraordinary emergency," which he concluded did not then exist. And so he canceled the whole program. On February 26, 1941, Standard's CEO received the memo explaining this, which included the claim that the RFC had accumulated a stockpile of natural rubber sufficient "to carry us for three years." This forecast was apparently developed by William L. Clayton, Jones's deputy, and was based on optimistic and, in the event, deeply unrealistic assumptions about how much supply could be drawn from South America, Africa, and reclaimed rubber (Herbert and Bisio, 1985, p. 48).[30]

The tire companies complained about the cancellation on the grounds that they needed experience both producing and working with the new synthetic materials. As a token response, on March 28, 1941, the RFC offered to fund four copolymerization plants, each with a capacity of 2,500 long tons per year, but with no provision for constructing butadiene production plants. On the table were small copolymerization facilities, where butadiene and styrene were to be combined to make GR-S, not plants to produce the butadiene, one of the two key ingredients in GR-S. Most industry specialists correctly anticipated the larger challenges to lie in making butadiene. Butadiene flows could not simply be diverted from other "nonessential" uses because, aside from the new interest in using it to make synthetic rubber, there were no other significant uses for the gas, and it was not being produced elsewhere in quantity. As Standard's Howard put it in his memoir, "Butadiene had no long-established background of commercial production in this country, and there were the widest differences of opinion as to how best to make it" (1947, p. 160).

In March 1941 Germany resumed offensive operations in North Africa, Yugoslavia, and Greece and increased U-boat operations, posing a challenge to those embracing complacency. On May 9, 1941, William Knudsen, the former Ford and GM executive who now headed the Office of Production Management (OPM), wrote to Jones resurrecting the 40,000-ton target for copolymerization facilities and indicating that planners should remain open to increasing this to 100,000 or 200,000 long tons. Jones had little choice but to accept this recommendation, and the interested companies (the four rubber companies, Standard, DuPont, and Union Carbide) met on May 21, 1941, to agree on plans to move forward. The copolymerization plants would be financed and owned by the Defense Plant Corporation but built and operated by the tire companies in return for costs and a fixed management fee, as laid out in a contract with the Defense Supplies Corporation. The plants producing the key inputs—butadiene and styrene—would also be financed and owned by the government but operated by oil or chemical companies.

On June 22, 1941, the Germans invaded the Soviet Union. Five and half months later, on December 7, 1941, the Japanese bombed Pearl Harbor. At that point, although some construction work had started on the copolymerization plants, no work had been done on any of the butadiene plants that would be needed to feed them.

On January 3, 1942, Roosevelt established by executive order the War Production Board (WPB), which replaced the Office of Production Management as well as the Supply Priorities and Allocation Board (SPAB), which had been created on August 28, 1941. Donald Nelson, former executive vice president of Sears, who had served as executive director of SPAB during its four-month existence, was appointed by the president to head the WPB. Four days later, January 7, in one of his first acts, Nelson directed the distilling industry to commit 60 percent of its capacity to producing industrial alcohol (ethanol), presaging a huge controversy that would develop over the next several months. On January 12 the WPB, acknowledging the gravity of the economic and military situation, increased the target output of the synthetic rubber program tenfold, to 400,000 long tons per year (Singapore would fall on February 15 after a week of fighting). Of the targeted 288,000 short tons annual output of butadiene that would be needed to make GR-S, less than 14 percent (40,000 tons) was to come from alcohol, and all of that from petroleum (these plants were to be built by Union Carbide).

Along the petroleum pathway, continuing conflicts over the best route to obtaining the butadiene (C_4H_6) surfaced at the January 12 WPB meeting. Some companies, such as Phillips, expressed concern that since butylene (C_4H_8) was needed for the aviation fuel program, butadiene should be manufactured instead by directly dehydrogenating butane (C_4H_{10}), which was in abundant supply. Standard (which largely prevailed) responded that its new fluid cracking process could increase the butadiene yield of butylene and avoid the need to invest in the equipment necessary for dehydrogenating butane. The different companies had different patent rights, different holdings of crude and natural gas reserves, and stakes in disposing of different byproducts. None could be expected to advocate in a disinterested fashion, and the government lacked the in-house technical competence to evaluate the different claims. That lacuna, and the development path that ensued, led to the 1942 political and production crisis that required the appointment of the Rubber Survey Committee.

In February 1942 the Soviet Union offered to share with the United States the technical knowledge it had accumulated from its decades-old synthetic rubber program, one that exploited the alcohol pathway to butadiene. The United States ignored the offer, an action strongly criticized in the Survey Committee Report (U.S. Rubber Survey Committee, 1942, pp. 50–51). In the same month, anticipating a critical shortage of butadiene in 1943, the Office of the Petroleum Coordinator (headed by Harold Ickes) proposed a "quickie program," in which the gas would be produced rapidly but at great expense, through converting existing refineries to allow the expanded exploitation of the previously used thermal cracking method (not the new and largely un-tested fluid catalytic cracking process). The thermal process would also yield scarce benzene (C_6H_6), toluene (C_7H_8, the chief ingredient in TNT), xylol (C_8H_{10}), and the isobutylene (C_4H_8) needed to make the butadiene (C_4H_6). Al-though never implemented because of conflicts between Rubber Reserve and the Office of the Petroleum Coordinator, its entertainment reflected the low ranking of enhancing productivity (as opposed to production) on war plan-ners' list of priorities. Cost (and therefore efficiency and productivity) was simply not an important consideration, particularly insofar as it applied to proposals involving the petroleum pathway. That attitude was not necessarily wrong given the commitment to the petroleum pathway and the critical need for rubber but reflected priorities consistent with declining manufacturing productivity during the war.

The Battle for Alcohol and Events Leading Up to Formation of the Rubber Survey Committee

On February 20, 1942, Senator Guy Gillette of Iowa, the number-one corn-producing state in the country, claimed in Congress that the United States Industrial Alcohol Corporation was blocking expansion of alcohol manufacturing facilities, out of a desire to preserve its market power in the distilling industry, and that Standard Oil was also involved in this conspiracy, in part because of its joint ownership of the IG Farben patents for the conversion of alcohol to butadiene. A Senate subcommittee (the Gillette Committee) was appointed, giving a platform to agricultural interests campaigning for a larger role for alcohol (especially alcohol from *plants*). The subcommittee began hearings on March 20. On May 8, 1942, in the heat of the tempest created by the Gillette Committee hearings, Standard offered royalty-free access to the alcohol-related patents for the duration of the conflict but indicated that it had made no effort to evaluate the IG Farben process and suggested that Union Carbide's process (the company would be operating two of the three alcohol-to-butadiene plants) might be superior (Solo, 1959, p. 14).

In March 1942 the War Production Board again raised the synthetic rubber annual production target, this time to 700,000 long tons. After declining precipitously, the annual production target had in one year increased seventy-fold from Jesse Jones's March 1941 dictum, reflecting recognition of the dire consequences of Japanese successes. Eight more oil companies eventually joined the program. Dow Chemical joined Union Carbide and Monsanto as an operator of government-owned styrene plants. And in the summer of 1942 three additional tire firms came in, each to operate 30,000-ton copolymerization plants.

In March as well the rubber program figured in testimony to both the Truman Committee and the Gillette Committee. The Truman Committee had been formed on March 1, 1941, with the aim of ferreting out waste and corruption in military contracting. In Truman Committee hearings, Assistant Attorney General Thurman Arnold accused Standard Oil of New Jersey of withholding details on its butyl rubber from U.S. military authorities during the 1930s while at the same time sharing them with IG Farben (as it felt it was contractually obligated to do, even when IG Farben was not living up to its side of the agreements). There was some truth to this, although, as it turned out, buytl would not be as useful during the war as the military hoped. In the Gillette Committee, agricultural interests pressed their case for the alcohol pathway and, pointedly, on the question of exactly how the division of butadiene production between the petroleum and alcohol pathways had been determined.

Ethanol, otherwise known as grain alcohol, is most commonly produced as the result of the fermentation of sugars, through processes familiar to manufacturers and consumers of beer, wine, and hard liquor. There are also ways to produce it synthetically as a byproduct of petroleum refining. In 1940 industrial alcohol in the United States came from three sources: 88 million gallons from molasses, 33 million from petroleum refining, and 17 million from grain (Solo, 1959, p. 31).[31] Molasses was the preferred feedstock for industrial uses because it was cheap, yielding ethanol at about a fourth the cost of alcohol derived from grains, which were reserved for production of spirits for human consumption. There was little doubt that butadiene could be derived directly from crude oil, avoiding alcohol as a precursor, and was likely to be more economical from this source over the long run and for large batches. But the processes were untested, and reverses, delays, and fine-tuning could be anticipated before they could be expected to operate at scale. The alcohol route to butadiene involved processes that were well understood.

Those advocating for the alcohol pathway made five interrelated claims. First, the country was sitting on an inventory of over a billion and a quarter tons of grain, accumulated as the result of agricultural price support programs in the 1930s, and indeed the surpluses were overflowing storage facilities. The grain was available, the costs of acquiring it had already been incurred, so whatever the relative prices of grain and petroleum might be in the future, at that historical moment the costs of acquiring the feedstock should be treated as sunk, and thus its effective price was zero. Second, substantial capacity for fermenting molasses lay idle, since the war had disrupted sugar imports, as German U-boats in the Caribbean and Gulf of Mexico and off the Atlantic Coast torpedoed not just oil tankers from the Gulf Coast, but also molasses shipments from Cuba. Sugar deliveries from the Philippines were also threatened and then completely cut off after the Japanese victories at Bataan and Corregidor in April 1942. The rationing of sugar (the first food item to be so controlled) began on May 5, 1942, and continued through 1947. The idle molasses-refining capacity could easily be converted to use grain as a feedstock.

Third, the liquor-distilling portion of the alcohol industry, which produced 276 million gallons of spirits in 1936, produced only 164 million gallons in 1940, so it also had excess capacity that could be used to produce alcohol from grain. The use of the molasses and grain spirits-distilling capacity, since it was already available, would not conflict with other war demands for equipment or construction manpower, and requirements for any new capacity would be modest. Fourth, making alcohol from plants was unlikely to conflict with the needs of the aviation fuel program. Finally, alcohol pathways for producing butadiene had been successfully exploited for years in the Soviet Union, Germany, and Poland, whereas the petroleum-to-butadiene pathways involved challenges that were likely to delay production. In sum, the alcohol pathways were simpler and there was considerable experience with them, the raw material inputs were in abundant supply, substantial refining capacity was already available, and if additional facilities were needed, they could be built more quickly with fewer requirements for equipment or building supplies that were or were likely to be in short supply (Solo, 1953, 1954).

Each of these claims was, or turned out to be, true, as was basically acknowledged in the Survey Committee Report. These arguments coincided with the political interests of senators from farm states and the economic interests of farmers in those states. But that did not necessarily make them wrong. Roosevelt's political instincts nevertheless made him suspicious, and this was likely a contributory factor in his vetoing of the Rubber Supply Act of 1942, although the veto was scarcely a surprise, since the act was a direct challenge to his authority, as it removed control from the executive branch agencies he had created. But Roosevelt understood the political maelstrom that had developed and recognized that there were serious technical questions that required evaluation by disinterested experts. Thus his appointment of the Rubber Survey Committee.

As of April 1942, only 80,000 short tons of the 550,000 short tons of butadiene needed to produce the then-targeted production of GR-S rubber was to be alcohol-based (that is, relying on butadiene made from alcohol) (Wendt, 1947, p. 211). Moreover, none of that alcohol was to come from plants: it was all to be produced from petroleum. In May 1942 the chemical branch of the WPB announced that it had made an error: the distilling industry actually had an annual capacity of 540 million, not 280 million gallons. This led the WPB to increase the planned alcohol-based share of butadiene output to 220,000 short tons.

That same month Dr. Chaim Weizmann, an Israeli chemist who would subsequently serve as president of Israel, met with two members of the WPB (he had been sent to the United States by Churchill). Weizmann had done pioneering work on the use of fermentation to produce acetone during the First World War, greatly facilitating Britain's manufacture of explosives during that conflict. He had figured out a new route along the alcohol pathway that used grain to produce pure butadiene and acetone (C_3H_6O), which could be manufactured into isoprene (C_5H_8). Between the pure butadiene and the isoprene (which could be mixed with it), he proposed to manufacture both the tire carcass/tread and the inner tubes (presumably a variant on the butyl recipe). The WPB officials saw no need to explore his proposals, and Weizmann remained bitter about the brush-off, which he attributed in his autobiography to his failure to be willing or politically savvy enough to overcome the

> vested interests of the great firms—particularly the oil firms. . . . I knew that large quantities of butadiene were already being made out of oil, but the trouble was, as far as I could gather, that the butadiene produced was not pure, and the purification was slow and costly, whereas the butylene produced by my process was chemically pure, and would lend itself more easily for conversion into a purer form of butadiene. But I had come too late, or at any rate, very late; the Government had already engaged the oil companies, and to initiate a process which had not the approval of the oil companies was almost too much of a task for any human being. (Weizmann, 1949, pp. 428–30)

Weizmann was also disappointed with his reception by the Rubber Survey Committee, during which Conant dismissed the process as "tedious and expensive" on the basis of his own research experience, but without having studied what Weizmann proposed. Weizmann received a somewhat more favorable reaction from Jeffers, the rubber czar, but no government commitment to use it, and ultimately Weizmann gave his process to "a firm in Philadelphia" (probably Publicker, which was the second-largest producer of industrial alcohol in the country), which "began to apply it during the war."

Weizmann was unhappy to be caught in the crossfire from the petroleum-alcohol battle, but the conflict continued, as companies like Seagram and Houdry took out newspaper ads to press their cases. Distilling companies such as Seagram complained that they were being cut out of the program, farm state senators on the Gillette Committee fumed, and a full-blown political crisis developed over which pathway and byway should be emphasized—but, more immediately, who or what organization was or should be making that decision? On July 22, 1942, both houses of Congress passed the Rubber Supply Act of 1942, which called for an agency independent of all executive branch organizations. The agency was to be charged with producing synthetic rubber using the alcohol pathway, but, more specifically, alcohol "produced from agricultural or forest products" (in other words, alcohol from petroleum need not apply).

Roosevelt vetoed the bill on August 6, 1942, but, acknowledging the political rebellion, he appointed the Rubber Survey Committee, chaired by Baruch. The president's veto message was carefully considered. As would the committee, he acknowledged uncertainty about the best route forward and the possibility of past errors:

> The processes for making synthetic rubber are now in a state of flux. Some of them are in the purely experimental stage, others have been demonstrated to have varying degrees of efficiency.
>
> It is obviously impossible to determine in advance just which process will eventually prove to be the most desirable, taking into consideration the elements of speed, efficiency of production, and consumption of critical materials. Even the processes for making synthetic rubber out of grain are several in number, and new ones are being presented from time to time. The whole question of which process to use is tied up with the question of the most strategic use of the materials which are at hand or which can be obtained. Determination in this more or less uncharted area should have the advantages of the flexibility of administrative action rather than be frozen by legislative mandate.
>
> It may well be that serious mistakes have been made in the past, based either on misinformation, misconception, or even partiality to one process or another. It may be that the present program of the War Production Board is not the best solution. If so, the facts should be ascertained and made public. This is particularly so, if it be true, as charged by some persons in the Congress and outside the Congress, that the manufacture of synthetic rubber from grain has been hamstrung by selfish business interests. (Roosevelt, 1942)

In the last sentence he acknowledged, without necessarily endorsing, the point of view of the Gillette Committee, after having earlier expressed concern that the bounty of stored grain available at that time might not persist were harvests in 1943 and 1944 poorer.

In testimony before the committee, one of the alcohol advocates, George Johnson, noted that forms filed with the WPB showed that the plants pro-posed to implement butadiene production along the petroleum pathway re-quired twenty-one times more steel, one hundred times more stainless steel, and eight and a half times as much copper as plants that would be needed should the alcohol pathway be pursued (Solo, 1959, p. 55). The petroleum path-way required 58,633 horsepower to drive compressors and blowers; the alcohol pathway required just 4,000 horsepower. The petroleum pathway butadiene plants were demonstrably more expensive to build per ton of rated or espe-cially actual capacity (see table 3.1).

Johnson also claimed that Department of Agriculture researchers in Peoria, Illinois, had found a way to ferment corn to produce butylene glycol ($C_4H_{10}O_2$) rather than ethanol (C_2H_6O), and the former was more cheaply convertible into butadiene. Johnson (along with the Seagram Company) recommended the program standardize on the butylene glycol method. A further advantage claimed was that 31 percent of the grain used in this process could then be turned into high-protein animal feed. Johnson pressed for small distilleries and small copolymerization plants to be built near the grain supplies in farm country (Howard, 1947, pp. 198–99). Wendt states that the butylene glycol pathway was subsequently found to be "impractical" (1947, p. 210) and what Johnson proposed was of course different from what Weizmann advocated, although both would use agricultural products as feedstock.

Part of the fog that the Rubber Survey Committee was intended to dispel resulted from myriad competing claims from both alcohol and petroleum ad-vocates about how best to produce butadiene. The committee was sympathetic to the general merits of including more alcohol-based production of butadi-ene and recommended a number of changes consistent with that. But, given the dire military situation, it was leery at that late date of endorsing new and largely untested processes as a substitute for previous commitments.

The Rubber Survey Committee also heard from Weizmann. Whereas John-son had rehearsed the arguments that the alcohol process would be cheaper and quicker because it used available raw materials and facilities and relied on known processes, Weizmann reemphasized the likelihood that reliance on the petroleum pathway would put the rubber program on a collision course with the 100-octane fuel program. Within the petroleum pathway, there was the fur-ther question of whether to travel the butane or the butylene route. Butane was abundant, and butylene was also needed to make 100-octane fuel. Weizmann was therefore confused as to why, six months into the program (June 17, 1942), the oil refiners had switched to the butylene byway, requiring retrofitting of all the refinery equipment. An examination of the disappointing output record of the petroleum-to-butadiene operator (Sun), which continued to work along the butane byway using the Houdry process, helps us understand why (see table 3.1 and figure 3.1). Houdry's catalytic cracking innovations made a major contribution to the production of aviation fuel, but not to butadiene and thus GR-S. The Phillips process worked somewhat better.

Nelson, the head of the WPB, protested to the Gillette Committee that he was open to considering different processes and described how, under his watch, the original targets of 350,000 tons of GR-S (Buna S), 40,000 tons of butyl, and 60,000 tons of neoprene had, for GR-S and butyl, been doubled (Solo, 1959, p. 68).

The Rubber Survey Committee completed its work in one month and in its report sharply criticized the administration of the rubber program. But it recommended no change in its basic direction. As noted, the committee acknowledged that there should have been a bigger stockpile, that construction of plants should have started earlier, and that the initial exclusive emphasis on petroleum had been a mistake, but it concluded that it was too late to make any radical changes. The committee accepted Rubber Reserve's claim that no more than 10 percent of final rubber products output would consist of natural rubber.

That percentage never got below 15 percent, even in 1945 (Herbert and Bisio, 1985, p. 126, figure 11.1). Truck tires require higher ratios of natural rubber because of its superior abrasion resistance. Natural rubber content could be reduced through the use of rayon cord, but a shortage of that material hampered substitution during the war (Solo, 1959, p. 91). The need for the abrasion resistance of natural rubber was even more acute in the production of airplane tires; the rubber content in such tires was and is almost entirely natural. The postwar development and diffusion of radial tires for passenger vehicles and trucks, which also required a higher fraction of natural rubber, is another reason the world continued and continues to rely on *Hevea* in the postwar period. In 2019 U.S. passenger tires contained 19 percent natural rubber and 24 percent synthetic, whereas truck tires contained 34 percent natural rubber and 11 percent synthetic (U.S. Tire Manufacturers Association, 2019). The remainders consisted of fillers, extenders, belts and cordage, and other specialized compounds.

Had the factors contributing to the continuing need for natural rubber been more realistically appraised, the committee might have concluded that the production targets for synthetic were in fact now too *high,* and that by 1944 there would be a surplus of synthetic at the same time there were shortages of critically needed rubber products (which turned out to be what happened) because of rapidly dwindling stocks of natural rubber needed as a complement. The failure to accumulate a larger strategic reserve or subsidize guayule production earlier ended up costing dearly here.

In the contexts of war mobilization and foreseeable shortages of a complementary input, setting a GR-S production target too high could be just as damaging to the war effort (because it wasted or squatted on critical inputs, making them unavailable for other purposes) as setting one that was too low (because it was inadequate to produce the materials needed for war goods). This underscores how important the gasoline rationing, thirty-five-mile-per-hour speed limit, and tire inspections were in allowing domestic transportation to limp through the war on tires that were at the margin of safety, which allowed military production and replacement to have priority.

The Rubber Survey Committee did express concern about the adequacy of the anticipated inventory of natural rubber at the end of 1943—224,000 tons. Like almost everything else about the forecasts for 1943, this turned out to be far too optimistic. End-of-year stocks were in fact 139,544 long tons, and in 1944 this dropped to a nadir of 93,650. Yet the committee recommended that the target for Buna S be increased even further, from 705,000 to 845,000 tons, and that the neoprene target grow from 40,000 to 60,000 tons. The military had originally argued that only neoprene was fully equal to natural rubber for military tires used in combat, and this view was fully endorsed in the Rubber Survey Committee's report (1942, p. 45). Subsequently, on February 18, 1943, the military concluded that neither butyl nor neoprene could be used for military tires except as a last resort (Solo, 1959, p. 91; see also Roth and Holt, 1944).

The synthetic rubber program was the most critical manufacturing initiative in the Second World War, more important than the Manhattan Project. The failure of the program in 1943 to produce promised levels of synthetic rubber could have had catastrophic consequences. At the same time, the escalation of production targets and the overemphasis on petroleum as a feedstock led to spending on facilities and equipment when the resources could have been better deployed elsewhere. Whereas raising production targets beyond the 10,000 long tons Jones had agreed to in March 1941 was obviously justified, it did not follow that, beyond a certain point, more continued to be better. The dwindling stocks of natural rubber placed a hard cap on how much final product could actually be produced in 1944.

To fully appreciate the problems created by the collision of private commercial interest with government oversight that was incapable or unwilling to deal with it effectively, one must again consider the strategic situation in 1942. German armies were on a tear. British and American planning assumed that the Soviet armies would eventually be crushed at Stalingrad. On December 4, 1941, three days before Pearl Harbor, the isolationist owner of the *Chicago Tribune,* Robert McCormack, published the Rainbow Five war plans, which had been leaked by Senator Burton Wheeler (Roosevelt's Victory Plan for economic mobilization derived from them). Those plans included the assessment that because of its state of preparedness, the United States would be able to mount an offensive campaign against Germany no earlier than July 1943. From February 1942 onward, the Allies planned on either a limited invasion of Europe in 1942 to take some pressure off the Soviet army (Sledgehammer), or a much larger cross-Channel invasion in the spring of 1943 (Roundup). The North Africa campaign of 1942 (Torch) was eventually substituted for the first option. After the Soviets prevailed at Stalingrad in January 1943, the cross-Channel invasion was postponed for a year, to the great discomfort of the Soviets. Given the rubber situation in the United States in 1943, that massive operation simply could not have gone forward then.

From the vantage point of 1942, war planners, including the members of the Rubber Survey Committee, anticipated huge needs for planes, tanks, aviation fuel, and rubber in late 1942 and particularly in calendar year 1943. The synthetic rubber program, as it went forward in 1942, promised 560,000 tons of synthetic rubber in 1943. Less than 40 percent of that—217,235 tons—was delivered, and of the butadiene needed to make the bulk of it, 83 percent (!) came from alcohol. As anticipated, concentrating on the petroleum pathway demanded capacity that required large amounts of scarce metals, components, materials, and construction labor at the peak of the building frenzy of the war during 1942. In addition, the petroleum pathway took precious time to work as desired, running into problems with the purity of butadiene and other issues. On top of that, the heavy emphasis on petroleum as the feedstock, and on butylene as the precursor, conflicted with the needs for producing 100-octane aviation fuel. Weizmann had warned of both problems (Solo, 1959, pp. 33–34).

The argument against the alcohol route was that in the long run the feedstock requirements were likely to be more expensive. After the war, with the plants that had by then been constructed, and given the price of grain or molasses feedstock, the marginal cost of producing butadiene from alcohol was indeed higher, and the alcohol-based plants were the first to be put on standby or mothballed (Solo, 1953, p. 32). But this argument was irrelevant if the reverse was true during the war and if an emphasis on the petroleum pathway caused the war to be lost. The government objective, and the rationale for government funding for the plants, was to win the war, not necessarily to lay the foundation for a postwar, commercially viable synthetic rubber industry.

Ultimately, the Defense Plant Corporation paid for the construction of thirty-eight plants costing at least $5 million each, and thirteen smaller plants, mostly producing specialty chemicals such as carbon black, for a total construction cost of $673 million. These included twelve plants for producing butadiene, nine using petroleum feedstock, and three using alcohol; five styrene plants; fifteen plants for copolymerizing the butadiene and styrene into GR-S rubber; two butyl plants; and one neoprene plant. All the petroleum-based butadiene plants were built and operated by large oil companies. The five styrene plants were built and operated by large chemical companies. The two butyl plants were built and run by Standard Oil of New Jersey (which had developed the butyl rubber process in the 1930s), and the neoprene plant was built and run by DuPont (which had developed neoprene in the 1930s). Finally, all but one of the copolymerization plants for combining the butadiene and styrene were built and operated by large tire companies.

Before the war, the rubber sector of U.S. manufacturing consisted almost entirely of the rubber products industry. As the war progressed, it came to have two parts: chemical synthesis and then copolymerization of the two key synthetic rubber inputs, and fabrication of crude and natural rubber into final products. In 1942 the rubber products industry in the United States faced strong negative supply shocks in the form of a sudden and forced change in the input mix coincident with the cutoff of most of the supply of a critical raw material. Even had the synthetic rubber program been planned and executed flawlessly, which it was not, the country would have expected productivity in fabrication to decline under these conditions.

But the ways in which the program was conducted imposed additional shocks on and unnecessarily distorted the economy. A substantial portion of the government expenditure for plant construction, including all the petroleum-to-butadiene plants, was unnecessary in order to pursue military objectives. The country should have had a larger strategic stockpile of natural rubber and would have benefited from Eisenhower's 1930 proposal to expand guayule production. The country should have relied more on butadiene from alcohol. Whatever the feedstock to be used, plant construction to build butadiene capacity should have started much earlier.

In the last third of 1944, reduced demand for aviation fuel, along with shortages of natural rubber that held back final product fabrication and contributed to the excess supplies of GR-S, led the alcohol-based production of butadiene to be cut back. In August 1944, before the cutback, alcohol-based production proceeded at the rate of 412,544 tons per annum (twice their rated capacity). Solo calculated that in order to produce butadiene at the highest level during the war (575,482 tons in 1945) an additional petroleum-based capacity of only 163,000 tons would have been needed, as opposed to the 415,000 tons of capacity actually contracted for and built. In less measured tones, he argues that if a small part of those resources had been used to build alcohol-based plants, no petroleum-based capacity at all needed to have been built. His conclusion: "From the point of view of war planning, nearly all of the vast expenditure of vital resources on the building of petroleum-butadiene capacity was waste" (1959, p. 89). Requiring the expenditure of hundreds of millions of dollars for unneeded production capacity was not a formula for boosting productivity. The 1942 increase of targeted neoprene capacity from 40,000 to 60,000 tons was also a waste, since the product was ultimately deemed unsuitable for military tires, although this error is perhaps more excusable since it was not so clearly anticipated.

The United States was engaged in a huge military, naval, and industrial construction program that was well under way in 1941 during the defense period.[32] The attack on Pearl Harbor caused an already large construction program to grow by another 25 percent in 1942 (from $10.758 billion to $13.434 billion). The construction sector's demands for materials that competed with materials needed for the concurrent production of munitions exacerbated the weaknesses of the priorities system, particularly in 1942. The introduction of the Controlled Materials Plan, to which so much credit has been given by authors such as Janeway (1951), coincided with an apparent amelioration of "priorities unemployment." But this was due in part to improvements in metals supply resulting from expansions of capacity[33] and in part to the tapering off of the construction program (total construction spending dropped to $7.732 billion in 1943). The falloff in construction claims reduced demand for materials, and some of the recently completed facilities devoted to smelting or refining enabled larger flows of supply of critical metals (Landon-Lane and Rockoff, 2013). The synthetic rubber program was a major claimant on construction resources. Total spending on industrial plant was $3.806 billion in 1942 and $2.198 billion in 1943. Over the two-year period rubber accounted for more than one-tenth of this.

A famous passage from the Bureau of the Budget's history of the war described the excesses of the construction program: "We built many new factories, and expanded many others which we could not use and did not need. . . . In the process we used up materials that might have gone into something else" (quoted in Janeway, 1951, p. 308; Lingeman, 1970, p. 66). Milward affirmed this judgment: "Completely new factories were built when there was no possibility that they would ever get the necessary raw materials to sustain their planned production" (1977, pp. 122–23). Though this was not a fate that befell the rubber plants, because they were so essential to the war effort and because the production of the required raw material inputs was prioritized over the vigorous objections of other claimants, unnecessary construction anywhere in the economy worsened priorities unemployment, and any such idleness depressed manufacturing productivity.

Grades

The wartime synthetic rubber program may in a sense have been well-oiled, but it did not operate like a well-oiled machine, and we can try to evaluate the performance of its different parts. Start with the two specialty rubbers. On the positive side, neoprene production had few major problems. DuPont was already producing the product commercially before the war and continued to do so during it. We can give it a letter grade of A-. The minus is because although production targets were largely met, those targets had been set too high, since in 1943 the War Department determined that neoprene could not in fact be used for most military tires.

Butyl production, as noted, never met production targets for reasons that are not clearly stated in the literature, but probably have to with the challenge of copolymerizing at 100 degrees or more below zero Fahrenheit. Also, despite Standard's hopes, butyl was not suitable for tire treads and carcasses. It gets a D.

The big enchilada was GR-S, and here it is useful to break down its manufacture into three parts: making butadiene, making styrene, and copolymerizing the two. As noted, the butadiene program was plagued with problems, most critically in the year 1943. It gets an F for that year. What was needed for the war could have been produced more cheaply and more rapidly had the alcohol pathway been emphasized from the start. Plants built were on average more expensive than they needed to be, took longer to come onstream than should have been the case, and involved more capacity than could ultimately be used in 1944 and 1945, at a cost to other programs. Overall grade: C-.

The other main ingredient for GR-S, styrene, in which there was prewar production experience, had fewer problems. Herbert and Bisio term styrene production "generally satisfactory and substantially free of operational difficulties," and they state that "the supply of styrene was at all times adequate to meet the needs of the rubber program except for a brief period in early 1943 when it was necessary to store some quantities of butadiene awaiting for the availability of styrene for conversion to GR-S" (1985, p. 129). Grade: A-.

Compared to the problems associated with butadiene production, the co-polymerization plants performed relatively well. It had been understood up front that copolymerization would be far simpler than obtaining the butadiene (Howard, 1947, p. 138). Production was limited in 1943, but this was because of the unavailability of butadiene. All fifteen plants were producing by the end of 1943. Five of the fifteen exceeded rated capacity in 1944, and all but one did so in 1945 (see table 3.2). Grade: B+.

Within the manufacture of final products, efficiency declined because it took more time to blend synthetic with natural than to use natural alone. This loss in productivity was unavoidable. Grade: B.

Summary

A useful way to think about foreign trade in this instance is that allowing exports to be swapped for imports provided the United States with a valuable "machine" for transforming grain and petroleum into crude rubber. The fall of Singapore destroyed almost all the transformative power of that machine for the duration of the war. This can hardly be considered a positive shock for the U.S. economy, any more than the events of December 7, 1941, represented a boost to the capabilities of the U.S. Navy. In its stead, the country had to spend $673 million to build fifty-one government-owned plants to produce an imperfect substitute for most of that rubber. As a means of transforming petroleum and grain into rubber, the synthetic rubber program was an expensive replacement for foreign trade. Even had the butadiene program been planned and executed well, the cutoff of natural rubber would have taken a toll in terms of the manufacturing sector's productivity.

And in the event, it was plagued with problems. The interaction of repeated plant construction delays with the heavy initial and continuing emphasis on the petroleum pathway resulted in a program that built large amounts of production capacity unnecessary for meeting immediate military requirements and, as will be discussed below, operated under patent and technical interchange agreements that eliminated almost all incentives for innovation. The program failed to deliver output when it might have been most needed (in 1943) and produced more than could be used in 1944.

In contrast to the aircraft industry, the rubber products industry did not experience a huge increase in its output or major changes in its final composition. In that sense it was something of an exception. Military uses soared, but demand from the civilian sector plummeted because of rationing of gasoline and tires and the cessation of production of new passenger vehicles. Overall rubber consumption (natural and synthetic) fell below 1941 levels in 1942, 1943, and 1944, surpassing 1941 levels only in 1945, but the products (tires, inner tubes, drive belts, rubber soles and heels) were mostly the same as in peacetime. Nevertheless, the shock of having to replace almost all the foreign trade sourcing with newly produced and constructed physical capital that did much the same thing was augmented by a negative effect associated with having to blend the synthetic with natural in making final products.

According to the 1942 Rubber Survey Committee's report, this resulted in a decline in efficiency in final product manufacture of approximately one-third. This is consistent with complaints from German rubber fabricators that working with Buna S (which they were forced by the government to absorb) required two to three times as much milling capacity as natural rubber (Howard, 1947, p. 44). Of course, it is likely that with experience some of this deficit would be, and was, recouped in both countries. The Rubber Survey Committee anticipated as much (and by 1939 the Germans were experiencing "less difficulty") (Howard, 1947, p. 60). Wendt indicates that the deficit for working with GR-S eventually narrowed to 10 percent (1947, p. 222n32). And those wishing to emphasize the positive could be excused for focusing on these or similar gains. But we should not imagine that such improvements overcame the negative effects of the initial shock.

If participants in the U.S. economy could have chosen between the actual course of events and the option of continued access to Southeast Asian supplies of rubber, as had been enjoyed during the First World War, there is no doubt which the tire makers would have preferred. The oil and chemical companies might have been somewhat more ambivalent, but they had their hands full with demands for aviation gasoline, explosives, and a host of other products, and they probably would have been more than content. From a national standpoint, in terms of its effect on production and productivity, it is exceedingly difficult to paint the consequences of the cutoff in supply of this critical raw material in a positive light.

To the two main shocks (on the costs of inputs and of fabrication) we can add the effects of gasoline rationing and the nationwide thirty-five-mile-per-hour speed limit. Both were the direct consequence of the rubber shortage. These restrictions created additional obstacles to getting to and from work in a labor market in which the physical location of jobs and the overall composition of output were experiencing radical changes. They also threatened the smooth movement of goods in what remained of the task of distributing civilian products and some intermediate goods to support the production of war materiel. To be sure, the economy learned to deal with these challenges, but, again, in considering the effects of the conquest of Singapore, we should not confuse the beneficial effects of that learning, which, considered by itself, represented improved efficiency, with the more significant and detrimental shocks that induced it.

Persistence of Learning Effects after the War

The remaining question to be addressed is whether the responses to adversity—the learning that took place as the economy responded to the cutoff of natural rubber supplies—had persisting benefits following the war. There are several related issues here. First, did the wartime experience accelerate the rate of technological progress in making synthetic rubber? Second, was that know-how and the physical capital accumulated beneficial after the war? The answer to the first question, I believe, is no. Indeed, the institutional arrangements during the war may have retarded such progress. The answer to the second question is more nuanced. The U.S. postwar synthetic rubber capability provided a bulwark against any future disruption of crude rubber supplies because of war or biological threats to natural rubber plants. That bulwark, however, came at a substantial cost.

The birth of the industry was heavily subsidized because the plants were paid for by the government and then eventually transferred, mostly to the wartime operators, at prices attractive to the firms. Knowledge asymmetries allowed the operators a far more accurate estimate of the commercial value of the plants, discouraging others from bidding, although a few of the plants did get competitive bids. Beyond that, and in anticipation of possible postwar privatization, operators had designed and fine-tuned the plants to take best advantage of their own patent portfolios and expertise. In retrospect, one might view what happened as the outcome of a successful industrial policy initiative, albeit one into which the country was reluctantly dragged. One's assessment of it may be influenced by how desirable one believes industrial policy to be. But it is also possible, perhaps probable, that private capital would have developed a synthetic rubber industry capability beyond specialty rubbers in the 1950s, particularly because the United States, unlike Britain, France, or the Netherlands, did not have a colonial legacy of Southeast Asian rubber suppliers that such a program could threaten.

On the first question, there is widespread agreement in the literature that the patent-sharing and technical interchange agreements entered into during the war and the federal sponsorship of industrial research during the postwar decade of government ownership did little to advance the state of technological knowledge. The standardization on the Standard Oil–IG Farben recipe for GR-S rubber may have been the right move in terms of maximizing the likelihood that the copolymerization plants operated smoothly and delivered GR-S without delays other than those associated with constructing the plants and obtaining adequate supplies of butadiene and styrene. But the arrangements had the effect of shutting down for the duration of the war the independent research programs previously pursued by Goodrich and Goodyear (Morris, 1989, p. 29).

The February 5, 1942, patent-sharing agreements reached between Rubber Reserve and the participating companies producing butadiene provided for payment by the government of a per-pound royalty to be shared among the companies according to a formula reflecting their use of patents owned by others. A similar patent-sharing and technical interchange agreement was made with respect to styrene on March 4, 1942. For the specialty rubbers, butyl and neoprene, whose manufacture was sole-sourced, agreements on royalty obligations were signed on May 15 and June 1, 1942. Finally, a June 15, 1942, agreement among the four tire companies and Rubber Reserve covered the art of compounding synthetic and natural rubber into final products and provided for limited technical interchange of jealously guarded trade secrets (Herbert and Bisio, 1985, p. 118).

Outside of copolymerization, where the recipe among the different operators was the same, and the plants were built to a common blueprint, companies had flexibility in selecting processes. This was especially true in butadiene production. Operators had little financial interest in using the lowest-cost processes (unless they had patent rights to it) because they were in any event being reimbursed for costs and doing so could reduce the share of the royalty payment they could retain. Moreover, since operators controlled the design of the government plants, they had a strong incentive to build along lines that would most benefit their own patent portfolio, even if doing so involved processes known not to be the most efficient. This would give the operator a strong bargaining position if and when the plants were privatized, and it would discourage others from bidding or, if a plant did go to a company that had not operated it during the war, put the original operator in a strong position to extract royalties from the processes locked into the plant design. The wartime royalty payment was also supposed to subsidize innovation and improvement, but it remained the same whether the operator made new process or product innovations or not (Solo, 1959). As far as innovation during the postwar decade of government ownership, Herbert and Bisio observed that "inasmuch as the cost-plus management fee was calculated as a percentage of the average of manufacturing costs and sales price, there was literally a *disincentive* to the operator to try to lower costs" because that would lower the management fee received (1985, p. 218; emphasis in original).

After the war, the government disbursed, through the year 1952, almost $41 million of funding to various universities, private corporations, and others for research and development of processes in the production of synthetic rubber and its use in fabrication of final products. Solo found that this program produced almost nothing of value (1954, p. 79). Herbert and Bisio (1985, pp. 156–57) reached similar conclusions.[34] As was true in much of the rest of the economy, patents granted in the area of rubber and plastics plummeted during the war, not returning to 1941 levels until 1951 (see chapter 7).

Companies used their own funds to pursue research along promising lines, given that only the results of that research could be patented and retained by the developer. In some instances companies built a Chinese wall between research conducted at the direction and with funding from the government and projects they pursued on their own account. An RFC report in 1953 claimed that government-funded research led to the development of "cold" rubber and oil-extended rubber. That is at best an exaggeration. Both "innovations" had their origin before the war or outside the government program, in research by General Tire and Rubber, Phillips, Dow, and Polymer Corporation, a Canadian Crown company.

Cold Rubber

If GR-S is copolymerized at colder temperatures, it is more flexible, wears better, and better resists extremes in temperature. In particular, "cold" GR-S is superior for car treads even when natural rubber is substantially cheaper, since it allows 10–30 percent greater tread wear. Goodrich had nine patents in this area before the war, but the process was not used initially in 1942 because of a shortage of refrigeration equipment and subsequently because the copolymerization operators did not want to change procedures at a time when continuity and throughput were of paramount importance. After the war, as an operator, Goodrich delayed pushing to implement or refine cold rubber until privatization, first because any fruits of government-funded research would need to be shared with all operators, and second because it was being reimbursed for its costs of manufacture in any case. Phillips, on the other hand, which operated a butadiene but not a copolymerization plant, the only company committed early on to developing a postwar integrated synthetic rubber operation, did not take government-provided research money. Building on German research, it developed the cold rubber processes to the point that the RFC jumped in and carried it further, challenging the Phillips patents on the grounds that the basic principles of cold rubber manufacture predated the war.

Oil-Extended Rubber

In a modern tire, typically one-quarter of the weight consists of fillers and extenders, such as carbon black (basically, soot, which gives the tire its coloring) or silica, which improves oil resistance. The use of mineral oil as an extender, which first required cold polymerized synthetic (Morris, 1989, p. 39), increased the plasticity of the GR-S rubber, making it easier to work with, but, more directly, cut the materials cost because it crowded out more expensive GR-S and thus reduced the demands for its ingredients, butadiene and styrene, which during the Korean War were once again in short supply. During World War II, even with access to cold rubber, there would have been no incentive to use the extender because the cost-plus-management-fee contracts meant that its introduction would have had zero effect on profits—or perhaps even reduced them.

After the Second World War ended, Congress terminated the various patent and technical interchange agreements, the GR-S agreement in 1946, styrene in

1948, butadiene and butyl in 1952. Once this happened, individual companies embarked on private research efforts, the uncertain outcome of which could make non-operators hesitant to bid for the plants and thus increase the bargaining power of the large operators. General Tire, working outside the government research program and in conjunction with Polymer, pushed forward with oil extension, then tried to sell it to the RFC. RFC, understanding the merits, then contracted with other companies to develop it in a non-infringing way. These other companies pointed to prior use of oil extension as a means of demonstrating that General Tire's processes were neither original nor patentable. General Tire then filed for patents, and litigation proceeded over their validity for the next two decades, ending only in 1974 with the Supreme Court's refusing to hear an appeal from the company over its loss in a suit by Firestone challenging validity on the basis in part of prior art (Solo, 1959, p. 102; Herbert and Bisio, 1985, pp. 152–53).

Rather than being the source of significant new product or process innovations, the development of the synthetic rubber industry both during the war and during the postwar decade of government ownership was based almost entirely on scientific and technological foundations established before the conflict in Europe began. That said, during the war U.S. petroleum companies did eventually became proficient in producing large quantities of butadiene from oil refinery gases, and tire companies gained experience in blending GR-S rubber with natural rubber and fillers such as carbon black in making tires. Whether this human capital would have value after the war depended on whether synthetic rubber continued to be produced. The fact that it took a decade before most of the government plants were privatized is testimony to how unsure about the future were industry players. The very real possibility that synthetic rubber would not be commercially viable is the reason private companies were loath to pay for the capital investment themselves and the federal government had to spend almost $700 million funding them. Both that physical capital and the human capital acquired in operating them might have had to be entirely written off, leaving no subsequent imprint on productivity data.

Between 1946 and 1949 the government-owned neoprene plant was sold to DuPont, and four of the five styrene plants were sold to large chemical producers. In these cases there were well-established prewar commercial uses for the outputs and, as noted, they were the plants that experienced the fewest operational difficulties during the war. Natural rubber is not a good substitute for neoprene (and vice versa), in part because of neoprene's superior oil resistance properties but natural rubber's superiority for tire treads and carcasses.

And styrene was and is widely used in the manufacture of a range of plastics. Between 1946 and 1949 the government also sold off the copolymerization plant in Louisville and five butadiene plants, four using the petroleum pathway and one an alcohol pathway, along with a bunch of smaller plants making fillers or catalysts. Original investment totaled $165 million, or about one-quarter of the total original investment of $673 million (Herbert and Bisio, 1985, p. 164, table 15.1). This left the bulk of the synthetic rubber industry in government hands, largely because of the great uncertainty about whether synthetic rubber would be commercially viable, combined with government concerns about preserving the capability in the event of another war.

Immediately after the war, an interagency policy committee (the Batt Committee) proposed maintaining a core of synthetic production capacity for strategic reasons. To that end, on July 22, 1946, it recommended that a minimum of one-third of peacetime rubber consumption be synthetic. In the Rubber Act of 1948 Congress cut this to 220,000 tons, which was less than the then-prevailing commercial demand and thus not binding because natural rubber prices remained elevated. The committee also recommended immediate privatization, but at the time there was relatively little appetite for this elsewhere in the political and commercial spheres.

Commercial interests were mixed in their desire that a government-owned synthetic capacity persist. Natural rubber producers, importers, and recyclers wanted privatization because they hoped it might lower the synthetic rubber output mandated for strategic purposes and as a result raise its price, from which they would benefit, since they would then provide a cheaper substitute. Also, there appears to have been some expectation that once plants were privately owned, the international rubber market, both natural and synthetic, could be recartelized (Solo, 1953, p. 35). This was unrealistic, since if under privatization the tire manufacturers owned the synthetic rubber plants, they were unlikely to conspire to jack up the price of their own raw materials.

The large tire manufacturers were content with their operating contracts, and the smaller tire companies feared that if the copolymerization plants were privatized in the hands of the large companies, the smaller fabricators might be squeezed by high synthetic rubber prices when natural rubber was in short supply. Congress was determined not to sell at fire-sale prices (no "giveaways"), and the plants seemed to be covering their costs, including beginning to pay down the costs of building them. For consumers of rubber—the tire makers and ultimately the final purchasers—synthetic rubber was preferred if natural rubber was more expensive. But a continuing synthetic rubber industry was also in consumers' interests because in the presence of an inelastic supply of natural rubber and with the prewar cartel not reestablished, some synthetic rubber production, even if apparently more expensive, could often depress natural rubber prices sufficiently that the overall costs per tire were actually lower if fabricators were forced to consume small amounts of synthetic (Solo, 1953, p. 36). The existence of a continuing synthetic rubber supply also tended to stabilize prices, a feature valued by the rubber manufacturers.

Through 1949, political instability in Southeast Asia as colonial empires dissolved kept natural rubber prices above those for synthetic, so commercial and natural security interests complemented each other in sustaining political support for continued government ownership. In 1949, however, natural rubber prices dropped below those for synthetic, and the requirement that those operating the synthetic plants buy a certain portion of the output for their own operations began, for the first time, to bind. During 1949 commercial users began advocating for shutting down or mothballing the plants. But then, thanks in part to the Korean War, which began on June 25, 1950, natural rubber prices shot up again, rising above synthetic. This price decline and then reversal, however, changed expectations about the future course of natural rubber prices, and companies besides Phillips now became more convinced of the longer-term commercial viability of a synthetic rubber industry. Natural rubber prices, which had fallen as low as $.14 a pound in 1949, rose to just under $.73 a pound in February 1951. Finally, refinements such as oil extension and the use of carbon black as a filler to increase abrasion resistance had improved the quality of products made with synthetic.

In 1950 the government still owned two butyl plants (built and operated by Standard Oil of New Jersey and its subsidiary Humble Oil), eight petroleum-to-butadiene plants (built and run by major petroleum companies), two alcohol-to-butadiene plants, one styrene plant (built and run by large chemical companies), and thirteen plants for copolymerizing styrene and butadiene into GR-S rubber (built and run by large tire companies, except one run by Phillips Petroleum) (Herbert and Bisio, 1985, p. 182). These plants had value only if synthetic rubber continued to be produced. From 1946 until 1950 disposal of the plants was not politically feasible because, although natural rubber prices remained elevated, all expectations were that cheap natural rubber would soon return, and no private company, with the possible exception of Phillips, was interested in taking the risks associated with acquiring the plants.

After considerable political back-and-forth, on November 18, 1953, the government advertised the plants, along with 447 pressurized tank cars, for sale.

The commission charged with sales sent out almost seven thousand brochures describing the plants and then toured all the facilities, noting in an interim report to Congress that "although the quality of synthetic rubber has been greatly improved and types developed such as cold rubber, in the past decade there have been no basic changes in the functional process of making rubber" (Herbert and Bisio, 1985, p. 183). The first part of the sentence must be taken with a grain of salt. As far as the second half of the sentence, there is widespread agreement on the relatively unchanged character of the basic technology during the years of government operation. Acquisition price during the war we can estimate at $508 million ($673 million less what had previously been sold off); total sales price was $260 million, although the price level had roughly doubled during the interval between acquisition and sale. So ended one of the most unusual episodes of industrial policy in the history of the United States.

Conclusion

The celebratory imperative reflected in the American Chemical Society's pamphlet actually predates the start of the synthetic rubber program. In 1940 Standard Oil of New Jersey confidently vowed that it could rapidly move production to scale as soon as it got the go-ahead from the government. A vice president at Goodrich predicted that synthetic rubber would rapidly replenish natural rubber inventories. U.S. Rubber boasted in September 1941 of the protection against catastrophe offered by its new synthetic rubber plant, and in newspaper advertisements Goodyear breathlessly highlighted technological advances in synthetic rubber (see Finlay, 2009, pp. 174, 288). Each of these statements was either wrong or reflected considerable exaggeration or wishful thinking.

The celebratory imperative and the prose to which it gives rise clouds our thinking about the economic history of the war. To talk repeatedly of miracles dulls our ability to think critically and crowds out efforts to find out what really happened. It creates a penumbra that shades and colors the interpretation of the supply-side consequences of the war. It can make data showing sharp declines in manufacturing productivity as the result of mobilization seem surprising.

Consider the potted history that appeared in 1956 in an article in *Scientific American*. According to the article, the history of the U.S. program *began* with the appointment of the Rubber Survey Committee (Baruch, Conant, and

Compton) in August 1942: "The committee and its experts recommended development and manufacture of a general-purpose rubber similar to Buna S. Under the leadership of William M. Jeffers, president of Union Pacific railroad, who was appointed rubber director, a staff of chemists and engineers, with only a general idea of how Buna S was produced, swiftly set up a process. In December 1943, the new rubber began pouring out of a new plant in Institute, W. Va. . . . In 1945 the production was 791,197 long tons" (Fisher, 1956, pp. 83–84).

Just like that! Almost as if a magician's wand had been waved!

In fact, the Rubber Survey Committee's charge was to resolve the political crisis surrounding the choice of feedstock for a program whose structure was in place by the end of 1940. The main rubber produced was not just similar to Buna S—it *was* Buna S, produced under royalty-free licenses to use the Standard Oil–IG Farben patents. The commencement of volume production at the *end* of 1943 is treated as unexceptional, rather than the reflection of delays that had potentially catastrophic consequences. It disguises the reality that the record of GR-S production in 1943 was an avoidable and potentially devastating failure. Government and private business decision makers bear responsibility for the flawed design and rollout of the program as much as they do for what was actually achieved. O'Neill's treatment of the rubber history (1993, pp. 91–92) is similarly superficial.

Although not as cavalier, Wendt, in his useful 1947 article, glosses over the implications of shortfalls in production in 1943, alluding to some "avoidable delays" early in the program, stressing the high level of output achieved starting in December 1943. He recognizes the overwhelming contribution of alcohol to butadiene production in 1943, but he immediately emphasizes the higher cost of alcohol as opposed to butylene feedstock, suggesting the alcohol-based butadiene was five times more expensive, although he acknowledges in a footnote that he had ignored the much higher physical capital cost per ton of demonstrated capacity for the petroleum-pathway plants. He states that "military requirements for rubber goods during the war years were fully met" and quotes the director of Rubber Programs in November 1945: "Broadly speaking, no vehicle, military or essential civilian, stood still for lack of tires and no military operation was delayed because rubber equipment was lacking (Wendt, 1947, pp. 225–26). This ignores the fact that the military had to accept vehicles without tires in 1944, and it ignores the impediments to the U.S. distribution system and the access of American workers to their places of employment resulting from nationwide gas and tire rationing and a thirty-five-mile-an-hour speed limit. Most important, it ignores the constraints posed on U.S. military options in 1943, and the resulting yearlong delay in the cross-Channel invasion. As the Rubber Survey Committee's report had stated in 1942, "We cannot base military offensives on rubber we do not have" (1942, p. 7).

Having considered the initiative's history, we are in a better position to respond to the question posed in the chapter title. Here is one answer: given the design of the program and the delays in building the plants, it was a miracle its execution did not lead to the loss of the war. Many feared in 1942 that that would indeed be the outcome. Without the ultimate success of the program, the U.S. economy along with its military capability would have ground to a halt as worn tires on civilian vehicles blew out, tanks, aircraft, and ships stood unfinished on assembly lines or on shipyard ways because of exhaustion of rubber supplies, factory equipment ceased to operate because of the lack of drive belts, and the existing military machine slowed down because of the absence of replacement tires, treads, hoses, and insulation.

The success of the synthetic rubber program in producing large quantities of GR-S was an important accomplishment. But that does not make it a miracle or absolve us of responsibility to evaluate its trajectory objectively. To describe something as miraculous is to suggest that we witnessed an outcome that could not be or was not reasonably expected or anticipated. Using this definition, it would be less of a stretch to apply the term to the Soviet victory at Stalingrad, which provided the breathing room for the rubber program to recover from its mistakes and for a successful cross-Channel invasion to be planned and, finally, in June 1944, carried out.

By cutting off access to rubber, the Japanese visited on the U.S. economy and its war-fighting capability a blow potentially more devastating than the attack on Pearl Harbor. The country addressed the threat to war-fighting ability and economic survival with a combination of demand suppression and supply enhancement. Pre–Pearl Harbor inaction left relatively unaffected the ability to suppress demand, but it had a big effect on the options available to enhance supply. Demand suppression alone, in any event, could not fix the problem since it could be applied only to civilian consumption and even in that sphere could not be pushed so far that it threatened military production by diminishing the ability of workers to get to and from work or the capabilities of moving goods around the country. The halting accumulation of a strategic reserve, the rejection of proposals to subsidize guayule production in the 1930s, the repeated cutbacks and delays in commencing construction on the facilities needed for a synthetic rubber program, and the initial decision to pursue a development path based on petroleum as the feedstock combined to determine a trajectory that was almost catastrophic.[35]

Far more than was true for other materials, dependence on imported rubber was the United States' Achilles' heel during the Second World War. In its statement of the problem, the Rubber Survey Committee's report was clear: "Of all critical and strategic materials, rubber is the one which presents the greatest threat to the safety of our nation and the success of the Allied cause. Production of steel, copper, aluminum, alloys, or aviation gasoline may be inadequate to prosecute the war as rapidly or as effectively as we could wish, but at the worst we are still assured of sufficient supplies of these items to operate our armed forces on a very powerful scale. But if we fail to secure quickly a large new rubber supply our war effort and our domestic economy both will collapse" (U.S. Rubber Survey Committee, 1942, p. 23). One may dismiss this language as hyperbolic, but it is hard to see how Conant or Compton, or Eberstadt, in his private communication to Baruch, had an incentive to exaggerate.

4 • Petroleum, Paukenschlag, and Pipelines

In 1946, as part of its closing act, the Petroleum Administration for War (PAW), the successor to the Office of the Petroleum Coordinator for War, commissioned a five-hundred-plus-page history of its accomplishments between 1941 and 1945. This history, while stuffed with encomiums to the self-sacrifice of members of the industry (so much oil company money spent on persuading the public not to buy its product!) also includes a wealth of useful information about the wartime challenges faced by the sector and how they were met. Still, unlike the American Chemical Society's celebration of the synthetic rubber program, the authors of the PAW history could not quite bring themselves to describe anything the oil industry did during the conflict as a miracle, or at least an unqualified miracle. Absent are suggestions, common in treatments of other sectors of the economy, that the experience of mobilization was somehow transformative, or that rising to the challenges of the war laid the supply-side foundations for postwar prosperity.

There is no five-hundred-plus-page authoritative government-sponsored treatment of the rubber program. Some of the difference in attention may be attributable to the forceful personality of the head of the PAW, Harold Ickes, a confidant of Roosevelt who continued as secretary of the Interior while heading this agency and its predecessor.[1] It was not until the appointment, following the Rubber Survey Committee's report, of William Jeffers as the first rubber czar that there was a public face and government-designated advocate for the rubber program. Ickes, a progressive politician who had often been at loggerheads with the oil industry during the 1930s, adopted a cooperative stance during the war, and there was little daylight between the agencies he ran and oil company viewpoints, which were well represented, carefully considered, and integrated into the process and substance of wartime administration.

Part may be attributable to the presence, in the case of petroleum but not of rubber, of a powerful industry in the United States devoted both to extracting the raw material and to refining and distributing it. Part also may be due to the continuing and growing geopolitical and strategic significance of petroleum, although in the 1940s the United States was a net exporter, and oil had not yet achieved the outsized influence on U.S. foreign policy it would come to exercise. Finally, part may simply be that it was easy to understand that planes, tanks, ships, military trucks, and jeeps could not operate without fuel, because people are reminded almost daily that if there is no gas in their tank, their car won't go. A vehicle's dependence on rubber is less obvious, its imperatives less frequent. One may fill a car with fuel every week but replace wiper blades only every year, tires every three or four, and the radiator hose or timing belt perhaps only every five. The PAW history appealed to these understandings of the immediacy of need, writing at the outset that "World War II from beginning to end was a war of oil" and "oil was *the* indispensable material" (U.S. PAW, 1946, p. 1; emphasis in original).

When factor proportions are fixed, as they commonly are in the short run, it becomes difficult to say what is truly indispensable, and, especially, what ranks *first* in indispensability. Not everyone shared the PAW's judgment, and the organization and its industry associates were quite unhappy—one might even say bitterly resentful—when the rubber program received priority access to scarce materials or equipment: "There were no delays more costly than those which resulted from the preferential treatment given to the rubber program as against the 100-octane program. PAW fought long and hard against this discrimination" (p. 209). Had the rubber program been executed in a different fashion and on a different timeline, the conflicts over materials and equipment, particularly in 1942, would have been less intense, but that leaves unresolved, and perhaps unresolvable, which input was more indispensable. What is certain is that, unlike rubber, there was never any danger that the country would run out of oil.

The PAW history complained repeatedly that almost everyone outside the agency or industry—both in the government and in the public—acted as if producing petroleum and refined products during the conflict was simply a matter of turning the spigots a little farther to the right. There was, however, some basis for that presumption. In contrast with rubber, the United States was extraordinarily well endowed with petroleum. Because of prewar discoveries and exploitation, particularly of the huge East Texas field, and because of efforts between 1924 and 1939 to curtail or restrict production to raise and help stabilize its price, the United States entered the war with an excess production capacity of 750,000 barrels of crude a day, representing what could easily be a 20 percent boost to production (U.S. PAW, 1946, p. 172). Before the war, the industry fueled the capability narrative by offering repeated assurances that it was "prepared to meet any demands placed on us" (Frey, 1941, p. 118).

To a considerable degree it was able to do so, and the PAW history was self-congratulatory, taking pride that it had breathed life into the popular wartime boast: "The difficult we do immediately; the impossible takes a little longer." But there is ambiguity in the nonchalance of this language, and the narrative in the history veers between emphasizing how easily challenges were overcome and belaboring how very difficult indeed were those challenges. If what the industry accomplished did not really require extraordinary efforts, its achievements cannot also have been a miracle. One sometimes has a sense reading the history that the industry felt it just had not gotten enough appreciation and love.

As for total output, between 1941 and 1945 average daily production increased from 3.84 million barrels to 4.89 million barrels, a rise of 1.05 million barrels a day. Roughly three-quarters of the increase represented exploitation of the 1941 gap between actual and potential output in the industry, and about a quarter million barrels a day an expansion of capacity. Exploration for new supplies continued during the conflict (although the rate of additions to proved reserves dropped off), and the economy remained almost entirely self-sufficient until 1944. By spring of that year most of the severe transportation and distribution problems in the East had been overcome, and U-boat predation along the Atlantic, Gulf, and Caribbean sea frontiers was more or less under control. But at that point there did begin to be pressure on supplies of petroleum products considered at the national level. Starting in June 1944, imports from Venezuela were necessary to deal with shortages of heating oil and bunker oil for the navy (U.S. PAW, 1946, pp. 6, 260).[2] And beginning in 1944Q3, some U.S. oilfields began to be pumped in a way detrimental to their long-run yield (U.S. PAW, 1946, pp. 444–45).

The pressures on overall supply in 1944 and 1945 resulted from the continuation and culmination of the Pacific campaigns along with the claims of the D-Day invasion, the continuing aerial bombardment of Germany, and the unexpected counterattack by Germany (the Battle of the Bulge) starting in December 1944. Still, even though the existing historiography makes it almost expected in treatments of the achievements of war mobilization, commentators who might otherwise have been so disposed could not quite bring themselves to describe the increase in output of crude as a miracle. A 1973 Library of Congress congressional research report, prepared at the time of the first OPEC oil crisis, when the country was once again considering rationing, described the World War II experience: "Fortunately, there was sufficient reserve production capacity from domestic oil fields so these priority demands could actually, almost miraculously, be filled" (1973, p. 179). Almost.

It is indisputable that petroleum products contributed in myriad ways to the war effort: not just motor gas and aviation fuel, but also toluene, the main ingredient in TNT, lubricating oils, bunker oil for navy and merchant ships, and asphalt for paving runways and building roads where the war effort demanded it. And, of course, the use of petroleum feedstock to make butadiene for the synthetic rubber program, although mention of this is conspicuously absent in the introduction to the PAW history. Between December 1941 and August 1945, the United States pumped 6 billion barrels (each 42 gallons) to supply itself and its allies—one-fifth of all the oil drawn from the ground from the birth of the industry in Pennsylvania in 1859 until VJ Day (U.S. PAW, 1946, p. 1).[3]

Beyond increasing the level of overall crude oil production by 27 percent and refinery output by 32 percent, two challenges and achievements during the war stand out. The first involved a continuing struggle to provide adequate supplies of crude and refined products to the Eastern Seaboard and European allies, particularly Britain. The second was addressing the unprecedented increase in demand for 100-octane aviation gasoline. This chapter considers the genesis of these challenges, the degree to which they affected supply capability (and thus productivity) during the war, and the extent to which responses to them may have influenced potential output in the postwar period. Persisting positive influences might have resulted from the accumulation of wartime physical capital useful after the war, know-how acquired through learning by the industry's workforce, or breakthrough technologies elicited under the pressures of wartime exigency.

Oil Supply and Demand in the Northeast

To understand the East Coast problem, one must begin with the fact that although well-endowed with petroleum, the country faced a geographical mismatch between the location of crude reserves, refinery capacity, and the locales of final demand. Some crude was pumped in as many as twenty states, but by the time of Pearl Harbor, most production came from Texas, California, Oklahoma, and Louisiana. Refinery capacity in the United States was concentrated in East Texas–Louisiana and California, in Chicago and St. Louis, and, in part for historical reasons, in the New York–New Jersey–Philadelphia area. The bulk of the country's population and industrial capacity was located east of the Mississippi, although by the time of the Second World War the oil fields of Pennsylvania and the Midwest were nearing exhaustion.[4] Outside the Mountain states, imbalances existed between where crude oil was pumped and where it was consumed, and to some degree where it was refined.

In the four states responsible for four-fifths of U.S. production, crude oil moved directly from oil fields to refineries through gathering pipelines.[5] These were small-diameter pipes that collected crude at the wellhead and then, along with other, similar pipes, routed it to the refinery. Refineries in the Chicago and St. Louis areas depended on river barges and larger-diameter pipelines that ran for longer distances, and in the New York–New Jersey–Philadelphia area, on oceangoing tankers. Before the war approximately 260 ships carried large volumes of crude and refined petroleum products from the Gulf Coast to the northeastern markets. Additional tankers took some California oil through the Panama Canal to the East, and U.S.-owned tankers flying Panamanian flags of convenience took product from Caribbean refineries in Aruba and Curaçao owned by U.S. and European oil companies. The bottom line was that deliveries to the Eastern Seaboard came approximately 95 percent by tanker; there was only a small (80,000 barrels a day) local production of crude. The Northeast of the United States was almost as dependent on inbound tanker shipments of petroleum and petroleum products as was Great Britain.

Where available, moving bulk cargo by water has always been the cheapest means because the energy required to overcome friction over water is so much less than is the case with land-based alternatives. This was true for the costs of transporting petroleum and petroleum products, with prewar rates in mills per ton mile of 1.25 by tanker, 3.2 by pipeline, and 8.3 by tank car (Maxwell and Balcom, 1946a, p. 562; a mill is one-tenth of a cent). The crude shipped from the Gulf fed the East Coast refineries, which distributed locally, reserved a portion for export, and then sent some refined products to the Midwest by rail tank car, pipelines, or river barges. This was a circuitous route for crude originating in Texas, Oklahoma, or even California, but testimony to the relative lack of friction in moving cargo over water, and thus the economic dominance of the Gulf–Atlantic Coast tanker "pipeline." In the prewar period, eastern refineries supplied about half of the regional demand for refined products; shipments of gasoline and other refined products from Gulf Coast refineries provided the rest. Deliveries of crude and fuel oil from foreign (mostly Caribbean) sources roughly balanced exports from the Eastern Seaboard (U.S. PAW, 1946, p. 83).

A second key point is that the petroleum industry depended (and depends) on a reliable and steady flow of crude to refineries and refinery products to distributors and final users. One way of ensuring against uneven or potentially disrupted flows is to hold large buffer stocks of crude or refined product at various points on the transshipment and distribution network. This solution is especially problematic for the oil industry, much more so than in the case of rubber. The best place to store petroleum is in the ground. Once pumped, stocks of crude or refined products are subject to evaporation, contamination, and the risk of fire. All parties in the production, refining, and distribution network, including final consumers, held (and hold) relatively small inventories, relying on a well-functioning transportation infrastructure to ensure an uninterrupted supply. The high premium placed on reliability meant (and means) a need for tight coordination, which explains in part why the large oil companies owned (and own) most of the tankers, barges, rail cars, and pipelines, along with the sources of crude and the refineries.

At the time of Pearl Harbor the United States possessed aboveground storage for a maximum of four months' consumption of crude oil and petroleum products. Ideally, storage would be zero; it existed (and exists) to cover small perturbations in the arrival of deliveries, to allow full-load tanker or tank truck deliveries in order to minimize transport cost, and to provide storage for the joint products of refinery runs when the seasonal demand for some may be low.[6] The inventory capacity referenced above includes oil in pipelines, at the bottom of storage tanks, and in so-called working tanks, and is thus a significant overestimate of what could actually be drawn down by final customers from local stocks, unless the entire industry was to be shut down and the ability to resupply terminated (U.S. PAW, 1946, p. 84). Even in peacetime, the large seasonal fluctuations in demand for such products as gasoline and fuel oil, the time it took for petroleum to get from wellhead to final consumer, and the limited buffer-stock storage meant that decisions on the composition of refinery runs had to be made as much as six months in advance of planned consumption, which created a delicate, somewhat fragile system.

At any moment of time the Northeast, which also, along with Halifax, served as points of origin for transshipments to Europe, possessed limited storage.[7] It took the form of above-ground tank farms, gas, diesel, or fuel oil reservoirs in cars, trucks, buses, locomotives and rail cars, fuel oil tanks in

homes, commercial buildings, or factories heated by oil, and stocks in transit in tankers, pipelines, railway tank cars, river- and oceangoing barges, and
delivery trucks. On average in 1941 the seventeen Eastern Seaboard states ran
through 1.5 million barrels of petroleum a day, roughly 40 percent of national
daily consumption. Of this, about 350,000 barrels a day fueled passenger vehicles, and about 550,000 barrels a day were used in industrial operations (U.S.
Civilian Production Administration, 1946a, p. 52). Without a well-functioning
infrastructure reliably resupplying these reservoirs, stocks would be quickly
diminished or exhausted, which at best (depending on the nature of rationing)
would lead to shortages that would make it difficult for people to get to and
from work, for goods and raw materials to reach their destinations, and for
factories, farms, and refineries to operate efficiently and without interruption.
Also, people might freeze in the winter.

In contrast to the situation in rubber, neither Germany nor Japan could
cut off supplies of a raw material in which the United States was almost entirely self-sufficient. Nor could they bomb or easily disrupt refinery operations
within the United States, although German submarines did go after Caribbean refineries owned by Standard and Royal Shell (Bercuson and Herwig,
2014), and on February 23, 1942, a Japanese submarine shelled a tank farm
near Santa Barbara, California, helping inflame the popular mood (but not
the tanks) and influencing the decision to intern Japanese Americans.[8] On
June 12, 1942, a German submarine landed four saboteurs on Long Island at
Amagansett, New York, and another submarine landed four more at Ponte Ve-
dra Beach in Florida. One member betrayed the group, all eight were captured
and tried, and six subsequently electrocuted. Their targets included aluminum and magnesium plants and other infrastructure but could have included
oil. After this failed mission, the Germans made no attempts at sabotage in
the United States during the war.

What Germany could effectively do, however, was shut down the tanker
route from the Gulf Coast to the Northeast. This its U-boat commanders
did with enthusiasm and abandon starting in mid-January 1942, torpedoing
almost sixty tankers between then and June. These attacks often took place
within sight of the U.S. coastline, where the absence of blackouts made it easy
to target the silhouetted ships, typically proceeding without escort and often
with their lights blazing.

Between January and June 1942, U-boats sank almost 400 ships in waters protected by the U.S. Navy, including 171 along the Atlantic Coast, 62 in
the Gulf, and 141 in the Caribbean frontiers (Gannon, 1990, pp. 388–89). At

its June 10, 1942, meeting, Ickes reported to the War Production Board that through May 1942, 59 tankers owned or controlled by the United States and supplying the East Coast were sunk by submarines along the Atlantic and Gulf Coast, which resulted in the loss "irretrievably" of 300,000 tons of steel, not much less than what would be needed for the Big Inch pipeline, the approval of which he was then seeking.[9] On two tours of duty originating from bomb-proof pens in occupied Lorient, France, one boat alone (U-123) sank twelve ships within one hundred miles of the U.S. Atlantic coast, and seven more on the outbound and return voyages (Gannon, 1990, p. 402). During the winter of 1942, tourists in Miami gathered each evening on the beach to watch torpedoed ships burn (Isserman, 1991, p. 55). In mid-June 1942 three submarines mined the approaches to Chesapeake Bay, destroying four ships in a spectacular display in full few of bathers at Virginia Beach (Offley, 2014, chs. 9–10). Within the first six months of 1942, approximately five thousand merchant seamen, civilian passengers including women and children, and a few military were killed in attacks on shipping along the Atlantic and Gulf seaboards and within the Caribbean. The original wave of U-boats consisted of only five vessels. At no time in the first half of 1942 were more than a dozen submarines manned by fewer than five hundred men operating in these theaters (Hickam, 1989).

The U.S. Navy covered its lack of preparation and negligence in dismissing British warnings with a withering public relations barrage. A release on April 1, 1942, stated that eighteen German submarines had been sunk, or presumably sunk. Was it an accident that this announcement took place on April Fools' Day? It echoed a similar November 21, 1941, claim by Secretary of the Navy Frank Knox that fourteen German subs had been either sunk or damaged in the North Atlantic. The correct number in both cases was zero. In late January the same public relations office made an embarrassed hero of a lone pilot who had dropped several ineffective depth charges in the vicinity of a U-boat; newspaper stories quoted an alleged report from the pilot that included the memorable line, "Sighted sub, sank same" (Gannon, 1990, p. 378; Offley, 2014, p. 123). The navy pushed a public service campaign reminding citizens that "loose lips sink ships." But the fact was that the unescorted and generally unarmed tankers and merchant ships moving along the coast and silhouetted against the bright lights of coastal tourist areas and automobile headlights provided such a rich range of targets that the U-boat commanders had no need of information on when their targets had sailed.

On January 23, 1942, a navy spokesman warned Americans that if they saw anything to say nothing, presumably so that such information would not provide confirmation to the Germans of the success of their predations; the statement helpfully suggested that what they might see is a German submarine being captured or destroyed. But the stories of rescued survivors could not be entirely suppressed, nor could the eyewitness accounts of the pyrotechnics associated with tankers burning not far from shore, the oil slicks that fouled the beaches from Long Island to Florida, and the debris and dead sailors washed ashore. Gannon argued that the little-known submarine campaign along the Atlantic Seaboard was "one of the greatest maritime disasters in history and the American nation's worst-ever defeat at sea" (1990, p. 389)

Before U.S. entry into the war, the petroleum industry and the East Coast of the United States got a taste of what might lie in store. In the spring of 1941, British oil inventories became dangerously low because of tanker losses (182 through April 1941), and the United States lent 50 tankers to Britain. They were lent in the sense that the ships were pulled from domestic supply and redeployed to move petroleum products from Gulf Coast or Caribbean oil fields or refineries to New York or Halifax, where their shipments could be picked up by British tankers for the trip across the Atlantic, cutting two weeks off the round trip. For the United States, however, this reduced by about 250,000 barrels a day the ability to move product from the Gulf to the Eastern Seaboard for domestic consumption. It was the immediate problem facing Harold Ickes as he stepped into his role as petroleum coordinator when the Office of the Petroleum Coordinator for War was established on June 19, 1941.[10]

This prewar challenge was addressed by improvising other means of getting supply to the East Coast, along with a failed initiative to encourage voluntary conservation. Tankers moving crude from California to Philadelphia were redeployed to move product from the Gulf Coast, which meant a shorter round trip, and thus a higher rate of product delivery. Toward the same end, efforts were made to reduce turnaround time in port. Westward shipments of product from eastern refineries were prohibited or at least strongly discouraged. Congress allowed higher load lines on the tankers, at some cost to safety, and the State Department permitted a similar relaxation on transatlantic shipments, which required a suspension of the International Load Line Convention of 1930.[11]

But the biggest initiative was to bring rail tank cars back into use for the long-distance transport of oil and oil products, regardless of the expense. Before the war, tank cars were being phased out as a means of moving crude or refined product because tankers and pipelines were so much cheaper. Many tank cars suffered from deferred maintenance, which had to be remedied as they were summoned back to intensive use. The country began the war with 145,500 cars. This included 105,600 that were normally used for petroleum, 1,600 pressurized tank cars for liquefied petroleum gas, 10,000 owned by railroads for their own use, and 28,300 used for vegetable oils and the industrial alcohol business, hauling molasses, alcohol, and other liquids (U.S. PAW, 1946, p. 90). Oil companies, which owned many of the cars, were asked, where possible, to switch to using them to move oil, but many resisted because the United States was still at peace, the cost per ton mile was almost seven times the tanker rate, and the companies would need to construct special facilities for emptying the cars when they arrived in the East for distribution of their contents to refineries or storage tanks.

The public saw no crisis, one reason the voluntary conservation program had so little effect, because the government could not reveal how desperate the situation was for Britain. Oil companies did manage successfully to pressure rail companies to lower tank car rates. Tank car deliveries to the East increased from 22,000 barrels a day in August 1941 to 141,300 in October at additional cost to the oil companies. The Office of Price Administration (OPA) allowed the price of oil to rise in partial compensation for higher transport costs, and ultimately the RFC provided funds to the oil companies to fully make up the difference, although the companies bore the cost of building the new facilities for unloading. Existing pipeline shipments increased from 40,000 to 65,000 barrels a day, and 6,000 barrels a day came by barge from Buffalo. These initiatives, which could be implemented without much delay, reduced the deficit from 250,000 to 175,000 barrels a day. In October and November 1941, as its antisubmarine efforts became more successful, Britain returned the tankers and they were restored to U.S. domestic service. The "phony" shortage ended (U.S. PAW, 1946, pp. 85–87). But it was a temporary respite.

On December 7 the Japanese bombed Pearl Harbor. On December 8 the United States declared war on Japan, followed on December 11 by a declaration of war against Germany and Italy. With U.S. entry into the war, the East Coast supply of crude and petroleum products was again vulnerable, although severe U-boat predation on U.S.-flagged and other vessels along the Atlantic coastline did not begin for another five weeks, in mid-January 1942. At the start of the war approximately 260 tankers ranging in capacity from 25,000 to 150,000 barrels moved oil and product from the Gulf Coast ports of Corpus Christi, Houston, and Port Arthur to East Coast destinations, with other, often foreign flagged tankers moving oil north from Caribbean refineries in Aruba and Curaçao. Together these fleets provided 95 percent of the East Coast supply (U.S. PAW, 1946, p. 89).

Once U-boat warfare commenced in earnest in these waters, the losses quickly mounted. The Germans sank almost sixty oil tankers between February and May 1942, often in sight of the U.S. coastline, killing crew members and despoiling beaches in New Jersey, Delaware, and Florida. A variety of statistics appear in the literature regarding tanker (and other ship) losses. The most complete are available at http://www.usmm.org/shipsunkdamaged. html. Counting tanker losses in the East Coast, Gulf of Mexico, and Caribbean, and including U.S.-owned tankers flying a Panamanian flag of convenience, this database shows four tankers lost in December 1941 and January 1942, rising to twelve in February, fourteen in March, eleven in April, fifteen in May, and thirteen in June. After June, the losses taper off (five in July, zero in August, one in September). June 1942 was the peak month for losses along these routes, and indeed for merchant ship losses in all theaters of the war.[12]

With a very few exceptions, the decline in losses over the Gulf-Atlantic route after June did not reflect the introduction of convoying. The reality was that in the face of skyrocketing insurance rates, growing shortages of ships, and discouragement from both German submarines and the U.S. Navy, fewer ships risked running the gauntlet, and the tanker route shut down almost completely for almost the entirety of the remainder of the war with Germany. By May 1942 average daily deliveries to the East Coast by tanker had fallen 82 percent compared with December 1941. They would reach their lowest point in April and May 1943, during which average daily deliveries were just 6.6 percent of what they had been the month Pearl Harbor was attacked (U.S. PAW, 1946, p. 87). Coastal and intracoastal shipping in the United States resumed in September 1945, following victory over Japan (U.S. Bureau of the Budget, 1946, p. 492).

Having initially ignored British warnings and spurned British advice, the U.S. Navy eventually did learn how to fight the U-boats, but Germany continued to build them and the climax of the Battle of the Atlantic did not take place until winter and early spring of 1943. Over a three-week period in March 1943, the Germans destroyed ninety-seven Allied ships, losing seven U-boats but taking delivery of fourteen more (Gannon, 1990, pp. 395–96). Tanker losses over the Gulf Coast–Atlantic traverse remained modest during these months, mostly because there were hardly any ships attempting it, a reality starkly reflected in the East Coast petroleum delivery statistics. Even in the first half of 1945, monthly deliveries by tanker to the Eastern Seaboard had recovered to barely a quarter of what they had been in 1941. Operation Paukenschlag (Drumbeat), as the Germans called their submarine offensive, was almost completely effective in severing the tanker "pipeline," and tanker shipments remained at low levels throughout the remainder of the war.

Because tankers were scarce, it made little sense to continue to use them on the Gulf Coast–Atlantic route, especially because alternative, if more expensive, overland routes were possible. Existing tankers and newly built ships were deployed to their highest-value use—on the North Atlantic run, where there was no alternative to moving over water. In contrast with the Eastern Seaboard routes, the convoy system helped greatly in reducing losses on the North Atlantic sea bridge. Indeed, without the tanker fleet built during peacetime for the Gulf Coast–Atlantic route, the United States would have been hard-pressed to help transport oil to its European allies.

But oil and petroleum products still had to get to the East Coast, not only so they could be transshipped to Europe, but also to satisfy domestic needs. Allied escort ships, prioritized for the North Atlantic, were scarce.[13] The convoy system worked better in the North Atlantic, where the great expanses of open sea made finding them difficult. The routes from the Gulf Coast and the Caribbean had more choke points where submarines could simply wait to ambush their prey (Bercuson and Herwig, 2014, p. 152). One of the most notorious was off Cape Hatteras, where the sixty-mile-wide Gulf Stream, moving north at about five nautical miles an hour, collides with the colder waters of the Labrador current, creating unstable and stormy conditions. Merchant ships had a thirty- to fifty-mile-wide corridor between the shoals nearer the coast and the Gulf Stream. Moreover, the continental shelf drops off very quickly in this region (as opposed to what is true along most of the Eastern Seaboard). The U-boats could rest submerged in deep waters during the day and then emerge at night to take their toll (Offley, 2014, pp. 3–4).

In January the British had given the United States advance warning of the arrival of U-boats off New England because they knew with a high degree of accuracy the location of each submarine. The U.S. Navy ignored the headsup, spending most of its energies suppressing information about the ensuing offshore destruction on the Eastern Sea Frontier. The challenge of combatting the U-boats became more difficult on February 1, 1942, when German commanders added a new four-rotor encryption machine for all communications to and from headquarters. British intelligence had previously reverse-engineered the three-rotor systems and broken the codes and could quickly decrypt communications; that was how they had been able to provide such accurate advance warning of the attacks. For the remainder of 1942, the United States and Britain no longer had highly accurate information on the location of each boat, although they could roughly plot positions by triangulation from high-frequency direction-finding equipment and photo reconnaissance. (The German submarines traveled fastest, and spent most of their time, on the surface of the water.)

An effective response to the U-boat threat on these routes awaited better training and tactics on the part of the navy and new tools such as the Leigh light, a twenty-four-inch floodlight mounted on the underside of an aircraft wing that allowed pursuers to keep track of a submarine after it dove, along with new ship-based antisubmarine ordnance, known as hedgehogs, which supplemented depth charges. In the meantime—and it was a long meantime, stretching well into 1944—the effect of this supply disruption was not simply to make matters uncomfortable during the winter for residents who heated with oil in the Northeast. The drawing down of inventories because of uncertain arrivals of new supply meant periodic spot shortages on the Eastern Seaboard— "one of the worst headaches of the war," as the PAW put it. These disrupted refinery operations and industrial production, as well as transportation and heating. In May 1942, one of the darkest months of the war, East Coast refineries could not get enough crude to operate at full capacity, which affected their efficiency, and oil wells in the Southwest had to stop pumping crude because they had no place to store it or ship it (U.S. PAW, 1946, pp. 3, 88).

Supply Restrictions and Rationing

End-user rationing during the Second World War in the United States affected gasoline and fuel oil and eleven other product categories: tires, automobiles, typewriters, sugar, bicycles, processed foods, meats, fats, oils and cheese, coffee, and shoes. Pursuant to a WPB directive of January 24, 1942, overall responsibility for implementing the programs lay with the OPA, working in conjunction with 5,600 local ration boards. Like draft boards, these were staffed mostly by volunteers, typically prominent members of the community. For all these products, including gasoline, the binding constraint on consumption was always on the supply side: the allocation decisions by the PAW whereby each refinery received a monthly allotment of crude and each wholesale and retail distributor an allotment of gasoline and fuel oil.

Operating the entire industry as if it were one large nationalized firm, the PAW planned and scheduled deliveries of crude and refined products by railway tank car, barge, tanker, and pipeline. These intended deliveries might be disrupted by inclement weather, derailments, or torpedoes. In any local market, the bottom line was that supply was what it was: aside from the black market, the short-run supply curve was vertical. End-user rationing aimed at influencing and indeed controlling how this limited supply was distributed. In particular, it aimed at reducing "nonessential" consumption so that prioritized uses and users could get all they needed.

The gasoline program was intended to limit "nonessential" use, while at the same time providing as much fuel as was reasonably justifiable to commercial or non-highway users. Owners of trucks, buses, taxicabs, and tractors and other commercial users, including agricultural users of gasoline-powered stationary machinery, could, upon receipt of a Certificate of War Necessity, receive ration coupons in whatever quantity they requested. These certificates, originally awarded by the OPA, were ultimately issued by the Office of Defense Transportation and also gave the holder preferential access to tires, spare parts, and replacement vehicles. Between 1941 and 1944 non-highway use of gasoline, for example by tractors, increased. Commercial use fell modestly (16 percent), mostly because of a reduction in the number of commercial vehicles on the road.

But the focus of curtailment was on passenger vehicle use. War planners reasoned that such curtailment was least likely to affect military production and fighting capability directly, and likely to be most effective in preserving the rapidly deteriorating installed stocks of rubber. Saving rubber, as opposed to a nationwide shortage of gasoline, was the rationale for introducing nationwide gas rationing in December 1942, following the Rubber Survey Committee's recommendations, but mandatory gasoline rationing had already begun with a card system in the seventeen Eastern Seaboard states on May 15, 1942, followed by a coupon system introduced on July 22, 1942. The makeshift card system was rushed into use before the coupon system was ready for rollout because of the mushrooming tanker losses and the continuing decline in retail deliveries in April. It was moderately effective initially but became less so as customers and retailers figured out its loopholes.

The eastern states, and perforce the overall war economy, faced severe regional shortages even when, nationally, petroleum and petroleum products were abundant. The implementation of end-user rationing had been preceded on March 19, 1942, by Limitation Order L-70 from the WPB, which reduced gasoline deliveries in the seventeen eastern states (PAW District 1) to 80 percent of their average 1941 levels, ratios that by subsequent orders were cut to 66.67 percent and then to 50 percent. These orders were a brute-force means of limiting consumption. In the context of fixed retail prices and high income and employment, the limitation orders and allocations resulted in excess demand at the announced money price. What ensued was a chaotic system, or lack thereof, for determining who actually got the fuel. These orders were an effective means for limiting total consumption but not for prioritizing it. Arbitrary rules or decisions by private distributors did not necessarily restrict consumption by nonessential users and prioritize it for essential uses.

The use of limitation orders alone could satisfactorily restrict consumption when the cuts were modest (say, 10 percent). Beyond that, the likelihood of political blowback and widespread complaints about favoritism and the principles and fairness of the distribution system required some sort of coupon-based system. The initial experience with petroleum products is reflected in the somewhat heated discussion of whether coal should be rationed and, if so, how, at the WPB's meeting of August 31, 1943; see also the discussion at the March 21, 1944, meeting (U.S. Civilian Production Administration, 1946a, pp. 272–75, 323).

The coupon-based rationing system had the benefit of some transparency in the logic of allocation. Operationally, the system advanced the principle of nondiscrimination: all customers arriving with cash and valid authorization for purchasing (coupons) should have access to gasoline on an equal footing. But rhetorically, this was somewhat misleading. Discrimination had not been eliminated. The difference was that its parameters were to be determined by government planners at the federal level, along with the local ration boards, rather than by private retailers.

Planned or intended deliveries of crude and refined products were not automatically realized. Actual flows of gasoline to filling stations, for example, depended both on how much refined product could be shipped in and on how much crude could be supplied to the regional refineries to supplement the 80,000 barrels a day from the largely exhausted eastern fields. The limitation orders to retail outlets were complemented by monthly PAW allocations of crude to refineries, including those on the East Coast. A prime objective was to keep all refineries in the country operating at or close to capacity. This required ensuring deliveries of crude and refined products to the Northeast. Despite the efforts of the PAW to ensure an adequate supply of crude, at the end of 1942 eastern refineries were operating on average at only 63 percent of capacity. Even had they been operating closer to 100 percent, the region needed refined products beyond what its own refineries could supply, and this also normally came mostly from the Gulf. If refined product such as gasoline or fuel oil could not be shipped, then the Gulf refineries had to cut back on their runs as they ran out of storage. Less than full-capacity operation of refineries in both regions seriously jeopardized the production of toluene (U.S. Civilian Production Administration, 1946b, March 10, 1942, meeting, p. 15).

Again, it is important to understand that the end-user rationing system did not control the total amount of crude and refined products flowing to the Eastern Seaboard. That was set by the WPB and the PAW, subject to the unpredictable vagaries of derailments, bad weather, and torpedoes. The end-user rationing system was intended to roughly match available supply with "valid" demands while at the same time segregating uses and users into those that were essential and those that were not, and, as much as possible, to provide unrestricted access to product for the former.

The allocation schedules and actual deliveries reduced supply compared to 1941, but, given the controlled price, without mandatory end-user rationing they did not reduce demand beyond what might be achieved through efforts to encourage voluntary cutbacks in use. This placed an unsustainable and politically explosive burden on wholesale distributors and retail outlets to decide who should and who should not get the product given an excess of orders over available supplies at the controlled price. Moreover, since the retail allocations were based on historical consumption levels, they did not reflect the changing geographical pattern of demand resulting from the flood of orders for war goods. Retailers used rules of thumb—supply product to longtime customers, limit purchases to two or three gallons. Persons without an established supplier were out of luck getting to work, or they might drive around wasting gas and rubber looking for stations with availability.

End-user rationing aimed to curtail demand among nonessential uses and users and thereby reduce and ideally eliminate excess demand. The intent was also to control black markets by requiring that coupons "flow back" through the distribution system: retail outlets had to present collected coupons to their wholesale distributors to claim their next deliveries. This requirement was also intended to encourage retailers to collect the coupons; under the original card system, they often neglected to punch the customer's card, meaning the customer retained the right to purchase.

The coupon system worked imperfectly. The WPB had delegated to the OPA the authority to administer a rationing program in the seventeen Eastern Seaboard states (PAW District 1) and allocate coupons for passenger vehicle use through local ration boards. At the same time, the Office of Defense Transportation and the War Food Administration were in the business of issuing

Certificates of War Necessity, which granted unlimited access to coupons for commercial and non-highway users. Supposedly, issuance required recipients to agree to abide by the thirty-five-mile-per-hour speed limit, keep vehicles fully loaded, and eliminate daily deliveries and other nonessential practices, but enforcement was limited (U.S. Bureau of the Budget, 1946, p. 122). Moreover, on the supply side, it was the PAW that allocated and scheduled deliveries of final product. Because the nondiscrimination rule required a retailer to sell gas to any customer with money and valid coupons, and because the PAW had pledged to allocate supplies to different companies' retail outlets in proportion to prewar usage, retailers might believe, based in part on coupons collected, that they had a claim on subsequent deliveries larger than they would in fact receive.

In the presence of price controls, curtailment of consumption resulted from an interaction of limitation orders and other supply disruptions that restricted deliveries and availability, and end-user rationing, which constrained purchases even when consumers had money and an intent to buy. Supply was always the binding constraint, and it remained particularly binding on the East Coast throughout the war. National statistics disguise substantial regional variation in the reductions in civilian consumption of gasoline, which was generally higher in the Northeast and lower in the Rocky Mountain and West Coast states. Since the bulk of American manufacturing and military production was in the Northeast and east north central regions and since the most severe shortages and rationing affected much of this area, it is here that supply interruptions had their biggest impact.

In the summer of 1942 pumps went dry all along the Eastern Seaboard. Most filling stations closed. Automobiles would tail a gasoline tanker truck until it stopped for a delivery, trailed by a string of desperate drivers. If word got out that a station had gas, lines of cars—as many as 350 of them—would form (Lingeman, 1970, p. 243). The disruptive effects rivaled and in some cases exceeded what Americans would experience in 1973–74.

Crisis conditions returned in October and November 1942, when inventories fell and could not be distributed evenly to retail outlets according to planned allocations. Critical war workers could not get to their jobs, and war production was disrupted (Maxwell and Balcom, 1946a, pp. 567–78). At an October 6, 1942, meeting of the WPB, Paul McNutt, chairman of the War Manpower Commission, noted that 500,000 workers were idle in New York City, while there were labor shortages in thirty-five other areas (U.S. Civilian Production

Administration, 1946a, pp. 132, 141). Again, idle labor and capital had corrosive effects on productivity and production.

Continuing difficulties in maintaining adequate deliveries to the Seaboard hindered attempts to establish a uniform nationwide gas-rationing program after December 1942. For the duration, District 1, designated the "Gasoline Shortage Area," was distinguished from the rest of the country by differences in the level of per-capita consumption allowed by gasoline production and delivery. In May 1943, at the nadir of tanker deliveries resulting from the U-boat offensive in the Atlantic, many filling stations again ran dry, which disrupted transportation and war production. The northern part of District 1— states north of North Carolina—was then designated the "Restricted Area," in which allocations of both gasoline deliveries and coupon claims were cut even further below those made available in the rest of the country. In the face of reduced supplies in the Gasoline Shortage Area and then in the Restricted Area, the OPA explored various remedies to maintain access for essential users by additional restrictions on nonessential use. These included after-the-fact devaluation of the gasoline value of coupons, extension of the number of months each coupon series was supposed to last, and an ill-fated attempt to ban "pleasure driving."

The OPA issued three types of coupons. The owner of a registered passenger vehicle received "A" coupon books, which provided a minimum allocation for driving not directly related to work or participation in an occupation. The books contained series of coupons, each valid (initially) for the purchase of four gallons over a period of two months. At fifteen miles per gallon, the coupons provided a monthly allowance of 240 miles. Upon application to the ration board, war workers who could show they engaged in carpooling on a regular basis (or that irregular work hours made this impossible) and that public transportation was not available, could obtain "B" coupons, which allowed up to a maximum of 320 additional monthly miles. Finally, certain categories of workers in five functional areas—government, education, public health and welfare, religion, and public information—could apply for preferred mileage ("C" coupons).

Within these areas, regulations specified favored occupational categories: government officers and employees and Red Cross workers; school officials traveling from school to school or transporting four or more students or teachers to or from school; wholesale deliverers of newspapers; telegram messengers; transporters of photographic equipment for newsreels; physicians, medical students, interns, and public health nurses; veterinarians; embalmers; clergy; transporters of farmworkers, marine workers, or farm materials; representatives of management and organized labor, including those recruiting labor; construction, maintenance, and repair service workers; those on duty in the armed forces; essential scrap dealers; and, finally, workers deemed essential to the war effort, including those in army and navy installations or hospitals, those working for common carriers or utilities, and those working in designated factories, farms, or extractive establishments (Maxwell and Balcom, 1946b, pp. 129–30).

Although the need for nationwide gasoline rationing up through 1944 can be laid at the feet of the Japanese, the severity of restrictions on consumption on the Eastern Seaboard and their effects on the U.S. economy in 1942, 1943, and the winter of 1944 were the direct consequence of German submarine warfare. Rationing in the last fifteen months of the war reflected a more general pressure of offensive military operations in both Europe and the Pacific on available supply.

Fuel (heating) oil consumption on the East Coast was also controlled through a combination of supply limitation and end-user rationing. In the first half of 1942, recommendations and orders from the WPB and the PAW cut deliveries to distributors, encouraged conversion of oil heaters to coal, prohibited the installation of new oil burners for home heating, and encouraged households to maintain nighttime temperatures no higher than 50 degrees Fahrenheit. Mandatory coupon rationing of fuel oil began on October 22, 1942. The fear and reality of fuel oil shortages persisted through most of the war. The most severe shortage hit the Eastern Seaboard in the winter of 1944. People shivered in their houses. Schools closed because they could not be heated. Businesses went on short weeks. James F. Byrnes, director of War Mobilization and "Assistant President" for domestic affairs, imposed an electrical brownout on the country to save fuel (Lingeman, 1970, p. 267).

If one just looks at the end-user rationing system, which prioritized agriculture, war industries, and other essential functions, one might conclude that it was impossible or unusual for factories or farms to have their operations disrupted because of lack of fuel. But this misses the duality of the systems aimed at curtailing consumption: the limitation orders, which restricted deliveries on the supply side, and whose effects could be amplified by severe weather, derailments, torpedoes, or a combination of these, and the end-user coupon system. If the supplies were not delivered, it did not matter if the entire population had unlimited money and unlimited coupons: the resources were simply not available. Once the barrel ran dry, as it were, essential and nonessential uses and users were on the same footing, and availability was now truly non-discriminatory. Spot shortages meant disruption of essential and nonessential activity. The former category included factories, farms, and refineries, along with much of wholesale and retail distribution. If the resource was not there, it simply was not there.

Consider crude oil, which had only one set of users: refineries. When deliveries of crude were insufficient, refineries could not operate at full capacity, which adversely affected their efficiency and their ability to supply byproducts for the manufacture of synthetic rubber, explosives, and many other products. Given the very limited storage facilities in the petroleum industry, the effects of this disruption spread: at refineries in East Texas and Louisiana, runs had to be cut back because there was no place to ship the product, and similarly, at wellheads in southwestern oilfields, the pumping of crude had to cease because there was no place to ship it and soon no place to store it.

Because of their effects on the transportation infrastructure, shortages of gasoline made it difficult for manufacturers to get deliveries of essential inputs, including raw materials, machinery, and subassemblies. Because intended curtailment cut so deeply into fuel available for passenger vehicles, when outages hit, the restrictions made it particularly challenging for workers to get to and from their places of employment. This affected absenteeism, labor turnover, and, ultimately, both production and productivity, which added to other forces that pushed these metrics in a negative direction. Reductions in average weekly work hours had historically been associated with increases in output per hour; the increase in average weekly hours during the war probably worked in the opposite direction. These effects were reinforced and compounded by the fact that when a nationwide labor shortage arrived sometime in late 1943 (see chapter 5), employers faced more difficulty getting workers in the numbers and with the skill, training, and experience desired. Work stoppages and unauthorized strikes also disrupted production. The regional shortage of petroleum for essential uses and users was one of several contributors to declining productivity. By causing these shortages and intermittently idle capacity, German submarines delivered an adverse supply shock to U.S. manufacturing, although one not as potentially devastating as what the Japanese had inflicted when they overran Singapore.

Despite its flaws, by 1943 the gasoline-rationing program achieved a 40 percent reduction in passenger car fuel consumption compared to average daily consumption in 1941 (Maxwell and Balcom, 1946b, p. 154). This was attributable to an intended reduction in average annual mileage per car combined with a decline in the number of passenger vehicles on the road, which fell 17 percent between 1941 and 1944, in part because tires were wearing out.

The devastating decline in tanker shipments of crude and refined products to the East Coast was in percentage terms similar to the decline of imports of crude rubber from Southeast Asia. Both represented adverse supply shocks for the economy. But remediating the effects of the petroleum disruptions ultimately proved easier. First, oil was available elsewhere in the country, and with logistical innovation and eventually with new pipeline construction it could be moved overland to the East Coast, albeit at greater expense. Rubber or rubber tree substitutes, on the other hand, could not be grown or had not been developed in the United States, and only limited quantities could be imported from elsewhere in the world. The complete lack of substitutes for rubber in some product areas—in particular pneumatic tires—made the threat especially serious and helps explain the near panic among military planners regarding the rubber situation in 1942. In 1944 General George Patton's 3rd Army ground to a halt in France because of a failure of petroleum supplies to match his pace of advance. He reportedly complained, "My men can eat their belts, but my tanks have gotta have gas." Patton's men, however, also needed tires, tank treads, radiator hoses, gas masks, and footwear. Absence of rubber or oil will ultimately bring a modern army to a halt.

Supply-Side Responses to the Destruction of the Tanker Pipeline

The bargain Ickes negotiated with industry leaders allowed the government agency, with input from councils of industry leaders, to run all four aspects of the petroleum industry—production, refining, transportation, and marketing/distribution—as if it were one large nationalized firm. No other major sector of the economy had such close integration of industry with government administration. The PAW program board, with input from the economics committee of the Petroleum Industry War Council, along with regional councils, mapped out strategy and tactics. Industry cooperation was the quid. The quo was suspension of antitrust action and the promise that the industry would continue to earn healthy profits throughout the war. What was good for the country would be made good for the oil companies. Although some companies had to make temporary sacrifices, Ickes persuaded them that he had their backs and was advancing agendas that benefited the country and, in most cases, the individual firms as well. In no other agency do we see businesses so closely integrated into the operation of a major sector of the economy, aside possibly from the reliance of the Office of Defense Transportation on private firms to run the railroads (U.S. Bureau of the Budget, 1946, p. 127).

The shortages in the fall of 1941 because of the temporary loan of fifty tankers to Britain had allowed the development and test implementation of a portfolio of initiatives to deal with the possibility of a disrupted Gulf Coast–Atlantic tanker pipeline, and so when U-boat predation along this route heated up in earnest in the first half of 1942, the playbook was ready. Moving to 24/7 operation of all aspects of the industry immediately increased transport capacity. Production and refining already ran on that schedule—but pressing trucks and rail car operation and loading and unloading to almost continuous operation effectively doubled the supply of trucks and cut the round trip for a tank car from thirty to twenty days, increasing capacity by 50 percent, from twelve to eighteen round trips a year (U.S. PAW, 1946, p. 91). This was coupled with efforts to ensure that capacity was actually used: pressing to have all transport vehicles fully loaded—and, with the relaxation of load line restrictions, allowing transport vessels over water to be overloaded.

Additional railway tank car capacity was effectively mobilized by encouraging and insisting that oil companies (which owned most of the cars) withdraw them, especially the large-capacity cars, from runs of less than one hundred, and later two hundred, miles, to make them available for long-distance hauls. Companies gathered crude at eight concentration points near the Texas and Oklahoma oil fields: Denison and Texarkana, Texas; Kansas City, Missouri; New Orleans and Shreveport, Louisiana; North Little Rock and Pine Bluff, Arkansas; and Tulsa, Oklahoma. Railways assembled tank cars at each of these points into symbol trains—often a mile long—which ran almost nonstop to East Coast terminals where they were unloaded, within twenty-four hours, and sent back empty for the return trip. When the first stage of the Big Inch pipeline was completed, companies assembled a pool of 10,000 tank cars to move product almost continuously from Norris City, in southern Illinois, to the East Coast. The first oil entered the Big Inch pipeline on December 31, 1942, and reached Norris City on February 19, 1943. War Emergency Pipelines completed construction on the second stage to a junction in Phoenixville, Pennsylvania, on June 19, 1943. A twenty-inch branch pipeline then took crude the remaining short distance to Philadelphia refineries and another ran eighty-eight miles to Linden, New Jersey, giving easy access to the New York and New Jersey refineries and storage tanks. The first oil reached the Eastern Seaboard on August 14, 1943 (U.S. PAW, 1946, p. 431). The supply situation in the East remained dicey, however; the use of box cars was resorted to at times to ship kerosene in fifty-five-gallon drums.

As was true during the prewar shortage, the PAW continued to discourage the shipment of refined petroleum products west from East Coast refineries. Instead of routing small numbers of partially loaded tank cars to multiple locations, massive tank car trains ran north and east. Pools of cars went back and forth between the same points on the long-distance shuttle routes. Trains were labeled with symbols, such as 28-G (thus the term *symbol trains*), which reflected their date of origin (28) and whether they were going (G) or returning (R). The system required that the exact route a train would take had to be specified in advance, along with the time allowed for the traverse of each segment. Telegraphic communication provided real-time information on the location of all trains, subjecting them to positive continual control (PAW, 1945, p. 92). Operational streamlining in the assemblage and routing of these trains reflected the serious attention given by the PAW at the national level to logistics.

The experience gained in this effort proved helpful in the last fifteen months of the war, when the demands of the Pacific campaign exceeded California supply, and product from the mid-country fields had to be shipped west—a real challenge since only seven rail lines crossed the Rockies, almost all of them single tracked. Before that, the West Coast and Rocky Mountains had escaped some of the tightened rationing that hit the East Coast on the grounds that any surplus production thereby freed could only with great difficulty be shipped east across the Rocky Mountains toward deficit areas.

Apart from some small western areas in these jurisdictions, PAW District 1 was coterminous with the seventeen Seaboard states. Tank car deliveries to the Eastern Seaboard increased to 585,000 barrels a day in April 1942 and 828,000 a day in September; deliveries peaked over several days during July 1943 at more than 1 million barrels. (Keep in mind that District 1 consumption was running at over 1.5 million barrels a day in 1941, 40 percent of the overall U.S. drawdown.) By summer of 1942 rail car deliveries had made up more than half the deficit created by the collapse of the Gulf Coast–Atlantic tanker pipeline and were delivering 70 percent of all product to the East Coast. Still, average daily deliveries in the second half of 1942 were in the 1.1 million barrels a day range and declining. Beginning in August 1943, as figure 4.1 shows, the share carried by pipeline began increasing because of the completion of the Big Inch pipeline. But it was not until March 1944, when the Little Big Inch pipeline became fully operation as well, that combined monthly deliveries of crude and refined products exceeded 1941 levels.

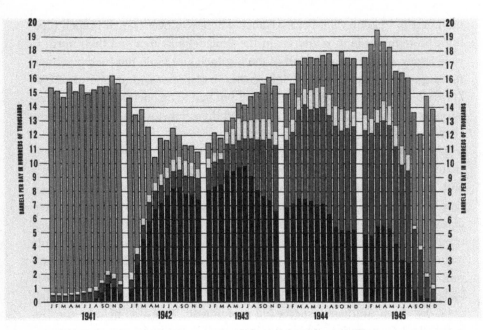

Figure 4.1. Deliveries of petroleum into PAW District no. 1. This is a stacked bar graph, illustrating the four modes of petroleum delivery to the Eastern Seaboard by month in the years 1941 to 1945, inclusive. From the bottom of each bar to the top, black = by rail, dark gray = by pipeline, off white = by barge, and light gray = by tanker. The figure illustrates the collapse of tanker deliveries (light gray) and the decline in overall deliveries in 1942, followed by the initial increase in rail deliveries (black) and the eventual contribution of the newly constructed Big Inch and Little Big Inch pipelines (dark gray) starting in August 1943 and dwindling as soon as the war ended and large-scale tanker deliveries resumed. Source: U.S. Petroleum Administration for War, 1946, p. 93.

The Big Inch and Little Big Inch Pipelines

The pipeline projects elicited romantic, almost mystical emotions from the public. When completed, they were the longest and largest-capacity pipelines in the world. Their appeal was powerful and almost visceral. As the PAW history put it, "There was a magic about Big Inch that captured the imagination of everyone" (1946, p. 104). In 1963 the Marx toy company put out a Big Inch construction set (available today to collectors on eBay).

The Big Inch pipeline ran 1,254 miles from near crude oil fields in Beaumont, Texas, north to Norris City, Illinois (the first stage of the project), and then east to Phoenixville, Pennsylvania, where two twenty-inch branch pipelines brought crude to refineries in the Philadelphia area and then north to New Jersey. Before construction of the Big Inch and Little Big Inch pipelines, the largest pipes were typically eight inches in diameter and could move 20,000 barrels a day. Larger pipes could be built but had to be operated at lower pressures (lest they burst), which thus reduced their flow rate and eliminated the advantage of the larger diameter.

During the interwar period, William Heltzel, a graduate of the Carnegie Institute of Technology and an engineer at the National Institute of Standards and Technology, developed usable flow formulas that provided the foundation for the use of higher pressures (and thus higher throughput) in larger-diameter pipes. Heltzel served as a consultant on the Big Inch project, which used twenty-four-inch pipes. The Little Big Inch had a diameter of twenty inches. The two lines, which for most of the distance used the same right-of-way, together cost $146 million. The Big Inch was designed to deliver 300,000 barrels of crude a day, the Little Big Inch about 200,000 barrels of refined product a day. Both ultimately succeeded in doing so. Title was held by the Defense Plant Corporation, which was responsible for financing construction. Operational responsibility lay with the Defense Supplies Corporation (another RFC subsidiary), which contracted with War Emergency Pipelines, a nonprofit corporation jointly owned by eleven oil companies.

Ickes's initial requests to the Supply Priorities and Allocation Board for priorities for steel to build the pipelines were rejected in September and again in November 1941. A third request was rejected by the Planning Committee of the WPB at its June 9, 1942, meeting on grounds that the steel could not be spared, that the project would not be completed in time to relieve the anticipated fuel oil shortage in the winter of 1942–43, that the navy should instead convoy tankers on the Gulf–East Coast routes, and that gas rationing should be implemented in the Midwest in order to free tank cars and barges to take it east. The Planning Committee's recommendation was overridden the next day at a full meeting of the WPB (see chapter 5). The board green-lighted funding and materials priorities for the Big Inch pipeline, and the first half, to Norris City, was completed in December of that year. Oil began arriving in Phoenixville, Pennsylvania, on August 14, 1943, nineteen months after the first U-boat attacks on the Atlantic Coast.

In April 1943 construction began on Little Big Inch, which ran 1,475 miles from refineries in the Houston–Port Arthur area of Texas to Linden, New Jersey, and was intended to carry refined products. Eleven months later, in March

1944, it began delivering heating oil to the East. Large rubber balls pumped through the line marked a switch from one refined product to another. In March 1944, when both pipelines were operating with a combined capacity of 500,000 barrels a day, the severe regional shortages created two years earlier by German submarines largely receded, and the use of tank car trains for the purpose of moving oil to the East began to wane.

The Severity of the U-boat Threat

The economic and military significance of submarine warfare along the Eastern, Gulf Coast, and Caribbean Sea Frontiers has not been fully appreciated. The historian Michael Gannon argued, "The U-boat assault on merchant shipping in United States waters during 1942 constituted a greater strategic setback for the Allied war effort than the defeat at Pearl Harbor." The ships damaged at Pearl Harbor were aged and obsolescent (battleships, not aircraft carriers), and putting them out of commission had no effect on the outcome of the pivotal carrier battles of Coral Sea and Midway (May and June 1942). By 1944, when battleships could be used effectively for shore bombardment in the Pacific campaigns, four of those damaged in December 1941 had been repaired and saw action, and by 1945 that number had increased to five. Gannon doubted that the ships, had they not been disabled in 1941 and under repair during 1942 and 1943, would have survived to see service in 1944 and 1945. While the losses and disabling of capital ships in the Pacific were remediated by 1944, this was not true for the disabling of the Gulf-Atlantic tanker fleet.

Unsparing in his critique of naval intelligence, Gannon argued that the United States was as unprepared for the attacks on merchant shipping along the Atlantic Seaboard as it had been for Pearl Harbor. As 1942 dawned, the U.S. Navy had only twenty small ships with poorly trained crews to protect the tankers. All were slower than a German submarine on the surface and equipped with inferior armament, and only two or three could be operational at any one time. Preparations to use aircraft to combat the threat were almost nonexistent. There were simply no well-developed plans for combatting the U-boats (Gannon, 1990, p. 176). As a consequence, the country suffered "a six-month-long massacre, compared with which the defeat at Pearl Harbor was but a rap on the knuckles" (p. 166).

Other knowledgeable observers expressed similar views at the time. On June 19, 1942, Army Chief of Staff George C. Marshall wrote, "The losses by submarines off our Atlantic Seaboard and in the Caribbean now threaten our entire war effort." In *The Hinge of Fate,* Winston Churchill observed, "For six or seven months, the U-boats ravaged American waters almost uncontrolled, and in fact almost brought us to the disaster of an indefinite prolongation of the war" (Gannon, 1990, pp. iii, xviii). Robert Nathan, the chair of the Planning Committee of the WPB, expressed deep frustration with the navy in a memo to Donald Nelson on May 16, 1942:

> The plain truth is that we are not currently producing ships as fast as they are being sunk. Seventy per cent of ship losses are from U-boats and seventy percent of U-boat losses this year have been in U.S. coastal waters. . . . The production of subchasers and escort boats is a function of the Navy, not the Maritime Commission, and the relative progress made by the Navy with this program is such as to make the performance on merchant shipping seem first class by contrast. . . . In spite of relative proximity to submarine bases there have been no ships sunk by submarines within 100 miles of the British Coast within a year. . . . There are thirty-six new wrecks charted by the Navy coastal survey as protruding from the water between Sandy Hook and Hatteras. (U.S. Civilian Production Administration, 1946b, pp. 131–32)

By disrupting the movement of crude oil and refined products to the Northeast, Germany inflicted a powerful adverse supply shock on the U.S. economy, not as potentially severe as what the Japanese had engineered in Southeast Asia, but one nevertheless more immediate in its effect.

The pipelines attracted a great deal of popular attention, and it was exciting to follow their progress to completion. By 1944 they were able to mitigate much of the damage to the economy inflicted by German submarines. What was their backstory? Before Pearl Harbor, Ickes was already pushing for the construction, perhaps with government financing, of new pipelines running north and east. He had written to Roosevelt on July 20, 1940, that "the building of a crude oil pipeline from Texas to the East might not be economically sound, but that in the event of an emergency, it might be absolutely necessary," views he reiterated to a congressional committee on October 1, 1941. Ickes acknowledged that, after the war, the industry would probably return to shipping product via tankers because it would be both cheaper and more flexible. The PAW history confirms these expectations about the postwar usefulness of the lines: "Alternatives devised to meet the situation—increased tank car and barge movement; the reversal and construction of thousands of miles of pipeline—could be made effective only through the expenditure of millions of dollars, only a very small proportion of which could be counted upon as an investment having peacetime utility" (U.S. PAW, 1946, p. 52).

It is important once again not to confuse the partial success of these re-mediation strategies—in themselves positive supply shocks during wartime operation—with the negative shocks that elicited them in the first place. The pipelines were intended to carry petroleum and petroleum products overland while the submarine threat persisted, which it did, albeit in diminished inten-sity, until the end of the war in Europe. It was universally expected that with the return of peace, the tanker pipeline would reopen, and there would be little need to use these capital improvements, at least for the purposes for which they were built and as they were used during the war.

Just as U.S. rubber fabricators would have much preferred a world in which the Japanese advance on the Malay Peninsula had been stopped, the oil com-panies and their customers would have much preferred a war without the disruption of tanker shipments along the Gulf Coast–Atlantic route, and with-out the pipelines, as opposed to the actual course of history, which brought with it both the challenge and the partially mitigating response. The pipelines, though they helped overcome the effects of the U-boat disruption, did not make the transportation of petroleum and petroleum products from the Gulf Coast to the East Coast cheaper, more reliable, or more efficient than had been true before the war.

By the standards of World War II, the lines were inexpensive—totaling $146 million, fronted by the government through the RFC. The United States spent $82 million alone building antisubmarine bases on the island of Trini-dad, one of the eight locations in which the country acquired a ninety-nine-year lease as a result of the September 2, 1940, destroyers-for-bases deal with England (Bercuson and Herwig, 2014, p. 30). And, as noted in chapter 3, the government spent $673 million on the synthetic rubber plants, a program de-signed to remediate the effects of another supply disruption.

The response by the PAW and industry to the loss of the Gulf-Atlantic pipe-line route necessitated, inter alia, the construction of two government-funded pipelines from East Texas to New Jersey, the mobilizing of mile-long tank car trains, and a tight integration of pipeline, barge, tank car, and trucks to move crude and refined products over land since they could no longer be easily sent by sea. This impressive achievement is described in the PAW history as a "vir-tual miracle" (p. 2). Again, although the authors of the history write in the celebratory spirit that informs so much else that has been written about the experiences and consequences of war mobilization, they could not quite bring themselves to describe the industry's success as a miracle, and indeed this is one of only two places in the entire opus where the freighted word appears (chapter 12 is titled "Miracles from Molecules," although the word never actually appears in its text).

The Disposition of the Pipelines

The pipelines survived and were used after the war, but for purposes different from what they were built for. They were instead used to carry natural gas. As different economic interests jockeyed for position, disagreement within government councils and Congress centered on three main options. The pipelines could be coated internally with an anticorrosion film, sealed, and then held in reserve by the government in case of another military emergency. Or they could remain open for the transport of petroleum and petroleum products under either government or private ownership. Or they could be converted for the transport of natural gas.

Immediately after the end of the war, the PAW recommended termination of use but then did not attempt further to influence their disposition. The last oil dribbled out in November 1945, the lines were sealed, and the pipelines were declared surplus. The pipelines were, however, worth more than their value as scrap, unlike, for example, the bombers and tanks lined up for demolition in Arizona boneyards (chapter 6). Could the lines be retained for the transport of crude oil and petroleum products and be competitive with tankers, earning a profit for their owners? Proponents maintained that they could. But the economic and financial analysis supporting this view assumed that the pipelines would operate at capacity, as they had during the war.

There were several reasons capacity operation was possible during the war and unlikely thereafter. First, during the war, tanker transport was, for the most part, simply not available. After the war it was. The oil industry greatly preferred tankers, even if the cost per ton mile were similar (which it was not), because they provided much greater flexibility along several dimensions: point of origin, point of destination, and products carried. Second, since the PAW ran the industry during the war as if it were one large nationalized firm, and since the tanker option was largely off the table, it was easy (by administrative fiat) to keep the pipelines full. After the war, the lines would be competing with tankers and, assuming the lines were operated as common carriers, would have highly variable loads, most of the time below capacity.

Since the pipelines had fixed costs of operation, this would reduce their efficiency and increase the per-ton mile charge needed if they were to be run profitably. It would be a race to the bottom as higher pipeline rates made tankers even more attractive, further reducing loads on the lines. This had all been anticipated before the war, as evidenced in Ickes's letter to Roosevelt and his congressional testimony. Private capital had been willing and indeed eager to use its own funds to build a natural gas pipeline in 1940 (tankers were a much less attractive option for transporting natural gas) but was not willing to do so to build the Big Inch projects during the war. Government ownership and financing are usually a tipoff that there was uncertainty about whether or to what degree assets would have economic value after the conclusion of the conflict.

Why natural gas? Before the war, a group of businessmen had recognized the profit potential in moving natural gas from Texas oil fields, where it had little or no value and was generally flared (burned off), to the city gates of East Coast municipal distribution systems, where it could replace manufactured or town gas if it could somehow be moved between the two regions. In urban areas gas was valued for cooking because, in contrast with a coal-fired stove, it was easier to use a gas range to regulate temperature or to turn the heat on and off quickly. And it was considered cleaner.

The problem in realizing these profits was that there was no economical way to store the gas, and without that there was no way to transport it other than through a direct connection from wellhead to user. Movement by tanker, rail car, barge, or tank truck all required liquefaction, which would necessitate compressing the gas to 1/600th of its original volume. Without compression, transport in any moving vehicle or container was prohibitively expensive. Chemical engineers understood that if the gas could be cleaned and then cooled, it would condense and could then be stored at a fraction of its original volume, and in fact this was already done in smaller quantities for liquefied petroleum gas. In 1940 the East Ohio Gas Company built a full-scale plant to do this at commercial scale with natural gas, but unfortunately the facility exploded in October 1944, killing 130 people. That accident set the liquefied natural gas industry back fifteen years. In the 1940s and 1950s, the only way to make this scheme work was to move the gas by pipeline.

In 1940 the Reserve Gas Pipeline Company filed applications with the Federal Power Commission for a certificate of public convenience to build an $80 million 1,500-mile line from Texas to New York to do this. The organizers had supply commitments for 4.5 trillion cubic feet of gas. They proposed to dispose of it in the East by connecting with existing municipal distribution systems that were currently being supplied by town gas manufactured by burning bituminous coal (U.S. Senate, 1941, p. 546; see also Dillard, 1944,

p. 120). They did not intend to sell at retail, but rather connect at the city gate—the portal to the local municipal systems.

As war clouds gathered, the prospects for advancing this project dimmed. The pipelines would require large quantities of increasingly scarce steel. Moreover, a natural gas pipeline would have to obtain rights-of-way. These would be expensive or almost impossible to obtain without federal backing, which would give a private company access to the legal remedy of condemnation. While there was great potential profit here, there was no particular merit in the project from a national defense perspective.

Ickes and others, however, anticipated the possible need for pipelines to move crude and refined oil in the case of war. The havoc that German submarines were visiting on British shipping, including tankers, was readily apparent. Even so, the competition for steel was already tight by 1941 and, as noted, Ickes was turned down twice by the Supply Priorities and Allocations Board and once by the Planning Committee of its successor, the War Production Board. With the overturning of the Planning Committee recommendation, the full board granted funding and priorities, and the lines were built. But with the coming of peace, as was true for so many other capital projects constructed during the war, there was little demand to use the assets for the purposes for which they had been constructed.

Nevertheless, the economics of the natural gas proposition remained very attractive. Coal interests in the state of Pennsylvania, however, were vehemently opposed, for understandable reasons. To build the Big Inch and Little Big Inch lines, the federal government through its agents negotiated with states and where necessary used the power of eminent domain against private owners to obtain the necessary rights-of-way. The Cole pipeline bill, passed on July 30, 1941, gave the president the power to designate any petroleum pipeline as necessary for the national defense, making possible condemnation proceedings even for privately funded projects (U.S. PAW, 1946, p. 102).

In congressional hearings regarding the postwar disposition of surplus property, Francis Walker, a representative from Pennsylvania, argued that the rights-of-way granted by his state were only for the purpose of conveying "petroleum or its byproducts," and legally, therefore, they could not be used for natural gas. Walker's position turned on whether natural gas, often found in petroleum wells, could be considered one of its byproducts (U.S. Congress, House of Representatives, 1947, p. 2217). Other opponents claimed that the lines were unsuitable for and could not easily be converted for the transport of natural gas.

In June 1946 the War Assets Administration (WAA) rejected as too low all bids from an initial auction of the now surplus pipelines. In December the agency leased the lines to the Tennessee Gas and Construction Company to determine on a trial basis whether they could be converted for the transport of natural gas (they could). The WAA held a second auction in 1947, and a newly chartered corporation, Texas Eastern Transmission, submitted a winning bid of $143,127,000. Texas Eastern went on to manage the pipelines for four decades, carrying mostly natural gas, although starting in 1958 the Little Big Inch again carried gasoline and other refined products. Neither pipeline, however, was ever again used to carry crude.

In cases where industrial or infrastructural capital was accumulated as the direct result of war mobilization and those assets continued to have value and thus make a contribution to postwar output, we must pose the counterfactual, and ask what would likely have happened in the absence of the conflict. The economics of the natural gas project were so attractive that in an alternative world a natural gas pipeline might have been developed earlier using private capital from the get-go. The intervention of the war delayed the scheme but rapidly overcame the right-of-way issues in coal country that might otherwise have bedeviled a private construction effort, particularly one aimed at moving natural gas. It is not clear that the Cole pipeline bill could or would have been invoked to support a natural gas project.

The pipelines did end up facilitating the penetration of natural gas on the East Coast as a substitute for town gas as a fuel for cooking and for coal and heating oil for space heating, and eventually as a fuel to drive power plants producing electricity. In 1945 there were about 11 million residential consumers of natural gas. A decade later there were over 26 million (U.S. Bureau of the Census, 1960, p. 732). By encouraging the shift from coal and fuel oil to natural gas in these areas, the initiative may be viewed as having had some beneficial environmental impact. As a fossil fuel, natural gas cannot really be called clean. But it is cleaner than oil or coal.[14]

The 100-Octane Program

The other main drain on PAW energy during the war was the 100-octane aviation fuel program. This required close to a billion dollars of investment in new refinery equipment, reconfiguration, and expansion, exceeding capital expenditures for the synthetic rubber program, and roughly half the cost of the Manhattan Project. Unlike both of those initiatives, however, much of this expansion was paid for by private capital, albeit partially assisted by government loans. Major refinery projects, not including facilities producing butadiene for the rubber program or toluene for explosives, cost $927 million to complete. Most of this involved adding specialized cracking and other processing units to existing facilities, rather than building new refineries, and the capacity of refineries to process crude went up little. The expenditures increased the range and flexibility of products that could be squeezed from a barrel of crude. About three-fourths was funded by firms (although almost a third of that was financed by government loans). The remaining quarter was funded and owned directly by the government and leased to operators (U.S. PAW, 1946, p. 193). A higher proportion of private funding reflected a higher *ex ante* probability that the assets would continue to have value after the war. A *Scientific American* article from 1944, discussing investments in 100-octane production facilities, reflected forecasts at the time: "It is to be expected that the greater number of the new plants will be diverted to other purposes once the war is over, but many will remain dedicated to their present uses" (Klemin, 1944, p. 262).

The high-compression aircraft engines to which the army and navy had committed in 1936 required 100-octane gasoline. In 1940 refining capacity for such fuel stood at about 40,000 barrels a day. The military services used one-tenth of this daily, and commercial and export demand took up perhaps one-third. There was substantial excess capacity. By 1944 domestic and military demand in all theaters of war had increased sixteen-fold to 636,000 barrels daily (U.S. PAW, 1946, p. 194). Domestic output (not including American-controlled refineries in South America and the Middle East) peaked at 514,000 barrels daily, almost a thirteen-fold increase. Since crude production increased over the course of the war by a little over one-fourth, the challenge was met largely by increasing the proportion of a barrel of crude ultimately refined into aviation gasoline. Between 1940 and 1944, the share of liquid petroleum products accounted for by aviation gas rose from 1 to 12 percent, while the share of motor gas fell from 49 to 42 percent (U.S. PAW, 1946, p. 191).

Producing 100-octane was like cooking, in the sense that there were different recipes. Particular refineries started with base stock, and then added blending agents, including tetraethyl lead along with isooctane or hydrocodimer. Adding refinery facilities to produce these agents was a big-ticket item and enabled petroleum engineers to slice and dice long-chain hydrocarbons in cracking units, and then, if desired, restitch them in different configurations in equipment designed for hydrogenation or polymerization. In high-compression engines these blending agents prevented heat and pressure from igniting the fuel before spark plugs fired.

In describing the one-year increase in 100-octane output between December 1941 and December 1942 from 46,000 barrels a day to 118,000, the PAW historians wrote: "It was a job which, in the beginning, had seemed physically impossible. Most people were sure it was impossible. But there it was, for all to see" (p. 191). And of course, that had to be multiplied several times to get to an average daily production of over half a million barrels by the end of the war. Again, the PAW history moved up to but did not quite cross the line to claim a miracle, which is literally what overcoming the impossible would have entailed.

In the case of both synthetic rubber and the 100-octane fuel program, the basic chemistry was well understood at the time of Pearl Harbor (U.S. PAW, 1946, p. 192). But the know-how gleaned from experience was much more advanced in the gasoline program since the product was already produced commercially. To make 100-octane fuel, one started with a good base stock of gasoline. The industry's maturation from a focus on kerosene at the turn of the twentieth century to a focus on gasoline had been made possible by improvements in cracking, which enabled the gasoline yield from a barrel of crude to increase substantially. Thermal crackers, which used heat, pressure, and catalysts to break down some of the heavier straight-run products into lighter distillates, were features of many of the four hundred–plus refineries in the country.

But one also needed antiknock compounds that could be blended with this base stock. The most well-known was tetraethyl lead (TEL), which, starting in the 1920s, had been produced in Ethyl Corporation plants jointly owned by General Motors, DuPont, and Standard Oil of New Jersey, and added to gasoline. Researchers in the 1920s had also discovered that adding ethanol to gasoline increased its octane rating, but TEL, unlike ethanol, had the advantage of being patentable. During the war some of the immediate increased output of aviation fuel was made possible by relaxing limits on the amounts of lead that could be added to base stock, but there were concerns about how far to push this, not so much because of the possible effect on pilot health, but because of worries that the accumulation of residues in engines would mean the need for more frequent maintenance.[15]

Reading the PAW history, one has the sense that the path forward was clear, and that the obstacles faced were largely those of obtaining the priorities necessary for the refinery expansions. In describing how the increase in aviation fuel production required "the surmounting of obstacle after obstacle," the emphasis is not, as was true in the rubber program, in getting the processes to work well, but rather on the political and other obstacles to obtaining the metals, the materials, and the equipment needed for the expansion, even after the financing had been arranged (U.S. PAW, 1946, p. 193). The much higher fraction of spending by the firms themselves is testimony to the belief that these facilities would continue to have value after the war, although the companies were not willing to use their own money until the expedient, agreed to on November 3, 1941, of the RFC or its subsidiaries signing long-term contracts for product; the RFC was to be reimbursed by the army and navy out of annual appropriations.

Adding the new equipment to refineries to assist in the production of blending agents took time, however, and the industry, operating under the PAW umbrella, embraced several immediate steps following Pearl Harbor to increase aviation gas availability. As noted, it persuaded the military services to accept an increase in allowable TEL in spite of concerns about the possibility of increased maintenance needs. Second, it embarked on a "quickie" program to boost output. As the PAW put it, the program "scorned the rules of economics, but . . . did get the gasoline produced in a hurry" (U.S. PAW, 1946, p. 198). The program was based on the proposition that more high-octane fuel could be produced if blending agents were transported to refineries whose base stocks could most readily complement them. This would "cost lots of money," would mean less output of other refinery products, was the opposite of a recipe for increased productivity, and was so acknowledged. The PAW summarized the underlying philosophy: "Forget economic considerations—forget everything except getting out more and more 100-octane as quickly as you can" (p. 199). Since the quickie program disrupted the product mix at individual refineries, imposing revenue losses on the companies, the Defense Supplies Corporation (DSC) agreed to reimburse them for the additional costs, and the army and navy then reimbursed the DSC. After January 1, 1943, all 100-octane fuel was bought directly by the DSC, rather than the individual services. The quickie program was a prime example of efficiency dropping to the bottom of a list of priorities when there was immediate need for a high-priority item.

In 1943 output increased by another 106,000 barrels a day, a jump that the PAW attributed one-third to new facilities finally online, and two-thirds to converted catalytic crackers, the production of new blending agents, and "a whole series of technical improvisations that bordered on sheer wizardry" (p. 202).[16] Despite that last comment, there is little evidence that efforts to produce

larger quantities of aviation fuel during the war resulted in major technological breakthroughs. Petroleum industry patenting declined during this period
(see chapter 7), and the PAW history gives no detail on the significance of these
improvisations in spite of its propensity to elaborate at length on almost every
other aspect of the industry's accomplishments. The fact was that the program
was based almost entirely on prewar chemistry and engineering knowledge.
The new facilities made the industry well-positioned to supply civilian and
military needs for a number of years in the postwar period. Eventually, however, 100-octane aviation fuel production dwindled to that demanded by small
general aviation propeller-driven aircraft. Jet engines required unleaded kerosene, not 100-octane gasoline.

Conclusion

The most serious challenge to the petroleum industry during the war came
from German U-boats, whose activities directly and indirectly threatened the
manufacturing heartland of the country and the strategic capabilities of the
United States and its allies. Dealing with East Coast supply was primarily a
distribution challenge, not a production or refining problem: "Certainly, more
than half the total energy expended by PAW and the industry during the entire
4 years was spent trying to bring enough petroleum to the Atlantic seaboard of
the United States, center of population and industry, and springboard to Europe and Africa." And the PAW history affirms that transportation problems
were "chronologically . . . the first, and throughout the war the worst, petroleum problems that had to be solved" (U.S. PAW, 1946, p. 82).

U-boat predation led to the construction of two pipelines from East Texas
to the Northeast, financed by the government. Once peacetime conditions
returned, these facilities could be competitive with tanker transport only if
they were operated at full capacity, which although achievable by directive during the war (and because the tanker route was blocked at least until 1944),
could not be after the war if private enterprise operated the lines as common
carriers. Individual oil companies much preferred to ship by tanker *even* if
costs were close, because of the greater flexibility offered for pickup and drop-
off points and the types of cargo carried. After a two-year postwar hiatus, the
pipelines were again used, but at that point to transport natural gas.

Before the war, the United States was already a leader in producing fuels
for high-compression engines. The large increase in the absolute and proportionate production of aviation fuel was achieved, as was true in all sectors of

the economy prioritized for the war effort, in a manner that reflected a low weight on efficiency. The imperative was to get the supplies, ideally yesterday, and cost be damned. With respect to production, the national shortages that began to be evident by spring of 1944 led to exploitation of existing wells in an uneconomic fashion. The six billion barrels of crude pumped, which supplied the country and its allies, hastened the exhaustion of existing fields and the country's future dependence on Middle Eastern oil. By the time the Big Inch pipeline started pumping, production in the East Texas fields, which produced a particularly desirable type of "sweet" crude, had begun to decline (U.S. PAW, 1946, p. 215), and during the remainder of the war refiners had to deal with the more sulfurous "sour" crude from West Texas and Venezuela.

The history of the petroleum industry between 1941 and 1945 is consistent with declining productivity in U.S. manufacturing. In responding to neither of the sector's main challenges did the exigencies of war lead to breakthrough technologies in the exploration for, production of, or refining of oil. The biggest problems were in transportation, and if there was useful learning, it was in the area of logistics. Although the particular circumstances of the war were never repeated, the experience may have contributed positively to postwar American leadership in intermodal transfer and the organization of distribution more generally (see chapter 9).

5 • From Priorities Unemployment to Labor Shortage

The conventional historiography of the Second World War emphasizes a large aggregate demand shock that closed the output gap remaining in 1941, along with a supply-side mechanism—learning by doing making planes, guns, and ships—that laid the foundations for increases in potential output after the war. The effects of the aggregate demand shock are uncontroversial. The claim that the learning effects laid the supply foundations for growth during the golden age (1948–73) is one this book questions. The United States was the world leader in manufacturing productivity in 1941. So was it in 1948. The war had little to do with this.

During World War II the United States was buffeted by a series of powerful supply shocks, and the learning effects served at best as a partial counterbalance to the resulting downward pressures on productivity within manufacturing. The negative shocks are critical in understanding why both labor productivity and TFP in the sector declined throughout most of the period between 1941 and 1945. Some of them were inflicted by enemy action, but much of the damage resulted from the nature and methods of economic mobilization for war itself. The radical, sudden, and forced change in the product mix led quickly to an economy plagued by shortages, resulting in the creation of agencies and mechanisms of administrative control that struggled to deal with them.

Beginning in 1942 and continuing with greater or lesser intensity throughout the conflict, the economy experienced raw material, machine tool, and subassembly and component shortages that gave rise to what came to be called, only partly in jest, priorities unemployment.[1] When other claimants stood ahead of a firm in line for necessary inputs, the firm's physical capital or labor stood idle or less than fully utilized. Production slowed, stopped, or simply did not start. If we think of production during the Second World War, images of factories running full bore, with double or even triple shifts, are likely to come to mind. It is true that the average workweek in manufacturing increased, and many operations ran multiple shifts when they could. But the lived experience of individual firms and sectors lacked continuity: periods of intense activity were punctuated by intervals of reduced effort or even shutdown, most frequently because of the inability to obtain complementary inputs.

Since output is the numerator in an efficiency calculation and since input flows are in the denominator, priorities unemployment meant falling productivity. Intermittent idleness of available inputs is the signature of a shortage economy. Shortages led to hoarding, which made the shortages worse. In the last two years of the war, widespread manpower deficiencies along with growing cancellations of war contracts added to the depressive forces, and the former emerged as the most powerful of several retardants to growth of manufacturing productivity.[2]

In his classic book, *The Visible Hand*, Alfred Chandler argued that the success of modern business enterprise in America depended on the ability of managers effectively to use reliable transportation and communication to ensure high rates of throughput, capacity utilization, and inventory turnover (Chandler, 1977; Field, 1987). The endemic shortages of an economy mobilized for war torpedoed this dynamic. Although the loci of the most severe deficiencies changed during the course of the conflict, the overall depressive effect on manufacturing productivity was never overcome, and in fact it worsened in 1944 and the first part of 1945, when labor became the scarcest of an already long list of difficult-to-obtain inputs. And labor was unlike other inputs: it had to be retained as well as obtained. A worker, unlike a machine tool, could walk away, fail to show up for work, go on strike, or get drafted.

From the beginning, and indeed throughout the war, the bulk of military contracts were negotiated, rather than awarded on the basis of sealed bids, as had been the practice during the 1930s. And they went for the most part to large firms with established engineering departments. Donald Nelson, the head of the War Production Board, explained the preference on the grounds that time was of the essence, that these businesses had the financial, managerial, and technical capabilities to deal with transitions to a new range of products, and that the transaction costs of dealing with a few well-known entities were far less than trying to contract with many small firms, whose participation could in any event be elicited via subcontracting. Military procurement officers emphasized a similar logic (Nelson, 1946, pp. 177–78, 269–89; Gropman, 1996, p. 65; Heath, 1972, pp. 298).

The bias in favor of established firms concentrated orders in centers of pre-war production that, as a consequence, suffered worsening shortages of housing, schools, and other social services, with predictable effects on worker morale. This contributed to absenteeism, labor-management conflict, and high turnover in defense plants, particularly in the later stages of the war, when the novelty (following the Depression) of steady employment at good wages began to wear off and the dawning appreciation of the inevitable temporariness of defense plant employment created incentives to find work in sectors where opportunities had a higher likelihood of persisting in the postwar period. From a systemwide perspective, the most important factors driving the growing manpower scarcities in the last two years of the war were the draft calls from the Selective Service System and the policies and cultural norms that influenced the sequence in which male labor pools were depleted.

The argument that the contracting pattern was justified because the urgency of immediate production trumped the pursuit of efficiency would have had more force if what was produced and in what order had been more carefully planned. But it is a mistake to believe that military procurement officers had considered the totality of the construction and military production they were ordering, or its scheduling, particularly during 1942 and the first half of 1943. Individual programs had champions and objectives. The overall war program did not. It was not well thought through, although Roosevelt's "must-have" list provided some aspirational goals.

By executive order on January 16, 1942, the president created the War Production Board (WPB) to "exercise general direction over the war procurement and production program" and appointed Donald M. Nelson as its first chair.[3] Nelson, formerly chief merchandising (purchasing) executive for Sears, Roebuck, had served as coordinator of defense purchases on the National Defense Advisory Committee (NDAC), which had preceded the Office of Production Management (OPM), in the Division of Priorities at OPM, and then as executive director of the Supply Priorities and Allocation Board (SPAB). OPM lasted just a year (it was established in January 1941), and SPAB barely four months. Roosevelt's action was precipitated by the impending release of a Truman Committee's report highly critical of the existing administrative structure, particularly within the OPM.

William S. Knudsen, a former Ford executive and CEO of General Motors from 1937 to 1940, had chaired the OPM. In that role Knudsen had been unable to achieve much overall control of the rearmament program, but he did succeed in accelerating the construction of government-owned plants that would facilitate the large expansion in aircraft production and other military durables and ordnance during the war, including smokeless powder, steel, and aluminum capacity. Augmenting this were foreign orders from Britain and, before its collapse, France, which paid not just for airplanes and other munitions but also for some expansion of facilities to produce them.

More than two full years elapsed between the German invasion of Poland in September 1939 and the Japanese attack on Pearl Harbor. During that period, construction began on entirely new government facilities designed specifically for defense work. Two notable examples, both reflecting the work of the industrial architect Albert Kahn, were the Detroit Tank Arsenal, which would be run by Chrysler, on which ground was broken on September 9, 1940, and Ford's Willow Run facility, started on April 18, 1941, which would take over $200 million and nineteen months to complete. Although the manufacture of automobiles proceeded without limitation through August 1941, Knudsen encouraged firms in the industry to begin considering how they could contribute to the manufacture of airframes, aircraft engines, military vehicles, tanks, guns, and other ordnance.

In contrast to the situation with respect to most other military durables, the country was already relatively well positioned in 1939 to build (and rebuild) ships and submarines. This was the result of the naval rearmament program that began in 1933 as Roosevelt pushed to expand the fleet. The Vinson-Trammel Act of 1934 gave the navy and Congress permanent authority to increase and maintain naval strength up to treaty limits and to maintain a balance between construction in naval yards and privately owned yards. At the outbreak of war in Europe (and in contrast to its position with respect to ground forces) the United States was one of the top three naval powers in the world and had in place much of the production infrastructure necessary to propel it to number one by the end of the war. After 1939, maritime ship production capacity also began to revive because of British and U.S. government orders (McGrath, 2019; Wilson, 2016, ch. 2).

All this activity notwithstanding, however, war spending before Pearl Harbor, including naval construction, the manufacture of aircraft, and the construction of new facilities, was a small fraction of what would follow, as figure 5.1 shows. The U.S. economy in December 1941, twenty-seven months after Germany crossed Poland's borders, was nowhere close to full industrial mobilization for war. As OPM closed up shop, the army commissioned

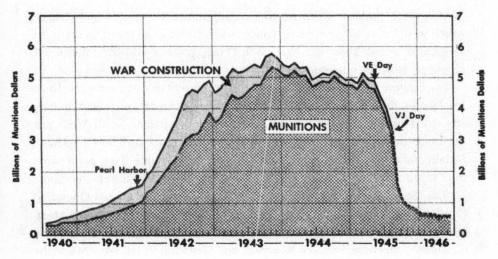

Figure 5.1. The rise and fall of U.S. war production, 1940–46. Source: U.S. Office of War Mobilization and Reconversion, 1945f, p. 2.

Knudsen as a lieutenant general, and he moved to the War Department, where he would serve as director of production in the office of Undersecretary of War Robert Patterson. As such, he would also have a seat on the WPB, but not as its leader. A key question as 1942 began was whether, as head of the new civilian production agency, Nelson would have more success than had Knudsen, while confronting issues that would rapidly become even more challenging.

Reckoning Potential and the Feasibility Debate

The attack on Pearl Harbor resolved any debate about whether the United States was or was not in the war. The U.S. manufacturing sector now faced an escalating range of demands: provide for the direct and indirect requirements of the military, produce ordnance and supplies for allies, particularly Great Britain and the Soviet Union, build the ships to move goods and troops across two oceans, and continue to manufacture consumer goods for U.S. civilians. There were limits on what the sector and the economy could produce in total, and the change in the final product mix and its uncertain evolution added additional challenges. During the twelve years before the Japanese attack, the economy had operated with a varying gap between actual and potential output (the former below the latter), and production was rarely limited by shortages of labor, raw materials, or other complementary inputs. That would now change, which would necessitate choices, consciously arrived at by planners or, in the absence of such deliberation, by default. Those choices could affect the course of and possibly the outcome of the war.

The biggest wild cards in trying to plan were military requirements. In an ideal world, these would have been deduced from a careful analysis of military strategy. This was impossible in 1942. The decision to invade North Africa was not made until August of that year.[4] There was no final agreement between Britain and the United States on overall Allied military objectives, particularly the timing and magnitude of a cross-Channel invasion of Europe, until the Tehran (Sextant) meetings in November 1943, when Stalin backed Operation Overlord, dashing Churchill's hope for more operations in the Eastern Mediterranean (Matloff, 1959, pp. 133, 362).[5] The matter had been discussed at the Casablanca meetings between Roosevelt and Churchill in January 1943, at the Trident Conference in Washington in May of that year, and at the Quadrant meeting in Quebec in August. At each of these, Britain seemed to endorse the idea, but that country had interests distinct from those of the United States, and the solidity of Churchill's commitment was never entirely certain, even after Tehran.

November 1943 was coincidentally the month when U.S. munitions production peaked. Consider what this meant: in a very real sense, U.S. economic mobilization for war was complete before agreement on Allied military objectives. In the months following Pearl Harbor, military planners did not know what kind of campaigns would be waged, where, or in what order.

Those uncertainties did little to arrest a frenzy of procurement activity in 1942: "The whole production build-up . . . was not and could not be, based on strategy. . . . We were manufacturing munitions 'for the shelf' . . . not for specific operations" (U.S. Bureau of the Budget, 1946, p. 131). Civilian planners, intent on benchmarking desired production against availabilities on the supply side, experienced frustration when they tried to get numbers out of the military. They were stonewalled whenever release of information was perceived as threatening military prerogatives, which was most of the time, and the information they got was quite frequently worthless (Brigante, 1947, pp. 90–91). In one case, Nelson had to go to Britain to learn about U.S. war plans that the military had refused to share with him. In other cases, the military would not divulge information that was publicly available.[6]

An agreed-upon and widely understood strategy would have enabled both military and civilian planners to make informed choices about what to manufacture and in what order. Earlier determination of strategy could have helped govern what in the event was a chaotic process of economic mobilization, particularly in 1942 and early 1943. The debacles of the priorities systems—the lack of centralized control over their granting and the resulting inflation of priority grades—were symptomatic of this chaos and a causal influence in their own right, as were the excessive commitments to construction programs in 1942.

On February 19, 1942, in an attempt to assist him in understanding the relationship between total proposed production in 1942 and 1943 and the economy's potential, Nelson established a Planning Committee, choosing as its chair Robert R. Nathan. Nathan had received a law degree from Georgetown in 1938 and a B.A. (1931) and M.A. (1933) in economics from the University of Pennsylvania, where he had taken two classes from Simon Kuznets. After assisting Kuznets with early national income estimates, he worked as chief of the National Income Division at the Department of Commerce's Division of Economic Research. Starting in 1940 he served as associate director of Research and Statistics for NDAC under Stacy May, a statistician who was also a member of the Executive Committee of the American Economic Association. Both men continued with similar responsibilities at OPM, and, in a sense, at the WPB, where, in addition to chairing the Planning Committee, Nathan reported to May as assistant director of the Bureau of Progress Reports.

The two other original members of the Planning Committee were Thomas C. Blaisdell Jr. and Frederick Searls Jr. Blaisdell had earned a Ph.D. in economics from Columbia, where he had also taught, and had served during the Depression as director of the National Resources Planning Board. After the war he worked on implementing the Marshall Plan, and then as a professor of political science at Berkeley. Searls was a former mining engineer and executive who continued during the war as industrial consultant to the Ordnance Branch of the War Department. Each of the three had been an all-outer during the defense period, pushing for more rapid conversion and a more rapid increase in military spending before Pearl Harbor.

As the key staff member, Nathan recruited Kuznets, his former professor, to serve as chief of the Planning Committee's Program Analysis and Research Section. Kuznets had done pioneering conceptual and empirical research on national income and product accounting during the 1930s, for which he would win the 1971 Nobel prize in economics. Another notable economist serving on the committee staff was Raymond Goldsmith, who had done seminal work on measuring U.S. saving flows and national wealth. The members of the

Planning Committee worked closely with May, who was both director of Statistics and director of the Bureau of Progress Reports at the WPB. To the extent that the United States had any civilian war-planning apparatus in the early stages of the war, this committee was its locus.

On July 9, 1941, following the German invasion of the Soviet Union (June 22, 1941), Roosevelt ordered his war and navy secretaries to work up a secret document that would identify the "overall production requirements required to defeat our potential enemies." Stimson and Knox delegated principal responsibility to Major Albert Wedemeyer; the report landed at the White House in late September, where it quickly became known as the Victory Program (Kennedy, 1999, pp. 485–90). The report, which detailed planning for a war the president was still promising the United States would not enter, remained secret until splashed across the pages of the *Chicago Tribune* three days before Pearl Harbor.

In the meantime, in November 1941, while still at OPM, Nathan and May estimated the dollar value of total requirements (adding up those of the army, navy, Maritime Commission, and Lend-Lease administration), combined these with estimates of necessary civilian consumption, and then benchmarked the total against what they thought was feasible.[7] Their calculations suggested the existence of a substantial gap between proposed targets and potential output: what was planned, they concluded, *fell substantially short* of what could be achieved. They therefore recommended that munitions programs for 1942 and 1943 be doubled. Their boss at OPM, Donald Nelson, agreed.

Two days after Pearl Harbor, at a December 9 meeting with President Roosevelt and defense officials, Nathan and May described their calculations, which underlay estimates of what the military's Victory Program would require and cost, and how quickly it could be achieved. Knudsen expressed reservations, believing that only 75 percent of what Nelson, May, and Nathan were recommending would be possible (Brigante, 1950, pp. 27–28). The president, however, was enthusiastic about the prospect of going big, and, through Harry Hopkins, Roosevelt's closest assistant, asked Nelson to come up with a set of "must-have" estimates. Nathan and May developed numbers they thought feasible, which were transmitted to the president, who on January 5 shared them with Knudsen and Sidney Hillman, then director and associate director, respectively, of the soon-to-be-defunct OPM. A day later, on January 6, 1942, Roosevelt delivered his State of the Union Address. He had, overnight, decided to go even bigger. Nathan and May's suggestion of 50,000[8] and 80,000 planes for 1942 and 1943 became 60,000 and 125,000. The tank "must-have" numbers went from 40,000 and 60,000 to 45,000 and 75,000. Merchant shipping went from 7 million tons to 8 million tons for 1942 and to 10 million tons for 1943 (Brigante, 1950, pp. 29–31).[9]

The military responded with considerable enthusiasm to these aggressive targets, anticipating much larger military forces and the ordnance that would be needed to support them. The challenge for the Planning Committee when it began meeting in February had come to be the reverse of what its members (and Nelson) had been trying to achieve just a few weeks earlier. Now the aggregate of proposed production threatened to exceed potential. One of the many difficulties to be faced in persuading both business executives and the military of the existence of supply-side limitations was that for the previous twelve years the economy had been operating below potential, and the ability to obtain materials and labor, given adequate financing and demand, had simply not been a serious constraint. The chief problem for the economy had been a deficiency of aggregate demand caused by a collapse of private-sector capital formation, exports, and spending on consumer durables, and for the military, difficulties in obtaining appropriations from a Congress reluctant to risk provoking war by appearing to prepare for one.

Even had some of the central strategic decisions been made earlier, and even had Nelson not, as one of his early acts, "delegated" contracting power to military procurement officers, much of the depressing effect on productivity during the first year was probably unavoidable.[10] Once inputs to production were rationed—necessary under the circumstances—priorities unemployment was practically inevitable, as were its consequences. A small manufacturer without a war contract was unlikely to obtain priorities for materials (Heath, 1972, p. 300). In extreme cases the result was bankruptcy, representing a loss of capacity and capability on the supply side.

How serious was this loss of capacity? Floyd Odlum, head of the Division of Contract Distribution, an agency set up to bring more small manufacturers into war production, estimated that of the nation's 184,000 manufacturing establishments, roughly 133,000 employed fewer than twenty workers, and of those, perhaps 45,000 could participate in war production (Klein, 2013, p. 258). Some of the remainder, and some of the larger firms, could continue to produce goods for civilians, but they would face many obstacles. At a June 26, 1942, meeting of the WPB's Planning Committee, members discussed a survey indicating that 24,000 establishments (13 percent), representing about 8 percent of prewar sales, would likely shut down by October 1 (U.S. Civilian Production Administration, 1946b, p. 66; Nelson, 1946, p. 279). The survey was mentioned again by Leon Henderson, a New Dealer who headed the Office of Price Administration (OPA), at a meeting of the full board on July 21, 1942 (U.S. Civilian Production Administration, 1946a, p. 101).[11] Given limitation (L) orders, which prohibited the production of certain goods, and conservation (M) orders, which prescribed allowable uses for certain raw materials, many of these firms would be unable to convert, or to continue to produce what they had made before.

These estimated failures in manufacturing are distinct from the shuttering of approximately 300,000 retail and service establishments in 1942 alone (Lingeman, 1970, p. 65; this is based on Department of Commerce data). In July 1942, more than two years after the fall of France, the production of all metal-intensive consumer durables was finally terminated, with disastrous effects for automobile and appliance dealers. The former could sell spare parts and do repairs, although few skilled mechanics were available. Appliance retailers did repairs, or tried to sell other goods, such as furniture or records (Lingeman, 1970).

A manufacturer might not be prohibited by a limitation order from continuing to make his product, but a conservation order might prevent the company from obtaining the inputs that had previously been used: "They were confronted with the choice of finding a substitute for the material (or a way to reduce the amount of it used in making the product) or going under. . . . As soon as a substitute metal was found, it too might well go on the critical list." Record makers needed shellac, which came from a beetle native to India, only intermittently available. Or consider hosiery. The United States had embargoed silk imports from Japan in July 1941. At that time 20 percent of stockings were already made from nylon, so industry tried to switch to that fiber entirely. But nylon was made from phenol, which was also a key ingredient in the manufacture of explosives. And nylon was needed by the military for parachutes, mosquito netting, and tents. Alternatives were rayon, which was eventually in short supply because it was needed for tire cords. That left cotton, but fine cotton was in short supply. "We could figure out a way to knit them with grass and the next day there would be a priority on grass" (Lingeman, 1970, p. 119).

Planning Committee members considered and rejected the idea that firms in distress because of the war effort should receive aid, recommending instead that they release their labor but could possibly rent out their equipment or their enclosed space for the duration. Henderson's view was that the government should either aid these firms financially or accept the responsibility for not doing so, but that the WPB itself could not take responsibility for the effects of some of its actions. Nelson expressed sympathy for the small companies but emphasized that the overriding objective had to be winning the war, not providing them with a safety net.[12]

Small businesses, however, had considerable support in the legislature, and on June 11, 1942, Congress passed the Smaller War Plants Corporation Act, intended to extend financial assistance to help small firms convert to war production. Subsequently the Planning Committee and the full board considered following British practice and encouraging concentration of limited civilian production in one establishment if others in the industry could be converted to war production. During the war, attempts were made to implement this practice through agreements and orders affecting the production of farm machinery, typewriters, and kitchen stoves, but ultimately the policy was abandoned (U.S. Bureau of the Budget, 1946, p. 434). Some businesses, barred from production of traditional civilian goods by limitation orders, were simply unable to participate in the war effort—another channel through which the altered output mix served to depress potential output during the war.

But the failure of these firms was likely less important in its effects on production and productivity than was the intermittent idleness of facilities and labor in firms that did participate. Priorities unemployment was severe in the early stages of conversion, when limitation orders mandated the shutdown of production of metals-intensive consumer durables, but factories, even if their owners had contracts to produce military goods, could not get the raw materials or other inputs they needed. The Fed's industrial production index was almost completely flat between March and April 1942. The "system" for granting materials priorities went through several iterations before being largely replaced by the Controlled Materials Plan in July 1943. But temporary idleness of labor or capital due to shortages of complementary inputs—the essence of priorities unemployment—remained endemic throughout the war, although the loci of its most severe manifestations changed. The uneven and unpredictable arrival and termination of war orders contributed additionally to the intermittency (Wilson, 2011).

The phrase "Hurry up and wait" originated during World War II as a caustic description of life within the U.S. military. It also had considerable applicability to the experience of firms engaged in wartime production. The idleness of productive inputs created by shortages of critical inputs was not always just for short periods. In his memoir Nelson noted that there were "a number of destroyer escorts . . . tied up for six months after launching because needed components had not been delivered." And he casually remarked, "There were times in 1942 when production in munitions plants was delayed a few months because copper was not available" (1946, p. 255).[13] The chaotic situation in 1942 is described in the U.S. Bureau of the Budget's history: "All semblance of balance in the production program disappeared because of the different rates of contracting and of production that resulted from the scramble to place orders. If there ever had been a planned balance between men, ships, tanks, planes, supplies, weapons, ammunition, and new facilities, and there is no evidence that there was, that balance disappeared in the differential time required to develop the orders, the differential energies of the various procurement officers, and the differential difficulties of getting production out" (U.S. Bureau of the Budget, 1946, p. 113).

This passage is followed by discussion of the "terrific waste in conversion" as locomotive plants were converted to making tanks, when the marginal benefit to the war effort of additional locomotives was greater, and truck assembly lines were hurriedly converted to making aircraft, laying the groundwork for a subsequent shortage of military trucks. Additional insight into the challenges of mobilization can be gleaned from the memoranda generated by members of the Planning Committee, the minutes of its meetings, and, finally, the minutes of the entire War Production Board.

One of the most important of the first was a March 14, 1942, report in which Kuznets addressed the feasibility of then-proposed military production levels for 1942 and 1943. After all-outers like Nelson, Nathan, and Henderson had pressed the military to be more ambitious in its requests during the defense period (between the fall of France in June 1940 and Pearl Harbor), Kuznets and Nathan now tried to deal with the reality that the proposed construction and munitions programs, and in many cases already contracted for, threatened the war effort by, in their totality, substantially exceeding the productive capacity of the economy.

Kuznets anticipated shortages in "rubber, nickel, TNT, and smokeless powder" (note rubber's pride of place), and "critical" shortages in aluminum, vanadium, wool, and toluene and a very tight copper situation as well (see also Nelson, 1946, p. 12). Kuznets wrote bluntly: "As for 1942, the war munitions program as presently designed seems to be impossible from the standpoint of raw material supply." He then described how limitations on the rate of expansion of the machine-tool sector, by constraining growth in the supply of new special-purpose tools, effectively limited the immediate production possibilities for military goods: "Many of our industrial facilities are special purpose instruments. . . . If one could disregard this problem of specific use, if one could proceed on the assumption that industrial facilities can be freely shifted from one use to another, the situation would be very simple indeed" (Kuznets, quoted in Lacey, 2011, p. 152).

The American system of mass production relied extensively on special-purpose machine tools, except in the machine-tool industry itself. The consequence was that most existing *facilities* (not just the machine tools within them) were not easily converted from producing their original outputs, one reason there was such a strong preference among operating firms to construct entirely new plants, such as Willow Run and the Detroit Tank Arsenal. As Charles E. Wilson, the General Electric CEO later recruited by Nelson to serve as vice chairman of the WPB, put it: "When you convert one of our factories, you move everything out and start with blank space. Out of a long row of intricate machines on the production line, a certain percentage may be used in the manufacture of a war product, depending on what the war product is. But the production line will necessarily consist mainly of new special purpose machines along with any of the old machines that can be rebuilt for the new manufacturing process" (quoted in Nelson, 1946, p. 218).

Trying to get firms to repurpose existing plants and, to the extent possible, reuse machine tools when making new products was a continuing struggle: the preference was almost always for a new special-purpose facility filled with new special-purpose tools, all paid for by the government, the plant being operated by the contracting firm.[14]

In its March 16, 1942, meeting, the Planning Committee discussed Kuznets' report and proposed cutting 1942 total munitions objectives from $62.6 to $42.6 billion dollars, with the largest cuts in ordnance, military construction, and industrial construction. This was coupled with a recommendation for an immediate moratorium on all new construction contracts or those requiring facilities that would need new tools (U.S. Civilian Production Administration, 1946b, p. 19). Nelson supported the proposal, and it was endorsed by the full board (U.S. Civilian Production Administration, 1946a, p. 41). The minutes of the March 31, 1942, Planning Committee meeting, however, indicate that although both Nelson, as chair of the WPB, and General Brehon Somervell, head of Army Services of Supply, had signed off on the moratorium, army procurement officers were still awarding construction contracts (U.S. Civilian Production Administration, 1946b, p. 32).

In the April 6, 1942, Planning Committee meeting, which Kuznets attended, Nathan stated unequivocally that the 1942 planned federal spending on industrial plants plus the $8.4 billion on direct military construction and defense housing were "beyond the bounds of feasibility, quite apart from any doubts as to the needs for such a large volume of construction." Other types of construction would add another $6 billion. Kuznets then stepped in to say that planned industrial plant and military construction would consume 13–14 million tons of steel, other construction another 4 million, or about one-fifth of overall capacity, and that this did not account for the derived demand for additional construction machinery and equipment, which would need steel as well. Kuznets also warned, since he forecast (correctly) that construction requirements would fall substantially in 1943, that "the direction of enormous quantities of men and equipment into the construction industry during 1942 and the rapid demobilization of the industry in early 1943 would result in great dislocation and waste" (U.S. Civilian Production Administration, 1946b, p. 38).[15]

In a private memo to Nathan dated April 13, 1942, Kuznets expanded on the general concept of feasibility. He emphasized that "an attempt to attain goals that are unattainable is likely to result in a situation which, for practical purposes, is worse than trying to attain more moderate but feasible goals. An attempt to secure unattainable goals is likely to result in an unbalanced performance in the sense that facilities will be built for which there are not enough raw materials; that semi-finished products will be produced which it will be impossible to finish; and that finished products will be produced for which indispensable complements will be lacking" (quoted in Lacey, 2011, p. 138; original in the National Archives, "Records of the Planning Committee," RG 179, box 4).

Nelson was of a similar mind (Nelson, 1946, pp. 379–81). If one hundred tanks were scheduled, it was better to complete eighty of them, rather than start work on all hundred, each of which would end up incomplete and none of which would be operable. Kuznets acknowledged that imbalances could be almost completely eliminated by setting production targets low enough, but, for obvious reasons, this was undesirable as well: "The real problem . . . is therefore to set your goals as high as possible, compatible with the attainment of a balance that is needed to assure usability of equipment and final products." High but attainable production should be aimed for at the likely expense of some shortages and imbalances, which invariably meant some losses in efficiency. Ambitious production goals might not ultimately be met, but Kuznets and Nathan hoped that by setting the goals high (thus accommodating the president) but not too high, the shortfalls could somehow be accommodated, so that the consequence was somewhat fewer than targeted completed planes, guns, and ships, but not large numbers of unfinished and unusable products. Exactly how this was to be accomplished was never precisely spelled out, although the hope apparently was that better control of scheduling could somehow ensure it (Kuznets, August 12, 1942, memorandum, pp. 5–9, summarized in Brigante, 1947, p. 34).[16] Bitter fights between the WPB and the military prevented much progress in this area until 1943, and how much improvement there was remains questionable. The final report of the Army Service Forces acknowledged this: "Even if unchanging requirements could have been established for a year in advance and there were no shortages of materials, facilities, or manpower, scheduling on the required scale would have been enormously difficult. The very nature of war made this impossible. Operating experience and unexpected strategic developments constantly required changes in items, specifications, and quantities. . . . Demands in many cases varied greatly from month to month; the resulting fluctuations in production schedules were of course not compatible with production efficiency" (U.S. Army Service Forces, 1948, p. 69).

The feasibility analyses conducted by Kuznets proceeded along four tracks. The first was similar to what Nathan and May had done in their November 1941 study for the OPM. It compared the dollar value of proposed civilian and military production with an estimate of the dollar value of potential output, checking to see whether the former was lower or higher than the latter. Because of the change in the output mix, however, this needed to be complemented by "qualitative" analyses of the ways in which availabilities of materials, facilities (structures and machine tools), and finally labor might impose stricter constraints. The national income approach was probably sufficient if one were studying a normal peacetime expansion as it closed an output gap. But, as has been noted, the alteration in the composition of final output operated like a negative supply shock and lowered potential output, even in the absence of changes in the underlying supply conditions for materials. It was by studying the effects of limitations on the supply of materials, machine tools and facilities, and labor (this was the "qualitative analysis"), that the magnitude of this effect could be more fully contemplated (Brigante, 1947, pp. 24–25; 1950).

The nesting of constraints was reflected in Kuznets' comments at the March 2, 1942, meeting of the Planning Committee. He suggested one should start with the national income approach, and if the total proposed production exceeded potential, the military plans should immediately be sent back for reduction. If proposed total production came in under potential using the aggregate analysis, it still needed to be subject to "qualitative" analysis, an exploration of the ways in which availabilities of raw materials, fabricated metals, machine tools, components, and specialized labor might place additional constraints on what was "feasible" (U.S. Civilian Production Administration 1946b, p. 10).

The Planning Committee was also deeply concerned that the program might succeed in producing large quantities of munitions that could not be moved to theaters of war because of shortages of shipping capacity. In 1942 German submarines were extracting a devastating toll on Allied shipping. The April 7, 1942, meeting noted that 670,000 tons of ammunition were then scheduled to be produced per month by 1943, that even if British ships carried away 20 percent of this production (rather than the then current 5 percent), the remaining output would be six times as much ammunition as the United States could move by ship to theaters of war. This helps explain why the Planning Committee advised (pressed) the military to lower the quantity of ammunition then scheduled for production in 1942 from $15.6 to $9.2 billion (U.S. Civilian Production Administration, 1946b, March 16, 1942, p. 19). The committee succeeded in this effort.

Minutes of an end-of-year meeting of the Planning Committee noted that the War Department had voluntarily agreed to abandon construction of projects with a value of $450 million, although, since two-thirds of the money had already been spent, the savings were only $150 million. Searls complained that in spite of pressure on the army to curtail its construction programs, delays had "resulted in a wastage of resources critically needed for the production of munitions" (U.S. Civilian Production Administration, 1946b, p. 107).

Through 1942 and, indeed, through most of 1943, the obstacles to production that depressed production and productivity did *not* take place within an economy experiencing an overall labor shortage. It is true that throughout the defense period and continuing through the first two years of the war, employers periodically complained of shortages of particular categories of skilled workers. In spite of the expansion of civilian employment and the drain of manpower to the military, however, the United States was not yet experiencing an economy-wide labor shortage. The reserves of the unemployed were still large in 1941. That pool, along with labor market entry of women, teenagers, older individuals, and marginally employed blacks and whites from the southern agricultural economy, postponed the arrival of labor shortage.

A WPB Planning Committee meeting on May 6, 1942, discussing the merchant shipping program reflected this: "Delays in the shipyards themselves are primarily due to individual errors of management. Labor has not been a bottleneck at any stage of the shipbuilding program. Delays due to strikes have been relatively minor, and the supply of general skilled labor appears to be adequate for the building of nine million tons of shipping in 1942" (U.S. Civilian Production Administration, 1946b, p. 55). In the May 12 meeting Searls expressed doubts that 8 million tons could be built, but it was the availability of steel plate (not labor) that would be the constraint.

Sir Walter Layton, chief advisor to the British minister of Production on Programs and Planning, joined the June 10, 1942, meeting. Edward T. Dickinson, executive director of the Planning Committee, contrasted the situation in the United States, where materials were in short supply but labor was not, with that in Britain, where he understood the reverse to be true. Layton clarified that some factories in Britain had in fact been idled because of lack of materials, although he agreed that manpower was indeed the more serious constraint. Dickinson remarked that in the United States, labor scarcity was not expected to arise "for some six to nine months," in other words in the third quarter of 1943, a forecast that proved remarkably prescient (U.S. Civilian Production Administration, 1946b, p. 65).

Frustration over the inability to get information out of the military about war aims in the context of an explosion in the totality of their procurement orders fueled a desire among Kuznets, Nathan, and other members of the committee for a Supreme War Production Council with a powerful leader. The WPB was not that council and Nelson was not that czar, although he had been granted considerably more authority by the president than he actually used. Nelson agreed with the Planning Committee on the conclusions of the feasibility analysis and what needed to be done about it, but he was less enthusiastic about the push for another agency, in part because it raised questions about his role and that of the WPB. That said, the politics were complicated, and the drumbeat for an all-powerful supreme industrial leader was also led by the army, which schemed to replace Nelson with Bernard Baruch, who had headed the War Industries Board during the final year of World War I. Nelson went out of his way in his memoir to be generous to all with whom he had worked, but he expressed some bitterness regarding the leaks to the press by army leaders as they fought jealously to preserve their power over procurement, even when it was likely such actions made it more difficult to achieve their goals.

The army evidenced great difficulty, for example, accepting the idea that a functioning rail system was essential to the military effort, needed to move troops, military goods, and supplies to ports where they could be transported overseas in support of allies and U.S. forces already in war theaters. It objected strongly to the preferences given to the synthetic rubber program, even though it was obvious that, without rubber, military operations, let alone the domestic economy, would grind to a halt. And it fought bitterly against cutting back direct military production even slightly to allow manufacture of replacement parts for agricultural machinery, locomotives, and buses. This was all viewed as coddling civilians, even though workers needed buses to get to defense plants, farmers needed operable machinery to produce food for the military and civilians, and the military needed trains to move troops and equipment as well as critical industrial materials to war plants and ports. Although Nelson had a generous and amiable personality, he sometimes did say no, and in his memoir he noted, "I had found one thing about the Army: the minute you start making decisions which they don't like, they complain that you are indecisive, and that the big trouble with you is that you can't make decisions" (Nelson, 1946, p. 384). Though Nelson worked hard to get along with people and did his best with the military brass, he was clear in his memoir about the necessity of retaining civilian control over war production in World War II and in any subsequent conflict.

In the army's defense, one can note that it was often preoccupied with maintaining Britain's sometimes halfhearted endorsement of the cross-Channel invasion first discussed for 1942 (Operation Sledgehammer; the purpose would have been to relieve pressure on the Soviets), then scheduled for April 1943 (Operation Roundup), and finally undertaken in June 1944 (Overlord; the buildup of troops and ordnance in Britain, as opposed to the invasion itself, was referred to as Bolero).[17] Churchill and British war planners had political objectives in the Eastern Mediterranean, and U.S. planners continually worried that the Mediterranean emphasis reflected in the North African campaign (Operation Torch), the invasion of Sicily (Operation Husky), and the subsequent invasion of the Italian mainland would expand in ways that would sap commitment and resources from preparations for Overlord.[18]

The army understood that men were needed to permit industrial production to continue at necessary rates, and it understood the existence of an overall manpower constraint. In 1943 the service settled on a budget for the ground forces of ninety divisions and an overall authorized strength of 7.7 million men, increased by 1945 to 8.3 million men and ninety-one divisions. From 1942 onward, army personnel were organized into ground divisions, air groups, and service forces, the last including the corps of engineers, quartermaster corps, medical corps, signal corps, chemical warfare unit, ordnance department, military police, and after July, transportation corps.

During 1942 economic planners needed to balance the immediate pressures for more munitions, emanating most forcefully from Roosevelt in the form of his "must-have" list, with a defense construction program that had begun in 1940 and that was by 1942 quite literally out of control (Lacey, 2011, p. 18). Nathan often did an even better job than Kuznets in articulating the trade-offs that needed to be made in planning the war. In his report to the critical War Production Board meeting of October 6, 1942, which drew on the April 13 memo to him from Kuznets and the follow-up study dated August 31, 1942, Nathan considered the plusses and minuses of an ambitious production program that ran ahead of the economy's potential output. In a nod to Roosevelt, Nathan acknowledged that such a call could rally energy and focus efforts on a set of concrete objectives. But he moved quickly to the downsides, which revolved, above all else, around imbalances:

> The easier parts of the program will be fully achieved, and unless tightly controlled, will run ahead of schedule or beyond objectives, at the expense of more difficult items. . . . It is impossible to avoid the development of excess fabricating capacity. Each procurement unit must establish facilities to achieve its objectives, and the net result is bound to be idle or only partly utilized plants. . . . Substantial excess capacity means wastage of materials. . . . Unless the program is now adjusted, we may be increasingly faced with the slowing down and closing of plants throughout the country. (Quoted in Lacey, 2011, p. 174)

It was at this meeting that the conflict between Nathan and Kuznets on the one hand and General Somervell, head of Army Services of Supply (renamed Army Service Forces in March 1943), on the other reached its climax. In a September 12 memorandum Somervell had responded derisively to a copy of Kuznets' August feasibility analysis, which had been shared with him. At a WPB Planning Committee meeting on September 17, 1942, Nathan mildly observed that Somervell's dismissal of Kuznets' memorandum "failed to recognize the great importance of bringing the war munitions program within feasible limits." Nathan and Searls reiterated that "unnecessary construction constitutes the most significant waste of economic resources," and Searls added that "unnecessary construction projects are a severe drain upon the supply of workers in critical war industry areas" (U.S. Civilian Production Administration, 1946b, p. 90).

Kuznets (under Nathan's signature) had provided a restrained but well-argued response to Somervell's memo. At the October 6 meeting, Somervell continued to push back against any diminution in scheduling of military construction or munitions production, or the construction of the industrial facilities and equipment production that would make possible increases in the latter.

A fundamental enemy of high or growing productivity is idle capacity or idle labor. The capital service flows from physical capital remain in the denominator of a TFP calculation regardless of the utilization level of the physical capital (OECD, 2001a, 2001b). In the short run, so too do the costs of labor, although unlike physical capital, labor can be laid off if the interruption persists. The inability to proceed with production because of the unavailability of complementary inputs drives down the numerator of the productivity ratio in the face of persisting flows in the denominator, and thus depresses its level. This is simply a matter of arithmetic.

During the years of the Great Depression, idle capacity was almost entirely a consequence of insufficient aggregate demand, and the cyclical effect of output decline on productivity between 1929 and 1933 is recognized and well understood. The declines in productivity in manufacturing between 1941 and 1945 were the result of an entirely different dynamic. Imbalances and shortages, not deficiency of demand, forced inputs to be periodically and intermittently idle. The war production program, led by the president, consciously aimed to drive the economy above potential; the resulting inflationary pressures were addressed through rationing, prohibitions on the production of consumer durables, price controls, and the encouragement of household saving via government bond drives. Accommodating the president was made more difficult because the "natural" level of total output (above which demand stimulus would accelerate inflation) had been reduced by its radically changed composition along with the external shocks delivered by the Japanese and Germans. This exacerbated, for any given level of total demand, the shortages and imbalances that led to priorities unemployment, generating a persistent drag on productivity within manufacturing that did not get better as the war continued.

During the first year of U.S. involvement in the war, the most serious problems involved shortages of materials. This is reflected repeatedly in the minutes of the meetings of both the board and its Planning Committee. A closely related syndrome, which affected holdings of components, machine tools, other equipment, and factory space as well as raw materials, bedeviled production throughout the war. It was individually rational for firms to hoard inventories in the face of uncertain supplies. But given that what was being hoarded was scarce and its availability uncertain (that was why it was being hoarded), the practice meant that other legitimate claimants could not get it. The more this happened, the more a high-priority rating deteriorated into a hunting license, and the greater the propensity of manufacturing labor or capital to stand idle. This drag on aggregate sectoral production and productivity was compounded by the challenges of producing technically complex products with which manufactures were unfamiliar or had little experience, aggravated in certain cases by pigheadedness (see, e.g., Henry Ford). At a May 12, 1942, meeting of the board, Undersecretary of War Robert Patterson attributed shortfalls in aircraft production to inadequate deliveries of engines, aluminum forgings, and aluminum sheet, but Nelson pushed back, questioning why airframe deliveries were running at just 40 percent of the rate of deliveries of aluminum (U.S. Civilian Production Administration, 1946a, p. 69).

The theme of idle or only partially utilized capital and labor recurs, as in the minutes of the June 16, 1942, meeting:

> Failure to utilize existing facilities to the fullest extent for war production continues as a major retarding factor in the production drive. In war industries such as shipyards, aircraft, and machine tool factories, machines stand idle for part of every week. The number of employees on the second shift is very much less than on the first shift, and in many cases negligible on the third shift. . . . The major reason given for underutilization of machine facilities is the lack of or delayed delivery of the necessary materials. . . . The second important factor frequently reported by the larger plants . . . is the lack of proper equipment to balance the production effort. (U.S. Civilian Production Administration, 1946a, p. 85)

At the August 18, 1942, meeting, May reported on the dynamics about which Nathan and Kuznets had expressed such concern and suggested that the hoarding problem went beyond inventories and also affected fixed capital:

> Analysis of the war program by items reveals clearly that the production forecast is seriously short of requirements for the year in many areas, while it is substantially in excess of requirements in other areas. . . . Lack of balance is characteristic of the production and use of . . . machine tools, and defects in present production controls contribute to the shortage of materials. . . . Only about two-thirds of the machine tool requirements for the new airplane projects will be provided on time. A number of these projects plan for a capacity far in excess of their production schedules, while others will have inadequate facilities under current

plans. . . . 43 airplane plants will have nearly 13 million square feet of productive floor space in excess of estimated requirements at the peak of scheduled airplane output in June 1944, while the area of 16 other plants will be about 10 million square feet below estimated requirements. (U.S. Civilian Production Administration, 1946a, pp. 118–19)

At the September 22 meeting May described disappointing munitions progress in August, and there were sharp disagreements between him and Somervell over whether targeted production for 1942 and 1943 was too high. In aircraft, May questioned feasibility on the basis of forecast machine tool and aluminum availability (bauxite imports from Dutch Guiana had been seriously disrupted by U-boats). May reported that shipyard facilities engaged in the naval vessel and merchant ships program were being operated at 43 percent of maximum capacity, and that half the yards building minor combat and landing vessels were not operating a second shift. Admiral S. M. Robinson attributed this to inadequate flow of materials and "housing and other problems." May also discussed severe shortages in torpedo production, due to lack of machine tools, and delays in the program to arm merchant vessels to protect them from submarines. And he provided more data indicating the severity of the inventory-hoarding problem, stating that many firms held stocks "substantially in excess of quarterly requirements." He recommended, as a disciplining device, cutting back deliveries, particularly of steel, copper, and aluminum to firms found to be stockpiling excessive quantities of materials.

At the climactic October 6 meeting, Nathan and Somervell disagreed over the feasibility of production targets. Nathan again pressed for an additional administrative structure—some sort of Supreme War Production Council favored by Kuznets (but not necessarily Nelson) that could combine considerations of strategy with those of production and adjudicate conflicts between them. Nathan was vigorously rebuffed by Somervell, who "failed to see what benefit would be derived from a board composed of an economist, a politician, and a soldier who does not know production" (U.S. Civilian Production Administration, 1946a, p. 141). Somervell was at the time engaged in battles within the military over the planning of production, and his visceral objection to Kuznets' concerns about feasibility was no doubt colored by the fact that the proposal for a Supreme Council threatened his own internal objectives. The meeting minutes present a somewhat sanitized version of what was in fact a very heated discussion (see Brigante, 1950, pp. 80–81).

The October 13 meeting, to which Nathan was not invited, concluded with a promise that Nelson would communicate with the Joint Chiefs that the combination of the president's "must-have" program and the military production targets was not achievable. In the aggregate they greatly exceeded productive capacity and promised critical shortages in copper, aluminum, and alloy steel (among other inputs), equipment needed for aluminum forgings and extrusions, and generators and compressors. Ultimately, they threatened a shortfall in usable military ordnance (U.S. Civilian Production Administration, 1946a, p. 145).

On the issue of feasibility, Roosevelt backed Nelson (and indirectly Nathan and Kuznets). Undersecretary of War Patterson wrote a memo to Somervell after the meeting indicating that they would need to compromise, and the military yielded to a moderated set of production goals for 1942 and for 1943. The face-saving compromise was to reduce the targets by pushing 1942 program completion goals into 1943, and 1943 completion goals into 1944, thus reducing the monthly production targets without apparently cutting the programs per se. For his part, Nathan refrained from pressing for a Supreme War Production Council, which did not, in any event, have Nelson's backing, since it drew attention to what the WPB was not, and some thought it should be (Durr, 2013, pp. 47–48). A subsequent effort by the Planning Committee to get the army to reduce its targeted head count for the end of 1943 below 7.5 million failed.

An attractive narrative (attractive to economists, at least) is that economists won the war by forcing the military to scale back unattainable targets for 1942 and 1943 (Lacey, 2011). There is some merit to this claim. But as Nathan's biographer suggests, it is an overstatement: the outcome was a compromise rather than a total victory (Durr, 2013). More significant than who won and by how much, however, is what the consequences were. It is important to acknowledge but not to exaggerate the significance of the lower production targets. Success in reducing monthly planned construction and munitions production reduced the negative pressures on production and productivity. But "victory" in the feasibility controversy meant only that the drags on production and efficiency anticipated by Kuznets and Nathan were partially weakened, not that they were eliminated. The imbalances that lay behind priorities unemployment—the inevitable consequences of still-ambitious production goals that aggravated shortages and required input rationing—were like a chronic inflammation that flared up in different places in the economy and with different intensities during the conflict. War planners learned to deal with the condition as best they could through better sequencing (scheduling) of production, but they could not make it go away. In his memoir, Nelson emphasized that "reduction of the program to manageable size . . . did not mean that our production problems were solved. . . . We had figured carefully when we set that top limit; it was the maximum attainable in 1943, but it could be reached only if everything went right" (Nelson, 1946, p. 381). And, of course, not everything went right.

At the November 24, 1942, meeting, Stacy May reported that October production was "disappointing in almost every category." Airplane production declined, army ordnance fell "sharply behind schedule," as had naval construction. Deliveries of merchant vessels "contributed the one bright spot in the month's production." May forecast that output of planes, ordnance, and naval ships would fall 25 percent behind schedule. He questioned whether the failure to meet scheduled production could be strictly attributed to shortages of materials, focusing again on the problem of materials hoarding. He compared statistics on increases in input deliveries during 1942Q1—44 percent for steel, 66 percent for copper, and 31 percent for aluminum—with the considerably lower increases in final output production from 1942Q2 to Q3—36 percent for total munitions, ships, and construction, 41 percent for ammunition, and 27 percent for aircraft (a one-quarter lag was assumed reasonable except for aircraft, whereas May allowed two quarters for the raw materials to find expression in finished goods) (U.S. Civilian Production Administration, 1946a, p. 159). Patterson and Knudsen countered by blaming materials shortages for production shortfalls, and Knudsen asked the foolish question, "What could have become of the available materials if they have not gone into production of finished items?" Nelson backed up May by saying what May had left unsaid, namely, that "a substantial quantity of materials has gone into badly distributed stocks of raw materials and into inventories of finished and semi-finished components which have been immobilized because of the lack of balance in output" (U.S. Civilian Production Administration, 1946a, p. 160).

May speculated that inflated output forecasts "in many cases" were an aspect of competitive expediting, an effort "to establish claims for materials and scarce resources in competition with other schedules." The failure to scrutinize these schedules "at a central point and to integrate them into a coordinated pattern has been a basic cause for disorderly production." Nathan piled on: combining high objectives and decentralized procurement resulted in "self-defeating competition for facilities and materials. Inadequate scheduling . . . immobilizes materials and components, wastes labor, results in construction of unneeded facilities, and makes the task of controlling the flow of materials increasingly difficult" (U.S. Civilian Production Administration, 1946a, p. 160). Nelson saw things similarly, in his memoir stating, "Every bit of evidence I had gathered showed that the companies which were producing ships, planes, high-octane gas, and synthetic rubber were hoarding components far in excess of their immediate needs"; he identified valves, heat exchangers, compressors, and motors as some of the scarcest and most critical components (Nelson, 1946, p. 383).

The problem of materials and components hoarding continued through 1942 and into 1943. The March 31, 1942, meeting of the board described efforts to uncover and unfreeze frozen inventories through a program of voluntary buybacks backstopped by the threat of requisition (U.S. Civilian Production Administration, 1946a, p. 38). It also described the work of the WPB regional offices in enforcing compliance with priorities (the Second War Powers Act, passed on March 27, 1942, made lack of compliance a misdemeanor).[19] At the April 14 meeting, May expressed concern that a number of manufacturers of critical products were receiving deliveries of copper, even though they already held substantial inventories (U.S. Civilian Production Administration, 1946a, p. 47). A September 24, 1942, meeting of the Planning Committee reported on a study of excess, idle, or frozen inventories, pointing out that since 1939 inventories had "increased at a rate not warranted by sales," but expressing some pessimism that the government had the tools necessary to control this (U.S. Civilian Production Administration, 1946b, p. 91). In the December 31, 1942, Planning Committee meeting, Searls stated that the strictness of "policing the inventory policy [no more than sixty days' worth] should vary directly with the effect of inadequate inventories on war production" (U.S. Civilian Production Administration, 1946b, p. 108).

At the December 1, 1942, meeting, General Lucius Clay reported that aircraft production for that year would fall substantially below the president's target of 60,000. He expected 49,000 to be completed (the actual number would be about 47,000). In explaining why, he suggested that "much of the deficiency results from shortages of materials." The minutes report that in July 1942, 66 percent of the airplane producers reported materials shortages; in August, 74 percent; in September, 80 percent; and in October, 84 percent; specific shortages of aluminum rods, bars, and extrusions were noted, although there was now more than enough aluminum sheet (U.S. Civilian Production Administration, 1946a, p. 166). In January 1943 two thousand telegrams were sent to manufacturers. Almost two-thirds replied that "the lack of materials and critical components were delaying production" (U.S. Civilian Production Administration, 1946a, p. 197). Materials shortages were a real and persisting problem, but reference to them also became a convenient excuse for poor results resulting from management failures and acted as a smoke screen to distract attention from the role of hoarding in worsening them.

The December 22, 1942, minutes of the board meeting contain the first direct reference to the military's agreement to cutbacks for 1943 (not counting unfulfilled production carried over from 1942). The $92.5 billion had been reduced to $80 billion.

After reading the record of the War Production Board's deliberations during calendar year 1942, it is hard to be surprised that measured labor productivity and TFP in manufacturing fell sharply in comparison with 1941. Table 5.1 provides another look at the year-over-year changes in labor productivity and TFP both immediately before and during the war. The declines between 1941 and 1945 almost entirely wiped out the gains experienced between 1939 and 1941.

The fall in labor productivity between 1941 and 1942—almost 6 percent—was the worst of the four annual percentage declines during the war. TFP fell almost as much in percentage terms, although the TFP drops would be larger in 1944 and 1945. The economists' efforts cannot have played much of a role in affecting the results for 1942, since the military did not accede to reduced production targets until late in October, by which time it was obvious the impossible was not going to be achieved in that year, whatever the outcome of the negotiations. There is more reason to credit the smaller labor productivity decline and the small improvement in TFP between 1942 and 1943 to the reductions in targets, although there were other forces at work as well, including diminution in construction spending, growing experience in mass-producing important wartime capital goods, and some progress in scheduling

Table 5.1 Year-over-Year Percentage
Change in Labor Productivity (LP) and
TFP in U.S. Manufacturing, 1940–45

Year	LP	TFP
1940	10.4	12.1
1941	5.2	8.9
1942	−5.8	−4.8
1943	−1.9	0.5
1944	−3.8	−6.6
1945	−3.6	−9.2

Source: Table 2.3.

and thereby sequencing production in a manner that increased capacity utilization and the rate of inventory turnover. This progress reduced but by no means eliminated the degree to which incomplete items remained frozen in the production pipeline while they awaited the arrival or availability of necessary complementary inputs.

Nathan and Kuznets had their greatest influence on the war effort early on in 1942. As Brigante wrote, "In the outcome of this story Nathan and Kuznets were among the expendables" (1950, p. 1). The last WPB meeting to which Nathan was invited was on December 1, 1942. Some of his enemies began publicly questioning why he was not serving in the military. On September 18, 1942, Nelson had brought in Charles E. Wilson, former CEO of General Electric, with instructions to tackle the problem of scheduling production already contracted for or in progress. In a reorganization in March 1943, Nelson ordered the Planning Committee to report directly to Wilson rather than to him. Wilson, who had been initially favorably disposed toward Nathan, began to sour on him. The feelings were to some degree reciprocated. In a 1989 oral history interview for the Truman Library, Nathan described Wilson as a "phony," someone who talked tough but then backed off when the chips were down.[20]

As Brigante (1947) details, Nathan and the committee had tried to throw their weight around on other aspects of mobilization, often without success. Sometime their failures were justified, generally because the committee members knew less about the situation than the actors whose behavior they were trying to influence (often because those actors would not provide them with the needed information). Their attempt to tell Petroleum Administrator for War Ickes how to manage a shortage of toluene left egg on Nathan's face. Their strong recommendation that requests for priorities for steel for the Big Inch pipeline project be rejected a third time—Goldsmith seems to have played an important role here—also fall into this category. Ickes was a competent administrator and made a compelling case, and after previous turndowns by both the OPM and the WPB, the WPB gave it the go-ahead.[21] In these instances members of the Planning Committee were not able to argue as effectively or marshal evidence as well as they had in the feasibility dispute.

At the final meeting of the Planning Committee, on April 1, 1943, Nathan announced that his deferment had been terminated at his request, and he would enter the military, and the remaining members of the committee announced their resignations. Stacy May stayed on with the board, as did Goldsmith and Kuznets (in a different capacity), but Kuznets, unlike May, was invited to board meetings only three times during 1943 (on January 26, August 24, and

November 30). May, in contrast, shows up in the minutes as attending four-teen times during that year.

The absolute and percentage increases in total industrial output were simi-lar in 1942 and 1943. But the absolute and percentage increases in *munitions* production were considerably larger during the first full year of the war (1942) than in 1943. This reflected a sharp reduction in the production of metals-intensive consumer durables along with the application of a firehose of labor and capital resources to defense output. It was not the result of a productivity miracle. The economy achieved an almost fourfold increase in production for the military during 1942, but this accomplishment was marked by chaos and rife with inefficiencies.

The War Production Board during the Climactic Year of Economic Mobilization

The 1943 minutes of the meetings of the War Production Board offer a re-markable you-are-there perspective on war planning and production, provid-ing running documentation of the pathologies, inefficiencies, and shortages characterizing a command economy during the race to peak industrial and military production. Recurring themes are severe shortfalls and imbalances in production coinciding with idle capacity, producer hoarding of materials and components, and the looming emergence of the widespread labor shortages that would be the primary disrupter of production during the final two years of the war.

At the first board meeting in 1943, on January 5, Nelson noted that the presi-dent viewed four programs as "imperative" for the coming year: destroyer es-cort vessels (for convoy duty), aircraft, high-octane gas, and rubber, although his directives did not indicate which among these should receive precedence. Nelson expressed confidence that raw materials "are now largely under con-trol" and the most serious problems had come to involve components such as boilers, valves, condensers, heat exchangers, and electrical equipment, for which each of these imperative programs competed (U.S. Civilian Production Administration, 1946a, p. 178).

The January 5 meeting showcased the parlous state of the synthetic rub-ber initiative as the year began. The minutes reflect the slow progress of the program, the threat posed to the U.S. economy and military capabilities by its prospective failure, and the resistance among skeptics in some quarters (such as the Petroleum Administration for War and the War Department) to provide priorities for synthetic rubber manufacture. Nelson stated that "until the new plants and processes are brought into successful large-scale operation, the synthetic rubber program must be recognized as in the most hazardous position." He reminded board members, "Failure of the program would impede the transportation of war workers, food, and other vital commodities with disastrous results on the conduct of the war" (U.S. Civilian Production Administration, 1946a, p. 178).

Undersecretary of War Patterson resisted, pushing back on granting top priorities to rubber, and the board agreed to kick the question up to the president for resolution. Roosevelt, more sensitive to the threat posed by the possible exhaustion of rubber supplies following the Rubber Survey Committee report and the explosive political conflicts over feedstocks of the previous year, backed Nelson. Nelson's memoir provides a fuller picture of this struggle to ensure sufficient production of a material critical for the success of the war.

The February 9 meeting included the first of several discussions that year of impending or actual manpower shortages and the threat posed for war production. The War Manpower Commission had estimated that during the 1943 calendar year 3.2 million individuals would need to transfer from less essential civilian activities to war industries. The magnitude of this number seems surprising at first, given that the absolute increase in munitions production in 1943 would be far less than what had taken place during 1942. This apparent paradox is resolved by examining the growth in military head count and corresponding increase in draft calls. More than 3.3 million inductions would take place during 1943, shrinking the total civilian labor force. Faced with a loss of workers to the military, and with insufficient new entrants to compensate, the only alternative was to pull labor from "nonessential" industries. But that of course pushed the problem to the "nonessential" industries. The minutes of the March 16 meeting, for example, refer to the resulting strain on railway operations, where a manpower shortage and inexperienced new workers reduced efficiency.

At the March 2 meeting, Wilson reported that recent progress had been "adequate" in some programs—tanks, self-propelled artillery, and heavy artillery—but not in the supply of necessary machine tools and the all-important aircraft sector. The problems in aircraft were mentioned repeatedly during WPB meetings in 1943, and one can see in real time the shift away from materials shortage as the number-one problem. The minutes of the March 30 meeting, still early in the year, emphasize the continuing challenge of stalled production and materials and components shortages and hoarding in the industry.

More than one-third more aluminum was going into the plants during the last half of 1942 than was contained in the completed planes and spare parts coming out of them. Patterson argued that the limiting factor was aluminum extrusions and, as he had done before, claimed that any shortfalls of actual relative to scheduled production of planes in 1943 would be due to materials shortages.[22] Wilson directly contradicted him, saying he was not prepared to predict how large the shortfall would be, but, whatever it was, it would not be because of a shortage of materials (U.S. Civilian Production Administration, 1946a, p. 210). Since Wilson did not bring up labor shortages at this point, the clear implication is that this was due to management failure.

The problems with copper were less severe than those with rubber because of greater possibilities for substitution, but this meeting's minutes do record that shortages of the metal were continuing to limit the ammunition program. (Nelson also alluded to this in his memoir.) The scarcity of copper led to efforts to recover and recycle brass cartridge cases from battlefields, and at one point to furloughing soldiers so they could return to work in the mines.

At the April 13, 1943, meeting, Paul McNutt, formerly governor of Indiana and at that point chair of the War Manpower Commission, noted that blanket deferment of farmers added to problems staffing defense plants (U.S. Civilian Production Administration, 1946a, p. 212).[23] Young men in defense plants were returning to farms while their fathers replaced them in the higher-paying defense jobs, both now protected from the draft (the latter by age). McNutt "pointed out that the careful efforts of the War Production Board to assure a steady flow of raw materials and semi-finished parts to war production will be vitiated if materials and parts are received by plants without a labor force large enough or good enough to fabricate them." Patterson also expressed concern about a growing reverse migration of workers from industry to farms (U.S. Civilian Production Administration, 1946a, pp. 212–13). McNutt and Patterson would reiterate their concerns on this account several times during the 1943 meetings.

The April 27, 1943, meeting minutes provide additional insight into the imbalances, pathologies, and shortages that plagued production throughout the war. Aircraft production again lagged behind schedule during the first quarter of 1943, as it had during the last quarter of 1942. More generally, many manufacturing plants were not using their facilities to the maximum: curtailed second shifts and the absence of a third shift were common. Some plants could not get enough orders to keep busy or large enough orders to schedule efficient runs. Favored plants that could do the most difficult work were tied up producing more easily produced goods, while others that could produce only the more easily manufactured items could not get enough work.

Machine tools also remained problematic, as had been noted almost two months earlier. Additional tools were being produced and installed even though in many cases those already in place required more labor and materials than were available. Yet procurement agencies continued to order 25,000 new tools each month. Wilson's deputy, Ralph Cordiner, who would succeed his boss as CEO of GE after the war, emphasized the need to prioritize tool production and focus on recruiting enough manpower for plants making critical items. He advocated "a drastic curtailment of facility construction programs," since the construction of new plants continued at a breakneck pace while completed facilities could not get the labor and materials they needed to operate (U.S. Civilian Production Administration, 1946a, p. 216).

At the May 25, 1943, meeting the problems created by shifting civilian labor from "nonessential" to "essential industries" were again mentioned. McNutt complained about difficulties staffing textile mills because of draft calls, higher wages in defense plants, and deferment of farm labor, because of which "nothing can be done to return workers from the farm to textile mills or other industrial plants except on a part time basis" (U.S. Civilian Production Administration, 1946a, p. 238).

The June 22 meeting turned to the toll taken on war production by labor strife. Coal strikes had already cost 50,000–60,000 tons. The steel industry had experienced 414 work stoppages and a loss of 660,000 man hours. Because of the continuing coal strike, "some Pittsburgh plants have already curtailed operations to 60 percent of capacity, which represents a daily production loss of about 10,500 tons." Without a resumption of coal deliveries, the steel industry would shut down in two weeks (U.S. Civilian Production Administration, 1946a, pp. 248–49).

The minutes again refer to the manpower problems of so-called nonessential industries. Pulp and paper shortages developed because that industry was losing workers to those offering higher wages and a draft deferment. Half of paper output was used in packaging raw materials and manufactured goods, where it was rapidly substituting for metal, wood, and glass; the industry was hardly nonessential for the war effort. McNutt expressed his desire to use prisoners of war (POWs) to address the shortages.

The WPB continued to struggle with inventory hoarding by surveying large users and cutting deliveries to those with large stocks.

The July 20, 1943, meeting focused on West Coast aircraft assembly, where production shortfalls were due to a shortage of both skilled and unskilled workers. Wilson complained that the drafting of skilled workers was "an increasingly difficult problem." He estimated that "in the next several months" Selective Service might take "22 percent of all male aircraft workers, including 31 percent of the engineering force and 19 percent of the tool makers." More generally, difficult housing conditions contributed to losing labor; in some plants turnover was at 100 percent per year. Absenteeism was a growing problem: there was great difficulty in getting workers to return to work after the July 4 holiday. The minutes reflect growing skepticism that the 1943 target of 95,000 aircraft could be reached. It was not: about 85,000 were produced. (U.S. Civilian Production Administration, 1946a, p. 257).

Conflict over the protected status of fathers and farm-sector workers again surfaced. Patterson stated that "Selective Service should induct fathers not engaged in essential production rather than trained aircraft workers, and that too many men of military age and fitness are returning to the farms and to the security which that occupation offers from induction." And the output of mines was threatened by manpower shortages: "Some mines are losing as much as 3 percent of their labor forces per month" (U.S. Civilian Production Administration, 1946a, pp. 258, 259).

The record of the July 27, 1943, meeting contains the first reference in the minutes to the link between battlefield victories and pressure to relax rationing and repeal some limits on the production of consumer goods (U.S. Civilian Production Administration, 1946a, p. 262). On the aircraft front, Knudsen reported on a trip to twenty-nine airframe and aircraft plants: "With the exception of aluminum forgings, he found no shortage of materials and the fact that production has failed to increase cannot be ascribed to that cause." He did express concern, however, that some firms were resisting maximum production for fear it would lead to cutbacks later: "Too many are confident of an early and easy victory" (U.S. Civilian Production Administration, 1946a, p. 264).

The August 24 minutes contained the first clear statement from Wilson that manpower had overtaken materials and components as the leading national constraint on production:

Manpower has replaced materials as the production bottleneck. . . . Nine million of the best male workers have been taken out of the production system by the Armed Forces and an adverse effect cannot be avoided. . . . The labor supply has now reached the stage of utilization where added increments become more and more difficult to obtain. . . . About 8 million have been drawn from the unemployed, . . . and very little more can be expected from the unemployed pool. The bulk of increasing employment has flowed into the chemicals and metals industries which essentially constitute the munitions group. . . . In aircraft and shipbuilding, . . . four workers must now be hired for every net addition of one to the labor force. (U.S. Civilian Production Administration, 1946a, pp. 269–70)

The West Coast situation was the most critical; aircraft plants were losing workers to shipyards, which had a higher pay scale that reflected prewar differentials. Even in the shipyards, "the quit rate has risen from one to five percent. Efficient operation under these conditions becomes impossible" (U.S. Civilian Production Administration, 1946a, p. 270).

McNutt, however, complained about aircraft plants and shipyards on the West Coast seeking blanket deferments for their workers, and he suggested that they were hoarding labor. Wilson pushed back, stating that he was convinced that unless very substantial deferments were granted to key workers in the aircraft plants, current scheduled production could not be met (Civilian Production Administration, 1946a, p. 270).

The War Manpower Commission sent Baruch and his aide John Hancock to investigate the West Coast situation, and they reported in August that it resulted "from the lack of any system of labor priorities and the hopelessly unbalanced production demands that have been imposed on the Pacific Coast. These demands for the next six months are so far in excess of the available labor supply that a disastrous breakdown of vital production programs all through the region is threatened" (Koistinen, 1973, p. 455)

At the August 24 WPB meeting, McNutt asked the production agencies to support his position that fathers should not be exempt from the draft if army draft calls could not otherwise be fulfilled. Wilson mentioned his hope that increased labor productivity could compensate for the manpower shortages, pointing to the records of some aircraft plants and the Liberty ship producers. But he also acknowledged that there was great variation among plants in how much productivity had grown. A week later, at the August 31, 1943, meeting, McNutt called attention to the 70 percent of the population that favored a National Service Act, but he hoped to deal with the West Coast manpower problem without resort to legislation.

The West Coast aircraft industry crisis would eventually be brought under control by an October 27, 1943, order from James F. Byrnes, director of War

Mobilization, granting "irreplaceable" workers a six-month deferment, renewable if they continued to be irreplaceable. The army and the navy, along with the aircraft contractors and subcontractors, assumed joint responsibility for certifying irreplaceability; information on individuals was then forwarded to the relevant local draft boards. This became known as the "West Coast Plan." Selective Service thought the deferment policy was too generous (U.S. Selective Service System, 1945, p. 84).

On October 12, 1943, Krug, reflecting on progress on the materials front, stated that although a year previously war production had been gravely threatened by shortages of aluminum, steel, copper, and rubber, materials supply was now largely under control. The main continuing threat, as in other parts of the economy, was manpower. Deficits in carbon steel remained a problem, as were shortages of lumber, which was "entirely" due to a shortage of labor.

In a somewhat puzzling comment during the November 30, 1943, meeting, McNutt remarked that the war manpower situation was now under control. It is true that this meeting took place at the end of the month in which wartime industrial and munitions production peaked, and there would be a slight relaxation of the pressure of production on the demand for industrial labor between then and March 1944. McNutt's confidence was premature, or perhaps he was just trying to defend the job his agency was doing. A multiplicity of evidence supports the view that labor shortage remained a critical problem up through the end of the war in Europe (May 1945).

The December 28, 1943, meeting acknowledged that the year would see the peak of Maritime Commission production of Liberty ships, and that 1944 would witness a shift to a less standardized range of ship output, which would result in lower productivity.

Construction Activity Tapers Off

Massive construction spending greatly aggravated shortages and imbalances during the first twenty months of U.S. participation in the war. The materials situation had been grave during 1942, particularly during the summer: "Scores of production lines were shut down" (U.S. Bureau of the Budget, 1946, p. 117). A year later the situation had improved in some areas (aluminum, magnesium, steel), but remained dicey in others: copper, zinc, some of the ferroalloys, and of course rubber. A major contributor to the gradual relaxation of materials supply constraints: by the middle of 1943, many of the biggest construction programs were nearing completion.

It takes time to build or manufacture plant and equipment. Wartime construction could not immediately add to the ability to train or administer military forces, operate or transport ordnance, or produce it. Construction did, on the other hand, make large claims on scarce inputs, including steel, aluminum, copper, and other inputs such as lumber, which, initially viewed as a good substitute for scarce metals, would itself become scarce. The magnitude of this drain resulted from, inter alia, a confluence of the army's drive to expand training and administrative facilities (camps, forts, airfields, depots) for what was correctly anticipated to be a much larger force structure, the Defense Plant Corporation's effort to build the production capacity that would be needed to meet Roosevelt's "must-have" targets, the navy's efforts to repair the damage inflicted by the Japanese at Pearl Harbor, and the Maritime Commission's program to maintain and increase the U.S. merchant marine by catching up with and then overtaking the monthly losses inflicted by German submarines. The construction efforts conflicted in their demand for resources with efforts immediately to increase the production of ordnance and supplies, both for hard-pressed Allies and for U.S. forces, all in the absence of an agreed-on Allied military strategy.

By 1943, however, the economy was over the hump in terms of the various wartime construction programs. Although the monthly peak in manufacturing (both total and war-related) occurred in November 1943, multiple statistical indicators show that the wartime peak in construction activity was reached in 1942. Expenditures on military and naval construction almost tripled between 1941 and 1942, from $1.756 billion to $5.060 billion. Between 1942 and 1943, they fell by more than half, and in 1944 plummeted to $720 million. The army's building of camps, training facilities, and airfields tapered off. Work began on the Pentagon on September 11, 1941, and the building was finished in January 1943. The naval construction program, smaller in dollar magnitude than the army's, also began to wind down, although not quite as rapidly. The number of combatant ships launched, which had risen from 128 in 1942 to 537 in 1943, declined in 1944 to 379. The peak in 1943, however, is somewhat misleading because much of the work on large vessels launched that year, particularly aircraft carriers and battleships, had actually been done in 1942. The biggest remaining gap for the navy—one that had been neglected by planners—was in landing vessels; production rose from 16,005 in 1943 to 27,388 in 1944 (U.S. War Production Board, 1945a, p. 107). In Maritime Commission production, the assembling of the famous Liberty ships ramped down after 1943: 1,238 in 1943, 722 in 1944. Tanker production dropped from

252 to 229, although the ships were larger on average, so total displacement increased by about 10 percent.

Government spending on industrial plant traced out a similar trajectory: $1.350 billion in 1941, $3.485 billion in 1942, $1.973 in 1943, and $748 million in 1944 (U.S. War Production Board, 1945a, p. 33). Overall construction spending for industrial purposes, which included smaller and declining amounts of private spending, grew from $2 billion in 1941 to $3.8 billion in 1942, and then fell to $2.2 and $1.0 billion in 1943 and 1944. Total construction spending in the United States expanded from $10.8 billion in 1941 to $13.4 billion in 1942, and then fell to $7.7 billion in 1943 and $3.4 billion in 1944 (U.S. War Production Board, 1945a, p. 33).

The decline in construction activity after 1942 is reflected in data on injuries and fatalities. The number (in thousands) of deaths and permanently disabling injuries in the sector fell from 3.6 in 1942 to 2.7 in 1943 to 1.2 in 1944. Manufacturing exhibited a different time profile: 2.8 in 1942, 3.4 in 1943, 3.2 in 1944, and 3.0 in 1945 (U.S. Bureau of the Census, 1947, p. 216, table 238). Finally, employment in construction, which held steady at about 2.1 million in both July 1941 and July 1942, by July 1943 had plummeted to 1.2 million, reflecting the tailing off of the big construction push (U.S. Bureau of Labor Statistics, 1944, p. 269). By April 1945 employment in the sector had declined by another half to 600,000 (U.S. Office of War Mobilization and Reconstruction, 1945b, p. 29).

The design of the Controlled Materials Plan (CMP), fully implemented in July 1943, was a significant improvement over the rationing schemes for producers that had preceded it. It focused on three critical metals—steel, aluminum, and copper—collected estimates of supply, and then allocated these to various claimant agencies (army, navy, Maritime Commission, Lend-Lease), who were then responsible for distributing the allocations to prime contractors, who in turn could distribute them to subcontractors. The system was not perfect—there were other materials (and eventually labor) in short supply, so imbalances were not eliminated. But the practice of competitive expediting was discouraged because there was now less to be gained from it. Still, as Landon-Lane and Rockoff (2013) have suggested, the problems the CMP were intended to address were becoming less acute by the second half of 1943 because of the waning of construction activity. This partly accounts for the amelioration for which the program is given so much credit.

The completion of big construction programs reduced demands for materials and in some cases expanded supply, particularly of steel, aluminum, and magnesium. After peaking in November 1943, munitions production continued at a high plateau through most of the remainder of the war. Its increase from January to November 1943 was less in both absolute and percentage terms than the increase from the beginning to the end of 1942. The combination of construction's declining claim on materials, the contribution of completed projects to the supply of materials, and the leveling off in the growth in overall munitions production softened but did not eliminate priorities unemployment or many of the other pathologies that pervaded the economy in the chaotic days of 1942 and the first part of 1943. Materials shortages remained a chronic inflammation, however, and the conflicts over components (which also required materials) became acute. Nevertheless, 1943 experienced some moderation in the imbalances and thus the downward pressures on productivity within manufacturing, along with success in mass-producing several important military capital goods.

See Figure 5.1 for an overview of the trajectory of wartime munitions production as well as the large role of military construction spending in 1941 and 1942 that so concerned Nelson and others at the War Production Board.

The Emergence of Labor Shortage and Nelson's Dissenting View

It is also true that during 1943 we begin to see the emergence of what would be the most critical shortage bedeviling production in the last two years of the war: manpower. Increasingly severe labor shortage was the major factor accounting for the resumption of steep declines in manufacturing productivity in 1944 and the continuation of this trend through the end of the war.[24] There is broad agreement among war planners and historians regarding the sequence of the most problematic imbalances and shortages as the war progressed: first materials, then subassemblies and components, and finally manpower. This order is reflected in August 1943 comments by Charles E. Wilson, who by that point was executive vice chair of the WPB. It is repeated in a 1945 retrospective by J. A. Krug, who took over from Nelson as head of the board in 1944. This chronology also shows up in remarks in 1945 by James F. Byrnes, who gave up a Supreme Court seat to become "Assistant President" when Roosevelt appointed him as head of a new "superagency," the Office of War Mobilization, in May 1943. It is consistent with Paul Koistinen's statement that "the nation's manpower pool was so large that labor supply set no major limits for production until mid-1943" (Koistinen, 1973, p. 454) and with language in the Bureau of the Budget's history: "In the earlier stages of the war, production had been limited primarily by shortages of raw materials. But now [the fall of 1943], labor supply began to act as the ultimate limit on production" (U.S. Bureau of the Budget, 1946, p. 429). The endemic labor scarcities did not begin to resolve themselves until after VE Day, as the 1945 annual report of General Somervell's organization—the Army Service Forces—makes clear:

> From the beginning of the fiscal year [July 1944] to May 1945, labor supply problems were a constant threat to the attainment of the Army Service Forces procurement program. . . . Many critical production programs were unable to meet delivery schedules because of manpower shortages. Moreover, these labor supply difficulties tended to become greater each month, until the cutbacks in production programs at the end of April [1945] eliminated many current and anticipated labor supply problems. . . . Labor shortages were widely recognized as the principal bottleneck to be broken if war production goals were to be achieved. (U.S. Army Service Forces, 1945, p. 205)

This was reiterated in the ASF's final report: "Shortages of industrial labor were the greatest single impediment to war production in the winter of 1944–45" (U.S. Army Service Forces, 1948, p. 210). At the beginning of 1945, industrial manpower problems were so critical that the army furloughed 4,500 soldiers to work in foundries, tire plants, and the manufacture of 105-mm shells.

Nelson's interpretation of labor supply conditions in the last half of the war stands out as an outlier. Nelson agreed with the early chronology but took issue with the view that the economy was afflicted by an "overall" labor shortage during the final two years of the war. He maintained that what was true in the first part of the war—labor shortages reflected localized scarcities of skilled labor—remained true in its later stages: "The 'manpower shortage' . . . was never an overall manpower shortage. America was not short of manpower; on the contrary, it was constantly getting on with fewer war workers from the fall of 1943 to the end of the war. What we had was a series of acutely localized manpower shortages, in some city, or in some industry; shortages of certain skills, shortages in certain trades—but never an actual overall shortage of manpower" (Nelson, 1946, p. 403).

It is hard to see how the fact that the country "was getting on with fewer war workers" proves the absence of widespread labor shortage. Nelson's memoir is a valuable historical record (and a pleasure to read). But some of his judgments are questionable. He overestimated, for example, the degree of standardization in German military production, and he glossed over the checkered history of Ford's Willow Run plant in a celebration of the achievements of a Ford engineer, Charles Sorensen (Nelson, 1946, pp. 49, 219–21).[25]

A related argument advanced by Nelson was that "the greatest labor shortages were not in temporary war industries, but in those industries that did, in fact, offer a peace-time future . . . in tire plants, in lumbering and logging, in textiles, in coal mines, and in railroads" (Nelson, 1946, p. 407). Again, the relevance of this argument to the question of whether the economy was experiencing nationwide labor shortage is unclear. The issue is not the relative scarcity of labor in different industries. It is whether it is meaningful to describe the economy as a whole as experiencing labor shortage.

War planners did all they could to prioritize labor for defense industries, and work there was generally better paid and often less dirty or dangerous. The "less essential" industries did not benefit from the same calibrated application of carrots and sticks by government planners.[26] Open positions remained unfilled longer. Earning differentials contributed to this outcome: ceilings on wages applied to work in "civilian" but not in "war" industries (Nelson, 1946, p. 407). Nevertheless, as labor shortage became more acute throughout the economy, managers, even in defense plants favored by these preferences, were forced to devote more and more time to maintaining head count. This is reflected in very high turnover rates, which cannot have been much better for productivity than a persistently high level of vacancies.

As draft calls increased, defense plants faced an exodus of workers not just to the military but to farm employments, not because those jobs paid more, but because such workers enjoyed an immunity from military service akin to what the ultraorthodox benefit from in Israel today. This reflected the power of the farm bloc and echoed William Jennings Bryan's view, reflected in his Cross of Gold speech, that agriculture was truly essential, whereas industry was less so. The II-C deferment for those in agriculture persisted through the war. By 1944 agricultural workers were passing up the higher wages in defense plants for fear of losing their deferment, and some draft dodgers were seeking farm employment for the same reason.

Nelson acknowledged problems of high turnover in defense plants but rejected the view that this was how labor shortage manifested itself in those industries, maintaining that the solution was to "treat each plant or city as a separate case, and to work out a solution on a local basis. Excessive turnover could always be checked if the trouble were taken to approach each problem individually" (Nelson, 1946, p. 405). Because of variation in local conditions, vacancies and localized labor scarcities will develop even in the worst depressions. And, correspondingly, even in the tightest national labor markets, pockets of serious unemployment will persist. During the worst years of the Great Depression, employers placed help wanted ads, and labor market accessions did not drop to zero.[27] Localized labor shortage, just as much as localized high unemployment, is structural, as are common remedies for them. Passing national service legislation would have created an industrial draft, but it turned out not to be politically possible to alter the institutional environment and its associated incentives in this manner.[28] We can acknowledge local variation and still conclude that there comes a point, as we consider progressively lower national unemployment rates, where it becomes reasonable to speak of widespread, even nationwide, labor shortages. Nelson did not, but almost all of his contemporaries did.

Shortages were driven by a cumulation of Selective Service draft calls, declining rates of entry by those not previously in the labor force, and an expansion of total industrial employment only partly compensated for by shrinkage elsewhere in the civilian economy. Although the United States entered the war with plentiful labor reserves, during 1942 the armed forces, including the marine corps and coast guard, grew from 2.2 to 7 million, increasing by another 3.5 million to 10.5 million during 1943, and to a peak of 12.3 million in June 1945 (U.S. Selective Service System, 1946, p. 154). Labor reserves were ample until they were not, given the country's political temperament and its unwillingness to impose an industrial draft. No knowledgeable observer identified labor as the primary source of bottlenecks or production constraints in 1942 or the first half of 1943. Early in the war, the most serious problems, as have been described, were in the sourcing, production, and transportation of sufficient quantities of materials to allow production of the new and radically altered final output mix.

In looking back on the war effort from the vantage point of October 1945, Julius Krug, the last head of the WPB, summarized the sequence of mobilization challenges faced by the country during the war: "In the effort to build up production, there were three basic problems with which we were continually struggling throughout the defense and war periods: (1) to provide the raw materials with which to fabricate military and essential civilian products; (2) to provide the plant and equipment to process these materials and assemble end items; and (3) to staff the plants adequately" (U.S. War Production Board, 1945a, p. 7).

Krug indicated that each of these challenges persisted "continually . . . throughout" the war. But the order in which they are listed reflected the chronology of their relative severity. Krug first described the struggles to respond to the initial two challenges, and then confirmed the emergence of labor shortage as the most serious systemwide challenge sometime in the last quarter of 1943: "Finally, as we increased supplies of industrial raw materials, and Selective Service took its toll on workers, it became increasingly difficult to find the men and women to feed these new supplies into the new machines." This challenge became steadily more severe: "By late 1944 the manpower recruitment drive was a race in a squirrel cage. . . . By early 1945, after the German offensive in the Ardennes and the step up in Selective Service withdrawals of previously deferred industrial workers, there was scarcely an industry that was not short of manpower. . . . The German collapse staved off what might have been a desperate manpower shortage" (U.S. War Production Board, 1945, pp. 8–9).

The final report of the Army Service Forces describes the same sequence: "In point of time, industrial labor shortages developed after the problems of raw materials and plant facilities had been largely solved. A surplus of labor existed at the time the United States started preparations for war. . . . Manpower shortages developed and became acute in 1944 and 1945, when the efforts of the Army and Navy and Industry were at their height. . . . If the war had not ended in Europe when it did, the situation would have become far more serious" (U.S. Army Service Forces, 1948, p. 68).

The U.S. Armed Forces counted 7 million in their ranks at the beginning of 1943 (5.4 million in the army and 1.4 million in the navy; the remainder were in the marines and coast guard). By the end of 1943, active-duty forces had increased to 10.5 million (7.5 million in the army and 2.8 million in the navy), and by July 1944, to 11.6 million (8 million in the army and 3.0 million in the navy) (U.S. Bureau of the Census, 1946, p. 221, tables 239 and 240). This meant that in the eighteen months between January 1943 and July 1944, the military withdrew a minimum of 4.6 million able-bodied men from the pool available for participation in the civilian labor force. This calculation does not take into account the growing number of military casualties, which required additional draft calls as replacements in order to maintain head count. In January 1944 the secretary of war forecast replacement needs for the army alone during that year at 750,000. Nor was it the end of the manpower buildup in the military. Force levels would peak at 12.3 million a year later, in July 1945.

All this coincided with the end of large inflows of women to the labor force. These had averaged 1.3 million a year between 1941 and 1943. The net inflow between 1943 and 1944 was just 250,000 (U.S. Army Industrial College, 1945e, pp. 10–11). It was not only women who had been drawn into the labor force. At the federal level, the 1938 Fair Labor Standards Act mandated that no child under sixteen could be employed in manufacturing, and no child under eighteen in dangerous occupations, but the act was weakly enforced. State child-labor laws had been relaxed. By 1944, 3 million workers between the ages of fourteen and seventeen participated. High school enrollments declined by 1 million between 1940 and 1943 (Lingeman, 1970, p. 161). Labor-force participation among the elderly also rose (Mulligan, 1997, p. 3).

The largest absolute and relative increases in active-duty forces took place during calendar year 1943, as the military began to gear up for the anticipated cross-Channel invasion, along with island-hopping campaigns in the Pacific and an eventual invasion (it was assumed) of Japan. By the start of 1944, these increased demands confronted the U.S. industrial system with the realities of a labor-shortage economy more severe than any it had experienced previously.

Since the decline of construction employment between July 1942 and July 1943 in principle freed 900,000 workers for use elsewhere (and would free another 600,000 by April 1945), and since munitions production and employment peaked in November 1943, one might have anticipated on this account alone that industrial labor shortages would subside rather than worsen in 1944. The explanation for why they did not subside may be found in the continuing appetite of the Selective Service System.

During the first twenty months of the war, the depth of labor reserves provided some cover for a multitude of planning sins as well as a rapidly expanding military head count. But sometime during the second half of 1943, the continuing demands of the military for both war goods and manpower, the depletion of the ranks of the unemployed, and the diminishing ability to draw workers from those not previously in the labor force created unprecedented labor scarcity. The civilian unemployment rate reached 1.9 percent in 1943 and then fell to an all-time low of 1.2 percent in 1944. The number of unemployed, which stood at 9.3 million in July 1940, 5.7 million in July 1941, 2.8 million in July 1942, and 1.2 million in July 1943, dropped below 1 million in July 1944, generally viewed as the peak of the combined industrial-military war effort (U.S. Bureau of Labor Statistics, 1944, p. 269).

Quarterly data from the 1946 *Statistical Abstract* round out the picture. They show the number of unemployed dropping to 900,000 in 1943Q4, rising to 1 million in 1944Q1, then returning to 900,000 through 1945Q2, except for 1944Q4, where it hit a low of 700,000. Between 1943Q4 and 1945Q2, the number of unemployed in a civilian labor force that ranged from 51.3 to 54 million over this period remained at 900,000 or below for all but one quarter (U.S. Bureau of the Census, 1946, p. 173, table 196).

Draft calls were the proximate cause. The male portion of the civilian labor force dropped 6.6 million from 40.3 million in 1942Q3 to 33.7 million in 1945Q1. This sharp decline was not the consequence of a sudden shift in work-leisure preferences. It is hardly coincidental that between the start of 1942Q3 and the end of 1945Q1, the armed forces of the United States grew by 8 million, from around 4 million to over 12 million. Over this same stretch of time, women in the labor force increased 2.2 million, from 15.5 to 17.7 million. Combining the effects of the drain to the military and the partial counterbalance of the increase in women and additional male entry, the civilian labor force shrank 4.4 million, from 55.8 to 51.4 million. The data summarized in the previous paragraph reflect a slight relaxation in the tightness of labor markets between November 1943 and March 1944, following the peak of total and war-related industrial production, and a temporary uptick in the number of unemployed. But the pause was modest and short-lived. The labor shortages that emerged during the last quarter of 1943 and were remarked upon by various war planners and historians remained severe until the war in Europe ended.

The procyclicality of productivity, particularly TFP, is a well-understood phenomenon. We expect measures of productivity to improve as an economy approaches potential output from below and the unemployment rate declines. But there is little reason to believe that this relationship continues to hold on the other side of potential output, where we can expect shortages and imbalances to develop and worsen. In peacetime these will be temporary and resolved, after a time, by an uptick in inflation, which neutralizes the stimulus from an aggregate demand shock that may initially have pushed the economy above potential. In the controlled wartime economy of the United States, the change in the output mix and other adverse shocks depressed potential output while, in spite of rationing and limitation orders, massive increases in military spending fueled growth in aggregate demand. Under these conditions we should anticipate adverse effects on productivity. Labor productivity in manufacturing declined 3.8 percent between 1943 and 1944, and TFP dropped 6.6 percent (see table 5.1).

Evidence of the growing stress in the labor market associated with an unprecedentedly low unemployment rate can be found in data on separations, turnover, discharges, and quits, as well as strikes, lockouts, and plant seizures. Within manufacturing, total separations between the beginning of 1943 and the end of the war ran at a rate twice that prevailing in 1939, although the composition changed drastically. Layoffs ran at about one-third the prewar levels, while separations due to the military draft were not a factor in 1939. Both quits and discharges, however, were more than five times what they had been in 1939 (figures 5.2–5.4).

Quits, which are voluntary, tend to vary inversely with the unemployment rate. On the basis of previous wartime experience, it had been anticipated already in 1940 that failure to provide adequate housing, schools, and social services near the burgeoning shipyards, aircraft plants, and other centers of war production would contribute to absenteeism and high turnover. In 1940 the Central Housing Committee of the Advisory Commission to the National Defense Council alerted Roosevelt that housing near these clogged centers needed to be expanded "in order to avoid the enormous labor turnover and hampering of production which was experienced in the last war" (U.S. Bureau of the Budget, 1946, p. 30). By the end of 1944 the National Housing Administration had "largely completed construction" of housing for 4 million temporary workers in defense plants, but this expanded supply was of varying effectiveness in alleviating what were often horrendous conditions (U.S. Office of War Mobilization and Reconversion, 1945a, p. 45).

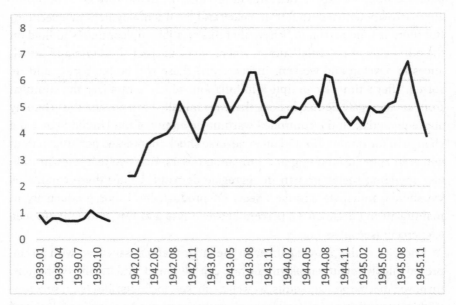

Figure 5.2. Monthly quit rate per 100 employees, U.S. manufacturing, 1939–45. Source: U.S. Bureau of the Census, 1945, p. 171, table 171; and 1946, p. 217, table 233.

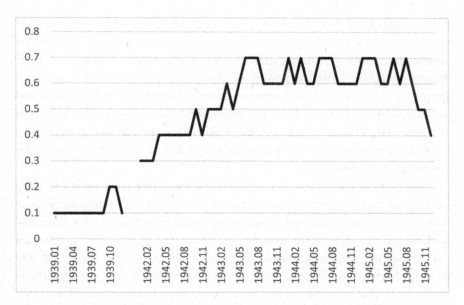

Figure 5.3. Monthly discharge rate per 100 employees, U.S. manufacturing, 1939–45. Source: U.S. Bureau of the Census, 1945, p. 171, table 171; and 1946, p. 217, table 233.

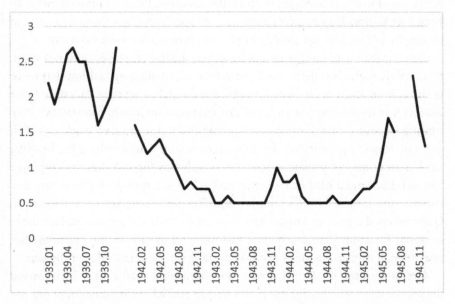

Figure 5.4. Monthly layoffs per 100 employees, U.S. manufacturing, 1939–45. Source: U.S. Bureau of the Census, 1945, p. 171, table 171; and 1946, p. 217, table 233.

Discharges are "terminations of employment initiated by the employer for such reasons as incompetence, violation of rules, dishonesty, laziness, absenteeism, insubordination, failure to pass probationary period, etc." (U.S. Bureau of Labor Statistics, 1976, p. 4). Rises in this rate reflect a variety of employee behaviors and performance found unacceptable by employers, and we would expect the rate to vary inversely with measured productivity. The discharge rate first reached a wartime peak in June and July 1943 at more than six times the average of 1939 and remained at or just below that rate for the remainder of the war.

Note that discharges are distinct from layoffs, where employees are let go because of factors affecting the firm as a whole, not necessarily because of unsatisfactory individual performance. We would expect layoff rates to decline with falling unemployment, and they did, dropping to .5 per 100 in February 1942 and remaining there or at .6 except for a brief rise from November 1943 through March 1944, following the peak of overall industrial and munitions production. The rate does not rise again above 1.0 until May 1945, following VE day (on the graph I have deleted the spike to 10.7 in August 1945 and 4.5 in September 1945, associated with the end of the war with Japan). The fact that the discharge rate was so high during a time of acute labor scarcity testifies to the seriousness of the challenges, such as absenteeism, faced by management. In June 1944 Willow Run could operate only by assuming that three thousand of its employees on average would simply not show up for work each day.

Discharges represent the loss of an employee the employer does not want, an employee who has performed in such an unsatisfactory fashion that he or is she is fired, even in an environment of severe labor scarcity. In a tight labor market it is in some sense an act of desperation—an attempt to staunch continuing losses in spite of the costs of hiring and training a new worker. A high quit rate impairs productivity for a different reason. Quits reflects the loss of a worker an employer prefers to keep (as revealed by the fact that the employer has not discharged him or her previously). Thus, a quit portends future disruption and losses, as the employer searches for a satisfactory replacement. Quits reached a peak in August and September 1943. The series displays more seasonal variation than discharges (people tend to quit in the summer) but remained at four to six times the 1939 average for the remainder of the war.

Overlaid on top of all of this were the continuing draft calls, which caused the loss of workers who did not prefer to quit and whom management did not prefer to fire.

Before the nationwide manpower shortage, when the problems were limited to materials and components, firms, including those operating government-owned plants, stockpiled or hoarded. Government war planners tried with mixed success to control the behavior. A complementary strategy was for managers to spend a great deal of time lobbying for priorities and then keep close tabs on suppliers and providers of transport services to encourage the timely arrival of needed inputs. If others engaged in this, self-preservation required a similar effort, leading to the collective behavior referred to as competitive expediting. Either strategy took its toll on a productivity metric, in the first instance because it deprived some firms of needed inputs and in others inflated capital stocks and storage costs (and thus estimates of capital service flows), and in the second because it diverted management time into what was ultimately an unproductive zero-sum activity. From the standpoint of an individual company, however, the potential benefit in each case was an uninterrupted flow of output.

Hoarding was a natural response to scarcity and paid dividends to those who practiced and got away with it. When the most critical shortages became labor, however, it became more difficult to follow the playbook, since head counts were vulnerable to voluntary quits and predations by the Selective Service System.[29] Physical inventories are subject to various forms of wastage and melt, including theft, fire, oxidization, mold, and other forms of contamination. But once the country moved more broadly into a labor shortage condition, the problems were qualitatively different. A stock of aluminum or copper could not move away on its own accord. In the absence of a slave system or industrial serfdom or an industrial draft, it is more difficult to physically or legally restrict workers to a plant or locality. Labor would not necessarily stay put, and without it, production could be and was interrupted or slowed down just as surely as was the case when the shortage was of materials, components, or fuel.

Additional evidence of stress and disruption comes from data on strikes and lockouts. In spite of labor's no-strike pledge, the number of such incidents increased from 2,968 in 1942 to 3,752 in 1943 to 4,956 in 1944. The number of workers involved more than doubled between 1942 and 1943, from 839,961 to 1,981,279, and increased further to 2,115,637 in 1944 (U.S. Bureau of the Census, 1946, p. 218, table 235). The number of man-days lost, however, peaked in 1943 at 13.5 million principally because of the lengthy and bitter coal strike that began that year. The president of the United Mine Workers, John L. Lewis, refused to honor the no-strike pledge. In April 1943, 500,000 miners walked out, and on May 1 Roosevelt issued an executive order directing the army to seize the mines. Resistance continued, and on May 6, 1943, Congress passed a law making it a criminal offense to instigate a strike in a mine taken over by the government. Mine workers shrugged and invited soldiers to come in and dig coal with their bayonets. The conflict, which dragged on for over a year, cost over 7.5 million man-days of idleness and 39 million tons of coal production. In June 1943 almost as many days were lost to strikes (4.7 million man-days) as was true at the height of the sit-down strikes six years earlier, in June 1937 (5.0 million man-days). By mid-August 1945, 9.6 million man-days had been lost in that year, which, had the war gone on, would have been the worst year of the war for this metric. Germany and the Soviet Union did not have such problems, although Britain did abide strikes, which were mostly resolved quickly.

Although labor did well financially during the war, business did better, and it would be a mistake to believe that after Pearl Harbor labor and management got together in a completely harmonious spirit to facilitate the industrial prosecution of the war. To quote the typically acerbic Eliot Janeway, "Labor spent the war in a state of sullen if prosperous resentment against being regarded as a necessary evil" (Janeway, 1951, p. 88).

Finally, the U.S. military had the authority, when so instructed by executive order of the president, to seize plants if a disruption of production threatened the war effort (table 5.2). The army did so twenty-nine times during the war, the navy fourteen times. And through authority delegated to him by the president, Harold Ickes did this ten times, five in his capacity as head of the Petroleum Administrator for War, and five, using executive orders, in his capacity as secretary of the Interior and administrator of the Office of Solid Fuels Coordinator. Between the army, the navy, and other agencies, the United States executed sixty takeovers of private businesses between June 1941 and VJ day, a record that belies the placid, smoothly functioning picture portrayed in corporate advertisements. In some cases the government seized multiple small businesses in an area; in others, multiple plants of a large enterprise. Many conflicts were resolved in part because of the credible threat of seizure.

After the relative calm of 1942, during which labor generally adhered to its no-strike pledge, labor unrest and the pace of takeovers increased, especially during the last two years of the war. The record for the War Department (army) shows two takeovers each in 1941, 1942, and 1943, fourteen in 1944, and nine in 1945 (table 5.2). Some of these seizures were single plants; others were much larger, including one in 1944 that involved 565 railroads and 1.8 million workers. The 1944 seizures also included the facilities of the Philadelphia Transportation Company, in response to a strike precipitated by the hiring of eight black motormen that affected the ability of 900,000 defense plant employees to get to work (August 3). In one of the most famous takeovers, Montgomery Ward was seized on December 28 because of the ongoing refusal by management to recognize a union. During an earlier seizure in April of that year, when CEO Sewell Avery refused to recognize their authority, two national guardsmen removed him, still sitting in his chair. On January 25, 1945, the Federal District Court in Chicago found the December seizure illegal, but this decision was reversed on appeal on June 8, 1945.

In the last three months of the war, the government engaged in an average of about one seizure a week as it struggled to maintain industrial peace. The takeovers sometimes, but hardly always, reflected state power coming down on labor on behalf of owners. For the army, roughly half the seizures were attributable to recalcitrance by management, roughly half by labor. For the navy, seven were due to production failures on the part of the company, one because of failure to comply with price regulations, and the remainder (six) due to labor issues, again, split equally between recalcitrance on the part of management and labor. Some conflicts were resolved quickly and property was returned to owners, but not all. When Japan officially surrendered in September 1945, six federal agencies continued to operate a total of twenty-four seized plants (Ohly, 2000, p. 25). Takeovers continued under President Truman until the landmark decision by the Supreme Court in June 1952 (*Youngstown Sheet and Tube v. Sawyer*) sharply limited exercise of this type of executive power. For more detail on the factors precipitating these takeovers, and many that nearly resulted in one, see Ohly (2000) and Wilson (2016, ch. 5).

The View from January 1944

As 1944 dawned, the process of economic mobilization for war was at an inflexion point. Most of the facilities construction was complete. Munitions production and overall industrial production had peaked. The armed forces were closing in on their then authorized strengths. The Soviet victory at Stalingrad, Allied successes in North Africa, the advance of U.S. forces into Italy, and U.S. progress in the Pacific had all led to a consensus that the Allies would win, and that the focus should begin to be on reconversion and how to avoid a postwar depression. And yet, from a military standpoint, one could argue that the war

Table 5.2 Plant Seizures by the U.S. Military and Other Agencies during World War II

War Department (Army Service Forces)

1941   North American Aviation, Inglewood, Calif. (June 1941)
        Air Associates, Bendix, N.J. (October 1941)
1942   S. A. Woods Machine Co., Boston, Mass. (August 1942)
        Fairport, Painesville, and Eastern Railroad, Painesville, Ohio (November 1942)
1943   13 leather-manufacturing plants in Massachusetts (October 1943)
        Western Electric, Point Breeze, Md. (November 1943)
1944   565 railroads (December 27, 1943–January 18, 1944)
        7 Textile mills, Fall River, Mass. (February 1944)
        Department of Water and Power, Los Angeles, Calif. (February 1944)
        Ken-Rad Tube and Lamp Co., Owensboro, Ky. (April 1944)
        Hummer Manufacturing Division, Montgomery Ward, Springfield, Ill. (May 1944)
        Philadelphia Transportation Co., Philadelphia, Pa. (August 1944)
        International Nickel Co. of Canada, W.Va. (August 1944)
        Cleveland Graphite Bronze Co., Cleveland, Ohio (September 1944)
        Hughes Tool Co., Houston, Tex. (September 1944)
        Twentieth Century Brass Co. Minneapolis, Minn. (September 1944)
        Farrell-Cheek Steel Co., Sandusky, Ohio (September 1944)
        8 plants affected by M.E.S.A. strike, Toledo, Ohio (November 1944)
        Cudahy Packing Co. Cudahy, Wis. (December 1944)
        Montgomery Ward and Co., Chicago, Ill. (December 1944)
1945   Cleveland Electric Illuminating Co., Cleveland, Ohio (January 1945)
        Bingham & Garfield Railway Co., Bingham, Utah (January 1945)
        American Enka Corp. Asheville, N.C. (February 1945)
        Coker Machine Foundry Co., Gastonia, N.C. (May 1945)
        Gaffney Manufacturing Co., Gaffney, S.C. (May 1945)
        Mary-Leila Cotton Mills Co., Greensboro, Ga. (May 1945)
        Diamond Alkali Co., Painesville, Ohio (June 1945)
        Springfield Plywood Co., Springfield, Ore. (July 1945)
        U.S. Rubber Co., Detroit, Mich. (July 1945)

U.S. Navy

1941   Federal Shipbuilding Co., Kearney, N.J. (August 1941)
1942   Brewster Aeronautical Corp., Long Island City, N.Y. (April 1942)
        General Cable Co., Bayonne, N.J. (August 1942)
        Triumph Explosives, Elkton, Md. (October 1942)
1943   Howarth Pivoted Bearings Co., Philadelphia, Pa. (June 1943)
        Remington Rand, Elmira, N.Y. (November 1943)

Los Angeles Shipbuilding and Drydock Corp., Los Angeles, Calif.
(December 1943)

1944   York Safe and Lock Co., York, Pa. (January 1944)

Jenkins Bros., Bridgeport, Conn. (April 1944)

104 uptown machine shops, San Francisco, Calif. (September 1944)

Lord Manufacturing Co., Erie, Pa. (October 1944)

1945   Goodyear Tire and Rubber Co., Akron, Ohio (1945)

United Engineering Co., San Francisco, Calif. (1945)

49 oil refineries and 3 pipelines (October 1945)

Department of Commerce

Montgomery Ward, Chicago, Ill. (April 1944)

Department of the Interior (Ickes, acting as head of the Petroleum Administration for War)

Cities Service, Lake Charles, La. (April 1945)

Humble Oil Corp., Ingleside, Tex. (June 1945)

Cabin Creek Oil Field of Pure Oil Co., Dawes, W.V. (June 1945)

Sinclair Rubber Co., Houston, Tex. (July 1945)

Texas Oil Corp., Port Arthur, Tex. (July 1945)

Department of the Interior (Ickes, acting as Solid Fuels Coordinator; all involved coal strikes)

May 1, 1943

November 1, 1943

August 1944

April 10, 1945

May 3, 1945

Maritime Commission

Three ships (1941)

Office of Defense Transportation

Toledo, Peoria, and Western Railroad Company, Chicago, Ill. (March 1942)

American Railroad Company of Puerto Rico (1943)

Midwest Motor Carrier Systems (1944)

81 Chicago area trucking companies, Chicago, Ill. (May 1945)

Scranton Transit Co., Scranton, Pa. (1945)

War Shipping Administration

Atlantic Basin Iron Works, Brooklyn, N.Y. (September 1943)

Note: EO = Executive Order

Sources: U.S. Army Industrial College (1946e, pp. 13–14); U.S. Army Service Forces (1948, p. 211); Ohly, 2000, pp. 25; 313–19; Wilson (2016, pp. 158–89).

had barely begun for the United States. Because of a shortage of shipping and landing craft and commitments to supply allies through Lend-Lease, in November 1943 fifty U.S. divisions—more than half the army ground forces—remained in the United States (Matloff, 1959, p. 362). More than 93 percent of all U.S. military fatalities were still to come. Roughly 28,000 had been killed up to that point; the deaths of roughly 379,000 lay ahead.

The January 11, 1944, WPB meeting recorded debate about relaxing rationing and restarting some consumer durables production. Steel and aluminum were now available "in such abundance that the War Production Board is immediately faced with the necessity of deciding whether to (1) shut down a portion of the producing capacity; (2) allow wider end use; or (3) increase stockpiles." Nelson responded that any relaxation "might be interpreted as meaning that the war was already won and that a back-to-normalcy movement was under way." He correctly pointed out that the war, for United States, had not yet entered its most violent stage. Nelson affirmed "that manpower is now one of the most critical factors of production" and asked McNutt for his views. McNutt was opposed to any relaxation of the limitations on civilian construction. Krug and James Forrestal, the undersecretary of the navy, agreed. Forrestal feared that relaxation could lead to firms declining war contracts in hopes of "getting back into peacetime production ahead of their former or potential competitors," although he thought that some of the proposed projects might be allowed through administrative discretion (U.S. Civilian Production Administration, 1946a, p. 299). Patterson was concerned that any relaxation on the home front could adversely affect troop morale. Knudsen also objected to any relaxation on the grounds that it would give rise to the belief that the war was over. (In retrospect, this discussion can be understood as taking place within a four-month temporary easing of the supply pressures following the peak of industrial production. Continuing draft calls would soon "rectify" this situation.)

Krug stated that the only remaining shortage in the controlled materials area was in capacity for making flat rolled steel products. Beyond the CMP's purview, cadmium was in short supply. The high-octane fuel program meant benzene was also short and, because of the heavy reliance of synthetic rubber on ethyl alcohol rather than petroleum feedstock, alcohol also was now scarce. But while, overall, availability in metals and chemicals continued to improve, the situation was moving in the opposite direction in "nonessential" industries such as lumber, leather, wood pulp, and textiles, and labor shortages were likely to further aggravate the situation (U.S. Civilian Production Administration, 1946a, p. 301).

At the February 22, 1944, meeting, Forrestal, Patterson, and Admiral Robinson restated opposition to resumption of previously limited civilian production. Patterson observed that the military challenges ahead were the "most formidable ever faced," and that reverses could be expected. Robinson noted that the military was "at present unable to fill its quotas for men" and that Selective Service would have to start drawing labor "in the lower-age group from manufacturing plants" (U.S. Civilian Production Administration, 1946a, p. 312). Nelson and Wilson countered that millions had been shifted into war production areas where housing and services were impacted, and that the resulting living conditions were "so inadequate as to constitute a limitation on war production." General Lucius Clay advocated holding the line on civilian production. The services did not want to get into vetoing specific programs, but he recognized that manpower was tight as both the military and industry struggled for head count. Wilson and Nelson argued that many of the items being held up by the "extreme opposition" of the services were, in effect, labor saving. It made no sense to deny expenditures for essential maintenance of the war supply infrastructure. General Young, something of an exception among the military members of the board, who were typically opposed to anything that smacked of "coddling civilians," argued that railroads and trucking were in a critical condition, could not employ women because the work was hazardous, and were in need of maintenance and repair in order to sustain the war effort (U.S. Civilian Production Administration, 1946a, p. 313).

At the March 7, 1944, meeting the rubber program reemerged as a topic of discussion, but the emphasis had now shifted away from concerns about raw material supplies. The downstream parts of the sector were heavily dependent on recently trained young men to make the changes necessary to fabricate tires and other products from synthetic rubber. Bradley Dewey (the rubber director who had succeeded Jeffers) pleaded with McNutt to protect these men from the draft. Ralph Davies, representing Ickes, made the same point about the 100-octane program as did Admiral Jones about the electronics industry. All objected to the policy of no deferments for men under twenty-six regardless of occupation, describing it as is a "tragic error." On the materials front, Charles Kohlhepp (director of the Program Bureau at the WPB) reiterated most of what Krug had said on October 12, 1943. The level of war production was no longer limited, he said, by the availability of steel, copper, and aluminum, but, notably, he dropped rubber from Krug's list. The problem was no longer synthetic rubber, which was more widely available, but the threat of completely running out of natural rubber (the nation's inventory, as well as rubber products manufacture, would reach their absolute nadirs in 1944). Still, Kohlhepp concluded that the most critical shortages were in manpower and certain components (U.S. Civilian Production Administration, 1946a, p. 319).

Two weeks later, on March 21, 1944, the board returned to the proposal to induct all physically fit men under twenty-six. Nelson referred to the presidential statement emphasizing the need to do so and stated that he (Nelson) had called the likely consequences of the implementation of this plan to the attention of the military. Patterson stated archly that the War Department "would not accept responsibility for inadequate war production arising from this new policy since the vigorous recruitment and training of workers by industry would offset any potential reduction in the war output attributable to the drafting of all men under 26." Nelson replied, quoting General George Marshall, that he (Marshall) was aware the policy might reduce production, and that "he accepted the need for sacrificing production in order to get the young men into the Services" (U.S. Civilian Production Administration, 1946a, p. 324).

Nelson stated that he was working with the Joint Chiefs to develop a plan to defer workers ages twenty-two to twenty-five employed "in the production of the most urgent war products." The essential programs were landing craft; synthetic rubber and 100-octane fuel; combat and heavy-duty truck and bus tires and tubes, including the necessary tire cord, fabric, and molds; high-tenacity rayon (needed for truck tires); certain aircraft; airborne radar; rockets; and submarines. Materials and components for these programs would receive the same protection. General Hershey (head of Selective Service) objected to Nelson's initiative on the grounds that it would receive too broad an interpretation. Nelson noted that in developing this plan, he had rejected preferential treatment for merchant shipping, rail transport, agriculture, coal mining, and other occupations central to the war effort (but not considered essential). Hershey wanted to know how many deferments there would be. He wanted a comprehensive plan, with a definitive number that would not subsequently be adjusted upward. Marvin Jones, the War Food Administrator, wanted preference for makers of agricultural machinery (U.S. Civilian Production Administration, 1946a, pp. 324, 325).

At the June 13, 1944, meeting, a week after the D-Day landings, manpower shortages remained the number-one problem: "The recruiting of able-bodied male workers is especially difficult for foundries and forge shops, rubber and tire production, logging and lumbering, and ship repairing. The same problem, although not so acute, is expected increasingly to limit the output of coal mines and industries manufacturing textiles and electronic equipment" (U.S.

Civilian Production Administration, 1946a, p. 339). This was the last meeting over which Donald Nelson presided as chair.

Labor Shortage, Draft Preferences, and the Push for National Service Legislation

The WPB minutes memorialize the chronology of challenges to war production. Materials shortages become less critical as we move through 1943 and into 1944. Multiple remarks refer to the emergence toward the end of 1943 of serious economy-wide challenges in attracting and retaining civilian labor. The manpower demands of the Selective Service System are mentioned several times, as are two controversial draft preferences: the almost complete protections against inductions enjoyed by farm-sector managers and workers, and the strong preference of local draft boards to protect fathers at the expense of nonfathers even if the latter were key employees in critical war industries. Both preferences were opposed by members of the military and civilian war planners (one of their areas of broad agreement), but they found strong support in Congress, and resolution of the controversies surrounding them aggravated the growing difficulties faced by manufacturing in retaining labor.[30]

Because these preferences affected the staffing of war industries, these difficulties fueled a desire among many of those who opposed them for national service legislation. Such legislation was seen by advocates as a move in the direction of more equal sacrifice and as a partial solution to labor shortages and high turnover in industry. But it was equally strongly opposed as forced labor by labor, agriculture, and many in Congress. Finally, better news from the battlefront in 1943 complicated the effort to sustain productive effort, since it fueled a narrative that the end of the war was in sight. War planners—both civilian and military—believed that the most intense efforts and the worst fighting still lay ahead, and they were right.

Labor productivity fell much more in 1944 than it had in 1943, and TFP resumed its downward trajectory. The fundamental explanation has to do with the exhaustion of labor reserves, the increased difficulties in attracting and retaining industrial labor, and the resolution of policy disputes over how to deal with this. The Budget Bureau's history, as has been noted, identified the fall of 1943 as the time when national labor shortage began to pinch. By this point, "the labor reserves with which the United States had entered the war had fully mobilized." Unemployment—9 million in July 1940—had fallen to 780,000 in September 1943. The number of women in the labor force had increased over the same period from 13.8 to 18.7 million, after which it leveled off. The average workweek in manufacturing had already gone up over seven hours since 1939; further increases were likely to lower output per hour. Participation of those under eighteen in the labor force had already risen. And inflows from agriculture were drying up. Indeed, in the wake of the initial success of the Italian campaign, a reverse flow seemed to have begun, as workers anticipated a swift conclusion to the war (U.S. Bureau of the Budget, 1946, pp. 431–32).

According to the Selective Service System, total inductions into the U.S. Armed Forces increased from 924,000 in 1941 to 3.033 million in 1942, and then to 3.324 million in 1943, the peak year. Inductions then fell by more than half, to 1.592 million, in 1944 and then to 946,000 in 1945 (U.S. Selective Service System, 2020). The big decline in monthly calls occurred after April 1944, when the army reached its then-authorized strength of 7.7 million men. At that point it switched to replacement demand (for which it estimated it would need 750,000 during the remainder of the year) and also implemented a major change of policy, by emphasizing a strong preference for men under twenty-six, who would best be able to endure the heavy fighting that was now anticipated. It is important to appreciate that at the start of 1943, of 7 million then in the U.S. Armed Forces, only 1.5 million were actually outside the country. This included only about 700,000 army and army air forces personnel, roughly equally split between the Pacific Theater and Britain–North Africa (Matloff, 1959, p. 15). During 1943, sixteen divisions would leave the country, but the military head count would be much larger, and at the end of the year more than fifty of ninety authorized divisions would still be in the United States. At the start of 1944, as noted, more than 93 percent of total World II U.S. fatalities still lay in the future.[31]

A real problem was that by the end of 1943, there was a widespread and growing popular belief (in contrast with 1942) that the Allies would win, and that it was simply a matter of perhaps six to eight months before Germany, at least, was defeated. In forecasting trends in labor force composition, the authors of the February 1944 issue of the BLS's *Monthly Labor Review* assumed that the peak of the war effort would come in July 1944, and that Germany would fall by summer or autumn of that year. They thought it necessary to note that, should surrender occur earlier, downward revisions of some figures might be needed, but they did not explore what might happen if the war dragged on (U.S. Bureau of Labor Statistics, 1944, p. 269). By July 1944, given the good news coming out of Europe following the D-Day invasion, even some war planners succumbed to the belief that the war in Europe would be over by the fall, turning attention to the challenges of reconversion, rescinding rationing of certain items, and ordering resumption of the production of some consumer durables.

The authors of the Budget Bureau's history appear to have reasoned that the decline in draft calls after April 1944 relaxed the scarcity of labor. This inference underlies the history's claim that "after the spring of 1944, labor shortages were not a major problem," although it allowed that "anxiety" increased again in December at the time of the Battle of the Bulge. The authors blamed impressions to the contrary on "an atmosphere of crisis . . . created by statements of military officials that the troops at the front were short of ammunition and supplies, that production programs were lagging, and that labor shortages constituted the most serious production problem" (U.S. Bureau of the Budget, 1946, p. 452). The views of the authors of the Budget Bureau's history were closer to Nelson's than those of most contemporary civilian and military leaders, although Nelson had gone much further, denying any period of nationwide labor stringency, not one that may no longer have been "a major problem" starting in the second half of 1944.

The Budget Bureau's history contains much valuable data and analysis, but it was written by a committee of eight authors, and problematic or puzzling assertions can be found interspersed with solid and often insightful analysis.[32] It might seem reasonable to expect that the decline in Selective Service withdrawals would have relieved some of the pressure on industrial labor supplies. It did not, as is evident in the quarterly unemployment data: the number of unemployed reached its lowest point in 1944Q4.

If there is slack in an economy and one is well below potential, large increases in spending are likely to show up in output and employment increases rather than in inflation. Similarly, so long as substantial reserves of labor remained, draft calls of 300,000 to 450,000 a month, as occurred in 1943, could proceed without producing stringency in the national labor market. Once slack was exhausted, however, every additional withdrawal meant an increase in the severity of labor market scarcity. It did not matter that calls were smaller than they had previously been. What mattered was the cumulative withdrawals by the military. Similarly, in peacetime, once one is in range of potential output, smaller spending increases can have a large effect on the price level.

Unlike a separation because of a voluntary quit, induction into the armed forces in most cases meant exit not just from a firm but from the civilian labor force for the duration of the conflict. Most of those returning home before VJ Day (aside from temporary furloughs as troops moved from the Atlantic to the Pacific after Germany collapsed) would be either dead or wounded. Thus, monthly inductions after April 1944 continued to tighten the labor market, even as inductions proceeded at a substantially reduced monthly rate.

It is true that employment in munitions declined slightly after the peak in November 1943. But that was compensated for by increased civilian employment in the federal government. The number of unemployed increased hardly at all until the fourth quarter of 1945. As the sum of military force levels, civilian employment in the federal government, employment in more and less essential manufacturing and the other sectors of the civilian economy increased, it began to strain the ability or willingness of the American population to supply labor, and those strains persisted until VE Day. Although November 1943 marked the monthly peak in munitions output, were we to consider annual data, the peak would be 1944 because high production and employment levels were sustained throughout the year.

Labor shortage drove a number of policy debates whose resolution affected the extent to which manufacturing productivity was as a consequence depressed. These controversies involved the protections against induction enjoyed by those working in agriculture, the resistance from local boards to drafting fathers ahead of single men employed in critical war industries, and the clamor by some and equally strong resistance by others for national service legislation.

Selective Service Manpower Policies

During the Second World War the sacrifice and risk of military service were shared more equally among different income and social strata and different groups within the occupational hierarchy than had been true in earlier conflicts (most notably the Civil War) or would be true in later ones, in particular Vietnam. The job of the Selective Service System was to provide manpower for the military, and the needs of the military were the number-one priority. At the same time, it was understood within the system and within the military that it would make little sense to classify and subsequently draft so many in Class I (available for training and service) that there were not enough workers left to operate the civilian economy and produce the military goods needed for the war effort. Thus, the system provided for deferments for those working in occupations or industries essential for the war (Class II, temporarily deferred because of occupation).

From the beginnings of the peacetime draft in 1940 through February 1943, four of five inductees were single men under thirty (U.S. Bureau of the Budget, 1946, p. 445). By spring, the supply of physically able men in this group was nearing exhaustion except in agriculture. In November 1942 Congress passed the Tydings Amendment, which gave special protections to any worker "necessary or regularly engaged in an agricultural occupation or endeavor." After passage, the Selective Service System published a table of agricultural outputs, each converted to standard "war units." For example, a milk cow was worth one war unit, as were twenty feedlot cattle, five acres in dry beans, one acre in carrots, or twenty acres in wheat. To justify an agricultural deferment, a man needed to be responsible for producing at least sixteen war units, although exceptions were made for seasonal work, and leniency was granted for those producing eight or more and trying to increase their output (U.S. Selective Service System, 1945, pp. 651–53).

By September 1, 1943, 7 percent of the male labor force aged eighteen to forty-four outside agriculture had an occupational deferment. Within agriculture, the percentage was 47 percent. Concerned about meeting the needs of the military both for men and for the equipment, food, clothing, oil, rubber, and ammunition needed to prosecute the war on multiple fronts, McNutt and those in the War Manpower Commission aimed both to weaken the preference for agriculture and do away with deferments for those with dependents, making occupation (work in an essential industry or occupation) the most important criterion for deferment. That agenda would be the most favorable for industrial production and productivity, because it would give the Manpower Commission a stick with which it could encourage able-bodied fathers to seek employment in occupations or industries the commission deemed critical. McNutt achieved some success with these efforts, but the victories were partial and often temporary, and manpower issues became especially challenging in both more and less essential industries from the latter part of 1943 until the end of the war.

The Selective Service System, reflecting in part the sentiments of local draft boards, distrusted the legitimacy of occupational deferments and, if necessary, preferred to draft men without children from critical war industries in lieu of fathers, regardless of their employment status. The army and the navy cared less about protecting fathers and farmers but shared some of the overall skepticism about the legitimacy of some of the occupational deferments.

It was obvious that manpower planning for the war needed to be integrated with consideration of draft policies and the armed forces' need for men.

McNutt's hand was strengthened when, by executive order on December 5, 1942, Roosevelt placed the Selective Service System within the War Manpower Commission. General Lewis B. Hershey, who headed Selective Service, would now report directly to McNutt. A possible resolution of the local board preference for protecting fathers was to insist that fathers accept employment in critical war industries if they wanted to retain their dependency deferments (the use of the term *dependency* is confusing: it meant that the men under draft board scrutiny had dependents, not that they themselves were dependent on others). To this end, on January 30, 1943, McNutt sent local boards a list of 35 industries and 120 occupations that were "nondeferrable" occupations that fathers would have to abandon if they wished to preserve their dependency exemptions (Selective Service System, 1945, pp. 650–51). The memo warned that men (including fathers) younger than thirty-eight had to be working in an essential industry or occupation by April 1, 1943, or they would lose their dependency exemption on May 1.

Congress was not happy, both at the prospect of fathers being drafted and by a sense that McNutt had overstepped his authority, particularly by identifying specific occupations as, on a blanket basis, nondeferrable. Senator Burton Wheeler introduced a bill that would have provided blanket deferments for fathers. This was vigorously opposed by Secretary of War Henry L. Stimson, who warned it could jeopardize the war effort or even affect its outcome. Although Wheeler's proposal was effectively blocked, legislation passed in November 1943 (Bailey-Clark) did the following: it required all nonfathers to be drafted before fathers, and it placed all men in a national pool, so that the pool of nonfathers had be exhausted nationally (rather than locally) before fathers were drafted. Second, it prohibited any reference to occupational groups in regulations governing who should receive an occupational deferment. This temporarily ended the pressure on men in nondeferrable occupations to switch to essential war work or face the draft. Finally, it punished McNutt for his "usurpation of power" by removing Selective Service from the War Manpower Commission (Geva, 2013, ch. 5). Roosevelt signed the bill in December, and, once again, Selective Service became an independent agency. (Hershey would go on to helm it through 1970.)

Before Pearl Harbor, there had been widespread opposition to the draft. Roosevelt managed to get the Selective Training and Service Act passed in September 1940, but not by large congressional majorities. The act required that all men between twenty-one and forty-five register, mandated a service term of twelve months for those inducted, and allowed for conscientious objectors.

In August 1941 Roosevelt asked that the term of service be extended to thirty months, or as many more months as the president might deem necessary for national security. The Service Extension Act of 1941 passed by one vote in the House; many of those already serving threatened to desert when their twelve-month term ended. Student deferments, for which the initial act had provided, went out the window on August 31, 1941.

After the Japanese attack, opposition to the draft receded, and voluntary enlistments increased. In a November 12, 1942, report, however, the Truman Committee recommended termination of recruitment and voluntary enlistment, stating that "unrestricted recruiting has seriously disrupted production" (U.S. Senate, 1942, p. 120). Voluntary enlistments to military service recruiters continued until the Executive Order placing the Selective Service System within the War Manpower Commission (December 5, 1942). After that date, all inductions had to proceed through the Selective Service System, not the individual service recruiters. Seventeen-year-olds, however, could still be recruited by the services, provided the recruits had parental permission.

Amendments to the Selective Service Act on December 21, 1941, required all men between eighteen and sixty-four to register, and those between twenty and forty-five were eligible to be drafted. The term of service became indefinite: a point six months following the conclusion of the war. This meant that once enlisted or drafted, a serviceman in most cases would not leave military service for the duration of the war unless killed or wounded, and he thus, unless specifically furloughed to work in a critical industry, would not be available to participate in the civilian labor force for the entire remaining duration of the conflict. On December 24, 1941, deferments for aliens were narrowed to those "unacceptable to armed services and other neutral nations." Subsequently, aliens were drafted with the promise that within ninety days they could become U.S. citizens.

On November 13, 1942, another amendment to the Selective Service Act made eighteen- and nineteen-year-olds fair game for induction. Five days later, boards also started drafting those twenty-eight and over. As the monthly draft calls increased in 1942, peaking at 450,000 in November and December, the percentage of the calls filled dropped precipitously, from 96.2 percent in October to 81.5 percent in November to 74.4 percent in December. After the monthly calls were cut back to a range between 300,000 and 400,000 during 1943, the fulfillment rate temporarily increased, but then again began to slide, reaching its lowest point (61.7 percent) in December 1943 (U.S. Selective Service System, 1945, p. 173).

Inductions met assigned calls in only fourteen of the forty-four months of the war. At the start of the war, the army rejected those illiterate, who couldn't speak English, or who had bad teeth or venereal disease. As inductions repeatedly fell short of calls, these standards went by the wayside. Those in the first two categories went through twelve weeks of training before assignment to the Army Service Forces. Those in the third category, if they had mild cases, received medical care after induction; 200,000 so-called venereals were inducted between October 1942 and June 1945. When the number of recruits fell short, the ground forces and the army air forces had priority over the third command, the ASF, which was charged with, among other duties, storing, shipping, and delivering troops and munitions to where they were needed (U.S. Army Service Forces, 1948, p. 107).

Local boards were also forced to yield on their preferences for deferring those with dependents. Most dependency deferments ended on December 11, 1943, although those working in agriculture who also had a dependency claim continued to receive favorable treatment until February 17, 1944. After that, dependency deferments were limited to cases of "extreme hardship and privation to wife, child, and parent." As Hershey's annual report for fiscal year 1945 put it, "The period after May of 1944 may be characterized as one when attention to deferment by reason of dependency was nonexistent outside of the field of extreme hardship. What is more, occupation other than agriculture steadily lost importance as a deferment factor except in relation to age" (U.S. Selective Service System, 1946, p. 48).

The progressive narrowing of deferment criteria, the moves to drafting both younger and older men, and the gutting of dependency deferments all reflected the press of necessity as calls continued and the pools of those eligible progressively dried up. The cumulative effect of inductions had predictable effects on the difficulty of running essential and nonessential industries. From the standpoint of McNutt's interest in maintaining military production, the decay of the protection for fathers was a win, but the resolution of his desired focus on occupation as the only criterion for deferment was at best mixed in terms of his objectives, given the continued (although weakened) protections for agriculture. The new focus on under-twenty-six draftees who were vigorous enough to shoulder the burdens of combat in the final and bloodiest months of the war made it necessary to fight rearguard actions to provide manpower for the more and less essential operations of the economy.

At the beginning of 1945, there were hardly any eighteen- to twenty-five-year-olds remaining to draft, except for 342,000 agriculturally deferred, and their deferments became subject to additional review. Roosevelt authorized reclassification of some of these workers, but the farm bloc's power led Congress to overrule him by passing a bill that Truman vetoed after Roosevelt's death and just shy of VE Day.

In January of that year, Hershey wrote local boards telling them they would have to begin taking twenty-six- to twenty-nine-year-olds, even though the military preferred younger men (U.S. Selective Service System, 1946, p. 17). A telling testimony to the overall shortage of manpower is this: in February 1945 the U.S. Armed Forces completely ran out of reserves, as the last tactical units shipped out (Gropman, 1996, p. 109). The well was dry. The divisions that as of December 1944 were held in reserve had been committed in response to German advances during the Battle of the Bulge, which cost the army 77,000 casualties, including 19,000 killed and over 23,000 missing in action. By April 1945 the remaining pools of manpower to satisfy replacement needs for soldiers, sailors, and airmen were so empty that the system had to start dipping into the thirty- to thirty-three-year-old group. Rationing, which had been lifted on some items during the summer of 1944, when the prospect for an early end to the European war looked good, was reimposed in late 1944 on all previously rationed consumer goods (Gropman, 1996, p. 88).

The Selective Service director's fourth annual report claimed that the shift to younger men after April 1944 "made for more liberal occupational deferment in the upper ages and thus tended to alleviate labor shortages. . . . Civilian manpower requirements were therefore met more satisfactorily from July 1944 to VE Day than during the year or so immediately preceding. . . . Between VE and VJ Day, cutbacks in war contracts eased the civilian manpower situation" (U.S. Selective Service System, 1946, p. 79). But the evidence is not consistent with this claim, which seems to echo that of the Bureau of the Budget history. According to the same Selective Service report, in July 1944, 50,000 workers were "urgently needed in ammunition factories" because of the depletion of stocks of heavy shells in Europe and the Pacific. The Manhattan Project needed 18,000, shipbuilding needed 40,000, ship repair needed 25,000 to 70,000, and airplane manufacture needed 40,000. And, according to the report, December 1944 saw "delayed deliveries in tanks, aircraft, heavy tires, cotton duck, aerial bombs, rockets, dry cell batteries, naval ammunition, heavy-duty trucks, aluminum sheet, field wire, heavy artillery ammunition, ship repair,

mortars, and mortar ammunition." Overall manpower shortages were estimated at 300,000 (U.S. Selective Service System, 1946, pp. 79–80).

Finally, the report included this clear-eyed description of the unrelenting
struggle for manpower in the last two years of the war:

> Just as civilian labor shortages caused industry and agriculture to exert
> pressure upon Selective Service for the occupational deferment of men
> aged 18–37 years, so the military needs of the War and Navy Departments
> made them urge the System to curb the deferments and fill the calls for
> induction which they placed upon it. The time of this report [July 1, 1944
> through December 1, 1945] saw no lessening in the intensity of the three-
> cornered struggle for registrants until the end of the war in Europe. It is
> true that monthly calls were smaller, but with more than half of the men
> of acceptable age already in the armed forces and almost another one-
> fourth rejected for military service, the problem of supplying inductees
> from the remainder assumed acute proportions. In addition, the situa-
> tion was further complicated by inadequate planning, maldistribution,
> incomplete utilization, hoarding, and rigid standards of personnel on
> the part of the Army and the Navy just as these factors operated similarly
> in relation to the manufacturing and farming enterprises of the country.
> (U.S. Selective Service System, 1946, p. 118)

The Selective Service struggled to fill even reduced draft calls. Because the
navy and some services of the army were still permitted to accept voluntary
enlistment (with parental permission) at seventeen, boards found that of the
roughly 100,000 men who turned eighteen each month, 20–30 percent were
already in the services (U.S. Selective Service System, 1946, p. 119).

The military skepticism regarding occupational deferments in industry
was ultimately addressed, following pushback from civilian war planners, by
extending the system originally developed at the end of 1943 to deal with the
West Coast aircraft plant problems (the West Coast Plan). The army and navy
worked together with contractors and subcontractors to certify the deferability
of an individual using Form 42a, which would be forwarded to the individual's
draft board. Eligibility for occupational deferments was thereby determined
jointly by the military and industry, but such deferments were not liberally extended. An enumeration as of August 1, 1945, shows a total of 225,860 certified
deferments (this excludes agricultural deferments and those for the merchant
marine) (U.S. Selective Service System, 1946, p. 94). Neither the civilian unemployment data, which remained very low into the second quarter of 1945,

nor the turnover, quit, and discharge data in manufacturing (see figures 5.2–5.4), which show no notable diminution between 1944 and 1945, suggest any great relaxation of labor market stress. Industry may have been able to secure deferments for its key workers, but the rules were strict, and managers continued to contend with high turnover of workers, many who quit, and many of whom had to be discharged. "Nonessential" manufacturing (about half the sector) was more likely to face prolonged vacancies. None of these conditions, as well as the increased number of strike actions and plant seizures in 1944 and 1945, was likely to be associated with rising productivity.

Selective Service draft calls and policies were the fundamental driver of a worsening nationwide labor shortage. The lower draft calls after April 1944 occurred within a context in which most of the available pools had been exhausted, and where the outcome of struggles over who should be drafted fueled problems of labor retention and turnover that grew in severity as the war careened toward its end.

The value of the WPB minutes in documenting production conditions begins to wane in mid-1944. This reflects personnel changes and the diminished importance of the agency. The last meeting at which Nelson presided was on June 13, 1944. For the next several meetings Charles E. Wilson, as executive vice president, presided, but then he was gone as well, and on September 5, 1944, J. A. Krug led the meeting as acting chair. Nelson, given by Roosevelt a face-saving mission to China, resigned on September 30. As of the October 3 meeting, Krug was chair, and he remained in that role until the agency was terminated at the end of the war.

The more informative commentary is now to be found in the quarterly reports of the director of the Office of War Mobilization (OWM; as of October 1944, the Office of War Mobilization and Reconversion), a superagency created by Roosevelt on May 27, 1943, and helmed by James F. Byrnes. The OWM functioned something like the Supreme War Production Council that Kuznets and Nathan had envisioned, a court of appeal to resolve conflicts between military and civilian war planners and different production programs. Except it was not a council. There was a twelve-member Advisory Board, but the decisions were Byrnes's. Roosevelt referred to him and allowed him to act as an "Assistant President," in that his decisions were generally final: there were few end runs around him to the president. Byrnes was disappointed, to put it mildly, when in 1944 Roosevelt dumped Vice President Wallace but picked Truman, rather than Byrnes, as his running mate.

The Campaign for a National Service Law

In July 1942 the War Department drafted legislation, introduced into Congress in January 1943, that would have created a universal service obligation for males eighteen to sixty-five and females eighteen to fifty. The legislation was backed by the navy and the Maritime Commission and supported by Grenville Clark's Citizen's Committee for a National War Service Act. Clark, a prominent corporate lawyer, advisor to four presidents, and close friend of Supreme Court Justice Felix Frankfurter, was chief drafter of the 1940 Selective Training and Service Act and a key figure pushing for national service legislation thereafter.[33] If necessary, according to the proposed legislation, the president could draft individuals to serve in particular war industries. Roosevelt was tempted to support national service, but he did not do so until his State of the Union Address in 1944. The main arguments advanced in favor were the principle of equality of sacrifice and the need to mobilize manpower for the war effort. Organized labor, the most vigorous opponent of national service, viewed the apparent labor shortages as the result of chaotic and poorly planned mobilization rather than a true labor shortage (Koistinen, 1973, p. 458).

In his January 1944 State of the Union Address, Roosevelt endorsed a National Service requirement. He did not push too hard, however, stating that he "believed" the war could be won without it, but that its enactment would ensure a quicker end, with less loss of American blood. He emphasized that the military services and the Maritime Commission supported it, that it was "the most democratic way to wage a war," and that there was still "a long, rough road ahead" and, as in all journeys, "the last mile is the hardest" (Roosevelt, 1944).

In April 1944 Henry Stimson, Frank Knox, and Emory Land, secretaries of war and the navy and head of the Maritime Commission, respectively, issued a cogently argued Statement on Demand for the Labor Draft. It began by anticipating a need by the end of 1944 to draft an additional 1.4 million men, most of whom would be currently employed, many in essential war industries. To deal with the shortages that would result, they proposed that initially, when an industry in a particular locality was short, a call for volunteers be posted, with the proviso that such volunteers had to come from nonessential employments. If the supply thus achieved was insufficient, then industrial workers would be drafted. By the end of 1944 the navy, marines, and coast guard would need 635,000 men (230,000 as replacements). The army would need 750,000 men, all as replacements (it was at its full complement). This minimum of just under 1.4 million men might have to be increased in 1945. The statement ran through a list of sectors with critical labor shortages, stated that the civilian labor force had shrunk by 1.5 million between March 1943 and March 1944,[34] noted that labor turnover had reached 6 percent a month, "three times the peacetime average," and complained that positive propaganda proclaiming successes in peripheral battles, by fueling the belief that the war was won, might "indeed imperil victory when we thrust at the war's heart" (*Washington Post*, April 21, 1944, p. 2).

In December 1944 Byrnes ordered that essential war industries make 30 percent of their male employees eligible for the draft. There were many objections, but Byrnes succeeded in making this stick (Gropman, 1996, p. 114). He also issued his "Work or Fight" order. The Selective Service would now draft men under thirty-eight who left employment in an essential war industry, or who switched jobs in such an industry without prior approval from their draft board. Byrnes had supported calls for national service legislation starting in late 1943 (Gropman, 1996, p. 110). In early 1945 Byrnes pressed for industrial draft legislation that would give him the power to order workers to critical war plants; noncompliers would face a fine of up to $10,000 and one year in prison.

In his 1945 State of the Union Address, Roosevelt again asked for a National Service Act—all men between eighteen and fifty could be drafted into any job for which they were needed or qualified. Those refusing would be sent to the army. Roosevelt also supported a labor freeze bill—giving Byrnes the authority to order any worker to stay on the job for any reason or for no reason (Gropman, 1996, p. 265). The bill died. In the speech Roosevelt also called for the power to induct nurses into the armed forces to deal with a critical shortage of medical personnel to care for the wounded, and he went on to describe the growing manpower crisis: "Many critical production programs with sharply rising needs are now seriously hampered by manpower shortages. The most important Army needs are artillery ammunition, cotton duck, bombs, tires, tanks, heavy trucks, and even B-29's. In each of these vital programs, present production is behind requirements. Navy production of bombardment ammunition is hampered by manpower shortages; so is production for its huge rocket program. Labor shortages have also delayed its cruiser and carrier programs, and production of certain types of aircraft. There is critical need for more repair workers" (Roosevelt, 1945).

He then described how the pool of men under twenty-six classified as I-A was "almost depleted," and that draft calls would now cut into those holding deferments because they worked in war industries. The armed services had to have priority, he argued, but the needs of war industry could not be ignored. He rejected arguments that it was too late in the war for a national service requirement. But the country was tired of war, having expected it to be over (at least in Europe) by autumn of 1944, and Congress would not go along with him. Unlike Britain, Canada, Australia, and New Zealand, the United States would not have an industrial draft. In a 1947 pamphlet describing the efforts to pass national service legislation, Grenville Clark claimed that its absence depressed potential output by 30–40 percent, prolonged the war, and resulted in military fatalities that otherwise could have been avoided (Clark and Williston, 1947, p. 79). The claims were that an industrial draft would have helped ensure that individual workers were assigned to jobs that would most effectively benefit the war effort and, within that category, where their marginal product would be highest. Turnover, absenteeism, and strikes would have been greatly reduced. The 30–40 percent increase in potential output in a hypothetical world with an industrial draft would have been due, arithmetically, to the extraction of a higher number of average hours per worker per week, an increase in the number of workers in the employed portion of the labor force, and an increase in output per hour (labor productivity) resulting from better matching of job requirements with worker capabilities.

To the argument regarding coercion, proponents responded that there was no difference between forcing men to work on local roads (a court case had ruled this constitutional) and a military draft, which the legislature had already approved. The most compelling rebuttal came from Norman Thomas, leader of the U.S. Socialist Party. Thomas pointed out that the proposed law would make it possible for the government to order individuals, under threat of jail time or a fine, to work on farms or in factories that were owned or operated by profit-making enterprises (Clark and Williston, 1947, p. 30). That, perhaps more than anything else, is what stuck in the craw of labor and led labor to raise the cry of slavery, distinguishing the idea of an industrial draft from compulsory military service in a national army or work on local public roads.

Proponents of national service made both work intensity and reallocation arguments in explaining why potential output would increase. If the United States had had an industrial draft, shortages of industrial manpower might not have been as severe, and the declines in manufacturing productivity during the war might have been less. Whether a negative effect on morale and effort would have offset the benefits of fuller and more efficient staffing, or whether the legislation itself would have had a positive effect on morale and effort is, of course, difficult to say. Janeway wrote that "the miracle of American production in World War II should not blind us to the greater miracles that the war could have produced if the crisis had forced upon the home front a sense of mass participation" (Janeway, 1951, pp. 89–90). Goldsmith believed that it would have been an easy matter to increase munitions production by another 10 or 20 percent in the United States by implementing a labor draft and wringing some of the inefficiency out of the U.S. production system (Goldsmith, 1946, p. 79). The historian John Morton Blum maintained that, "unlike any other belligerent, the United States never reached the point of total mobilization during World War II" (Blum, 1968, p. 318).

As Kuznets noted in his feasibility memos, the potential output of a country is influenced by factors other than simply its accumulated capital stock, the size of its population, and its scientific and technological foundations. Its laws, institutions, politics, and cultural and social norms also matter. Robert Nathan made the same points in a September 19, 1942, memo to Nelson as the feasibility debate spilled over into conflicts about what would happen in 1943: "The fundamental bases for formulating the production program . . . are a combination of strategic, economic, and political considerations. The strategic relate to the general balance among broad categories of weapons and complementary items; the economic to the productive resources available in the country and the extent to which they can be shifted to military production on a given time schedule; and the political to the extent of indicating how far we can go in changing the existing institutional setup under which the economy operates" (U.S. Civilian Production Administration, 1946b, p. 157).

The eventual support by the president of calls for national service during 1944 and 1945 and the arguments made for it by proponents speak to the acute manpower situation faced by the industrial economy as it battled toward the conclusion of an epic struggle with a war-weary populace primed to think that victory was at hand, at least in Europe. But heavy fighting dragged on, active force numbers continued to increase, more and more troops were shipped overseas, casualties soared, and draft notices continued to deplete the ranks of workers in the industrial labor force. Nevertheless, although the country exploited POW and prison labor during the war, it balked at an industrial draft.

Secondary Product Mix Effects

In November 1943 total munitions production peaked, and then remained at a high plateau for most of the rest of the war. In 1944 and until the end of the war, however, the economy did not simply continue producing at slightly lower rates the same mix of goods with which manufacturers had become experienced. Before November 1943, there was no agreed-on Allied strategy with respect to the war in Europe (strategy with respect to Japan was never fully resolved until the end of the war). Goods were produced "for the shelf." The year-over-year change in manufacturing productivity between 1941 and 1942 was sharply negative.

TFP declined less between 1942 and 1943 than during other wartime intervals before resuming its sharp downward trajectory in 1944 and 1945 (see table 5.1). In 1943 U.S. industry succeeded for the first time in mass-producing important wartime capital goods. Contractors began making large numbers of Liberty ships, B-24 bombers, and Sherman tanks using assembly techniques that permitted efficiency to approach what in prewar times had been realized in the production of automobiles, washing machines, and refrigerators. The year 1943 saw peak production of Liberty ship: triple-digit output in eight of twelve months. It was also the year evidencing the largest productivity gains in their manufacture. The average number of labor hours required to build a ship declined 31 percent between 1942 and 1943. Year-over-year decline continued between 1943 and 1944, but at a much slower rate, 4 percent. Liberty ship production dropped from 1,238 in 1943 to 722 in 1944 (U.S. Bureau of Labor Statistics, 1945, pp. 1135–36). As the December 18, 1943, minutes of the WPB anticipated, shipyards' switch in 1944 to a less standardized range of ships reduced overall output per unit input in vessels produced for the Maritime Commission.

The same plateauing of productivity is evident in aircraft production in 1943. Ford's Willow Run plant produced a grand total of twenty-four or fifty-six aircraft in 1942 (depending on the source; see chapter 6), and these were primarily incomplete kits that had to be trucked to assembly plants operated by Douglas Aircraft and Consolidated Aircraft in Tulsa and Fort Worth.[35] By the end of 1943, Ford was finally succeeding in rolling out B-24s on a regular basis. They still needed to be sent to modification centers to be readied for combat, but at least they were flyable. The year-over-year increase in output per unit input between 1942 and 1943 was very great, mirroring trends in the aircraft sector as a whole. This can be appreciated by examining monthly data on pounds of airframe produced per worker, adjusted for subcontracting (this was the aircraft industry's preferred productivity metric). As figure 5.5 shows, the big acceleration took place between the start of 1943 and March 1944, after which the metric, aside from minor fluctuations, stopped increasing, even though the overall production of aircraft did not.

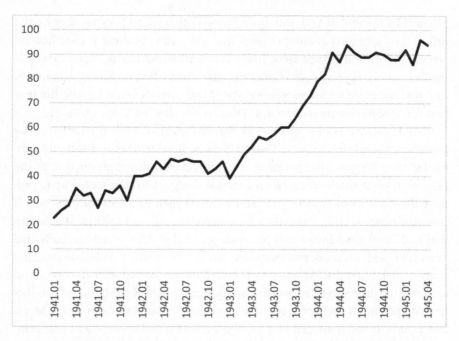

Figure 5.5. Pounds of airframe per worker, United States, January 1941–April 1945.
Note: data refer to airframes accepted for delivery, and labor input is adjusted to take
account of subcontracting. Source: Aircraft Industries Association of America, 1953,
table 2-15; based on BLS data.

By September 1944 Ford had produced its 6,000th bomber and was looking
forward to knocking out 650 a month. The B-24 could fly from bases in Britain or Italy to Germany and back, but now the need was for a longer-range
machine that could take the war to Japan. The B-29 could carry eight tons
of bombs 1,500 miles, drop them, and then return. The War Department cut
back the B-24 program, and in 1944 and on into 1945 spending on B-24s was
eclipsed by spending on the B-29, a plane that cost three times as much and
was plagued by production delays and disastrous crashes.

Many of the same dynamics evident in the checkered production history
of the B-24 persisted with the B-29. The demand for change orders slowed
production so much that General Hap Arnold pressed to freeze the design;
he hoped the plane could be used "in this war rather than the next." Data on
hours required per unit show the standard learning curve progress: a decline
from 157,000 for the first one hundred units to 78,000 for the next one hundred,
to 57,000 for the third one hundred, eventually plateauing at around 30,000

per unit by the end of 1944. But again, these data mislead because they do not reflect the enormous amount of work that still had to be done at modification centers before the planes were ready for combat. As late as April 1944, this involved an average of 61,000 hours per plane and often took longer than two months. An army air forces general stated the obvious when he said the process was "extremely uneconomical" (Vander Meulen, 1995, pp. 34–35, 45.

This trajectory is also evident in the evolution of tank production. The government built the massive Detroit Tank Arsenal in 1940 and 1941 and contracted with Chrysler to operate it. The army first ordered production of the M2, an obsolete machine based on a prewar design. Chrysler tooled up to produce the tank, its engineers puzzled by details such as volute springs, which they had never seen before—they were based on railroad springs of a design that had been abandoned two generations earlier. After machine tools had been designed, ordered, and installed, but before production had begun, the army realized that the M2 was poorly suited for warfare against Germany and canceled the order. Deferring to the military, members of the Office of Production Management had not scrutinized the plans handed to them by the army, and Knudsen had managed to get Chrysler, which had an excellent engineering department, to produce it. Janeway summed up the problem: "Vast new arsenals were committing precious machinery and materials and manpower and time to the production of ordnance that was farcically obsolete before it went on the drawing boards" (1951, p. 217).

After acknowledging its mistake, the army ordered Chrysler and others to build the M3 (Grant or Lee),[36] a modified M2 with better armament that had limited success against German Panzers in North Africa. A total of 6,258 M3s were manufactured between August 1941 and December 1942. As in the case of Ford's B-24 efforts, the 1942 record in mass-producing one of President Roosevelt's "must-have" items was disappointing.

While M3s were produced as an interim solution, the army worked with Chrysler to design a medium tank—the thirty-ton Sherman (M4), which proved to be a mass-production success. First built in February 1942, it quickly became the workhorse of the U.S. Army and was widely used by British and Soviet forces as well. The Sherman was reliable and cheap, and Chrysler and other contractors built more than 49,000 of them—almost eight times as many as the M3. More than half the output was in 1942 and 1943, the high point of production. The biggest year-over-year increase in productivity occurred between 1942 and 1943.

In 1944 overall tank production declined sharply, from 29,497 in 1943 to 17,565 (U.S. War Production Board, 1945a, p. 109), and the composition of reduced unit totals changed. Production of the heavier (forty-six-ton) Pershing began in November 1944 and continued into 1945. (The new model ended up playing little role in World War II combat.) The rate of change of productivity in making Shermans probably continued to improve but at a lower rate between 1943 and 1944, and the relative importance of M4s in the product mix declined, reflecting the gearing up for the heavier, more expensive Pershing (of which 2,202 were made) and the overall drop in tank production.

The *Second Report by the Director of War Mobilization and Reconversion* (April 1, 1945) detailed these changes and their productivity consequences: "Many items, such as the B-29 Superfortress and the General Pershing tank, have come into production to supplant requirements for B-24 Liberators and General Sherman tanks. The supplanted items were in volume production and schedules could be met with relative ease. Mass production of new items required retooling, retraining, and many changes in design before assembly lines could operate smoothly. We exchanged quantity for quality; we lost volume" (U.S. Office of War Mobilization and Reconversion, 1945b, p. 4).

Whether it involves annual model changeovers in peacetime automobile production or wartime production of ships, planes, or tanks, retooling in the American system for mass-producing metal-intensive durables always took a toll on productivity.

Consider one more poster child for the production miracle narrative: the Oerlikon 20-mm antiaircraft gun. Nelson devoted a whole chapter to Pontiac's role in the successful reengineering and mass production of this armament, originally of German-Swiss design and manufacture. Walton (1956, pp. 84–87) also featured its history in his narrative. By 1944, however, Oerlikon guns were being replaced by Bofors 40-mm guns, and 1944 production of all antiaircraft guns was declining. Both the change from 20-mm to 40-mm guns and the decline of antiaircraft guns in the output mix reduced the degree to which strong productivity performance in Oerlikon production could counteract the effects of other forces depressing productivity.

The contribution of the manufacture of any one military good to sectoral productivity growth depended on the rate of change of productivity within its manufacture and on any change in its relative importance in the output mix. In each of these instances, the effect of mass production on the growth of sectoral productivity between 1942 and 1943 was dissipated thereafter by a slowing of productivity gains and by declines in the relative importance of these goods. Production shifted to different and more complex ships, planes, tanks, and guns with which manufacturers, again, had less experience—or toward other types of goods entirely.

In the absence of known or agreed-upon military strategy, early production "for the shelf" was not a recipe for total disaster, since many military goods and much ordnance could be used in a variety of different environments and contexts. But there were limits to fungibility, and certain operations had very specific requirements. Following the meetings between Allied commanders in Cairo and Tehran in November 1943, military planners could finally look ahead with more clarity to the nature and order of subsequent campaigns. That clarity powerfully concentrated minds. Much of what was needed had been produced, in some cases much more than could ever be used. But important items were missing.

The most critical shortage was of landing craft. Once it became clear that every major military operation planned or under serious consideration would require amphibious assaults, a severe shortage of these boats became apparent. These included larger LSTs (Landing Ship, Tank) and LSIs (Landing Ship, Infantry) and smaller vessels, LCTs (Landing Craft, Tank) and LCIs (Landing Craft, Infantry). All these vessels had shallow drafts and a bow door that opened forward from the bottom, which allowed them to be driven onto a beach and then quickly disgorge troops or motorized equipment. LSTs for example, could carry about twenty tanks or other motorized vehicles or equipment. Such boats were essential for the Italian campaign, for the continued initiatives in the Pacific, for Anvil, the plan to invade southern France, largely with French troops the U.S. had been equipping in North Africa, and most important, for Overlord, the cross-Channel invasion. The shortage of landing craft imposed hard constraints on Allied military capabilities and led Roosevelt to insist that they be given priority in production above all else. In April 1944, in a letter to U.S. Army Chief of Staff George Marshall, Prime Minister Churchill lamented the situation in which the Allies found themselves: "How it is that the plans of two great empires like Britain and the United States should be so much hamstrung and limited by a hundred or two of these particular vessels will never be understood by history" (quoted in Matloff, 1959, p. 426).

Partly this was attributable to lack of interest from the navy, which assumed that operable ports would quickly be secured following initial assaults, which would allow men and material to be easily unloaded. The marines, anticipating island-hopping campaigns in the Pacific, had a more continuing interest

(Klein, 2013, p. 189). If the United States had been able to transform just one of the eight new battleships launched or scheduled for launch after Pearl Harbor into landing craft, it would have been a godsend. The great vulnerability of battleships to torpedoes and carrier-launched aircraft made their military utility questionable, whereas the landing craft were indispensable for what would be the greatest amphibious assault in history as well as operations in the Pacific and elsewhere. The country would eventually spend $5 billion on these ships—more than was spent on the Manhattan Project and the B-29 programs combined—in a procurement program that dwindled quickly after D-Day (Wilson, 2016, p. 153).

The improved clarity on battle plans meant cutbacks in items that had been overproduced, the replacement of ships, planes, and tanks by different models, and an increase in production of items, some technologically complex, some mundane, the demand for which could now more easily be foreseen. Total munitions production, measured in standard (1943) munitions dollars, including aircraft, ships, guns and fire control equipment, ammunition, combat and motor vehicles, communication and electronic equipment, and other equipment and supplies, peaked in the last quarter of 1943 but remained at high levels, declining only about 5 percent in real terms over the next year (U.S. War Production Board, 1945a, p. 105).[37]

As 1943 neared its end, huge numbers of American servicemen were still stationed in the United States. During that year sixteen army divisions left the country, five to the Pacific, five to North Africa, and six to Britain. Still, as of November, of the ninety then-authorized army divisions, just twenty-eight had been sent abroad (Matloff, 1959, p. 267). In the first eight months of 1944, more than twice as many divisions were committed overseas as in all of 1943. Between January and September 1944, a total of thirty-three divisions shipped out: eighteen to Great Britain, three to North Africa, one to Italy, and five to France (in September, after the Mediterranean landings in August, which were a follow-up to the Overlord landings in Normandy in June). Just six went to the Pacific. In October 1944 the country sent more soldiers to Europe than during any previous month (Matloff, 1959, pp. 551–52). By February 1945, following the German counterattack in December (the Battle of the Bulge), all U.S. combat divisions had been committed.

The worst fighting involving U.S. troops occurred after many Americans expected or had decided it was time for the war to be over. The military goods produced during 1944 differed in important respects from those manufactured in 1943 and earlier, and not just in the variety and complexity of the major capital goods. The heaviest ground fighting and most of the fatalities occurred in 1944 and 1945: servicemen needed ammunition, equipment, clothing, and supplies. Deliveries of clothing to the Army Service Forces peaked in 1942Q4 and then again in 1945Q2, but within the category, the composition changed. More than 97 percent of all the combat boots produced during the war were manufactured in 1944 and 1945. Similarly, in 1943, 253,000 wool sleeping bags were manufactured; 1944's production was 5,749,000. Field jacket production went from 275,000 to 7,470,000. On the other hand, manufacture of items issued to servicemen during basic training decreased.

Deliveries of weapons (not self-propelled) to the army peaked in 1943Q4. The production of most small arms declined, with the exception of pistols and revolvers. A very sharp decline in light and medium artillery production after 1943Q3 was partially compensated for by an increase in heavy artillery manufacture in 1944 and 1945. Heavy field artillery increased from 2,660 pieces to 3,384, along with comparable growth in production of replacement parts. For naval guns, production of five-inch and over increased while four-inch or below decreased.

Bazookas were a new antitank weapon, designed and introduced in 1942, and subsequently copied by the Germans and Japanese. Manufacture of bazooka rocket launchers more than doubled between 1943 and 1944, from 98,000 to 215,000, and flame throwers, used extensively in the island-hopping campaigns against dug-in Japanese in the Pacific, grew from 6,000 to 21,000.

Ammunition production, in spite of cutbacks in production targets resulting from resolution of the feasibility battles, increased dramatically between 1943 and 1944. Surging deliveries of artillery shells in the last two years of the war led to an overall peak in ammunition deliveries to the army in standard munition dollars in 1945Q1. Reflecting the rising intensity of combat in the last two years of the war, output of ground artillery shells almost doubled, from 799,850 to 1,447,016 short tons between 1943 and 1944. Mortar shells doubled, from 70,928 to 141,729 short tons. Grenade production rose from 24.981 to 40.654 million.

Production of aerial bombs (to be dropped by either army or navy planes) increased by a smaller percentage, from 1.548 to 1.953 million short tons. But the composition changed. These totals reflect an almost sevenfold increase in fragmentation bombs (from 67,000 to 453,000 short tons) and a more than doubling of incendiary bombs (from 176,000 to 407,000 short tons). The growth in the quantities and changes in composition of aerial bombs reflected the increased brutality of the latter stages of the war, particularly the targeting of civilian populations. Incendiary bombs were used by Allied forces in the firebombings of Hamburg, Dresden, Tokyo, and dozens of Japanese cities. The Hamburg raid probably killed 35,000 people. The attack on Dresden was immortalized in Kurt Vonnegut's novel *Slaughterhouse Five*. The raid on Tokyo on March 9–10, 1945, killed roughly 100,000 Japanese and destroyed sixteen square miles of the city.

Production of ammunition and rockets for naval guns soared from 277,300 to 524,058 short tons. Roughly 90,000 tons of the increase was for antiaircraft ammunition. Torpedo production increased from 15,599 to 24,015, and depth charge production grew about 15 percent, from 147,340 in 1943 to 169,652. These changes reflected an increase in offensive submarine operations in the Pacific and the growing success of antisubmarine warfare in the Atlantic.

In contrast, deliveries of small arms ammunition to the army peaked in 1943Q3 before falling off dramatically and never recovering. Annual production plummeted from 19.8 million in 1943 to 6.6 million rounds in 1944, presumably because of the availability of excess inventories at the end of 1943.

Reflecting increased activity in the Pacific, production of atabrine (antimalarial) tablets jumped from 1.3 to 2.2 million between 1943 and 1944. As penicillin production appeared for the first time in noticeable quantities, sulfa drug production fell more than 30 percent. Radio production fell slightly but expenditures on radar increased by more than 50 percent in dollar terms.

Total aircraft production peaked in 1944 at 96,318, up from 85,898 in 1943, but, as already noted, there were changes in the composition of output. These production numbers were buoyed by the ramping up of the long-range B-29 program and medium-range four-engine bombers (9,383 in 1943 and 14,884 in 1944). And fighter plane output grew dramatically: 23,988 to 38,873. The production of most other plane categories, as well as other military vehicles, however, declined after 1943. The drop-off in tank production (from 29,497 to 17,565 in 1944) was particularly pronounced. Truck production declined modestly, although within this category, production of heavy-heavy (over two-and-a-half-ton) vehicles increased (U.S. War Production Board, 1945a, pp. 107–9; Crawford and Cook, 1952, pp. 6–7).

These data reveal important changes in the composition of military output following the peak of munitions output in November 1943. More was cumulatively produced in 1944 than in 1943, but the output mix changed. These alterations resulted from final agreement on Allied military aims in Europe, which clarified equipment and ordnance requirements and the overseas deployment of multiple divisions still in the United States at the end of 1943. Experience in battle and changes in enemy tactics and equipment (the development of heavier tanks by the Germans, and kamikaze attacks by the Japanese beginning in October 1944) also fueled them. The last half of the war saw major disruptions in both the durable and nondurable military production mix, a factor that worked alongside worsening labor scarcity in depressing productivity levels.

After VE Day and especially after VJ Day, manufacturing productivity got pummeled again by the (reverse) product mix effects associated with demobilization. As the director of the Office of War Mobilization and Reconversion correctly forecast in a report dated August 15, 1945, after it became clear the war was over, "The sudden termination of the major portion of war contracts will cause an immediate and large dislocation of our economy" (U.S. Office of War Mobilization and Reconversion, 1945e, p. 1). Between 1944 and 1945 manufacturing TFP declined 9.2 percent.

Conclusion

U.S. economic mobilization for the Second World War was a production success. The country manufactured enough military goods to enable the United States and its allies to defeat their enemies. The achievement was not, however, the consequence of a productivity miracle. In the aggregate, output per unit of input in manufacturing declined throughout the conflict and by the end had almost completely erased the 1939–41 gains. Radical changes in the output mix forced some producers to fall by the wayside and many others to make products with which they were initially unfamiliar. Subsequent improvement in their abilities to do so only partially counterbalanced powerful forces depressing productivity. Shortages of materials and subassemblies, aggravated by producer hoarding, drove the priorities unemployment that was a signature feature of production during the first half of U.S. participation in the war. After 1943, severe labor shortage and a secondary product composition effect added to the mix. Throughout the war, these strains periodically caused productive capacity to remain idle, sometimes for extended periods.

Perhaps these disappointments in the productivity sphere were inevitable. We can consider and debate what might have been avoided. What we must not do is whitewash the historical and empirical record in a perhaps understandable desire to emphasize and reinforce the feel-good narratives engendered by Allied victory.

The Truman Committee, formally known as the Senate Special Committee to Investigate the National Defense Program, was established in 1941 to provide oversight of U.S. mobilization for war. During the committee's life, it conducted a series of noteworthy investigations; its role in critiquing the operation of the Office of Production Management and in exploring conditions at Ford's Willow Run plant has already been mentioned. By all accounts it did an impressive job, and its tenure was marked by a notable absence of scandal. It was the vehicle that catapulted its leader into the vice presidency and ultimately the presidency.

Its *Third Annual Report* reflected on both the accomplishments and the failures of the committee from the vantage point of March 1944. The last sentence of its last paragraph emphasized an enduring truth about a conflict that consumed so much of the country's (and the world's) blood and treasure: "This committee has noted many decisions that were hastily and sometimes foolishly made, and many mistakes that were continued long after they should have been rectified. . . . No task of such magnitude can ever be accomplished at such speed without enormous waste. War is waste—waste of manpower and of material" (U.S. Congress, Senate, 1944, p. 4).

That is the nature of the enterprise. There is little reason in the aggregate to expect such an effort to enhance efficiency in the short or long run. In spite of increased government ownership of the means of production, expanded presidential and federal government power, and a rudimentary planning apparatus, the U.S. economy during the war never came close in its institutional features to those of the country's Soviet ally. Contrary to what some of his enemies suggested, and notwithstanding the First and Second War Powers Acts, Roosevelt was not a dictator. But the characteristics and pathologies of the wartime U.S. economy—the coexistence of often superb engineering with shortages, hoarding, and a poor productivity record—are indeed reminiscent of some of the distinctive features of former Eastern bloc command economies (Kornai, 1980).

6 · Bright Shiny Objects

Learning by Doing and Postwar Potential Output

Much of what economists believe is known about the supply-side effects of U.S. mobilization for the Second World War derives from two famous papers published in the 1960s (Arrow, 1962; Alchian, 1963). The foundation for each was empirical evidence underlying the learning curve: data showing that, in mass production, the number of labor hours required to complete the assembly of metals-intensive wartime ordnance, especially aircraft and ships, declined systematically as a function of the number of units previously completed. Unit labor requirements in building Liberty and Victory ships, tankers, and destroyer escorts, for example, fell 16–22 percent with each doubling of completed output. In negotiating contracts, army estimators assumed, as a rule of thumb, that, after an initial few hundred units of a new product, direct labor requirements would decline by one-fifth every time the number of completed units doubled (U.S. Bureau of Labor Statistics, 1945, p. 1132; Hyde, 2013, p. 79; Wright, 1936).

Airframe data, buttressed by widely publicized information on the reduction over time in the number of days required to assemble a Liberty ship, were then generalized into more encompassing propositions about the effects of war mobilization on productivity, both during the war and after. The most dramatic and well-known stories apply to the largest categories of wartime military spending: aircraft and ships. The narratives and the conclusions drawn from them have influenced and undergirded conventional interpretations of the effects of World War II on economic potential.

These narratives raise two important questions. First, how do we square them with the chapter 2 data on the wartime productivity record in manufacturing? Second, even if positive learning effects were insufficient to counterbalance the negative influences associated with the wartime product mix and raw material shocks, what of their legacy for the postwar period? This chapter focuses on both questions and their interrelation.

Learning by doing is central to the claim that World War II production experience had persisting positive effects on aggregate supply. References almost always begin with the Liberty ships and go on to cite examples of the inverse relationship between cumulated output and unit labor requirements for B-24s, C-47s, or Oerlikon antiaircraft guns.[1] To the extent these oft-reported gains were real (some require qualification), they were, nonetheless, associated with striking declines in overall manufacturing productivity during the war. This chapter explores why this was so and also why that experience did little to boost either military or civilian capability after the war. The main explanation for the limited postwar impact is that the manufacture of most of the products in question ceased even before the end of the conflict or, if not, soon after. In contrast with what was true during the war, postwar military hardware had limited production runs and much higher costs per unit. And learning to produce a sequence of military durables had an important opportunity cost: it disrupted advance in the manufacture of metals-intensive consumer durables.

Although some of the narratives lose their luster when examined closely, they are, by and large, not fake news. They can be likened, however, to shiny objects, and, like all such objects, they distract, making it more difficult for us to see the larger picture.

Aircraft

Well-funded efforts at persuasion—advertising and other activities—have shaped narratives regarding U.S. aircraft production during the war, and these have exercised a persisting influence on treatments of the economic effects of mobilization. This is most evident in the case of Ford, the fourth-largest military contractor during the war. Thanks to an active and effective public relations apparatus, Ford was, in the eyes of the public, number one in terms of contribution to the overall war effort. (General Motors was in fact the leading contractor, by a sizable margin.) Much of this misimpression was attributable to the massive Willow Run plant—when first completed, the largest manufacturing plant in the world. The plant had a mesmerizing effect on almost all who saw it. During most of the interval between groundbreaking in April 1941 and the end of the war, press coverage of the facility was overwhelmingly positive. The exception was a yearlong hiatus running roughly from August 1942 through July 1943, during which more critical coverage broke through.

Government planners originally intended Ford's factory to produce parts for Consolidated Aircraft's plant in Fort Worth and the Douglas plant in Tulsa, both of which opened in 1941. But Henry Ford persisted in pursuing his vision of an entirely integrated operation—what he had come close to achieving in car production. The idea was that the plant would both manufacture parts and components from materials like aluminum sheet, and also assemble them into complete aircraft. Although Willow Run's initial output was indeed parts for other plants, Ford overcame War Department resistance, and the facility set out to assemble aircraft that could fly directly away from the Willow Run airfield. In order to achieve an approximation of what he desired, Ford's vision had eventually to be compromised in two important ways.

First, though the planes that eventually rolled off the assembly line were *flyable*, they were not *combat-ready* and had first to be sent to modification centers, to make the changes necessitated by what the army air forces had learned operating them in a theater of war. Thus, it is not quite right to say that the flyaway planes were *complete*. As the planes returned from bombing runs (or did not), much was learned about their vulnerabilities, and the military ordered alterations. This was not what Ford had in mind, and the company pushed back against the steady stream of change orders and finally refused to accommodate more of them. To resolve an impasse that threatened an already poor production record, the War Production Board allowed Ford to freeze the design for lengthy intervals. As planes rolled out of the facility, they were flown immediately to modification centers (eventually twenty of them), run initially by commercial aviation contractors, ultimately by army air forces personnel. Newly installed equipment was ripped out and replaced, and other changes made, some that customized the aircraft for its intended theater of operations (Walton, 1956, p. 249; Klein, 2013, p. 532), but many because mass manufacture as Ford had envisioned it was simply not compatible with the frequency of change requests desired by the military.[2]

In peacetime, car companies tooled up for a year's production and made no significant alterations until retooling during the annual model change the following year. As far as military durables were concerned, one could get away with freezing the design of a jeep or an M1 rifle for the duration of the conflict. But not a B-24 or other large, complex durables, which the army considered works in progress as feedback arrived from combat experience. Huge backlogs developed at the modification centers, which had extensive work to perform, so actual delivery to the military services often lagged far behind the figures on factory output (Milward, 1977, p. 192).

The conflict created by Ford's resistance to change orders was the partial consequence of the company's insistence, against much contrary advice, on using hard steel dies. These worked well on steel automobile parts and lasted longer and meant cheaper costs at high volume. But they often deformed the softer aluminum metal that made up most of an airplane and were difficult and expensive to modify. The compromise was part of what allowed the apparently high rates of throughput achieved in 1944 and 1945. The B-24 design was frozen for long periods so that Ford could reap the economies from stamping out identical parts from the dies. But the economies were in a sense illusory since whole sections of the planes had to be deconstructed and rebuilt at the modification centers.

Aside from the agreement on freezing design, production at Willow Run really began to accelerate only when, under government pressure in the first months of 1943, the company gave up on its aspirations to build complete planes and began allowing up to a third of components and parts production to be subcontracted to other plants in the Detroit area. Ford could claim that the company produced complete planes at Willow Run. But that misled, both because only part of the value was added at the plant, and because the flyaway planes required modification before they could actually be used by the military. Ford was both stubborn and grandiose in his aspirations. He had promised in 1940 to build one thousand planes a day, an unreasonable prospect and an accomplishment he never came close to realizing. But during 1941 and the first eight months of 1942, the awe and veneration inspired by Ford himself and the company he had built resulted in enormous and highly positive attention to the Willow Run plant and inflated expectations about what it could and would do. *Business Week* opined that "the nation had come to expect production miracles from Ford as routine" (Lewis, 1976, p. 348).

The plant began limited parts production in November 1941. But through early 1943, the factory was in chaos, as custom-built, special-purpose machine tools arrived and Ford managers tried to set up an aircraft assembly line that could produce planes the way Detroit built cars. Charles Lindbergh, hired as a consultant by Ford in March 1942, confided to his diary, after being told that the first bombers would be produced in May, that "it would be little short of a miracle if the actual production of four-engine bombers is under way in April" (quoted in Baime, 2014, p. 152). The problems in the plant were overlooked or ignored by the American press, which lavished superlatives on the enterprise.

Some of the frequently used adjectives and descriptors: "the greatest," "largest," "most enormous," "marvelous," "amazing," a "U.S. miracle," "Henry Ford's miracle," "one of the wonders of the world," "one of the seven wonders of the world," "the greatest show on earth," "the damndest colossus the world had ever seen"—the last from the conservative journalist and Roosevelt antagonist Westbrook Pegler (see Lewis, 1976, p. 349).

Prophecies of the time schedule and quantity dimensions of bomber production at Willow Run were equally glorious. Fully assembled bombers would be rolling off the assembly line "before June 1," "shortly," "soon," "this spring," "next month," "in a few months," or "early in the summer." A radio broadcast to Manila Bay, obviously intended to buck up the spirits of U.S. and Filipino servicemen fighting the Japanese, was thinly disguised propaganda, reporting that Ford was already manufacturing "astronomical" numbers of aircraft (Lewis, 1976, p. 349).

Other reports allowed that while Ford might not yet be making flyable aircraft, once it began doing so, production would be "unprecedented," "unbelievable," "one every two hours," "one per hour," "two per hour," "dozens daily," "en masse," "one every few minutes." The *New York Herald Tribune* stated that annual production at the plant would be "tens of thousands, and eventually, if required . . . hundreds of thousands." Scripps-Howard newspapers were equally over the top: production "could easily add up to more bombers of this type in a year than there are now in the whole world" (Lewis, 1976, p. 349–50).

The War Department's Bureau of Public Relations added fuel to Ford's PR fire by announcing falsely on May 14, 1942, that Willow Run had begun "the actual production of bombers." Newspaper after newspaper hailed this "industrial miracle." A discordant voice was that of J. H. Kindelberger, CEO of North American Aviation, a critic of encouraging the automobile industry to enter the aviation industry. Kindelberger stated that Detroit "had not delivered a single aircraft part in 16 months." Aside from coverage in the *Ann Arbor News*, critical analysis was drowned out in a flood of hosannas (Lewis, 1976, pp. 354–55).

The truth was that Lindbergh's fears had been fully justified. In May 1942 no flyable aircraft had come off the Willow Run assembly line. One hand-built plane had been put together for "educational purposes," using parts mostly shipped from Consolidated's San Diego plant. Assembly of "Bomber Ship 1" was actually done not at Willow Run but twenty miles away at the old Dearborn airport, and then flown to Willow Run for display. This was what underlay the War Department's May press release. The *Ann Arbor News* was gentle when it referred to that announcement as "deliberately misleading."

In February 1942 Ford had promised two planes by May. It delivered neither. The first commitment was for a set of parts that could be shipped to
the Douglas plant in Tulsa for assembly. Ford failed to meet this deadline,
and the Douglas facility had to shift to other work. The first such kit was not
trucked into Tulsa until July; by October Ford had delivered just four. The
second promise was for a "flyaway" plane, but the plane displayed in May, as
noted, was a sham. The first flyaway actually assembled at Willow Run was
completed on September 10, 1942, and accepted by the army on September 30.
After flying one of these planes, Lindbergh described it as "the worst piece of
aircraft construction I have ever seen. . . . Rivets missing, rivets badly put in,
rivet holes started and forgotten, whole lines of rivets left entirely out, wrong
sized rivets, lopsided rivets, badly formed skin, corner cuts improperly made,
cracks already started, soft metal used where hard metal is essential, control
holes left out, pilot's escape hatch badly constructed" (Baime, 2014, p. 176).

Ford's public relations bonanza was temporarily derailed in August 1942
with the publication of a critical article in *Life* magazine, which was widely
cited in other publications, and additional caustic commentary from Kindelberger, who with some justification lambasted the aircraft displayed in May
as a public relations stunt, shipped to the plant "for the benefit of photogra-
phers." Charles Sorensen, the industrial engineer responsible for the plant's
design, pushed back with bravado, promising to name the first completed B-24
bomber as it rolled off the line the Kindelberger.

Following an inspection of the facility in October 1942, Roosevelt happened
to remark to reporters that the Willow Run plant was not yet in production.
When asked by reporters why his remark had been censored, and thus blocked
from transmission to Britain, the president could offer no explanation. He
"supposed that everybody in Detroit knew the same thing he did about the
plant" (*New York Times*, October 16, 1942, p. 28). On December 5, 1942, the *Times*
reported cryptically that B-24Es were "being delivered" to the army from Willow Run.

On January 30, 1943, the WPB released a statement acknowledging that
"there have been many disappointments in connection with the Willow Run
operation and the plant, even now, is far from peak production" (*New York
Times*, January 31, 1943, p. 17). On February 13, 1943, the War Department's
Office of War Information felt it necessary to issue a statement about low
production in the plant "because of widespread conflicting stories reporting the output all the way from ridiculously small to fantastically large numbers." The report implicitly acknowledged the slow ramp-up of production

and suggested several explanations. These included materials shortages and difficulties in hiring and retaining labor. It also acknowledged that Ford's insistence on using hard steel dies both delayed initial production and made it much harder to make changes in design as information from the field flowed in. "It is much more difficult and time consuming to make changes under Willow Run's tooling methods than under those of other aircraft plants," and "There is no question that production could have been started at Willow Run many months sooner had more conventional methods of tooling been followed" (*New York Times*, February 14, 1943, p. 25; *Washington Post*, February 14, 1943, p. 1).

On February 15, 1943, Truman announced that there would be a full-scale investigation of Willow Run, along with the Curtiss-Wright plant in Columbus, Ohio, stating, "There has been so little production at either plant as to amount to virtually none" (*Washington Post*, February 16, 1943, p. 5). A March 14, 1943, story reported that the Truman Committee was pressing the Willow Run plant, which had delivered only a "handful of planes in 1942," to increase its output "or else" other management would be brought in (*New York Times*, March 14, 1943, p. 18). It was in this context that the company surrendered much of its vision, allowing the facility to become primarily an assembly plant, reliant on subcontracts with other facilities for many parts and components. This retreat was one reason employment in the plant peaked at 42,000, and never came close to the 100,000 originally anticipated (Mawdsley, 2020, p. 313).

On July 10, 1943, following visits to the plant and testimony in Washington, the Truman Committee released its report on Willow Run. It acknowledged that the plant had made "great progress" and that substantial numbers of aircraft were by then being completed, although it faulted the facility for, among other things, trying to use an assembly line modeled on car production to build planes, which was "probably a mistake." There were many other serious mistakes associated with Willow Run: its location, thirty miles from downtown Detroit, which required a long commute for many workers; housing conditions, and Ford's opposition to attempts to improve them; the insistence on using hard steel dies, which were cheaper for volume production but expensive if changes were needed; the insistence, as a consequence, that change orders be limited, necessitating the use of the modification centers; Ford's demand that the plant produce entire aircraft, which was stubbornly adhered to as an objective until February 1943.

Ford used hard steel dies for his tooling, despite repeated warnings that the need for change orders would suggest using softer dies, which, though less durable, could be more easily and cheaply replaced. He also insisted on building the factory—the largest in the world, in an L shape, with expensive turntables to rotate assemblies. To have built in a straight line would have pushed the revenue-generating plant out of Washtenaw into Wayne County, controlled by liberal Democrats, whom Ford detested (Baime, 2014, pp. 101, 172). Labor relations were anything but harmonious. Ford anticipated employing almost 100,000 (although peak employment was much less) but would not allow war housing to be built near the factory, lest Washtenaw County voter rolls be diluted by an influx of pro-union Democrats. Average commutes for half the workers who could not find local housing were forty to seventy miles round trip a day at a time when gasoline, tires, and cars were in very short supply. Labor turnover and absenteeism were extraordinarily high, even by wartime standards (see also O'Neill, 1993, pp. 218–21).

Care must be exercised in interpreting Willow Run production statistics because the facility produced both flyaway planes and parts kits that were assembled elsewhere, because flyaway planes were not in fact complete, since they had to go to modification centers, and because planes delivered after February 1943 included an increasing volume of parts and components whose production had been subcontracted to other plants in the Detroit area. As for 1942, there is lack of agreement about the actual number of aircraft Ford produced. The Aviation Industries Association of America credited the company with 24 of the 47,386 produced in the country that year: .05 percent, although .2 percent by airframe weight (Aircraft Industries Association of America, 1953, tables 2-13 and 2-14). Lewis states that there was "net" production of 56 planes in 1942 (Lewis, 1976, p. 357). My guess is that the discrepancy reflects different allowances for or treatments of parts shipped for assembly to plants run by other companies in Oklahoma and Texas. Whichever number one prefers, it is a disappointing performance given the hundreds of millions of federal dollars invested in the Willow Run plant and equipment and the tens of thousands by then employed.

Production began to accelerate in 1943: 31 in January, 75 in February, 148 in April, 190 in June. Even as late as September 1943, however, frustrated with the slow pace of delivery, the Army Air Forces Material Command proposed taking over the management of the facility from Ford (Hyde, 2013, p. 101).

Only in the last months of 1943 did the facility begin to approach fulfillment of its promise. On November 20, 1943, Ford for the first time received permission from the War Department to release production statistics for the plant and announced that over 1,000 B-24s had been delivered, not counting knockdown sets trucked for assembly elsewhere (*New York Times*, November 21, 1943, p. 45). On March 26, 1944, Ford announced that a total of 2,000 flyway bombers had been completed at Willow Run (plus another 1,000 knockdown kits) (*Washington Post*, March 27, 1944, p. 11). As Ford production finally accelerated, overall output of aircraft in the country peaked and began to decline. March 1944 was the all-time monthly peak for the nation: 9,113 aircraft produced by U.S. manufacturers and accepted by the military (Aircraft Industries Association of America, 1955, p. 17).

By the beginning of July 1944, Ford recorded that a total of 5,000 bombers had been produced, although this did not distinguish between knockdown kits and flyaways (*Washington Post*, July 8, 1944, p. 5). In September 1944 Ford produced its 6,000th bomber, at which point the army cut back B-24 orders in favor of the B-29, and the rate of production slowed. On April 17, 1945, the U.S. Army Air Forces announced that production of the B-24 would cease by August. It reported that 8,000 bombers had been produced to that date and indicated that the reductions would affect 21,731 workers at Willow Run, and more than 9,000 additional workers at Ford plants in the Detroit area (*Washington Post*, April 18, 1945, p. 4). Those employment numbers reveal the extent to which parts and components construction had been subcontracted to other Ford facilities and subcontractors.

After freezing the design and yielding to subcontracting for parts and components, Willow Run assembled aircraft in quantity, and by the time production was terminated in August 1945, it credited itself with 6,972 flyaways, along with another 1,893 kits to be assembled elsewhere, for a total of 8,865 (Klein, 2013, pp. 531, 675). But it took more than two and half years after groundbreaking before the plant came close to producing at scale. On October 25, 1943, the War Production Board announced a plan to improve efficiency in airplane plants by focusing on the productivity laggards in the industry. In motivating the initiative, it cited the huge improvement over the previous year in output per worker hour at Willow Run: "Willow Run is now using its manpower about 40 times more efficiently than a year ago" (*Washington Post*, October 26, 1943, p. 2). A large multiple, however, is not difficult to achieve if one starts from a level close to zero.

By the fall of 1943, when it finally did appear that the corner had been turned on volume production, the press coverage reverted to 1942-level paeans to the magnificence of what Ford had accomplished. In April 1944, the plant announced it had reached a production rate of one bomber an hour. This was hailed as "the war production miracle that has been wrought in Detroit," "a symbol of American ingenuity," "a product of inventive genius," "one of the world's great monuments of productive genius," "a production miracle," "the miracle production of the war," "Willow Run has to be seen to be believed" (Lewis, 1976, p. 361).

The plant eventually assembled thousands of aircraft and built parts for other plants. It was able to do so as the result of huge expenditures on what was when completed the world's largest manufacturing plant, a myriad of special-purchase machine tools, and hundreds of thousands of labor hours. For a two-year period, the production and productivity record was abysmal. Willow Run's eventual achievements can be ascribed to a productivity miracle only if one compares performance in 1944 and 1945 with the production and productivity levels experienced through the first months of 1943. At the national level, once production shifted to the B-29, the largest single weapon system in the war by cost, sector productivity levels were again adversely affected by a program on the early segments of its learning curve.

Willow Run proved that it was possible to mass-produce four-engine bombers using manufacturing methods that bore some resemblance to those used to make cars and refrigerators. What learning took place, however, had little relevance for the postwar period because it was almost entirely specific to the product (as was the tooling) and because the country never again mass-produced aircraft in these quantities. And it came at the cost of suspending improvements in the production of consumer durables.

Contributions of Wartime Learning in Aircraft Production to Technological Advance

Learning by doing as a contributor to declining production cost at the product level would seem an attractive explanation for rises in manufacturing TFP. But as the data in chapter 2 reveal, the level of sectoral TFP declined between 1941 and 1948, and even more sharply between 1941 and 1942, 1943, 1944, or 1945. To understand why, we must identify where the technological progress is claimed to have been most concentrated and consider why it might not have benefited sectoral productivity in the war years and the postwar period.

The most frequently cited examples of such success involve stories of the declining unit cost of ships, planes, tanks, and other ordnance. The "miraculous" effects of learning by doing during the war are well known to economists, largely as the result of Kenneth Arrow's 1962 article in the *Review of Economic Studies* and Armen Alchian's 1963 article in *Econometrica*. Citing work by

Wright, Verdoorn, and Lundberg, Arrow noted that it was well established that the number of labor hours required to complete an airframe dropped predictably with the number of previously completed airframes, and that the Horndal ironworks in Sweden had experienced a 2 percent annual increase in labor productivity over a fifteen-year period in the absence of any new physical investment. He then explored the theoretical implications of these observations.[3] Alchian also took the effects of learning by doing as well established and explored how reliable were statistically estimated learning parameters in airframe production in predicting the decline in labor requirements per pound of aircraft (the inverse of physical productivity) as a function of cumulated output (he found that there was considerable variability across models).

Aircraft production (airframes and engines) absorbed one-quarter of all wartime spending on munitions ($45 billion) (Koistinen, 2004, p. 38). Learning by doing might have generated three types of advance that could have contributed to a residual measuring "technological" progress in manufacturing between 1941 and 1948 and on into the postwar period: (1) gains in producing a particular type or model of aircraft; (2) broader gains in the understanding of how to produce large quantities of aircraft within a very short time frame; and (3) gains that might have applied to manufacturing more generally.

The war was undoubtedly associated with advances in many military technologies, including the beginnings of the move from piston-driven to jet aircraft, the supplanting of the battleship by the aircraft carrier, the development of rocketry, and the atomic bomb. Nuclear power, of course, did have civilian applications, but its benefits in the postwar economy were mixed and, given the prewar state of scientific and technical knowledge, it would have arrived eventually, and probably sooner rather than later, with or without the war. It took Enrico Fermi and his colleagues at the University of Chicago less than a year following Pearl Harbor to produce the world's first controlled nuclear chain reaction.

On the basis of the English experience, Davies and Stammers suggest that advances in gas turbine technology may have been an area in which the war genuinely advanced a useful postwar technology (1975, p. 515). But production experience building piston-driven aircraft can have had little to do with this. Moreover, we can only speculate about the counterfactual. It is possible that jet engines would have arrived as quickly in the absence of the conflict. Aircraft and aircraft engine design was advancing rapidly during the 1930s, contributing to a very rapid rate of obsolescence. By 1938 U.S. commercial aviation already transported more than 1 million passengers a year, a carriage that had increased more than twenty-fold over the previous decade (Holley, 1964, pp. 11–12).

The B-29 was the single most expensive weapons system in the Second World War (more than $3 billion as compared with $2 billion for the Manhattan Project). It was entirely pressurized and boasted a state-of-the-art fire-control system, and its design advanced monocoque technique—the external skin of the plane contributed to its structural integrity. But that concept went back decades—and the last generation of bombers with propellers most likely would have had it with or without the war. And, as was true for every other aircraft discussed below, design work had been completed before Pearl Harbor, and the first orders placed in May 1941 (Herman, 2012, pp. 293–96). Although the B-29's advanced airframe design was reflected in postwar planes, including parts of the Boeing 747, it is hard to credit this influence to design or production experience gained during the war itself.

With the exception of approximately 14,000 gliders, all of the 276,000 military aircraft produced between 1942 and 1945 were piston driven. A 1971 Smithsonian Institution study documents that most of the technical improvements in such engines predated 1940 (Taylor, 1971; see especially p. 84, fig. 71). That is in part because development work shifted to jet engines, but it is also illustrative of the fact that the production of hundreds of thousands of aircraft engines under wartime conditions did not magically lead to major improvements in their performance or reliability. That said, the army air forces' combat experience generated a steady stream of change orders, and incremental improvement meant that piston-driven aircraft produced later in the war differed significantly from those produced earlier.

The United States produced approximately 276,000 aircraft between 1942 and 1945, and over 300,000 between 1940 and 1945, and over those years, the U.S. military took delivery of more than 800,000 aircraft engines (Klein, 2013, p. 505). Productivity gains in category 1 were large.[4] Wartime exigency, however, forced a dramatic change in output mix. One would expect productivity measures for the goods newly produced in quantity to have experienced gains, but from initial low levels. Consider Detroit's shift from making cars, where there was significant cumulative experience, to building airplanes and tanks, where there was little, or the Frigidaire plant in Dayton, Ohio, which transitioned from making refrigerators to assembling 50-caliber machine guns and airplane propellers (General Motors Corporation, n.d.). Or consider the tens of firms manufacturing fractional-horsepower electric motors. Before the war, 90 percent went into household appliances (washing machines, kitchen mixers, vacuum cleaners). During the war, a similar fraction went into mechanized weapons (more than three hundred in a B-29 alone). Motors produced for these military applications had to be smaller, lighter, more rugged, and run on direct rather than alternating current. Making them required major changes in design and tooling and the learning of new skills by workers (U.S. War Production Board, 1945a, pp. 103–4). Outputs produced during the war were not just different, they were often more complex and typically involved many more individual parts. A 1941 Ford automobile required approximately 15,000 parts, a B-24 bomber, in contrast, about 1,225,000 (Ford Motor Company, 1945).

If the sharp decline in sectoral productivity during the war seems puzzling, it is because we are distracted by the reductions from high initial levels in the unit costs of producing the new goods. As Kuznets noted in 1945, "There is no inconsistency in assuming a rapid rise in the relative efficiency of resource use in munitions and war construction and a low level compared with the efficiency" in those industries in the prewar period (1945, p. 51).[5] The data are dominated by the negative compositional effect resulting from the forced shift into the production of goods in which manufacturers had relatively little experience.

Corporations like Ford, GM, and Chrysler eventually succeeded in manufacturing military goods in quantity using an approach successfully exploited to make cars and refrigerators in the 1930s. The American system of mass production featured custom-designed, special-purpose machine tools fabricating interchangeable parts that were then assembled along a moving line (Evans, 1947, p. 217). But in no case was the transition easy. Postwar demand for the new products was highly uncertain and most likely to be low. To produce goods in which they had little experience, private corporations demanded tax subsidies in the form of accelerated amortization (before Pearl Harbor), and, after full-scale mobilization began in 1942, they insisted that the government provide (and own) the physical capital.

Operating contracts were typically cost plus a fixed fee (CPFF). As Secretary of State Henry Stimson commented early in the process, "If you are going to try to go to war or to prepare for war in a capitalist economy, you've got to let business make money out of the process or business won't work" (quoted in Gropman, 1996, p. 5). Flat-price contracts with competitive bidding, the norm during the interwar period, gave firms an incentive to economize on resources, thus targeting efficiency and putting a premium on improved productivity. Cost plus a percentage of cost, the prevailing contract in World War I, gave firms an incentive to waste resources. Cost plus a fixed fee (the

World War II norm) did not provide the same egregious incentives to waste inputs. Neither, however, did such contracts provide incentives to economize on them.[6]

In a CPFF contract, let us say for a certain number of aircraft and spare parts, the government and the contractor would agree on an estimated unit cost and, depending on the number of units, total contractor costs. These costs, which would include purchased materials and assemblies, engineer and production worker salaries and wages, and depreciation on any company-owned plant and equipment used in the process, were reimbursable. The contractor's fee was then calculated as 6 percent of this total (Vander Meulen, 1995, p. 17). The fee was considered by the company to be profit (return on capital), but since the factory building and much or even most of the equipment was provided by the government, it was really a management fee. The fee would not rise if costs exceeded those estimates. If costs declined over time as determined by government auditors, however, reimbursements based on the original cost estimate would be clawed back through a process of renegotiation. But the fee remained fixed. A particularly rapid decline in costs was one factor that might reduce the size of the negotiated clawback, offering the contractor a slight additional benefit.[7] But overall, as a Government Service Administration website providing guidance to procurement officers stated in 2021, CPFF "provides the contractor only a minimum incentive to control costs" (U.S. Government Service Administration, 2021).

Lawrence Bell, CEO of Bell Aircraft, explained the consequence of CPFF:

I don't like it, but for a rush job, it's the only thing. Of course it contributes to waste. For maximum economy, go flat price. If you want maximum output, you have to go fixed fee. The volume of our business is more than a hundred times the capital invested. On flat price, it would take a small error to wipe us out. The whole staff would be frightened of going broke, and production would be secondary.

On the flat price I'd want to do a smaller business and watch it to the last detail. In this way [fixed fee] every official can give his whole attention to the volume of the product. Net result—the unit cost may be less in the long run because you divided it between bigger output. (Quoted in Lingeman, 1970, pp. 110–11)

The last line reflects a theme the learning narratives tried to amplify: that reduction of costs through volume could (somehow, ultimately, perhaps) make up for the profligacy in the use of plant, equipment, labor, and materials (the "it" in the last sentence of the quote). As firms scrambled to generate the output on which they would earn their fee, they hoarded materials, machine tools, plant capacity, and ultimately labor because they did not want the absence of any required input to cause deliveries of output to slow or come to a halt. But what one firm had, another did not. The face of waste was not just profligacy in raw material use, but the resulting temporary idleness or underutilized service flows from physical capital and labor that were a signature feature of a shortage economy. Bell starts by acknowledging that the contract form contributed to waste, the enemy of efficiency and high productivity. The organizers of wartime production willingly traded off the latter in hopes this would enable high volume, delivered quickly.

In writing about Henry Kaiser and the production of the Liberty ships, Eliot Janeway described similar trade-offs, in this case involving quality as well:

> It was unbelievably extravagant at cost plus—but it paid for itself in time saved and security won. . . . Kaiser hired the people, bought the materials, and sent the Government the bill. Everyone who read the newspapers knew what his results were, and only a few Government comptrollers knew what his costs were. They philosophized that the men who got results are invariably men who break rules, and they hoped that come "I-Day"—Investigation Day—Congress would agree that the results *at the time* were worth the price.
>
> By normal standards of value, the product was not worth the price. . . . Kaiser bought time at the expense of durability. But this was realistic. All through 1942 and 1943 the chances were that every Kaiser ship launched would be sunk before it could be repaired. (Janeway, 1951, p. 251)

Landon-Lane and Rockoff (2013) describe the generous terms on which the government invited private corporations to build war goods as creating an environment akin to that of the California gold rush. This is attributable largely to the switch from fixed cost awarded through competitive bidding to CPFF. Businesses earned profits, understood as a return to capital, even when they risked none or little of their own (Gordon, 1970, p. 942; Higgs, 1993). Milward estimates that pretax industrial profits rose 350 percent during the war (120 percent after taxation), as opposed to considerably smaller percentage gains for labor (Milward, 1977, p. 67). Such arrangements may have been necessary to get military goods out the door quickly, but, in contrast with competitive bidding or fixed price contracts, they did not prioritize efficiency (U.S. Bureau of the Budget, 1946, p. 140). Efficiency in the production of some items improved with experience, but this did not mean the sector as a whole enjoyed rising productivity during the war.

The Postwar Legacy of Manufacture for the Military

From the standpoint of longer-run questions about economic growth, we need to ask why manufacturing TFP was lower after demobilization in 1948 than it had been in 1941, and why it grew more slowly thereafter than had been true during the interwar period. To answer, we must consider in more detail how much relevance wartime learning had for manufacturing—either civilian or military—after the war. We can begin by examining the production history of aircraft, the largest category of World War II military spending in the United States.

Wikipedia has compiled a list of most-produced aircraft, enumerating those with total production runs greater than 5,000 (Wikipedia, 2021a, 2021b). Twenty-one World War II aircraft in the United States meet this criterion: five bombers (two heavy, two medium, one light), eight fighters, three dive or torpedo bombers, three trainers, a transport aircraft, and a glider. These are described below, with production totals in parentheses, along with information on the year in which production ceased.

Increasing the production of heavy bombers was the centerpiece of Roosevelt's mobilization strategy. On May 4, 1941, roughly a year after he had announced a goal of producing 50,000 military and naval planes, he wrote that "the effective defense of the country and the vital defense of other democratic countries required" this (Baime, 2014, p. 73). The two heavy bombers were the Boeing B-17 Flying Fortress (12,731) and the Consolidated B-24 Liberator (18,482).[8] The two medium bombers were the North American Mitchell B-25 (9,984) and the Martin B-26 Marauder (5,288). The light bomber or intruder aircraft was the Douglas DB7 (A-20 Havoc) (7,478). Production of all of these aircraft ceased in 1945, with the exception of the Douglas, for which production ceased in 1944. Each of these aircraft had been fully designed, tested, and flown before Pearl Harbor (Wilson, 2016, p. 58).[9] These bomber production runs exceeded by two orders of magnitude those common in the postwar period.[10]

A similar pattern is evident in the fighter category: very high production runs that ended in 1945 or shortly thereafter. Eight World War II fighters had production runs of more than 5,000: the Grumman F4F Wildcat (7,885), the Curtiss P-40 Warhawk (13,738), the Chance Vought F4U Corsair (12,571), the Grumman F6F Hellcat (12,275), the Lockheed P-38 Lightning (10,037), the Republic

P-47 Thunderbolt (15,660), the North American P-51 Mustang (15,586), and the Bell P-39 Airacobra (9,584). Production of all these aircraft had ceased by the end of 1945, with the exception of the Mustang and the Corsair, which remained in production until 1951 and 1952, respectively. All these aircraft had been designed before the war. With the exception of the P-47, F4U, and F6F, all had flown before Pearl Harbor.

And the same pattern is evident for other types of aircraft: dive bombers, military transports, and training craft. The Douglas SBD Dauntless dive bomber (5,938), the Curtiss SB2C Helldiver (7,140), and the Grumman TBF Avenger torpedo bomber (9,836) ceased production in 1945. All three had flown before Pearl Harbor. The Douglas C-47, the military transport version of the DC-3, remained in production until 1952, but the rate of production slowed greatly after the war. Total production was 16,079, including 607 civilian versions (DC-3s completed in 1942 or earlier), 10,048 C-47s built in the United States during the war, and 4,937 under license by the Soviets (Wikipedia, 2021a, 2021c). Three small training aircraft also continued to be built after the war. The North American T-6 Texan (15,495) remained in production into the 1950s. The Vultee BT-13 Valiant (11,537) ceased production in 1947, and the Fairchild PT-19 (~7,700) in 1948. Finally, about 13,900 Waco CG-4 gliders were produced before production ceased in 1945.[11]

A commonly cited statistic is that during 1944, the United States completed an airplane on average once every five and a half minutes (Walton, 1956, p. 540).[12] But the war did not effect a dramatic acceleration of the design process. Every military aircraft experiencing significant World War II deployment had been designed before the war and, as noted, all but four (the B-29 and the three fighters mentioned above) had been flight-tested or were already in active service before Pearl Harbor. None of the experience acquired in producing these models—and incrementally improving their design in response to flight and combat experience—can have had much direct bearing on U.S. productivity levels and growth in the postwar period because production of almost all ceased before or shortly after the end of the war.

What about category 2—gains relevant perhaps not to the manufacture of specific aircraft per se, but to the manufacture of aircraft more generally? This was, after all, an industry in which the United States became a world leader after the war, with consequences that stimulated regional economies, particularly in the West, although, as Rhode (2003) notes, the aircraft industry was already well established in that region in the prewar period. It is important in this regard to appreciate the unusual and indeed unique characteristics of

World War II aircraft manufacture. The country—indeed the world—never again produced such vast quantities in a similarly compressed time frame. In the postwar period, a very small number of aircraft models approached or exceeded cumulative production runs of 5,000, and most of those that did were small, single-engine, piston-driven aircraft produced for the general aviation market: Beechcraft, Cessnas, Pipers, and Aeroncas.

Following World War II, only four military aircraft experienced production runs greater than 5,000 (Wikipedia's threshold in the previous analysis). These were the North American F-86 Sabre (9,860; 1947–56), the Republic F-84 Thunderjet (7,524; 1946–53), the McDonnell-Douglas F-4 Phantom II (5,195; 1958–81), and the Lockheed T-33 Shooting Star jet trainer (6,557; 1948–59). The subsonic heavy bomber, the B-52, originally built between 1954 and 1963 (and scheduled to remain flying, after extensive modification, until 2050), had a cumulative production run of 742. Only one U.S. commercial aircraft exceeded cumulated output of more than 5,000 in the postwar period. Production of the Boeing 737 began in 1967, and on March 13, 2018, surpassed 10,000. That cumulative output, however, took place over half a century, not two or three years. As of April 2020, Boeing had built 865 707s, 1,832 727s, 10,576 737s, 1,557 747s, 1,050 757s, 1,186 767s, 1,633 777s, and 1,000 787s; most of these production runs took place over multiple decades.

Disrupted Technical Advance in Consumer Durables

During the postwar period, the consumer sector experienced limited beneficial spillovers from the wartime experience of mass-producing military goods. Moreover, whatever gains accrued as the result of learning by doing in military production came at the cost of advances in the production of metals-using consumer durables. For three and a half years U.S. manufacturing shifted from cars, refrigerators, and washing machines to planes, tanks, ships, and machine guns. Then it shifted back. The temporary diversion of resources to the manufacture of ordnance disrupted a robust peacetime trajectory of learning and technical advance in making consumer durables—one that involved both product improvement and cost reduction—that was a key feature of the Depression years. The goods whose production was shut down during the war lost the benefits of product development and experience effects during the hiatus. The net impacts were not devastating, but neither were they positive.

Then, as now, the most important of these goods was automobiles. In 1939 the car industry consumed 18 percent of the steel, 75 percent of the plate glass,

80 percent of the rubber, 34 percent of the lead, and 10–14 percent of the copper, tin, and aluminum in the U.S. economy. Largely because of the industry's customary annual model change, it was, before mobilization, the machine tool industry's largest customer (Klein, 2013, p. 64). Output and sales of passenger vehicles rose rapidly in 1940 and 1941, as growing defense spending along with foreign orders primed the pump of an economy finally emerging from a decade of depression. As monthly production between September 1940 and July 1941 pressed against peak 1937 (but not 1929) levels, all-outers became concerned that, if war came, rising demands for consumer durables and military hardware could not both be accommodated without exacerbating developing shortages in steel, machine tools, and other key inputs.

Those who believed war inevitable concluded that, in order to maximize production of aircraft, tanks, and ships, the United States needed to terminate, or at least dramatically curtail, the production of metals-intensive consumer durables, particularly automobiles and white goods (refrigerators, washing machines, and other large appliances), as well as metal office furniture. Before Pearl Harbor industry leaders resisted curtailment, arguing that only a small part of its plant and equipment could be converted to military production. They were joined by officials in the Office of Production Management (OPM), who echoed industry fears. After a decade of depression, their concern was that factories and workers might sit idle during an interval between curtailment and a stream of military orders whose size and timing remained uncertain, and that some might never find a use in war production. These concerns were not unfounded. Those resisting conversion also had unpleasant memories of what had happened after World War I and feared an overhang of excess capacity after the war. The president, economists such as Robert Nathan, Leon Henderson, and other New Dealers, meanwhile, pushed for speedier reductions in civilian metals-intensive production (Koistinen, 2004, pp. 130–32).

In October 1940 the automobile industry agreed to suspend annual model changes (Herman, 2012, p. 115), although, since one had just been completed, this would have no practical significance until the following fall. The intent was to make it easier for the machine tool industry to supply the aircraft industry, a sector in which employment would increase from roughly 40,000 to more than 2 million between 1939 and 1944. Over the same period, the industry would rise in rank by value of production from forty-fourth to first and, by January 1944, employ 12.4 percent of all workers in U.S. manufacturing (Ballard,

1983, p. 140; Aircraft Industries Association of America, 1945, tables 3.1, 3.2, 3.4). In April 1941 William S. Knudsen, the head of OPM, secured an agreement with car manufacturers for a 20 percent cutback in output, which took effect in August 1941 (U.S. Bureau of the Budget, 1946, p. 60). Reinforcing the agreement's intent, the Federal Reserve issued Regulation W, restricting installment loans to no more than eighteen months, and requiring a down payment of at least one-third for car purchases (Klein, 2013, pp. 169, 172; U.S. Bureau of the Budget, 1946, p. 264).

The commencement of war for the United States in December dramatically accelerated curtailment. Effective January 1, 1942, all sales of as well as the delivery of previously ordered cars, trucks, and parts were prohibited. Effective February 22, 1942, the production of all U.S. passenger vehicles, commercial trucks, and auto parts ceased. Half-finished assemblies, along with some of the specialized tools and dies, were sent to salvage to be melted down and recycled. Most of the rest of the machine tools were stored in anticipation of the resumption of production after the war (Ballard, 1983, p. 137). Car dealers retained an inventory of 532,000 1942 model vehicles produced but not yet sold; those with a permit from a local ration board could purchase one during the war.[13] Design work on new models ceased completely for thirty months, resuming again in the fall of 1944, subject to the restriction that it not interfere with ongoing war work. Production of new vehicles recommenced in October 1945. Passenger vehicles produced for the 1946 and 1947 model years were little changed from those manufactured during the 1941 and abortive 1942 model years.[14] Similarly, in May 1941, nine months before the cessation of automobile production, General Electric shut down all civilian radio and television R&D in order to focus on military orders (Klein, 2013, p. 105).

The suggestion that experience gained building B-24s or Sherman tanks generated major beneficial spillovers in civilian production after the war is inconsistent with the sectoral productivity data. Nor is it supported by what we know qualitatively about the evolution of technologies in these sectors. The 1930s were a fertile period for automotive engineering, during which the industry introduced many modern features, including automatic transmission, power steering, and the V-8 engine. The 1940s were largely a lost decade: the 1948 and 1949 model years finally reflected new vehicle designs. During the 1950s and 1960s the industry settled into a marketing-infused senescence distinguished by planned obsolescence, a continuing emphasis on annual model changes, many of which did little to improve functionality or performance, and deteriorating quality, which ultimately left it at the mercy of foreign competitors (Zeitlin, 1995, p. 75).[15] Raff and Trajtenberg contrast the vibrancy of the pre-1940 period with the "tight oligopoly and dull performance of the post–World War II decades" (1997, p. 72).

The story was not noticeably different in the appliance sector. Refrigerator and appliance production, including washing machines, cookstoves, metal office furniture, and vacuum cleaners became subject to limitation orders in the fall of 1941 and ceased entirely during the war. As in the case of the automobile industry, most of the specialized machine tools were mothballed in anticipation of the end of the war. Commercial television, developed during the 1930s, was introduced at the 1939 New York World's Fair, but the war delayed large-scale production and take-up for at least six years. Production of TV sets was completely prohibited between April 1942 and August 1945.

Ships

Airplanes and ships together accounted for almost 46 percent of total munitions spending between July 1, 1940, and July 31, 1945 (U.S. War Production Board, 1945a, p. 105; expenditure flows have been reckoned in Standard Munitions Dollars, based on August 1945 unit costs; see Fesler, 1947, p. 961). After airplanes, a close runner-up in broad categories of military spending was ships, and a reexamination of learning by doing in the sector leads to conclusions very similar to those reached for aircraft. The most famous case was the Liberty ships. Between 1941 and 1945 eighteen shipyards in the United States produced 2,710 of these vessels. No other ship model before or after approached this record of cumulated output. (The ship was based on an 1879 British design.) The gains in labor productivity were partly enabled by replacing rivets with welds; the remainder has traditionally been attributed to more quotidian learning by doing. As in the case of aircraft, the Liberty ships narrative requires some qualification. Thompson (2001), in particular, suggests that much of the measured labor productivity improvement over time was attributable to quality deterioration and capital deepening, rather than advance in TFP. The quality deterioration was evident in the more than one hundred Liberty ships that sank within ten years of launch because of hull or deck fractures resulting from poor welds.

Analyzing a larger shipbuilding data set from World War II, Thornton and Thompson (2001) were more optimistic about the role of learning by doing. Even if we acknowledge significant contributions from this source, such knowledge was of questionable value after the war because the U.S. economy was never again faced with the challenge of producing so many similar ships in such a short period.

U.S. shipyards, including those owned and operated by the U.S. Navy, also produced a prodigious number of naval vessels between 1941 and 1945 inclusive: 31 aircraft carriers, 6 battleships, 42 battle, heavy, and light cruisers, 302 destroyers, 191 submarines, and 78,242 landing craft (U.S. Bureau of the Census, 1947, p. 222, table 247). Here also there were learning effects, as labor productivity improved with cumulated output (see Gemery and Hogendorn, 1993, for evidence on destroyer production). The relevance of this to the postwar economy, civilian or military, however, is also questionable. As in the case of aircraft, in the postwar period the U.S. built many fewer but far more expensive combat vessels.[16]

We can conclude that the gains in category 1 (production of a particular model) were significant, in category 2 (production of aircraft or ships more generally) moderate, and in category 3 (manufacturing more generally) almost entirely absent.

Gains in category 3 had the greatest potential for persistence and general applicability. But there is scant evidence that organizational breakthroughs during the war, which would show up in TFP, help explain success after it, at least within manufacturing. We can get some perspective on this by examining the changing share of "other transportation equipment" (all transport equipment except automobiles) in U.S. manufacturing. In spite of Lend-Lease, foreign aircraft orders, and pre–Pearl Harbor increases in military spending, the category represented just 2.2 percent of total manufacturing output in 1941. At its peak in 1944 that share had risen to 20.7 percent of a considerably expanded manufacturing sector. By 1948 it had fallen back to 2.7 percent (see also Field, 2011, tables 3.3 and 3.4). Even at the height of the Korean War in 1953, the share rose only to 6.9 percent of manufacturing output, or 2.4 percent of the private nonfarm economy (U.S. Department of Commerce, 1966, p. 19, table 1.12).

Automatic Guns

The most compelling learning-by-doing narratives involve not planes and ships but smaller items, such as the Oerlikon and Bofors antiaircraft guns, which Pontiac and Chrysler copied from Swiss and Swedish designs, respectively, or the Browning automatic rifle, which the Saginaw steering division of GM copied from Colt. In each case, by applying techniques used in automobile parts manufacturing, the contractors were able to manufacture the weapons more cheaply as they gained experience. Because of the smaller physical scale of the items (in contrast to B-24s or Liberty ships), these transitions did not require the construction of massive new special-purpose manufacturing facilities (or new shipways), and the need for custom-designed machine tools and stamping presses was almost certainly less than was the case in the manufacture of the larger military durables.

For the 20-mm Oerlikon antiaircraft gun, Pontiac reduced direct labor hour requirements from 428 to 346, and thus cut the cost of the gun from $7,000 to $5,355. For the Bofors, the 40-mm antiaircraft gun that supplanted the Oerlikon in production toward the end of the war, Chrysler, producing at scale, was eventually able to manufacture a gun using ten hours of semiskilled labor, whereas in Sweden the weapon had been handcrafted at a cost of 450 hours of skilled labor. There are several other commonly cited examples of Detroit auto manufacturers engineering dramatic reductions in unit costs. After studying how Browning machine guns had been made by Colt, the Saginaw division of GM drove the original cost of $667 down to $141 (Janeway, 1951, pp. 213–14; Lingeman, 1970, p. 130). Dodge reduced the costs of a gyrocompass by 45 percent and shortwave radar systems by 57 percent over an eighteen-month period (Baime, 2014, p. 259). These examples illustrate the successful application of 1930s mass-production techniques to new products. But it is hard to make an argument that the experience did or should have had a lasting effect on postwar capability. The demand for and production of antiaircraft guns and machine guns plummeted after the war.

The Temptation to Generalize from the Learning Narratives

In his restatement of the war-benefits-aggregate-supply thesis as it applied to the Second World War, Gordon claimed that its "most novel aspect" was "its assertion that World War II itself was perhaps the most important contributor to the Great Leap," by which he meant the rapid rise in U.S. productivity during the second quarter of the twentieth century. As he developed his argument, he abandoned the hedging reflected in his initial inclusion of the word *perhaps:* "In fact . . . the case is overwhelming for the 'economic rescue' interpretation of World War II along every conceivable dimension" (Gordon, 2016, p. 537). There is little doubt that Gordon intended "every conceivable dimension" to refer to aggregate supply as much as aggregate demand.

The tendency in discussions of the supply-side effects of the war to move enthusiastically from qualified speculation to unqualified certainty was not new. In a short book criticizing Alvin Hansen's theory of secular stagnation published in 1945, George Terborgh included this aside: "Incidentally, the march of invention has probably been stepped up on balance by the impact of the war, which has in many cases telescoped into a few years what would otherwise be the product of decades. We face the postwar era with an unprecedented accumulation of new materials, new techniques, and new products, that will create hundreds of new industries and revolutionize scores of old ones. Never in history have we had so huge a backlog of invention awaiting practical application" (Terborgh, 1945, p. 90).

The passage evidences the same transition from qualified uncertainty ("probably") in the first sentence to the expansive and confident certainty ("Never in history") in the final two sentences. Both Gordon's and Terborgh's transitions represent leaps of faith. They are not based on evidence. Terborgh's language is not so different in its enthusiasm from promises in the 2020s about what artificial intelligence combined with big data would deliver, or the breathless commentary that exploded during the peak of the dot-com boom in the last half of the 1990s. From the standpoint of 2022, the case for AI involved mostly speculation as to what its ultimate effect would be. In contrast, we have available an empirical record with which to assess the supply-side impact of World War II economic mobilization, as well as, insofar as the promises of the dot-com boom are concerned, the contributions of information technology to productivity growth after 2005. Terborgh was writing *ex ante*.

Gordon (2016) went on to argue that the "economic rescue" represented by production and productivity growth during the Second World War propelled TFP to a permanently higher level and was largely responsible for setting the stage for the golden age (1948–73). This is essentially the same position taken by Klein and Herman and the other authors cited in chapter 1. Gordon explained the logic: "The most obvious reason why productivity remained high after the war is that *technological change does not regress*. People do not forget. Once progress is made, ... it is permanent."[17] After the war, "as they struggled to fill orders that seemed almost infinite, they adopted all that they had learned about efficient production in the high-pressure economy of World War II" (2016, p. 550; emphasis in original). He repeated the oft-cited examples of learning by doing in building airframes and Liberty ships, and then argued that "the shipyard example can be generalized to the entire manufacturing sector" (p. 549), and that "every part of the postwar manufacturing sector had been deeply involved in making military equipment or its components, and the lessons learned from the war translated into permanent efficiency gains after the war" (p. 550).

Here Gordon channeled the immediate postwar optimism of writers like Terborgh. A more detailed but equally optimistic assessment of the likely contribution of wartime learning to postwar prospects is found in Julius Krug's 1945 report *Wartime Production Achievements and the Reconversion Outlook:*

> We have come out of the war knowing a great deal more about how to produce efficiently, speedily, and cheaply than we knew when we went in. Much of this knowledge which we gained from war can serve us well in peacetime.
>
> The miracle of atomic fission, the spectacular achievements of radar, have tended to make us forget the more prosaic developments in science and industry in these past few years. I am thinking, for example, of such things as the education of many hundreds of manufacturers in the techniques of working to very close tolerances, or the speeding up of metalworking by the widespread use of tungsten carbide cutting tools. The tremendous development of the electronics industry in process control and inspection operations; the advances in production volume and fabricating know-how in the light metals; the widespread experimentation with substitutes for scarce items which led to the development of new, and in many cases superior, raw materials (such as plywood or plastics, for example), the tremendous improvement in packaging and shipping techniques—these are only a few of dozens I could mention. (U.S. War Production Board, 1945a, pp. 21–23)

Krug wrote in the warm glow that suffused the country only a month after VJ Day. Given the widespread fears about the possibility of a postwar depression, he naturally wanted to project an air of optimism as he looked forward. He included here the most compelling examples he could think of to reinforce his supply-side optimism (although given the concerns about technological unemployment during the 1930s, it is not clear that an emphasis on the longer-run effects of wartime technological advance would necessarily dispel depression fears).

That same year, Vannevar Bush published *Science, the Endless Frontier,* a work often viewed as distilling the lessons and achievements of the war into an actionable blueprint for postwar science and technology policy. But, as David Mowery noted in 1977, "The Bush report consistently took the position that the remarkable technological achievements of World War II represented a depletion of the reservoir of basic scientific knowledge" (1997, p. 26). This view is echoed in Conant's recollection after the war that "the basic knowledge at hand had to be turned to good account. For the duration further advances in pure science for the most part were suspended" (1947, p. 203).

And much of what Krug suggested on the applied side suffers from exaggerated novelty or excessive optimism about its postwar relevance. Consider just a few of his examples. Tungsten carbide cutting tools were introduced commercially in 1927 in Germany and diffused widely in the United States during the 1930s. Plywood had been manufactured industrially for almost a century, and many of the wartime innovations in its use reflected responses to shortages of aluminum and steel. These new recipes were of little value once those materials were no longer in short supply.

Or consider Krug's enthusiasm for wartime advances in packing and packaging that helped protect military goods from damage during shipping. Packing and packaging might seem more prosaic upon first consideration than manufacturing, but that reaction unfairly diminishes their importance. If consumables were ruined, if metals-intensive ordnance rusted, if goods were sent to the wrong port, if space was wasted in the holds of ships, if goods were improperly labeled, if parts of complex equipment could not be located and brought together for assembly, then all the mightiest achievements in manufacturing were for naught: the goods and supplies might as well not have been produced in the first place.

At the end of the First World War, military packaging mirrored commercial practice of the time, utilizing rugged wood boxes, barrels, kegs, and crates. During the 1920s and the 1930s, commercial packaging in the United States shifted increasingly to corrugated and solid cardboard, and the railroads (in 1914) and the trucking industry (in 1935) modified their regulations to allow use of these lighter and less expensive packing materials. Another trend in commercial packaging involved the wrapping of individual units of consumables. Assuming that the time spent between production and consumption would be short, and that products would be protected from moisture during transit, cellophane and glassine materials came to be used frequently to wrap product.

In calm and nonextreme conditions in a joint army-navy-marine training exercise at New River in North Carolina in August 1941, a troubling outcome (one of many) ensued: "Boxes of ammunition and rations, handed from the boats to men standing in the surf, were usually saturated. Cardboard cartons of C rations, stacked on the beach, disintegrated, 'and the cans of vegetable hash mingled with the cans of beef stew in a tall silver pyramid which glistened in the sunlight, but which was difficult to distribute to kitchens.' Equipment rusted ashore because lubricants had been stowed deep in ships' holds" (Leighton and Coakley, 1955, p. 67).

In the same month in 1941 in Iceland, when U.S. marines landed to take over garrisoning duties from the British, and even more so at Guadalcanal in the Solomon Islands in 1942, the use of prewar commercial packaging in extreme environments proved catastrophic: cardboard boxes fell apart and perishables were destroyed because of inadequate moisture barriers. More generally, goods, once delivered to their port of debarkation, were often stored in open dumps, where cardboard deteriorated and metal parts corroded with exposure to moisture and salt (see chapter 9). The military responded to these disasters in several ways: first, by developing V-board, a corrugated fiberboard with a waterproof asphaltic barrier sandwiched between the layers, with sisal fiber added to the kraft paper to strengthen it. After a shortage of such paper resolved itself, the military began using V-board, which came in three grades, in the spring of 1943.

Second, the army and navy worked out uniform packaging specifications for different categories of goods. Third, the services developed procedures and regulations involving packing goods strapped onto pallets, some of which were fitted with skids, so they could be dragged across beaches in amphibious landings. Depending on the circumstances, palletization could either facilitate or hinder loading and unloading. Because of the large, fixed shape of the pallets, regulations mandated that no more than a quarter of a ship's load could be palletized; a hold could be more fully filled using smaller packaging units, although that advantage was negated if needed supplies could not be easily accessed when needed. The final area of innovation involved labeling or marking of packed materials, which were stenciled with a uniform five-part code, conveying information about destination, priority, contents, and originating depot. The result of all this work was a detailed codification of military packaging requirements and procedures, which military contractors were required to adhere to.

There is little evidence that these practices had much influence on the evolution of commercial packaging after the war. The biggest postwar innovation—containerization, which had huge beneficial impacts on the costs of intermodal transfer—appears to owe little or nothing to wartime experience for its inspiration and implementation. The development of substitute packaging materials during the war was largely irrelevant afterward with the return of peacetime availabilities and less extreme transportation and storage environments.

The requirements and regulations for the delivery of goods that would enter military distribution, however, persisted. A half century later, in the 1990s, they came under attack, when pressure arose to allow the services to buy off-the-shelf commercial products for many supply needs. The response to packaging disasters early in the Second World War had, according to those supporting this initiative, ossified into a bureaucratic straitjacket unnecessarily inflating the costs of military procurement (U.S. Defense Logistics Agency, 1996). Chapter 8 examines the productivity history of sectors other than manufacturing during the war, and chapter 9 discusses in more detail the legacy of wartime military distribution.

Because the needs and hazards were so different in the commercial arenas, small container packaging for the civilian economy continued to evolve according to its own dynamic after the war, relatively uninfluenced by what had been accomplished by the military during it (U.S. Defense Logistics Agency, 1996). Birdseye had introduced frozen foods in the 1920s. Tin-plated steel beverage cans arrived in 1935; aluminum cans were not introduced until 1959 by Coors. The pull-tab beer or soda can arrived during the late 1960s. PET plastic drink containers first appeared in 1977.

Similarly, Krug alludes to wartime experience in machining metal to finer tolerance and advances in the application of statistical process control in U.S. electronics. The central figure here was W. Edwards Deming, who championed systems developed by Walter Shewhart at Bell Laboratories during the 1920s. Deming's influence after the war, however, was much greater in Japan, which eagerly embraced his gospel, than in the United States, a country in which manufacturing backslid. Deming always emphasized that the route to productivity advance ran through an unrelenting focus on quality, not cost cutting. It is difficult to see a link between experience achieving finer tolerances and applying statistical process control in munitions production and a positive effect on the growth rate of postwar manufacturing productivity. In the United States the lessons learned appear to have faded from memory as the pressures from the emergency conditions receded.

Understanding the Wartime Productivity Data

The learning-by-doing narratives apply to the manufacture of products that were initially new or unfamiliar to the firms making them. Many and in some cases all the firms making aircraft, Liberty ships, or the Oerlikon antiaircraft guns had shifted from making goods in which they had a great deal of experience to producing those in which they had little. The immediate effect was a sharp reduction in output, and, since labor and capital service inputs continued and in many cases increased, a decline in productivity. The likelihood of adverse effects on productivity when firms shifted to making unfamiliar goods was well understood and anticipated in the Educational Orders Act (June 16, 1938), which provided funds for modest contracts intended (in the language of the act) to "familiarize private manufacturing establishments with the production of munitions of war of special or technical design, noncommercial in nature."

The share of war production that would involve unfamiliar goods was widely invoked as one of the justifications for shifting away from fixed-price competitive bidding to negotiated contracts for cost plus a fixed fee, combined with a statutory requirement for renegotiation (U.S. Army Industrial College, 1946c). In 1945 Krug alluded to the asymmetry between mobilization and demobilization: "Despite all our problems in reconverting to peacetime production, the very fact that it is reconversion—a going back to the things we know best how to do—makes it a far less difficult task than the one we have performed so well in the past five historic years" (U.S. War Production Board, 1945a, p. 1).

The learning curves document partial recovery from these initial setbacks. Achieving high rates of improvement was helped by starting from low levels. The sectoral productivity numbers are adversely affected by the compositional effect of the shift in product mix, which forced some firms to start trying to produce goods with which they had little experience. This effect was especially pronounced in 1942, when, during conversion, the labor and capital of many firms stood idle after production of civilian goods had ceased in response to limitation orders but, even where contracts for war goods were in hand, priorities could not be obtained for the materials or machine tools required to start production of the new goods (see chapter 5).

Much of what was learned making military goods during the war was worth little afterward because the country never again produced these goods in such quantities. In particular, the country never again produced piston-driven bombers and, more generally, never again produced 300,000 aircraft over a five-year period, as it did between mid-1940 and mid-1945 (approximately 276,000 between Pearl Harbor and VJ Day). One might argue that there was option value in access to this learning, even if it was never used again. But even this must be questioned. Because much of the learning involved was embedded in the brains and improved dexterity of managers and workers, rather than formally codified, its value deteriorated with nonuse, and as those who had acquired it eventually retired and died (see Benkard, 2000).

Another type of learning involved the development of processes and products that enabled substitution for materials that were in short supply. Examples would be innovations in the use of wood or prestressed concrete in lieu of steel, which needed to be husbanded for guns, tanks, ships, and aircraft engines. During the construction frenzy of 1941 and 1942, firms faced with shortages of structural steel developed kiln-dried wood forms called, because of their shape, thunderbirds. These served as effective roof-bearing substitutes in many of the one-story factory buildings hastily erected by the federal government (Walton, 1956, p. 214; Klein, 2013, p. 532). In 1943 a Douglas Aircraft assembly plant in Chicago opened, featuring laminated wooden columns and trusses, the latter spanning 150 feet. The navy used similar materials and designs in constructing huge hangars for blimps, featuring spans as long as 246 feet (Albrecht, 1995, pp. 54–55, 66). The enthusiasm for such substitution dampened in 1942 as a serious lumber shortage developed, one that persisted for the duration of the conflict, although that shortage was driven in 1943–45 more by the need for packing and crating material than by construction, along with the drain of workers from lumbering and lumber products to the higher-paying war plants.

These innovations, as well as substitution of prestressed concrete for steel, were responses to materials shortages that would not persist. They might be more easily codifiable than bomber assembly knowledge but would be of little relevance in the postwar period, when materials previously in short supply, in this case steel, once again become widely available and cheap.[18] A limited exception to this pattern may be found in the use of plastic as a substitute for metal, rubber, or other materials subject to conservation or limitation orders: "In a number of instances, plastic substitutes for orthodox materials were so superior to the original that no return to the latter was contemplated when it should again become abundant" (Risch, 1953, p. 92). Another example (not mentioned by Krug in the passage quoted earlier) might be learning in tire plants how to blend synthetic with natural rubber in fabricating tires, which continued to be of value in the postwar rubber industry (see chapter 3).

The Legacy of Wartime Capital Accumulation

The war resulted in an enormous accumulation of physical capital in the form of military hardware, producer durables such as machine tools and dies, and industrial structures such as the massive Willow Run facility, the Chrysler tank-production facility and Chicago aircraft engine assembly plant, and the Geneva integrated steel mill in Utah. In addition, the country experienced a large increase in physical capital associated with military command structures, forts, and bases. The utility of this capital after the war is an important issue, in cases both where the capital might contribute to postwar nonmilitary production, and where it could be used only for military purposes. In the latter case, suppose that a large accumulated stock of military ships, tanks, aircraft, hardware, and structures produced or constructed during the war made it possible subsequently to devote a smaller share of U.S. production capability to the manufacture or construction of such goods. Reduced postwar spending for such hardware could have crowded in more postwar spending on government infrastructure complementary to private production, or the production and acquisition by the private sector of more physical capital useful in civilian production because of smaller government deficits and lower interest rates.

With the temporary exception of B-29 bombers, however, most of the aircraft produced during the war were, at its conclusion, deemed surplus: obsolete or unneeded. Tens of thousands were flown to boneyards in Arizona: air bases such as Kingman and Davis-Monthan. Engines were removed for steel scrap and the airframes guillotined, fed immediately into onsite smelters where the metal reemerged as aluminum ingots. Toward the end of the war some aircraft were flown directly from the factory gate to Arizona for disassembly and recycling. Many aircraft operating overseas were never repatriated. They were abandoned in their theaters of operation. It was simply not worth the cost in fuel and manpower to fly them back to the United States so they could be scrapped. Similar fates befell Liberty ships (scrapped and recycled for the steel), tanks, and other military equipment.[19] These goods had been produced to fulfill an extraordinary need. When the war ended, so did most of that need.

It was not just aircraft and freighters. A veritable flotilla of military ships, including two aircraft carriers, four battleships, thirteen destroyers, five submarines, and multitudinous other naval vessels were destroyed or made so severely radioactive in the North Pacific that almost all had to be scuttled. This was the result of two atomic blasts (Operations Crossroads), an air blast on

July 1, 1946 (Able), and a spectacular underwater detonation on July 26, 1946 (Baker). Several vessels sank immediately at Bikini as the result of the explosions. Most of the rest were towed to Kwajalein (about four hundred kilometers) for tests and then scuttled. A few were taken to Pearl Harbor or West Coast U.S. harbors before being used for target practice and then sunk. Two submarines and four smaller ships were successfully decontaminated and sold for scrap. The tests had been designed to demonstrate that naval vessels could survive nuclear bombs, thus countering claims that such ships were obsolete in the atomic age. The tests demonstrated that ships could not withstand nuclear blasts and still operate, and the third planned atomic blast was canceled. At the time, some members of Congress complained that tons of steel that could otherwise have been recycled went to the bottom of the ocean (Weisgall, 1994, pp. 77–78, 317–22).

As thousands of tons of obsolete or no longer needed military equipment lay parched on the Arizona desert, as hundreds of rusting Liberty and naval war ships prepared for scrappage or served as targets for atomic bombs or conventional ordnance, the knowledge that was acquired in building these durables also dissipated. Creative destruction is a feature of production knowledge as much as it is of products or firms and was particularly severe under the extraordinary conditions of World War II production and its aftermath.

What of the enormous production of machine tools paid for by the government? Machine-tool output increased by two orders of magnitude during the war (see chapter 2). There was indeed a huge investment in plant and equipment by the federal government. But the mass-production techniques that made volume production of tanks and aircraft possible in the United States relied overwhelmingly on special-purpose machine tools, and the majority of these tools and related jigs and frames were scrapped with reconversion.[20] The United States did use multipurpose machine tools, which could more easily be repurposed, but this was principally in the shops producing machine tools.

Already in 1944 the country confronted serious surplus and scrappage issues. By early 1945 disposal agencies had surplus inventories of roughly $2 billion—equivalent to the entire cost of the Manhattan Project. By VJ Day that had risen to $4 billion, and ultimately to a peak of $14.4 billion in mid-1946 (Cook, 1948, pp. 10–11). Most military hardware, with the exception of jeeps and trucks, was not dual-use. Automobile manufacturers, in any event, lobbied against repatriation of such vehicles, concerned they would spoil the postwar market. A few tanks were converted to tractors or bulldozers. Overall, recycling and disposal posed huge logistical challenges.

More generally, what of the billions of dollars of government-funded equipment and structures built to produce all the military hardware? Valued at cost of construction, government-owned plant included about $3 billion in aircraft, aircraft engine, and aircraft accessory plants, $900 million in steel facilities, $800 million in aluminum and aluminum fabrication, and about $700 million in synthetic rubber plants (the bulk of which were not sold off until 1955).[21] A large fraction of the government investment in plant and equipment was of relatively little value in the postwar period. As John Sumner wrote in 1944, "Many plants are so specialized in war equipment or so situated with respect to markets or sources of material as to be comparatively inefficient from the standpoint of postwar production" (p. 464). In his final report, the WPB's chair, Krug, observed: "The proportion of government-financed construction was naturally heaviest in those categories where there was the least assurance of postwar absorption of the facilities by the industrial economy. This means that a good deal of the federally financed plant is in a marginal position" (1945a, p. 35). That is why so much of it was scrapped or sold for pennies on the dollar in the postwar period (see also Jaszi, 1970, p. 936).

A competing narrative suggests these were giveaways, sweetheart deals for large military contractors. A careful reading of the literature suggests that the prices at which industrial plant was disposed of were generally reasonable. Disposal took place amid significant antimonopoly sentiment and political currents favoring the encouragement of small business. The aluminum industry, in particular, was restructured on a more competitive basis than had been the case before the war, an outcome expected from the start. Unlike other government-owned, contractor-operated agreements, Alcoa's had not included an option to buy the new government plants it operated, and after the war it faced a new competitor in the form of the Reynolds Aluminum Corporation.

The problem of scrappage extended not just to the tools of war but also to the tools and parts that made them. Often the cost of scrappage was greater than the quantity of recoverable materials. But inaction was not an option because unless somebody cleared out and disposed of the obsolete or no longer needed parts and equipment, machine tools and dies, and finished or partly finished tools of war, they would clog production facilities and adversely affect the revival of civilian production. Scrappage was already a serious challenge before VJ Day. Assembled parts, tools, jigs, and frames, as well as completed units, could be instantly rendered obsolete by change orders for tanks or bombers. Mass-production techniques pioneered in the 1920s and 1930s and used to build military equipment in the 1940s relied on single- or special-purpose jigs, frames, and machine tools. These were of no more use after the war than most of the military equipment they had helped produce. Whereas many of the jigs, frames and machine tools used to produce cars and refrigerators had been covered in oil or wrapped in brown paper in 1942 and then stored in anticipation of a postwar resumption of production of similar products, the mass production of propeller-driven aircraft was a one-off event. These tools had value only as scrap.

Government plants were frequently sold for a fraction of their construction cost in part because they were often not ideally suited to the needs of postwar production. There was often only a single bidder. Plants had been constructed to manufacture a product mix some of which would never return. Some were not built to last more than a few years. Within individual aircraft production facilities, structures were uneconomically dispersed, to make the facility less vulnerable to air attack. More generally, they were sometimes dispersed around the country to protect them from bombing, a questionable precaution given the new realities of military technology. A prime example was the Geneva steel mill built in Vineyard, Utah, a heavily polluting white elephant operated by U.S. Steel during the war.[22] In 1945 the WPB considered its postwar fate uncertain (1945a, p. 36), but it was bought by the operating company in 1946 for what critics said was a fraction of its worth. After being sold in 1987, it ceased operations in 2002. Government-built industrial facilities after the war did have value, but it was on average a fraction of their cost of construction.

The conflict also left the country with a vastly expanded network of military structures, a physical plant substantially in excess of the country's needs in the postwar period. The Pentagon, completed in 1943 at a cost of $78 million, was the small tip of a very large iceberg. As of June 30, 1945, the army had spent within the United States $7.2 billion on command (nonindustrial) plant. This total compares with a total of $8 billion for industrial facilities, of which $7 billion was for government plants and $1 billion for equipment in privately owned plants. Along the way, the army acquired ownership of additional acreage in the country exceeding the combined area of the six New England states (Smith, 1959, pp. 441, 444, 447). Once built, new forts and bases created political coalitions in favor of their retention. It took decades, including the establishment of multiple Base Realignment and Closure Commissions, for the country to make a dent in that surplus.

Other Influences on Potential Output

The immediate postwar impact of the war on potential hours was clearly negative: 407,000 mostly prime-age males never returned. Most would have been alive in the absence of the war. There were another 607,000 casualties. To this one must add the 8,651 deaths in the U.S. Merchant Marine resulting from sunk cargo ships.[23] As Alan Milward put it, "The only recurrent demographic phenomenon relating to all or most wars is the fact that war kills many people" (1977, p. 209).[24] The 50 percent wartime rise in female labor-force participation (Schweitzer, 1980, p. 90; Rose, 2018) largely dissipated during the immediate postwar period.

The counterfactual with respect to capital is more complex. The country emerged in 1948 with, inter alia, a vastly expanded aluminum production industry and a reduction in its industrial concentration, increased capacity in steel and magnesium, a synthetic rubber capability that had been developed basically from scratch, and the Big Inch and Little Big Inch pipelines, bringing crude oil and refined petroleum products from East Texas to the East Coast.[25] But both public and private capital accumulation in areas not militarily prioritized had been repressed. Wartime priorities starved the economy of government investment in streets and highways, bridges and tunnels, water and sewage systems, hydro power, and other infrastructure that had played such an important role in the growth of productivity and potential across the Depression years. These categories of government capital complementary to private capital grew at a combined rate of 0.15 percent per year between 1941 and 1948, as opposed to 4.17 percent per year between 1929 and 1941 (U.S. Bureau of Economic Analysis, FAT 7.1 and 7.2).

Portions of the private economy not deemed critical to the war effort also subsisted on a thin gruel of new physical capital. Trade, transportation, and manufacturing not directly related to the war are cases in point. Private nonfarm housing starts, which had recovered to 619,500 in 1941, still 34 percent below the 1925 peak (937,000), plunged to 138,700 in 1944, barely above the 1933 trough of 93,000.[26] All "nonessential" construction in the country was restricted effective October 9, 1941 (U.S. Bureau of the Budget, 1946, p. 83; Herman, 2012, p. 153).

Abramovitz and David wrote that "the war . . . imposed restrictions on civilian investment, caused a serious reduction in private capital accumulation and retarded normal productivity growth" (2000a, p. 6). These effects were most pronounced in manufacturing and construction, the sectors most heavily disrupted during the war.[27] Higgs (2010) supplied an additional twist to this argument by emphasizing the wear and tear on the capital stock caused by double and triple shifts, and the understatement of depreciation allowances caused by the repressed inflation during the war. Once price controls were removed and inflation accelerated between 1945 and 1950, those allowances were inadequate to repair the ravages of intensive wartime utilization. On the other hand, investments by the Defense Plant Corporation added significantly to manufacturing capacity in war-prioritized sectors, so it's not absolutely clear how significant this effect was.

Because the effect on potential hours was so clearly negative and because the effect on capital services, although more complex, was probably mildly retardative, any argument that the war accelerated the advance of potential output must rely on a strong persisting boost to TFP. TFP in manufacturing declined between 1941 and 1948, and it is in that sector that we would most have expected to see longer-run consequences of the wartime production experience. The learning narratives have distracted us from this larger picture.

Conclusion

There are two types of shiny objects: those inherently shiny that attract our attention, and those that have been fabricated and deliberately placed in our line of vision with the intent to mislead. For the most part, the learning narratives are of the first type. That is important to know because false narratives often spread more quickly than those that are true (Vosoughi, Roy, and Aral, 2018, cited in Shiller, 2019). Nevertheless, the learning narratives are deeply implicated in what most economists and many historians think is known (wrongly) about the economic effects of the war, and either type can distract. Their shininess, sometimes unconsciously abetted by natural biases or efforts at persuasion, has diverted attention, and has allowed sideshows to be confused with the main story.

7 • Are Patent Data Consistent with the Productivity Numbers?

The labor productivity and TFP data in chapter 2 suggest that mobilization and demobilization for war between 1941 and 1948 disrupted a strong trajectory of technological advance prevailing during the interwar period, particularly the Depression years (1929–41). This chapter asks whether patent data can be interpreted as consistent with this narrative. For aviation and shipbuilding, patenting rates were stable compared to those in the prewar period, but there were declines for chemicals, and even sharper declines for petroleum, rubber and plastics, instruments, fabricated metals, and other machinery, particularly when comparing 1941–48 with 1932–1940. Similar declines are evident in consumer-oriented sectors where production was eliminated or sharply restricted during the war, including motor vehicles, electrical appliances, and radios and televisions. Existing explanations for weak wartime patenting focus on "economic conditions" and judicial decisions—particularly compulsory licensing decrees in the late 1930s—along with an intellectual and political environment that allegedly weakened the economic value of patents. The explanation advanced here is that, with a few exceptions, patentable inventive activity declined as a direct consequence of economic mobilization for war.

There are many reasons to be cautious in interpreting trends in patents as indicators of technological innovation. Some patents are more important and valuable than others, so aggregate counts combine apples and oranges. There are alternative ways of protecting intellectual property, including secrecy and the exploitation of first-mover advantages. Moving first, even without patent protection, may allow the accumulation of non-codifiable know-how that gives a firm a production cost advantage vis-à-vis competitors. The relative attractiveness of these different means of protection may vary over time, across countries, across industries, and according to the type of invention. Process inventions, for example, are easier to protect using secrecy than product inventions because the latter can be bought, disassembled, and reverse engineered. The intellectual, political, and judicial environment can influence patenting propensities, depending on whether changes in that environment strengthen or weaken patent rights, or for other reasons.

In spite of these cautions, scholars have continued to look toward patent data for clues as to the course and sectoral location of innovative activity. In a 1990 survey article, after casting doubt on the reliability of conclusions drawn from TFP calculations ("the use of various, only distantly related, 'residual' measures"), Zvi Griliches summarized the continuing siren song of patent data: "In this desert of data, patent statistics loom up as a mirage of wonderful plentitude and objectivity. They are available; they are by definition related to inventiveness, and they are based on what appears to be an objective and only slowly changing standard. No wonder that the idea that something interesting might be learned from such data tends to be rediscovered in each generation" (Griliches, 1990, p. 1661).

This is rhetorically clever, on the one hand characterizing a research environment without patent data as a desert (in other words, there is nothing else out there), while on the other, in describing patent data as a mirage, appealing to those who might doubt the ability of such data to reveal much about rates of innovation. Ultimately, of course, one cannot have it both ways: either patents can tell us *something interesting* about technological change and productivity, or they cannot, a position essentially endorsed by Boldrin and Levine (2013). To his credit, Griliches did ultimately choose and endorsed the former position, arguing that patents are "interesting, in spite of all the difficulties that arise in their use and interpretation." Later in his survey, he made an even stronger statement: "I will argue below that patents are a good index of inventive activity" (1990, p. 1663). Almost a quarter century later, Petra Moser wrote: "In the absence of economy-wide data on the quantity of innovations, patent counts have become the standard measure of innovation" (2013, pp. 23–24). Still, the usefulness of such data as an empirical measure of inventive activity remains controversial, particularly with respect to the explosion of patenting since 1980. While acknowledging grounds for caution and retaining some skepticism, this chapter proceeds under the working assumption that patent counts may be able to tell us *something interesting* about technological change. It examines data on patents granted in the United States between 1919 and 1960 across a number of important manufacturing industries. It focuses on trends and levels during the years 1941–48, spanning the periods of both economic mobilization for the Second World War and demobilization. Labor productivity and TFP data (chapter 2) indicate that mobilization and demobilization disrupted a strong trajectory of technological advance prevailing during the interwar period, particularly the Depression years. The concern here is whether it is possible to read patent data as consistent with this narrative, in spite of "all the difficulties . . . in their use and interpretation."

The data are from *Historical Statistics of the United States: Earliest Times to the Present* (Carter et al., 2006). The series referenced classify patents granted according to their sector of origin, which may overlap to a greater or lesser degree with their sector of use. Because these are grant data, they reflect applications filed some number of months or years earlier.

We begin with aircraft and engines, which, as has been noted, accounted for a quarter of all military spending during the conflict. The relevant statistical series is aerospace (figure 7.1). The series shows a sharp peak in aviation patenting during the years 1930, 1931, 1932, and 1933, followed by a return to annual levels between 200 and 300 from 1934 until the end of demobilization

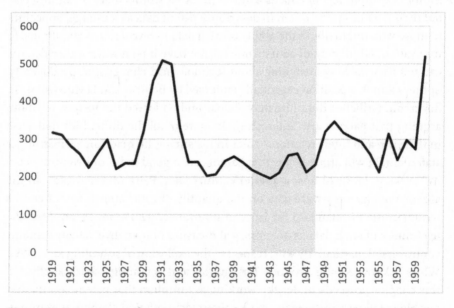

Figure 7.1. Patents granted, aerospace, United States, 1919–60. Note: shaded area indicates years of World War II and demobilization (1941–48). Source: Carter et al., 2006, series Cg51.

in 1948. Suppose we take the peak as indicative of a surge in technological advance in aviation, which is consistent with other evidence. I do not mean to suggest, here or elsewhere, that severe recession is necessarily a good means of stimulating innovative activity. There may be instances in particular industries where there is a positive influence, but these tend to be the exception rather than the rule (see Field, 2011, ch. 12). A more likely explanation is simply that aviation was a technological paradigm ripe for exploitation, and that these advances would have occurred irrespective of the stage of the business cycle. The extraordinary patenting in this sector during the worst years of the Depression is therefore probably coincidental. It should be kept in mind as well that because of the lag between application and grants, some (but not all) of this surge can be attributed to applications filed in the late 1920s.

The war period does not witness a noticeable downturn in patenting in aircraft, but neither is it marked by an uptick. Levels during war and demobilization were roughly identical with those in the six years preceding, averaging 232 between 1934 and 1940, and 225 between 1941 and 1948. These numbers suggest that the war neither stimulated nor disrupted a healthy prewar rate of advance in this sector. This finding is consistent with the Davies and Stammers claim (1975, p. 515) that wartime advances, particularly in the area of jet propulsion, may have been one of the few areas yielding a significant positive supply-side legacy for the postwar period, for civilian or military production. Although the war does not appear to have disrupted the pace of patenting in this sector, the absence of an increase might be considered surprising given the enormous resources allocated to airframe and aircraft engine production between 1941 and 1945.

Although the levels are considerably lower, the data on patenting in ships trace out a similar pattern (figure 7.2). The series shows a spike at the end of World War I, and another spike (as in aircraft) during the years 1930–32. Average levels comparing 1934–40 with 1941–48 are virtually identical (73), although there is a noticeable uptick in 1943, 1944, and 1945, and a falling off thereafter. Again, we can say that the wartime mobilization that led to the huge naval construction program, in part to remedy the damage from the attack on Pearl Harbor, along with the mass production of Liberty ships, Victory ships, and tankers, neither stimulated nor disrupted a prewar rate of technological advance, at least insofar as this is reflected in patenting data. This likely left a minimal postwar supply-side legacy, however, because the economy never again undertook a naval construction program of this magnitude and never mass-produced merchant ships again. And, in contrast with aircraft jet engine

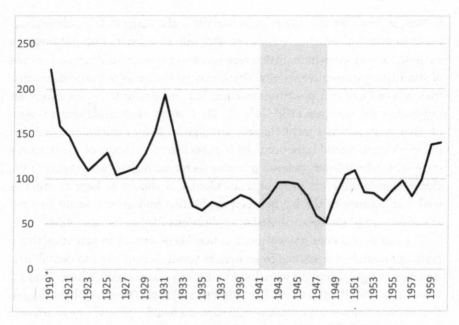

Figure 7.2. Patents granted, ships, United States, 1919–60. Note: shaded area indicates years of World War II and demobilization (1941–48). Source: Carter et al., 2006, series Cg53.

developments, postwar naval propulsion systems were not as revolutionary, save for the use of nuclear fuel to generate steam.

As has been noted, we cannot say whether the advances in jet propulsion occurred because of or in spite of the war. The postwar supply legacy is not plausibly connected to learning by doing in producing World War II aircraft, since no U.S. aircraft in the Second World War used jet propulsion. Indeed, the larger military contractors preferred to focus their development efforts on refinements to piston technology. Advances in jet propulsion appear to have come more frequently from smaller companies.

The data for both aviation and ships, however, are significant because they show that the major declines in patenting in other sectors documented below cannot simply be attributed to a shortage of patent lawyers or a breakdown of the operations of the U.S. patent office during the war and immediately after, or some other ad hoc explanation. Within sectors that identified patentable inventions or innovations, individuals or companies went ahead and obtained legal protection for their intellectual property, in spite of wartime exigencies.

Once we move away from planes and ships, which together accounted for almost half of U.S. World War II military spending, the effect of the war on patenting rates begins to look consistently and sharply negative.

Chemicals was an especially innovative sector during the Depression years, with huge increases in R&D spending and personnel, bolstered by émigrés from Nazi Germany (figure 7.3). Chemicals are also an industry where patents are considered the most effective means of protecting intellectual property (Moser, 2013). Patents granted increased by two-thirds between 1929 and 1932, and then remained at high levels through 1941. There is a noticeable downward trend during mobilization and demobilization. Patents granted averaged 3,260 per year between 1932 and 1940 inclusive, and 2,976 between 1941 and 1948.

Sharper declines are evident in petroleum (figure 7.4). Patents granted doubled between 1929 and 1933. Some of those gains are given back during the later years of the Depression, although levels remain considerably above those experienced in the 1920s. Between 1941 and 1948, however, patenting levels plunged. Patents granted averaged 107 per year between 1932 and 1940 inclusive, and 72 between 1941 and 1948.

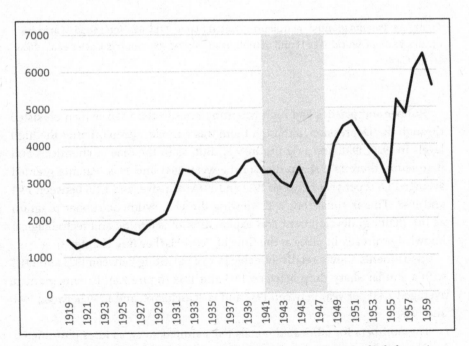

Figure 7.3. Patents granted, chemicals, United States, 1919–60. Note: shaded area indicates years of World War II and demobilization (1941–48). Source: Carter et al., 2006, series Cg48.

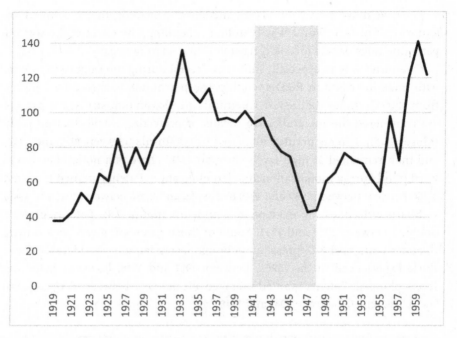

Figure 7.4. Patents granted, petroleum, United States, 1919–60. Note: shaded area indicates years of World War II and demobilization (1941–48). Source: Carter et al., 2006, series Cg50.

Rubber and plastics had high patenting rates in the 1920s, which persisted through the Depression, although there was a modest drop-off after the high levels in 1930, 1931, and 1932 (figure 7.5). But, as in the case of chemicals and petroleum, there is a sharp drop-off between 1941 and 1948. Patents granted averaged 1,852 per year between 1932 and 1940 inclusive, and 1,116 between 1941 and 1948. This is consistent with viewing the U.S. synthetic rubber program as the (halting) development and exploitation of scientific and technological knowledge already in place at the time of Pearl Harbor (see chapter 3).

Instruments show a relatively stable rate of patenting between 1925 and 1941, with a similar sharp drop between 1941 and 1948 (figure 7.6). Patents granted averaged 2,431 per year between 1932 and 1940 inclusive, and 1,759 between 1941 and 1948.

The numbers for fabricated metals tell a similar story, as rates plummeted between 1941 and 1948 (figure 7.7). Patents granted averaged 4,586 per year between 1932 and 1940 inclusive, and 2,761 between 1941 and 1948.

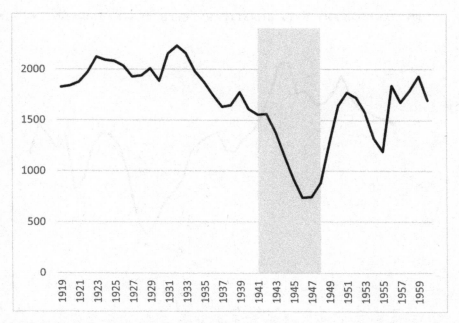

Figure 7.5. Patents granted, rubber and plastic, United States, 1919–60. Note: shaded area indicates years of World War II and demobilization (1941–48). Source: Carter et al., 2006, series Cg64.

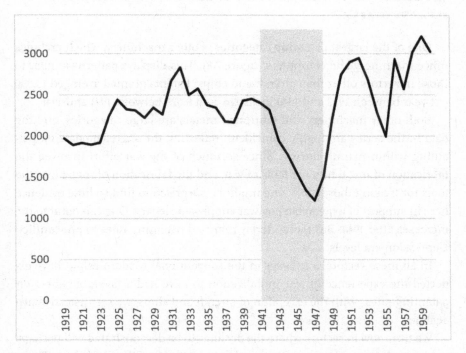

Figure 7.6. Patents granted, instruments, United States, 1919–60. Note: shaded area indicates years of World War II and demobilization (1941–48). Source: Carter et al., 2006, series Cg53.

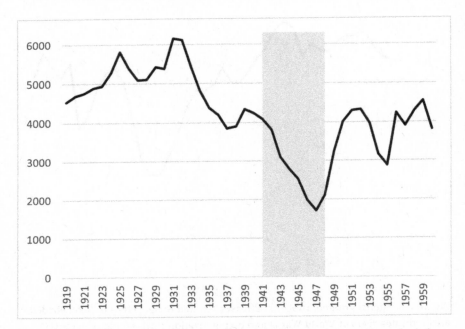

Figure 7.7. Patents granted, fabricated metals, United States, 1919–60. Note: shaded area indicates years of World War II and demobilization (1941–48). Source: Carter et al., 2006, series Cg57.

One of the largest patenting categories is other machinery, which excludes office machinery and computers (figure 7.8). This displays patterns similar to those in sectors other than aircraft and ships. Patents granted averaged 13,590 per year between 1932 and 1940 inclusive, and 8,629 between 1941 and 1948.

Both other machinery and fabricated metals are large categories, and the data in the series are highly coincident, reflecting the aggregate data on patenting within manufacturing. Since so much of the war effort involved the fabrication of metal into the tools of war, and the fabrication of metal into the tools for making those tools, one might be surprised to find so little evidence here in support of a favorable postwar supply-side legacy. One can point to the increases after 1948. But these merely returned patenting rates to pre-conflict, Depression-era levels.

In all these sectors, a believer in the conventional wisdom might have expected the experience of war mobilization to have had a favorable effect on patenting rates. With the exception of aircraft and ships, we see instead sharp declines.

We turn now to sectors where the declines to be demonstrated will perhaps not be as surprising, even to those endorsing the conventional wisdom. These are (largely) consumer-oriented sectors where both R&D and production shut down from the first half of 1942 through the fourth quarter of 1945.

First we look at motor vehicles (figure 7.9). The data show relatively high rates throughout the interwar period, consistent with the Raff and Trajtenberg (1997) narrative, which views the product and industry as relatively mature by 1941. Patenting then declines precipitously between 1941 and 1948. Patents granted averaged 2,411 per year between 1932 and 1940 inclusive, and 1,393 between 1941 and 1948. An obvious explanation is the cessation of both R&D spending and production, which could have produced innovations as the result of learning by doing. As described in chapter 6, automobile production ceased in February 1942. Design work on new models ceased completely for thirty months, resuming again in the fall of 1944, when it was subject to the restriction that it not interfere with ongoing war work. Production of new vehicles recommenced in October 1945. Passenger vehicles produced for the 1946 and 1947 model years were little changed from those manufactured during the 1941 and abortive 1942 model years.

Electrical appliances show a relatively stable rate of patenting from 1924 through 1941, followed by a sharp drop between 1941 and 1948 (figure 7.10).

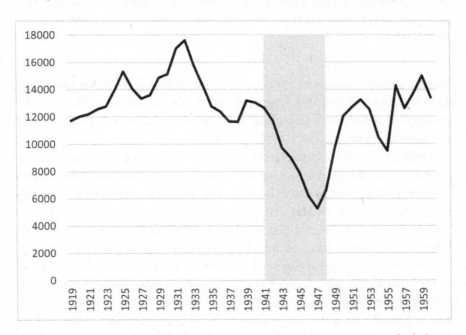

Figure 7.8. Patents granted, other machinery, United States, 1919–60. Note: shaded area indicates years of World War II and demobilization (1941–48). Source: Carter et al., 2006, series Cg61.

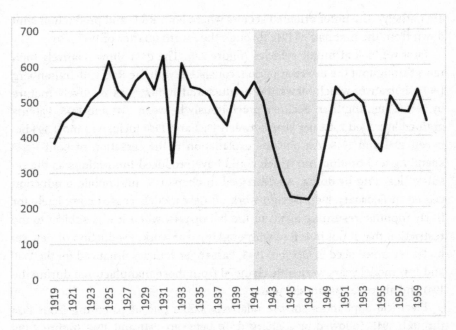

Figure 7.9. Patents granted, motor vehicles, United States, 1919–60. Note: shaded area indicates years of World War II and demobilization (1941–48). Source: Carter et al., 2006, series Cg52.

Patents granted averaged 2,394 per year between 1924 and 1940 inclusive, and 1,759 between 1941 and 1948. The explanation here is similar to that for cars: production and research on consumer electrical appliances ceased for most of the duration of the war.

Finally, the radio and television series display a rising trend over the interwar period, followed by a very sharp drop between 1941 and 1948. Patents granted averaged 184 per year between 1932 and 1940 inclusive, and 133 between 1941 and 1948. In May 1941, nine months before the cessation of automobile production, General Electric shut down all R&D on civilian radio and television in order to focus on military orders (Klein, 2013, p. 105).

Griliches asked, "What can one use patent statistics for? Can one use them to interpret longer term trends? If so, did inventiveness really decline in the 1930s and early 1940s, as indicated by such statistics?" (1990, p. 1662). Unfortunately, he made no real effort to answer any of these questions, including the last, which would require one to consider the Depression years and the war years separately. F. M. Scherer tried, arguing, "The sharp decline in patenting

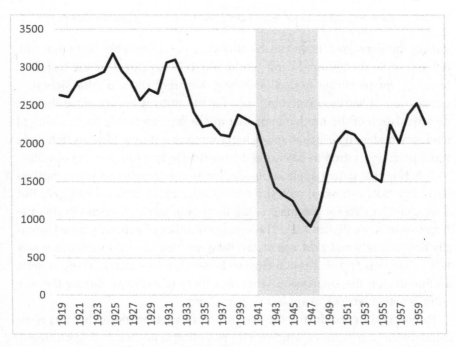

Figure 7.10. Patents granted, electrical appliances, United States, 1919–60. Note: shaded area indicates years of World War II and demobilization (1941–48). Source: Carter et al., 2006, series Cg42.

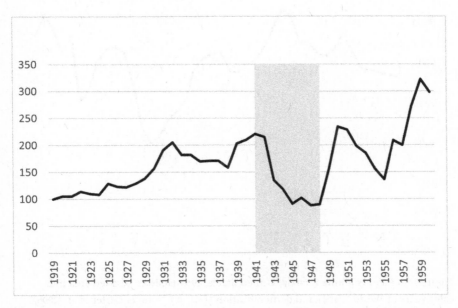

Figure 7.11. Patents granted, radios and televisions, United States, 1919–60. Note: shaded area indicates years of World War II and demobilization (1941–48). Source: Carter et al., 2006, series Cg69.

during the depressed 1930s can be attributed to unfavorable economic conditions, while the slump during World War II is explained by the historical tendency for patenting to decline during wartime" (1959, p. 130). Scherer's explanation of wartime patenting data for the 1940s is empty, since there is no articulation of the mechanisms that might be responsible for this alleged tendency, and both Griliches and Scherer write as if it were obvious that there was a precipitous drop in patenting during the Depression. It is not obvious.

It is true that patent applications decline in the Depression years, particularly after 1930, compared with the 1920s (Carter et al., 2006, series Cg27). But if we consider data for patents *granted*, there is in fact an increase during the Depression years (figure 7.12). The average number of patents granted annually between 1919 and 1929 was 41,224. Between 1930 and 1941 inclusive it was 44,077. Between 1942 and 1948 inclusive, however, it was 27,132. There is *not* a decline during the Depression years, but there is a decline during the war years, whether we look at applications or grants.

Patenting dropped during the war. Scherer's explanation is that this is attributable to "the historical tendency for patenting to decline during wartime."

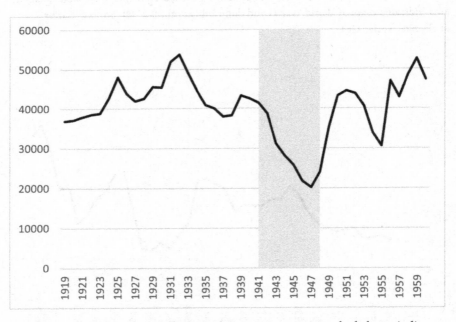

Figure 7.12. Patents granted, totals, United States, 1919–60. Note: shaded area indicates years of World War II and demobilization (1941–48). Source: Carter et al., 2006, series Cg27.

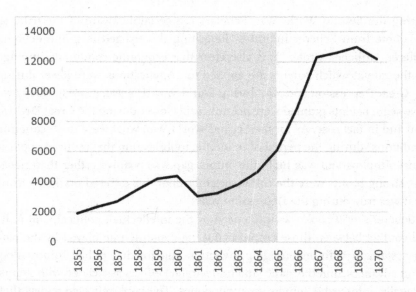

Figure 7.13. Patents granted before, during, and after the Civil War, United States, 1855–70. Note: shaded area indicates Civil War years. Source: Carter et al., 2006, series Cg27.

That is hardly an explanation! It was moreover not true during the Civil War (see Carter et al., 2006, series Cg27 and Cg30). The average number of patents granted between 1855 and 1860 inclusive was 3,156. Between 1861 and 1865 inclusive it was 4,162. It is true that patents awarded dropped by about a quarter during the first two years of the war but then recovered sharply; numbers in both 1864 and 1865 were higher than any previously recorded (figure 7.13). The decline during the first two years of the war can be partially attributed to the withdrawal of inventors resident in the Confederate States from engagement with the U.S. Patent Office, or its refusal to grant patents to those who were so resident (the Confederate Patent Office issued 266 patents between 1862 and 1865).

For a detailed discussion of changes in the types of patenting during the conflict, in particular a redirection of inventive activity toward military technologies and inventions that remediated the damage of war, such as better prostheses, see Khan (2020, p. 210–11). The overall rise in patenting during the nineteenth-century conflict might make one somewhat more sympathetic to claims about the positive supply-side effect of the Civil War (see chapter 10). But it also brings us back to the lack of an adequate explanation for the drop during the Second World War. Scholars are certainly aware of the data, as the quote from Scherer indicates. Repeating the stylized fact, and echoing Scherer, Griliches wrote: "It is also clear that economic conditions impinge on the rate at which patents are applied for. Applications were lower during the Great Depression and also during World War II" (1990, p. 1663). But as we have seen, patents granted were *not* noticeably lower during the Great Depression and in fact rose. As for the Second World War, what were the "economic conditions" during the period of economic mobilization that reduced applications? Employment was high, the output gap was positive rather than negative, strong profits were the rule—certainly all of this differed markedly from what was true during the Depression years.

Scherer's 1959 book was influenced by the intellectual, political, and judicial conflict between those emphasizing the dynamic role played by the patent system in both encouraging invention and making public information about advances, and the static (and undesirable) effects associated with grants of legally enforceable temporary monopolies. The book reflected a view that compulsory licensing decrees, an intellectual environment increasingly hostile toward patents because of their abuse and monopolistic features, and the anticorporate sentiments encouraged by the Temporary National Economic Committee (TNEC) hearings all served to reduce the economic value of patents and discourage patenting. But the TNEC operated only from June 1938 through April 1941, and Roosevelt's rhetorical attacks on "economic royalists" faded quickly in the light of the looming conflict with Germany and Japan. In 1977 Scherer questioned whether compulsory licensing adversely affects patenting. Moreover, if a judicial and intellectual attack on the sanctity and value of patent protection was as effective as some patent lawyers and academic clearly felt, we would not expect rates to have rebounded after the war, as they clearly did.

The patents literature suggests that after these Second New Deal attacks on patent rights, an era of "strong" protection for patent rights reemerged only in the early 1980s, with the creation in 1982 of a centralized appellate court, the Court of Appeals for the Federal Circuit (Hall and Ziedonis, 2001, p. 101). There is strong circumstantial evidence that strengthening patent rights did succeed in increasing patenting, but much less evidence of demonstrably positive effects on innovation or productivity. Boldrin and Levine concluded that "it is fair to say that the sector-level, national, and cross-national evidence fail to provide any clear empirical link from patents to innovation or to productivity" (2013, p. 7).

So we come back to this: scholars have noted the downward trend in both applications and grants during the Second World War, but they have not provided a satisfactory explanation. It is possible, of course, that "economic conditions" or some other type of shock associated with wartime reduced the propensity to patent for a given level of innovation. But it is also possible that the explanation is simpler: with a few exceptions, patentable inventive activity declined as a consequence of an overall discouragement of innovation during a period when the economy was mobilized for war.

The war shifted the balance in R&D heavily toward development, a change in balance that persisted after the war in comparison with what had been true during the Depression years. In the private sector, expenditures on basic research are typically quite moderate because of *ex ante* uncertainty about whether these explorations will lead to patentable and commercially exploitable inventions. Only after some of this uncertainty is resolved will businesses commit large amounts of money to development. At that stage, R&D workers may not be able fully to describe the final product or processes, but they are reasonably confident there is a path forward that will eventually lead to success: "The risks of complete technical failure have been minimized. Although the technical problems which remain are often difficult, capable scientists and engineers know that they can be solved." Scherer offered the history of the invention and development of nylon and time pattern of expenditures at DuPont on this synthetic fiber as an illustration. The same language can characterize the creation of the U.S. synthetic rubber industry. Scherer noted in his summary of the R&D process that initial productivity levels in new products are usually low and remain so for some time: "As a rule, the first innovated items are produced under conditions of inefficiency which are eliminated only slowly" (Scherer, 1959, pp. 29–36).

The Second World War involved huge expenditures on development of processes that built on existing foundations of basic research. This was true even in the case of the Manhattan Project: "Most of the essential basic discoveries, conceived at relatively low cost in university laboratories and private foundations, were in hand when the Manhattan atomic bomb project commenced during World War II" (Scherer, 1959, p. 35). Again, with the possible exception of jet propulsion, the overwhelming urgency of pushing forward the mass production of military goods placed a lower premium on basic research. Echoing this perspective, in the introduction to its five-volume report submitted in 1952, the President's Materials Policy Commission included this aside: "Men far wiser than this Commission in the affairs of science warn us that, particularly since 1940, we have been far more industrious in putting our scientific facts to work than in increasing the store of fundamental knowledge, and that we need to take vigorous steps to bring the effort we devote to the search for more knowledge into better balance with the manpower and treasure we apply to making use of what we already know" (U.S. President's Materials Policy Commission, 1952, p. 16).[1]

Daniel Gross makes a similar observation: "Aggregate patenting declined by nearly 50% by the height of the war in 1943, as resources were diverted away from invention and into war and military production" (2019, p. 12). Gross's paper is about a patent secrecy program that covered areas considered critical to national security. Initially these orders were predominantly for innovations in the chemical industry, later in the war for advances in communications and electronics. The effect of the patent secrecy program on the data analyzed in the chapter is, however, likely to have been small. Whereas monthly patent applications fell from a peak of over four thousand in April 1940 to a trough of just over two thousand in August 1943, close to the peak of industrial mobilization for war, the monthly number of patent applications with a secrecy order never exceeded two hundred (Gross, 2019, fig. 1).

What about the Civil War? If we stipulate that the conflict appears to have had at best a small negative effect on the advance of technology and overall some net positive effects, we are compelled to ask why this experience is so different in the Second World War. The explanation probably comes down to these contrasts. Most of the weaponry (rifles, artillery pieces, and ammunition) produced during the Civil War was manufactured in government-owned armories, and the military technology of the time did not require the huge numbers of tanks, aircraft, and other motorized vehicles of World War II. In that sense it was qualitatively different. Large increases in the production of wool blankets and uniforms (but not cotton goods), boots and saddles, canvas tents, and horse-drawn carts took place in the North, but this did not represent a radical shift toward the temporary mass production of goods in which the manufacturing sector had little experience. With the exception of artillery, rifles, and ammunition, which were almost entirely produced in state and federal armories, the wartime output mix did not involve products noticeably different from those produced in the years immediately preceding, although the quantities demanded of certain products—wool uniforms and blankets, canvas knapsacks and haversacks, horses, oxen, mules, wagons, leather boots, saddles and harnesses, and food for both men and animals—increased (Wilson, 2006). As Stanley Engerman observed, "It is crucial to note that the industries most frequently cited as affected by the Civil War do not fit into the category of war-related industries as that term is customarily used. Rather, they are consumer goods industries" (1966, p. 181).

There was nothing comparable to the Defense Plant Corporation's funding of billions of dollars of new facilities, many of which, it was understood, would be of questionable value after the conflict. The manufacturing sector did not undergo a huge expansion followed by shrinkage similar to that experienced between 1941 and 1948. Nor during the Civil War was there anything comparable to the wholesale conversion of a mature automobile industry producing millions of vehicles annually in very large assembly and parts fabrication facilities to the production of military goods in which it had little or no experience. In sum, the contrasts between "old" and "new" goods were much less stark than was true between 1941 and 1948.

Both Scherer and Jacob Schmookler looked at patent applications, which do decline more than grants during the 1930s, and attribute this to a changed judicial environment and a greater frequency of compulsory licensing orders. But if those changes were associated with a drop in frivolous applications or those with a lower probability of being granted, what is the explanation for the increase in the number of patent grants? Do we conclude that the increase during the worst years of the Depression was because of greater leniency on the part of patent examiners? This makes no sense if the argument is that the government interest in protecting intellectual property waned during the Depression. One can acknowledge that the lags between application and granting of a patent complicate the interpretation of these data, while still maintaining that the data on patents actually granted constitute the more meaningful measure of new patentable processes or products likely to have economic value.

It should be remembered, of course, that patentable product or process breakthroughs are only part of the knowledge accumulation that may be reflected in (and influence) productivity advance. For example, much of the informal knowledge among managers and production workers that allowed unit costs to drop systematically with cumulated output might not be codified or codifiable. But this was of course also true before economic mobilization for war.

The overall picture here is one in which increases in military spending associated with a radical shift in the manufacturing output mix adversely affected patenting. This is not consistent with the Civil War experience but is consistent with an effect identified by Griliches in a regression explaining the log of U.S. domestic patent applications between 1953 and 1987 (Griliches, 1989,

p. 310). The rate of growth of the national defense component of real GDP and its lagged value both had large, robust, and statistically significant *negative* effects on patent applications. A 10 percent increase in real defense spending was associated with a 5 percent decline in domestic patent applications.

Finally, a number of recent empirical papers have attempted to separate out more important from less important patents, which has led to refined time series that deal more effectively with the heterogeneity in the scientific and commercial value of different patents. The most ambitious of these is a paper by Kelly, Papanikolaou, Seru, and Taddy (2020). (The published and highly trimmed version is available as Kelly et al., 2021). These authors used textual analysis to measure the similarity of different patent pairs and, on the basis of these measures, identified what they considered to be the most important (breakthrough) patents. Breakthrough patents are those that are distinct from (dissimilar to) earlier patents, and thus novel, but similar to subsequent patents, and thus influential. Their research required digitizing close to the entire corpus of U.S. patent grants from 1840 to 2010, and then quantifying the similarity of texts in each pair of patents. They started by calculating, for each patent, how frequently each word appeared in the text. To put more weight on terms that were less common in earlier patent grants, they multiplied this frequency by the backward inverse document frequency, the log of the ratio of the total number of patents granted before the one in question to those in that set containing the term in question. Thus, for each patent, words with high scores were those mentioned frequently in the patent in question but infrequently in the universe of earlier patent grants.

For each patent they created a vector containing the scores for each word. They then measured the similarity of every pair of patents in their study, recalculating the vector for the more recent patent using the backward inverse document frequency for the older of the two. The two vectors were multiplied together and their cosine similarity calculated and used as a measure of similarity. Cosine similarity is easy to understand for two dimensions but becomes almost impossible to visualize for higher-dimensionality vectors such as these; one can think of it as something like a correlation coefficient for two vectors. This exercise produced a 9-million-by-9-million matrix (30 terabytes of data). To reduce the computational burden, they threw out pairs with less than 5 percent similarity.

The authors then selected "breakthrough patents," which were both novel at the time they were granted and influential afterward (figure 7.14). To measure the novelty of a patent grant, they calculated the inverse of the sum of

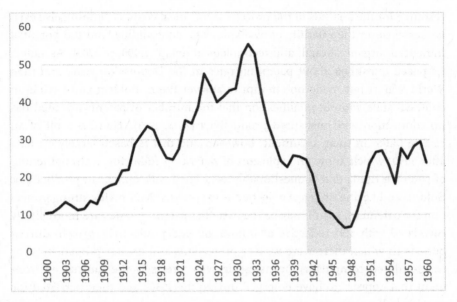

Figure 7.14. Breakthrough patents, United States, 1900–1960. Note: shaded area indi-cates 1941–48. See text for definition of breakthrough patents. Source: Kelly, Papaniko-laou, Seru, and Taddy (2020), fig. 7, panel A; underlying data made available by and used with permission of the authors

the similarity scores of that patent with all patents granted in the previous five years (backward similarity), and then calculated forward similarity by aggre-gating the similarity scores for all patents granted in the next 10 calendar year. Patent significance (quality) was defined simply as the ratio of the forward similarity score for the patent to its backward similarity, net of year fixed ef-fects: significant patents are those that have high forward similarity and low backward similarity.

Breakthrough patents are those with quality scores in the top 10 percent of the distribution of all patents. Kelly et al.'s long time series of per-capita breakthrough patents shows a sharp peak during the worst years of the Great Depression and a collapse during the period of war mobilization and demo-bilization (1941–48), which is consistent with the message that the productiv-ity data in chapter 2 convey. Note also the decline in breakthrough patenting between 1916 and 1920, coincident with the period of U.S. involvement in the First World War.

Near the end of his survey article, Griliches reaffirmed the importance of patent data: "In spite of all the difficulties, patents statistics remain a unique resource for the analysis of the process of technical change. Nothing else even comes close in the quantity of available data, accessibility, and the potential industrial, organizational, and technological detail" (1990, p. 1702). As noted, he posed questions about patenting rates in the Depression years and then World War II but made no attempt to answer them. Boldrin and Levine, in contrast, state without qualification that the number of patents awarded has no connection with measured productivity (2013, p. 3). There is a bit of an escape hatch in their argument, however, one that is based largely on data after 1980, which show an explosion of patenting following a strengthening of patentee rights that is questionably associated with upticks in productivity. Boldrin and Levine's biggest objection is to systems that provide strong protection for patentees. It still may be the case that patenting rates are more highly correlated with and reflective of innovation and productivity growth during periods in which there were weaker protections and greater propensities for court-ordered compulsory licensing decrees, precisely the judicial environment that appears to have emerged during the 1930s and then persisted for roughly half a century.

This chapter asked whether patent data could be read in a manner that supported the impression of overall wartime technological stasis evident in labor productivity and TFP data. The counts do appear to have *some* connection to measured productivity growth rates, correlating, roughly, with high TFP growth between 1929 and 1941 and weaker (negative in manufacturing) TFP growth between 1941 and 1948. And the trends within particular sectors are generally consistent with what we know of the evolution of these industries during the war. There is no reason here or elsewhere that should require us to treat patent data as dispositive with respect to rates of innovation. But when examined in the light of other evidence, they provide additional support for a narrative emerging from analysis of these sources.

We have known at least since the cited works of Griliches and Scherer that World War II saw a decrease in the frequency of overall patenting. Griliches offered no explanation, and Scherer's was not much better: "the historical tendency for patenting to decline during wartime." World War II is widely understood in the United States as a period in which the exigencies of military conflict created a premium on development rather than research. For World War II, the effects of disruption in raw material supplies, particularly rubber from the Far East and oil and oil products from the Gulf Coast to the Eastern Seaboard, combined with radical changes in the output mix along with extraordinary time pressure to meet production targets, are likely to explain both sharp declines in labor productivity and TFP and lower patenting rates.

Conclusion

A large literature celebrates wartime cooperation among industry, government, and universities, the increased funding and mobilization of research and development under federal government auspices in areas outside agriculture, the achievements of U.S. scientists and engineers during the war, and the growing share of extramural funding for universities (Margolin, 2013; Gross and Sampat, 2020a, 2020b). The emphasis placed on the work of the Instrumentation and Radiation Laboratories and on servomechanisms at MIT, Howard Aiken's development of computers at Harvard, Enrico Fermi's construction of atomic piles at Chicago, Ernest Lawrence's pursuit of separation of uranium isotopes at Berkeley, and Robert Oppenheimer's work in leading the Manhattan Project are typical. Radar, proximity fuses (at Johns Hopkins), the atomic bomb, computers and electronics, magnetic tape recording, the bazooka (based on an early design by Robert Goddard), napalm, the improved manufacture of atabrine and development of chloroquine (antimalaria drugs), and mass production of penicillin are some of the advances frequently cited.

In placing these contributions in perspective, it is important to keep several points in mind. First, the years preceding U.S. entry into the war were an extraordinarily fertile period for basic research and product and process innovations, a period that left a strong imprint on both patenting and productivity data. The years between 1929 and 1941 saw a substantial increase in potential output, almost all of which can be attributed to TFP advance. All of that growth took place in the absence of war, with limited government research funding outside of agriculture, and in the context of a rump military establishment, aside from the navy. Almost all can be attributed to TFP advance; in earlier work I termed the Depression years the most technologically progressive decade of the century (Field, 2003). The level of scientific, technological, and organizational knowledge in place in 1941 was the foundation upon which World War II innovation was built and a critical factor contributing to Allied victory.

Gross and Sampat argued that Office of Scientific Research and Development contracts, which funded wartime research with military applications, were responsible for three thousand patents. But they also admitted (in the first version of their working paper) that they "lack a counterfactual" against which to benchmark wartime achievements (2020b, p. 30). Comparing wartime patenting trends with what took place during the preceding decade, in spite of all its limitations, is a start. U.S. scientists and engineers achieved memorable successes during the war. So too did they during the Depression, with cumulatively greater effect on potential output.

The United States participated in the Second World War for less than four years; mobilization took place over twenty-two months. In crediting an innovation to mobilization, one must always pose the counterfactual, as has already been done with respect to advances in jet engine technology. What would have taken place in the absence of the war? How much would have happened anyway, or perhaps with a slight delay? We can give credit to the work of scientists and technologists, but also acknowledge that many technological paradigms were ripe for exploitation, and some of what was achieved during the war was the result of pushing on open doors. The emphasis was on applied work—development rather than basic research. Arguing that the war opened up "entire new fields of research" can also be read as an attempt to put a positive spin on the disruption and distortion of research trajectories imposed by the urgency of focused wartime research efforts. In reckoning the wartime influence on the postwar growth of potential, opportunity costs—the negatives—also need to be acknowledged.

Although some wartime innovations had applications in peace, the overriding objective of R&D workers was to win the war, which in most instances meant creating or developing better, more efficient means of destroying buildings, infrastructure, machines, and raw materials, and maiming, burning, and killing enemy soldiers and civilians. An exception was medical research focused on keeping Allied soldiers alive and able to fight: improved methods for treating battlefield trauma, malaria, and bacterial infections, including venereal diseases. These benefited the health and welfare of the civilian population after the war, although it may appear a questionable bargain when weighed against the more than 1 million U.S. military casualties or what the trajectory of pharmaceutical development would have looked like in its absence. Finally, while government spending on R&D added to available sources of finance, the war crowded out private research in areas without wartime application, shut down production and improvement of many consumer durables for at least thirty months, and for several years diverted the cream of American science and engineering talent away from what they might otherwise have discovered or developed.

8 · Productivity Growth in the Rest of the Economy

The empirical work in chapter 2 and much of the subsequent analysis in this book has focused on the manufacturing sector. The learning-by-doing narratives imply that it is here that we should expect to find the putative beneficial effects on productivity of mobilization for war. This chapter considers productivity growth between 1941 and 1948 in nine sectors other than manufacturing. Sectoral TFP growth rates along with their shares in the national economy are used to apportion national economy productivity growth among the different sectors. The chapter then compares TFP advance in the private domestic economy in the 1929–41 and 1941–48 time periods and provides a reconciliation of the Field and Gordon views of comparative rates of advance in the two intervals, identifying why there are differences.

As in chapter 2, we require estimates of sectoral real value added: gross sales less purchased materials and services, where both output and inputs are adjusted for price changes. Identifying the "correct" procedure for deflation is fraught: a voluminous theoretical literature on the subject sometimes offers conflicting guidance. The Bureau of Economic Analysis's preferred method in the "GDP by Industry" section of its website is to deflate the nominal value of gross sector output by its price, deflate the nominal value of intermediate inputs (purchased materials, energy, and services) by their prices, and treat the difference as real value added. This practice is called double deflation, as contrasted with single deflation, where the same deflator is used for sector output and for purchased materials and services.

Here is an argument for preferring double deflation. Consider businesses that buy grain and use employed labor and owned capital to mill grain into flour. Suppose the price of grain declines because of an improvement in farming technology, but the price of flour does not. With single deflation by the price of flour, the "real" amount of grain input will appear to have declined while the "real" amount of flour output has not, even though the physical quantity of each is unchanged. Productivity (and real product) in milling would apparently have risen, even though there had been no identifiable change in the organization of production or physical output per unit input in the milling industry.

Deflating the nominal output flow by the price of flour and the nominal input flow by the price of grain would leave the real values unchanged. The TFP measure would then correctly register no change and avoid inappropriately crediting to the milling industry a productivity improvement that in fact took place in agriculture. When input prices are rising more rapidly than output prices, single deflation of value added using the price of output would, in contrast, underestimate real output growth, and therefore productivity growth in the sector in question (Alexander et al., 2017). This example, however, assumed implicitly that the requirements of grain per unit of flour were fixed. In cases where there are greater possibilities for input substitution, double deflation can produce apparently anomalous results, including negative value added.

The merits and defects of double deflation notwithstanding, data availability before 1947 precludes its application. Its use requires tailored deflators that apply specifically to the goods or services being produced and those that serve as inputs. In most cases such detailed and specific deflators are simply not available. As in chapter 2, we will use a form of single deflation to calculate output and, in the decomposition exercise, output shares. The approach followed, in instances where output growth rates do not rely on index numbers available in Kendrick (1961), is to deflate nominal income in a sector by a price index, creating a sectoral real output series that can meaningfully be compared over time and used for productivity calculations.

Combining the real output measures with data on full-time equivalent workers (FTEs) and estimates of capital input, and assuming a 70 percent income share for labor and 30 percent for capital, allows calculation of a sector's rate of TFP growth. This still leaves open the question of which deflator to use for a sector's nominal output or nominal income (the two are in principle equivalent). Within the constraints imposed by data availability, the decision is not always obvious or simple, even to experienced empirical economists. As the calculators available at www.measuringworth.com show, the choice can exercise a sizable influence on comparisons of value added over time. For more perspective on the challenges of selecting deflators that produce meaningful real value series, see Hanes (2006).

The contribution of a particular sector to economy-wide TFP growth depends on its TFP growth rate and on the sector's relative importance. High rates of TFP growth in a small sector may excite our attention, but if the share of total value added remains small, its effect on overall TFP growth is also likely to be small. In calculating contributions to TFP growth between two years, sectoral shares are likely to have changed. An average of nominal income (value-added) share in the initial year and in the end year is used to determine weights for the different sectoral growth rates.

These procedures allow decomposition of an economy-wide TFP growth rate into the percentage point contributions of different sectors. Because of the obstacles to using double deflation we cannot expect the weighted sum of TFP growth rates necessarily to equal that for the national economy.[1] The estimates of productivity growth in the residual sectors of the economy in this exercise are therefore particularly unreliable. The exercise can, however, provide broad insight into which sectors were most responsible for economy-wide rates of productivity advance.

Keynes observed in *The General Theory* that there is an "unavoidable element of vagueness" in such concepts as real output. These ambiguities should not, nevertheless, he suggested, "prevent us from making approximate statistical comparisons, depending on some broad element of judgment. . . . Their purpose should be to satisfy historical or social curiosity, a purpose for which perfect precision . . . is neither usual nor necessary" (Keynes, 1936, pp. 39–40, quoted in Hanes, 2006, p. 153). It is in that spirit that the calculations and decomposition in this chapter are offered.

According to Field (2011, p. 59, table 2.5), manufacturing, wholesale and retail trade, and railroad transportation accounted for over 90 percent of total TFP growth in the private nonfarm economy (PNE) between 1929 and 1941.[2] Because the exercise on which we now embark also includes agriculture, the national aggregate referenced is the private domestic economy (PDE; the entire economy less government). For 1941–48, agriculture, wholesale and retail trade, railroad transportation, and electric and gas utilities contributed positively to economy-wide TFP growth. As we have seen in chapter 2, manufacturing did not. Table 2.1 shows manufacturing TFP declining at 1.40 percent per year between 1941 and 1948. Because of that high rate of decline and manufacturing's large share in the economy, the sector subtracted .48 percentage points per year from PDE TFP growth between 1941 and 1948.

Construction

The other serious drag on advance was construction, a sector in which, between 1941 and 1948, TFP fell at an even more rapid rate: 2.71 percent per year. Real value added in the sector (output) is calculated by deflating nominal income by a price index for total structures (U.S. Department of Commerce, 1966, p. 18, table 1.12, and p. 165, table 8.7). FTEs are from the same source, table 6.4. Capital input is from the U.S. Bureau of Economic Analysis, FAT 2.2, line 29, Construction Machinery.

The 2.71 percent per year decline in TFP between 1941 and 1948 disguises considerable variation over the seven-year period, which is characteristic of a historically volatile investment goods sector. Output soared 35 percent in 1942 (simple percent). This reflected big increases in military base, airfield, and industrial facility construction. FTEs increased 20 percent (simple percent), yielding an 11.4 log percentage point increase in labor productivity and a 16.1 log percentage point increase in TFP. But 1941–42 was the only annual interval between 1941 and 1948 during which TFP rose. Between 1942 and 1944, construction output plummeted (42 percent simple percentage decline), and labor input fell by almost half, although capital declined more moderately. TFP fell. FTEs in the sector then more than doubled between 1944 and 1948 with the end of the war and the onset of the postwar construction boom. Between 1945 and 1946 alone, FTEs jumped 53 percent (simple percent). Starting in 1944, there was also a large increase in equipment available to the construction sector. These input increases overwhelmed output growth, causing precipitous declines in TFP between 1944 and 1947. Factoring in its share of national income, construction subtracted .13 percentage points per year from PDE TFP growth between 1941 and 1948.

Table 8.1 presents data on the construction sector in a format used consistently in this chapter. Four columns present growth rates of real output, labor input, capital input, and TFP. Labor productivity growth is easily calculated by subtracting labor input growth from output growth. Rates are reported for 1929–41, 1941–48, and annual intervals between 1941 and 1948. The sources and assumptions underlying the data calculations are described in the text. All rates of growth in these tables are continuously compounded.

Wholesale and Retail Trade

Between manufacturing (–.48 percentage points per year) and construction (-.13 percentage points per year), national economy TFP growth started off in

**Table 8.1 Rates of Growth of Output, Inputs, and TFP,
1941–48 Construction Sector, United States**

	Output	Labor	Capital	TFP
1929–41	0.0058	0.0149	0.0086	−0.0072
1941–48	0.0337	0.0357	0.1192	−0.0271
1941–42	0.2976	0.1834	−0.0016	0.1698
1942–43	−0.2670	−0.3081	−0.0488	−0.0367
1943–44	−0.2784	−0.3442	−0.0058	−0.0358
1944–45	−0.0057	0.0223	0.2700	−0.1023
1945–46	0.2886	0.4267	0.2368	−0.0811
1946–47	0.0800	0.1704	0.1962	−0.0981
1947–48	0.1206	0.0996	0.1876	−0.0054

Sources: See text.

the hole to the tune of .61 percentage points per year between 1941 and 1948. These declines had to be balanced by positive contributions made by other sectors in order for PDE TFP to show positive movement over this interval (which it did). The most important of these was wholesale and retail trade. We adopt a similar approach to calculate productivity change in the sector. Nominal income is from Department of Commerce, 1966, p. 18, table 1.12, and is deflated by the personal consumption expenditure—services (PCE-S) deflator (Department of Commerce, 1966, p. 158, table 8.1).[3] Real output grew 3.1 percent per year between 1929 and 1941, and 7.2 percent between 1941 and 1948. For labor input, FTEs for both wholesale and retail trade are drawn from the same source (p. 102, table 6.4; see also U.S. BEA NIPA table 6.5A, which provides the same data). Labor input grew 1.5 percent per year between 1929 and 1941, and 3.4 percent per year between 1941 and 1948, although most of the increase over the latter period took place during demobilization (1945–48); labor input declined between 1941 and 1944. Labor productivity grew 1.57 percent between 1929 and 1941 and 3.80 percent between 1941 and 1948.

Capital input is from U.S. BEA FAT 2.2, lines 44 (multi-merchandise shopping structures), and 47 (other commercial structures).[4] Their growth rates are weighted to construct a combined physical asset (capital) input growth rate, the weights based on FAT 2.1, which provides the current cost, by year, for each of the two relevant asset categories. Capital input grew −.4 percent per year between 1929 and 1941, and −.5 percent between 1941 and 1948. Assuming a capital share of .3, TFP increased 2.15 percent per year between

1929 and 1941, and 4.96 percent per year between 1941 and 1948 (see table 8.1). Factoring in the sector's share in national income, wholesale and retail trade contributed .97 percentage points to national economy PDE TFP growth rates between 1941 and 1948, the largest sectoral contribution, and one that more than compensated for the subtractions emanating from manufacturing and construction.

In spite of rationing, price controls, and the unavailability of some goods, real output in wholesale and retail trade grew 24 percent (simple percent) between 1941 and 1943. Labor input, however, declined at an annual rate of about 2.5 percent across the two years, and capital input declined 1.8 percent between 1941 and 1942, and then 2.5 percent between 1942 and 1943. This reflected the drain in manpower to war production and the military, and the low priority accorded the sector's requests to add to or even maintain its existing capital stock. The consequence of rising output and declining input was that TFP grew dramatically between 1941 and 1942 (10.3 percent) and even more so between 1942 and 1943 (10.8 percent).

Output grew at a slower rate between 1943 and 1944 (3.7 percent), but it regained momentum in 1944–45, and then soared in 1945–46 with demobilization and the transition to a civilian economy. Labor input bottomed out in 1944, grew 4 percent between 1944 and 1945, and then jumped 17 log percentage points between 1945 and 1946, retreating to a growth of 5.4 percent between 1946 and 1947, and then declining 2.5 percent between 1947 and 1948. The large influx of labor between 1945 and 1947 reflected the release of millions from the military and their partial reabsorption in a sector starved of inputs during the war. Capital input growth finally turned positive in 1945–46. The rise in inputs depressed productivity growth between 1945 and 1947.

In contrast to manufacturing, labor input in trade declined through 1942 and 1943 before beginning to recover, although FTE levels in both wholesale and retail trade were still lower in 1945 than they had been in 1941. Also in contrast to manufacturing, capital input declined. In distribution, learning by doing *without* appears to have been a powerful stimulus to advance. Moreover, the tasks demanded of wholesale and retail distribution persisted after the war, unlike the mass production of Liberty ships and B-24 bombers, which were one-off historical events.

The data included in these calculations apply to privately owned capital and privately employed labor within the United States, and a significant portion of wholesale and retail distribution during the war is not reflected in these numbers. It involved the supply and provisioning of U.S. armed forces on

Table 8.2 Rates of Growth of Output, Inputs, and TFP, 1941–48
Wholesale and Retail Trade, United States

	Output	Labor	Capital	TFP
1929–41	0.0311	0.0153	−0.0040	0.0215
1941–48	0.0718	0.0338	−0.0050	0.0496
1941–42	0.1030	−0.0251	−0.0181	0.1259
1942–43	0.1083	−0.0259	−0.0249	0.1339
1943–44	0.0370	−0.0016	−0.0236	0.0452
1944–45	0.0628	0.0398	−0.0161	0.0397
1945–46	0.1455	0.1703	0.0253	0.0187
1946–47	0.0021	0.0541	0.0064	−0.0377
1947–48	0.0442	0.0252	0.0158	0.0217

Sources: See text.

multiple continents and was almost entirely a government operation, using government-owned capital (particularly ships) and government manpower: conscripted labor serving in the Army Service Forces (ASF) and civilian labor employed by that organization. Most manufacture was government owned but contractor operated. This, however, was government owned and government operated. At home, across the oceans, through the air, overland in foreign territory, the supply of trucks, military vehicles, construction equipment, ammunition, artillery, aircraft, rations, housing, port facilities, runway materials, and a multitude of other goods and services was the principal responsibility of the ASF, helmed by Kuznets' nemesis, General Brehon Somervell, although the navy, the War Shipping Administration, and the Maritime Commission also played roles. An important question, addressed in the next chapter, is whether experience in government-operated wholesale and retail distribution resulted in learning with persisting benefits for the postwar period, or whether, like so much of wartime manufacturing, it was of little relevance because these challenges were unique to the war.

Several other sectors also boosted aggregate TFP growth between 1941 and 1948 which, although positive, did not rise as rapidly as it had during the 1929–41 period, or as it would during the golden age (1948–73). Advance took place in such sectors as wholesale and retail trade, agriculture, electric and gas utilities, and railroad transportation, sectors starved of both manpower and replacement physical capital during the war. It did not take place in the heavily resourced manufacturing sector.

Agriculture

Agriculture is often excluded from or treated separately in productivity studies because output (and thus productivity) can be affected so strongly by supply shocks that have little to do with technical change as commonly understood. These include temperature and rainfall fluctuations, floods, and insect and other biological infestations that can cause substantial variation in output unrelated to factors appealed to in studies of other sectors. This was as true between 1941 and 1948 as it had been before or as it would be after. Output increased seven log percentage points in 1942, reflecting the abundant harvests that underlay some of the pressure to use alcohol rather than petroleum as the feedstock for butadiene in the synthetic rubber industry (chapter 3). Three years—1943, 1945, and 1947—experienced somewhat poorer harvests, although in 1948 output increased 8 log percentage points.

Because agriculture remained an important part of the economy and the war effort (9 percent of private-sector output in 1941; 10.5 percent in 1948), the sector is included in this decomposition (figure 8.3). I rely on Kendrick for net output and hours (1961, p. 364, appendix table B-1), and the U.S. BEA for capital: FAT 2.1 and 2.2; lines 28 (agricultural machinery) and 65 (farm structures). Growth rates of the FAT 2.2 net stocks are weighted by current costs of the two components (FAT 2.1), with equipment given a 2.5X multiplier, to create a combined measure of the growth of capital input.[5] The additional weighting on equipment is based on the assumption that the annual service

Table 8.3 Rates of Growth of Output, Inputs, and TFP, 1941–48 Agriculture, United States

	Output	Labor	Capital	TFP
1929–41	0.0115	−0.0120	−0.0035	0.0209
1941–48	0.0054	−0.0227	0.0255	0.0136
1941–42	0.0690	0.0385	0.0087	0.0394
1942–43	−0.0466	−0.0078	−0.0212	−0.0348
1943–44	0.0093	−0.0101	0.0358	0.0057
1944–45	−0.0449	−0.0691	0.0406	−0.0087
1945–46	0.0210	−0.0358	0.0391	0.0343
1946–47	−0.0505	−0.0463	0.0787	−0.0417
1947–48	0.0803	−0.0280	0.0999	0.0700

Sources: See text.

flow from equipment represented a higher proportion of its stock than was true for structures. Based on these series and again using a capital share of .3, agricultural TFP increased respectably between 1941 and 1948: 1.36 percent per year, but not quite as rapidly as between 1929 and 1941 (2.09 percent per year).

Because of its approximately 10 percent share in the PDE, agriculture contributed .13 percentage points per year to PDE TFP growth between 1941 and 1948. Some of this, of course, may have reflected the good fortune of relatively favorable harvests.

Railroad Transportation

For railroads, a sector that, in contrast with 1917–18, performed well during the war, productivity growth remained about as high between 1941 and 1948 as it had been between 1929 and 1941. The huge loads carried during the war were their swan song, at least with respect to passenger traffic, which began dwindling in the 1950s until all that remained were a few subsidized routes run by Amtrak. But productivity growth in freight transportation after the war remained robust (Field, 2011, pp. 112–15).

During the war, faced with exceptionally strong demand, tight labor availabilities, and very limited abilities to replace or augment physical capital, the sector was able to extend the notable trajectory of TFP advance displayed between 1929 and 1941 (2.91 percent per year), and return 2.67 percent per year between 1941 and 1948 (table 8.4). The Depression years had seen a shift toward diesel electric motors and progress toward unlimited freight interchange, and systematic rationalization in which hours, locomotives, and rolling stock all declined by one-quarter or one-third, while output changed hardly at all.

In the case of railroad transportation we have good physical metrics for output—freight-ton miles and passenger miles. Kendrick extended Barger (1951), who constructed a combined output measure by weighting the two main products by unit revenues (Kendrick, 1961, p. 508). I have not tried to improve on Kendrick's output estimates (pp. 544–45, table G-III): they are likely to capture trends in real railroad sector output better than deflating nominal income generated in the sector either by the PCE-S or the PCE for railway passenger transportation (U.S. Department of Commerce, 1966, p. 162, table 8.5, line 50). For labor input I use FTE data from the U.S. Department of Commerce, 1966, p. 102, table 6.4.

The source for capital is the U.S. BEA's FAT 2.2, line 25, Railway Equipment, and line 64, Land Transportation Structures (a footnote to the table

**Table 8.4 Rates of Growth of Output, Inputs, and
TFP, 1941–48 Railroads, United States**

	Output	Labor	Capital	TFP
1929–41	0.0045	−0.0301	−0.0119	0.0291
1941–48	0.0422	0.0224	−0.0004	0.0267
1941–42	0.3385	0.1062	−0.0049	0.2656
1942–43	0.1918	0.0709	−0.0088	0.1449
1943–44	0.0313	0.0521	−0.0018	−0.0046
1944–45	−0.0705	0.0074	−0.0006	−0.0755
1945–46	−0.1849	−0.0401	−0.0033	−0.1558
1946–47	0.0269	−0.0135	−0.0003	0.0364
1947–48	−0.0374	−0.0263	0.0154	−0.0236

Sources: See text.

states that these "consist primarily of railroads"). To obtain a combined capital
input growth-rate measure, the growth rates of these two asset categories are
weighted by the shares of the two asset classes in the net current cost of the
total (from U.S. BEA FAT 2.1), with a double weight for line 25 (equipment).
The IRS (2019) treats railway equipment as having a class life of fourteen to fifteen years, and railway structures thirty years; a double weight for equipment
is used to approximate the higher service flow per dollar of the stock.

Although the labor input and capital input series for railroad transportation
differ from those used in Kendrick, there is no net effect in calculating TFP
growth over the 1929–41 interval (2.91 percent per year). The Kendrick series
shows a slightly larger drop in labor input (3.14 percent per year across the
Depression years versus 3.01 percent per year in the source used here) but a
smaller decline in capital services input (−.47 percent per year versus −1.19 percent per year). Remarkably, the TFP growth rate between 1941 and 1948 is quite
close using either of the approaches (2.56 percent per year in Kendrick). The
year-to-year increments differ, but the differences in annual labor and capital
input flows cancel out. Taking into consideration the size of the sector, railroad
transportation contributed .10 percentage points per year to PDE TFP advance
between 1941 and 1948.

Electric and Gas Utilities

The calculations for the electric and manufactured and natural gas industries are based entirely on the work of Kendrick. Kendrick's output measures

Table 8.5 Electric and Gas Utilities, United States

	Output	Labor	Capital	TFP
1929–41	0.0415	−0.0172	0.0039	0.0478
1941–48	0.0769	0.0222	0.0095	0.0601
1941–42	0.1064	−0.0778	−0.0149	0.1549
1942–43	0.1255	−0.0660	0.0210	0.1450
1943–44	0.0484	−0.0035	−0.0247	0.0563
1944–45	0.0073	0.0262	0.0039	−0.0049
1945–46	0.0205	0.1032	−0.0076	−0.0268
1946–47	0.1333	0.1069	0.0338	0.0582
1947–48	0.0967	0.0667	0.0551	0.0382

Sources: See text.

are again founded on physical metrics: kilowatt hours of generated electricity or cubic feet of gas manufactured or transmitted. Both subsectors experienced respectable TFP growth between 1929 and 1941: 5.55 percent for electric and 3.33 percent for manufactured and natural gas. Between 1941 and 1948 advance in electric utilities continued at roughly the same rate: 5.87 percent, but the rate of TFP growth in manufactured and natural gas almost doubled, to 6.28 percent per year. Within this interval, the preponderance of advance for both sectors was between 1941 and 1944.

Table 8.5 weights these subsector growth rates and the corresponding input growth rates by the number of employed persons in the respective subsectors in 1929 (Kendrick, 1961, p. 598, table H-X)[6] to yield TFP growth of combined utilities of 6.01 percent per year, the highest rate of advance among the individual sectors considered in this chapter. Even though the sector was roughly half the size of railroads, the high rate of TFP advance meant that utilities contributed .12 percentage points to PDE TFP growth between 1941 and 1948, as compared with railroads' .10 percentage points. Shortages of domestic generating capacity (naval ships represented a huge competing demand for boilers and turbines) led to innovations in distribution that improved the efficiency of the national electrical grid (see U.S. War Production Board, 1945a, pp. 40–41). Again, the lasting benefit can be interpreted as the consequence of learning by doing without.

Telephone and Telegraph

For communications (table 8.6), nominal income in telephone, telegraph, and related services (U.S. Department of Commerce, 1966, p. 18, table 1.12,

Table 8.6 Rates of Growth of Output, Inputs, and TFP, 1941–48
Telephone and Telegraph, United States

	Output	Labor	Capital	TFP
1929–41	0.0044	−0.0244	0.0210	0.0152
1941–48	0.0891	0.0617	0.0527	0.0301
1941–42	0.1354	0.0520	0.0182	0.0935
1942–43	0.0929	0.0332	−0.0041	0.0709
1943–44	0.0338	−0.0082	0.0531	0.0236
1944–45	0.0416	0.0284	0.0617	0.0032
1945–46	0.1260	0.2038	0.0560	−0.0334
1946–47	0.0312	0.0478	0.0908	−0.0294
1947–48	0.1626	0.0749	0.0854	0.0846

Sources: See text.

line 44) is deflated by the personal consumption expenditure deflator for telephone services (U.S. Department of Commerce, 1966, p. 192, table 8.6, line 43) to generate a series on real output. FTEs are from the same source, p. 102, table 6.4, line 44. Capital input is from U.S. BEA FAT 2.2, line 53 (Communication Structures) and line 6 (Communication Equipment); the growth rates of the two components are weighted by their current costs (FAT 2.1), and a 2.5X boost to the equipment component to approximate the higher proportionate service flow from shorter-lived assets.[7]

The bottom line is that communications TFP grew overall between 1941 and 1948 at about 3.01 percent per year, in contrast to 1929–41 (1.52 percent per year). Advance was sharp between 1941 and 1942, owing to very strong growth of output, and it continued positive in the next two annual intervals. It declined between 1944 and 1947, but then grew smartly between 1947 and 1948. Taking into account its share of national income, it contributed .04 percentage points per year to PDE TFP growth between 1941 and 1948.

Trucking and Warehousing

Trucking and warehousing (table 8.7) takes nominal income from Department of Commerce, 1966, p. 18, table 1.12, and deflates with the PCE-S index (Department of Commerce, 1966, p. 158, table 8.1). Employment is FTEs from the same source (p. 104, table 6.4, line 31). Capital is from U.S. BEA FAT 2.2, line 19 (trucks, buses, and light trailers), and line 46 (warehouses). The growth

Table 8.7 Rates of Growth of Output, Inputs, and TFP, 1941–48
Trucking and Warehousing, United States

	Output	Labor	Capital	TFP
1929–41	0.0596	0.0333	0.0116	0.0327
1941–48	0.0632	0.0355	0.0549	0.0219
1941–42	0.0907	0.0543	−0.1286	0.0913
1942–43	0.0502	−0.0051	−0.1101	0.0868
1943–44	−0.0046	−0.0127	−0.0221	0.0110
1944–45	0.0119	0.0203	0.1616	−0.0508
1945–46	0.1336	0.1003	0.1505	0.0182
1946–47	0.0801	0.0466	0.1809	−0.0068
1947–48	0.0808	0.0445	0.1562	0.0027

Sources: See text.

rates of these components are weighted by the current cost of these components from FAT 2.1, with the weight on equipment (line 19) increased by a factor of six, to reflect higher service flows (the adjustment is approximate; trucks are assumed to have a class life of five years and warehouses thirty years). These data show TFP growth retreating from the torrid advance between 1929 and 1941 of 3.27 percent per year to a still very strong 2.19 percent per year between 1941 and 1948. Taking into account its share of national income, the sector contributed .02 percentage points per year to PDE TFP growth between 1941 and 1948.

Mining

For mining I again rely on Kendrick for output because I am not confident the nominal income approach will produce a more meaningful result, given the deflators needed to aggregate such varied activities as oil pumping and coal mining. U.S. Department of Commerce, 1966, table 6.4 provides FTEs (labor input). Capital input is from the U.S. BEA's FAT 2.1 and 2.2, lines 30 (mining and oilfield machinery) and 54 (mining exploration, shafts, and wells), combining the growth rate of these two components using the net costs of the two stocks from FAT 2.1, with a 2X boost to the equipment component to adjust for higher service flow. The IRS indicates that the class lives of mining and petroleum exploration structures are substantially shorter than structures in other sectors. Based on these sources and assumptions, TFP growth rose

Table 8.8 Rates of Growth of Output, Inputs, and TFP, 1941–48 Mining, United States

	Output	Labor	Capital	TFP
1929–41	0.0052	−0.0015	0.0149	0.0019
1941–48	0.0321	0.0033	0.0259	0.0220
1941–42	0.0305	0.0102	0.0037	0.0223
1942–43	0.0287	−0.0715	−0.0020	0.0794
1943–44	0.0609	−0.0423	0.0218	0.0840
1944–45	−0.0185	−0.0586	0.0472	0.0083
1945–46	−0.0171	0.0494	0.0253	−0.0593
1946–47	0.0883	0.0741	0.0309	0.0272
1947–48	0.0516	0.0620	0.0503	−0.0069

Sources: See text.

from .19 percent per year between 1929 and 1941 to 2.20 percent between 1941 and 1948. Taking into consideration the size of the mining sector, we have a contribution of .06 percentage points to PDE TFP growth across the war years.

Decomposition of National Economy TFP Growth

The calculated growth rate of national economy TFP between 1941 and 1948 depends on the method used to deflate nominal magnitudes. There is no one "best" measure of the "true" rate of growth of TFP over these years (or any interval). For this exercise an important consideration is that the rate be measured using procedures similar to those used in estimating the sectoral output and TFP growth rates. For agriculture, railroads, electric and gas utilities, and mining, I rely on Kendrick. The remaining subsector calculations rely on nominal income converted to real using deflators based on the 1958 structure of prices and production.

Compared to estimates based on deflators reflecting prices in earlier years, this will tend to return lower rates of real output (and thus productivity) advance before 1958 because the goods and services that have increased most as a share of national output will tend to be those in which prices have fallen (or risen more slowly). In contrast, real output series in Kendrick (1961) are premised on prices prevailing in 1929 and will therefore tend to show higher real output growth rates because the goods and services that have increased most in volume will receive higher weights, which reflects their higher relative prices in the earlier period. Real output growth calculated using chained index methods may be higher still. The final section of this chapter looks at the Field and Gordon estimates of TFP growth rates during the Depression and across the war years, and why they differ with respect to which intervals experienced higher TFP growth rates. For those estimates both Gordon and I start with aggregate output measures that are based on chained index measures, which the U.S. BEA started using in 1995.

For each pair of adjacent years, one calculates real output growth first using initial-year prices and then using end-year prices, and then takes a geometric average of the two. Abandoning fixed-weight output series avoids the necessity of deciding between different histories depending on which deflators are used, or retrospectively rewriting our account of the past every time the base year is changed. Although the U.S. BEA has extended chain-linked indexes of annual real output back to 1929, it has done so for specific industries only as far back as 2005. The absence of sectoral data before 2005 precludes using this method to make sectoral productivity calculations for the period 1941–48, whose aggregate TFP growth we are now interested in decomposing (table 8.9).[8]

The main consequence for table 8.9 of the choice of method for estimating PDE output growth is its influence on the relative contribution of the residual services category to total economy TFP growth. If the method chosen yields a higher PDE growth rate then that residual contribution will be higher. After due consideration I've stuck with Kendrick's index numbers for PDE output growth (Kendrick, 1961, pp. 334–45, table A-XXII). FTEs are from U.S. Department of Commerce, 1966, p. 162, table 6.4. FTEs in government are subtracted to get totals appropriate for the PDE. The source for capital input is the U.S. BEA's FAT 2.2, line 1 (Private Fixed Assets), with an adjustment for the private capital stock level in 1948 that is based on the reality that government-built wartime industrial facilities are not adequately reckoned in the 1948 U.S. BEA data on manufacturing fixed assets (Gordon, 1969).

This adjustment has already been discussed in chapter 2. According to those calculations, the 1948 manufacturing sector capital stock is underestimated in the U.S. BEA data by about 32 percent. The U.S. BEA's FAT 6.1 estimates the current cost of private-sector fixed assets in that year as $562.2 billion, of which $55.4 billion was in manufacturing. Thirty-two percent of $55.4 is $17.8 billion, which, added to the $562.2 billion, increases it by 3.16 percent. The index number for private-sector fixed assets in 1948 is therefore multiplied by 1.0316. Continuing to use .7 and .3 for the respective shares of labor and capital income yields 1.63 percent per year PDE TFP growth for 1929–41, and 1.02 percent per year for 1941–48.

The absolute values of the national economy growth rates depend heavily on the deflators used and therefore have an inherent element of arbitrariness.

Table 8.9 Sectoral Contributions to TFP Growth within
U.S. Private Domestic Economy, 1941–48

	1941 Share of Nominal Income	1948 Share of Nominal Income	1941–48 Sector TFP Growth (% per year)	1941–48 Percentage Point Contrib. to PDE TFP
Negative Contributors				
Manufacturing	0.354	0.331	−1.40	−0.48
Construction	0.045	0.052	−2.71	−0.13
Positive Contributors:				
Wholesale and Retail Trade	0.186	0.204	4.96	0.97
Agriculture	0.090	0.105	1.36	0.13
Electric and Gas Utilities	0.022	0.018	6.01	0.12
Railroads	0.040	0.035	2.67	0.10
Mining	0.025	0.026	2.20	0.06
Telephone and Telegraph	0.012	0.014	3.01	0.04
Trucking and Warehousing	0.011	0.011	2.19	0.02
TOTAL of Above	0.786	0.796		0.83
Residual Services				
FIRE	0.099	0.090		
Other transport services	0.016	0.017		
Services n.e.c.	0.095	0.095		
TOTAL Residual Services	0.210	0.203	0.94	0.19
TOTAL PDE	0.995	0.999	1.02	1.02

Notes: Sector percentage point contribution = sector TFP growth rate × sector share.
Sector share = (average of 1941 and 1948 nominal income)/(income in all sectors less government).
FIRE stands for finance, insurance, and real estate. Services n.e.c. refers to services not elsewhere classified.
Because of rounding, some totals may differ slightly from the sum of the separate figures.

Source: Shares of private domestic economy: US Department of Commerce, 1966, table 1.12.

What is of interest here are the relatives over different time intervals, and the conclusion that private-sector TFP grew more slowly between 1941 and 1948 than was true during the Depression is almost assuredly robust to the choice of different methods of deflation. Since there is no cyclical correction for any of the sectoral productivity growth measures, none is made for the aggregate economy measure.

Summing the percentage-point contributions to PDE TFP growth of the nine sectors considered above, we have .83 percentage points per year: a debit of .61 percentage points from manufacturing and construction, and a counterbalancing positive contribution of 1.44 percentage points per year from the other seven sectors; .97 percentage points came from wholesale and retail trade alone.

Between 1941 and 1948 the biggest percentage point contributors to PDE TFP growth were wholesale and retail trade, agriculture, electric and gas utilities, and railroads. Trucking and warehousing, telephone and telegraph, and mining made smaller positive contribution. Collectively, these sectors were more than enough to compensate for the retrogression in productivity levels in manufacturing and construction, leaving a net positive balance of 1.02 percentage points per year. The remainder of the private domestic economy is split among finance, insurance, and real estate (9.5 percent), transportation services other than railroads and trucking (1.6 percent), and other services not elsewhere classified (9.5 percent), for a total of roughly 21 percent of the PDE. A residual calculation suggests that these sectors collectively contributed an additional .19 percentage points per year to PDE TFP growth.

Comparing Aggregate TFP Growth across the War Years and the Depression

The decomposition exercise and the procedures that underlie it indicate that aggregate economy TFP growth between 1941 and 1948 was positive, but lower than between 1929 and 1941. We now focus more explicitly on comparing aggregate TFP growth rates in the 1941–48 period with what was achieved between 1929 and 1941 and understanding why Gordon and I have a different take on the relative rates of advance over the two intervals.

Switching to chained index measures for output and making a cyclical adjustment for the 1941 level of TFP, I have private domestic economy TFP growth at 3.07 percent per year for 1929–41, and 2.01 percent per year between 1941 and 1948. Gordon (2016), starting with the same U.S. BEA chained index measures of output, offers a comparison between TFP growth over the Depression and across the war years that is almost the reverse of mine.[9] His figure 16-5 appropriately highlights the generally strong advance between 1920 and 1970, as compared with the decades before and following these years. Figure 16-5 is a symmetric bar graph showing TFP growth rates peaking in the decade of the 1940s and falling off monotonically in the decades immediately preceding and following. The peak total economy TFP growth rate for the decade bracketing the war is the principal, indeed the only, quantitative evidence for his interpretation of the beneficial supply-side effects of World War II mobilization and demobilization.

Gordon's figure 16-5 suggests TFP growth in the 1940s almost twice as high as during the 1930s: 3.4 versus 1.8 percent per year. These numbers are almost the reverse of those I calculated for slightly different intervals, 1929–41 and 1941–48. I am grateful to Bob Gordon for sharing his spreadsheets with me, making it possible to identify and quantify the reasons for our differences. Here are some of the most important. We measure over slightly different time intervals (1929–41 and 1941–48, versus 1930–40 and 1940–50). I make a cyclical correction for the level of TFP in 1941. The adjustments for labor quality differ and, although we both start from U.S. BEA Fixed Asset data on private-sector capital growth, Gordon makes several adjustments that raise his capital input growth rates, especially for the earlier interval. Those adjustments depress his estimate of TFP growth during the decade of the 1930s.

Table 8.10 summarizes the sources of our differences and their relative importance. The row labels describe how one gets from Field to Gordon, but the table can be read from top to bottom or from bottom to top, moving from Field to Gordon or vice versa. The first two columns of figures show growth rates for 1929–41 and 1941–48, respectively (these are boldfaced), and the third shows the percentage point spread between the former and the latter. The first row includes my estimates, and the last row is from the spreadsheet underlying Gordon, figure 16-5. For each adjustment, the percentage point effects on the growth rates for the intervals are shown in the first two columns of figures and the combined effect on the spread is shown in the far-right column.

We begin at the top (row 1) with a 1.06 point spread in favor of 1929–41 (Field), and end at the bottom (row 19) with a 1.57 point advantage for the 1940s as compared with the 1930s (Gordon). Rows 2 and 3 show the effect of removing my cyclical adjustment for the level of TFP in 1941. That adjustment is based on a regression of the change in the natural log of TFP on the change in Lebergott unemployment rates in percentage points, which is then used to adjust the 1941 level of TFP to what it would have been had unemployment in 1941 been at the low 3.8 percent rate of 1948. This adjustment is the most important contributor to the differences in our bottom lines and warrants further discussion.

Table 8.10 Field-Gordon TFP Growth Reconciliation, 1929–41 and 1941–48 (National Economy)

	1929–41	1941–48	% Point Difference
1 **Field Table 2.1 (growth rates are for 1929–41 and 1941–48)**	3.07	2.01	−1.06
2 Remove cyclical correction for level of 1941 TFP	−0.50	0.85	1.35
3 Subtotal	2.57	2.86	0.29
4 Use Gordon (GDP) rather than Field (PDE) output growth	0.27	−0.18	−0.45
5 Subtotal	2.84	2.68	−0.16
6 Use Gordon labor input growth (including quality adjustment)	−0.57	0.32	0.89
7 Subtotal	2.27	3.00	0.73
8 Use Gordon measure of "official capital"	0.03	0.02	−0.01
9 Subtotal	2.30	3.02	0.72
10 Include Gordon's variable retirement adj. to capital growth	−0.30	−0.02	0.28
11 Subtotal	2.00	3.00	1.00
12 Include adj. to capital growth for growing equipment share	−0.08	−0.16	−0.08
13 Subtotal	1.92	2.84	0.92
14 Include Gordon adjustment for government capital	−0.13	−0.03	0.10
15 Subtotal	1.79	2.81	1.02
16 Measure 1930–40, 1940–50 rather than 1929–41, 1941–48	0.04	0.58	0.54
17 Subtotal	1.83	3.39	1.56
18 Statistical Discrepancy	−0.01	0	0.01
19 **Gordon Table 16–5 (growth rates are for 1930–40 and 1940–50)**	1.82	3.39	1.57

	Growth Rates							
	Labor Input		Capital Input		Output		TFP	
	Field	Gordon	Field	Gordon	Field	Gordon	Field	Gordon
1929–41	−0.06	0.76	0.25	1.85	2.60	2.87	3.07	1.82
1941–48	1.71	1.26	1.57	2.19	4.52	4.34	2.01	3.39

Note: Gordon's growth rates apply to 1930–40 and 1940–50. For purposes of comparability, Field follows Gordon and assumes a capital share of .3. Sources: Table 2.1; see text; Gordon (2016, table 16-5).

The Output Gap Redux

A key premise of this book has been that a substantial output gap remained in 1941. The argument was introduced in chapter 1, and note 10 in that chapter referenced unemployment data, the principal support for the view. Dissenters claiming that the gap remaining in 1941 was minimal might appeal to evidence that inflation rates or real wage growth was accelerating as we approached Pearl Harbor.

The GDP deflator in 1941 was indeed higher than it had been in 1940. After four years it had finally caught up with and then risen above where it had been in 1937, and it stood 3.9 percent above its level in that year. In 1937, in comparison, the deflator was 13.6 percent higher than it had been four years earlier (U.S. BEA NIPA table 1.1.9). In December 1941 the wholesale price index was up a dramatic 22.7 percent from the previous December. But the level in that month reflected an annual increase of only 1.4 percent per year from the previous peak in July 1937. The fact that inflation was much higher over the four years preceding 1937 does not mean that the U.S. economy was closer to potential in 1937 than it was in 1941. Nor does the fact that inflation was positive in 1941 and virtually nonexistent in 1929 mean the country was closer to potential in 1941 than it was in 1929. Although accelerations of the inflation rate are commonly identified as an indicator that potential output has been exceeded, the relationships are not as reliable or stable as our textbooks might suggest.

Hourly wages (nominal) in U.S. manufacturing also rose in 1941: up seven cents an hour (10.6 percent) from 1940, and up 17.7 percent (eleven cents) from 1937. In 1937, however, hourly wages were up seven cents from 1936 (a 13 percent increase) and up eighteen cents from 1933 (a 43 percent increase) (Carter et al., 2006, series Ba4361). Moreover, the GDP deflator increased only 3.7 percent between 1936 and 1937, versus 6.8 percent between 1940 and 1941, so the increase in real wages in manufacturing was larger between 1936 and 1937 than it was between 1940 and 1941.

Indicators other than unemployment are also consistent with an economy in 1941 with substantial remaining excess capacity. Monthly auto production peaked in June 1941 at 419,000, 5 percent below output in April 1937, and still 22 percent below peak production in April 1929. And single-family private non-farm housing starts in 1941 remained 32 percent below their peak in 1925.[10]

Rows 4 and 5 in table 8.10 factor in the effect of switching to Gordon's measure of output (GDP), as opposed to my estimate for the private domestic economy (PDE).[11] Rows 6 and 7 show the consequences of switching to Gordon's labor input series. Gordon starts with total economy hours from

Kendrick (1961, table A-X), and then adds a labor quality adjustment based on Goldin and Katz's calculation that educational quality improved at a rate of .50 percent per year between 1915 and 1940 and .49 percent per year between 1940 and 1960 (2008, p. 39, table 1.3). Field starts with Kendrick's hours for the PDE (1961, table A-XXII) and then includes Kendrick's labor quality adjustment. Gordon's labor input rises substantially more rapidly than Field's over the 1929–41 period (see the bottom panel of table 8.10), but more slowly than Field's in the 1941–48 interval, thus relative to Field, depressing Gordon's TFP growth in the earlier period by .57 percentage points but raising it in the latter by .32 percentage points. Since the Goldin-Katz rate of educational quality improvement is approximately constant over the entire period 1915–60, Gordon's inclusion of this adjustment has little effect on the relative TFP growth rates he calculates across different time periods, so the effects of the different treatments of labor quality relative to Field have to do mostly with Kendrick's larger labor quality adjustment for the 1941–48 interval as compared with 1929–41.[12]

The Capital Input Adjustments

Rows 8 and 9 deal with the slight differences between our measure of "official BEA capital" in the private economy (my source is U.S. BEA FAT 2.2, line 1). Rows 10–17 cover the effect of the three adjustments Gordon made to capital input. The most empirically significant is "variable retirement" (rows 10 and 11). Gordon observed that because gross investment was low during the Depression years, the average age of both structures and equipment increased. He then noted that the BEA, employing perpetual inventory methods (gross investment added, depreciation subtracted) in constructing its estimates of net fixed assets, used fixed depreciation schedules, ignoring the fact that assets fully depreciated according to its conventions often continued in place. In other words, assets fully depreciated by the BEA were not necessarily retired. Consequently, he argued, we need to adjust upward the implied flow of capital services from the BEA stock estimates across the Depression years.

We do not know, however, the extent to which this dynamic may have been operative in other periods. Gordon writes that when "gross investment was high, depreciation was also high" (2016, p. 662), by which he seems to mean that *actual* retirements were high. But this is simply asserted.[13] It may well have been true that during the 1940s, for example, previously produced assets also remained in place even after they were fully depreciated according to

U.S. BEA conventions. This is most likely to have been the case in sectors of the economy not directly involved in the production of war goods, which had extremely limited access to the resources needed to replace existing structures or equipment. More generally, such possibilities are suggested by Gordon's remarks about the almost infinite life of some residential and nonresidential structures (2016, p. 663). To be comfortable with this adjustment, we would need to have detailed information about how the incidence of this variation in service lives affected different intervals.

An additional concern is this. To the degree that we worry about unmeasured quality improvement in capital goods, the slowdown in replacement of vintages during the 1930s would suggest an adjustment in the opposite direction (Abramovitz and David, 2000, pp. 28–29; see also Field, 2011, pp. 29–30). This concern is typically motivated by reference to machinery. But the change in the optimal layout of factory buildings and shift away from multistoried construction associated with replacing the means of internally distributing power in the 1920s suggests it might have been applicable to structures as well. For 1941–48, the variable retirement adjustment makes little difference for a TFP growth rate calculation. But it makes a significant difference for 1929–41 (.30 percentage points), again depressing the estimate for that interval finally arrived at by Gordon.

Gordon's second adjustment to BEA capital addresses the growing share of equipment in the fixed asset stocks (rows 12 and 13). Since machinery has a higher annual user cost per dollar of net stock than structures, changes in shares of fixed assets may require adjustments to the estimate of service flows if we are using data on the value of capital stocks as proxies for those flows (see chapter 2 for further discussion). This adjustment has relatively little effect on the difference between the growth rates in the two intervals.

Gordon's third adjustment is based on the possible effect on private-sector productivity of government capital that might be complementary to private production (rows 14 and 15). The logic here is sound, even if we are interested in PDE rather than total economy output (see also Field, 2003, 2011, pp. 27–30). But the implementation raises concerns. Somewhat surprisingly, given the subject of his 1969 AER article, Gordon does not include government-owned manufacturing plant and equipment. He argues persuasively that most military hardware should be excluded, but he includes military structures. Many should probably be excluded on the same grounds as are bombers, aircraft carriers, and fighter airplanes.

Finally, rows 16 and 17 show the effect of shifting to Gordon's 1930–40 and 1940–50 intervals. Kendrick (1961), Abramovitz and David (2000), Field (2003, 2011), and Gordon all operate within a National Bureau of Economic Research (NBER) tradition emphasizing the desirability, to the extent possible, of estimating trends in macroeconomic series by measuring between peaks. We cannot expect census years necessarily to coincide with business cycle peaks, and in most instance they do not. The closest we can get to full employment before the economic distortions associated with full-scale war mobilization is 1941. For the postwar peak, 1948 is preferable to 1950—since the unemployment rate was lower in 1948 and thus any negative output gap was probably smaller than was true in 1950. November 1948 is an NBER business cycle peak.

As for the pre-Depression peak, 1929 is preferable to Gordon's sometime preference for 1928; since unemployment was lower in 1929 in the absence of any evidence of goods and services price inflation. Either should be preferred to 1930, which had an 8.7 percent unemployment rate. The use of 1940 as a benchmark is the most problematic. Because of the procyclicality of TFP, measured productivity levels were substantially lower in 1940 than in 1941, reducing a calculated growth rate to 1940 and increasing a calculated growth rate from 1940, as compared with calculations that measure to and from 1941, even without a cyclical adjustment. As a consequence, rates of TFP growth between census years are unlikely to be good proxies for peak-to-peak measures, especially for the decade that brackets the war years.

The case for preferring my estimates to those offered by Gordon is based on reservations about some of the adjustments he makes, combined with arguments in favor of those I make. I remain particularly concerned that the use of Gordon's adjusted capital input may move us away from rather than toward more informative TFP growth rates for the two intervals in question. But the case for preferring my estimates, and what they imply about relative productivity growth rates across the Depression and war years, is based as well on the argument that my numbers are consistent with the historical narrative and other evidence developed and discussed in this book and earlier writing (Field, 2003, 2011) in ways that Gordon's simply are not. Ultimately, readers will make their own judgments. In doing so, they should also consider again the Kelly, Papanikolaou, Seru, and Taddy (2020) study, which develops a quality-adjusted time series of U.S. patents. Their series on breakthrough patents, as excerpted in figure 7.14, shows the early 1930s to be a peak period for influential patenting, after which rates fell off rapidly during the war and demobilization.

Conclusion

We should acknowledge again the merits of Keynes' remarks. The choices and assumptions made in these calculations can be second-guessed and correspondingly adjusted; we should be alert to the fallacy of misplaced precision. That said, the analysis here supports two important generalizations. First, aggregate TFP growth was relatively higher in the 1929–41 period than in the 1941–48 period, a conclusion that appears to be robust to the choice of different deflators to calculate real output growth. The second generalization applies to the 1941–48 interval. In sectors outside manufacturing, a combination of strong aggregate demand, scarce labor, and (in most cases) meager capital growth seems to have been a more powerful stimulus to TFP advance over the course of wartime mobilization and demobilization than conditions faced within manufacturing, where wartime declines in TFP dragged down the PDE TFP growth rate in comparison with the interwar period. Manufacturing experienced the disruptions of a transitory new product mix along with massive government infusions of physical capital and priority access to materials and labor. Output went up, but TFP declined, and the sector made a large negative contribution to national economy productivity advance.

These conclusions echo those reached by Julius Hirsch in 1947 in a study focusing only on labor productivity. Hirsch attempted to compare 1946 output per person with data from 1939. He found the strongest increases in agriculture, although noting that some of that was because of a remarkable string of good weather across those seven years.[14] He then went on to report labor productivity increases in mining, transportation and other utilities, and trade, which were several times higher than those in manufacturing. He commented and summarized: "This picture will be a surprise to many onlookers. It means that the increase in our productivity has taken place to an overwhelming part in agriculture, mining, transportation and retailing, wholesaling, and other service trades, but only to a very minor degree in the more than one-quarter of our economy which embraces the manufacturing industries" (1947, p. 401).

Hirsch based his conclusions on productivity information available at the time. He was puzzled, and perhaps troubled, by his findings: "I wonder if the statistical picture will not look considerably different when the transition of our economy from a wartime to a peacetime basis has been completed. The great influx of capital and improved technique which took place in the last seven years is bound to show up" (1947, p. 401).

In fact, manufacturing productivity growth in the postwar period continued not only to be slower than it had been during the interwar period, but also to be slower than the rates of advance in other important sectors of the postwar economy (table 2.1; Field, 2011, ch. 4). The reference to "the great influx of . . . improved technique" and the faith that its putative benefits were "bound to show up" are testimony to how powerfully the belief in a strong postwar supply-side legacy due to spillovers from wartime learning had fixed itself in the minds of scholars and the general public.

Table 8.9 suggests that the popular learning-by-doing narratives, the "bright shiny objects" of chapter 7, have caused us to look in the wrong places. The record of productivity advance before, during, and after the war makes it difficult to argue that longer-term supply-side benefits from mobilization are to be found in manufacturing. It may be more fruitful to look more carefully instead at distribution and logistics.

9 • Military Distribution and Its Legacy

From a statistical standpoint, the productivity record of wartime manufacturing is reflected, however imperfectly, in the national income and product accounts and the productivity data in chapter 2. That is because almost all U.S. goods production was conducted within privately owned and operated or government-owned but contractor-operated facilities. The few exceptions were government arsenals, armories, and naval yards, and some (but not all) of the facilities associated with the Manhattan Project. These were owned and operated by the federal government and staffed with government employees.

In the case of trade, the situation was markedly different. Wholesale and retail distribution to the civilian U.S. population continued during the conflict, the prewar privately owned and operated sector starved of both labor and infusions of new or replacement physical capital. It is primarily those operations that are reflected in the chapter 8 sectoral calculations. The exemplary productivity record reflected in these data is perhaps best understood as reflecting *learning by doing without.*

An important component of wartime distribution, however, is not included in these data. These were operations conducted by or under the direction of the U.S. military. The United States faced the unprecedented (and perhaps never to be repeated) challenges of supplying the ordnance and supplies necessary to support combat operations on multiple continents, as well as those of our allies, including especially Britain and the Soviet Union. And so a critical question is whether distribution internalized within the military generated learning of persisting relevance for the postwar period.

There is a plausible case that, as in the instance of manufacturing, it did not, that the wartime experience was sui generis and without lasting implications

344

for the golden age of U.S. economic growth (1948–73). There is also a counter case suggesting that the logistics experience, even if not a postcard illustration of efficiency and high productivity, nevertheless laid the groundwork for and stimulated advances in the postwar period, particularly in civilian distribution.

In March 1942 the U.S. Army reorganized its personnel into three commands: the Army Ground Forces, the Army Air Forces, and the Army Services of Supply (later to be renamed Army Service Forces). The official responsibilities of the ASF were to provide "services and supplies to meet military requirements" (Millett, 1954, p. 53). The ASF were responsible for procuring, warehousing, and shipping munitions, food, clothing, medicine, and equipment (along with additional or replacement troops themselves) to U.S. tactical forces around the world. They organized the assembly of troops in staging areas and their embarkation across two oceans. They ran the vast network of forts, camps, airfields, and cantonments that trained and housed troops in the Zone of the Interior,[1] along with the post offices and PXs (post exchanges) and other ancillary services that each of these installations required. They used force where necessary to assure their sources of supply, seizing U.S. manufacturing, transportation, mining, or public utility facilities when commanded to do so by executive order of the president. And, as they rapidly became the largest user of the nation's merchant marine, they sent supplies to multiple fronts around the world. Without the military's delivery of the right munitions, equipment, and supplies in the right quantities when and where they were needed, the manufacturing achievements of U.S. industry would have been for naught.

In his 1945 biennial report as army chief of staff, General George C. Marshall described the enormous range and volume of ASF responsibilities. It "supplied food, clothing, munitions, transportation," operated a fleet of 1,537 ships, managed 3,700 post or cantonment facilities in the Zone of the Interior, operated huge port facilities in Boston, New York, Hampton Roads, New Orleans, Los Angeles, San Francisco, and Seattle, operated 791,000 hospital beds, and managed PXs doing $90 million of monthly sales (quoted in Millett, 1954, p. 2).

In addition to its troops, the ASF employed more than 1 million civilians, and several million more through contracting. Indeed, during the war the ASF became the largest single employer in the nation's history (U.S. Army Service Forces, 1948, p. 112). Between enlisted men and civilians, more than 2 million employees (this does not count contractors) handled upwards of 4 million tons a month within the Zone of the Interior. ASF direct employment can be compared with the roughly 6.6 to 7 million FTEs in wholesale and retail trade within the portion of trade broken out in the National Income and Product Accounts. A smaller logistics operation supported the navy's needs for fuel, maintenance supplies, and ammunition (Connerly, 1951), but the ASF was the dominant organization in military distribution. We can, on the basis of these numbers, say with some confidence that more than one-fourth of all distribution activity during the war was embedded within military spending totals and not readily visible for those interested in studying productivity trends.

A wide variety of evidence suggests that the record of U.S. military distribution, like so many other aspects of military activity, was not one efficiency experts should be proud of. The ASF's final report described duplication and dysfunction in wartime operations:

> Logistic organization and procedures within and between the military forces were far from perfect during the recent war. Too much of our success was accompanied by inefficient practices. Too much was accomplished only by placing terrific strain upon the energies of our logistic leadership. Not enough can be attributed to sound organization and efficient procedures. The many self-contained procurement and supply agencies, eight in the War Department and eight in the Navy Department, had an adverse effect on both industrial mobilization and the supply of combat forces. Duplicating supply lines and different standards of service among the Army, the Navy, and the Air Forces complicated and slowed logistic operations. Within the War Department itself two logistic organizations developed, one for supporting the Army Ground Forces and another for the Army Air Forces. (U.S. Army Service Forces, 1948, p. 247)

Military distribution was responsible for spectacular failures that internal critics retrospectively blamed on the scant attention to logistics in officer training. An illustrative instance: in 1943, when a general in the Zone of the Interior was begging for enough ammunition to allow the ground troops he was training to practice firing their individual weapons and thereby become qualified in their use, "almost a billion and a half rounds of small arms ammunition were piled in depots and dumps in North Africa." For that same North Africa campaign—the first projection of U.S. ground combat troops across the Atlantic in the conflict—tons of equipment and supplies prepositioned in England in anticipation of an eventual cross-Channel invasion could not be accessed because they were buried too deeply in British warehouses or military supply officers did not know where they were. In another instance, vast stocks of blankets in Rangoon, destined for the China-Burma-India theater, were slowly consumed by white ants as large deliveries continued to replenish their food supply. And in a final example, the military relied religiously on standard tables mandating the required equipment complement for an army or marine corps division, so troops destined for the Pacific received the standard allocation of trucks, even when the islands where the troops were to operate had no roads (Leighton and Coakley, 1955, pp. 306, 527, 638).

Somervell—commander of the ASF—had repeated difficulty securing what he viewed as sufficient manpower (Millett, 1954, p. 59). The ground forces command was skeptical of the need to train and deploy so many noncombat troops; their view was that wars were won by troops that fought and, given legislatively approved caps on the total size of the army, more troops to the ASF meant fewer available for combat. On the basis of the documentary record, it appears that ground forces commanders generally dealt with supply issues simply by assuming they would be resolved: God or, if not God, Somervell would provide. His position was that without an organization that could supply food, clothing, ammunition, heavy equipment, and medical services and supplies to the troops in war theaters, combat forces could not fight effectively.

The ASF operations were not very efficient in the conventional sense in part because its leader did not hold efficiency in high regard. Harry Truman observed: "I will say this for General Somervell, he will get the stuff, but it is going to be hell on the taxpayer. He has a WPA attitude on the expenditure of money." Somervell had in fact been in charge of the New York office of the Works Progress Administration during the 1930s. Immediately before commanding the ASF, he had responsibility for building cantonments for the new soldiers drafted starting in August 1940 under the Selective Training and Service Act. He got them housed, but at the cost of a $100,000,000 overrun. His view then, as it was throughout the war, was that time was more valuable than money (Millett, 1954, pp. 5, 7).

Modern supply-chain management depends on an IT infrastructure providing real-time data on inventory stocks at various locations from the point of production to the point of sale. A fundamental problem with wartime distribution was the inadequacy, at least until well into 1944, of procedures or technology to support anything close to "just-in-time" inventory control. Without a semblance of up-to-date reporting of stocks at dumps and depots in the war theaters, the training camps, and the embarkation points, it was simply not possible to run a distribution system lean in its holding of inventories. This mattered because the conceptually simplest way of improving efficiency in distribution is to reduce the ratio of the stocks of physical capital (structures, equipment—including railcars, trucks, and ships—and inventories) to the flows of sales, shipments, or deliveries. An inadequate information infrastructure combined with continuing uncertainty about where and when the enemy would be engaged made this difficult. To avoid costly and possible deadly outages, military commanders competed to maintain large stocks of material and ammunition along the supply chain, a dynamic that, as we have seen, also sapped productivity within U.S. manufacturing.

The practice of holding large buffer stocks risked not only wastage from deterioration and theft but also traffic jams at pinch points, particularly port facilities where supplies were unloaded. The ASF did succeed in avoiding the colossal Zone of the Interior congestion of World War I, which resulted at one point in 44,000 rail cars backed up all the way to Pittsburgh and Buffalo as they vied for access to East Coast ports. In spite of the seizure of the railroads by government troops during that conflict, the congestion was so bad that little ordnance made it to Europe before the war ended, and soldiers in the American Expeditionary Forces had to rely on the British and French for most of their equipment and ammunition. The United States did succeed in supplying its troops with food, clothing, and motor transport, but, for example, only 160 of the 2,000 75-mm field guns its forces used made it. The remainder and all of the 155-mm howitzers came from the British and French, along with 1,000 pursuit planes provided by the French (Millett, 1954, p. 13).

Rail congestion was better managed during World War II—the fact that it was a two-ocean war made operations somewhat easier by reducing the backhaul problem—but ships could (and did) stack up outside harbors waiting to take on cargo, and they did at destinations as well. Congestion at intermodal transfer points could be reduced by tolerating less than carload arrivals of railcars and by sending out less than fully loaded ships. Releasing half-empty ships clearly wasted capacity. But putting a premium on full loads wasted capacity in a different way if it contributed to traffic jams at ports and increased average turnaround time. In principle, efficient distribution benefited when rail cars, trucks, and ships were fully loaded. But they needed to be loaded quickly with the right supplies and be heading to the right destinations at the right time. Aside from the obvious challenges in getting this all right, full loads were difficult to achieve because military cargo was inherently wasteful of space owing to its irregular shapes and high ratios of bulk to weight (Leighton and Coakley, 1955, p. 617).

Attempts to overcome that reality, which would facilitate economizing on space, could lead to other problems. This became particularly apparent with respect to trucks, which were large, bulky, and needed to be transported in very large numbers. Shipping them completely knocked-down (CKD) made the most efficient use of space. But this required trained mechanics at the destination to assemble the vehicles correctly. Where CKD assembly facilities and labor were not available, the optimum trade-off was found to be the twin-unit pack (TUP) or medium knocked-down pack. These expedients allowed trucks to be shipped in two to five packages, and although not as space-efficient as a CKD pack, took up about one-third the volume of a fully assembled truck. A TUP could be assembled by two mechanics assisted by eight inexperienced helpers and did not require heavy tools (Leighton and Coakley, 1955, p. 640).

The supply challenge—balancing the needs of U.S. troops in training with those in theater—was complicated by the role of Lend-Lease. Britain had mobilized a larger fraction of its population for war fighting, on the basis of the expectation that it could rely on the United States as its backup warehouse and arsenal, providing critical supplies, equipment, and raw materials. The strategic objectives of Britain, which included defending an empire on which the sun never set, were not identical to those of the United States. This tension continued to be evident in discussions among the combined chiefs of staff and bedeviled the series of wartime conferences devoted to hammering out Allied military strategy. Commitments to supplying Britain and the Soviet Union along with distribution failures increased the frequency with which troops training in the United States were unable to practice with the equipment and munitions they would eventually use. This was particularly so in 1942, when one-quarter of all munitions production was diverted to Lend-Lease.

Troops about to ship out were supposed to arrive at ports of embarkation fully equipped. But that was not always the case, which required the Army Service Forces to maintain embarkation depots with deep inventories that could fill in gaps. A related debate was whether troops should travel with their equipment, or whether final outfitting should be completed when they arrived in theater, which of course would require depots at that end with inventories. The War Department was, however, loath to build up deep overseas inventories in support of operations that might never in fact be undertaken, one of the many ways in which uncertainties about overall military strategy sapped efficiency in distribution. Still, trying to economize outside the Zone of the Interior risked troops landing in theater without the food, fuel, clothing, equipment, and ammunition needed to fight. Screwups were frequent and often monumental, and today's civilian complaints about delayed baggage from airplane flights are a faint echo: "The equipment of one antiaircraft regiment that went overseas in summer of 1942 was loaded haphazardly on fifty-five separate vessels calling at several different ports" (Leighton and Coakley, 1955, pp. 344–45). On the other hand, the apparently desirable principle that troops be shipped with their equipment conflicted with the need not to waste cargo space by sending out less-than-fully loaded vessels. The bottom line is this: efficiency in distribution could not be achieved simply by focusing on any one particular indicator. The conflict between imperatives not easily reconciled meant that equipment and supplies would often catch up with troops weeks or months after embarkation from the United States—and sometimes never.

Throughout the war, unloading operations in the Pacific suffered disproportionately because of the lack of adequate port facilities and other infrastructure in the region. Inadequate packaging and poor stowage in the holds of ships contributed to near disasters at Nouméa, Guadalcanal, and Espiritu Santo in 1942. The principle of block stowage seemed to make sense, as supplies for a single destination were stored in one hold. In practice, however, "light and flimsy packages loaded beneath heavy ones were crushed; paper bags containing cereals, flour, and sugar tore and their contents spilled; cardboard cartons containing rations disintegrated when exposed to heavy moisture; paper labels on cans disappeared leaving their contents a mystery to the recipients; exposed parts of equipment and machinery corroded and rusted when not heavily sprayed with cosmoline" (Leighton and Coakley, 1955, p. 404).

In the later stages of the war, particularly in the Pacific, ships were used as floating warehouses; lighters ferried supplies and ordnance to shore as needed. This solution limited deterioration and theft of supplies, to be sure, but at the severe cost of immobilizing scarce shipping capacity for weeks or months (Coakley and Leighton, 1968, p. 451).

Although port facilities were generally better in the European and Mediterranean theaters (when they had not been sabotaged by retreating German forces), that availability could not compensate for other failures of logistics. In preparation for Operation Torch (November 1942), the first projection of American ground forces across the Atlantic in the conflict, "hundreds of thousands of tons of material already shipped to the United Kingdom were buried too deeply in British warehouses to be retrieved in time for the impending operations." Unloading at Casablanca was also not a model of superior logistics. Boxes were simply piled one on top of another. Thousands of barrack bags lay interspersed with loose grenades. The ASF had shipped the wrong types of ammunition, along with large quantities of unauthorized or superfluous equipment, while needed fire-control equipment was missing. Again, as in the Pacific, cardboard cartons disintegrated, and metal-strapped wooden crates broke when improperly and roughly handled. Theft led to additional wastage. Eisenhower, the general in command of U.S. forces in Torch, wrote in December 1942 that the logistical operations of the campaign "have violated every recognized principle of war, are in conflict with all operational and logistical methods laid down in textbooks, and will be condemned in their entirety by all Leavenworth and War College classes for the next twenty-five years" (Leighton and Coakley, 1955, p. 455). Operation Torch was a "supply nightmare" (Millett, 1954, p. 113).

The biggest logistical story of the war, of course, was the buildup of men and material in England—often thought of by U.S. planners as a large floating aircraft carrier—in anticipation of a cross-Channel invasion repeatedly delayed until finally executed on June 6, 1944. The long delay was reflected in multiple operation names, all referring to variations on the same basic agenda. Before Overlord, there was Roundup, and before that Sledgehammer. By October 1942, in anticipation of the possibility of Sledgehammer, there were already more than a quarter million U.S. troops in Britain. But as Operation Torch redirected attention to the Mediterranean—a British priority, but one about which the Americans had serious reservations—U.S. troop strength in Britain fell by more than half, to 105,000 in February 1943. Construction and other preparations slowed; preparation became a standby operation with a skeleton crew (Leighton and Coakley, 1955, p. 480). The mixed record of the ASF in operating efficiently during the war should be understood in the context of the environment in which it operated during the first two years of the war. In particular, the absence of a clearly defined military strategy, lack of consensus between the Americans and the British, and constantly changing timetables and plans would have presented severe challenges to even the most experienced distribution organization.

Both labor and physical capital were used inefficiently in military distribution, particularly during the first two years of the conflict. For enlisted men in the ASF, as for those in the ground or air combat forces, much of the experience of life in the military consisted of long spells of relative idleness interspersed with periods of intense activity. The Service Forces (and other army) personnel faced the worst underemployment in 1943, as the wherewithal to move troops and supplies into theaters fell far short of the forces that had been trained (Leighton and Coakley, 1955, p. 210). "Hurry up and wait" were the watchwords. Inventory to "sales" ratios were high because of the imperatives felt by military commanders to maintain large buffer stocks to deal with unexpected surges in demand or cutoff in supply. Ships were used inefficiently— sent out partially loaded, immobilized for use as floating warehouses, sent to the wrong destinations with the wrong supplies. Warehouses and depots were used inefficiently, and supplies could not be accessed when needed because they were buried, because systems had lost track of what was stored where, or because items were poorly or improperly labeled. These obstacles were overcome by directing massive quantities of ammunition, equipment, and supplies to stock inventory reserves, massive quantities of shipping tonnage to compensate for inefficient use and losses from German submarines, and massive supplies of personnel to provide the surge capacity when and where needed.

The tendency for ships to become immobilized as warehouses was evident both in the Pacific and in the European Theater of Operations, particularly in late 1944, when the reconstruction of Cherbourg lagged behind the rapid advance of Allied forces to the French border in the east. The ASF had planned to be able to unload seventy-five ships in the first two weeks of October. The actual total was fifteen (Millett, 1954, p. 85).

These realities and others are abundantly evident in the more than two thousand pages of the three principal sources on which this chapter's account is based: *Logistics in World War II: Final Report of the Army Service Forces* (1948; 297 pages), and the two massive volumes by Coakley and Leighton (*Global Logistics and Strategy: 1940–1943* and *1943–1945; 1955* and *1968; 807* and *916* pages, respectively). These often critical accounts were written by military staff or official military historians. They questioned the relevance of whatever learning might have taken place in the process, either for future military operations or for civilian distribution more generally. In the foreword to the 1993 reprint of the final report, General Harold Nelson, chief of military history, acknowledged, "Many of the logistical problems faced in World War II may never need to be addressed by a future army," and he went on to ask, "If the Army Air Forces dropped two million tons of bombs on our enemies in World War II, and if that quantity of destructiveness could now fit on a single ICBM, what was the relevance of the massive munition production, storage, and transportation experience of that prior war?" Leighton and Coakley, speculating on the implications of nuclear weapons, wondered, since the outcome of future wars "might be won or lost within the first few days or even hours," whether the whole problem of military supply (let alone industrial production), which had determined the course of conflict so often in the past, might now be irrelevant (1955, p. 8). Nuclear weapons, however, played a role only in the closing days of World War II and, they noted, were not used in Korea. Since they wrote, we can add Vietnam, Iraq, Afghanistan, and a variety of other conflicts where this has remained true. Nevertheless, none of these conflicts involved supply challenges comparable to those faced by the military between 1941 and 1945. The United States has never again fought a war like World War II, and probably never will. It is fair to say that the learning that may have arisen from wartime experience in logistics and distribution was of questionable value for the exclusively military challenges that lay in the future.

On the civilian side, the negative conclusion is less clear. When the United States entered the war in 1941, it already led the world in manufacturing productivity—by a substantial margin. The country continued to dominate in the immediate postwar period. But that dominance had little directly to do with the war except to the degree that destruction put a damper on the capabilities of Germany, Japan, and other combatants who would subsequently, along with China, South Korea, and other countries, become formidable competitors. The U.S. never again manufactured the wartime product mix, and the learning obtained in doing so was of questionable value. The capability of the sector after the war largely reflected what had been achieved in the preceding two decades.

As we have seen, the productivity record of military distribution, like that of manufacturing for the military, was often disappointing. In both cases, impressive output metrics reflected the deployment of even more impressive quantities of labor and physical capital, much of which lay intermittently idle or inefficiently used. As in the World War II manufacture of weapons of war, much of military distribution responded to a unique set of demands that would not be repeated.

And yet the magnitude of the demands faced—particularly by the army— brought into sharp relief the complicated challenge of operating efficiently a large international distribution system. It implicitly posed questions about how this might be done better. In particular, could one move beyond ad hoc and sometimes conflicting rules of thumb to a more comprehensive consideration of how complex distribution tasks might be executed? There were some operational improvements in the last two years of the war, but no fundamental changes in planning and operating procedures. Nevertheless, the war stimulated the search for better solutions and provided funding for researchers who pursued them. The fruits of this groundwork were realized largely after the war with benefits that persisted, particularly in civilian distribution.

The most compelling illustration of this involves the development and subsequent use of activity analysis or, as its originator preferred, programming within a linear framework. The requirements of military distribution during the war presented optimization challenges that were far from simple. The objective functions to be maximized had multiple, rather than one or only a very few, arguments. (During the war no one used such language or posed matters in these terms.) It could seem obvious that ordering port managers to fully load ships, or promoting this as a desirable rule of thumb, would enhance the efficiency of distribution. But this might not be true if it resulted in ships remaining in port for longer periods. It might not be true if it meant that critical goods took longer to reach their destination. It might not be true if it resulted in more goods going to the wrong destinations. It might not be true if it meant that ships had to spend more time and fuel delivering their cargoes to multiple locations. It might not be true if it led to more goods damaged in transit, or if it meant that it took longer for high-priority items to reach fighting forces because the items were buried in the bottom of a hold.

Or it could seem obvious that maintaining ships offshore as floating warehouses was more efficient than unloading them in locations with inadequate port facilities and storage facilities, risking spoilage, theft, deterioration, and other forms of wastage. But this might not be true if the practice effectively removed a freighter from the available transport fleet for weeks or months.

Under these circumstances, what rules of thumb should guide port officers or planners? Reduce the turnaround time for ships? At the cost of sending out half-full vessels, carelessly loaded, resulting in damage to goods during transit and multiple errors in destinations? To make the process more efficient, one certainly needed officers better trained in logistics who could analyze operations at the macrolevel, not just the individual components piecemeal. But one needed more than this: these officers needed a means for systematically and quickly evaluating huge numbers of potential programs (coordinated or sequenced activity levels) on the basis of how well they met identified goals. Whereas U.S. manufacturers for the most part entered the war with a highly advanced understanding of relevant production technologies, the tools that would allow the quick evaluation of different activity programs were then

unavailable or only in their infancy. Transportation and distribution challenges played a central role in motivating the search for them.

In a 1939 paper ignored by Soviet authorities and little known elsewhere
until the 1960s, the economist Leonid Kantorovich distinguished between

> two ways of increasing efficiency of the work of a shop, an enterprise,
> or a whole branch of industry. One way is by various improvements in
> technology, that is, new attachments for individual machines, changes
> in technological processes, and the discovery of new, better kinds of raw
> materials. The other way, thus far much less used, is by improvement
> in the organization of planning and production. Here are included such
> questions as the distribution of work among individual machines of the
> enterprise, or among mechanisms, orders among enterprises, the cor-
> rect distribution of different kinds of raw materials, fuels, and other fac-
> tors. (quoted in Dantzig, 1963, p. 22)

Kantorovich's comments were couched in the language of manufacturing,
and it is easy for this to mislead; we need to interpret the use of words like
industry with care. The tendency of economists and others to write as if the
factory is the canonical locus of production and equipment the canonical capital good has a very long history (Field, 1985). Writing in *Operations Research*
in 1963, Norman Barish felt it necessary to note that "the term industrial engineering is used very broadly to include service, distributive, governmental,
medical, agricultural, military, and many other types of activity. Industrial
engineering and operations research are thus not confined to the factory"
(1963, p. 391).

Kantorovich was in fact concerned in this article with a transportation problem: how to calculate the optimal (cost-minimizing) movement and routing
of freight where there were n origination points with known capacity and m
depots with known demands. In reviewing this precursor to advances in activity analysis and linear programming, George Dantzig noted that Kantorovich
wrote "in a nontechnical manner, so as to encourage those responsible for
routing freight to use the proposed procedures."

Tjalling Koopmans, who shared the 1975 Nobel Prize in economics with
Kantorovich, was also inspired by the wartime search for solutions to transportation problems. Koopmans served as a member of the (American-British)
Combined Shipping Board, where he aimed to use mathematical analysis to
reduce overall shipping times in order to alleviate the shortage of cargo ships

then plaguing the Allied war effort. Dantzig attributed Koopmans' "rapid development of the economic theory . . . to the insight he gained during the war with a special class of linear programming models called *transportation models*" (Dantzig, 1963 pp. 18, 300; emphasis in original).

During the war, Dantzig worked at the Pentagon within (and eventually as head of) the combat analysis branch of Headquarters Statistical Control for the Army Air Forces. In the process (according to his recollection), he became skilled at using desk calculators to solve programming-planning models. "Solving" such models involved identifying which among programs (sets of coordinated or sequenced activity levels) was likely to be most effective in meeting specified goals or objectives.[2]

Dantzig returned to Berkeley in 1946 to complete his doctoral dissertation (he had been on leave at the Pentagon). The Berkeley Math Department offered him an academic position (financially unattractive), and to retain him, his superiors in the Pentagon countered, asking him to return to Washington to "find a way to more rapidly compute a time-staged deployment, training and logistical supply program" (Dantzig, 2002, p. 42). Grappling with the challenge, Dantzig formulated a powerful new procedure, the simplex algorithm, which could be used for identifying efficient solutions to transportation problems and many other isomorphic challenges that could be described in a similar fashion. He published details of the method in 1947.

Linear programming could be (and has been) applied to challenges in manufacturing per se (and in agriculture, petroleum refining, and many other areas).[3] But wartime problems in transportation and distribution provided a particularly powerful stimulus to its postwar development, and it is in these areas that it has likely had its most lasting impact. In Dantzig's 1963 textbook, the very first challenge discussed is a transportation and distribution problem (pp. 2–3). Many of his published papers focus specifically on transportation problems (Cottle, 2005). At Stanford University his eventual appointment was as an endowed professor of transportation services.

Within manufacturing, activity analysis is applicable to the second category of challenges identified by Kantorovich. Specific knowledge developed in sequencing and scheduling of production was of relatively little value after the war since the wartime product mix did not persist. In contrast, the postwar period experienced a huge expansion of international trade amid the dawning of the second great age of globalization, and challenges similar to those faced (and only imperfectly met) by the ASF continued to present themselves, to some degree to the military (as in the Berlin airlift), but eventually and more importantly to managers in the civilian economy.

In the transportation problem and the many others to which activity analysis or linear programming could be applied, there were typically a very large number of programs that might be run, and even with the development of electronic digital computers, a brute-force approach to evaluating them was (and is) simply not practical. Dantzig described how this was dealt with before 1946: "In place of an explicit goal or objective function, there were a large number of ad hoc ground rules issued by those in authority to guide the selection" among multiple possible programs (2002, p. 43). The simplex algorithm made possible what was otherwise impractical: it enabled decision makers to zero-in quickly on which coordinated or sequenced set of activity levels (program) was most likely to minimize or maximize some objective function.

The Department of Defense's official definition of operations research is "the analytical study of military problems undertaken to provide responsible commanders and staff agencies with a scientific basis for decision on action to improve military operations" (quoted in Shrader, 2006, p. v). There is widespread agreement that the discipline of operations research (OR) resulted from the challenges and research generated by the war effort. The wartime funding environment produced advances in the theoretical understanding of the principles of supply-chain management and halting progress in its actual practice, particularly during the last two years of the conflict. In both the theory and the practice, the United States emerged in the postwar era as a leader. The journal *Operations Research* and the Operations Research Society of America (ORSA), the organization that publishes it, date from 1952.

OR has nevertheless sometimes struggled for academic legitimacy since it appears to contain a grab bag of different techniques. It has sought to distinguish itself from (and claim more prestige than) industrial engineering, even though similar challenges are addressed in both areas (Barish, 1963). Some of the differences have been cultural: OR departments have been more hospitable to mathematicians and economists and those with interests in theory; industrial engineering has had a more practical focus, with a greater emphasis on the codification of procedural knowledge (Dantzig served in the Industrial Engineering Department at Berkeley and what became an Operations Research Department at Stanford).

On the basis of an analysis of the first generation of OR textbooks, Johnson (1997, p. 913) identified probability and statistics, linear programming, queuing theory, and game theory as core subject matter areas. Linear programming stands out among these because (a) it posed puzzles that interested mathematicians, (b) it was genuinely new, and (c) it had practical applicability. Probability and statistics and queuing theory were certainly of interest to mathematicians but were not new areas of inquiry. Game theory probably has the closest claim to having had a similar developmental path. As John von Neumann noted when Dantzig first discussed his work with him, it used some of the same mathematics. It also experienced analytical advances in the immediate postwar period, particularly with the work of John Nash, which allowed the analysis of non-zero-sum games, expanding beyond the zero-sum games analyzed by von Neumann and Morgenstern. In contrast to activity analysis, however, it is very hard to claim that game theory, although it also advanced theoretically in the immediate postwar period, has contributed much to advancing U.S. productivity over the subsequent seven decades.[4]

The army was a "late starter" in terms of its interest in operations research (Johnson, 1997, p. 897). Of its three commands after the Marshall reorganization of 1942 (Service Forces, Ground Forces, and Air Forces), the army air forces (which became a separate military service, the U.S. Air Force, in 1947, when the Department of Defense came into being) laid the most groundwork for the development of useful new techniques, and it was within this command that Dantzig worked. One of the army air forces' signal achievements was the development of a reporting framework (the Statistical Control System) that enabled close to real-time monitoring of personnel, supplies, and operations. As noted previously, improved efficiency in distribution required advances in and investment in a smoothly functioning information infrastructure.

Dantzig described what he saw as the practical contributions of what he had helped develop:

> Prior to linear programming it was not meaningful to explicitly state general goals and so objectives were confused with the ground rules for solution. Ask a military commander what the goal is and he will say "The goal is to win the war." Upon being pressed to be more explicit, a Navy man will say "The way to win the war is to build battleships," or, if he is an Air Force general, he will say "The way to win is to build a great fleet of bombers." Thus the *means becomes the objectives* and these in turn spawn new ground rules as to how to go about building bombers or space shuttles that again become confused with the goals, etc., down the line. *The ability to state general objectives and then find optimal policy*

solutions to practical decision problems of great complexity is a revolutionary development. (Dantzig, 1981, p. 11; emphases in original)

He also described how the war created a fertile environment for developments that would come to fruition afterward: "The advent or *rather the promise* of the electronic computer, the exposure of theoretical mathematicians and economists to real problems during the war, the interest in mechanizing the planning process, and the availability of money for such applied research all converged during the period 1947–1949. The time was ripe. The research accomplished in these two short years, in my opinion, is one of the remarkable events of history" (Dantzig, 1981, p. 7; emphasis in original).

The major sources of TFP growth during the golden age of U.S. economic growth (1948–73) are to be found in distribution rather than in manufacturing (Field, 2011, ch. 4). These gains were facilitated by theoretical breakthroughs, as practical applications (such as Dantzig's simplex algorithm) and continued growth and improvement in the technologies underlay the nation's information and transportation infrastructures. Walmart, founded in 1950, stands out as an exemplar of an organization that successfully took advantage of both. The signature technological and organizational innovation of the postwar period was arguably not just the shipping container but the complementary investments in railcars, trucks, freighters, and port facilities that *together* (as a system) revolutionized how goods were distributed in the United States and around the world (Levinson, 2016). Just as the telegraph and the railroad transformed American distribution in the last third of the nineteenth century (Chandler, 1977; Field, 1987), computerization and the growing speed of data transfer protocols, combined with big gains in the efficiency of intermodal transfer, made possible modern supply chain management.

Activity analysis or linear programming was not strictly a technological improvement. What it did is make available a tool to arrange labor and physical capital so that their service flows could be more efficiently used. It can be thought of as a facilitator of organizational improvement. Cooper and Charnes indicate that the procedure was first used by the air force in planning and scheduling the Berlin airlift in 1949 (1954, p. 21). Dantzig dates the start of its use in industry (broadly understood) to 1951 (Dantzig, 1991, p. 28). He describes its application in petroleum refining and the routing of tanker ships. Metalworking industries used it for job scheduling. Paper mills used it to decrease trim losses. In 1953 a major producer of catsup used it to determine optimal shipping of catsup from six plants to seventy warehouses (1991, p. 29).

Whenever one attributes a development to the war experience—technological or organizational—one must consider the counterfactual: would these
advances have occurred even in the absence of the war? In the case of linear
programming, perhaps eventually. But there is a case to be made that the war
accelerated its progress and that advances in developing and applying these
methods had benefits for civilian production persisting in the postwar period.
This was particularly so in the areas of logistics, the management of global
supply chains, transportation, and wholesale and retail distribution. Companies in these areas (and in IT production) have been strong performers since
the end of the war. When one compares the postwar and prewar periods, technological and organizational improvement within U.S. manufacturing is not
as striking.

    U.S. TFP growth rates after 1973 proved disappointing, with the exception of
the information technology boom between 1995 and 2005. U.S. manufacturing
continued to shrink as a proportion of the economy, and the most progressive
sectors of the economy were those that produced the information technology
and exploited it to manage distribution networks. The three-quarters of a century following the end of World War II eventually saw a return to the frequent
dominance of suppliers (manufacturers) by distribution companies (such as
Amazon, Costco, Target, Home Depot), a situation not unlike what had prevailed in the 1870s, 1880s, and 1890s with the rise of department stores like
Macy's and large mail-order houses such as Sears, Roebuck and Montgomery
Ward. If we are to argue that mobilization for war ended up having lasting
beneficial effects on U.S. productivity, there may be a stronger case that it was
in these service sectors as opposed to goods production (manufacturing) per
se. There is a plausible case that the distinctive competencies of many large
American firms in the twenty-first century have their roots in responses to
the logistical and distribution challenges posed during the Second World War.

10 • Do You Believe in Magic?

Do you believe in magic?
I'd like to . . .
But I don't.
At least not in my academic work.

When John Sebastian penned the lyrics to his classic song with this chapter's title (Sebastian, 1965), he obviously was not concerned with why people believed what they did about U.S. mobilization for World War II. But he was celebrating human proclivities for abandoning critical thinking, for embracing warm feelings, admittedly in a very different context, that help explain the widespread acceptance of what became and continues to be the conventional wisdom. One word appears again and again in descriptions of U.S. manufacturing during the Second World War: *miracle*. Few who employ the term would admit that they mean or meant it literally. But its use finds ready and often enthusiastic acceptance as it both builds upon and triggers the warm feelings associated with "the Good War," "the Greatest Generation," and, from the Allied perspective, unconditional victory. An appeal to miracles celebrates the ability of the country to produce thousands of Liberty ships, tens of thousands of tanks, hundreds of thousands of aircraft, jeeps, trucks, and guns to supply the soldiers, sailors, and airmen of the United States and its allies while at the same time sustaining domestic consumption. The use of the word suggests that this achievement so far exceeded what could reasonably be expected, given the country's knowledge base and its ostensible labor and capital reserves, that the only way to "explain" it is by invoking the supernatural. That is literally what it means to describe something as a miracle.

As humans we have probably evolved to be receptive to such appeals. Steve Jobs loved to surround Apple's technology creations with the aura of the mystical and was famous for his ability as a persuader to gin up "reality distortion fields." The science fiction writer Arthur C. Clarke captivated many with his claim that "any sufficiently advanced technology is indistinguishable from magic." It must be the case that such invocations tap into something deep within our psyche.

But the norms of scientific inquiry differ from those of science fiction and make it generally inadvisable to use the word *miracle,* except to caution against doing so. More often than not it is an invitation to suspend critical judgment, or an indication that such judgment has been suspended. Ultimately it is an encouragement to make leaps of faith. We discipline such proclivities by examining evidence, and by reminding ourselves that believing something does not necessarily make it so. In important realms progress depends on adopting a more dispassionate attitude and resisting inclinations to be swept along on seas of enthusiasm.

I'd like to believe in magic. I try not to in my academic work. As the previous chapters have argued, there is no need to appeal to magic to explain the increase in manufacturing output during the war. From an accounting perspective, it can be explained by the increase in inputs. Indeed, it can be more than explained by increases in inputs, which is to say that efficiency within the sector declined. It declined because of radical changes in the output mix, because of adverse resource shocks, and because of the behavioral pathologies engendered by shortages and the rationing systems to which they gave rise.

The Second World War did leave significant institutional, normative, and economic legacies for the United States. It solidified a compression of wages and a reduction in overall income inequality that endured for three decades, and this included new opportunities for black workers to move from unskilled to semiskilled occupations, opportunities that might not otherwise have been available (Ferrara, 2018). Many veterans pursued a college education or bought a house, benefiting from the provisions of the GI Bill. Experience with high and progressive tax rates and the introduction of withholding gave the federal government expanded fiscal capacity. Controls on wages during the war led inadvertently to the U.S. system of largely employer-provided health-care insurance. Aside from the aluminum industry, procurement practices reinforced, or at least did not lessen, tendencies toward economic concentration. And the war presaged, after a brief lull, permanently higher levels of military spending, which had persisting regional economic effects (Garin, 2019; Wright, 2017; but see also Rhode, 2003; Lewis, 2007; and Jaworski, 2017, who are more skeptical about the longer-term effects).

The war was not, however, associated with a political revolution or fundamental changes in the instrumentalities of government. There was no significant expansion or contraction of the franchise (Ferejohn and Rosenbluth, 2017). Nor, aside from the destruction on the island of Oahu and possibly the wear and tear on plant and equipment resulting from running double and triple shifts (Higgs, 2004, pp. 504, 515–16), did the war damage infrastructure within the United States and its territories. Appeals to "prairie fire" explanations of the benefits of war emphasize how armed conflict can clear the ground for new growth by burning away retardative institutional structures or destroying outmoded productive capacity, thus paving the way for improved productivity in the future. Prairie fire argument may be applicable at other times or in other places, but it has little relevance in understanding the consequences of what transpired in the United States between 1941 and 1945. The legal and institutional rules governing the operation of the economy changed after Pearl Harbor, but those changes lacked permanence. Most were unwound quickly (some have argued too quickly) with the coming of peace.

This book has questioned the attribution of positive long-term supply-side benefits to U.S. economic mobilization for the Second World War. The evidence in previous chapters speaks against prairie fire reasoning. Yet the thesis survives, and it is worth asking why. Previous discussion has already referred to some of the psychological mechanisms that may bias our receptivity to the argument. The roots of this apparently indestructible optimism can also be found deep in the historiography of U.S. military conflict and economic growth.

An interpretation of the American Civil War known as the Beard-Hacker thesis played an important role. In 1927, in *The Rise of American Civilization*, Charles and Mary Beard argued that the political consequences of that conflict established conditions necessary for rapid economic development in its aftermath, particularly in the manufacturing (industrial) sector and more generally in the North and West. Thirteen years later, in *The Triumph of American Capitalism* (1940), Louis M. Hacker refined and developed the Beards' thesis and, drawing on his interpretation of European and U.S. evidence, set forth a more general claim about war. The experience of the U.S. Civil War loomed front and center in his thinking, as it had for the Beards. Hacker was enthusiastic about the propulsive impact of the conflict over slavery: "Under the leadership of the new and vital force released by the Civil War and Reconstruction measures, American industry strode ahead on seven-league boots" (p. 401). He argued that "railroading, like industrial production, was . . . transformed in the fires of the Civil War" (p. 227). Speaking of the effects of the Napoleonic Wars on England and the Civil War on the United States, he suggested more broadly that "as far as capitalism has been concerned, modern war (while it lasts) has been an unmixed blessing" (p. 250).[1]

Since the end of the Second World War, the thesis that war benefits aggregate supply has, in the U.S. context, been supported primarily by claims about the consequences of economic mobilization for that conflict. But, obviously, before 1941, the thesis could not have drawn sustenance from that source. It was instead the Civil War that proponents repeatedly referenced. Considering combined drafts on blood and treasure, these two conflicts, both lasting roughly four years, stand out as the largest and most costly in U.S. history, so it is perhaps not surprising that promoters of the thesis have appealed to them. World War II was more expensive in purely financial terms. Because it required the production of much greater quantities of military equipment, U.S. expenditures were roughly fifty times larger (when measured in 2001 dollars) in comparison with combined Union and Confederate spending during the earlier conflict. Benchmarked against contemporaneous productive capacity, the difference is smaller but still dramatic: peak annual military expenditure was roughly three times as large relative to potential output in the 1940s as compared with the conflict in the first half of the 1860s.[2] The Civil War, on the other hand, was more devastating demographically. Union and Confederate military deaths of 650,000 (or more) dwarf the 407,000 attributable to World War II and were much greater relative to population: about 2 percent on a base of 31 million as opposed to .3 percent on a base of 140 million for the twentieth-century conflict.

The mechanisms purportedly linking wartime experience with postwar growth also differ. The Beards and Hacker placed considerable weight on institutional change, including pro-growth legislation for the North and West and the elimination of slavery and the plantation system and the growth of sharecropping in the South; they placed less emphasis on advances in techniques or new products specifically attributable to wartime production. As Stanley Engerman noted, most of the industries affected by the Civil War produced consumer goods. For the Second World War, the relative influences are reversed, reflecting the lack of truly dramatic and persistent institutional change, as well as the much greater role of materiel and military capital goods in that conflict. The main focus has been on wartime learning by doing in manufacture for the military, and on its alleged legacy.

Since Hacker published, the supply-side claims about the direct effect of the Civil War on industrialization in the United States have been vigorously disputed (e.g., Cochran, 1961; Engerman, 1966; Goldin and Lewis, 1975; Lindert and Williamson, 2016). It has been easy to show that, on balance, the immediate effects of the war were to disrupt industrial advance in the North. (The wool and metalworking industries may have benefited from the demand for uniforms and guns, but the cotton famine starved New England cotton textile mills.) The political component of the Beard-Hacker thesis—the idea that the Civil War and its aftermath constituted a Second American Revolution—and its implied counterfactual—has proved more difficult to dismiss. The Beards and Hacker emphasized that with Southerners out of Congress, Republicans in 1862 pushed through legislation that included the Pacific Railway Act, which provided subsidies for building a transcontinental railway, the Morrill Act, which established land-grant universities to focus on agriculture and the mechanical arts, and the National Banking Act, which affected the U.S. financial sector for decades to come, all of which they interpreted as pro-growth, at least for the North. Engerman (1966) nevertheless disputed whether any of this played a decisive role in fostering U.S. industrialization in the North and Middle West (his claim was that it would have happened anyway).

Both wars reduced potential output while under way. During the Second World War the economy reeled from resource shocks and a radical change in the product mix. Because the changes were temporary, the experience of wartime production gave little long-run boost to potential output. During the Civil War, the mix of products changed much less relative to that prevailing during peacetime. The drop in wartime potential was due principally to blockades and other transport disruptions that cut off access to inputs such as cotton in the North. Patenting data (chapter 7) caution against entirely dismissing a longer-run boost to potential output attributable to production for the military during the Civil War, possibly because of the greater continuity in the product mix in peacetime and war.

The political components of the Beard-Hacker thesis are part of a larger class of arguments focusing on the influence of war on political systems, legislation, and institutions. Within this class the most powerful is a strain metaphorically describable as prairie fire. Prairie fires blacken grasslands, but in so doing clear the ground of obstructions, allowing regrowth ("green shoots") and possibly even superior yields in the future. Because of its potentially disruptive political effects, it is argued, war can burn away retardant institutional structures or corrupt institutions and thus pave the way for faster growth. War might also have had a large and persisting positive effect on potential output by destroying infrastructure, plant, or equipment, allowing it to be replaced or rebuilt along more efficient lines. These two varieties of prairie fire explanation suggest that in spite of, indeed, because of, its destructive power, war can clear paths for modern, more dynamic growth.[3]

But since both channels were weak or nonexistent in the case of the United States in World War II, the argument about effects on potential output must turn on something other than prairie fire reasoning: longer-run effects on TFP growth or the growth of hours and physical capital services. In other words, it must turn on more straightforward growth-accounting considerations.[4] And these provide a thin reed.

If neither the Civil War nor World War II offers much support for the thesis, what remains? Peter Lindert and Jeffrey Williamson (2016, ch. 4) conclude that the Revolutionary War was retardative, although, to be honest, in this instance no one has really claimed otherwise. Perhaps the Mexican War, which concluded with the treaty of Guadalupe Hidalgo in 1848, is a good candidate. It added 60 percent as much territory to the United States as had the Louisiana Purchase and, therefore, in an arithmetic sense, increased potential output. But we should probably exclude wars of conquest from these considerations. Proponents of the war-benefits-aggregate-supply hypothesis in the United States have not invoked territorial aggrandizement, instead claiming a boost within the boundaries within which the country began the war.

What of other post–Civil War conflicts? Hacker had virtually nothing to say in his book about developments after 1870 and, in particular, nothing to say about the First World War. One of the striking features of the case for the positive supply-side effects of war based on the U.S. experience is the almost complete absence of references to that conflict, the third-bloodiest in the country's history. Various realities have probably contributed, including the relatively short period of U.S. involvement (barely a year and a half), the disastrous rail and truck transportation bottlenecks that developed, and the failure of the country to produce important munition items in time for actual use during the war. (American troops relied on the British and French for aircraft and other heavy equipment, and government efforts to produce smokeless powder and armor plate in-house reached fruition too late to do much good.)[5]

The conflict left a sour taste in the body politic, fueled by narratives of trench warfare immortalized by Erich Maria Remarque and, on a larger plane, disappointment with Wilsonian ambitions and the rhetoric of making the world safe for democracy. The Senate rejected joining the League of Nations, pacifism enjoyed remarkable popularity (no one referred to the 1917–18 conflict as "the Good War"), disarmament remained a central feature of both domestic and foreign policy, and the country retreated into an isolationism that Roosevelt struggled with difficulty to overcome, with an eventual assist from the Japanese. Finally, the Merchants of Death (Nye Committee) hearings in 1936 made it virtually impossible to develop or sustain a narrative emphasizing the heroic contributions of U.S. industry during the conflict, even had there been more basis or enthusiasm for making that claim, or receptivity in the country to it. Whatever the reasons, purveyors of the war-benefits-aggregate-supply thesis are almost entirely silent about the First World War.

Nevertheless, the thesis did not die and was poised to reemerge with the arrival of more favorable environmental conditions. World War II apparently provided these, and Hacker's optimism about the longer-run positive effects of war was almost immediately taken up by influencers during the conflict the United States was poised to enter as he published. In 1943, summarizing a wartime survey he had conducted, W. B. Donham, dean of the Graduate School of Business Administration at Harvard, wrote, "All the record of history points to the notion that wars set in motion great technological changes and encourage great bursts of productivity. The full impact of these changes and the enhancement of productivity comes in the period after the war is over" (Liberty Bank of Buffalo, 1943). We have already seen similar speculation advanced in the 1940s by George Terborgh (1945) and Julius Krug (U.S. War Production Board, 1945a).

But we now have three-quarters of a century of postwar economic history with which to evaluate those optimistic claims. In considering the survival of the thesis, it is important to appreciate that beyond analysis of data and documents such as those cited in this book, other factors have influenced the historiography of World War II. These have included organized campaigns of persuasion (advertising and, frankly, propaganda), which complemented all-too-human predispositions to allow the warm feelings engendered by military victory to spill over into romanticized views of what had happened during the conflict, and the appealing nature of the oft-repeated stories about learning by doing.

The celebratory imperative is common in countries that aspire to be or have been victorious in war. It afflicts journalists, historians, and many others, and it spills over into a sense of obligation to paint all aspects of a nation's efforts in a rose-colored light, glossing over or ignoring inconvenient features. It easily metastasizes into hosannas of praise, crowding out critical analysis. Emerging out of natural human inclinations, it can be powerfully reinforced by those with a vested interest in establishing particular narratives.

The "economic miracle" narrative, with which this book has taken issue, emerged against the backdrop of a continuing contest over how to organize, characterize, and credit the production successes. The use of the word *miracle* to describe U.S. war mobilization took shape in 1942 in an address by Eugene Wilson, CEO of United Aircraft. Picking up on this theme, the Ford Motor Company ran advertisements describing its production efforts as "the greatest miracle of mass production the world has ever seen," language echoed in the firm's film about the Willow Run plant and in much of the journalistic treatment of what was happening within the factory (Wilson, 2016, p. 106; Ford Motor Company, 1945). President Roosevelt used similar words in his January 1943 State of the Union Address, referring to the "miracle of production" (Roosevelt, 1943).

The spread of this language was in part the result of efforts led by the National Association of Manufacturers and the U.S. Chamber of Commerce to ensure that private enterprise got all or most of the credit for winning the war, even though most production took place in government-owned and government-built factories, and armies of government employees, both civilian and military, supervised and monitored what was taking place. Business was determined to reestablish and reassert a dominant status from which it had been, in its view, temporarily and unfairly dislodged during the New Deal.

This narrative was reflected and reinforced in Francis Walton's *The Miracle of World War II: How American Industry Made Victory Possible* (1956) and many other publications, including Arthur Herman's 2012 best seller, *Freedom's Forge: How American Business Produced Victory in World War II*. The reality is that even beyond the government-owned and government-operated navy yards and army arsenals and proving grounds,[6] production took place largely within plants and facilities owned by the U.S. government, which by the end of the war accounted for roughly a third of U.S. manufacturing capacity (see chapter 2). Hundreds of thousands of U.S. government employees, both military and nonmilitary, negotiated contracts, assigned priorities (or, eventually, raw material allocations), audited books, inspected output, and, in some cases, with the backing of arms, took over production facilities where labor or management recalcitrance threatened the war effort.[7] Even after paying excess profit taxes, business did well during the war while risking little (Higgs, 1993).

The campaign to ensure that private enterprise, not government or labor, got credit for the success of economic mobilization was relentless and disciplined, funded, by some estimates, to the tune of a half billion dollars a year.[8] There was, it is true, minor concern within the National Association of Manufacturers about possibly offending the military if business tried to claim too much credit for victory. And business leaders were so focused on who should get credit for the production achievements that they eventually began expressing unease about references to "miracles." Their concern was that such language did not adequately credit the contribution of the production experience gained in "150 years of free enterprise" before the war, as the president of the National Association of Manufacturers put it in a speech in December 1943 (Wilson, 2016, pp. 106, 124, 129).

While the repeated insistence by private-sector leaders that achievements had been made despite bureaucratic hamstringing by government officials and that obstruction by labor was self-serving, their claim that success depended on previous production experience and their misgivings about appeals to the supernatural can be endorsed. We should be skeptical of magical thinking in explaining World War II production successes, just as we are of mystical (and mythical) evocations of the "Greatest Generation" (Klein, 2013). As the official government history of economic mobilization put it:

> There was terrific waste in conversion. After a tragically slow start, many a plant was changed over to war production when its normal product was more needed than its new product. . . . We built many factories, and expanded many others, which we could not use and did not need. Many of these new factories we could not supply with labor or with raw materials, or if we had we would not have been able to fly the planes or shoot the ammunition that would come out of them. But in the process we used up critical material which could better have gone into something else. (U.S. Bureau of the Budget, 1946, pp. 113–14)

It is unlikely that either the National Association of Manufacturers' public relations staff or the hundreds of corporations sponsoring print and other advertisement were thinking ahead to how academic economists and historians would analyze productivity growth decades later. But in advancing the narrative that business deserved exclusive credit for production success, they could not help but also promote the view that productivity growth was consistently and persistently positive. Business leaders feared the exercise of federal power in seizing private property, particularly when doing so supported unions. In general, business had few qualms about criticizing such action and was quick to do so. But when armed troops seized mismanaged businesses whose performance jeopardized the war effort, protests were muted or absent, lest calling attention to these failures might darken the carefully cultivated image of private business (and private business leaders) as visiting efficiency miracles wherever they engaged (Wilson, 2016, p. 201).

Much as we may be tempted to view U.S. economic mobilization for the Second World War through tinted glasses, bequeathed to us as the legacy of private-sector wartime public relations efforts, this was the reality: lack of systematic planning and scheduling led to multiple claimants for limited resources. "During the summer and fall of 1942 scores, if not hundreds, of production lines were closed down for brief periods when the flow of materials ceased" (U.S. Bureau of the Budget, 1946, p. 280). The feasibility debate reached crisis proportions with the October 6, 1942, report by Robert Nathan. That the country was able to proceed in the fashion it did and still win the war was a reflection of the level of its scientific, technical, and organizational capability in 1941 as well as its unrealized potential at the time of Pearl Harbor. It was not a productivity miracle quickly incubated during the months of mobilization, and its successes were the result of civilian and military public-sector leadership as much as that of the private business sector.

The sheer quantity of production should and must be acknowledged. William O'Neill mentioned the "production miracle" but gently added, "if not always so efficiently achieved as memory would have it" (1993, p. 234). Others confronted the narratives more directly. In particular, historians employed by or closely associated with the military have been more careful in avoiding the celebratory imperative and have offered a more balanced evaluation of the success of the production of war goods and its legacy, eschewing references to miracles except in passages cautioning against an easy appeal to them. This probably reflects the attitudes of many in the military itself. Paul Koistinen concluded, "When placed in the proper context, the American production record appears neither exceptional, miraculous, nor prodigious" (1984, p. 101). Alan Gropman, another skeptic, echoed this view. In a 1996 National Defense University publication, *Mobilizing U.S. Industry in World War II: Myth and Reality,* he carefully distinguished between the production and productivity record: "The prodigious arms manufacturing capability of the United States is well known. . . . But myths provoked by sentimentality regarding United States munitions production have evolved in the half century since the war ended. . . . United States industrial production was neither a 'miracle' nor was its output comparatively prodigious given the American advantages. . . . The halo that has surrounded [U.S. production] needs to be examined, because there were enormous governmental, supervisory, labor-management, and domestic political frictions that hampered the effort" (1996, p. 3).

The general claim about war and aggregate supply suffered or should have suffered in the 1950s with the Korean War, which killed almost 37,000 U.S. military and led to a negotiated truce, rather than, as had been true in the preceding conflict, an unconditional surrender of adversaries. It was a much smaller conflict, did not have a decisive conclusion on the battlefield, and, like the First World War, did not engender encomiums to the role of U.S. industry in supporting its successful prosecution. Nor were there claims of major war-related technological advances that contributed to spillovers in civilian production. Nevertheless, the application of the war-benefits-aggregate-supply thesis insofar as it applied to World War II remained robust in post-Korea publications such as Walton's *The Miracle of World War II* (1956).

The general proposition, insofar as it applied to the United States, should have taken a further hit with the Vietnam War, which killed over 50,000 American service people and was arguably lost. The conflict was associated with low unemployment (although, in contrast with World War II, this predated the big upsurge in war spending and ground forces) and an upsurge in inflationary pressures and was followed by a decade marked by economic downturns and almost a quarter century of sluggish productivity growth. Not all of this can be attributed to the conflict in Indochina—two oil shocks in the 1970s certainly played a role, but one might have thought that the history of the Southeast Asian conflict would have put a damper on the war-benefits-aggregate-supply generalization. A variant, however, found support among champions of the space race—admittedly a manifestation of a cold rather than hot war, but one that, in contrast to the concurrent conflict in Vietnam, had a triumphant climax with the landing of a man on the moon in July 1969. Much was made of Tang and Teflon and advances in electronics and computerization, although, of course, it was tough to know how much of this would have happened in the absence of the spending on Saturn Vs.

For the United States it remains the experience of the Second World War that looms largest in fueling the war-benefits-aggregate-supply thesis. In 2007 Keith A. Crawford and Stuart J. Foster observed that the United States "cannot escape the powerful hegemonic hold that World War II has on us; it is part of our everyday discourse and its presence is visible all around us in ideological, political, and academic debates as well as in myriad popular cultural relics, monuments, and memorabilia" (2007, p. 10).[9] This is true even among those of us who are scholars and fancy ourselves immune to such influences. For economic historians and time series econometricians, the Second World War often remains a cipher, a series of years to be omitted from regressions or otherwise passed over. But it continues to play an important role in the macro-economic narrative of the twentieth century—both in closing the output gap remaining in 1941, and in (allegedly) laying the groundwork on the supply side for postwar advance.

In 1948 the United States stood astride the world, both militarily and economically. Japan, having endured two atomic bombings and the earlier fire-bombing of Tokyo and most of its larger cities, lay prostrate. Germany and much of Europe were in ruins. The Soviet Union had suffered 20 million war-related deaths. England had sold off much of its remaining overseas economic empire to pay for military spending. The United States appeared relatively unscathed, and it was easy to connect the country's success in producing hundreds of thousands of aircraft and other military hardware with the level of its potential output after the war and the large productivity gap between the United States and the rest of the world then evident. But the connection is a mirage. The economy's postwar capabilities are almost entirely attributable to conditions already in place in 1941.

The military conflict and the economic mobilization for war that it necessitated diverted energies and disrupted the growth of potential. Although World War II did leave the economy with assets that benefited postwar production capability, it distorted physical capital accumulation, crowding out investment in sectors of the economy not critical for the military effort. The United States suffered more than 1 million military casualties.[10] On the home front, the increase in the female labor force between 1940 and 1944 proved to be a flash in the wartime pan. The country achieved production success, but this was not the consequence of a productivity miracle. Between 1941 and 1948 TFP declined in manufacturing and construction and, in the aggregate, grew more slowly than had been true between 1929 and 1941.

When subject to critical analysis, the learning-by-doing narratives, which seem so compelling on their face, break down as an explanation for an alleged boost to postwar TFP advance not obviously evident in the data. We have looked in depth at the case of aircraft (the largest category of spending on munitions during the conflict) and the Liberty ships. The learning that took place during the war was largely irrelevant afterward because the output mix was different and the country never again mass-produced such large quantities of aircraft or ships in such a limited time frame. Creative responses to shortages of critical raw materials such as aluminum and steel were mostly irrelevant after the war, when more "normal" peacetime availabilities and factor prices returned.

Not all wars are wars of choice. But whatever the objectives for which they are fought, and whatever their merits, they are always and everywhere a waste of human and physical resources. Faced with horrific carnage and destruction, we may be predisposed to search for silver linings. That is probably part of the reason why economists, historians, and much of the general public have often been sanguine about the economic benefits of war, emphasizing its role not only in closing output gaps, but also in accelerating the growth of potential output. This has been particularly so for the United States.

But for the country and its economy, as for other combatants, the Second World War was a detour.[11] The government investment during the 1930s—the highways, municipal airports, bridges, dams, hydroelectric facilities, and rural electrification—complemented private-sector labor and capital and raised potential output in a way that not only made possible the production successes of the Second World War but also established the supply-side foundations for the golden age (1948–73) (Field, 2011). In contrast, the wartime spending on structures and equipment to produce munitions and military durables—which was in total of a similar magnitude—had relatively little long-term value.[12] The war greatly distorted production for a period of several years, as sectors critical to the war effort expanded severalfold and then as rapidly shrank. The effect on the growth of U.S. potential output of this unique and never-to-be-repeated experience was, on balance, almost certainly retardative.

If we must celebrate the achievements of mobilization, we might instead emphasize this. Despite the rampant dysfunctionality, a heavily regulated economy produced and distributed what was needed to defeat the Axis powers. Controls brought with them inefficiency and likely retardation in the long-run growth of productivity and potential output. There was no magic to them any more than there was to what private contractors accomplished on the factory floor. But without "interference" in the operation of the "free" market by those who devised and implemented these controls, the production accomplishments would not have been possible and the war could not have been won.

In an emergency, some goals are more important than long-term growth, and the experience of the Second World War was a reminder of what government could do when prepared to take over from the private sector control of investment, production, and allocation. The fear that the American public might draw the wrong conclusions from the experience of mobilization helps explain the relentless push of business propagandists to denigrate and indeed erase the role of the public sector in winning the production battles.

In mid-1942 Donaldson Brown, a corporate director of DuPont and General Motors, expressed concern that the "public has not come to distinguish between the necessity of central planning and regimentation in time of war, and the exercise of corresponding functions on the part of government in time of peace." He worried that interested parties with "ulterior motives" might argue that this same apparatus "could be applied with equal benefit and effectiveness in the post-war economy." And at the National Association of Manufacturer's annual meeting in December 1942, H. W. Prentis, the chair of its executive committee, spoke disdainfully of the "childlike" faith too many had placed in government: "It is not government that has wrought the miracle that is being accomplished today in the production of war materials, but the initiative, ingenuity, and organizing genius of private enterprise" (Fones-Wolf, 1994, p. 26). These quotes from early in the U.S. war effort reinforce Mark Wilson's conclusion that "the business community had already decided what lessons Americans should learn from industrial mobilization even before the arsenal was up and running" (Wilson, 2016, p. 105).

It is unlikely that the United States will ever again confront a military challenge whose breadth, intensity, and duration are comparable with those faced in World War II. In the nuclear age, conflicts will either be over quickly or be limited in their geographical scope. That said, in 1950 the Defense Production Act (DPA) placed on the books authority to reinstate almost the entirety of the World War II administrative machinery.[13] In cases of national emergency, the legislation gave the president or his or her delegates power to set priorities or allocate materials (Title I), requisition materials or facilities (Title II), subsidize the expansion of facilities or materials supply (Title III), control wages and prices (Title IV), order settlement of labor disputes (Title V), regulate and control credit (Title VI), and suspend antitrust enforcement, allowing what might otherwise be illegal cooperation among private companies (Title VII).

Congress allowed titles II, IV, V, and VI to lapse at the end of the Korean War, but titles I, III, and VII remained in force in the 2020s. Title I permits

government orders to jump the queue, ahead of a firm's other supply obligations. Title III authorizes the encouragement of domestic production via loans
or loan guarantees, subsidies, long-term contracts, or purchase and installation of equipment in government-owned or privately owned facilities. Title VII
allows suspension of antitrust enforcement, enabling competitors to cooperate in producing needed goods or materials.

The challenges presented by the 2020–22 pandemic differed in important
respects from those seven decades earlier. But in both cases, a crisis exposed
vulnerabilities resulting from reliance on global supply chains. During the
war this involved access (most importantly) to natural rubber, but also to tin,
chromium, manganese, mica, tungsten, silk, and manila fiber, and during
the pandemic, to personal protective equipment, ventilators, and materials
for vaccine production. The policy dilemma was similar: how to balance the
benefits of cheap foreign sourcing against the costs of stockpiling or providing
backup production capability as insurance against the possibility of a cutoff.

In 2020 the federal government used some of the authority granted to it
in the DPA to encourage the production of ventilators, prevent hoarding of
personal protective equipment, obtain equipment and supplies needed for
vaccines, and subsidize their production. Resort to the act was, nevertheless,
marked by an absence of unity of administrative action, criticized by the Congressional Research Service as "sporadic and relatively narrow," and reflecting the unpredictable enthusiasms of the nation's chief executive (Karbassi,
2021). President Trump invoked the DPA on March 18, 2020, but four days later
expressed reluctance to use it, equating it with "nationalizing our business"
(Farley, 2020).

The successor administration expressed less ambivalence about the desirability of federal involvement or the invocation of the DPA. For example,
President Biden used the act to give Pfizer priority access to special syringes
needed to extract an extra dose of vaccine from the vials in which its vaccine
was shipped (Arnsdorf and Gabrielson, 2021). Building domestic capacity to
address or protect against sudden increases in demand for critical materials or
disruption of heretofore reliable foreign supply, stockpiling large reserves of
wasting inventories, requiring existing producers to give priority to some customers and thus depriving others of prompt fulfillment—all of these actions
have downsides. None is likely, over either the short or the long run, to improve efficiency, raise productivity, or reduce costs in the industries affected.
In combatting a pandemic, as much as in fighting a world war, these are not
primary objectives. Nor should they be.

The ideological conflicts that marked political discourse during the war (and earlier) have persisted and will persist. The ideas, values, and indeed slogans permeating conflict in the 1930s, the 1940s, and the postwar period are remarkably similar to those expressed in the third decade of the twenty-first century. The deepest cleavages remained the respective roles of government and the private sector in addressing opportunities for and threats to the nation. They are not less important today than they were seven decades earlier.

As the war came nearer to its end in 1944, Everett Hagen and Nora Kirkpatrick attempted to forecast 1950 U.S. potential output. They did so in part by extrapolating postwar productivity growth on the basis of trends before Pearl Harbor and anticipated two possible criticisms: that the war was either "(1) so accelerating or (2) so retarding the rate of technical progress that estimates of advance . . . based upon pre-war trends will not be applicable to the postwar period." In calling attention to these contrasting objections, they acknowledged the wide differences in opinion about the effects of mobilization on productivity as wartime manufacture peaked. Hagen and Kirkpatrick then identified two types of evidence they saw as underpinning the accelerationist view: first, data on the rise in GNP since 1941 (which would not in itself be dispositive since it could and did result from large increases in inputs), and second, "the frequent mention in current news and advertisements of great advances in techniques and in productivity in the production of war goods" (Hagen and Kirkpatrick, 1944, p. 488).

It is that combination of appeals that has sustained the positions so many have held and continue to hold: on the one hand, references to the indisputable increases in manufacturing and total output, and on the other, narratives about trends in productivity promulgated by those with interests in shaping our beliefs or who have just been swept along by an appealing, emotionally satisfying story. In its wartime public relations campaigns, business fostered a disciplined, consistent narrative: productivity was growing by leaps and bounds. It is revealing, however, that in the immediate postwar period, when labor pressed for wage increases based on this same claim, management began to argue the opposite, that productivity had in fact declined. These wage demands took place in the context of a historic strike wave that crested in February 1946; 22.9 million man days were lost that month because of strikes or lockouts.[14]

It is only a modest simplification to say that during the war business took the public position that productivity as well as production was soaring, and that this was more or less entirely attributable to the efforts of business, not labor or government (see Herman, 2012). When the war ended, management then claimed (correctly, in my view, but not, as in the earlier claims, in full-page magazine ads) that productivity had in fact been falling. Whereas the purported increase during the war had been credited to the efforts of business, the decline was now attributed almost exclusively to the efforts, or non-efforts, of labor, acting both individually and collectively. A 1946 survey found that 73 percent of executives explained declining wartime labor productivity as primarily the result of "a general indifference on the part of the workers" (Fones-Wolf, 1994, p. 72). One manager complained specifically about "absenteeism, tardiness, disinterest in application to the job, lessened pride of workmanship, and just plain soldiering" (Harris, 1982, p. 63). Such grumbling is common in the history of industrial relations, but tight labor markets did give individual workers more bargaining power and reduced the fear of leaving or losing a job. The very low wartime unemployment rates contributed to what business perceived as a "loss of control and productivity at the workplace."

This weakening of shop floor control was, however, viewed as temporary and likely to be reversed with the return of higher unemployment after the war. The situation was tolerated during the first two years of mobilization because of the urgency of meeting wartime production deadlines and the high profits to be made by doing so. When in 1944 it became clearer that the war would be won, business began preparing for the postwar political battles that would lead, among other successes, to the passage of the Taft-Hartley Act. The adoption of a more aggressive posture toward worker discipline in that year led to an uptick in wildcat strikes, presaging a much more extensive wave of strikes during the eight months following V-J Day (Harris, 1982, pp. 60–63).

Change in the attitude and behavior of employees in an extremely tight labor market was, however, at best only one of many factors contributing to lower productivity. Others, discussed in this book, included radical changes in the output mix, resource shocks due to enemy action, a recurring inability to obtain complementary inputs in a timely fashion, producer hoarding, poor management, and, most generally, the relative lack of priority accorded during the war to efficiency improvement. These realities are reflected in comments by a vice president of the American Management Association: "Production costs are relatively unimportant during a war. . . . Military products wholly new to industry are placed in production with little or no idea of what they should cost, and the customer cares little about their actual cost so long as the goods are delivered. . . . The manufacturer is usually assured the return of the full cost, regardless of inefficiency, with a fixed profit to boot. Renegotiation confiscates a major share, if not all, of the reward for reduced costs. These conditions soon destroy the cost-consciousness of any organization" (Hill, 1945, p. 7, quoted in Harris, 1982, pp. 62–63).

In maintaining that productivity had risen, labor could reasonably argue that it was merely repeating what business had claimed publicly during the war. Management's new posture now produced sharp differences between the two parties about what had actually happened between 1941 and 1945. In response, the Bureau of Labor Statistics and the Bureau of the Budget convened a special conference in October 1946 to try to resolve the empirical question (Hirsch, 1947, p. 397).[15]

The passage of the Taft-Hartley Act was one marker of an often successful postwar agenda pursued by business and those aligned with it. The use of language was an integral part of that campaign. During the war, Senator Robert Taft, one of the sponsors of the act, echoed a rhetorical position shared with much of the business community when he worried that government-owned industrial facilities would not be "returned to private industry" at its conclusion. Taft's phrasing reflected a strong sense of business entitlement. Such facilities could not literally be "returned" to the private sector at war's end because at that point they had never been part of it (Taft, 2001, p. 310, quoted in Wilson, 2016, p. 251).

In 1953 Congress appointed a second Hoover Commission, charged, as was the first, with improving the efficiency of executive branch operation by, among other things, "eliminating nonessential services, functions and activities which are competitive with private enterprise" (Divine, 1955, p. 264). Mirroring concerns and a point of view similar to that articulated by Taft, a subcommittee report on Defense Department business enterprise opposed the military's continued ownership and operation of large industrial facilities manufacturing ordnance because these facilities "constitute[d] a substantial encroachment upon our private enterprise economy." The report went on to object to continued operation of the ten surviving naval shipyards on the grounds that they represented "an alarming intrusion into the private shipbuilding industry." (U.S. Commission on Organization of the Executive Branch of the Government, 1955, pp. 34, 41; Wilson, 2016, p. 275).

The United States had operated government-owned shipyards and arsenals since the late eighteenth century and public enterprise had long played a dominant role in naval construction Six of the ten yards were eventually shut down or privatized; the remaining four were converted to a maintenance-only role. It may or may not ultimately have proved cheaper to produce vessels in private yards. In terms of the simple meaning of words, however, the reduction in public capacity did not take place because naval shipyards were an "intrusion into the private shipbuilding industry," any more than government-owned industrial facilities built during the war could be "returned" to the private sector.[16]

Reflecting on the success of public relations campaigns in discouraging critical inquiry, Senator Claude Pepper (D-Florida) observed in a 1946 speech that "we have almost enshrined the words 'free enterprise'—propagated by the National Association of Manufacturers . . . into a national taboo beyond the reach of inquiring minds" (Wilson, 2016, p. 270).

In asking readers to examine and perhaps discard deeply held views, I am asking that we consider what it means to embrace the miracle narrative, and why we might be receptive to it. My answer is in part that we are human (it makes us feel good), in part that business spent hundreds of millions of tax-deductible dollars during the war to cement an often misleading and at best woefully incomplete narrative that encouraged us to do so, and in part that many writers and influencers after the war embraced and reinforced this feel-good narrative, oblivious to or ignoring what management claimed in postwar labor negotiations.

In thinking about the war, no less than in understanding the political terrain of the second half of the twentieth century and navigating that of the twenty-first, we must continue to be sensitive to the ways in which interested actors work and have worked, often with a deep understanding of human behavior and psychology, the use of language, and techniques of persuasion, to shape narratives about the present and the past.

Notes

Chapter 1. The Impact of War Mobilization on Economic Potential

1. Ruttan went on to argue that "military and defense-related R&D and procurement has been a major source of technology development across a broad spectrum of industries that account for an important share of U.S. industrial production" (p. 5), emphasizing computers and the internet, but he passed lightly over the histories of electricity and the internal combustion engine, which owed little to stimulus from military conflict, although in the long run they have probably been more important in contributing to the growth and development of the U.S. economy.

2. In a *New York Times* opinion piece in 2014, "Lack of Major Wars May Be Hurting Economic Growth," Tyler Cowen surveyed broader historical treatments and made similar arguments. His emphasis was on the claim that war focused national attention on big projects, a focus that might be lacking in peacetime.

3. Gordon originally settled on One Big Wave as his way of calling attention to the strong TFP growth that characterized the half century between roughly 1920 and 1970. In *The Rise and Fall of American Growth* he abandoned this catchphrase and adopted instead a Great Leap Forward. The idea of applying this language to TFP growth in the 1930s originated with me (2011). In explaining his appropriation, Gordon cited Baumol (the quote given earlier) as evidence that the idea of a "great leap" was current in the literature a quarter century before I published (Gordon, 2016, pp. 706–7). But Baumol used the words to apply to a period after 1941, accepting what was then conventional wisdom that productivity advance was below trend between 1929 and 1941. His view, roughly the opposite of what I had argued, epitomized what has for decades been the conventional view of the Depression and the war.

4. Bakker, Crafts, and Woltjer (2019) are of little help in adjudicating these differences since they don't explore growth across the war years. They argue that the postwar period (1948–73) was the locus of the most rapid TFP growth, a position that Gordon

endorsed beginning around 2000 but subsequently abandoned. Most recently, Gordon has stepped back from discussion of individual subperiods and instead focused broadly on the half century 1920–70 (Gordon, 2016, 2018). But calculations over shorter intervals remain important. They can powerfully affect our understanding of different subperiods by directing our attention toward additional evidence and influencing how we interpret it.

5. The output gap closed substantially between 1938 and 1941, and Christina Romer (1992) stressed the role of expansionary monetary policy in bringing this about. With the coming of war and Fed commitments to peg short- and long-term government borrowing rates and thus monetize growing government deficits, monetary policy starting in July 1942 became even more expansionary, as is evident in data on the monetary base (Federal Reserve Bank of St. Louis, "St. Louis Adjusted Monetary Base," https://fred .stlouisfed.org/series/AMBSL).

6. Baumol speculated that "perhaps the accumulated innovative ideas, unused because of the depression, as well as frustrated savings goals, fueled an outburst of innovation and investment when business conditions permitted" (1986, p. 1082).

7. In the case of Germany and Japan it is sometimes argued that the *destruction* of plants by Allied bombers enabled replacement with newer vintages of factories and equipment in the postwar period, facilitating growth of product and productivity. But this argument is different from one based on learning by doing during wartime production.

8. It may seem jarring to think of demobilization beginning already in 1944. According to annual data, munitions production peaked in that year. Monthly data, however, show the peak in November 1943. After the Soviet victory at Stalingrad in January 1943 and Allied military progress in North Africa, Sicily, and Italy, as well as in the Pacific, there was by late 1943 a consensus that the Allies would win and increased pressure to reopen civilian production lines and reduce or eliminate rationing. Limited moves in that direction early in 1944 were reversed following the German offensive late in that year (the Battle of the Bulge).

9. The Selective Training and Service Act reintroduced the draft in September 1940, and active-duty military increased by a factor of five between 1939 and 1941. But this was from a very low level—345,000 to 1.8 million—far from the peak of 12.2 million in 1945. In comparison, Germany in 1941 had more than 7.2 million men in uniform. Looking backward from the end of the war, rather than forward from 1939 to Pearl Harbor, gives a very different perspective. Less than 5 percent of total inflation-adjusted military spending between 1940 and 1945 had been incurred by the end of 1941 (Field, 2003, p. 1403; 2011, p. 85). The upward inflexion point in munitions production in 1942 (see figure 5.1) marked a qualitative change in the nature and intensity of mobilization and coincided with a sharp reversal of productivity trends in manufacturing, from strongly positive between 1939 (or indeed 1929) and 1941 to strongly negative from 1941 through 1945.

10. The most widely cited annual unemployment estimates are from Lebergott (1964), and they put the civilian unemployment rate at 9.9 percent that year. Darby (1976) argued that federal emergency workers should be considered employed, which would bring the rate down to 6 percent, but the claim is controversial, since it presumes that, had those workers not had government relief jobs, they would have been working in the private sector. DeLong and Summers (1988, p. 467) argued that five-sixths of the Depression-era decline in output per working-age adult relative to trend had been reversed before Pearl Harbor, but this is based on the extrapolation of trend growth rates before 1929, which are not necessarily a good guide to what happened across the Depression years. Potential output grew exceptionally rapidly between 1929 and 1941 and more slowly between 1941 and 1948, and the output gap remained substantial in calendar year 1941. Romer expressed a similar view: in spite of the rapid growth after 1938, "it is certainly the case . . . that . . . output remained substantially below normal until 1942" (Romer, 1992, p. 760).

11. Inventory buildup is treated by national income and product accountants as "purchases" by firms of their own output, which guarantees (subject to statistical discrepancies) that gross domestic expenditure equals gross domestic product and income at all moments in time. Many people wonder how, if this is so, aggregate demand can ever fall below output, thus (allegedly) dragging it into recession. The answer is that aggregate demand is understood to include only *intended* inventory accumulation. Firms respond quite differently to inventory changes that are unintended, and they will cut output and employment when inventory buildup is unplanned.

12. That is one reason estimates of government-spending multipliers during the war at the national level are unlikely to be reliable policy guides during periods of economic slack, when interest rates are at or close to the zero lower bound, even though the clear exogeneity of the World War II military spending increases provides an attractive solution to the identification problem.

13. Natural resources also influence an economy's ability to produce. So long as availabilities are relatively unchanged, they have little influence on the conduct and interpretation of growth accounting as described above. To the degree they do change, the effects will show up in the residual. Discoveries of new resources can be thought of as an addition to knowledge, improvements in extraction processes are a form of technological change, and disruptions of supply through international trade, a negative influence, can be analogized to loss of a technology for transforming domestic goods or services into the desired import.

14. In explaining growth of output, increases in available labor or capital services or improvements in knowledge are positive supply shocks. When growth accounting is done in terms of output per person, the relevant factors are capital deepening (rises in the capital-to-labor ratio due to growth of capital services faster than growth of labor input) and improvement in knowledge. Ditchdiggers with access to power machinery move more cubic meters of earth per hour than those using only hand tools. Those

with better knowledge of excavation procedures or how best to organize a work brigade do so as well.

15. Both labor productivity and TFP, particularly TFP, are procyclical: the measures tend to rise as an economy comes out of a recession and decline going into a recession. These cyclical effects are overlaid on longer-term trend growth rates of productivity (see Field, 2010).

16. Their analysis is based on data in Richard Duboff's 1964 Ph.D. dissertation.

17. National Bureau of Economic Research, "Automobile Production, Passenger Cars, Factory Production for United States," https://fred.stlouisfed.org/series/M0107 AUSM543NNBR.

Chapter 2. Manufacturing Productivity Before, During, and After World War II

1. The assembly line methods used to produce Liberty ships mark a permeable boundary between manufacture and construction. Building vessels is commonly described as maritime construction, although construction strictly defined is limited to goods that remain fixed in place. Ships move, and war planners considered them part of overall munitions production.

2. This formulation elides the distinction between embodied and disembodied technical change. And, while acknowledging the role of serendipity, economists do not literally believe TFP growth falls from the sky. In the case of World War II, the main mechanism allegedly responsible for the purported advance in manufacturing TFP was learning by doing, including scale effects. Investigations of other periods have quantified expenditures on R&D as a separate input to the production function. The reference to manna from heaven, although widely attributed to Solow, cannot actually be found in either Solow (1956) or Solow (1957).

3. General government is excluded from the PNE and the PDE. But government enterprises that cover a substantial portion of operating expenses by selling goods and services to the public, most importantly the Post Office, are included in these national economy aggregates. For purposes of productivity analysis, excluding general government makes sense since the value of its output in the national accounts is measured by the value of compensation. Given this method of reckoning output, productivity in general government cannot grow. See Kendrick (1961, appendix K) for discussion.

4. Although the growth rate of productivity can be calculated without price data in this manner, the *level* of productivity in the multiproduct environment cannot meaningfully be characterized except as an index number.

5. I have left the influence of possible changes in labor quality to be picked up in the residual factor. To the degree that the rate of improvement or change does not differ greatly across time periods, it will not affect the ordinal ranking of TFP growth rates in different intervals.

6. Backman and Gainsbrugh wrote that "man-hour data are homogeneous, easily measured, and common to all industry, in contrast to the diverse nature of machines and equipment" (1949, p. 165).

7. Assume that the bulb burns just as brightly from the day it is installed until the day the filament breaks and that there are no repair and maintenance costs until the bulb burns out and must be replaced (no service flow deterioration).

8. One-hoss-shay deterioration is a reference to a poem by Oliver Wendell Holmes about a two-wheeled, horse-drawn carriage that worked perfectly for a hundred years and then fell apart all at once at the end of its life. Bridges and dams are examples of long-lived public assets that approximate one-hoss-shay deterioration profiles.

9. The more one believes overall deterioration profiles approach this pattern, the stronger the case for preferring a gross to a net stock measure as a proxy for a productive stock and the flow of capital services. The Bureau of Economic Analysis's (BEA's) efforts are largely directed at constructing net wealth measures.

10. A related convenience is that deterioration or depreciation for a given year can be easily calculated knowing only the value of the stock at the start of the year, since it will always be a constant percentage of that number, regardless of the vintage demography of the stock. For other age-efficiency profiles, deterioration cannot be calculated without knowing the history of past annual new investment.

11. Only the third of these claims can be considered uncontroversial. What does it mean to say that the assumption is "conceptually correct"? Hyperbolic age-efficiency profiles have also been used by the Australian Bureau of Statistics, Statistics New Zealand, and the OECD (OECD, 2001a, p. 19; 2009, p. 92).

12. The main example, also described in section 4.3 of the manual's second edition (p. 42), involves an asset cohort with different linear age-efficiency profiles for each member of the cohort and shows that the integrated profile of the cohort will be pulled toward convexity (convexity toward the origin means that the asset type loses a large percentage of efficiency in the initial years). The case illustrated assumes a cohort with a range of service lives, and efficiency deteriorating at different rates even before the asset is retired (see also Hulten, 1990, p. 126). The results are considerably less dramatic if one makes the more reasonable assumption that the deterioration profiles for the individual assets are identical even if the retirement dates are not. Finally, the decision to populate the example with linear rather than hyperbolic age-efficiency profiles also makes the argument appear more compelling than perhaps it should be.

13. The agency assumes that an asset's original purchase price represents the discounted present value of the stream of expected benefits to the owner during the interval between installation and retirement. The main components of property income are corporate profits, net interest, and depreciation. Property income also includes rental income of persons (rent accruing to commercial real estate companies shows up as corporate profits) and a portion of proprietors' income (income to unincorporated

businesses, partnerships, and cooperatives). Corporate profits resolve themselves into dividends, retained business earnings, and taxes. The estimates of rate of return also incorporate the effects of taxes and changes in the nominal prices of a new asset over time, per the full Hall-Jorgenson theory. The approach requires the assumption of long-run equilibrium in the markets for both constructing and renting capital goods.

14. A note on philosophy: It is better, in my opinion, to be approximately correct than precisely wrong, and better to stick with calculations that can be easily understood using data that can be easily sourced and therefore easily replicated. Bespoke adjustments and imputations should be kept to a minimum. They are often little more than educated guesses, and with too many it becomes almost impossible to judge the reliability and meaningfulness of the resulting TFP numbers. This may help explain, for example, why Denison's work (1962, 1974), which included many such adjustments and imputations, although widely cited when first published, has been less influential in recent years. References in the Google Ngram Viewer collapse after 1980.

15. If one believes age-efficiency profiles are generally hyperbolic (service flow deteriorates slowly initially, then rapidly at or toward the end of the asset's life), and if one is forced to choose between a gross or net wealth stock as a proxy for a productive stock, a gross stock is preferable, since assets are subtracted only upon retirement. Solow's 1957 calculations, based on net wealth data, were gently criticized by Hogan on this basis. In his reply, Solow was dismissive of the potential empirical significance of the issue (Hogan, 1958; Solow 1958). Kendrick used gross stocks.

16. Although Gordon (2016) identified the 1940s as the decade during which U.S. TFP growth was fastest, in 1969 he expressed some concern that the U.S. "Wirtschaftswunder" (alleged wartime productivity advance) was overstated because of the failure to include government-provided physical capital in official fixed asset data (1969, p. 226). The vast majority of military goods were produced in government-owned but contractor-operated facilities; contractor-employed workers and the value of production from these facilities are included in the output and labor input data.

17. The 1948 calculation may be biased upward, since some of the government-funded and government-owned manufacturing assets had been sold off and were already included in the private-sector totals at their sales prices, which represented a heavy discount from their cost of construction.

18. The measurement of capital and labor shares involves difficult decisions about how proprietors' income is allocated and whether and for what purposes gross as opposed to net (of depreciation) measures are to be preferred (Rognlie, 2015). Capital shares commonly used for this period vary between one-quarter and one-third. The 1929–41 calculation is insensitive to differences within this range, since labor and capital input growth rates were quite similar. For 1941–48, assuming a capital share of .25 would imply TFP growth within the sector of −1.34 percent per year.

19. The manufacturing annual output growth rate between 1929 and 1941 calculated here (4.43 percent) exceeds that from Kendrick's table D-II (3.81 percent), which was

used in Field (2011); thus the higher reported TFP growth rate. For 1941–48, the 1.98 percent per year output growth calculated here is slightly less than a rate based on Kendrick's output index, which grows at 2.20 percent per year over that period. The major contributor to the difference is the adjustment to capital input for government-owned, contractor-operated capital described in the text.

20. Massell (1960, charts 1 and 4) also found stagnation in both labor and TFP across the war years, although he used a gross output measure, rather than value added, a procedure he acknowledges may introduce an "unknown bias" in his results (p. 183).

21. The labor productivity numbers in table 2.3 are consistent with Krug's claim, if we are prepared to view a .8 percent annual rise from 125.9 in 1939 to 131.1 in 1944 as "sharp." Measuring from 1941, both labor productivity and TFP declined during the war.

22. In 2020–22 the world experienced a global pandemic that forced millions of teachers to embrace online instruction. Some optimistically proclaimed that the crisis would bring long-run benefits for pedagogy. After more than a year under the new regime, most instructors (and many of their employers) were of the opinion that online teaching for most courses could not end soon enough, and that much of the skill acquisition, which had real opportunity costs, would decay from nonuse and have little long-run value.

23. Recall that the fundamental growth-accounting equation using only K and L as inputs can be rearranged to decompose the growth of labor productivity into a portion due to TFP growth (a) and a portion attributable to physical capital deepening: $y - n = a + \beta(k - n)$, where β is capital's share. The larger the economic aggregate, the more we can justify focusing simply on K and L inputs.

24. National Bureau of Economic Research, "Electric Power Production for United States," https://fred.stlouisfed.org/series/M0128AUSM247NNBR. Blunt-force rationing of electric power occurred once, when James Byrnes, director of the Office of War Mobilization, ordered a nationwide electrical brownout to cope with a severe shortage of fuel oil on the East Coast of the United States in the winter of 1944 (Lingeman, 1970, p. 267).

25. Before 1947 the BEA does not provide information on the makeup of nonresidential fixed assets or the fixed asset composition of (private) physical capital within manufacturing.

26. There is one additional caveat about capital inputs during the war for the metalworking industries, which were devoted almost exclusively to military goods between 1942 and 1944. The BEA numbers probably include the automobile- and appliance-maker equipment mothballed for the duration of the conflict. A category of capital goods "temporarily obsolete" because the goods to whose production they were specialized temporarily stopped is unusual. We have added in the government-provided machine tools for making the war goods. One might argue that since the mothballed tools were useless in producing the war goods (and not available at production sites), capital input

is slightly overestimated during the period of economic mobilization. But any such effect is probably swamped by other factors attributable to the use of net wealth stocks that result in an understatement of capital service flow growth.

27. This calculation is based on the table 2.3 index of labor productivity for 1941 and 1944, and an assumed war manufacturing labor force of 16.6 million in 1944.

Chapter 3. What Kind of Miracle Was the U.S. Synthetic Rubber Program?

1. The ability to lay waste to Japanese cities depended on long-distance bombers (B-29s) capable of carrying large payloads. The March 9–10, 1945, air raid on Tokyo, which relied entirely on conventional ordnance (incendiary bombs), was more devastating than either Hiroshima or Nagasaki and remains the most destructive bombing raid in human history. It killed approximately 100,000 Japanese civilians and leveled sixteen square miles of the city. Another raid on Tokyo on May 25–26, 1945, leveled an additional seventeen square miles, and at least sixty-five other Japanese cities experienced major damage as the result of incendiary bombs (Wilson, 2011; Vander Meulen, 1995, p. 8). Had more raids of this nature not forced Japan to surrender, U.S. military forces would almost certainly have been capable of a successful land invasion, which had always been the anticipated endgame. The atomic bomb hastened Japan's surrender because of the efficacy of its destructive power and its psychological impact. One plane with one bomb leveled four square miles in Hiroshima, whereas it took 279 planes and tons of conventional ordnance to level sixteen square miles in the March Tokyo raid. The two atomic bombs used against Japan each weighed about five kilotons but had an explosive yield of fifteen and twenty-one kilotons of TNT, respectively. One B-29 could carry a payload of up to eight kilotons of conventional or atomic ordnance to Japan, so it took three or four aircraft to carry conventional ordnance equivalent in explosive power to Fat Man or Little Boy. Atomic bombs, once built, were a more efficient means of killing people and destroying physical capital, but that did not make them indispensable for U.S. victory.

2. The British long ton (2,240 pounds) differs from the U.S. (short) ton (2,000 pounds). For historical reasons, imports of natural rubber are reckoned in long tons, whereas production of synthetic rubber is measured in short tons.

3. The argument is not that nations or firms (or individuals) should not or do not learn from adversity. The claim is rather that in most cases the net effect is to leave the affected actors worse off than if they had not experienced the adverse shock. In part this is because time and energy spent learning to deal with conditions that may never recur combines limited and uncertain future benefits with nonnegligible opportunity costs.

4. Such contracts were, however, superior to cost plus a percentage of cost (the norm in World War I), which provided clear incentives to inflate costs.

5. After the war, piston-driven engines faded in importance, and the country never again mass-produced airplanes in World War II–level quantities. See chapter 6.

6. Rubber blankets were, nevertheless, an essential item in the equipage of Civil War soldiers (Wilson, 2006, pp. 17–18).

7. The top-six producing countries in 2017 were, in order, Thailand, Indonesia, Malaysia, China, India, and Vietnam. Ironically, plantation cultivation of rubber never succeeded in Brazil.

8. The U.S. continued to receive a trickle of imports from Ceylon (Sri Lanka), which has sometimes, although not usually, been considered part of Southeast Asia. Ceylon remained under British control during the war.

9. This is another illustration of how the uncertainties and disruptions of war lowered productivity. Initially, capital productivity went down because of pressures for the accumulation of larger inventory stocks, which meant higher ratios of inventories to production and thus reduced output per unit input. Ultimately, both labor and capital productivity were affected if, in the event, the stocks proved insufficient given the actuality of supply disruptions, and production requiring them was slowed or halted.

10. The contracts struck between Rubber Reserve and the International Rubber Regulation Committee on June 29 and August 18, 1940 were contingent on an open market price within a very narrow range. If the price was above that, the U.S. would not buy (U.S. Tariff Commission, 1940, pp. 27–28). "Jones, formerly a smalltime banker, hoarded the Rubber Reserve Corporation [sic] fund, searching for bargains that did not exist because war was inflating commodity prices" (O'Neill, 1993, p. 79). When a warehouse in Fall River, Massachusetts, burned down on October 12, 1941, destroying at least 15,000 tons of crude rubber, Jones reportedly exclaimed, in a remarkable display of nearsightedness, given how critical the size of the stockpile would be less than half a year later, "Good thing we have it insured" (New York Times, October 13, 1941; Janeway, 1951, p. 82). Herbert Feis wrote that he and others at the State Department wished to pursue purchases more aggressively but were thwarted by Jones, who placed sharp limits on what Rubber Reserve would pay (Feis, 1947, cited in Rockoff, 2000).

11. By 1941 rubber companies, increasingly fearful of a cutoff of supply, were bidding against each other and against Rubber Reserve (Rockoff, 2000, p. 11). This change gave the company (and Jones) power to act monopsonistically, as sole purchasing agent for all the rubber fabricators (the Purchasing Committee consisted of a chair and purchasing agents from the five largest rubber product manufacturers) (Rubber Reserve Company, 1945, pp. 15–16). Monopsony power would be worthless less than a year later, when supply was completely cut off.

12. According to a report of the U.S. Tariff Commission, tires made from crude rubber ran for 25,000–30,000 miles; those using reclaimed rubber without addition of crude ran for less than half that (1940, p. 50). An attempt to make an all-reclaimed tire in the last quarter of 1942 was a costly disaster (Wendt, 1947 p. 218). Nevertheless, after

the Stevenson Plan pushed up world prices in the 1920s, reclaimed rubber came to provide the raw materials for a sizable fraction (on average about one-fifth) of U.S. rubber product manufacture. An industry rule of thumb was that it took 1.82 pounds of reclaim to substitute for a pound of virgin rubber. In 1940 the U.S. used 190,000 tons of reclaim, equivalent to 105,000 tons of a total consumption (measured in virgin rubber equivalent) of 757,000 tons that year (Stocking and Watkins, 1946, pp. 56, 75).

13. A Truman Committee report from 1942, however, stated that the plantation, "for the first time, is expected to yield up to 1,000 tons" (U.S. Senate, 1942, p. 43).

14. See Frank Swain, "The Wonder Material We All Need but Is Running Out," BBC, March 8, 2021, https://www.bbc.com/future/article/20210308-rubber-the-wonder-material-we-are-running-out-of for discussion of this concern.

15. Spending on the Haitian project totaled $6.9 million; it was abandoned in February 1944 because of bad weather (drought), insect pests, the absence of an efficient extraction process, and the availability by that time of significant quantities of U.S. synthetic rubber. Between March and July all the *Cryptostegia* acreage was burned (Hubert, 1947, p. 282; Wendt, 1947, p. 209). During the war 47,000 acres—one-twentieth of Haiti's arable land—was planted in U.S.-sponsored rubber projects, which also included *Hevea*. Despite the early termination of the *Cryptostegia* project, more rubber from that source was exported than from *Hevea* trees.

16. This is based on converting the metric tons (2,204 pounds) into long tons (2,240 pounds) and dividing by the 775,000 long tons consumed in 1941.

17. Even after Pearl Harbor, Brazil remained neutral, although increasing losses of freighters to U-boats gradually pushed the country into the American orbit. On May 23, 1942, while still neutral, it signed the Brazil–United States Political Military Agreement, one component of which anticipated natural rubber exports to the U.S. of 45,000 long tons a year. The Brazilian government forcibly enlisted tens of thousands of impoverished citizens to serve as "Rubber Soldiers." Many died, and the increase in exports from Brazil was modest and did not approach the target. Brazil declared war on Germany and Italy on August 22, 1942. U.S. Vice President Henry Wallace had an almost romantic vision that necessary replacements for the lost imports from Southeast Asia could come from Latin America, while at the same time bolstering democracies in the region. The need for synthetic rubber was therefore, in his mind, questionable (Janeway, 1951, p. 342).

18. A 1940 U.S. Tariff Commission Report stated that crude rubber was "indispensable" in the manufacture of "motor vehicles, airplanes, balloons, gas masks, electric motors, ships, railroad trains, street cars, electric lights, telephones, typewriters, erasers, printers' rolls, wireless apparatus, radios, medical goods, hospital sheeting, jar rings, fire hose, garden hose, orchard spray tubing, milking machines, athletic goods, overshoes, and tennis shoes." It was used, but not indispensable, in the production of "transmission belting, packing, gaskets, shoe heels, raincoats, mats and matting, smokers' articles, toys, and in the sealing of tin cans" (1940, pp. 1–2). The concept

of indispensability acquired something of a bad name among economic historians because of the role it played in the debate about the contribution of the railroad to nineteenth-century U.S. economic growth (Rostow, 1960; Fogel, 1964). But sometimes indispensability means just that: in the case of tires and other products, there were no available alternatives and none reasonably foreseeable that could substitute for the functions rubber performed. There were alternative sources of elastomers—loosely cross-linked polymers with elastic mechanical properties—as the synthetic rubber program and the processing of guayule demonstrated.

19. "There have been many adjustments and readjustments in the synthetic rubber program. Some were inevitable. Some appear to be the result of bad administration" (Rubber Survey Committee, 1942, p. 13).

20. The rubber situation was part of a larger set of constraints. General George Marshall "became aware immediately before the Casablanca conference that the munitions production he expected the United States to produce in 1943—the basis of his strategy—would not be available until June 1944. Therefore an invasion in 1943 was impossible" (Lacey, 2011, p. 4). The Casablanca conference (January 14–24, 1943) brought Roosevelt and Churchill together to plan Allied strategy.

21. The initial downturn in the second half of 1941 was partly due to the 20 percent cutback in automobile production starting in August negotiated by William Knudsen, then head of the Office of Production Management (see chapter 5).

22. Carothers, who had recently been recruited from Harvard's Chemistry Department, would go on to develop nylon before, despondent about his future creativity, committing suicide in 1937.

23. Cracking is rarely carried to that extreme, since heavier fractions such as fuel oil and asphalt are also in demand. In the twenty-first century a forty-two-gallon barrel of crude is refined to yield on average nineteen gallons of gasoline and ten gallons of diesel fuel.

24. All the hydrogen-carbon bonds in saturated hydrocarbons are single. Unsaturated hydrocarbons have double or in some cases triple bonds and are more reactive. An alkane is a class of unsaturated hydrocarbons with formula C_nH_{2n+2}. An alkene is a class of saturated hydrocarbons with formula (C_nH_{2n}). Monomers are molecules that can be linked together by covalent bonds (sharing an electron) in long chains, forming polymers. A copolymer is a polymer composed of more than one monomer. Isomers are compounds with the same molecular formula but different structure and characteristics.

25. Unlike other chemicals, there was no other significant demand for butadiene, so existing production—say, to serve consumer needs—couldn't simply be diverted to the synthetic rubber program.

26. In 1945 Rubber Reserve claimed that the gradual addition of this capacity was entirely due to new information on the availability of industrial alcohol as an input, as opposed to political pressure (Rubber Reserve Company, 1945, pp. 21–22).

27. The natural stock was not in fact exhausted in 1943. It appears the Rubber Survey Committee's estimate of military and other essential consumption between July 1, 1942, and December 31, 1943—842,000 long tons—was too high by perhaps 140,000. This may be partly attributable to the postponement of the cross-Channel invasion, which at the time the committee wrote was still tentatively planned for 1943. Because of the shortfall in hoped-for GR-S production in 1943, however, the year-end stock of natural rubber dropped precipitously, from 422,714 long tons at the end of 1942 to 139,594 long tons at the end of 1943. At the end of 1944 it was dangerously low: 93,650 long tons (U.S. Rubber Survey Committee, 1942, p. 5; Rubber Reserve Company, 1945, p. 58).

28. "In brief, Standard Oil had agreed, beginning in the early 1930s, not to develop processes for the manufacture of synthetic rubber in exchange for the German firm's commitment not to compete in the American petroleum market" (Finlay, 2009, p. 176).

29. Aside from styrene and acrylonitrile, no other compounds have been found that copolymerize with butadiene to make satisfactory synthetic rubber.

30. Reclaimed rubber is an imperfect substitute for natural rubber, as it wears out about twice as quickly when used in tires. An important obstacle in using reclaimed is the need to remove the fibers in the fabric cord used to strengthen and shape the original tire. Reclamation involves grinding up old tires, removing fibers and other foreign substances, and then adding plasticizers and fillers like carbon black (U.S. Senate, 1942, p. 46).

31. The industry was dominated by five companies, which controlled 80 percent of the alcohol-distilling capacity. Some of the heat emerging from the Gillette Committee reflected conflict between these large producers and farm interests advocating for smaller, local distilleries. Carbide and Carbon Chemical Company (Union Carbide) produced 20 percent; Publicker Commercial Alcohol, 18 percent; U.S. Industrial Alcohol Corporation, 17 percent; DuPont, 13 percent; and Commercial Solvent Corporation, 12 percent. See "Alcohol Trust Investigated, Says Arnold," *Washington Post*, May 8, 1942, p. 31.

32. In the historiography of U.S. mobilization for the Second World War, the term *defense period* sometimes denotes the interval between the German attack on Poland (September 1939) and the Japanese attack on Pearl Harbor (December 1941). See Connerly (1951, p. ix) or Crawford and Cook (1952, p. 1). More often it refers to the months between the fall of France (June 1940) and Pearl Harbor (December 1941). See Fairchild and Grossman, 1959, p. 73; Harris, 1982, p. 30. That latter interval is also sometimes called the *emergency period*. See Risch, 1953.

33. Risch claimed: "In general, by the end of 1943 shortages of most metals had disappeared. . . . The story of metal conservation was one of famine followed by feast." Although the situation had undoubtedly improved, this is an exaggeration. The same source refers to late summer of 1944 as when increased supplies of aluminum and stainless steel could be resubstituted in the production of various items of military equipage, and some shortages recurred in late 1944 (1953, pp. 65–66, 172).

34. For a more favorable view of the outcome of the research program, see Morris, 1989, p. 55. Morris does allow that "solving production bottlenecks and improving the quality of the rubber were important, perhaps more important than innovation during World War II" (p. 27).

35. In his 1946 memoir, Donald Nelson, who had served as head of the WPB, recollected, "To this day I do not understand the difficulties we encountered in building up stockpiles of rubber prior to Pearl Harbor or in erecting synthetic rubber plants" (Nelson, 1946, p. 290).

Chapter 4. Petroleum, Paukenschlag, and Pipelines

1. Ickes served as Interior secretary from 1933 through 1946, the longest tenure of anyone in that role. The title of the agency he headed changed from Office of Petroleum Coordinator for War to Petroleum Administration for War (PAW) on December 2, 1942.

2. The largest refinery in the world at the time, owned by Standard Oil of New Jersey, was located in Aruba, a Dutch-owned island close to the Venezuelan mainland that processed much of the Venezuelan crude.

3. It is fair to say that for the U.S. economy, and for other combatant countries as well, protection of the environment had an even lower priority than efficiency during the war. A comparison of annual average global temperatures with the 1901–2000 average shows that there is in fact a substantial positive anomaly for each of the years 1940–45. Indeed, 1940 is the first positive anomaly in the time series going back to 1880, and all six of the anomalies are the largest until 1973 and 1978 and the rapid acceleration beginning in the 1980s (Lindsey and Dahlman, 2019). The interpretation of the wartime anomalies is, however, controversial. Thompson (2008) attributes them to a measurement issue resulting from the different methods used by British and U.S. ships to ascertain ocean temperatures, and the drop in the share of British ships contributing such measurements during the war. Still, the greenhouse gases produced by burning petroleum during the war cannot have been a long-term positive as far as climate change.

4. In 1941 the seventeen states on the East Coast (PAW District 1) consumed 1.5 million barrels of petroleum and petroleum products a day, most of which was shipped in by tanker from the Gulf Coast. Only 80,000 barrels of crude were pumped locally in District 1 (Maxwell and Balcom, 1946a, p. 561).

5. Over the years 1941–45, approximately four-fifths of U.S. crude production came from Texas, California, Louisiana, and Oklahoma (U.S. Bureau of the Census, 1955, p. 750).

6. The demand for gasoline tends to be high during the summer travel season, but some of the crude refined to produce gasoline will also yield heavier fractions such as fuel oil, which will not be in strong demand until the winter.

7. Petroleum and petroleum products accounted for more than half the total tonnage shipped overseas from the United States during the war (U.S. PAW, 1946, p. 1).

8. The Japanese had planned but did not follow through on a third wave of attacks on Pearl Harbor intended to destroy the tank farm and 4.5 million gallons of fuel oil south of Hickam Field. Gannon argued that had the Japanese gone after the port facilities, including repair yards and the submarine pens, it would have taken another year before the navy could have been active again in the Pacific (1990, p. 390). Admiral Chester Nimitz is on record stating that blowing up the fuel storage tanks would have prolonged the war by two years.

9. Thomas Blaisdell, a member of the WPB's Planning Committee, had opposed the pipeline on the grounds that scarce steel would be better deployed by raising and repairing the sunk tankers. Indeed, the entire Planning Committee, including its chair, Robert Nathan, opposed the pipeline.

10. Roosevelt had appointed him petroleum coordinator for national defense on May 28.

11. Load lines are marks on the exterior of a vessel indicating how low in the water the vessel can safely settle. In other words, they specify a ship's maximum draft and are intended to limit the weight of the cargo it can carry.

12. U-boats also sank over 50 percent of the original fleet supplying bauxite from Dutch Guyana to the United States and Canada (U.S. Civilian Production Administration, 1946a, August 25, 1942, meeting, p. 120). Again, the navy could not or would not provide adequate convoy protection, which led both Undersecretary of War Robert Patterson and the full WPB to express deep concern and petition the Combined Chiefs of Staff to provide convoy protection for imports of a material critical for airplane production.

13. "Allied sinkings were particularly heavy in Atlantic waters. Because of a deficiency in escort vessels, the United States Navy was not prepared to perform an adequate job of convoying. For some months the fate of the war hung in the balance. . . . The long tanker haul from the Gulf of Mexico had to be given up because escort vessels could not be spared from convoy duty in the Atlantic and Pacific" (U.S. Bureau of the Budget, 1946, pp. 135–36, 155). Thus, claims by Kennedy and other authors that the reduction in coastal sinkings after May 1942 was due to the introduction of an "Interlocking Convoy System" are questionable (Kennedy, 1999, p. 570). A more plausible explanation is simply that there were few remaining targets. Figure 4.1, for example, shows that there was hardly any recovery of tanker deliveries of petroleum to PAW District 1 until fall 1943, and then the increase was quite modest until the end of the war in Europe.

14. Per million British thermal units (BTUs), natural gas produces 117 pounds of CO_2; oil, more than 160; and coal, more than 200. And the contribution to global warming is less if the gas is burned, producing CO_2, than if the unburned gas (mostly

methane) is simply flared—allowed to escape, uncombusted, into the atmosphere (U.S. Energy Information Agency, 2019).

15. Before the war refiners had also perfected alkylation techniques, whereby light hydrocarbons—olefins like propylene and butylene, as well as isoparaffins such as isobutane, were put into a catalytic reactor to produce isooctane, another important antiknock additive. And refiners had developed experience with catalytic polymerization and hydrogenation to produce other blending agents. One area where processes could have benefited from more road testing before the war was the new fluid catalytic cracking process, also critical to the rubber program.

16. Again, up to, but not quite over the line into magic.

Chapter 5. From Priorities Unemployment to Labor Shortage

1. *Priorities unemployment* refers to the temporary or permanent idleness of productive inputs caused by lack of access to or unavailability of complementary inputs, including raw materials, machine tools, subassemblies such as valves or heat exchangers, or, toward the end of the war, labor. Priority rankings determined the order in which firms were supposed to fulfill orders from their customers; a high priority allegedly took you to the head of the line. Henry J. Kaiser quipped: "A priority is something which gives you an option to ask for something which you know you're not going to get anyhow" (Lingeman, 1970, p. 112).

2. Throughout the war the government abruptly terminated contracts as designs were deemed obsolete, materials were in short supply, the product was no longer needed because the desired product mix changed, or the end of the war was forecast (rightly or wrongly) to be within sight. As early as 1941 the army canceled a large contract with Chrysler to build tanks based on an outmoded design. Steel shortages in 1942 led to termination of a contract with Higgins Industries in New Orleans to build Liberty ships (Klein, 2013, p. 452). The concern here is with the supply-side effects of contract terminations. After peaking at the end of 1943, aggregate spending on munitions didn't decline sharply until the second quarter of 1945, following VE Day. But the continuing changes in military demands spread intermittent idleness and periods of low productivity throughout the economy on a persisting basis. These effects accelerated as the product mix continued to change and the end of the war was glimpsed in 1944 and 1945.

3. The WPB was the immediate successor to two other Executive Office agencies, the Office of Production Management (OPM) and the Supply Priorities and Allocation Board (SPAB), both of which were then abolished, although the WPB inherited many of the staff and most of the responsibilities of these two entities, as had OPM from NDAC. The authority to establish each of these agencies derived from the passage of the Administrative Reorganization Act of April 1939, which created an Executive Office

of the President, for the first time giving the presidency its own administrative machinery (see Klein, 2013, pp. 18, 123, 156).

4. Operation Torch, which began in November 1942, represented the first deployment of U.S. combat troops in the European or Mediterranean theater.

5. Even then, Churchill's embrace of the cross-Channel plan was reluctant, and after the successful invasion of Sicily (July–August 1943; Operation Husky) there was enthusiasm among some Allied war planners for concentrating forces in a march up the Italian peninsula, at the expense of the buildup of forces in the United Kingdom that would be necessary as preparation for Overlord—the cross-Channel invasion then planned for May 1944.

6. Some of the stonewalling on what was needed reflected the fact that in the first two years of the war, the Army Service Forces—helmed by General Brehon Somervell—did not have any better idea than the WPB about what types of campaigns were to be waged, and where and when. This passage is from the ASF's final report: "During the early stages of the war, the Army Service Forces had little or no guidance from the War Department General Staff or Theatre Commanders in computing these requirements. This was understandable because the strategic plans being considered at the highest government levels were constantly changing" (1948, p. 59).

7. The Maritime Commission was responsible for building the merchant shipping, most owned by the U.S. government, that would supply Allies and move military ordnance and sometimes troops to theaters of war. The Victory Program, which called for an army of 215 divisions by summer of 1943, assumed that the Soviet Union would by then have been defeated by the Germans, its worst forecasting error.

8. In a speech before Congress on May 16, 1940, after the invasion of France, Roosevelt floated a goal for the country to have a fleet of 50,000 military aircraft, and an annual production capacity of the same number. This seemed a stretch at the time given that the total number of planes on hand at the end of 1939 was 1,800 (Leighton and Coakley, 1955, pp. 21, 29; Klein, 2013, p. 37).

9. These targets were aspirational. Merchant shipping exceeded them: 8.09 million deadweights tons in 1942; 19.296 million in 1943. Aircraft came close: 47,836 and 85,898 in 1942 and 1943, respectively. Tanks never came close: 23,884 and 29,497 in the two years (U.S. War Production Board, 1945a, pp. 107–9).

10. In his memoir, Nelson defended his decision not to take purchasing authority away from army, navy, and Maritime Commission procurement officers. He argued that even though he had the authority and the experience to execute such a transfer, there was not time, that it would have taken six weeks to set up an effective purchasing organization within the WPB, and that civilians freshly drawn from the private sector would be especially vulnerable to criticisms of favoritism in the award of huge military contracts. Nelson was able to appoint some of his own men (people who had worked closely with him) to the military procurement bureaus (Nelson, 1946, pp. 188–89; Connery, 1951, pp. 147–48).

11. Nelson referred to estimates of total business failures between Pearl Harbor and the end of the war as between 500,000 and 650,000, claiming that the casualty rate was "not greatly above that of normal peacetime years" (Nelson, 1946, p. 270). For descriptions of the uneven effects of war mobilization and the coexistence of soaring orders and profits in some sectors and businesses with fears of idleness and unemployment in others, see Klein (2013, pp. 243–47.)

12. The Office of Small Business Activities (OSBA) had operated under Nelson when he served as coordinator of National Defense Purchases on the NDAC, which had preceded OPM, which had preceded the WPB. When OPM replaced NDAC (January 1941), the OSBA was renamed Defense Contract Services, and renamed again the Division of Contract Distribution in September 1941 (Heath, 1972, pp. 297–99).

13. The shortages of copper, unlike those of aluminum and magnesium, remained serious throughout the war. Huge scrap drives and subsidization of production in marginal mines were some of the methods used to try to overcome them. In midsummer of 1942, the army furloughed 4,000 soldiers who had previously worked in mines, allowing them to return to digging ore (Nelson, 1946, p. 173). At the October 27, 1942, meeting of the WPB, General Somervell stressed the critical importance of conserving copper, and May urged Somervell to implement programs to recover scrap from battlefields where possible (U.S. Civilian Production Administration, 1946a, p. 150). Brass shell casings would have been a particular target. In the early stages of the war, steel scrap was also a concern since it is used to charge open-hearth furnaces. Planners failed to anticipate that shutting down passenger vehicle production would sharply curtail the availability of scrap.

14. "American production, for the most part, was based upon special purpose tools, which frequently made it impossible to transfer machine tools constructed for one type of work to some other more urgent use" (U.S. Army Service Forces, 1948, p. 66).

15. In the event, reabsorption does not appear to have been a great problem, given draft calls and the continuing need for manufacturing workers.

16. Kuznets mused that in the final analysis, "better production and scheduling control rather than securing a more feasible set of production objectives" was paramount, although both were important.

17. Plans for a cross-Channel invasion were considered as early as April 1942 by Roosevelt and U.S. and British military advisers. Bolero eventually came to refer to logistical preparation, whereas Roundup applied to planning for tactical execution in 1943 (Ross and Romanus, 1965, p. 17).

18. The Americans and the British differed greatly on the merits of Torch in ultimately defeating Germany. The British knew that the brunt of any cross-Channel invasion in 1942 would be borne by British troops. The country had less rosy recollections of the Western Front in World War I than did the Americans, and the memory of Dunkirk was still fresh in their minds (Isserman, 1991, p. 60). By clearing German submarines out of the Western Mediterranean and removing the military threat to the Suez Canal,

Allied success did have the economic benefit of reopening the preferred route to India, cutting a month off a round trip between Britain and its colony. This added the equivalent of a million tons of shipping that could be redeployed in part to the North Atlantic run, over which the United States was supplying its ally with oil, ordnance, and foodstuffs (O'Neill, 1993, p. 187).

19. The act also gave the army and navy authority, under threat of condemnation, to acquire land for military or defense purposes, made it easier for aliens serving in the military to become citizens, and repealed the confidentiality of census data, allowing the FBI to round up Japanese citizens and residents on the West Coast for internment.

20. In contrast, Nathan viewed Nelson as "one of the brightest" and "liked him very much," but he saw him as "somewhat soft. . . . The military never forgave the civilians for getting as much power in the war as they did. . . . Somervell would come along and stick a knife in Don's back, and Don would reach around and pull it out and say, 'Pardon me, General, is this yours?' and Somervell would say, 'Oh, yes, thank you. Thank you, Don.' Then he'd turn around and stick it in the other side of Don's back and Don would reach out and say, 'Pardon me. General, isn't this yours?'" (Nathan, 1989).

21. In a December 1942 report, the Truman Committee criticized earlier rejections of priorities for the project. The OPM had given as a reason the need to economize on steel, but the Truman Committee argued that any such savings were almost certainly less than the metal lost in sunk tankers (U.S. Senate, 1942, p. 135).

22. Extrusions are made by pushing hot metal through a die with a shaped opening, creating a piece with a uniform cross section. Other means of fabricating metal include casting (pouring liquid metal into molds), forging (hammering, pressing, or rolling), and milling (shaving off tiny pieces until the desired form is attained).

23. The War Manpower Commission had been formed in April 1942 with McNutt heading it.

24. Significant mid-war changes in the military output mix during that year also contributed, and the annual data for 1945 were affected by the disruptions, including strikes, associated with demobilization.

25. Nelson claimed that "eleven months after ground was broken at Willow Run [which would have been March 1942] the first four-engine Ford-made Consolidated bombers were assembled" (1946, p. 220). This is terribly misleading. These were incomplete kits that were trucked to assembly plants run by other companies in Tulsa and Fort Worth. It was not until well into 1943 that Ford had a full-scale assembly line producing operable planes. And Nelson glosses over the consequences of Ford's insistence on hard steel dies and standardized design, which necessitated major work by modification centers to prepare the planes for combat. There is no evidence for Kennedy's statement that in December 1941, eight months after groundbreaking at Willow Run, "the first of the plant's eighty-five hundred B-24 bombers rolled off the end of the mile-long assembly plant" (Kennedy, 1999, p. 653).

26. The standard terms were *essential* and *non-essential*, but at the WPB, Vice President Henry Wallace pushed for different language: *more essential* and *less essential* (Nelson, 1946, p. 169). For the purposes of writing economic history, if not for writing bright-line government regulations, there are grounds for preferring Wallace's terminology.

27. For example, see *Washington Post*, February 25, 1933, p. 16, or any similar date during the worst year of the downturn.

28. Britain, Canada, Australia, and New Zealand all implemented comprehensive industrial drafts. In Britain, the National Service Act (December 1941) made all men under fifty and all women under thirty subject to assignment by government to industrial or other jobs. With combinations of carrots and sticks, the United States moved a considerable distance in that direction, even without new legislation. For example, on September 7, 1942, the War Manpower Commission issued a "freeze" order preventing employees in the Pacific Northwest lumber industry from leaving their employment to work elsewhere (U.S. Senate, 1942, p. 147).

29. A concern with labor hoarding is mentioned as early as November 1942 in a Truman Committee report (U.S. Senate, 1942, p. 122).

30. The preference of draft boards to spare fathers, evident soon after the passage of conscription in September 1940, was associated with a half million more marriages in 1940 and 1941 than would otherwise have been expected, and an upsurge in births in 1941 and 1942 (O'Neill, 1993, p. 87).

31. Casualty data through November 15, 1943, show 14,321 army killed, and 13,160 navy, marine, and coast guard dead, for a total of 27,481. During all of 1943, the army experienced 74,150 battle casualties, including 15,399 killed in action. In 1944 these annual totals increased by a factor of more than six: 530,344 battle casualties, of which 96,699 were killed in action. Total battle casualties for 1945 were 301,271, of which 49,992 were killed in action. The estimate of fatalities remaining at the start of 1944 is based on adding to the November 15 numbers the additional 1,083 army fatalities and an estimate of an additional 1,000 fatalities for the navy, marines, and coast guard for the last month and a half of the year and dividing by the approximately 407,000 total fatalities for the war (which includes military deaths not battle related). Had the war concluded at the end of 1943, it would have been, in terms of fatalities, a relatively minor conflict in the annals of U.S. military history (U.S. Selective Service System, 1945, pp. 10, 26; U.S. Army Service Forces, 1946, p. 211).

32. The authors included the economists Clarence H. Danhof and Lloyd G. Reynolds, as well as the political scientist V. O. Key.

33. As a member of the Harvard Corporation, he was primarily responsible for the appointment of James Conant as the university's president. After the war, believing that the United Nations charter did not go far enough in creating a world government, he was one of the founders of the World Federalist movement.

34. The Bureau of the Census's 1946 *Statistical Abstract* (p. 173, table 196) shows a decline in the civilian labor force from 52.5 to 51.3 million between 1943Q1 and 1944Q1.

35. "B-24 Bomber Assemblies Being Loaded into a Trailer, Willow Run Bomber Plant, circa 1943," Henry Ford Collections, https://www.thehenryford.org/collections -and-research/digital-collections/artifact/217082/.

36. The tanks were called Lees in the United States and Grants in Britain.

37. In this and many other government publications one finds references to Standard Munitions Dollars. Crawford and Cook include this note to a similar enumeration: "Data were computed from physical quantities delivered and standard dollar weights which for the most part were unit costs as of 1945 (1952, p. 20). See also Fesler, 1947, p. 961. But the *First Report of the Director of the Office of War Mobilization and Reconversion* includes a note that total munitions spending is reckoned in August 1943 prices (1945a, p. 1). Subsequent reports include a chart of the breakdown of annual munitions production in "Billions of Dollars—August 1943 Prices." And Copeland, Jacobsen, and Lasken, in describing their construction of the WPB Index of War Production, state that for the most part it is an aggregated physical volume index, and "the weights are unit costs, most of them as of August 1943" (1945, p. 146). My conclusion is that standard munitions dollars were initially reckoned on the basis of prices in August 1943, but in publication, roughly from 1947 onwards, in August 1945 unit prices.

Chapter 6. Bright Shiny Objects

1. Roosevelt's "must-have" list of January 6, 1942, announced unit production targets for 1942 and 1943 in four categories: planes, tanks, antiaircraft guns, and merchant ships (Edelstein, 2001, p. 60, citing Smith, 1959, p. 141). Planes and ships were, overall, responsible for the largest categories of hardware spending in the U.S. war effort (Smith, 1959, p. 7). Because the impetus to expanded production is so clearly exogenous (the increased military spending), experience in the United States during World War II is a particularly attractive venue within which to explore the effects of cumulative output on costs, one reason the learning narratives have had such salience. During peacetime, technological improvements attributable to sources other than production experience can lower costs, shifting out the supply curve, and, given sufficient demand elasticity, lead to increases in output. But the greater production experience will not have caused the cost reductions; indeed, it will have been the reverse, and simple regressions of costs on cumulative production will bias upward the estimate of the coefficient on the learning proxy. See Nordhaus (2014); Lafond, Greenwald, and Farmer (2020).

2. Ferguson (2005) provides a nuanced treatment of the different approaches to production taken by aircraft manufacturers and General Motors as opposed to Ford. He makes it clear that, contrary to Ford's optimistic assertions, the manufacture of aircraft bore little relation to that of automobiles.

3. As Scott-Kemmis and Bell (2010) observed, Arrow's argument emphasized a stimulus given to the development and improvement of capital equipment resulting from experience in production. Most of the learning-by-doing literature, however, has

emphasized the pure effects of learning and experience, presumably with a fixed set of capital goods.

4. There are differences over how much this should be attributed to learning by production workers with unchanged equipment and physical plant, as opposed to improvements in the kind and quality of equipment and the organization of production, which should be credited to mechanical, electrical, and industrial engineers (see, in particular, Thompson, 2001, and Scott-Kemmis and Bell, 2010).

5. According to Kuznets, and as discussed in chapter 5, munitions producers hoarded labor and capital and behaved in other wasteful ways that reduced efficiency. See also Rockoff (1995, p. 5). Milward (1977, p. 73) argued that productivity was higher in the armaments sector in the United States (presumably he means higher than in other sectors) but provided little empirical foundation for his claim, which would imply that the expansion of military production should have raised rather than lowered productivity levels in the manufacturing sector as a whole. He claimed that in 1945 U.S. industries were operating "at higher levels of efficiency than ever before" (1977, p. 93). His source appears to be U.S. War Production Board (1945b, p. 9), but the higher efficiency estimate is offered without much evidence or analysis ("apparently") and seems to be heavily influenced by the gains within the munitions sector. Note that Milward also states that "there is no convincing evidence that the overall speed of technological advance was greater in wartime" (p. 180), and that even in military goods, there were "at least as many forces inherent in the armaments and munitions industries in wartime retarding technological innovation as stimulating it" (p. 193).

6. Shortly after Pearl Harbor, Morris Copeland, an economist and statistician working at the WPB, wrote, "We have avoided the incentives to inefficiency and even corruption which were involved in the cost-plus-a-percentage arrangement, but we have done relatively little to develop positive incentives to efficiency" (1942, p. 99).

7. Critics complained that CPFF did not incentivize innovation. But neither did it penalize it. See Wilson (2010).

8. These two aircraft models delivered 43 and 30 percent, respectively, of the 1.5 million tons of bombs dropped within the European theater during the war (Klein, 2013, p. 657).

9. See also Herman, 2012, pp. 87, 116. This useful book is nevertheless marred by its ideological slant, reflected in repeated swipes at labor unions and government bureaucrats. The only heavy bomber that had not flown before Pearl Harbor was the B-29, 3,970 of which were built. This was the aircraft used to drop atomic bombs on Hiroshima and Nagasaki, as well as the Able air blast at Bikini Atoll in July 1946. Production of B-29s ceased in 1946.

10. The B-52, produced between 1952 and 1962 (742); the B-1A and B, produced between 1973 and 1974 and then again between 1983 and 1988 (104); the B-2, produced between 1987 and 2000 (21). Here are comparable numbers for postwar military transport aircraft, along with years of production: Lockheed C-141 Starlifter, 1963–68 (285);

Lockheed C-5 Galaxy, 1968–73, 1985–1989 (131); Boeing C-17 Globemaster III, 1991–2015 (279). All data are from Wikipedia entries for the individual aircraft models.

11. See Smith (1959, p. 27) for statistics on army aircraft production that are in close agreement with the comparable numbers from Wikipedia.

12. The U.S. produced 301,572 aircraft between 1940 and 1945; 6,086 were produced in 1940, and 19,433 in 1941. Peak production was in 1944, when the U.S. manufactured 96,318 (Wikipedia, 2017b). There are 525,600 minutes in a year, and 525,600/96,318 = 5.45, the basis for the statistic cited by Walton.

13. Permits were available for doctors, first responders (police and fire department employees), critical war workers, and traveling salesmen, although the last group lost access in January 1944. Only 47,000 of the initial inventory remained as of May 1944 (Snyder, 2011).

14. "The 1946 and '47 Chevys were just '42s with new grilles and trim." The source is a vintage car dealer quoted in Snyder (2011). The situation with respect to truck tech-nology is somewhat more nuanced. Between 1942 and 1945 the U.S. produced for the military close to 2.4 million light, medium, light-heavy, and heavy-heavy trucks (Smith, 1959, p. 9). There may have been more learning by doing relevant for the postwar era in these product lines. See Milward, 1977, pp. 191–92, for a description of the special capabilities of the two-and-a-half-ton truck produced for the U.S. Army. This vehicle, as well as the iconic jeep, was designed by the army's Quartermaster Corps (not private businesses), and both were in production before Pearl Harbor. It is not clear how much or how quickly many of their features (such as four-wheel drive) made it into postwar U.S. truck production.

15. "In the United States . . . wartime aircraft production appears to have had little impact on domestic manufacturing practice outside of the industry itself" (Zeitlin, 1995, p. 75). Those effects were limited, moreover, since the industry never again mass-produced aircraft on such a scale.

16. Klein (2013, pp. 516, 825), citing data from Darman, 2009, provides somewhat different numbers, noting in a footnote that "here, as elsewhere, the figures for total production vary widely among sources and cannot be reconciled." In 2022 the U.S. Navy operated eleven aircraft carriers.

17. Actually, people do forget, and organizations "forget" because of deaths, retire-ments, or rapid turnover of key employees. There is a well-developed psychology lit-erature on the former, and a management literature on the latter (see Benkard, 2000). Some discoveries may be well documented, codified, or patented, and they will not be forgotten when the processes are used on a continuing basis. But the type of knowl-edge acquisition to which appeal is made in the learning narratives is particularly sub-ject to decay, especially when the relevant products are no longer made.

18. A similar dynamic was evident in America's wartime kitchens, as cooks inno-vated, modifying recipes in response to the limited availability of some ingredients. Surely this was learning, but of what relevance to culinary productivity in the postwar

period, aside from some option value in a dark future, assuming the formulas had not been forgotten? See Civitello (2017, p. 131) for description of how this played out in World War I, when wheat and sugar were in short supply and cooks experimented with substitutes, after which the recipes, which "made passable cakes and cookies . . . were retired when the war ended."

19. Weyerhauser maintained a small fleet of Liberty ships after the war, but surplus Liberty ships made more of a contribution to the postwar Greek and Italian merchant marines than they did to that of the United States. Aristotle Onassis got his start by acquiring several. Most of the remainder were mothballed and ultimately scrapped.

20. Klein described the experience in Evansville, Indiana: "Here, as elsewhere, conversion foundered on the plethora of single-purpose machines used by the plants. Studebaker, for example, undertook to manufacture Wright airplane engines only to find that only 414 of its 3,000 machines could be adapted to the new product, and all but 64 of them were simple drill presses. . . . American factories were themselves huge single-purpose machines designed to turn out one special product in enormous quantities" (2013, p. 388). See Ferguson (2005, p. 166) for a nuanced discussion of variation among manufacturers in their practices. See also Milward (1977, p. 188).

21. Figures are from a statement by Hans A. Klagsbrunn, executive vice president, Defense Plant Corporation, on April 12, 1944, U.S. Congress, Senate, Committee on Military Affairs, *Problems of Contract Termination, Hearings before a Subcommittee of the Committee of Military Affairs,* 78th Cong., 2nd sess., 1944, p. 868. Quoted in Ballard, 1983, p. 159.

22. The mill covered 1,600 acres and included eleven miles of railroads (White, 1980, p. 74). The commitment to geographical dispersal of industrial facilities was reaffirmed in the 1950 Defense Production Act (U.S. Congressional Research Service, 2020, p. 5).

23. Kendrick, 1961, p. 466, table D-II, and p. 545, table G-III; Carter et al., 2006, series Ba4742, Ba4678, Ba4679.

24. Surgical and other improvements in treating trauma resulting from experience with battlefield injuries had persisting benefits in the postwar period, but this was at best a mild offset.

25. Between 1939 and 1943, capacity in the aluminum industry increased sevenfold, from 325 million pounds per year to 2.3 billion pounds per year. This contributed critically to U.S. dominance in military and commercial aviation after the war. The new synthetic rubber industry was created in response to the loss of natural rubber supplies from the Far East during the war. The Big Inch and Little Big Inch pipelines transported fuel without exposing it to the risk of submarine predation along the Gulf and Atlantic coasts. See chapters 3 and 4.

26. National Bureau of Economic Research, "Number of New Private Nonfarm Housing Units Started for United States," Federal Reserve Bank of St. Louis, https://fred.stlouisfed.org/series/A0261AUSA610NNBR.

27. While endorsing for the most part Abramovitz and David's conclusions about the war, I take issue with their broader characterization of the twentieth century as reflecting a dependence on knowledge-based growth that differed fundamentally from what had been true in the nineteenth. Abramovitz and David generalized from the high TFP growth of the first half of the twentieth century, a generalization that does not hold up when data from the entire second half of the century are examined. TFP growth in the last third of the twentieth century in the United States was lower than it had been during the comparable period in the nineteenth.

Chapter 7. Are Patent Data Consistent with the Productivity Numbers?

1. In January 1951 President Truman appointed the commission, which included among its five members the Harvard economist Edward S. Mason, and was headed by William S. Paley, chairman of the CBS broadcasting network.

Chapter 8. Productivity Growth in the Rest of the Economy

1. In principle, the consistent use of double deflation could ensure that suitably weighted growth rates of industry real output equaled the growth rate of national economy output, and that the same would be true of the relationship between calculated industry TFP growth rates and TFP growth rates for the national economy (see Oulton, Rincon-Aznar, Samek, and Srinivasan, 2018).

2. The PNE consists of the entire economy less agriculture and government.

3. As is often the case, the choice of a deflator matters. Because the PCE-S rises more slowly between 1941 and 1948 than does the overall PCE deflator, the use of the latter results in a slower estimate of real output growth in the sector and a slower estimated TFP growth rate (2.56 percent per year vs. 3.80 percent per year over the seven-year period). Wholesale and retail trade is, however, part of the service, not goods-producing, sector of the economy, although it involves the distribution of goods. PCE-S would seem, therefore, to be the more appropriate choice.

4. A footnote to the table indicates that the "other commercial structures" consist of "buildings and structures used by the retail, wholesale, and selected service industries, . . . auto dealerships, garages, service stations, drug stores, restaurants, mobile structures, and other structures used for commercial purposes. Bus or truck garages are included in transportation." Warehousing (line 46) is conventionally included in transportation, along with trucking, rather than as part of wholesale and retail trade, and that practice is followed here.

5. The IRS treats agricultural machinery as having a class life of ten years and agricultural structures twenty-five years (U.S. Internal Revenue Service, 2019, table B-1).

6. The weights are .6523 on electric and .3477 on gas.

7. The IRS (2019, table B-1) gives a class life of forty-five years for Telephone Central Office Buildings, and eighteen years for Telephone Central Office Equipment.

8. A peculiarity of chained indexes is that if the resulting indexes are used to construct dollar values of sectoral output starting from an initial year, the sum of sector dollar values will deviate from the dollar value of the real series for the national economy constructed in a similar fashion. The deviations are generally small initially but can cumulate.

9. *The Rise and Fall of American Growth* brought to a popular audience as well as many economists an interpretation of the broad contours of U.S. economic growth since 1870. Gordon considered the evolution of productivity, consumption, and more generally the U.S. standard of living from the end of the Civil War to the present day. Although the research was determinedly historical—sixteen of eighteen chapters focused principally on the past—it was the pessimistic forecast for the future developed in previous working papers and summarized in chapters 17 and 18 that generated the lion's share of critical discussion and commentary. The debate featured dueling TED talks from Gordon, on the one hand, and Eric Brynjolfsson and Andrew McAfee, on the other (both 2013), as well as optimist rebuttals to Gordon from his colleague Joel Mokyr (2016), Deirdre McCloskey (2016), and others.

10. National Bureau of Economic Research, "Automobile Production, Passenger Cars, Factory Production for United States," https://fred.stlouisfed.org/series/M0107AUSM543NNBR; National Bureau of Economic Research, "Number of New Private Nonfarm Housing Units Started for United States," https://fred.stlouisfed.org/series/A0261AUSA610NNBR.

11. Gordon used a total economy measure based on GDP as opposed to the PDE. In his 1969 article, he noted that the value of government output is measured by labor compensation and cannot (from a statistical perspective) experience productivity improvement. Therefore, "the government sector . . . must be excluded in any project which intends to study productivity change" (Gordon, 1969, p. 222). Including government actually worsens the picture for 1941–48, as one would expect from adding output and input in a sector in which, because of the way data are constructed, productivity can't increase.

12. Kendrick's labor quality adjustment is based on weighting labor hours within different industries according to relative wage rates in those industries. Since wages in essential war industries were less controlled than those in nonessential industries, the shift into higher-paying industries may overestimate the wartime growth in labor quality.

13. Since rises in gross investment presumably followed a period of low gross investment, and thus slow or even declining net stocks of capital, it is quite likely that BEA depreciation was relatively low when gross investment was high.

14. Agriculture was also something of an exception since, with the exception of 1943, it suffered less from wartime restrictions on access to new machinery (Vatter, 1985, p. 53).

Chapter 9. Military Distribution and Its Legacy

1. Zone of the Interior was that area of the United States not included in a theater of operations; in other words, the continental United States, excluding the territories of Alaska and Hawaii (U.S. Army Service Forces, 1948, p. 74).

2. Robert McNamara, future CEO of Ford, President Kennedy's secretary of defense, and later World Bank president, also worked in this office. One successful project toward the end of the war was to reconfigure fueling routes in a way that allowed B-29s to spend 30 percent more time in the air on bombing missions. See Kaplan, 2020, p. 32.

3. Examples of the widespread application of linear programming and other operational research techniques can be found in *Interfaces,* an INFORMS journal that began publication in the 1970s.

4. I know some of my colleagues who work in this area may take exception to this, but I think it is true and have difficulty making the counter case.

Chapter 10. Do You Believe in Magic?

1. In 1977 Alan Milward used language more modest and not so metaphorically colorful. But his argument was, if more restrained, similar in its conclusions. Synthesizing a perspective that drew on both European and American experience, he wrote: "War itself was an important stimulus to technological development in many industries in the late nineteenth century such as shipbuilding, the manufacture of steel plate and the development of machine tools (1977, p. 2).

2. The Civil War calculation is based on Union spending and Union potential output; see Daggett, 2010.

3. These ideas draw strength from an older and highly evocative tradition that sees war as rejuvenating. Theodore Roosevelt was a notable exponent. The "benefits" of destroyed infrastructure as well as reconfigured institutions are often mentioned as partially explaining rapid growth in Germany and Japan in the thirty years after the Second World War. The role that different political conditions can play in restraining or fostering growth has been analyzed by Olson (1993).

4. Prairie fire effects might, of course, ultimately be reflected in any of the components of a growth-accounting exercise.

5. A 1946 Bureau of Labor Statistics study reported that overall output per man hour in manufacturing was lower in 1919 than it had been in 1914 (U.S. Bureau of Labor Statistics, 1946, p. 895). The underlying data are from Fabricant (1942).

6. In contrast to the situation today, the U.S. Navy built roughly half its warships in its own government-owned and government-operated shipyards, and the U.S. Army controlled arsenals where design, testing, and production of weaponry, particularly artillery and small arms, took place.

7. The War Production Board, which had 6,000 employees when first established in 1942, had 18,000 by midyear (Vatter, 1985, p. 67) and 22,591 at its peak (Klein, 2013, p. 357).

In 1942 the Office of Price Administration had 6,500 employees and 20,000 volunteers, eight regional and twenty-five district offices, and 8,000 local ration boards (Klein, 2013, p. 425). Over a quarter million civilians and 325,000 enlisted men worked for the Army Ordnance Department (https://goordnance.army.mil/history/ORDhistory.html). At its peak, the armed services directly employed more than 2 million civilian employees (U.S. Bureau of the Budget, 1946, p. 176). Roughly 30,000 civilians worked at the Army Air Forces' Materiel Command at Wright Field in Ohio (Wilson, 2016, pp. 89, 127).

8. The Treasury Department determined that "ordinary and necessary" advertising was an allowable cost under CPFF contracts. In each of the years 1943, 1944, and 1945, Boeing spent more than $1 million on print advertising, almost as much as it spent on R&D (Wilson, 2016, p. 91).

9. If one has doubt about this, watch or rewatch the opening and closing sequences in *White Christmas* (1954), or any of dozens of other Hollywood films sentimentalizing the war, some much more egregiously.

10. Other countries suffered more, both in absolute terms and in relation to their size. The argument here is with the optimistic view of the war's effect on U.S. aggregate supply.

11. Kaldor (1945) provides an authoritative treatment of the German experience based on data from the Strategic Bombing Survey, along with comparisons to Britain. The productivity record in Germany was mixed, its dynamics in some ways similar to those experienced in the United States affecting efficiency. The totalitarian nature of the German political system, however, dragged down public-sector performance. All its stumbling and fumbling notwithstanding, the U.S. public sector performed relatively better: "Not that German industry was uncompetitive commercially. The problem lay in adopting the same practices in the armaments factories. Not only was this slow to happen, but those commercial firms brought into war work also became infected by the incompetence and inflexibility of the system" (Overy, 1982, p. 287).

12. As for innovation, many of the important wartime advances, such as sonar, radar, and the proximity fuse, should be primarily credited to Britain, not the United States (O'Neill, 1993, p. 215).

13. Much of the language in a number of titles was borrowed with little change from the Second War Powers Act of 1942, which had lapsed, as legislatively mandated, six months after the end of the war (Field, 1950, p. 1). As of 2020, the DPA had been reauthorized fifty-three times, most recently for FY2019 (U.S. Congressional Research Service, 2020, p. 2).

14. Based on this metric, the postwar strike wave was the most severe in U.S. history. See https://fred.stlouisfed.org/series/M08257USM552NNBR. On the merits and limitations of treating the business community as a cohesive, unitary actor, see Harris, 1982, pp. 10-13.

15. A December article in the *Monthly Labor Review* summarized BLS thinking on the matter (U.S. Bureau of Labor Statistics, 1946). Its efforts to compare manufacturing

productivity trends before and during the war were inconclusive because of its reliance on output measures based on physical units alone.

16. Nine government owned naval shipyards operated at the start of the Second World War. Boston, Brooklyn, Philadelphia and Portsmouth dated from 1800 or 1801, during President John Adams's naval buildup, Norfolk from before the Revolution (1767). Mare Island in Vallejo, California, opened in 1854, and Charleston, Puget Sound, and Pearl Harbor between 1901 and 1908, helping to support President Theodore Roosevelt's Great White Fleet. Hunters Point (San Francisco) became a U.S. naval shipyard in 1941. A tenth government yard, Long Beach, opened in 1943.

BIBLIOGRAPHY

Abramovitz, Moses. 1956. "Resource and Output Trends in the United States since 1870." *American Economic Review* 46 (May): 5–23.

———. 1962. "Economic Growth in the United States." *American Economic Review* 52 (September): 762–82.

Abramovitz, Moses, and Paul David. 2000a. "Two Centuries of American Macroeconomic Growth: From Exploitation of Resource Abundance to Knowledge-Driven Development." SIEPR Discussion Paper no. 01-05. Stanford University.

———. Abramovitz, Moses, and Paul A. David. 2000b. "American Macroeconomic Growth in the Era of Knowledge-Based Progress: The Long-Run Perspective." In *The Cambridge Economic History of the United States,* vol. 3, *The Twentieth Century,* edited by Stanley L. Engerman and Robert E. Gallman. Cambridge: Cambridge University Press, 1–92.

Aerospace Industries Association of America. 1958. *Aerospace Facts and Figures,* 1958. Washington, D.C.: American Aviation Publications.

———. 1962. *Aerospace Facts and Figures,* 1962. Washington, D.C.: American Aviation Publications.

———. 1971. *Aerospace Facts and Figures,* 1971–72. New York: McGraw-Hill.

Aircraft Industries Association of America. 1945. *Aviation Facts and Figures,* 1945. Washington, D.C.: American Aviation Publications.

———. 1953. *Aviation Facts and Figures,* 1953. Washington, D.C.: Lincoln Press.

———. 1955. *Aviation Facts and Figures,* 1955. Washington, D.C.: American Aviation Publications.

Albrecht, Donald, ed. 1995. *World War II and the American Dream.* Cambridge: MIT Press.

Alchian, Armen. 1963. "Reliability of Progress Curves in Airframe Production." *Econometrica* 30 (October): 679–93.

Alexander, Thomas, Claudia Dziobek, Marco Marini, Eric Metreau, and Michael Stanger. 2017. "Measure Up: A Better Way to Calculate GDP." IMF Staff Discussion Note SDN/17/02.

American Chemical Society. 1996. "The Houdry Process: From the Catalytic Conversion of Crude Petroleum to High-Octane Gasoline." https://www.acs.org/content/dam/acsorg/education/whatischemistry/landmarks/houdry/the-houdry-process-catalytic-conversion-commemorative-booklet.pdf.

———. 1998. "United States Synthetic Rubber Program, 1939–1945." https://www.acs.org/content/acs/en/education/whatischemistry/landmarks/syntheticrubber.html.

Arnaud, Benoit, Julien Dupont, Seung-hee Koh, and Paul Schreyer. 2011. "Measuring Multifactor Productivity by Industry: Methodology and First Results from the OECD Productivity Database." Working paper, Organization for Economic Cooperation and Development.

Arnsdorf, Isaac, and Ryan Gabrielson. 2021. "Why We Can't Make Vaccine Doses Any Faster." ProPublica, February 19. https://www.propublica.org/article/covid-vaccine-supply.

Arrow, Kenneth. 1962. "The Economic Implications of Learning by Doing." *Review of Economic Studies* 29 (June): 155–73.

Automotive Manufacturers' Association. 1950. *Freedom's Arsenal: The Story of the Automotive Council for War Production.* Detroit: Automotive Manufacturers' Association.

Backman, Jules, and M. R. Gainsbrugh. 1949. "Productivity and Living Standards." *Industrial and Labor Relations Review* 2 (January): 163–94.

Baime, A. J. 2014. *The Arsenal of Democracy: FDR, Detroit, and an Epic Quest to Arm an America for War.* Boston: Houghton Mifflin.

Bakker, Gerben, Nicholas Crafts, and Pieter Woltjer. 2019. "The Sources of Growth in a Technologically Progressive Economy, 1899–1941." *Economic Journal* 129 (August): 2267–94.

Ballard, Jack Stokes. 1983. *The Shock of Peace: Military and Economic Demobilization after World War II.* Washington, D.C.: University Press of America.

Barger, Harold. 1951. *The Transportation Industries, 1889–1946: A Study of Output, Employment, and Productivity.* New York: National Bureau of Economic Research.

Barish, Norman N. 1963. "Operations Research and Industrial Engineering." *Operations Research* 11 (May–June): 387–98.

Barro, Robert J. 1998. "Notes on Growth Accounting." NBER working paper 6654 (July).

Basu, Susanto, John Fernald, and Miles Kimball. 2006. "Are Technology Improvements Contractionary?" *American Economic Review* 96 (December): 1418–48.

Baumol, William J. 1986. "Productivity Growth, Convergence, and Welfare: What the Long-Run Data Show." *American Economic Review* 76 (December): 1072–85.

Beard, Charles, and Mary Beard. 1927. *The Rise of American Civilization.* 2 vols. New York: Macmillan.

Benkard, C. Lanier. 2000. "Learning and Forgetting: The Dynamics of Aircraft Production." *American Economic Review* 90 (4): 1034–54.

Bercuson, David J., and Holger Herwig. 2014. *Long Night of the Tankers: Hitler's War against Caribbean Oil.* Calgary: University of Calgary Press.

Bernanke, Ben. 1983. "Nonmonetary Effects of the Financial Crisis in the Propagation of the Great Depression." *American Economic Review* 73 (June): 257–76.

Bernstein, Barton J. 1965. "The Removal of War Production Board Controls on Business, 1944–1946." *Business History Review* 39 (Summer): 243–60.

Block, Fred, and Gene A. Burns. 1986. "Productivity as a Social Problem: The Uses and Misuses of Social Indicators." *American Sociological Review* 51 (December): 767–80.

Blum, John Morton. 1968. "The Cold War." In *The Comparative Approach to American History,* edited by C. Vann Woodward. New York: Basic Books.

———. 1976. *V Was for Victory: Politics and American Culture during World War II.* New York: Harcourt Brace Jovanovich.

Boldrin, Michele, and David Levine. 2013. "The Case against Patents." *Journal of Economic Perspectives* 27 (Winter): 3–22.

Brigante, John E. 1947. "The Planning Committee of the War Production Board: A Chapter in American Planning Experience." Ph.D. dissertation, Princeton University.

———. 1950. *The Feasibility Dispute: Determination of War Production Objectives for 1942 and 1943.* Washington, D.C.: Committee on Public Administration Cases.

Brynjolfsson, Eric, and Andrew McAfee. 2013. "The Key to Growth? Race with the Machines." TED talk. https://www.ted.com/talks/erik_brynjolfsson_the_key_to _growth_race_with_the_machines.

Bush, Vannevar. 1945. *Science, the Endless Frontier: A Report to the President.* Washington, D.C.: Government Printing Office.

Cardozier, V. R. 1995. *The Mobilization of the United States in World War II: How the Government, Military, and Industry Prepared for War.* Jefferson, N.C.: McFarland.

Carter, Susan B., Scott Gartner, Michael Haines, Alan Olmstead, Richard Sutch, and Gavin Wright, eds. 2006. *Historical Statistics of the United States: Earliest Times to the Present.* 5 vols. New York: Cambridge University Press.

Catton, Bruce. 1948. *The War Lords of Washington.* New York: Harcourt, Brace.

Chalk, Frank Robert. 1970. "The United States and the International Struggle for Rubber, 1914–1941." Ph.D. dissertation, University of Wisconsin, Madison.

Chandler, Alfred M. 1977. *The Visible Hand: The Managerial Revolution in American Business.* Cambridge: Harvard University Press.

Christensen, Laurits R., and Dale W. Jorgenson. 1969. "The Measurement of U.S. Real Capital Input, 1929–1967." *Review of Income and Wealth* 15 (4): 293–320.

Civitello, Linda. 2017. *Baking Powder Wars: The Cutthroat Food Fight That Revolutionized Cooking.* Urbana: University of Illinois Press.

Clark, Grenville, and Arthur L. Williston. 1947. *The Effort for a National Service Law in World War II, 1942–1945: Report to the National Council of the Citizens Committee for a National Service Act*. Dedham, Mass.: N.p.

Coakley, Robert W., and Richard M. Leighton. 1968. *Global Logistics and Strategy: 1943–1945*. United States Army, Center of Military History: Washington D.C. https://history.army.mil/html/books/001/1-6/CMH_Pub_1-6.pdf.

Cochran, Thomas. 1961. "Did the Civil War Retard Industrialization?" *Mississippi Valley Historical Review* 48 (September): 197–210.

Cohen, Avi J., and G. C. Harcourt. 2003. "Whatever Happened to the Cambridge Capital Theory Controversies?" *Journal of Economic Perspectives* 17 (Winter): 199–214.

Conant, James B. 1947. "The Mobilization of Science for the War Effort." *American Scientist* 35: 195–210.

Connerly, Robert H. 1951. *The Navy and the Industrial Mobilization in World War II*. Princeton: Princeton University Press.

Cook, James Allan. 1948. *The Marketing of Surplus War Property*. Washington, D.C.: Public Affairs Press.

Cooper, William W., and Abraham Charnes. 1954. "Linear Programming." *Scientific American* 191 (August): 21–23.

Copeland, Morris A. 1942. "Production Planning for a War Economy." *Annals of the American Academy of Political and Social Science* 220 (March): 94–105.

Copeland, Morris A., Jerome Jacobson, and Herman Lasken. 1945. "The WPB Index of War Production." *Journal of the American Statistical Association* 40 (June): 145–59.

Cottle, Richard W. 2005. "George B. Dantzig: Operations Research Icon." *Operations Research* 53 (November–December): 892–98.

Cowen, Tyler. 2014. "The Lack of Major Wars May Be Hurting Economic Growth." *New York Times*, June 14. https://www.nytimes.com/2014/06/14/upshot/the-lack-of-major-wars-may-be-hurting-economic-growth.html.

Crawford, Keith A., and Stuart J. Foster. 2007. *War, Nation, Memory: International Perspectives on World War II in School History Textbooks*. Charlotte, N.C.: Information Age.

Crawford, Richard H., and Lindsley F. Cook. 1952. *The United States Army in World War II: Statistics: Procurement*. Washington, D.C.: Department of the Army. http://www.alternatewars.com/BBOW/Stats/USA_in_WW2_Stats-Procure_9-APR-52.PDF.

Creamer, Daniel, Sergei Dobrovolsky, and Israel Borenstein. 1960. *Capital in Manufacturing and Mining: Its Formation and Financing*. Princeton: Princeton University Press.

Daggett, Stephen. 2010. *Costs of Major U.S. Wars*. Washington, D.C.: Congressional Research Service. https://fas.org/sgp/crs/natsec/RS22926.pdf.

Dantzig, George B. 1963. *Linear Programming and Extensions*. Princeton: Princeton University Press.

————. 1981. "Reminiscences about the Origins of Linear Programming." Technical Report SOL 81-5. Systems Optimization Laboratory, Department of Operations Research, Stanford University.

————. 2002. "Linear Programming." *Operations Research* 50 (January–February): 42–47.

Darby, Michael R. 1976. "Three-and-a-Half Million U.S. Employees Have Been Mislaid: Or, an Explanation of Unemployment, 1934–1941." *Journal of Political Economy* 84 (February): 1–16.

Darman, Peter. 2009. *World War II: Stats and Figures.* New York: Metro Books.

David, Paul. 1977. "Invention and Accumulation in America's Economic Growth: A Nineteenth-Century Parable." In *Carnegie-Rochester Conference Series on Public Policy,* edited by Karl Brunner and Allan Meltzer, vol. 6. New York: Elsevier, 179–228.

David, Paul, Herbert S. Gutman, Richard Sutch, Peter Temin, and Gavin Wright. 1976. *Reckoning with Slavery: A Critical Study in the Quantitative History of American Negro Slavery.* Oxford: Oxford University Press.

Davies, D., & Stammers, J. 1975. "The Effect of World War II on Industrial Science." *Proceedings of the Royal Society of London. Series A, Mathematical and Physical Sciences* 342 (1631): 505–18.

Dechter, Aimee R., and Glen H. Elder Jr. 2004. "World War II Mobilization in Men's Work Lives: Continuity or Disruption for the Middle Class?" *American Journal of Sociology* 110 (November): 761–93.

De Long, J. Bradford, and Lawrence H. Summers. 1988. "How Does Macroeconomic Policy Affect Output?" *Brookings Papers on Economic Activity* 2: 433–80.

Denison, Edward F. 1962. *The Sources of Economic Growth in the United States and the Alternative before Us.* New York: Committee on Economic Development.

————. 1969. "Some Major Issues in Productivity Analysis: An Examination of Estimates by Jorgenson and Griliches." *Survey of Current Business,* part II (May): 1–27.

————. 1972. "Final Comments." *Survey of Current Business,* part II (May): 95–110.

————. 1974. *Accounting for United States Economic Growth, 1929–1969.* Washington, D.C.: Brookings Institution.

Devine, Warren D. 1983. "From Shafts to Wires: Historical Perspective on Electrification." *Journal of Economic History* 43 (June): 347–72.

Dillard, Dudley. 1944. "Big Inch Pipelines and the Monopoly Competition in the Petroleum Industry." *Journal of Land & Public Utility Economics* 20 (May): 109–122.

Divine, William R. 1955. "The Second Hoover Commission Reports: An Analysis." *Public Administration Review* 15 (Autumn): 263–69.

Duboff, Richard. 1964. "Electric Power in American Manufacturing, 1889–1958." Ph.D. dissertation, University of Pennsylvania.

Durr, Kenneth. 2013. *The Best Made Plans: Robert R. Nathan and 20th Century Liberalism.* Rockville, Md.: Montrose Press.

Edelstein, Michael. 2001. "The Size of the U.S. Armed Forces during World War II." *Research in Economic History* 20: 47–97.

Eiler, Keith R. 1997. *Mobilizing America: Robert F. Patterson and the War Effort*, 1941–1945. Ithaca: Cornell University Press.

Engerman, Stanley. 1966. "The Economic Impact of the Civil War." *Explorations in Economic History*, 2nd series, 3 (Spring–Summer): 176–79.

Engerman, Stanley L., and Robert E. Gallman. 2000. *The Cambridge Economic History of the United States*, vol. 3, *The Twentieth Century*. Cambridge: Cambridge University Press.

Evans, W. D. 1947. "Recent Productivity Trends and Their Implications." *Journal of the American Statistical Association* 42 (June): 211–23.

Fabricant, Solomon. 1940. *The Output of Manufacturing Industries*, 1899–1937. New York: National Bureau of Economic Research.

———. 1942. *Employment in Manufacturing*, 1899–1939: *An Analysis of Its Relation to the Volume of Production*. New York: National Bureau of Economic Research.

Fairchild, Brian, and Jonathan Grossman. 1959. *The Army and Industrial Manpower*. Washington, D.C.: U.S. Department of the Army. https://www.google.com/books/edition/The_Army_and_Industrial_Manpower/D-hmAAAAMAAJ?hl=en&gbpv=1.

Farley, Robert. 2020. "Trump, Biden, and the Defense Production Act." FactCheck .org, April 2. https://www.factcheck.org/2020/04/trump-biden-and-the-defense-production-act/.

Feis, Herbert. 1947. *Seen from E.A.: Three International Episodes*. New York: Alfred A. Knopf.

Ferejohn, John, and Frances McCall Rosenbluth. 2017. *Forged through Fire: War, Peace, and the Democratic Bargain*. New York: Liveright.

Ferguson, Robert G. 2005. "One Thousand Planes a Day: Ford, Grumman, General Motors and the Arsenal of Democracy." *History and Technology* 21 (June): 149–75.

Ferrara, Andreas. 2018. "World War II and African American Socioeconomic Progress." CAGE working paper series 387. https://ideas.repec.org/p/cge/wacage/387.html.

Fesler, James W. 1947. *Industrial Mobilization for War: History of the War Production Board and Predecessor Agencies. Volume 1: Program and Administration*. Washington, D.C.: Government Printing Office for the Civilian Production Administration.

Field, Alexander J. 1985. "On the Unimportance of Machinery." *Explorations in Economic History* 22 (October): 378–401.

———. 1987. "Modern Business Enterprise as a Capital-Saving Innovation." *Journal of Economic History* 47 (June): 473–85.

———. 2003. "The Most Technologically Progressive Decade of the Century." *American Economic Review* 93 (September): 1399–1414.

———. 2008. "The Impact of the Second World War on U.S. Productivity Growth." *Economic History Review* 61 (August): 672–94.

———. 2010. "The Procyclical Behavior of Total Factor Productivity in the United States, 1890–2004." *Journal of Economic History* 70 (June): 326–50.

———. 2011. *A Great Leap Forward: 1930s Depression and U.S. Economic Growth*. New Haven: Yale University Press.

———. 2018. "Manufacturing Productivity." In *Oxford Handbook of American Economic History*, edited by Louis P. Cain, Price Fishback, and Paul Rhode. Oxford: Oxford University Press, 213–34.

———. 2021. "Abramovitz lecture." Stanford University. December 6. https://www.youtube.com/watch?v=D_dkxmf8wgy.

Field, Richard H. 1950, "Economic Stabilization under the Defense Production Act of 1950." *Harvard Law Review* 64 (1): 1–26.

Finlay, Mark R. 2009. *Growing American Rubber: Strategic Plants and the Politics of National Security.* New Brunswick: Rutgers University Press.

———. 2011. "Behind the Barbed Wire of Manzanar: Guayule and the Search for Natural Rubber." https://www.sciencehistory.org/distillations/behind-the-barbed-wire-of-manzanar-guayule-and-the-search-for-natural-rubber.

Fisher, Harry L. 1956. "Rubber." *Scientific American* 195 (November): 74–92.

Flynn, George Q. 1979. *Manpower Mobilization in World War II.* Westport, Conn.: Greenwood.

Fogel, Robert. 1964. *Railroads and American Economic Growth: Essays in Econometric History.* Baltimore: Johns Hopkins University Press.

Fogel, Robert, and Stanley Engerman. 1974. *Time on the Cross: The Economics of American Negro Slavery.* Boston: Little, Brown.

Fones-Wolf, Elizabeth. 1994. *Selling Free Enterprise: The Business Assault on Labor and Liberalism,* 1945–60. Urbana: University of Illinois Press.

Ford Motor Company. 1945. "The Story of Willow Run." YouTube, 34 minutes. https://www.youtube.com/watch?v=p2zukteYbGQ.

Foster, Karen R. 2016. *Productivity and Prosperity: A Historical Sociology of Productivist Thought.* Toronto: University of Toronto Press.

French, Sidney J. 1942. "Gasoline Miracles." *Scientific American* 166 (April): 167–70.

Frey, John W. 1941 "Petroleum Utilization in Peacetime and in Wartime." *Annals of the Association of American Geographers* 31 (June): 113–18.

Galbraith, John Kenneth. 1941. "The Selection and Timing of Inflation Controls." *Review of Economics and Statistics* 23 (May): 82–85.

Gannon, Michael. 1990. *Operation Drumbeat: The Dramatic True Story of Germany's First U-Boat Attacks along the American Coast in World War II.* New York: Harper and Row.

Garin, Andrew. 2019. "Public Investment and the Spread of 'Good Paying' Manufacturing Jobs: Evidence from World War II's Big Plants." Working paper (April 1). https://drive.google.com/file/d/1B-5V02IEARt4di13ANm602nBK-sGk3Oe/view.

Gemery, Henry A., and Jan S. Hogendorn. 1993. "The Microeconomic Bases of Short-Run Learning Curves: Destroyer Production in World War II." In *The Sinews of War: Essays on the Economic History of World War II,* edited by Geoffrey T. Mills and Hugh Rockoff. Ames: Iowa State University Press, 150–65.

General Motors Corporation. n.d.; probably 1945. "These People: War Manufacturing Scenes Photographed in Plants of Frigidaire Division." https://www.youtube.com/watch?v=dUQzzdSDn0E.

Geva, Dorit. 2013. *Conscription, Family, and the Modern State: A Comparative Study of France and the United States.* New York: Cambridge University Press.

Goldin, Claudia, and Laurence Katz. 2008. *The Race between Education and Technology.* Cambridge: Harvard University Press.

Goldin, Claudia, and Frank Lewis. 1975. "The Economic Cost of the American Civil War: Estimates and Implications." *Journal of Economic History* 35 (June): 299–326.

Goldsmith, Raymond. 1946. "The Power of Victory: Munitions Output in World War II." *Military Affairs* 10 (Spring): 69–80.

Gordon, Robert J. 1969. "$45 Billion of U.S. Private Investment Has Been Mislaid." *American Economic Review* 59 (June): 221–38.

———. 1970. "$45 Billion of U.S. Private Investment Has Been Mislaid: Reply." *American Economic Review* 60 (December): 940–45.

———. 2000. "Interpreting the 'One Big Wave' in U.S. Productivity Growth." In *Productivity, Technology, and Economic Growth,* edited by Bart van Ark, Simon Kuipers, and Gerard Kuper. Boston: Kluwer, 19–66.

———. 2013. "The Death of Innovation, the End of Growth." TED talk. https://www.ted.com/talks/robert_gordon_the_death_of_innovation_the_end_of_growth.

———. 2016. *The Rise and Fall of American Growth: The U.S. Standard of Living since the Civil War.* Princeton: Princeton University Press.

———. 2018. "Declining American Growth Despite Ongoing Innovation." *Explorations in Economic History* 69 (July): 1–12.

Grandin, Greg. 2009. *Fordlandia: The Rise and Fall of Ford's Forgotten Jungle City.* New York: Henry Holt.

Greider, William. 1987. *Secrets of the Temple: How the Federal Reserve Runs the Country.* New York: Simon and Schuster.

Griliches, Zvi. 1989. "Patents: Recent Trends and Puzzles." *Brookings Papers on Economic Activity, Microeconomics,* 291–330.

———. 1990. "Patent Statistics as Economic Indicators: A Survey." *Journal of Economic Literature* 28 (December): 1661–1707.

Gropman, Alan N. 1996. *Mobilizing U.S. Industry in World War II: Myth and Reality.* Washington, D.C.: Institute for National Strategic Studies, National Defense University.

Gross, Daniel P. 2019. "The Consequences of Invention Secrecy: Evidence from the USPTO Patent Secrecy Program in World War II." Harvard Business School, working paper 19-090.

Gross, Daniel P., and Bhaven N. Sampat. 2020a. "Inventing the Endless Frontier: The Effects of the World War II Research Effort on Post-War Innovation." Harvard Business School, working paper 20-126 (June).

———. 2020b. "Organizing Crisis Innovation: Lessons from World War II." NBER working paper 27909 (October).

Gullickson, William, and Michael J. Harper. 1987. "Multifactor Productivity in U.S. Manufacturing, 1949–1983." *Monthly Labor Review* 110 (October): 18–28.

Hacker, Louis M. 1940. *The Triumph of American Capitalism: The Development of Forces in American History to the End of the Nineteenth Century.* New York: Columbia University Press.

Hagen, Everett E., and Nora Boddy Kirkpatrick. 1944. "The National Output at Full Employment in 1950." *American Economic Review* 34 (September): 472–500.

Hall, Bronwyn, and Rosemary Ham Ziedonis. 2001. "The Patent Paradox Revisited: An Empirical Study." *RAND Journal of Economics* 32 (Spring): 101–28.

Hall, Robert E. 1968. "Technical Change and Capital from the Point of View of the Dual." *Review of Economic Studies* 35 (January): 35–46.

Hanes, Christopher. 2006. "Prices." In *Historical Statistics of the United States: Earliest Times to the Present,* edited by Susan B. Carter et al. 5 vols. New York: Cambridge University Press, 3:147–57.

Hansen, Alvin H. 1941. "Defense Financing and Inflation Potentialities." *Review of Economics and Statistics* 23 (May): 1–7.

Harper, Michael J. 1982. "The Measurement of Productive Capital Stock, Capital Wealth, and Wealth Services." Working paper 128 (June). U.S. Department of Labor, Office of Productivity and Technology.

———. 1999. "Estimating Capital Inputs for Productivity Measurement: An Overview of U.S. Concepts and Methods." *International Statistical Review* 67 (December): 327–37.

Harris, Howell John. 1982. *The Right to Manage: Industrial Relations Policy of American Business in the 1940s.* Madison: University of Wisconsin Press.

Harrison, Mark. 1988. "Resource Mobilization for World War II: The U.S.A., U.K., U.S.S.R., and Germany, 1938–1945." *Economic History Review* 41 (May): 171–92.

Heath, Jim F. 1972. "American Mobilization and the Use of Small Manufacturers, 1939–43." *Business History Review* 46 (Autumn): 295–319.

Herbert, Vernon, and Attilio Bisio. 1985. *Synthetic Rubber: A Project That Had to Succeed.* Westport, Conn.: Greenwood.

Herman, Arthur. 2012. *Freedom's Forge: How American Business Produced Victory in World War II.* New York: Random House.

Hickam, Homer H. 1989. *Torpedo Junction.* Annapolis: Naval Institute Press.

Hicks, John R. 1981. *Capital and Growth.* Oxford: Oxford University Press.

Higgs, Robert. 1993. "Private Profit, Public Risk: Institutional Antecedents of the Modern Military Procurement System in the Rearmament Program of 1940–41." In *The Sinews of War: Essays on the Economic History of World War II,* edited by Geoffrey T. Mills and Hugh Rockoff. Ames: Iowa State University Press, 166–98.

———. 2004. "Wartime Socialization of Investment: A Reassessment of US Capital Formation in the 1940s." *Journal of Economic History* 64 (June): 500–520.

———. 2010. "Private Capital Consumption: Another Downside of the Wartime 'Miracle of Production,'" Foundation for Economic Education, March 24. https://fee.org/

articles/private-capital-consumption-another-downside-of-the-wartime-miracle
-ofproduction/?utm_medium=popular_widget.

Hill, L. Clayton. 1945. "How Can We Meet This Challenge—'Higher Wages, No Price
Increases?'" In *Developments in Production and Management Engineering no. 162.*
New York: American Management Association.

Hirsch, Julius. 1947. "Productivity in War and Peace." *American Economic Review* 37
(May): 397–411.

Hogan, Warren P. 1958. "Technical Progress and Production Functions." *Review of Economics and Statistics* 40 (November): 407–11.

Holley, Irving Brinton, Jr. 1964. *Buying Aircraft: Material Procurement for the Army Air
Forces.* Washington, D.C.: Office of the Chief of Military History, Department of the
Army.

Howard, Frank. 1947. *Buna Rubber: The Birth of an Industry.* New York: Van Nostrand.

Hubert, Giles A. 1947. "War and the Trade Orientation of Haiti." *Southern Economic
Journal* 13 (January): 276–84.

Hulten, Charles R. 1990. "The Measurement of Capital." In *Fifty Years of Economic Measurement: The Jubilee of the Conference on Income and Wealth,* edited by Ernst R. Berndt and Jack E. Triplett. Chicago: University of Chicago Press, 119–58.

Hulten, Charles R., and Frank C. Wycoff. 1981. "The Measurement of Economic Depreciation." In *Depreciation, Inflation, and the Taxation of Income from Capital,* edited by
Charles R. Hulten. Washington, D.C.: Urban Institute Press.

Hyde, Charles K. 2013. *Arsenal of Democracy: The American Automobile Industry in World
War II.* Detroit: Wayne State University Press.

Isserman, Maurice. 1991. *World War II.* New York: Facts on File.

Janeway, Eliot. 1951. *The Struggle for Survival: A Chronicle of Economic Mobilization in
World War II.* New Haven: Yale University Press.

Jaszi, George. 1970. "$45 Billion of U.S. Private Investment Has Been Mislaid: Comment." *American Economic Review* 60 (December): 934–39.

Jaworksi, Taylor. 2017. "World War II and the Industrialization of the American South."
Journal of Economic History 77 (December): 1048–82.

Johnson, Stephen B. 1997. "Three Approaches to Big Technology: Operations Research,
Systems Engineering, and Project Management." *Technology and Culture* 38 (October): 891–919.

Jorgenson, Dale. W., and Zvi Griliches. 1967. "The Explanation of Productivity Change."
Review of Economic Studies 34 (July): 249–83.

Jovanovic, Boyan, and Peter Rousseau. 2005. "General Purpose Technologies." In *Handbook of Economic Growth,* edited by P. Aghion and Steven M. Durlauf. Amsterdam:
Elsevier, 1:1181–1224.

Kaldor, Nicholas. 1945–46. "The German War Economy." *Review of Economic Studies* 13
(1): 33–52.

Kaplan, Fred. 2020. *The Bomb: Presidents, Generals, and the Secret History of Nuclear War.*
New York: Simon and Schuster.

Karbassi, Shayan. 2021. "Understanding Biden's Invocation of the Defense Production Act." *Lawfare Blog*, March 4. https://www.lawfareblog.com/understanding-bidens-invocation-defense-production-act.

Kelly, Bryan, Dimitris Papanikolaou, Amit Seru, and Matt Taddy. 2020. "Measuring Technological Innovation over the Long Run." NBER working paper 25266 (November).

———. 2021. "Measuring Technological Innovation over the Long Run." *American Economic Review: Insights* 3 (September): 303–20.

Kendrick, John W. 1961. *Productivity Trends in the United States.* Princeton: Princeton University Press.

Kennedy, David. 1999. *Freedom from Fear: The American People in Depression and War, 1929–1945.* New York: Oxford University Press.

Keynes, John Maynard. 1936. *The General Theory of Employment, Interest, and Money.* New York: Harcourt, Brace.

Khan, Zorina. 2020. *Inventing Ideas: Patents, Prizes, and the Knowledge Economy.* New York: Oxford University Press.

Kimble, James J. 2018. "The US Home Front: Archetypal Opposition and Narrative Casting as Propaganda Strategies in World War II." In *World War II and the Cold War: The Rhetoric of Hearts and Minds,* edited by Martin J. Medhurst. East Lansing: Michigan State University Press.

Klein, Maury. 2013. *A Call to Arms: Mobilizing America for World War II.* New York: Bloomsbury.

Klemin, Alexander. 1944. "High-Octane Gas." *Scientific American* 170 (June): 262–64.

Koistinen, Paul C. 1973. "Mobilizing the World War II Economy: Labor and the Industrial Military Alliance." *Pacific Historical Review* 42 (November): 443–78.

———. 1984. "Warfare and Power Relations in America: Mobilizing the World War II Economy." In *The Home Front and War in the Twentieth Century: The American Experience in Comparative Perspective: Proceedings of the Tenth Air Force Academy Military History Symposium,* edited by James Titus. Washington, D.C.: Office of Air Force History.

———. 2004. *Arsenal of World War II: The Political Economy of American Warfare, 1940–1945.* Lawrence: University Press of Kansas.

Kornai, János. 1980. *Economics of Shortage,* vols. A and B. New York: Elsevier-North Holland.

Krebs, Michelle. 1993. "Model A Is a Smashing but Short-Lived Success." *Automotive News,* June 16. https://www.autonews.com/article/20030616/SUB/306160740/model-a-is-a-smashing-but-short-lived-success.

Kuznets, Simon. 1945. *National Product in Wartime.* New York: National Bureau of Economic Research.

———. 1952. "National Income Estimates for the United States prior to 1870." *Journal of Economic History* 12 (Spring): 115–30.

Lacey, Jim. 2011. *Keep from All Thoughtful Men: How U.S. Economists Won World War II.* Annapolis: Naval Institute Press.

Lafond, François, Diana Greenwald, and J. Doyne Farmer. 2020. "Can Stimulating Demand Drive Costs Down? World War II as a Natural Experiment." Working paper.

Landefeld, Stephen J., and Robert J. Parker. 1997. "BEA's Chain Indexes, Time Series, and Measure of Long-Term Economic Growth." *Survey of Current Business* (May): 58–68.

Landon-Lane, John, and Hugh Rockoff. 2013. "The Paradox of Planning: The Controlled Materials Plan of World War II." NBER historical working paper no. 83.

Lebergott, Stanley. 1964. *Manpower in Economic Growth: The American Record since 1800.* New York: McGraw-Hill.

Leighton, Richard M., and Robert W. Coakley. 1955. *Global Logistics and Strategy, 1940–1943.* Washington, D.C.: Government Printing Office. https://history.army.mil/html/books/001/1-5/CMH_Pub_1-5.pdf.

Levinson, Marc. 2016. *The Box: How the Shipping Container Made the World Smaller and the World Economy Bigger.* Princeton: Princeton University Press.

Lewis, David L. 1976. *The Public Image of Henry Ford.* Detroit: Wayne State University Press.

Lewis, Robert. 2007. "World War II Manufacturing and the Postwar Southern Economy." *Journal of Southern History* 73 (November): 837–66.

Liberty Bank of Buffalo, Research Advisory Service. 1943. "When the Defense Boom Ends: Industry Plans for after the War." https://fraser.stlouisfed.org/archival/1343/item/468508.

Lindert, Peter H., and Jeffrey G. Williamson. 2016. *Unequal Gains: American Growth and Inequality since 1700.* Princeton: Princeton University Press.

Lindsey, Rebecca, and LuAnn Dahlman. 2019. "Climate Change: Global Temperature." https://www.climate.gov/news-features/understanding-climate/climate-change-global-temperature.

Lingeman, Richard R. 1970. *Don't You Know There's a War On? The American Home Front, 1941–1945.* New York: G. P. Putnam's Sons.

Magdoff, Harry. 1939. "The Purpose and Method of Measuring Productivity." *Journal of the American Statistical Association* 34 (June): 309–18.

Margolin, Victor. 2013. "The United States in World War II: Scientists, Engineers, Designers." *Design Issues* 29 (Winter): 14–29.

Massell, Benton F. 1960. "Capital Formation and Technological Change in United States Manufacturing." *Review of Economics and Statistics* 42 (May): 182–88.

Matloff, Maurice. 1959. *Strategic Planning for Coalition Warfare.* Washington, D.C.: Office of the Chief of Military History, Department of the Army.

Mawdsley, Evan. 2020. *World War II: A New History.* 2nd ed. Cambridge: Cambridge University Press.

Maxwell, James, and Margaret Balcom. 1946a. "Gasoline Rationing in the United States. I." *Quarterly Journal of Economics* 60 (August): 561–87.

———. 1946b. "Gasoline Rationing in the United States. II." *Quarterly Journal of Economics* 61 (November): 125–55.

McCloskey, Deirdre. 2016. "Relax, Economic Pessimists, the Sky Will Not Fall." *Prospect*, February 18. http://www.prospectmagazine.co.uk/magazine/relax-economic -pessimists-robert-gordon-lawrence-summers-economic-growth-not-over.

McGrath, Jamie. 2019. "Peacetime Naval Rearmament, 1933–39: Lessons for Today." *Naval War College Review* 72 (Spring): 83–103.

Millett, John D. 1954. *The Organization and Role of the Army Service Forces*. Washington D.C.: Center of Military History, United States Army. https://history.army.mil/ html/books/003/3-1/CMH_Pub_3-1.pdf.

Milward, Alan. 1977. *War, Economy, and Society: 1939–45*. Berkeley: University of California Press.

Mokyr, Joel. 2016. "Technology and Economic Growth." Project Syndicate, November 29. https://www.project-syndicate.org/commentary/technology-and-economic -growth-by-joel-mokyr-2016-11.

Moretti, Enrico, Claudia Steinwender, and John Van Reenen. 2019. "The Intellectual Spoils of War? Defense R&D, Productivity, and International Spillovers." NBER working paper 26483 (November).

Morris, Peter J. K. 1989. *The American Synthetic Rubber Research Program*. Philadelphia: University of Pennsylvania Press.

Moser, Petra. 2013. "Patents and Innovation: Evidence from Economic History." *Journal of Economic Perspectives* 27 (Winter): 23–44.

Mowery, David C. 1997. "The Bush Report after 50 Years: Blueprint or Relic?" In *Science for the 21st Century: The Bush Report Revisited*. Edited by Claude E. Barfield. Washington, D.C.: American Enterprise Institution, 24–41.

Mulligan, Casey. 1997. "Pecuniary Incentives to Work in the U.S. during World War II." NBER working paper 6326 (December).

Nathan, Robert R. 1989. Oral history interview by Niel M. Johnson for Truman Library, June 22. https://www.trumanlibrary.gov/library/oral-histories/nathanrr.

Nelson, Donald M. 1946. *Arsenal of Democracy: The Story of American War Production*. New York: Harcourt, Brace.

Nordhaus, William. 2014. "The Perils of the Learning Model for Modelling Endogenous Technological Change." *Energy Journal* 35 (1): 1–13.

Offley, Ed. 2014. *The Burning Shore: How Hitler's U-Boats Brought World War II to America*. New York: Basic Books.

Ohly, John H. 2000. *Industrialists in Olive Drab: The Emergency Operation of Private Industry during World War II*. Edited by Clayton D. Laurie. Washington, D.C.: United States Army, Center of Military History. https://history.army.mil/html/books/070/ 70-32-1/CMH_Pub_70-32-1.pdf.

Oliner, Stephen D., and Daniel E. Sichel. 2000. "The Resurgence of Growth in the 1990s: Is Information Technology the Story?" *Journal of Economic Perspectives* 14 (4): 3–22.

Olson, Mancur. 1993. "Dictatorship, Democracy, and Development." *American Political Science Review* 87 (September): 567–76.

O'Neill, William L. 1993. *Democracy at War: America's Fight at Home & Abroad in World War II*. New York: Free Press.

Organization for Economic Cooperation and Development. 2001a. *Measuring Capital: Measurement of Capital Stocks, Consumption of Fixed Capital, and Capital Services*. Paris: OECD. http://www.oecd.org/sdd/na/1876369.pdf.

———. 2001b. *Measuring Productivity: Measurement of Aggregate and Industry-Level Productivity Growth*. Paris: OECD. http://www.oecd.org/sdd/productivity-stats/2352458.pdf.

———. 2009. *Measuring Capital*, 2nd edition. Paris: OECD. https://www.oecd.org/sdd/productivity-stats/43734711.pdf.

Oulton, Nicholas, Ana Rincon-Aznar, Lea Samek, and Sylaja Srinivasan. 2018. "Double Deflation: Theory and Practice." ESCoE discussion paper 2018-17 (December). https://www.escoe.ac.uk/wp-content/uploads/2018/12/ESCoE-DP-2018-17.pdf.

Overy, R. J. 1982 "Hitler's War and the German Economy: A Reinterpretation." *Economic History Review*, n.s., 35 (May): 272–91.

Pelley, John J. 1943. "American Railroads in and after the War." *Annals of the American Academy of Political and Social Science* 230 (November): 22–28.

Phillips, Charles F., Jr. 1960. "The Competitive Potential of Synthetic Rubber." *Land Economics* 36 (November): 322–32.

Raff, Daniel, and Manuel Trajtenberg. 1997. "Quality-Adjusted Prices for the American Automobile Industry, 1906–1940." In *The Economics of New Goods*, edited by Timothy F. Bresnahan and Robert J. Gordon. Chicago: University of Chicago Press, 71–108.

Rhode, Paul W. 2003. "After the War Boom: Reconversion on the Pacific Coast, 1943–49." In *History Matters: Essays on Economic Growth, Technology, and Demographic Change*, edited by Timothy Guinnane, Warren Whatley, and William Sundstrom. Stanford: Stanford University Press, 187–220.

Risch, Erna. 1953. *The Quartermaster Corps: Organization, Supply, and Services*, vol. 1. Washington, D.C.: Government Printing Office. https://history.army.mil/html/books/010/10-12/CMH_Pub_10-12-1.pdf.

Ristuccia, Cristiano Andrea, and Adam Tooze. 2013. "Machine Tools and Mass Production in the Armaments Boom: Germany and the United States, 1929–44." *Economic History Review* 66 (4): 953–74.

Rockoff, Hugh. 1995. "From Plowshares to Swords: The American Economy in World War II." NBER historical paper no. 77.

———. 2000. "Getting in the Scrap: The Salvage Drives of World War II." Working paper (March 15).

———. 2012. *America's Economic Way of War*. Cambridge: Cambridge University Press.

Rognlie, Matthew. 2015. "Deciphering the Fall and Rise in the Net Capital Share: Accumulation or Scarcity?" *Brookings Papers on Economic Activity* 46 (Spring): 1–19.

Romer, Christina D. 1992. "What Ended the Great Depression?" *Journal of Economic History* 52 (December): 757–84.

Roosevelt, Franklin D. 1942. "Veto of a Bill Promoting the Production of Synthetic Rubber from Grain Alcohol." https://www.presidency.ucsb.edu/documents/veto-bill-promoting-the-production-synthetic-rubber-from-grain-alcohol.

———. 1943. "State of the Union Address." https://millercenter.org/the-presidency/presidential-speeches/january-7-1943-state-union-address.

———. 1944. "State of the Union Address." https://www.presidency.ucsb.edu/documents/state-the-union-message-congress.

———. 1945. "State of the Union Address." https://www.presidency.ucsb.edu/documents/state-the-union-address.

Rose, Evan K. 2018. "The Rise and Fall of Female Labor Force Participation during World War II in the United States." *Journal of Economic History* 78 (September): 673–711.

Ross, William F., and Charles F. Romanus. 1965. *The Quartermasters Corps: Operations in the War against Germany.* Washington, D.C.: U.S. Government Printing Office. https://history.army.mil/html/books/010/10-15/CMH_Pub_10-15.pdf.

Rostow, W. W. 1960. *The Stages of Economic Growth: A Non-Communist Manifesto.* Cambridge: Cambridge University Press.

Roth, Frank L., and William L. Holt. 1944. "Measuring the Rate of Wear of Tire Treads." *Journal of Research of the National Bureau of Standards* 32 (February): 61–65.

"Rubber Plants Sale." 1955. *Congressional Quarterly Almanac,* 1955, 11th ed. Washington, D.C.: Congressional Quarterly, 429–30.

Rubber Reserve Company. 1945. *Report on the Rubber Program, 1940–1945.* Washington, D.C.: Rubber Reserve Co.

Ruttan, Vernon. 2006. *Is War Necessary for Economic Growth? Military Procurement and Economic Development.* Oxford: Oxford University Press.

Scherer, F. M., et al. 1959. *Patents and the Corporation.* 2nd ed. Boston: James Galvin & Assoc., 1959.

Scherer, Frederic M. 1977. "The Economic Effects of Patent Compulsory Licensing." New York University, Graduate School of Business Administration, Center for the Study of Financial Institutions.

Schlaifer, Robert, and S. D. Heron. 1950. *Development of Aircraft Engines and Development of Aviation Fuels: Two Studies of Relations between Government and Business.* Boston: Graduate School of Business Administration, Harvard University.

Schmookler, Jacob. 1966. *Patents and Economic Growth.* Cambridge: Harvard University Press.

Schweitzer, Mary. 1980. "World War II and Female Labor Force Participation Rates." *Journal of Economic History* 40 (March): 89–95.

Scott-Kemmis, Don, and Martin Bell. 2010. "The Mythology of Learning-by-Doing in World War II Airframe and Ship Production." *International Journal of Technological Learning, Innovation, and Development* 3 (1): 1–35.

Sebastian, John. 1965. "Do You Believe in Magic?" On *Do You Believe in Magic?* Kama Sutra Records.

Shatnawi, Dina, and Price Fishback. 2018. "The Impact of World War II on the Demand for Female Workers in Manufacturing." *Journal of Economic History* 78 (June): 539–74.

Shiller, Robert. 2019. *Narrative Economics: How Stories Go Viral and Drive Major Economic Events.* Princeton: Princeton University Press.

Shrader, Charles R. 2006. *History of Operations Research in the United States Army,* vol. 1, 1942–1962. Washington D.C.: United States Army. https://history.army.mil/html/ books/hist_op_research/CMH_70-102-1.pdf.

Smith, R. Elberton. 1959. *The Army and Economic Mobilization.* Washington, D.C.: Government Printing Office.

Snyder, Jesse. 2011. "No New Cars, but That Didn't Stop U.S. Automakers, Dealers, during WWII." *Automotive News,* October 31. http://www.autonews.com/article/ 20111031/CHEVY100/310319970/no-new-cars-but-that-didnt-stop-u.s.-automakers -dealers-during-wwii.

Solo, Robert A. 1953. "The Sale of the Synthetic Rubber Plants." *Journal of Industrial Economics* 2 (November): 32–43.

———. 1954. "Research and Development in the Synthetic Rubber Industry." *Quarterly Journal of Economics* 68 (February): 61–82.

———. 1959. *Synthetic Rubber: A Case Study in Technological Development under Government Direction.* Study of the Committee on the Judiciary, U.S. Senate, 85th Cong., 2nd sess. Washington, D.C.: Government Printing Office.

———. 1980. "The Saga of Synthetic Rubber." *Bulletin of the Atomic Scientists* 36 (April): 31–36.

Solow, Robert M. 1956. "A Contribution to the Theory of Economic Growth." *Quarterly Journal of Economics* 70 (February): 65–94.

———. 1957. "Technical Change and the Aggregate Production Function." *Review of Economics and Statistics* 39 (August): 312–20.

———. 1958. "Technical Change and the Aggregate Production Function: Reply." *Review of Economics and Statistics* 40 (November): 411–13.

Sparrow, James. 2011. *Warfare State: World War II Americans and the Age of Big Government.* New York: Oxford University Press.

Stocking, George W., and Myron W. Watkins. 1946. *Cartels in Action: Case Studies in International Business Diplomacy.* New York: Twentieth Century Fund.

Stout, Wesley. 1946. *Tanks Are Mighty Fine Things.* Detroit: Chrysler Corp.

Sumner, John. 1944. "The Disposition of Surplus War Property." *American Economic Review* 34 (September): 458–71.

Taft, Robert A. 2001. *The Papers of Robert A. Taft,* vol. 2, 1939–1944. Edited by Clarence E. Wunderlin. Kent, Ohio: Kent State University Press.

Taylor, C. Fayette. 1971. *Aircraft Propulsion: A Review of the Evolution of Aircraft Piston Engines.* Washington, D.C.: Smithsonian Institution Press.

Terborgh, George. 1945. *The Bogey of Economic Maturity.* Chicago: Machinery and Allied Products Institute.

Thompson, David W. J., John J. Kennedy, John M. Wallace, and Phil D. Jones. 2008. "A Large Discontinuity in the Mid-Twentieth Century in Observed Global-Mean Surface Temperature." *Nature,* May 29. https://www.nature.com/articles/nature 06982.

Thompson, Peter. 2001. "How Much Did the Liberty Shipbuilders Learn? New Evidence for an Old Case Study." *Journal of Political Economy* 109 (February): 103–37.

Thornton, Rebecca, and Peter Thompson. 2001. "Learning from Experience and Learning from Others: An Exploration of Learning and Spillovers in Wartime Shipbuilding." *American Economic Review* 91 (December): 1350–68.

Triplett, Jack E. 1997. "Concepts of Capital for Production Accounts and for Wealth Accounts: The Implications for Statistical Programs." Working paper (March). http://www.oecd.org/sdd/na/2666700.pdf.

Tully, John. 2011. *The Devil's Milk: A Social History of Rubber.* New York: Monthly Review Press.

Tuttle, William M., Jr. 1981. "The Synthetic Rubber 'Mess' in World War II." *Technology and Culture* 22 (January): 35–67.

United States Army Industrial College. 1946a. "Study of Experience in Industrial Mobilization in World War II: Allocation of Transportation and Other Public Utilities." Washington, D.C.: Industrial College of the Armed Forces, Department of Research.

———. 1946b. "Study of Experience in Industrial Mobilization in World War II: Development of Submarginal Resources." Washington, D.C.: Industrial College of the Armed Forces, Department of Research.

———. 1946c. "Study of Experience in Industrial Mobilization in World War II: Handling of Material." Washington, D.C.: Industrial College of the Armed Forces, Department of Research.

———. 1946d. "Study of Experience in Industrial Mobilization in World War II: Development of Clauses to Adjust Fixed Price Contracts to War Conditions." Washington, D.C.: Industrial College of the Armed Forces, Department of Research.

———. 1946e. "Study of Experience in Industrial Mobilization in World War II: Manpower in Industrial Mobilization." Washington, D.C.: Industrial College of the Armed Forces, Department of Research.

United States Army Service Forces. 1945. *Annual Report of the Director.* Washington, D.C.: Government Printing Office

———. 1946. *Statistical Review: World War II.* Washington, D.C.: Government Printing Office.

———. 1948. *Logistics in World War II: Final Report of the Army Service Forces.* Washington, D.C.: Government Printing Office. https://history.army.mil/html/books/070/70-29/CMH_Pub_70-29.pdf.

United States Bureau of Economic Analysis, National Income and Product Account Tables, (referred to as NIPA tables) and Fixed Asset Tables (referred to as FAT). Both at http://www.bea.gov.

United States Bureau of Labor Statistics. 1944. "Factors Determining Postwar Job Transfers and Unemployment." *Monthly Labor Review* 58 (February): 269–79.

———. 1945. "Productivity Changes in Selected Wartime Shipbuilding Programs." *Monthly Labor Review* 61 (December): 1132–47.

———. 1946. "Productivity Changes since 1939." *Monthly Labor Review* 62 (December): 893–917.

———. 1976. *BLS Handbook of Methods, Bulletin* 1910. Washington, D.C.: Government Printing Office.

———. 1983. "Trends in Multifactor Productivity, 1948–1981." Bulletin 2178. September. Washington, D. C. Government Printing Office.

———. 1997. *BLS Handbook of Methods, Bulletin* 2490. April. Washington, D.C.: Government Printing Office.

———. 2004. "Multifactor Productivity in U.S. Manufacturing and in 20 Manufacturing Industries." February 10.

———. 2007a. "BLS Handbook of Methods. Chapter 10. Productivity Measures: Business Sectors and Major Subsectors." April. https://www.bls.gov/opub/hom/pdf/msp-19970714.pdf.

———. 2007b. "Technical Information about the BLS Multifactor Productivity Measures." September 26. https://www.bls.gov/mfp/mprtech.pdf.

———. 2017. "Overview of Capital Inputs for the BLS Multifactor Productivity Measures." June 2. https://www.bls.gov/mfp/mprcaptl.pdf.

United States Bureau of the Budget. 1946. *The United States at War: Development and Administration of the War Program by the Federal Government.* Washington, D.C.: Government Printing Office.

United States Bureau of the Census. 1946. *Statistical Abstract of the United States.* Washington, D.C.: Government Printing Office.

———. 1947. *Statistical Abstract of the United States.* Washington, D.C.: Government Printing Office.

———. 1955. *Statistical Abstract of the United States.* Washington, D.C.: Government Printing Office.

———. 1960. *Statistical Abstract of the United States.* Washington, D.C.: Government Printing Office.

United States Civilian Production Administration. 1946a. *Minutes of the War Production Board, January 20, 1942, to October 9, 1945.* Washington, D.C.: Government Printing Office. https://play.google.com/books/reader?id=MVgUAAAAIAAJ&pg=GBS.PA5.

———. 1946b. *Minutes of the Planning Committee of the War Production Board, February 20, 1942, to April 1, 1943.* Washington, D.C.: Government Printing Office. https://babel.hathitrust.org/cgi/pt?id=uiug.30112074256261&view=1up&seq=8.

United States Commission on Organization of the Executive Branch of the Government. 1955. *Subcommittee Report on Business Enterprises of the Department of Defense.* Washington, D.C.: Government Printing Office.

United States Congress, House of Representatives. 1947. *Hearings before the Select Committee to Investigate Disposition of Surplus Property.* Part 4, Hearings on Disposition of Big Inch and Little Big Inch Pipe Lines. 79th Cong., 2nd sess. Washington, D.C.: Government Printing Office.

United States Congress, Senate. 1941. *Hearings before the Special Committee to Investigate Gasoline and Fuel-Oil Shortages.* 77th Cong., 1st sess. Washington, D.C.: Government Printing Office.

———. 1942. "Investigation of the National Defense Program." Report 480, part 7. 77th Cong., 2nd sess.

———. 1944. *Third Annual Report of the Special Committee to Investigate the National Defense Program.* 78th Cong., 2nd sess., March 4.

———. 1945. Committee on Military Affairs. "Wartime Technological Developments: A Study Made for the Subcommittee on War Mobilization." https://babel.hathitrust .org/cgi/pt?id=uc1.$b75655&view=1up&seq=1.

United States Congressional Research Service. 2020. "The Defense Production Act of 1950: History, Authorities, and Considerations for Congress." March 2. https://fas .org/sgp/crs/natsec/R43767.pdf.

United States Defense Logistics Agency. 1996. "The History and Significance of Military Packaging." By Joseph C. Maloney Jr. https://apps.dtic.mil/sti/citations/ADA307293.

United States Department of Agriculture. 2017. "Guayule's Past Meets Its Future." *AgResearch Magazine*, March. https://agresearchmag.ars.usda.gov/2017/mar/ guayule/.

United States Department of Commerce, Office of Business Economics. 1966. *The National Income and Product Accounts of the United States,* 1929–65. Washington, D.C.: Government Printing Office.

United States Energy Information Agency. 2019. "Natural Gas and the Environment." https://www.eia.gov/energyexplained/natural-gas/natural-gas-and-the-environ ment.php.

United States Government Services Administration. 2021. Federal Acquisition Regulation. "Cost-Plus-Fixed-Fee Contracts." https://www.acquisition.gov/far/16.306.

United States Internal Revenue Service. 2019. "Publication 946: How to Depreciate Property." https://www.irs.gov/publications/p946#en_US_2019_publink1000107774.

United States Library of Congress. 1973. "United States Experience with Voluntary and Mandatory Rationing of Gasoline and Fuel Oil in World War II." By Francis A. Gulick. Congressional Research Service, November 20. In *Hearings before the Committee on Governmental Relations,* U.S. Senate, 93rd Cong., 1st sess., 178–202.

———. 2015. "Technical Reports and Standards: The Synthetic Rubber Project." http:// www.loc.gov/rr/scitech/trs/trschemical_rubber.html.

United States Office of War Mobilization and Reconversion. 1944. *Report on War and Post-War Adjustment Policies*. By Bernard Baruch and John M. Hancock. Washington, D.C. https://babel.hathitrust.org/cgi/pt?id=mdp.35128000132801.

———. 1945a. *Problems of Mobilization and Reconversion. First Report by the Director of War Mobilization and Reconversion*, January 1. Washington, D.C. https://babel.hathitrust.org/cgi/pt?id=osu.32435064206576.

———. 1945b. *War Production and VE-Day: Second Report by the Director of War Mobilization and Reconversion*, April 1. Washington, D.C. https://babel.hathitrust.org/cgi/pt?id=osu.32435064206576 (begins on #73).

———. 1945c. *The War: Phase Two*, May 10. Washington, D.C. https://babel.hathitrust.org/cgi/pt?id=mdp.39015031925905.

———. 1945d. *The Road to Tokyo and Beyond. Third Report by the Director of War Mobilization*, July 1. Washington, D.C.: Government Printing Office. https://babel.hathitrust.org/cgi/pt?id=osu.32435064206576 (begins on #129).

———. 1945e. *From War to Peace: A Challenge*, August 15. Washington, D.C. https://babel.hathitrust.org/cgi/pt?id=mdp.39015074872659.

———. 1945f. *Fourth Report by the Director of War Mobilization and Reconversion*, October 1. https://babel.hathitrust.org/cgi/pt?id=osu.32435064206048.

United States Petroleum Administration for War. 1946. *A History of the Petroleum Administration for War, 1941–1945*. Washington, D.C.: Government Printing Office. https://babel.hathitrust.org/cgi/pt?id=mdp.39015019963779&view=1up&seq=5.

United States President's Materials Policy Commission. 1952. *Resources for Freedom.* 5 vols. Washington, D.C.: Government Printing Office.

United States Secretary of the Treasury. 1959. "Final Report on the Reconstruction Finance Corporation." Washington, D.C.: Government Printing Office.

United States Selective Service System. 1945. *Selective Service as the Tide of War Turns: Third Report of the Director of the Selective Service System*. Washington, D.C.: Government Printing Office.

———. 1946. *Selective Service and Victory. Fourth Report of the Director of the Selective Service System*. Washington, D.C.: Government Printing Office. https://babel.hathitrust.org/cgi/pt?id=mdp.39015029400861&view=1up&seq=1.

———. 2020. Induction Statistics. https://www.sss.gov/About/History-And-Records/Induction-Statistics.

United States Special Committee to Study the Rubber Situation. 1942. *Report of the Rubber Survey Committee*. https://babel.hathitrust.org/cgi/pt?id=mdp.39015031328209&view=1up&seq=3.

United States Tariff Commission. 1940. "Crude Rubber: A Brief Summary of the Present Situation Respecting Crude Rubber with Special Reference to the Effects of War Conditions on United States Imports." Washington, D.C. https://babel.hathitrust.org/cgi/pt?id=uiug.30112069790712&view=1up&seq=5.

United States War Production Board. 1945a. *Wartime Production Achievements and the Reconversion Outlook: Report of the Chairman.* Washington, D.C.: War Production Board.

———. 1945b. *American Industry in War and Transition, 1940–1950: Part II: The Effect of the War on the Industrial Economy.* Washington, D.C.: War Production Board.

U.S. Tire Manufacturers Association. 2019. "What's in a Tire." https://www.ustires.org/whats-tire-0.

Vander Meulen, Jacob. 1995. *Building the B-29.* Washington, D.C.: Smithsonian Institution Press.

Van Harmelen, Jonathan. 2021. "The Scientists and the Shrub: Manzanar's Guayule Project and Incarcerated Japanese American Scientists." *Southern California Quarterly* 103 (Spring): 61–98.

Vatter, Harold. 1985. *The U.S. Economy in World War II.* New York: Columbia University Press.

Vosoughi, Soroush, Deb Roy, and Sinan Aral. 2018. "The Spread of True and False News Online." *Science* 359 (6380): 1146–51.

Wallace, Max. 2004. *The American Axis: Henry Ford, Charles Lindbergh, and the Rise of the Third Reich.* New York: St. Martin's.

Walton, Francis. 1956. *The Miracle of World War II: How American Industry Made Victory Possible.* New York: Macmillan.

Weizmann, Chaim. 1949. *Trial and Error: The Autobiography of Chaim Weizmann.* New York: Harper & Brothers.

Wendt, Paul. 1947. "The Control of Rubber in World War II." *Southern Economic Journal* 13 (January): 203–27.

Weisgall, Jonathan. 1994. *Operation Crossroads: The Atomic Tests at Bikini Atoll.* Annapolis: Naval Institute Press.

White, Gerald T. 1980. *Billions for Defense: Government Financing by the Defense Plant Corporation during World War II.* University: University of Alabama Press.

Wikipedia. 2021a. "List of Most-Produced Aircraft." https://en.wikipedia.org/wiki/List_of_most-produced_aircraft.

———. 20217b. "World War II Aircraft Production." https://en.wikipedia.org/wiki/World_War_II_aircraft_production.

———. 2021c. "Lisunov Li-2." https://en.wikipedia.org/wiki/Lisunov_Li-2.

Wilson, Mark R. 2006. *The Business of Civil War: Military Mobilization and the State, 1861–1865.* Baltimore: Johns Hopkins University Press.

———. 2010. "'Taking a Nickel Out of the Cash Register': Statutory Renegotiation of Military Contracts and the Politics of Profit Control in the United States during World War II." *Law and History Review* 28 (May): 343–83.

———. 2011. "Making 'Goop' Out of Lemons: The Permanente Metals Corporation, Magnesium Incendiary Bombs, and the Struggle for Profits during World War II." *Enterprise and Society* 12 (March): 10–45.

———. 2016. *Destructive Creation: American Business and the Winning of World War II*. Philadelphia: University of Pennsylvania Press.

Wood, Edward W., Jr. 2006. *Worshipping the Myths of World War II: Reflections on America's Dedication to War*. Washington, D.C.: Potomac Books.

Wright, Gavin. 2006. *Slavery and American Economic Development*. Baton Rouge: Louisiana State University Press.

———. 2017. "World War II, the Cold War, and the Knowledge Economies of the Pacific Coast." Working paper, Stanford University.

Wright, T. P. 1936. "Factors Affecting the Cost of Airplanes." *Journal of the Aeronautical Sciences* 3 (February): 122–28.

Zeitlin, Jonathan. 1995. "Flexibility and Mass Production at War: Aircraft Manufacture in Britain, the United States, and Germany, 1939–1945." *Technology and Culture* 36 (January): 46–79.

INDEX

Abramovitz, Moses: 1930s capital input data, 340–41; pioneering work on growth accounting, 4, 23; twentieth century growth knowledge based, 404n27; World War II retarded productivity growth, 294

acrylonitrile, 112. *See also* rubber, synthetic, Buna-N

adversity as possible stimulus to innovation, 73, 75, 133, 388n3

advertising, 261, 367, 369; costs allowable under CPFF contracts, 407n8

aggregate demand: can drive output above or below potential, 7; can fuel or moderate inflation, 8; closes output gap remaining in 1941, 181; collapse responsible for Great Depression, 1, 48, 189, 200. *See also* consumption, household; fiscal policy; investment, private domestic; monetary policy

aggregate supply: can fuel or moderate inflation, 7; can increase or decrease potential, 8; economy is not supply constrained during Depression, 185; economy is supply constrained during World War II, 189; and growth accounting, 10. *See also* supply shocks, negative; supply shocks, positive

Agricultural Adjustment Act (1933), 86

agriculture: draft deferments, 64, 210–12, 219, 234–35, 238–39, 242– 244; effects on manufacturing labor supply, 210, 236; Emergency Rubber Project, 86–87; farm machinery shortages, 191, 198; productivity growth, 325–27, 334–35, 342

Aiken, Howard (computer pioneer), 337

aircraft, Boeing, postwar commercial production data, 277

aircraft, military: B-17 (Flying Fortress), 67, 69, 275; B-24 (Liberator), 3, 14, 18, 19, 66, 261–69, 275; B-25 (Mitchell), 275; B-26 (Marauder), 275; B-29 (Superfortress), 15, 19, 251, 253, 269, 271; B-52, 67, 277; Bell P-39 Airacobra, 276; C-47 (military version of DC-3), 3, 18, 261, 276; Chance Vought F4U Corsair, 275; Curtiss P-40 Warhawk, 275; Curtiss SB2C Helldiver, 276; Douglas DB-7, 275; Douglas SBD Dauntless,

431